The Development of the USSR

AN EXCHANGE OF VIEWS

The Development of the USSR

AN EXCHANGE OF VIEWS

Edited by Donald W. Treadgold

University of Washington Press Seattle 1964

The essays in this book originally appeared in the Discussion section of the *Slavic Review,* copyright 1961, 1962, 1963, 1964, by the American Association for the Advancement of Slavic Studies, Inc.

Contents

v

PART IV: RUSSIA BETWEEN EAST AND WEST

Introduction

DONALD W. TREADGOLD

This book is made up of a series of exchanges of differing views among some of the West's foremost specialists on Russia. Certain fundamental issues are singled out for examination, ranging over the organization of the political system and the economy of the USSR, the development of Russian literature, and the various historical stages through which Russia and two non-Russian areas, the Ukraine and Belorussia, have passed. In each case one scholar advances a thesis, two others consider it critically, and the original writer replies to the criticisms. The result is a thoroughgoing assessment of a spectrum of views held by the best Western students, based on the best scholarship produced in all countries, concerning the development of the USSR to the present day.

Ever since Herodotus inquired into the way the Scythians milked mares, Westerners have maintained an interest in events on the territory of what is today called the Soviet Union. The first state of the Eastern Slavs, Kievan Rus (*ca.* 850–*ca.* 1200), was frequently visited by travelers and traders from Western Europe. After Russia was conquered by the Mongols in 1240, some foreigners still occasionally reached the country despite difficulties. When the Russians succeeded in gaining their independence of the Mongols, shortly before 1500, Western envoys began regular visits or periods of residence in Moscow, capital of the new state. Many of these visitors put their observations in writing, and beginning with Sigismund von Herberstein, ambassador of the Holy Roman Empire, some wrote lengthy "voyages to Muscovy." This genre, of great interest and historical value, has continued to win readers down to the time of John Gunther. Many Western visitors made penetrating observations about the institutional patterns, cultural traditions, and psychological traits of the state and peoples of Russia. Even the best-informed and most reflective journalism, however, has its limitations. The journalist can report what he sees, and if he is an experienced observer well trained in the complexities of what he is observing, will penetrate appearances to reach reality. But his profession lays emphasis on personal confrontation rather than on reading

ix

and analyses of documentary material, and he seldom has enough time for the latter even if he is trained in the use of it.

The scholar may make his personal observations, but he relies for proof on analysis of all the evidence, written, oral, and other; and his profession does not admit the excuse that he did not have time to do so. Through the work of the properly trained scholar, possessing knowledge of all the necessary languages and techniques, access to original materials, and all the conditions necessary for research, we come as close as we can expect to accurate and balanced understanding of human affairs.

Western scholarship, which has set the standard for men and women of all countries in our own time, has been more or less fully and systematically developed only in the last century or two. In the maturing of certain disciplines, such as history, law, and political economy, Russians of the nineteenth century shared fully. It was Germans (Schlözer, Müller, and others) who in the eighteenth century began in earnest the spadework for modern historiography dealing with Russia. With the emergence of such great historians as Sergei Soloviev (d. 1879) and Vasilii Kliuchevsky (d. 1911), Russians forged into the lead, and became the chief authorities on the history of their country. After the Revolution of 1917, they faltered, confused, while the Soviet regime pondered what the received doctrines of Marxism-Leninism required of scholarship, and what rewards and punishments ought to be meted out as fearful scholars sought to work within the shifting limits of official orthodoxy. From the 1920's at least until the death of Stalin, objective and reputable scholarly writing on Russia could be and was conducted in the West almost exclusively.

During these decades, when Western studies of Russia were reaching new heights of sophistication and skill, great changes in Russia itself were taking place and many more data on the Russian past were becoming available to specialists. The character of the Soviet political system was coming to be recognized as different from both Russian tsarism and Western absolutism. A series of notable theorists argued that along with German naziism and perhaps Italian fascism it constituted a type of system unique in world history, which they called totalitarianism, characterized by total concentration of political, economic, and cultural power in a single center, atomization of social structure, and the imposition of a single set of all-encompassing beliefs, or ideology, in a fashion requiring active and overt adherence from the entire population. Was it in fact different from the China of the Mings, the France of Louis XIV, the Russia of Ivan the Terrible? If so, how?

The kind of economy being built up as a result of the sweeping transformation of Russian society by the Communists was obviously of great interest, but it became much harder to study as the Soviets attempted to conceal their failures by ceasing to publish data. The economists were therefore compelled to use all sorts of indirect methods and interpolations. When starting in 1956 economic data and statistical information began to be published in quantity again, the economists hastened to evaluate it and to take account of its implications for their cautious findings during the era of statistical black-out. How far had the Soviet economy achieved results? Through what sacrifices? By the use of what methods?

The position of literature had deteriorated very seriously along with that of the arts generally. In the nineteenth century, Russia had produced a series of fairly lonely geniuses in belles-lettres; in the early twentieth century, fewer geniuses but a far larger number of capable writers. Under Soviet rule, there had been an early literary response to the revolution perhaps more impressive in quantity than in quality, but in the late twenties and thirties Russian literature had dwindled and all but perished, except for the work of Russian writers abroad. In the last two centuries Russian literature had reached a position of at least matching the best the West could produce, before the stifling effect of the Stalin period in Russia. Had these achievements been accounted for by Russia's own literary forces, or were they mainly successful borrowings from the West? Was the Stalin period an end to their brilliant development, or did Soviet writers have the potentiality to lift Russian literature again to the heights of world literature?

The USSR's historians had reinterpreted the past in various ways. Michael Pokrovsky, during the 1920's, had denigrated the personalities and achievements of the tsars and lumped prerevolutionary Russia with the other imperialist powers; at the behest of Stalin and others, Pokrovsky's successors had found virtue in Ivan the Terrible and Peter the Great, and asserted that Russian conquest had been beneficial to a number of backward nationalities, at least to the East. Several such questions had long persisted in the minds of Western historians. Did Peter the Great begin to civilize Russia by bringing her in closer contact with the West, or was the indigenous Russian cultural tradition a vital and creative one? Was the Russian Empire that Peter founded a modernizing and reforming institution, or was the autocracy in St. Petersburg a brake on Russian economic, social, and political development?

The Ukraine and Belorussia had never managed to establish themselves during modern times for any substantial period as independent states. For centuries they had been mostly under the rule of the Polish-Lithuanian Commonwealth *(Rzeczpospolita)*, but in 1654 and afterward they had gradually come under Russian rule. Was this a fraternal and harmonious reunion of the Eastern Slavs, or a subjection to oppressive foreign domination? Was there a "Ukraine" that could be identi-

fied as a self-conscious ethnic entity, and if so could its history be traced
to the nineteenth century, the seventeenth century, or perhaps all the
way back to the Kievan state?

Finally, what was Russia's place in world history? Was she properly
to be regarded as one of the family of Asian systems, as one of the
European polities and societies, a variant of either, or as entirely *sui
generis*, belonging neither to Europe nor Asia?

Especially after World War II, Western scholarship on Russia came
to be largely concentrated in the United States. American scholars
moved to expand Slavic studies greatly in the 1940's. The result was
noteworthy: the quantity and quality of American scholarly publication on Russia increased in nearly geometrical progression (for an
evaluation of this body of work, see Harold H. Fisher, ed., *American
Research on Russia*, Bloomington, 1959).

In 1960 the American Slavists founded a new membership organization, the American Association for the Advancement of Slavic Studies,
and they decided to expand and reshape the former *American Slavic
and East European Review* as the organ of this body under the name
*Slavic Review: American Quarterly of Soviet and East European
Studies*. At that time some of us thought it wise to try to take stock
of the new knowledge and new ideas produced during the previous
two decades or so. It was decided to attempt to foster an exchange of
views among American (and also foreign) scholars concerning some of
the broader and more fundamental questions in the field of Slavic
studies. In each case a scholar was invited to write an article in which
he would attempt to define the issue proposed by the managing editor of the *Review*, relate it to the best and most recent scholarship,
and in so doing present his own conclusions on the problem. Two other
scholars were enlisted to comment on his essay and to advance views of
their own. The author of the original article was then sent the two commentaries and wrote a reply. The article, commentaries, and reply
were published together in a new section of the *Review* entitled "Discussion." In the initial series there were eleven sections; the first was
published in October, 1961, the last in March, 1964.

Two of the eleven sections dealt almost entirely with territory outside Russia or the USSR, and it was regretfully decided to omit those
two from this volume when the question arose of defining the character
of the volume and its probable readership. We may hope that the
number of East Europeanists among the membership of the AAASS
will grow and that Eastern Europe outside of Russia will one day
command the extent of interest that Russia past and present has gained
in this country.

The book is divided into four parts, dealing with the Soviet Union,
prerevolutionary Russia, Russian borderlands, and Russia's place in

the world. There is a systematic effort to examine the questions mentioned above. The first section discusses the Soviet system. Professor Brzezinski argues that the limits of change within the USSR are set by the organization of totalitarianism; Professor Meyer compares the Soviet system to an American corporation; Professor Tucker examines the category of "totalitarianism" critically. In assessing the Soviet economy, Professor Grossman investigates the concrete limitations the "command economy" of the USSR has set on the satisfaction of the economic needs of the Soviet state and peoples; Professor Chambre points out certain similarities between the Soviet and Western economies; Professor Granick questions whether the structure of the "command economy" is as restrictive in its effects as Grossman contends. The development of the modern Russian literature of the USSR is examined by Professor McLean against a background of the development of a Russian literature in West European genres; Professor Mathewson emphasizes Russia's debt to Western Europe in its literary growth; and Professor Struve lays stress on the contribution of the many gifted Russian writers who live outside their homeland.

"Old Russia," in the second part, refers to all of pre-Soviet history. The period of Kiev and Muscovy is treated by Professor Florovsky with special consideration of the cultural problem: did Russia before Peter the Great (1682-1725) develop a real culture of its own? Professor Florovsky tends to emphasize its achievements, concentrating on its religious basis; Professor Andreyev deals more extensively with the fine arts; Professor Billington regards the culture of Muscovy more critically. Professor Likhachev, in the only supernumerary contribution, written some months later, adds his support to the view that extensive cultural foundations were laid before Peter I. In considering the imperial period, which lasted from Peter until the Revolution of 1917, Professor Black works within a framework of a general analysis of "modernization" in all societies. Professor Seton-Watson suggests that modernizing intelligentsias of today can afford to study the positive and negative sides of the Russian example; Professor Riasanovsky is more inclined to consider imperial Russia as an active participant in Western history than as a passive recipient of Western influences.

Russia's Western borderlands next receive attention. Professor Rudnytsky, in dealing with the role of the Ukraine, lays stress on the consequences of the growth of the Ukrainian national movement in modern times. Professors Pritsak and Reshetar find the beginning of Ukrainian national consciousness a good deal earlier; Professor Adams takes a more reserved view. The entire section ought to contribute substantially to the clarification of the use of the word "Russia" in connection with all or part of the territories inhabited by the Eastern Slavs throughout history. The Ukraine and Belorussia were under the rule of Poland or what has sometimes been called Poland-Lithuania for centuries, and Professor Backus questions the durability of the federative arrangements that existed in this prenationalist, multinational state; Professor Halecki argues in favor of durability; Professor Jakstas takes into account the position of the Lithuanians under largely Polish leadership. The relations of the Poles to the Lithuanians, Belorussians, and Ukrainians of course also bear on the Polish–Great Russian relationship, both during the period of the Muscovite state and later.

The final section is an attempt to assess the over-all position of Russia in world history. Professor Wittfogel argues the similarities of Russian state and society to those of the Far East, laying stress on the Mongol conquest as a source of such similarities. Professor Riasanovsky questions the significance of the Mongol heritage; Professor Spuler asks what light the comparison with Middle Eastern societies throws on the position of Russia. In investigating the relationship of Russia to the West, Professor Roberts advances to the task in full consciousness of the fact that the question has probably been debated more extensively, both by Russians and Westerners, than any other single issue of Russian history; he therefore makes a special effort to re-examine the methodological foundations of the question before undertaking to draw some lines of similarity and difference. Professor Raeff emphasizes the way in which consciousness of this relationship changed among educated Russians over the century or so during which it preoccupied them; Professor Szeftel warns lest contemporary interests prejudice the consideration of the problems of the past. To the last point Professor Roberts replies that the past and present cannot be separated; we can only try, he believes, to examine all issues and periods in their own terms, recognizing human fallibility.

The fundamental questions concerning the development of the USSR today are far from being exhausted in the symposia offered here. For the identification, let alone the solution, of some, more research will be needed; for more than a few problems, the lack of surviving source material probably dooms us to perpetual ignorance. One interesting fact seems to be that the amount of research done does not necessarily permit us to anticipate how clearly the issues may be described. Some of the relatively little-debated problems are here approached swiftly and pungently; some of the much-mooted ones evidently still need further conceptual clarification. Such a book as this can promise neither uniform depth nor uniform clarity. It can only reflect the state of the art at a given moment, disregarding whether for all sorts of temporary and accidental reasons a certain person was as ready to write the essay requested as he might be ten years from now or as he felt himself to be ten years ago.

The contributors include men born in a dozen different countries and presently citizens of five (the United States, England, France, Germany, and the USSR), adhering to a variety of political and religious positions (or none), having suffered oppression at the hands of several different regimes or known freedom under others, but all speaking the international and supranational language of scholarship and concerned with the quest of that elusive but compelling human value—truth. Even if scholars know the facts, their conclusions may diverge—even very widely, enough for sustained and even impassioned discussion, but yet within the limits set by the facts established by means generally accepted by the scholarly community of all times and places. Through divergence of conclusions and exchange of views among specialists, the public may be better informed, students better instructed, and, perhaps, future scholars inspired to write more careful, more searching, and more balanced works. On the really important problems of mankind, many important things were said centuries ago; but the last word will never be said as long as humanity endures.

Part I

THE SOVIET UNION

ONE

The Nature of the Soviet System

ZBIGNIEW BRZEZINSKI

"If the mind is obligated to obey the word of command, it can at any rate feel that it is not free. But if it has been so manipulated beforehand that it obeys without even waiting for the word of command, it loses even the consciousness of enslavement." All modern societies involve mass manipulation, especially now since the masses have become economically and politically important. Whether it is an election or merely a matter of consumption, the crucial factor is the behavior of the activated mass. Motivation research and public opinion polls are a way of gauging the anticipated reaction of the consumer and the voter. The asymmetry in decision-making between the masses and the businessman or the politician is thus diminished.

André Gide, the writer quoted above, had, however, something far more ominous in mind. He was pointing to the possibility of a society's maintaining a total political-social conformity, wherein the leadership does not just anticipate the mass reactions but the masses in effect almost anticipate the desires of the leadership. A self-enforcing unanimity and conformity would be the consequence. But for such a condition to arise, there would have to be some overt, systematized framework of socially instilled values, which could guide—almost without command —the behavior of the masses. And if that were to come to pass, perhaps one would be safer not to raise the baffling question whether such a society was in fact free or enslaved. Compared to it, Nazi Germany and Soviet Russia of the nineteen-thirties and China of today would be examples of admirably simple tyrannies, with the continuous use of force leaving little doubt as to the internal essence of their systems.

I

The most prevalent form of political system has always been one or another type of authoritarianism, although the scope of arbitrary power has often varied according to circumstances, local traditions, the nature

MR. BRZEZINSKI *is professor of public law and government and director of the Research Institute on Communist Affairs at Columbia University. He wishes to acknowledge his obligation to the Russian Institute at Columbia for facilitating his work.*

3

of social-political alliances supporting a given regime, and the vitality of institutional and legal customs. Furthermore, with very few exceptions, such regimes tended to be conservative, adopting major reforms usually only in response to social-economic pressures or political unrest, rarely actually initiating them. In the event of occasional reform drives, the usual pattern was one of temporary bursts of initiative, followed by lengthier relapses into conservative passivity.

Regimes of this sort could endure as long as the masses of the population remained politically neutral and passive. A variety of well-known factors undermined this neutrality and passivity. Rapid social-economic changes brought about by the machine age, literacy, and nationalism have all contributed to the politicization of the masses and have made the politics of mass consciousness a feature of our age. Practically all contemporary leaders have to shape and appeal to popular sentiments and organize various forms of mass action in order to wield power effectively.

The extent of the appeal and of the manipulation depends on the nature of the objective for which power is wielded and on the susceptibility of the given society to a more or less extensive domination of the masses by an elite. In cases of widespread social disintegration because of war or social-economic crises, the opportunities for the emergence of extremist elites and for the direct domination of the masses are at an optimum. The weakening or disappearance of intermediary pluralistic forms of social organization allows for the consolidation of centralized power and for the eventual use of that power to effect large-scale societal reconstruction. To do the latter, both the ruling elite (organized into a revolutionary movement) and the masses must share certain general notions of what was wrong with the past society, as well as an action-program for the building of a better one.

The political systems established by movements of this sort discussed above differ profoundly from old-fashioned dictatorships. Instead of using societal pluralism to manipulate various interests in order to maintain power, these movements take advantage of the occasional weakness of such pluralist groups to seize power and then use that power, first, to eliminate all intermediary groups, and then to construct a new society reflecting the movement's ideology. Such elimination can take place with particular thoroughness and intensity if the given society happens to have lagged behind in the process of modernization. In that case, the construction of a new order can be linked to rapid social-economic and technical development. In our age, force and progress make a formidable combination.

Because of the unprecedented total social impact of these regimes, they have been labeled "totalitarian." The word is used to suggest that at some point the scope of arbitrary power and the domination of society by a political elite, especially one that tolerates no barriers between itself and the population, becomes so extensive that differences of degree become differences of kind. Although it is often difficult to define that point with great precision (as is also true in defining "democracies"; for example, is Mexico or France a democracy?) , it may be suggested that the totalitarian systems differ in kind from other forms of authoritarian regimes, either traditional dictatorships, or what Moore calls the "totalitarian elements in pre-industrial societies,"[1] or the contemporary nationalist single-party regimes because: (1) their ideology provides a total critique of the antecedent form of societal organization and a prescription for a complete reconstruction of society and man; (2) owing to the absolutist character of their ideology, the movements feel themselves free of any moral or traditional-legal restraints on their power and consider themselves justified in undertaking even the most ruthless steps to consolidate their power and execute their ideology; (3) the combination of these two factors, linked to the urgent belief of the committed members, produces within the movement an *organizational compulsion* for ideologically focused and ideologically compatible action (ideology-action) to absorb or destroy all social groups that might even constitute passive obstructions to the movement's dynamic need to subordinate society totally to its power. This organizational compulsion absorbs both the leadership and the membership. This inbuilt pressure toward action, operating within the Soviet Communist Party, caused Lenin no little difficulty in his attempt to effect a temporary truce between the party and the Russian society it ruled; by the mid-twenties the pressure had become almost impossible for the leaders to resist.

The character of totalitarianism emerges even more sharply when a totalitarian movement begins to implement its ideology, thereby subverting established limitations on political power. In the broadest sense, three types of restraints on the arbitrary exercise of political power can be said to exist in any organized society: direct restraints, usually formal, constitutional, or legal in character; indirect ones, rooted in the existence of multiple intermediary social groups which have interests of their own, compete on their own behalf, and thereby articulate a variety of societal claims on the body politic—in a word, pluralism; and the natural ones arising from human nature, national character, and national values. Any dictatorial movement has to subvert the first in order to seize and maintain power. So does a totalitarian movement; this was the aim, for example, of the Enabling Acts of 1933 in Germany. In time a totalitarian movement attacks the second by isolating and then destroying all independent social groups and institutions, such as the church or professional groups, and finally comes into conflict with the third. It is when the second has been sub-

[1] See Barrington Moore, Jr., *Political Power and Social Theory* (Cambridge, Mass., 1958), chap. ii.

verted that one may say that the totalitarian system, and not just a totalitarian movement in power, has finally been consolidated. A traditional dictatorship rarely goes beyond the first, while the contemporary and more revolutionary nationalist regimes generally have so far come into only a partial conflict with some of the second.

II

The Soviet system has now existed for more than forty-three years, and its political history has been closely identified with three major Communist leaders, each of whom symbolizes a distinct, but also a related, stage of development of that system. Broadly speaking, the phase of Leninism after 1917 can be said to have involved primarily the consolidation of the Communist Party's rule over society and the internal transformation of the party from a revolutionary vanguard into a more disciplined ruling elite. While some small measure of internal diversity remained within the party, especially at the top, perhaps the most enduring achievement of Leninism was the dogmatization of the party, thereby in effect both preparing and causing the next stage, that of Stalinism.

The Stalinist phase, particularly during the years 1928-41, was the time of what might be called the totalitarian "break-through," that is the all-out effort to destroy the basic institutions of the old order and to construct at least the framework for the new. The postwar period, that is, 1945-53, was in some respects a repetition of the preceding period and an extension of it. The process of postwar reconstruction again meant a conflict with society, destruction of established ways, and an extension of earlier efforts to build "socialism" in agriculture, through industrialization, in the arts and sciences, and so forth. The political consequences of these efforts, especially as they were shaped by Stalin's own personality, were the decline in the importance of the party, the personalization of leadership, the growth of the secret police, and the reliance upon terror as the crucial, most characteristic feature of the system. Indeed, Stalin's totalitarian edifice could be said to have rested on three supporting columns: the secret police, the state bureaucracy, and the party, with all three co-ordinated by the old dictator's personal secretariat. At the same time, the party reached perhaps its lowest point since the seizure of power. Weakened and demoralized by the purges, it became less and less the instrument of social revolution. Decline in zeal, dogmatic stagnation, and bureaucratization were the familiar consequences.

During the fourth phase, which began with several years of instability within the Kremlin but can still be associated with the name of Khrushchev, there occurred a gradual lessening of the conflict between society and the regime coupled with a certain maturation, and social acceptance, of the new order. This phase was made possible by the

Stalinist liquidation of all nonpolitically-directed social groups, and hence the regime could afford the luxury of diminished violence. Thus Stalinism paved the way for the relative leniency of the post-Stalinist phase. It has been characterized by the re-emergence of the party apparatus as the dominant political force and by Khrushchev's increasing emphasis on linking technical-economic achievement with broad and intensive ideological indoctrination. The revitalization of the party and the renewed emphasis on ideology marked an effort to make the system "move again" (to borrow a phrase made popular in the recent election), and the personal success of Khrushchev is in large part due to his instinctive perception of the organizational compulsion of the party towards ideology-action. Stagnant in Stalin's later days, the party almost naturally responded to a man whose appeal involved a reactivation of the party's historical role.

As the preceding remarks suggest, Khrushchev's political system is not the same as Stalin's, even though both may be generally described as totalitarian. Therefore, the next step in examining the nature of the Soviet system of 1960-61 is to find clues to important continuities and changes by looking more closely at certain key dynamic aspects of its political regime. Three seem to be most revealing: the role of the party; the role of ideology; the role of violence. (Because of limitations of space, each will be considered very briefly and only certain issues highlighted.)

Perhaps the most important single development of the last few years in Soviet politics has been the revitalization of the party and the reassertion of its dominant position in Soviet life. One by one, the secret police, the state administration, the army, as well as the planners, the intelligentsia, and the youth learned—sometimes painfully—this lesson. A direct relationship between the leadership and the masses has thus been reasserted—the relationship of access and mobilization.[2]

But the implications of the recent assertion of the party's role may be broader still. Certain conclusions reached by sociologists concerning the comparative roles of specialized experts and managers in large-scale American enterprises may be highly relevant to the Soviet totalitarian system. These studies have implied that experts are unable to provide the "integration" which a large-scale, diversified organization requires, since such integration is often incompatible with the narrower, highly specialized focus of the expert and requires a high degree of skill in human relations which an expert rarely possesses. Studies of the two groups have further suggested the following important differences between them: personality types; background and promotion procedures; orientations and goals.[3]

[2] For a theoretical analysis of this relationship see William Kornhauser, *The Politics of Mass Society* (Glencoe, Ill.: Free Press, 1959).

[3] For discussion see Amitai Etzioni, "Authority Structure and Organizational Effective-

It would not be far-fetched to suggest that the role of manager in the Soviet system, if that system as a whole is seen as a large goal-oriented enterprise, is performed by the *apparatchiki* of the party. They are the ones who are skilled in human relations or in social organization; they are the ones who have a sufficiently wide perspective (if one can call their ideology that) to provide broad integration; they are the ones who rise from the ranks with their minds and skills focused on the over-all objective of the organization—the fulfillment of its historical purpose. They thus enjoy an inherent advantage over the expert, whether he is a technocrat or a professional bureaucrat. This picture is confirmed by the valuable studies of Soviet political and managerial elites carried out in recent years by Armstrong and Granick.[4]

A certain amount of technical expertise does not handicap a manager, but rather makes him more able to cope with his sometimes recalcitrant experts. This is true also of the party. The growing penetration of its ranks by technically and professionally trained persons will not necessarily transform its organizational values or sap its vitality. A local party secretary who can now deal with a recalcitrant expert by cajoling and arguing with him may get better results than his ignorant predecessor of twenty-five years ago achieved by threats and curses. What is essential, however, is that this political goal-orientation of the party be maintained. The recent intensification of indoctrination within the party suggests that the leadership intends to maintain it. The stress on *agitprop* activity and the size of the staffs engaged in it indicate the importance attached to this task by the regime. Technical proficiency and doctrinal sophistication were secrets of the Jesuits' success. It is important and revealing to note the CPSU's efforts to use the same methods.

In discussing the changing role of the party, it is also revealing to touch on the problem of leadership conflicts within it. The character of the contestants, the issues over which they fought, and the methods used to resolve the struggles cast light both on continuities and changes within the party and the system. In this connection, it is instructive to ask: who, what about, and how? For example, take the difference between some of the major party opponents of Stalin and Khrushchev. Trotsky symbolized the revolutionary, almost anarchistic, traditions of communism. To defeat him, Stalin skillfully exploited the instinct of self-preservation of the party, which was far from willing to sacrifice

---

ness," *Administrative Science Quarterly*, Vol. IV, No. 1 (1959), as well as the following sources cited therein: Robert Dubin, *Human Relations in Administration* (New York, 1951); Melville Dalton, "Conflicts Between Staff and Line Managerial Officers," *American Sociological Review*, Vol. XV, No. 3 (1950); A. W. Gouldner, "Cosmopolitans and Locals: Toward an Analysis of Latent Social Roles," *Administrative Science Quarterly*, Vol. II, No. 3 (1957) and No. 4 (1958).

[4] John A. Armstrong, *The Soviet Bureaucratic Elite: A Case Study of the Ukrainian Apparatus* (New York, 1959); David Granick, *The Red Executive* (New York, 1960).

itself on the altar of world revolution. No contrast could be sharper than that between the flamboyant revolutionary and the quiet, dull Malenkov—a party *apparatchik* who perhaps in spite of himself became the symbol and maybe even the spokesman of the managerial technocracy. Similarly, when the time came for Stalin to move forward with domestic reforms, he was opposed by the brilliant and articulate Bukharin. Is it just a coincidence that his counterpart thirty years later was the hulking, sullen, and anything but effervescent Kaganovich? The change that has taken place within the top elite is well symbolized by the men who failed in the struggle for power; and this change is as significant as any of the similarities that one might find between the victors.

The "what about" of the conflicts is also revealing. The issues at hand no longer involve basic questions of the very survival of the Communist regime. The problem now is how to promote a venture that has been eminently successful but that cannot stand still (much like a prospering business in a competitive environment). Domestically, the major challenge to the ruler's power does not come from the visionaries and revolutionaries. To succeed, a challenger must be able to work within the ruling organization, and this successful organization, even while compulsively requiring ideology-action, does not wish to undertake reckless adventures. The greater threat comes from the dogmatic conservatives and the undogmatic managerial and technical intelligentsia. To the former, all necessary wisdom of theory and practice is to be found in the experience of the years 1928-53. The latter tend to equate the construction of "socialism" with the process of building a technically advanced industrial society, and to consider that after the process is completed, the further operation of society can be handled by the technical cadres of experts and specialists. But to each group the other group is a greater threat than the Khrushchev leadership, and hence the two neutralize each other, much in the same way that the Left and Right did in Stalin's early days. Nonetheless, the characteristics of both groups indicate that the ruling party is no longer faced by fundamental questions of life and death, that the revolutionary phase of the great dilemma of principle and practice is finished.

The "how" of the conflicts serves, however, as a timely warning against premature conclusions concerning any fundamental change in the internal political practices of the party. In both cases, the victorious contestants skillfully combined their perception of the innate collective interest of the ruling elite with effective manipulation of the party's *apparat,* particularly through the secretariat. It would be misleading, however, to attribute Khrushchev's success merely to his control of the secretariat. After all, his opponents were strong in it as well. The case was similar, as Deutscher shows in his *Prophet Unarmed,* in Stalin's struggle with Trotsky. Khrushchev as well as Stalin employed muted appeals for support and perceptive appreciation of the dominant aspirations of the ruling elite. And in both cases there were inherent pressures towards centralization of power in the hands of a single individual, pressures which he could exploit but which he alone could not have generated. Considering Khrushchev's age, it is well to be alert for signs of the struggle for succession that is likely soon to begin or has already begun, and in doing so one can learn a great deal not only about the power struggle itself but also about the *Gestalt* of the ruling party.

A discussion of the role of the party as a dynamic factor in Soviet politics leads directly into a consideration of the political function of ideology.[5] One of the most distinctive features of the Soviet system, and particularly of its ruling regime, is its conscious purposefulness. Everything it does—in fact, its very existence—is related to a conscious striving towards an announced but not exactly defined goal. Since this action is focused necessarily on the immediate task facing the party, whether it is collectivization and class struggle or the further limitation of the individual's opportunity for personal ownership, different aspects of the ideology may be emphasized at different times. These varying emphases provide clues to the changing preoccupations of the regime. As noted above, much of the ideological emphasis today is centered on making Russia a highly advanced, technically skilled nation, and the party a rational, efficiency-oriented organization. But it is one thing for the party to be "rational" in its operations and another thing if this rationality begins to affect the utopian ends of political action and makes the efficient functioning of the system an end in itself. It is the party and the ideology together that provide the system with its inbuilt momentum. The decline of either would force the regime to rely almost exclusively on terror, as Stalin did, or face the prospect of far-reaching transformation of the system.

Internal indoctrination within the party is therefore a prime necessity. It is important that power within the party should not gravitate into the hands of "experts," but that broad purposeful "generalizers" remain at the helm, assisted on the one hand by loyal party "experts" (Gosplanner or manager) and on the other by the watchdogs of ideological purity. The split between these extremes is more "objective" than "subjective." Both are loyal and dedicated, but with the modernization and development of Soviet society the party, as noted, has necessarily absorbed the new, highly trained elite, with the concomitant danger of gradual change of orientation within its ranks. In part to balance this, in part almost by a process of reaction, there has

---

[5] I have tried elsewhere to define what I mean by ideology and in what way I think it affects the conduct of Soviet leaders. I will not therefore cover the same ground here. See chapter xvi of my *The Soviet Bloc: Unity and Conflict* (Cambridge, Mass., 1960), and "Communist Ideology and International Affairs," *Journal of Conflict Resolution*, September, 1960.

developed within the party a professional cadre of "ideologues," a group of specialists in doctrinal matters, who bear little resemblance to the creative revolutionaries of the twenties. Yet the growth of the *agitprop,* its professionalization, is in itself an indication of the process of change which, in this case, involves strenuous efforts to maintain the commitment of the party membership to the party ideology and to express that commitment in action.

At the risk of excessively speculative generalization, one may perhaps suggest that the present relationship between the party members and the ideology is as follows: the very top of the party hierarchy is generally staffed by "ideology-action generalizers," men like Khrushchev, Aristov, Kozlov, with the extremes of technical "experts" (who may be said to specialize in aspects of action alone) and of "ideologues" (who specialize in ideology) represented. It would appear that among the probable successors to Khrushchev the ideology-action generalizers still predominate. (Of the various individuals that one may mention, Kozlov, Polyansky, Brezhnev, Aristov, or Suslov, only the last one is an ideologue, and none are narrow experts of the Kosygin type.)[6] On the intermediary level, we can note two broad categories: the professional party bureaucrats, the *apparatchiki,* from among whom the top level "generalizers" eventually emerge, but to whom on the whole the ideology has become internalized and is not a matter of continuous preoccupation; and, secondly, the large staffs of the *agitprop,* containing the often dogmatic, doctrinaire, and conservative professional ideologues. They are the ones who most often view any new departure as a betrayal. In the lower echelons, it is more a matter of simple stereotypes and formulas than fanatical commitment, although some cases of the latter can be observed even by a casual visitor to the USSR. However, it is to be remembered that all three levels operate within a system whose institutions already reflect the basic notions of the ideology and that therefore a more assured mood prevails than in the period of struggle against the old order.

Another aspect of the role of ideology is the almost frenetic effort of the regime to indoctrinate the masses. It is not an exaggeration to say that indoctrination has replaced terror as the most distinctive feature

---

[6] It may be tentatively posited that the ideology-action generalizers at the apex are usually in a closer relationship to the ideologues than to the more subordinate experts. On lower levels, the party *apparatchiki* are usually in a closer relationship to *agitprop* than to the experts. (By closer relationship is meant less direct subordination of latter by former.) In revolutionary times (in early post-1917 Russia or even in China today) there tends to be a relative fusion between the ideology-action generalizers and the ideologues (symbolized by Lenin or Mao Tse-tung). With stability a process of differentiation took place, and in some respects the *apparatchiki* came closer to the experts. In recent years Khrushchev has been trying to counteract this process by stimulating increased activity by the *agitprop* and by assigning greater responsibility to the *apparat,* thus compensating for the necessarily greater importance of the experts, given Soviet industrial-technical development.

of the relationship of the regime to society, and perhaps even of the system itself as compared to others. With the completion of the destruction of organized intermediary groups between the regime and the people, with the basic outlines of the new society erected, the emphasis on class struggle has given way to a massively organized effort to instill in the Soviet people the values of the ruling party. The closer one studies the Soviet political system, the more one becomes impressed by the totality of the effort and the energy and resources committed to it. There is just no example elsewhere comparable to this total effort (in *Pravda's* words on September 14, 1960) "to rear the new man." While the party meets often with major difficulties because of boredom, hostility towards uniformity and absence of free contacts with the West, disbelief or just formal acquiescence, it is able to exploit a very great advantage, namely, that it is in a position to link the process of ideological indoctrination to technical modernization of society, which in our age has become the universally accepted good. It is not an accident that in all recent discussions of propaganda the party, as already noted, has been stressing the need to link the two, and because of its monopoly of power the party can make modernization appear to be the consequence of its ideologically inspired action. The organizational compulsion of the party for ideology-action thus becomes the source and the means of modernization, thereby strengthening the party's social legitimization.

Ideology has thus the important effect of transforming the party's power into authority, and of replacing terror as a major buttress for the party's power. This is a major change from Stalin's days. It is now clear that terror has to be seen as a manifestation of a particular stage in the development of the system. In its most intense form, terror manifests itself during the "break-through" stage of totalitarianism, when the old order is being destroyed and the new erected. At that stage, the secret police emerges as the crucial organ of the regime, dominating the political scene. Given the objective of total reconstruction, terror quickly pervades the entire society and the police becomes supreme. If the dictator is inclined to a personal appreciation of violence, such terror can be in some respects even more extreme and sadistic. However, it is doubtful that the social impact of Soviet terror in the thirties would have been much less even if Stalin did not, as has been alleged, derive enjoyment from the physical liquidation of his enemies and friends. As terror mounts, the apparatus of violence becomes institutionalized and develops a vested interest in continuing its own operations. Terror is therefore difficult to halt suddenly; the ruling elite is naturally aware of the accumulation of social hostility that has been aroused and becomes fearful that abandoning terror might bring about a violent upheaval. Terror thus tends to perpetuate itself even after the regime's felt need for it recedes.

The abandonment of terror was facilitated by the involvement of the terror machine in the struggle for succession after Stalin's death. Although it is likely that terror would have declined anyway, the desperate need to decapitate the secret police lest it decapitate the various heirs-apparent precipitated a more rapid decline of the secret police than perhaps would otherwise have been the case. It is quite conceivable that Stalin's successors were pleasantly surprised to find that their system could work, and work as well or even better, without terror, and that the social response was not a revolution but gratitude. They thus pushed the process forward, and today one may justifiably say that terror is no longer a dominant feature of the system. To be sure, the potential is there and it acts as a restraining force. But it no longer pervades society, and it is certainly no longer one of the central means for effecting social change.

Instead, organized coercion performs the function of enforcing societal conformity. The acceptance of the new forms of society by a large part of at least the urban population permits the regime to utilize social orthodoxy for the purpose of enforcing ideologically desirable behavior. The Comrades' Courts, the Citizens' Militia, staffed by narrow-minded and intolerant low-level activists, are all forms of organized mass coercion designed to stifle politically dangerous individualism which might threaten the pattern of positive indoctrination discussed earlier. For that purpose, the potential of political terror in the background and organized social intolerance in the forefront is sufficient. A voluntarist totalitarianism can be far more effective than a terrorist one.

The theme running through the three aspects discussed earlier is the organizational compulsion of the party towards enforcing social integration around its overt dogmatic beliefs. To abandon these efforts to "ideologize" society, even if this process is already highly ritualized and may no longer involve general individual commitment, would signal the first real step in the direction of the transformation of the system. The regime has shown that it can rule with far less violent means than were used under Stalinism, but the kind of power it needs to continue changing society, even if at a decreasing pace, demands a degree of social integration that can be achieved only if a sense of purpose, organizationally expressed, is energetically maintained.[7] Only then can the emergence of alternative values be avoided; only then can the appearance of groups showing alternative goals be prevented. Only then can the individual be faced with this politically paralyzing dilemma of the one alternative—to be against the regime is to be against everything and for nothing.

---

[7] One may add that an older example of the expression of the survival instinct of a goal-oriented movement through such organizational compulsion towards indoctrination and social integration is provided by church history.

III

In recent years a great deal has been said about the socio-economic development of Soviet society. It has been argued that the achievement of the highly literate and economically mature society would necessarily cause a profound transformation of the political order, and in this connection the words "liberalization" or "democratization" have often been used. It has been suggested in the preceding pages that politics are still supreme within the Soviet system, but such political supremacy cannot be viewed as existing in a vacuum, independent of the socio-economic context. The role of the dynamic factors in shaping Soviet politics must be seen within a framework which relates them to the significant changes that have taken place in the USSR over the last few decades, and the preceding discussion has borne that in mind.

There can be no doubt that several sectors of Soviet society have particular relevance to a discussion of the Soviet political system and pose special problems for it. The relationship between the regime and four such sectors, namely, agriculture, the industrial organization, the intelligentsia, and the evolving public organizations, deserves special note.

In recent years agriculture has been in the forefront of domestic policy discussions. The failure of Stalinist policies to improve appreciably agricultural production forced the succession leadership to re-examine some hitherto sacred tenets concerning the untouchability of the MTS's and to adopt urgent measures to expand the acreage of arable land, to improve productivity, to increase individual incentives for the deplorably underpaid *kolkhozniki*, and last but not least to strengthen the direct control of the countryside by the party. Both the extremity of the crisis as well as the fluid situation in the leadership quickly led to the emergence of alternative positions, and the Central Committee plenums which attempted to deal with the situation (starting with the September, 1953, plenum and including both the 1958 and the 1959 meetings) also became arenas of bitter political conflict, with consequent political casualties at the very top. However, what is particularly interesting is that, although ample evidence has been cited by the Soviet leaders as well as by the recent statistical yearbook to show that productivity on private plots far outdistances the "socialist sector," all the solutions offered, both the conservative and neo-Stalinist as well as the innovating Khrushchevist ones, specifically excluded any alternative which could increase agricultural production at the cost of the ideology. Furthermore, the least controversial measures have been those which resulted in the taking of highly successful steps to politicize fully for the first time the agricultural sector. The present trend toward the amalgamation of collective farms, their increasing formation into state farms, and the liquidation of private plots and livestock, suggests that efforts to improve production and the lot of the collective farmer by making him in essence like an industrial worker, involve conscious political direction based on ideological considerations. In effect, the way of life of roughly 50 per cent of the Soviet population is still being actively and profoundly changed by political action.

The situation in the industrial sector is somewhat different. Here, too, the question of reforms was linked with serious political conflict, as was openly admitted after the July, 1957, plenum, particularly at the December, 1958, plenum. However, the policy issues and the measures taken in the industrial sector were much less, if at all, related to the dilemma of ideology versus efficiency, and brought no further politically directed changes in the way of life of the urban proletariat. Instead, the issues centered on the problem of planning and managerial organization, and their relationship to effective party control. The solution adopted, namely the system of *sovnarkhozy,* is familiar. In many individual cases it certainly involved important changes in the accustomed mode of life. A bureaucrat's family, moving from Moscow to Irkutsk, may have perhaps reflected, in the course of the long train ride on the Siberian railway, on the relationship of political decisions to their way of life. However, a more significant consequence of the reforms was that increased efficiency of operations (achieved, it is claimed, by debureaucratization and decentralization) was linked to a consolidation of direct party control over the industrial sector. The party remained as the only source of social and political cohesion in Soviet society, and on all levels of the industrial organization direct party participation in the decision-making process was assured. A party secretary, Brezhnev, personally supervised the reorganization, and it is the responsibility of republican and regional party secretaries to make certain that increasingly frequent manifestations of *mestnichestvo* are subordinated to over-all national objectives as set by the top leadership.

The relationship with the intelligentsia is more difficult to define. As a group it enjoys special privileges, and many of its members, particularly among the intellectuals, have direct access to the leadership circles. As a result, it can make its influence felt perhaps even to a disproportionate degree. Furthermore, the experience of recent years, particularly of 1956-57, shows that there is restlessness and even dissatisfaction among a great many Soviet students, writers, and poets. The intellectuals have always been the carriers of new ideas, either indigenously conceived or adopted from abroad. However, in order to disseminate ideas on a politically significant scale, they must live in an environment which is actively, or at least passively, receptive.[8] By and

[8] By the former is meant that type of community which because of a continuous and often competitive interplay of groups is necessarily responsive to the impact of new ideas. New York and Paris are good metropolitan examples of actively receptive communities. By a passively receptive society is meant one which does not set up purposeful impediments to the inflow of new ideas.

large, one is forced to conclude that those intellectuals who are inclined to question the existing taboos have not found the Soviet Union to be either actively or passively receptive. With the possible exception of the small artistic communities in Moscow and Leningrad (within which a novel like *The Trial Begins* could be created) , the regime has so far been able to prevent the development of anything like the intellectuals' clubs of Warsaw or Budapest, and it has successfully maintained its general monopoly on all means of communication.[9] Furthermore, the first generation of urban dwellers of the USSR are not paragons of intellectual tolerance; and the regime successfully appealed in 1956-57 to the anti-intellectual bias of the masses when it needed to intimidate the intellectuals. Beyond that, party control over *nomenklatura,* over publications, rewards and awards, has served to contain occasional individual violations of the politically determined limits.

Insofar as the intelligentsia as a whole is concerned, the prevalent tendency seems to be towards professionalization, towards a compartmentalization of interests. An engineer or a doctor is given relatively unlimited opportunities for advancement on the basis of merit, provided he meets certain minimum political criteria. Party membership, but not necessarily activism, is often a necessary condition for a position of major professional responsibility, but as long as formal behavior is in accord with the political norm and the expected degree of ideological competence is demonstrated, the regime does not impose heavy and objectionable demands. To the extent that such a relationship can be appraised, it would appear that there is at present mutual satisfaction with this arrangement.

A relatively new phenomenon in the regime-society relationship is the emphasis placed on the public organizations which are to absorb certain state functions in view of the latter's gradual "withering away" in the course of the transition to communism. Although as yet little of major significance has passed into the hands of such "public organizations," there appear to be three major objectives for stressing them: to revitalize public zeal and to stimulate interest in the transition to communism; to develop through popular participation a form of citizen's control over bureaucratic operations; to enforce societal conformity over wayward behavior. All three suggest that the regime is increasingly confident that it enjoys some measure of popular support and that if it is to increase the scope of social initiative, it will do so at the bottom, where ideological intolerance and social conformity are probably the strongest. At the same time, the regime will be in a better position to appraise popular moods (recent Soviet interest in public

---

[9] The political experience of intellectual unrest in Hungary and Poland on the one hand and in China on the other might be relevant here. In the former it was closely associated with demoralization in the party and led to an eruption. In the latter it did not penetrate the party and the regime could quickly suppress it.

opinion polls is revealing) and will therefore be better prepared for the difficult task of both running and changing a large and at least a semi-modern society.

The Soviet political system thus involves one-party dictatorship, with its outstanding characteristic being the active indoctrination of the society in the party's ideology and the shaping of all social relations according to that ideology. For this reason, words such as "liberalization" and "democratization" are somewhat misleading. They are, after all, terms used to describe a process of political, social, and economic change that took place in Western societies under entirely different conditions—organically, often spontaneously, usually pluralistically.

Any consideration of the process of change within a totalitarian society must take into account the means used to modernize the existing society, since the means that have been used tend to affect the longer-range patterns of development. In the Soviet Union, a primitive society was to a degree industrialized and modernized through total social mobilization effected by violent, terroristic means wielded by a highly disciplined and motivated political elite. The very nature of this process is inimical to the emergence of a separate managerial class (not to speak of the even more amorphous concept of a "middle class"), which would be a first step toward limiting of the party's power. Furthermore, a society that has developed under total political direction has a need for continued political integration on a national scale since the liquidation both of the private economic sector and of all informal leadership groups creates a vacuum that must be filled. In such conditions, the party—its discipline, morale, and zeal—remain the determinants of change.

Assuming that this ruling party desires to maintain continued mobilization of society, it may even be argued that a modern industrial society provides that party with the most sophisticated tools of social control available and permits it to maintain that mobilization. Indeed, one may even say that the more modern and developed the society, the more malleable it is. Terror and violence may be necessary to change rapidly a primitive, uneducated, and traditional society. Persuasion, indoctrination, and social control can work more effectively in more highly developed societies. Czechoslovakia as compared to Poland and Hungary would be a good example. Students of Soviet scientific development have already noted ominous indications that even more sophisticated techniques of psychological and social manipulation are in the offing. Gide's observation, cited at the beginning of this essay, remains applicable.

The present Soviet discussions of what the future Communist society will be like offers us a revealing picture which, if past experience is a guide, should not be ignored. Professor S. G. Strumilin, the Soviet expert on the transition to communism, assures us (in *Novyi mir,* July,

1960) : "Any Soviet citizen who enters the world will automatically be enrolled in a nursery, transferring to an established children's home and then, according to age, placed in a boarding school. His transition to productive life or to further special studies will also be arranged." The Professor adds: "Too much parental love often has catastrophic results for the children, hindering the development of the children. We are absolutely opposed to the old tradition which regarded children as the 'property' of the parents." People will live together in large communes, eating together; their children will play only with communal toys: "personal property in toys, ice skates, bicycles, and so forth will not be recognized in the commune. All gifts received by the children will go into the 'common pot' and be there for everybody." Everyone will be dedicated; behavior will be enforced by the sheer weight of communal orthodoxy, which necessarily excludes individual self-assertion. Dachas and automobiles will no longer be the objects of an individual's ambition, and public servants will toil with a dedication deeply rooted in the Communist ideology.

It may be comforting to dismiss all this as sheer fantasy, but to the extent that the stability of the present regime depends on the continuous, even if gradual, implementation of the ideology, such descriptions are a good guide to the understanding of the goals of a party ruling an increasingly mature and voluntarist totalitarian system. They suggest that the CPSU has not yet resigned itself to playing the role merely of a Soviet Chamber of Commerce! Indeed, all indications are that Soviet society is again on the eve of momentous changes, the execution of which is not likely to weaken the party's power.

It is at this point that a consideration of the interaction between external and domestic affairs becomes particularly relevant. Many past cases of such interaction can be cited: for instance, in 1926, the China policy and the domestic struggle for power; in 1936, the mounting war threat and the domestic purges; in 1946, Stalin's conviction of the West's basic hostility and his decision to give the Soviet society another taste of "war communism," that is, radical political and economic policies; in 1956, the general situation in the Soviet bloc and anti-Stalin campaign. It could be argued, however, that in some ways the relationship is becoming increasingly significant. In the past Stalin's regime was basically inward oriented and isolationist, but today the USSR is deeply involved both in world politics and in the complex process of running an international Communist empire. This involvement on the one hand strengthens the role of the ruling party, since it seems to demonstrate its claim that it is leading the USSR to greatness. At the same time, what happens abroad is now much more relevant to domestic Soviet politics. That is why Kennan's thesis that political containment could lead to a domestic mellowing or breakdown of the Soviet system was at least premature. It assumed a relationship between external affairs and domestic politics that did not exist in Stalin's time. It exists today, however, but in a much different way.

The emerging diversity within the Communist orbit, and the necessary Soviet adjustment to it, means that the hitherto uniform ideology tends increasingly to be expressed and emphasized in different ways. Furthermore, the recent admonition that war is not inevitable and that a nuclear war would be a universal catastrophe necessarily challenges the conception of an immutable and objective historical process and makes a subjective and perhaps even an irrational factor, namely, someone's decision to start a war, a deciding factor in the historical process. The domestic ideological uniformity of the system may thus be threatened either by the penetration of competitive ideas or by the relativization of the ideology as a result of its varied interpretations in different Communist states. In either case, there is a danger of the gradual domestic erosion of the absolutist ideological commitment. The officially admitted fear of war, stemming in large part from the objective "factor"—the destructiveness of nuclear weapons, is closely related to the increasing domestic social desire to enjoy the "good life." In the history of the regime there has always been a tension between the regime's genuine desire to improve the lot of society and its fear that doing it too quickly would be politically and economically disastrous. With the "victory" of socialism in the USSR finally assured, the regime finds itself increasingly able to respond to social pressures for a better life. However, it would be politically very dangerous if both at home and abroad a mood of general social relaxation were to prevail. The sense of dynamism must be preserved. The need for the party's dictatorship and therefore for its ideology-action must be demonstrated.

The present response is a compromise both at home and abroad. It is no longer a matter of violent large-scale social revolution at home, but "the extensive transition to communism," with its hopes for the good life, does mean that the march forward is being continued. And abroad, it is not a matter of outright violent hostility towards the enemy, since that carries with it the danger of total destruction. Rather again a compromise: acceptance of the "peaceful co-existence" of systems but an offensive in ideology, including the encouragement of radical nationalist revolutions that are made possible by the peaceful and paralyzing mutual nuclear blackmail of the USSR and the United States. Peace with victories will serve to strengthen the party's claim that history is still unfolding, that it must continue its mission, that there is no fraternization with the enemy—but all without war.

Nonetheless, relativization of the ideology is implicit in such adjustments and carries with it dangerous internal implications. The domestic power of the totalitarian system depends on the commitment to an absolutist ideology. But such conviction cannot be provided by an ideology which is right only in some places for some people and at some times. If the ideology becomes a relative one, it will be deprived of the fanaticism and dogmatic conviction which provided the momentum for sacrifice, forceful action, and internal unity. History teaches that relativization is the first stage in the erosion of dogmatic ideas.

The appearance of diversity within international communism, a diversity that the Soviet regime initially desired to restrict to institutions and not to extend to ideology, carries with it the danger that varying ideological emphases may result either in splits within the bloc or in the development of a silent agreement to disagree. That is a novel situation for a movement that has matured in the belief that ideological unity and organizational unity are absolutely essential. It also suggests that if gradual erosion of either kind of unity is to take place, and if as a result the Soviet political system is to change fundamentally, the change will have to come primarily from the outside and not from the inside. Originating in bona fide Communist states and formulated within the framework of the common ideology, alternative and more tolerant notions might gradually penetrate the ruling elite and only afterwards affect the society as a whole.[10] However, if one considers what it took and how long it took for foreign ideas to penetrate the far less controlled Tsarist Russia, to merge with domestic trends and eventually to emerge supreme, and weighs all this against the power of the Communist regime, one may well be justified in cautioning that this erosion must be awaited with a great deal of patience.

[10] There might be an analogy here to the political history of religiously oriented societies. It was only after the Protestant and Catholic states learned to coexist with one another and, for that matter, with non-Christian states, that Protestants, Catholics, and others learned to live with one another *within* given states. An "interfaith council" in the United States is thus not only an example of conscious toleration but also of a decline in absolutist commitment.

USSR, Incorporated

ALFRED G. MEYER

To summarize the nature of an entire social system in one brief article is a truly forbidding task; but to criticize such an effort is equally difficult. There is much in Zbigniew Brzezinski's essay with which I agree; and for the article as a whole I am inclined to express admiration. There are some statements with which I do not agree, some that I would express differently, and some things which I think are essential enough to have been added. In order to make it easier for me to state my views systematically, I propose to begin by indicating how I would have written an outline sketch of the Soviet social system. We shall then see where major disagreements or shifts of emphasis are located.

The Soviet Union, it seems to me, is a society governed by what C. Wright Mills calls a power elite. In the USSR this elite is composed of industrial and administrative executives; military and security officers; leading scientists; opinion makers (including both social scientists and journalists); and, finally, professional politicians, who constitute the party *aktiv*. Although relations between the various elements have fluctuated in the past and can be expected to do so in the future, one might generalize that in governing the society the professional politicians must carefully steer a middle course by balancing various groups of experts against each other as well as against the hard-shell ideological dogmatists. Their problem is somewhat similar to that of professional politicians in constitutional governments who steer between various interest groups and the watchdogs of democratic and constitutional purity.[1]

Within the complex structure of the power elite, the party *aktiv* has regained supremacy, not to say sovereignty. If we compare the corporate structure of the USSR with a Western corporation, the party leadership today represents the Board of Directors, i.e., the major shareholders or owners. Although our knowledge of the *aktiv* as a distinct social group is still very inadequate, we can define it as the group which behaves as if it owned the Soviet Union, and which, therefore, in fact does own it. Meanwhile, the rank-and-file members of the party are almost as powerless within the total corporate structure as the Western possessor of a single share. At the same time, there are significant dif-

MR. MEYER *is professor of political science at Michigan State University.*

[1] The conflicts between a Suslov and a Malenkov might be rather similar to the disagreements between a Senator Goldwater and a Governor Rockefeller.

ferences between party members and stockholders, which limitations of space forbid me to develop.

Struggles within the party leadership and major changes in policy are often followed by shake-ups in the ranks of management or by major reorganization of the administrative structure. The top management is free to tinker with all elements of the corporation.

The sovereignty of the party is at times obscured by the overlapping of functions. Just as the functions of ownership and management have tended to merge in Western corporations, so there is a considerable merger of personnel in the highest reaches of all the Soviet power hierarchies, a certain mobility between the different structures. Such mobility has also been attributed to the power elite of the United States. To the average citizen, incidentally, the relations within the power elite are very obscure and of only the slightest concern; it may be legitimate to question how important they are to the social scientist trying to analyze the total system. We should beware of dealing excessively with the fate and relations of the leading personalities, while neglecting the society as a whole.

The whole society is a bureaucratic command structure, with all of the features familiar to students of bureaucracy. The most striking of these features is perhaps the high degree of specialization of functions that has been instituted, and the consequent multiplication of agencies and jurisdictions. Every citizen is a civil servant; and many if not all of them belong to a number of bureaucratic agencies. In any event, every citizen faces a multiplicity of authorities in daily life; and yet all these agencies are parts of the same corporate structure. Life for the Soviet citizen is in many respects similar to life on a military post or in a company town.

A. G. Frank has developed an interesting model of public administration which is based on this proliferation of functions and agencies.[2] Its central feature is the selective enforcement of conflicting standards of performance. This permits the Directors to maintain the fiction of continuity even while they are changing the course of their policies. At the same time, many of the risks of choosing between policy alternatives fall on the middle ranks of management, whose objectives, set by their superiors, are always beyond reach. Success in this agonizing rat race goes to those with one or another special advantage: one of these is contacts in high places, which provide bargaining power as well as advance information on how the political wind is blowing; another is the complex combination of skills and personality attributes that Deans of Students and ROTC colonels like to call leadership ability.

Although the administrative dilemmas of middle-rank managers are

2 See Andrew Gunder Frank, "The Organization of Economic Activity in the Soviet Union," in *Weltwirtschaftliches Archiv*, LXXVIII, No. 1 (1957), 104-56. Frank's article draws heavily on the works of Granick and Berliner.

those arising from the complexities of managing any modern industrial society, the system as a whole must make broader decisions about the over-all objectives of government. To take only one example: In setting the tasks for the Soviet economy, the power elite must balance the requirements of rapid economic growth with those of military preparedness, international economic warfare, consumer satisfaction, and the rational allocation of resources. We have only the foggiest notions about the manner in which such problems are solved and conflicts settled. The locus of decision-making on highest policies is probably a kitchen cabinet within the Central Committee. Its membership can only be surmised. We know next to nothing about avenues of access to this body or about the way in which subordinates may take the initiative in presenting proposals or criticism. Nor do we know the range of the circle within which there is freedom of discussion; and we can, so far, only make cautious guesses concerning the formation and functioning of anything resembling pressure groups or interest groups, such as, for instance, the physicists.

We compared the USSR to a company town because all organizations and associations have become company organizations. All organized life—political, economic, cultural—goes on within the framework of institutions created and managed by the party; and the leaders have striven to destroy all organized life not so dominated. This process of *Gleichschaltung* has not been completely successful as long as such primary ties as the family, the church, the nationality, and that vague thing which we might call the "peasant way of life" have not been either annihilated or made completely subservient. At present, the attempt to eliminate all associations and activities not in keeping with the industrial way of life continues. At the same time, just because industrialism is developing apace, society is growing rapidly more complex, and there is a trend toward greater autonomy for various essential groups of experts. The more they succeed in destroying resistance to their revolution, the more the leaders will be faced with the difficulty of controlling the new society they have constructed.

As a giant industrial bureaucracy, Soviet society is governed by the principle of careerism; and its educational system is geared to this. Upward mobility is an accepted value. There is a good deal of room at the top. To the ambitious and talented, the USSR is an open society. Although the existence of vested interests makes for a certain amount of corruption, there is a growing trend toward equalizing opportunities of advancement. Status and other rewards go to each according to his ability, application, and success. One further principle of selection for advancement is conformism. In the bureaucratic society the organization man wins out over the creative, autonomous personality.

The careerist system not only serves in recruiting younger members for the elite. It also serves the broader purpose of educating the entire population for life in industrial society and thus carries out the process that Lenin called the "cultural revolution." In its political overtones, this educational process accomplishes not only the elimination of troublemakers but also the political socialization of the entire population. Although we might refer to this as indoctrination, it may also spell the end of ideology; for the organization man, in the USSR as well as elsewhere, is other-directed. He takes his cues from his superiors. He has indeed internalized the basic tenets of the ideology, but these are so broad and may have become so meaningless that they cannot serve him as a guide to action.

For those who move up, the careerist system doubtless is a source of gratification. In addition, it may satisfy all those who believe in the Horatio Alger myth that Soviet society promotes and rewards those who deserve it, even if the believer himself has not succeeded. At the same time, control over training and assignment is a method of over-all social control and a means of ensuring political stability. Because the party is, in the final analysis, the sole employer, dissent is sharply discouraged. We have mentioned universal organization as another method of control. In comparison with those methods, violence and terror have decreased in importance. Perhaps we ought to compare the genteel methods of labor relations between USSR, Inc., and its staff with the goon tactics used by that and other corporations a few decades ago. The reason for the change in method is a marked decrease in the mutual hostility between bosses and workers. Both have learned to accept rather than hate or fear each other.

One further means of ensuring political stability is the party's control over communications, including not only the mass media, but also all intellectual and scientific discourse, all entertainment, all cultural pursuits. In the Soviet Union all communication is at least partly a matter of public relations. All communication is ideological; and the function of ideology is to legitimize the system. It does so by appealing to values which, at the same time, it tries to instill in all the citizens, and by veiling unpleasant features of the system in a fog of magical formulas. In the early decades of the regime, resistance to the system was more serious than it is today. Consequently, the compulsion to eliminate all and any communication that violated the magical formulas of the official litany was very strong. But now, when Soviet citizenship training has succeeded and the basic tenets of the ideology have been internalized, the regime can afford to allow a modicum of sophistication to be manifested. Today, an increasing proportion of the citizens identify their individual aspirations with those of the successful enterprise with which they are associated. Their frustrations may be numerous. Their participation in public life may be no more meaningful than the American citizen's contribution to the Community Chest. Individuals may escape into apathy, cultural nonconformism, or some other form of inner emigration. There are, moreover, important segments of the population that have not yet transformed their way of life to fit the desired pattern. But for the Soviet citizen there is no possibility of escaping the system itself. You don't quit your job at USSR, Incorporated.

Brzezinski has pointed to some similarities between Soviet society and Western corporations, and I have spelled out the parallels more carefully, in order to emphasize important features of the Soviet system. The scholars who accept C. Wright Mills's method of analyzing American society will see significant similarities here as well. Finally, I should like to suggest similarities between Soviet society and the age of absolutism, royal or puritan. Both systems arose out of the ruins of another social order. Both established themselves as a result of revolution and ideological (religious) warfare; and both attempted the total indoctrination of their subjects. The Church became the *agitprop-otdel* of royal absolutism. Absolutism, like Soviet communism, attempted to infuse all human endeavors with bureaucratic control. Finally, in both systems we note a decided stress on promoting progress in science, learning, technology, and productivity. In both systems the prime purpose of government seems to have been accumulation.

It seems to me that Brzezinski has paid insufficient attention to the importance of accumulation (industrialization) as the driving force of the Soviet system. Does it not explain most of the outstanding features of the society? Once the decision was made to undertake a crash program for industrialization, a regime of consumer austerity followed logically. So did, under Russian conditions, an absolute dictatorship; and although the web of lies fabricated for the purpose of domestic and world-wide public relations was not inevitable, it certainly was functional to the overriding purpose of rapid economic growth. Finally, the massive attempt to shape peasants and nomads into industrial workers and professional experts was a *sine qua non* of industrialization; and with it came inevitably the acute conflict between generations and the sharp contrast between city and country that mark Soviet society.

At the same time, the successful accomplishment of industrialization is the basis for whatever changes have occurred in the social system within the last five or ten years. I should reject as naive the suggestion that industrialization would lead to democratization. I would, on the contrary, argue that this accomplishment is likely to lead Soviet society out of one variety of totalitarianism into another: While the adoption of a crash program of industrialization requires the application of Stalinism, the totalitarianism of achieved industrialism conforms, roughly, to the modern corporation as a form of government.

Expressing this differently, I should argue that modern industrial society is characterized by the prevalence of certain totalitarian features, some of which are explained by the organizational requirements of industrial production, and some by the newly discovered possibilities for manipulation. Among them I should list the following: (1) the growing trend toward the strict and hierarchic organization of human activities; the growing independence of top managers from control by the constituents; (2) the increasing importance of, and rule by, experts in material and human engineering; (3) the steady effort to induce the masses into participation in public life, and the increasing meaninglessness of such participation for purposes of actual decision-making; (4) the standardization and bureaucratization of work, career lines, consumption patterns, leisure-time activities; the transformation of the individual into a set of categories and test scores which can be punched on an IBM card or filed in a police dossier; (5) the attendant erosion of our notions of due process; finally (6) the imposition of ceaseless social change unwanted by the constituents. Brzezinski, incidentally, seems to think that this last item is a characteristic feature only of Soviet society. He is correct as long as he speaks about "politically directed" changes in the social structure and the way of life, and argues that in the USSR "the state" is stronger than "society." Against this, I should argue that the state is a part and function of society; and that, moreover, we should look at the society which is affected by technological and organizational change, not at the locus of decision-making. To the citizens who are affected by ceaseless change on the part of the bureaucrats, it does not matter whether the bureaucrat belongs to the party *aktiv* or to the management of General Motors. The family of an economic planner transferred from Moscow to Irkutsk is in the same situation as the family of the automotive engineer whose assembly plant has been transplanted from Michigan to Alabama.

It is obvious from the remarks above that my definition of totalitarianism differs from Brzezinski's. Now, since his definition is so closely tied up with his views regarding the functions of ideology, I must express disagreement on this score as well.

Brzezinski sees the present-day structure and the policies of the Soviet regime as an effort to spread the ideology among the people. The entire society is seen almost as an outgrowth or product of the ideology. It provides the system with its inbuilt momentum. Moreover, he thinks of ideology as he once thought of terror: in his view it is essential to the survival of the system.

My own view is as follows: I agree that, to a considerable extent, the ideology, critical of the past and advancing utopian goals, provided the *original* momentum of the Soviet regime. Moreover, communism is still the announced goal of its policies; all actions of the regime are justified by reference to the doctrine. But this does not necessarily mean any more than that the ideology provides the regime with a doctrine of legitimation. It legitimizes not only the very existence of the regime but also its current policies, whatever they be; because all temporary tasks and practices will be fitted into the broader goals, as implementation. Ideology furthermore serves as the language of communication; and this means that it provides the frame of reference which Soviet citizens and leaders will use in analyzing reality. In other words, Soviet society and its members orient themselves in their environment in terms of the ideology. Although the ideology may serve the purpose of Soviet citizens in analyzing the non-Soviet world moderately well, it can be used for the purpose of analyzing the Soviet system itself only with very great difficulties. The reason for this is that one of the chief functions of Soviet ideology has been, and still is, to veil the reality of the Soviet social system. Ideology is to hide the fact that the very goals of the revolution are being violated. It serves as a set of magic formulas for the purpose of creating a fictitious image of Soviet society as the best of all possible worlds. It has set up numerous taboos by closing entire areas of inquiry or making meaningful analysis of social relationships impossible. Although this kind of litany does indeed provide the system with a certain integration, I do not agree that it does very much any longer to provide the system with its inbuilt momentum. Instead, I should argue that such momentum would be present even if the ideology were not as all-pervasive. And the integration that the myths of Soviet ideology are to provide has, by and large, been achieved. By now it only needs to be refreshed occasionally and passed on, as a matter of routine, to each new generation. Soviet ideology, in other words, is gradually turning into a Sunday sermon or a July Fourth oration. It is taken for granted, and its expressions become hollow phrases.

We might draw a parallel between the present Soviet system and the European working class movement around the turn of the century. In both cases there was at first a period in which the leaders undertook intensive indoctrination of the masses. In both cases the effort was crowned with success: the labor movement turned Marxist, and the Soviet citizens internalized the doctrine. In both cases, however, the doctrine was accepted not for its own sake, but because the masses had come to accept the system (or the Social-Democratic movement). In both cases, indoctrination succeeded at a time when the need for indoctrination was no longer compelling. And indeed, my own view is that indoctrination is no longer promoted so frenetically today as it still was in the days of Zhdanov. The self-enforcing conformity of today is not the same as the "overt systematic imposition of values." The values now do impose themselves in routine fashion, if only because the effective emergence of alternative values has become virtually impossible. In short, while Brzezinski states that "indoctrination has replaced terror as the most distinctive feature of the system," I should argue that the acceptance and internalization of the central principles of the ideology have replaced both terror and frenetic indoctrination. Considerations of space prevent me from drawing fascinating comparisons between the Soviet scene and a Midwestern university campus concerning the internalization of social doctrines and the reinforcement of spontaneous totalitarianism through the work of compulsively orthodox guardians of righteousness.

The success of the regime in indoctrinating its citizens not only permits the transformation of the doctrine into a Sunday sermon; it also permits a certain growth of sophistication, which, in turn, erodes the ideology. This erosion is due not only to the strong impetus from Western Marxists, but also to the growing need for more operational or realistic work in natural and social science, even if such work comes in conflict with hitherto cherished dogmas. At least some members of the elite seem to have discovered that differences in scientific method or (in the cultural realm) differences in taste are not necessarily subversive. The resultant erosion of doctrine does not, however, spell the end of ideology, but only its sophistication. Basic positions remain. A Kremlin ruler would no more readily plan the extension of private farming plots than a President of the United States could seriously intend to nationalize our railroads, even though both methods might be advisable from the point of view of efficiency.

The erosion of ideology is connected with a much broader pattern of changes in the entire social system. I should summarize these changes by saying that the achievement of industrialization and the internalization of the doctrine by the urban population argue for changes in existing institutions, personnel, ways of doing things, and problems faced by the regime, and that resistance to these changes should be explained by considerations of power (in all its manifestations) and temperament. Tension has been relaxed in the last five years, not because Stalin destroyed all autonomy, but because Stalin's aims of economic growth and ideological conversion were attained and because, consequently, the Soviet citizens have become more satisfied, loyal, and co-operative. Further changes are likely to come in the wake of a shift in the proportion of work and leisure; and again we can expect conflicting trends. On the one hand, we can expect a growth of diversity and permissiveness in art, culture, and sex life. On the other hand, we should expect resistance against such sophistication on the part of the older generation brought up with the Victorian outlook of the Stalin period.

The Question of Totalitarianism

ROBERT C. TUCKER

Professor Brzezinski's paper moves along a number of planes of discourse. Some of it is describable as general theory of modern dictatorship, some as analysis of a particular political order, that of Russia, and some as discussion of current Russian political affairs and tendencies. In these necessarily rather brief remarks, I shall be concerned chiefly with issues that arise under the first two headings.

In Section I, where the notion of totalitarianism is expounded as a comprehensive conceptual key to the nature of the Soviet and other like systems (presumably both Communist and Fascist), Professor Brzezinski stresses the difference in kind between "traditional" or "old-fashioned" dictatorship and modern totalitarian dictatorship. The nub of the difference is that the traditional dictatorships "tended to be conservative," whereas the modern totalitarian ones are dynamic and revolutionary, recognize no limits to the extension of their power throughout society, and have an "organizational compulsion" to "ideology-action." In passing I must observe that the idea of an "organizational compulsion" remains obscure to me, for a "compulsion" seems to be a psychological force or condition that has its locus in individual human beings rather than in organizations or movements. For the same reason, I am troubled by such a phrase as *"the movement's* dynamic need to subordinate society wholly to its power" (italics added).

The distinction between traditional conservative and modern revolutionary dictatorship is familiar and has its uses. But the historian, and particularly the Russian historian, may well demur. Although Russian Tsarism did become a generally conservative, change-resistant political force during the greater part of the nineteenth century, especially towards its close, Tsarism had shown a great and at times a positively revolutionary dynamism during much of its earlier career from the fifteenth to the eighteenth centuries. Kovalevsky, for example, calls Peter I "the greatest of Russian revolutionists,"[1] quite correctly suggesting by this phrase that Peter was not the only tsar-revolutionary. In general the Tsarist autocracy emerged in Muscovy as a dynamic political organization that carried out, occasionally by forcible means

MR. TUCKER *is professor of politics and director of the Program in Russian Studies at Princeton University.*

[1] M. M. Kovalevsky, *Russian Political Institutions* (Chicago, 1901), p. 100.

and in the case of Ivan IV by a sort of blood purge of leading boyars, a series of revolutions from above in Russian society. Dynamic dictatorship was thus a very important fact of the earlier post-Kievan Russian political tradition. On the other hand, the modern Stalinist totalitarian autocracy became, in its final phase between 1945 and 1953, highly conservative and change-resistant in very many ways. Clearly, then, the distinction between revolutionary and conservative dictatorship is one that confronts us in both Tsarist and Soviet Russia. But if so, it cannot, as such, serve to differentiate either the old from the new Russia or a peculiarly modern totalitarian sort of dictatorship from the older variety.

This is not to imply that the Soviet dictatorship is simply a continuation of the Tsarist under a different name. There are genuine and significant differences, particularly if the Tsarist system is compared with the Soviet system in its Leninist phase. Speaking more broadly, it is undeniable that the twentieth century has seen the rise of authoritarian or dictatorial systems of a distinctively new kind, and that the Russian Communist political system is one of these. The crucial question is this: how are we to conceive and describe this new type of authoritarianism? And further: what characteristics are common to all of its varieties, and in what ways do the different varieties of it differ? According to the school of thought to which Professor Brzezinski adheres, what is distinctively new in this century is the totalitarian dictatorship as seen in Soviet Russia, Nazi Germany, and Fascist Italy, and what is demanded of political science, therefore, is above all a theory of totalitarianism.

The work that has been done toward creating such a theory has been useful in many ways. But for reasons explained at some length elsewhere,[2] I do not believe that the concept of totalitarianism as so far elaborated by this school of thought serves as an adequate base-concept for a comparative politics of the new type of dictatorship. For one thing, the theory of totalitarianism has tended to blur significant differences between the Communist and Fascist varieties of the new type. At the same time, it has tended to set these two varieties apart as *the* subject of inquiry, with the result that we have generally failed to extend the analysis to a third variety that needs to be included in our comprehensive theoretical scheme—nationalist revolutionary regimes of single-party complexion. What seems to me to be needed, therefore, is a base-concept that is at once wider in range or generality than that of totalitarianism and at the same time more concretely descriptive of the phenomenon. It should direct our attention to *all* the principal vari-

[2] In a paper presented at the meeting of the American Political Science Association in New York, September, 1960, a revised version of which was published in *American Political Science Review* for June, 1961, under the title "Towards a Comparative Politics of Movement-Regimes."

eties of the new type of political formation, while inviting analysis of the qualitative differences between them. I have suggested for this purpose the concept of "movement-regime," this term being an abbreviation for "revolutionary mass-movement regime under single-party auspices." The distinctively new development in the politics of authoritarianism in the twentieth century appears to be the movement-regime, of which three principal species may be distinguished: the Communist, the Fascist (or Führerist, to use a more accurate generic term), and the nationalist.

To illustrate the potential usefulness of the concept of movement-regime, we may return briefly to the problem of differentiating the Soviet political system from its Tsarist predecessor. As was explained, the dichotomy of dynamic or revolutionary versus conservative dictatorship is of little help to us here, since the dictatorships in both old and new Russia have exhibited both dynamic and conservative phases. However, the movement-regime as described above *is* something new, distinctively Soviet and non-Tsarist in Russian political experience. We might perhaps consider Ivan Groznyi's *Oprichnina* an historical intimation of a modern revolutionary party (Stalin evidently did), but the Tsarist political tradition was, on the whole, foreign to such essential features of the modern movement-regime—in this instance Communist—as the "vanguard" political party and the involvement of masses of people in the politics of revolution.

All this is not to suggest that there is no legitimate place in political science for a concept of totalitarianism. Though the term itself was not popularized by political scientists but by totalitarians—Mussolini in particular—it has become virtually indispensable in today's political discourse. And though it is often used rather nebulously, it need not be. A clear and useful working definition of it has been suggested, for example, by Professor Hans Kelsen, for whom totalitarianism is synonymous with extreme etatism. It is used with reference to the *scope* of the state order, meaning the relatively centralized coercive order under which certain behavior is prescribed or proscribed by governmental authority on pain of legal sanctions. If the scope of the state order is total or approximately total, i.e., if virtually every aspect of the life of the citizens is subject to regulation under the coercive order, then it may be called a totalitarian order.[3]

So defined, totalitarianism is not an innovation of politics in the twentieth century. Totalitarian tendencies, at any rate, are age-old, although this century of modern technology and communications has seen the most rapid and disturbing development of the phenomenon and its most extreme manifestations. The scope of certain state orders of the past, such as those of the great oriental despotisms of antiquity, has been such as to warrant our describing them as totalitarian or

[3] Hans Kelsen, *The Political Theory of Bolshevism* (Berkeley, 1948), p. 6.

proto-totalitarian.[4] Moreover, the concept of totalitarianism has a certain applicability to at least certain periods in the history of Tsarist Russia. In the reign of Nicholas I, for example, the Russian state order verged on the totalitarian. This was in every sense a police state, even school children being recruited into the network of secret agents,[5] and the scope of the coercive order was virtually unlimited, extending to culture, art, intellectual life, and likewise to the serf economy ruled by landlords who formed, in the words of the sovereign, a corps of "free police chiefs."

Totalitarianism in the sense defined above is not, then, something quite novel in the Soviet period of Russian history, and we cannot employ this concept as the main means of differentiating the Soviet from the Tsarist Russian political systems. It is true, on the other hand, that totalitarian tendencies have attained their most extreme development in Russian experience under the novel movement-regime that was established in 1917. But even in speaking of Soviet totalitarianism, we must always be aware of highly significant differences in degree. The scope of the coercive order in Russia under NEP was far less extensive (in relation, for example, to the peasantry and its mode of economic life) than it became in Stalinist Russia after NEP. Professor Brzezinski recognizes this fact, or seems to, when he says that Stalinism involved a "totalitarian break-through." The implication would appear to be that Stalinist Russia was *more* totalitarian than Leninist Russia had been. But if this is admitted, we are brought back once again to the limitations of the notion of totalitarianism as a *base-concept* for describing the Soviet political system.

This fundamental theoretical difficulty shows up again in Professor Brzezinski's discussion—which is penetrating in places—of changes in Russian government and politics since the death of Stalin. On the definition of totalitarianism that I have been employing here, one would be inclined to say that Khrushchev's Russia of 1960 is somewhat *less* totalitarian than was Stalin's of 1950, for there has been a small (very small to be sure) recession of the scope of the state order—accompanied, however, by a corresponding expansion of the scope of what might be called the "party order." One of the principal manifestations of this change is the decline of terror as a normal instrument of government—a phenomenon to which Professor Brzezinski, quite rightly in my opinion, attaches very serious importance. Since, however, he is committed to the use of the concept of totalitarianism as the comprehensive category and the description of the Soviet system per se, he

---

[4] The historical applicability of the concept of totalitarianism has been argued by Karl Wittfogel in his *Oriental Despotism* (New Haven, 1957) and other writings. See also Bertram Wolfe, "The Durability of Soviet Despotism," in *Soviet Conduct in World Affairs,* comp. Alexander Dallin (New York, 1960).

[5] Michael T. Florinsky, *Russia: A History and an Interpretation* (2 vols.; New York, 1953), II, 772.

interprets the change or the tendency as a shift from a "terrorist" totalitarianism to a "voluntarist" one. The notion of totalitarianism tends in this way to become positively protean, and in any event to lose what value it might have as an instrument of political analysis. The Soviet system becomes, as it were, the definition of totalitarianism—and we are still left with the need of defining the nature of the Soviet system.

Towards the close of the paper, Professor Brzezinski suggests the following definition or description: "The Soviet political system thus involves one-party dictatorship, with its outstanding characteristic being the active indoctrination of the society in the party's ideology and the shaping of all social relations according to that ideology." Ideological indoctrination is unquestionably an important facet of the Soviet system, though I would not consider it the outstanding or definitive one. As to the shaping of all social relations according to the ideology, it might also be held that the ideology has been shaped (or at any rate reshaped) according to the social relations. The main point, in any case, is that one-party-dictatorship-with-a-big-stress-on-ideology is not an adequate conceptualization of the system. It would equally apply, for example, to various non-Soviet or non-Communist one-party dictatorships.

In Section II of the paper, Professor Brzezinski suggests that an historical approach is desirable. He points out that the system itself, and not simply the regime, has had a history, and this he divides into the Leninist, the Stalinist, and the post-Stalinist (or Khrushchevian) phases. With this general view I am in full agreement, having been propounding it myself for some years. Indeed, I should go so far as to say that what we carelessly call "the Soviet political system" is best seen and analyzed as an historical succession of political systems within a broadly continuous institutional framework.[6] If we adopt this historical approach, the first big task is to define the nature of the system, or form a conceptual picture of it, in its original Leninist form. On this point, however, Professor Brzezinski has very little to say. He writes that Leninism "involved primarily the consolidation of the Communist Party's rule over society and the internal transformation of the party from a revolutionary vanguard into a more disciplined ruling elite." This, again, is to define the Leninist system as a one-party dictatorship, and, as already indicated, that is not an adequate definition. It does not, in other words, represent a satisfactory statement of the defining characteristics of the system *as a political system*.

In effect, Professor Brzezinski has chosen to tackle the last task first. The great bulk of the paper has to do with changes after Stalin, and the question of the nature of the Soviet system becomes that of the nature of the *present* Soviet system. I do not question the legitimacy of this interpretation of the question. But it seems to me that if one

[6] Some of the reasoning underlying this position is presented in the paper cited in note 2.

wishes to follow the historical approach and analyze the Soviet system as a succession of Leninist, Stalinist, and Khrushchevian systems, it is important, indeed essential, to begin with an analysis of the Leninist version and to build the rest of the analysis upon this foundation, layer by layer. But this brings me to my own starting point and interpretation of the task—and consequently to the end of my comments on Professor Brzezinski's.

Reply

ZBIGNIEW BRZEZINSKI

Professors Meyer and Tucker raise a number of very important issues, and their commentaries are both provocative and thoughtful. They take the form not only of amending or rejecting some of my propositions but also of suggesting interesting alternative approaches to the study of the *contemporary* Soviet system, the task put before me by the Editor.

In responding to them, I am tempted to categorize Meyer's approach as a "rightist" critique and Tucker's as a "leftist" challenge. In my view, Meyer exaggerates the elements of "corporate" stability in the Soviet system, places undue emphasis on economic determinism, thereby underestimating the role of political "consciousness" or purpose, represented by a dynamic and ideologically oriented party, and he presents an essentially static analysis of "USSR, Incorporated." Tucker, on the other hand, in the course of developing his rather generalized concept of "movement-regime," denies that modern Soviet totalitarianism is a new political phenomenon by the device of defining it in Kelsen's essentially legalistic terms even though arguing at the same time that the movement-regime is a novel form of government, and that fascism and communism are two of its three species. By not sharply differentiating mass revolutionary action from elite-controlled mass action, he underestimates the distinctive total social impact of a revolutionary ideology embraced by a bureaucratized and ideologically oriented ruling party. The historically minded reader will perhaps forgive me if I reverse Stalin's sequence and first liquidate the "rightist" threat before disposing of the "left."

Meyer's argument is a brilliant application of C. Wright Mills's concept to the Soviet system, applied within an essentially economic determinist framework. Thus Professor Meyer views the social, economic, and political revolution which the CPSU under Stalin's direction carried out in Russia as involving the elimination of "all associations and activities not in keeping with the industrial way of life," since these conflict with the concept of the "company town" applied on the scale of Russian society. It is precisely here that the analogy breaks down: The concept of company town does not involve the annihilation of the church or the subordination of the family, and so on, since the functional requirements of the company are far narrower than the demands of the revolutionary party with an ideology

35

of total social and individual change, going far beyond the demands of merely "the industrial way of life." Similarly, to speak of Soviet efforts to inculcate on the masses the official Communist ideology, with its broad philosophical assumptions as well as with its implications for the perception that the average Soviet citizen acquires of contemporary international affairs, as involving "educating the entire population for life in industrial society" is to miss perhaps the most important and ambitious aspect of the relationship between the elite and the masses. What, then, is it that makes this educational process different from the Japanese or the contemporary Indian efforts to socialize their populations for life in an industrial order? Or is it the same?

Far be it from me to defend either a modern corporation or even some of its academic variants, but even here I must demur. These are still limited undertakings—limited not only in their actual scope but, more important, in their own aspirations. The latter are limited because, by and large, those who control them realize that the acquisition of unlimited control over the total way of life of those associated with the corporation would significantly impair its functioning. The limits may vary, and in some cases they may be very elastic indeed. Nonetheless, it is extremely difficult for these organizations to develop an overt justification for total control, and this fact by itself hampers the inclination that may exist here and there to acquire such control. I do not discern this particular difficulty in "USSR, Incorporated."

As far as the ruling elite and its ideology are concerned, I am compelled to note that the application of Mills's framework to the Soviet rulers is not any more successful than it was in the case of America itself. As Talcott Parsons accurately observed, Mills is concerned with the distributive aspect of power and does not tell us very much about how power is generated. Since Professor Meyer correctly notes that only the party elite wields power, it is not helpful to speak of various other groups, some of which can influence policy, often by the process of "anticipated reaction," as part of the "power elite." Furthermore, whence is the party elite's power derived? Here, I think, we have to consider the role of rapid social change, of the ideology that justifies this change, legitimizes the power of those who sponsor it, and also in turn stimulates them to undertake this change. As long as this rapid social change continues, the ideology is much more than a July Fourth oration. To roughly 50 per cent of the Russian population—the collective farmers—it means the immediate prospect of major, revolutionary changes in their way of life. To the ruling party bureaucracy, it is the very basis of their claim to power. In his analysis Professor Meyer nowhere mentions the 22nd Party Congress and what it portends. I submit that the relationship between power and ideology, between an ideologically oriented power elite and the masses, is still a vital one. The reader of this exchange will be able to verify directly whether the 22nd

CPSU Congress justifies comparing the Soviet ideology to a Sunday sermon.

For the foregoing reasons, I will also comment briefly on two minor but illustrative examples on which Professor Meyer and I disagree. The difference between a Soviet executive's moving to Irkutsk and his American counterpart's moving to Alabama is that in the former case evasion immediately acquires harmful political and ideological connotations. In the latter, it is much more a matter of the availability or nonavailability of alternative employment. Similarly, I would not compare the Soviet unwillingness to extend private farming with the unwillingness of a United States President to nationalize the railroads. For one thing, the latter strikes me as much more likely than the former if it were shown to be economically desirable, as the extension of private farming in the Soviet Union would almost certainly seem to be. Beyond that, the United States has undertaken on occasion such ventures as the TVA, which indicates a willingness to move into direct state economic undertakings when economics, and not ideology, seems to justify it.

Lastly and very briefly, Professor Meyer and I would probably differ on the relationship of politics to an industrial society. He attaches great significance to certain political imperatives which an industrial society produces, and sees these manifesting themselves both in the United States and the Soviet Union in the shape of "certain totalitarian features," which he lists. I would argue, on the other hand, that some of those he lists have little to do with totalitarianism, that furthermore an industrial society also produces new forms of pluralism (e.g., trade unions), and finally that it is not the industrial society that produces some of the totalitarian features but the nature of the process of industrialization. If these processes of industrialization are similar, certain common political features are likely to be present in the societies involved. If, however, they differ—and I would argue that they differ profoundly in the Soviet and the American cases (one being rapid, forceful, politically directed, and based on purposeful social homogenizing; the other originally organic, spontaneous, and pluralistic, with political co-ordination emerging at a far later date, when social, economic, and political pluralism had already taken firm root)— then the political systems that come with it, and interact with it, are likely to be divergent, at least in the foreseeable future. That perhaps is the most fundamental difference between us.

Professor Tucker's commentary is a stimulating and in places penetrating effort to develop a common framework which would embrace various revolutionary regimes of the twentieth century. Professor Tucker begins by expressing some uneasiness over my use of such terms as "organizational compulsion," which I applied to the CPSU's commitment to action which is either ideologically focused or ideologically compatible, on the grounds that we are dealing in such a case with individual psychological forces and not political organization. I must confess some surprise, since most political scientists and sociologists would agree that different types of organizations create different forms of conditioning and operational style, which both limit action alternatives open to these organizations and induce marked preferences in them for one kind of action over another. Studies of such diverse organizations as the United States Senate, the Catholic Church, the trade unions, the officer corps, or even the bureaucracy as a whole, provide ample documentation, and it would be most surprising if the actions of a disciplined movement, which is so overtly built around certain proclaimed ends and certain very specific categories for analyzing reality and acting on it, were suddenly to be evaluated primarily on the level of individual psychology.

More important, however, is his critique of my use of the concept of totalitarianism.[1] Professor Tucker argues that in Russian history there are already precedents for justifying the application of the term totalitarianism to such regimes as Peter's or Nicholas I's, and that hence the term does not distinguish the new from the old. I would argue, first of all, that differences in degree do become differences in kind, and that there is no parallel in the past to the extensively developed ideology of total social change and to the degree to which this ideology has been applied in practice. Arbitrary modernization is indeed nothing new. But the execution of premeditated and total social change (which in some cases may involve modernization and in others may not; e.g., Communist Czechoslovakia or Nazi Germany), including even the conditioning of the individual, by a purposeful political elite organization, which sees itself as a special agent of history and maintains power by stimulating continuous change, strikes me as a phenomenon particularly peculiar to our age if for no other reason than the availability to such elites of modern technology.[2]

Actually, I believe that Professor Tucker agrees with me, since he does observe that regimes which combine a "vanguard" movement with mass action are a "distinctively new development." He prefers, however, to label these regimes differently, under a broader category which includes not only the Nazi and Communist varieties but also

[1] I have defined it elsewhere as ". . . a system where technologically advanced instruments of political power are wielded without restraint by a centralized leadership of an elite movement, for the purpose of effecting a total social revolution, including the conditioning of man, on the basis of certain arbitrary ideological assumptions proclaimed by the leadership, in an atmosphere of coerced unanimity of the entire population."

[2] For this reason it is inaccurate to think of Stalin's postwar regime as merely a conservative regime. On the level of innovation, it was; on the level of action it was not, since Stalin was in effect repeating the revolution of the thirties which the war had pushed back. For a full airing of the differences between Tsarism and Soviet totalitarianism, see Part II of *The Transformation of Russian Society*, ed. Cyril E. Black (Cambridge, Mass., 1960).

the modern revolutionary nationalist regimes. Since subsequently he refers to the Soviet regime as totalitarian, he in effect is saying that one form of the movement-regime, which according to him is distinctively new, is not new—which creates certain problems! But to point out this contradiction in his reasoning is not to deny the potential usefulness of the concept that he is developing and which, in my judgment, can contribute to a better understanding of the varieties of revolutionary, social, economic, and political actions of our times. However, for the concept to be useful analytically it should differentiate between mass-action movements and those which involve both the mobilization and control of the masses as well as efforts to mold the masses, i.e., totalitarian movements. (Kornhauser in his *The Politics of Mass Society* develops some distinctions which could be helpful here.) Otherwise we run the risk of lumping Red China, Castro Cuba, and Tunisia together on the grounds that their one-party regimes favor mass movement. It seems to me that, for all its shortcomings, the concept of totalitarianism as defined above can more meaningfully subsume regimes superficially as different as those of Russia, China, Nazi Germany, and, probably, Castro Cuba, and differentiate them from other mass-action movements of the twentieth century.

The above leads me to reject Kelsen's definition of totalitarianism which Professor Tucker favors. To talk of "state order" in which a "governmental authority" is prescribing behavior "on pain of legal sanctions" is indeed tantamount to describing the Tsarist autocracy. It tells us next to nothing about Soviet Russia or Nazi Germany, where non-state organs reign supreme, where non-legal sanctions are applied. Above all, it does not even mention the Herculean efforts of the ruling party elites to destroy old forms of social life and to construct new ones, on the basis of a utopian ideology. It does not focus on the vital task of destroying all intermediary social forms of organization, which distinguishes a totalitarian regime from merely a nationalist revolutionary one. The latter can become the former, as has occurred, for example, in Cuba. However, it would not be helpful to analyze this change in Professor Tucker's category since his three types are merely external labels and do not tell us anything about the internal structure and dynamics of the political system. This difficulty can be avoided by distinguishing between a mass-action movement and a totalitarian movement which controls the masses. Such a distinction allows us to account for the transition of the mass-action regime into a totalitarian one, instead of being limited by the theoretically inadequate options of having to say that a nationalist regime has become either a Communist or Fascist one, which are the only two other alternatives available in Professor Tucker's terms.

The totalitarian efforts to build a new society must be viewed in a developmental perspective, and I am not troubled by the notion that

Stalinist Russia was more totalitarian than Leninist any more than I might be by the generalization that England in 1920 was less democratic than in 1950. Admittedly and even inevitably, the importance of various instruments inducing change can increase or decline with social, economic, and political development, and I argued that today, in Khrushchev's Russia, indoctrination superimposed on technical modernization is overshadowing crude terror. This in turn led me to apply the one-sentence description of the Soviet political system which Professor Tucker criticizes towards the end of his commentary. The sentence was not meant to be an over-all "conceptualization of the system" but rather an attempt to sum up a previous argument on behalf of the proposition that indoctrination as well as the ideologically rooted social changes constitute the central aspects of today's regime-masses political relationship in the USSR. Professor Tucker points out that this may be true of other regimes also. In reply, I would say, yes, efforts to reshape all social relations might be true of other *totalitarian* regimes, and I think he would agree that the loose concept of movement-regime would not be meaningful here.

His final criticism is concerned with my failure to deal adequately with the Leninist phase. I am not quite certain what methodology is involved in progressing "layer by layer" from Lenin to the present, as he recommends. I would add, however, that sometimes the past is better understood by examining the present and then defining the relationship of the present to the past. With forty-four years of Soviet experience already behind us we should have some basis for generalizing about the political consequences of the dynamic interaction between socio-economic change and politically directed social revolution. This to me is the key question of the type of politics which we are witnessing today in the Communist world, which we witnessed in the Nazi and Fascist varieties some decades ago, and which we may still see elsewhere under different ideological inspiration. It is Professor Tucker's failure to tackle this crucial issue which prompts me not to favor his approach.

TWO

The Structure and Organization
of the Soviet Economy

GREGORY GROSSMAN

I

An economist has little reason to dispute a political scientist's appraisal of the 1961 Program of the CPSU as a "credo of conservatism,"[1] although the economist might qualify the conservatism as a dynamic one. While aiming at the eventual creation of full communism, for the near future the Program eschews all radical departures from established rates and directions of growth and from prevailing socio-economic institutions or the current tendencies in the evolution of these institutions. In this sense the Program codifies the present and projects it into the future. "Maximal Growth with Minimal Change" could well be the epigraph of its economic section.

It is perhaps no surprise that the economist finds no major surprises in the Program. Conservatism is said to have two sources: not wanting change and not knowing how to bring it about. Both partially apply in this case. Surely the progress of the Soviet economy since 1953—the basis for economic comparisons in the USSR nowadays—has been such as to make the party doubt the wisdom of changing courses, and at the same time the difficulties of the Soviet economy are so deeply rooted in its present institutions that any fundamental reform would not be easy to design. Indeed, like any established regime, the post-Stalin Soviet regime has been assiduously avoiding radical solutions. Except possibly for some of the measures in the agricultural sector, such as the abolition of the MTS, its institutional and organizational reforms have tended to be chiefly of a "patchwork" character when minor (e.g., the various measures to spur technological progress), or essentially conservative.when major (as in the 1957 reorganization of industry and construction).[2]

MR. GROSSMAN is professor of economics and chairman of the Center for Slavic and East European Studies at the University of California, Berkeley.

[1] Robert C. Tucker, "A Credo of Conservatism," Problems of Communism, X, No. 5 (Sept.-Oct., 1961), 1-4.

[2] Cf. Oleg Hoeffding, "The Soviet Industrial Reorganization of 1957," American Economic Review, XLIX, No. 2 (May, 1959), 65-67.

That the Program's conservatism is more than matched by the continuity and persistence of the economy's problems is forcefully brought out if one looks back a full quarter of a century. True, the economy's scale is quite different at the end of 1961, the time of this writing, than in 1936-37. Taking the average of the two earlier years as the base, we find that agricultural production has nearly doubled (though the territory has of course expanded), and industrial production has increased by a factor of about nine according to the official index, and by around half as much according to independent estimates. Yet there is hardly an economic problem that preoccupied the regime twenty-five years ago which does not preoccupy its successor today, or indeed has not plagued the economy and its rulers continuously for at least three decades. The list is a long one; there is no need to recite it fully here. But we may take a look at the more important problems, grouping them in an arbitrary fashion.

(1) Problems pertaining to agriculture: its pronounced lag behind the rest of the economy, its sluggish response to many of the remedial measures, the low productivity of labor, the great dispersion of peasant incomes around a relatively low average, the contrasts between the socialized sector and the private plot.

(2) Overcentralization and bureaucratization of the whole economy, with attendant delays, inefficiencies, and political problems.

(3) Deficiencies of planning: cumbersomeness, great delays in the plans reaching the executants and their frequent revisions; their imperfect internal consistency and balance; poor articulation between production (or investment) planning, supply planning, and financial planning.

(4) Inadequate attention to economic efficiency (optimization) in planning and management; related problems in pricing.

(5) Chronic and general supply difficulties with regard to producer goods, including equipment; and, as the other side of the coin, poor quality, improper assortment, incomplete assembly, and many other defects of the goods themselves.

(6) Obstacles to innovation, whether owing to "friction" in the bureaucratic hierarchies or to resistance from below.

(7) "Localism" and "departmentalism" of varying degrees of enlightenment or selfishness; neglect and pilferage of socialist property; self-serving acts of the greatest variety and ingenuity, not to say ubiquity; and widespread deception of superiors.

(8) The many ills of the construction industry, such as dispersion of funds and resources among too many projects, building without blueprints, great delays in completion and frequent partial noncompletion (the notorious *nedodelki*), a very large amount of resources frozen

in the "unfinished construction" and "uninstalled equipment,"[3] and the generally low quality of the product. When, at the 22nd Party Congress, Mr. Khrushchev characterized the performance of the construction industry as "the problem of problems,"[4] he was merely attaching a new—and since much popularized—label to a decades-old headache.

(9) The consumer's well-known woes: shortages of consumer goods and interruptions in their supply, their poor quality and limited variety, the lack of both service and services, and the ever-present housing shortage.

While a quarter of a century ago one could attribute these difficulties in good measure to the workers' and peasants' "darkness" (as the Russians might say) and to the planners' and managers' greenness, today their children are hardly wanting in the experience, training, education, indoctrination, and tools to do a much better job of it. The persistence of the problems is strong evidence that they are a systemic phenomenon.

II

Economic systems are best known by the institutions they keep. The undogmatic student nowadays realizes that all classifications are no more than constructs and abstractions, that their function is to be tools of analysis and not its master, and that therefore they ought to be adapted to the object of his study. In examining economic systems from a dynamic standpoint it is useful to look at the factors conditioning their motion in particular phases of their histories, namely, their ideologies (or the ideologies of their governing elites) and the points in economic-historical development marking the beginning of these phases. The latter of course determine the resources on hand, while the ideologies bear on the directions and speed of development, the degree of pressure on the available resources, and the political restraints that might or might not be placed on the single-mindedness of the advance.

Some — notably Alexander Gerschenkron[5] — would argue that the nature and intensity of the ideological commitment to industrialization

---

[3] As of January 1, 1961, the volume of unfinished construction was 21.4 billion (new) rubles, and the increment for the preceding year was 2.4 billion rubles (*Экономическая газета*, Sept. 4, 1961, p. 14). The total of construction by the state, centralized and decentralized, in 1960 was 19.3 billion rubles. The amount of uninstalled equipment as of May 1, 1961, on enterprises subordinated to republic Councils of Ministers (accounting for 94 per cent of gross industrial production in the country) was 2.47 billion rubles (*Экономическая газета*, Dec. 18, 1961, p. 7). Total investment in machinery in the state sector during 1960 was about 9.3 billion rubles. 1960 data from *Народное хозяйство СССР в 1960 г.* (Moscow: ЦСУ СССР, 1961), pp. 591-92.

[4] *Правда*, Oct. 18, 1961, p. 6.

[5] See particularly his "Economic Backwardness in Historical Perspective" in Bert F. Hoselitz, ed., *The Progress of Underdeveloped Areas* (Chicago, 1952).

is related to the country's relative economic backwardness at the beginning of the relevant phase; in other words, that the march of Economic History is not an orderly procession but a grand and inexorable game of catching up. Be that as it may, the USSR can be seen as a special case of a country that despite considerable economic backwardness relative to the other great powers (1) enjoyed a favorable resource endowment and had already had its industrial "take-off" decades earlier (in this regard it is very different from many an underdeveloped country today), (2) has been, for various reasons good or bad, in an enormous hurry to industrialize and to build up its military might, and (3) has had a polity providing few checks on the urgent and single-minded policy of industrialization. It is not necessary to accept the dubious thesis that the actual Soviet pattern of development, including its noneconomic aspects, was the only possible one in order to see that this pattern was a consistent product of the logic of haste under conditions of relative backwardness and (to put it mildly) within a highly authoritarian political milieu. The logic of haste is above all a powerful centralizing force in social affairs. In the Soviet instance "centralism" found a ready and most convenient ally in "socialism," however incompatible with some of the European intellectual roots of socialism the total social mobilization in the Soviet case may have been.

The Soviet—or, more exactly, Stalinist—formula for industrialization is by now well known. One of its cornerstones has been, of course, the collectivization of agriculture, which permitted a large unrequited extraction of agricultural surplus while avoiding (or so it was thought) a large-scale withdrawal of effort by the peasants, as happened during War Communism. The extraction of the agricultural surplus in turn allowed a very high rate of investment out of the national product. Physical resources have been "mobilized" for capital construction by virtue of central planning and a tight control over the allocation of materials and foreign exchange. Western technology has been taken over on a vast scale and injected into the economy from above under constant pressure. A large training program has been conducted. Material benefits and social privileges have been offered in a highly selective and differentiated way in order to stimulate labor to maximum self-improvement and best performance on the job. But direct controls were exercised over labor for a long time, too.

Money, of course, remained in use, but in the production sector more "passively," to control compliance and constrain independence, than "actively," to guide performance.[6] The economy has not only

[6] On active and passive money in alternative economic systems see, for example, P. J. D. Wiles, "Rationality, the Market, Decentralization, and the Territorial Principle" in G. Grossman, ed., *Value and Plan* (Berkeley and Los Angeles, 1960), esp. pp. 188 ff.

been planned centrally (although all effective national planning is by definition "central," and no planning is entirely centralized), and not only has the volume and distribution of investments been centrally determined, but the economy has also been *centrally managed* by dint of a plethora of production directives and allocation orders *in natura*. It is primarily the last of these three features of central direction, rather than the first two, that sets the Soviet-type economy apart from other planned economies such as the Indian, Norwegian, or Yugoslav, and which has produced such appellations as "command economy" and *Zentralverwaltungswirtschaft*. (The Soviets have no name for their own type of economy except "socialist," which is of course quite imprecise.) A command economy, in contrast to a market economy, allocates resources and attempts to attain balance between requirements and availabilities by means of commands (orders, directives) from the center, rather than by the mutual interaction of many decentralized economic units linked together by a market (price) mechanism. A command economy must also be a planned one in the sense that a certain minimal amount of co-ordination between the directives is required lest the economy break down. While a command economy need not be socialist—the Nazi war economy is frequently cited in evidence of this—it is difficult to imagine one except in a highly authoritarian milieu. On the other hand, a market economy can be both planned and socialist, as these words are commonly understood in the West. The Yugoslav economy, and the Soviet economy itself during the NEP era, are the most outstanding examples of "market socialism" with central planning.

It is only with reference to the logic of haste under conditions of relative economic backwardness and of political dictatorship that one understands those crucial features of Soviet industrialization (and the later Chinese industrialization) which go completely counter to Western experience. If in the West industrialization was associated with commercialization and a great extension of the scope of the market mechanism, Soviet industrialization, as we have just seen, all but abolished the market mechanism. If in the West there was a parallel monetization of the economy, the Soviet economy was to a considerable degree demonetized. If in the West, and even in Tsarist Russia, restrictions on labor mobility were progressively removed and the individual's relation to society tended to shift "from status to contract," in the Soviet case there was a marked return to restrictions on labor mobility, paternalism of a sort, and even labor adscription within the new institutional context. The functional role of the three "M's" of Western industrialization—the market, money, and mobility—are well known: in brief, they afforded the greatest scope and incentive for innovation, accumulation, and growth under essentially decentralized initiative and decision-making. *Laissez-faire* is the name we use for the more extreme form of such decentralization. It was only later in the West (at least in the Anglo-Saxon world) that substantial curbs came to be placed on the working of the market mechanism, and trade unions came to impart status privileges to labor as the production ethic gave ground to considerations of welfare, social justice, and economic stability.

Ideologically rooted in the nineteenth-century revolt against *laissez-faire* and politically committed to dictatorship as it was, the new Soviet regime could hardly have been expected to opt for rapid industrialization within a decentralized framework, not to say with private initiative and private property in industry. The rate of accumulation, and hence the rate of growth, and the pattern of investment, and hence the direction of development, could hardly have been left to the despised and dreaded *stikhiinost'* (spontaneous and atomized decision-making). But—not to mention coercion and terror—it is questionable that the (socialist) market mechanism had to be destroyed, the economy partially demonetized, and labor mobility impaired, to the extent that they were. And it is quite understandable that these three "non-M's" would tend to come into progressively sharper conflict with the very development of the economy that they originally were intended to spur—a conflict whose manifestations were repressed by Stalin, but which, together with the closely related problem of agriculture, has dominated the *Problematik* of the post-Stalin era. The fact is that the three "non-M's" clash with some of the most fundamental requirements of a modern economy and society. The lack of a market mechanism, that is, the command principle, obstructs decentralization and thus conflicts with a modern economy's enormous complexity, the need for dispersed initiative to take full advantage of industrialism's productive and growing potential, and the modern consumer's quest for quality and variety of goods and services. Demonetization, albeit partial, stands in the way of effective decentralization and bars the use of a rational calculus even within the framework of the command economy. And lastly, direct controls over labor—trained and educated labor at that—offend against human dignity and the sense of justice. In terms of the historical contrast with the West, the wheel is set for another turn.

III

Labor.—The breaking of the autonomy of the Soviet trade unions at the outset of the Five-Year Plans—more precisely, at the 16th Party Conference in April, 1929—was essential for the consolidation of Stalin's power. Their concern with living standards and distributive justice would have stood in the way of Stalin's industrialization. What followed is well known. Less than a year later began the collectivization drive, a kind of mass enserfment in the name of socialism, an adscription of the peasantry to state-controlled (if not formally state-owned) estates complete with *barshchina* (*corvée*).[7] The impressing of millions into forced labor camps or work at places of banishment was an even harsher kind of adscription, though primarily to industrial and building enterprises. The structure of wages was revised to reward contribution to the industrialization drive above all other considerations.

Toward the end of the first decade of the Plan Era came the notorious measures aimed at limiting the mobility and controlling the activity of free nonpeasant labor: the introduction of labor books on December 20, 1938, penalties against absenteeism and loafing on December 28, 1938, and prohibitions against voluntary quitting and much stiffer penalties against absenteeism on June 26, 1940. In October of the same year appeared decrees empowering authorities to transfer skilled and technical personnel regardless of the individual's wishes and establishing a labor draft (State Labor Reserves) for youths. During the war additional restrictions on labor mobility were decreed in the face of the new and grave emergency.

One must also bear in mind that in all these cases it was the individual's mobility that was being curbed; the state's freedom to move labor was in no way limited. On the contrary, it was enhanced. Where in the West the individual had to be freed to be drawn into new forms of life in the course of industrialization, in the Soviet Union the conflict between curbs on mobility and industrialization did not appear, at least not at that stage. The adscriber and the industrializer were one and the same.

If we cannot approve these developments on ethical grounds, we can at least understand some of them with reference to the logic of haste operating in the particular milieu. But the controls over labor—and especially the concomitant drop in living standards (including "leisure") and the brutalities of the collectivization drive and of the forced labor camps—had a great and lasting negative impact on two of the regime's prime long-run goals: the re-education of man according to the Communist model, and productivity (particularly in agriculture).

More gradually and less dramatically, but in the long run possibly of no smaller importance, there also appeared a situation in which the life of the individual urban worker or employee—not to mention the peasant on the kolkhoz—became closely tied in very many ways to his immediate employer and the closely-related trade union. The individual came to depend largely on the employer and the trade union for

---

[7] It is said that some peasants deciphered the then initials of the party, VKP(b), as *Vtoroe krepostnoe pravo (bol'shevikov)* ("The Second Serfdom, that of the Bolsheviks").

housing, recreation, vacations, medical care, cultural activities, and further technical or professional training. This tended, and still tends, to "pigeon-hole" the individual in society along the lines of his job and profession to a greater extent than is usually the case in other industrial systems. In a sense, the regime has striven to maintain some aspects of a rural social structure as well as a village morality while industrializing and urbanizing at unprecedented speed. Convenient as this may have been for the regime for political, educative, and economic purposes, one wonders how well it accords with a more highly developed, urban, industrial society. Or, alternatively, whether it might not hide the seeds of a certain particularism along economic lines.

The post-Stalin developments with regard to labor are far from consistent. In some respects the direct controls over individuals have been tightened, despite the over-all relaxation of terror in the country. This is especially true of the peasants, by now of course a much smaller proportion of the population.[8] Although criminal prosecution for failure to work the required minimum for the kolkhoz was apparently abandoned in October, 1953, beginning with mid-1954 the minimum itself was sharply increased on a farm-by-farm basis. Certain new sanctions were introduced to enforce compliance with the minimum work norms, the most important of which seems to be the curtailment or complete recapture of the private plot. But at the same time, in the usual "carrot and stick" fashion, work for the kolkhoz has been made materially much more attractive. The direction (largely through the Komsomol) of many hundreds of thousands for settlement in the "virgin lands," annually for harvesting, and for construction projects in the East, are other instances of retained or even enlarged direct controls over labor. Graduates of various technical and professional schools are apparently also still administratively assigned to their first jobs. And last, but certainly not least, there are now the "antiparasite laws," adopted by the various republics in somewhat varying form between 1957 and 1961, and aimed against those deemed not to engage in socially useful activities.[9]

On the other side of the ledger the two major developments are (1) the transformation of at least a large part of the forced labor camps into "correctional labor colonies" and apparently a very large reduction in the number of persons undergoing forced labor, and (2) the repeal in April, 1956, of the 1940 decrees pertaining to penalties for absenteeism and the compulsory transfer of workers. The latter,

---

[8] According to the January, 1959, census, *kolkhozniki* engaged in "social production" represented just under one-third of the total active population (excluding that engaged in private subsidiary agriculture).

[9] See R. Beermann, "The Parasites Law," *Soviet Studies*, XIII, No. 2, 191-205.

however, apparently merely recognized the *de facto* situation, since the decrees had not been really enforced for quite a number of years. Simultaneously, a thoroughgoing wage and income reform has been carried out, chiefly for the benefit of the lowest paid workers and employees and of pensioners. Its effect has been to reduce very markedly the extent of income inequality in the nonpeasant sector and, with the relative pulling up of the peasants' earnings, in the society as a whole. The fact that the reduction in wage inequality coincided with the abolition of certain direct controls (outside the village) only served to underline how anachronistic the latter had become by the mid-fifties.

Thus, what a Western economist would consider a rather "normal" labor market has emerged (always excepting the kolkhoz sector). True, the total supply of labor in this market is subject to much greater social and political pressure than exists in other industrial systems, as, for instance, through the medium of the anti-parasite laws.[10] Moreover, chiefly because of inertia, labor exchanges have not yet been organized, though the matter is apparently receiving attention on the part of some economists. Although rate setting is still formally a centralized function, the allocative function of Soviet wages is on the whole the same as in any labor market, and in their slow way they tend to move accordingly.

It is therefore not surprising that the factory trade union committees should be significantly revitalized and should become more actively concerned with questions of fairness as they affect the individual worker. At the same time, the range of these questions is being significantly broadened as mechanization and automation begin to release substantial numbers of workers from their jobs.[11]

But effective trade union independence or local workers' management are something else again. Both imply a degree of pluralism in the society of which there seems to be no sign on the horizon, least of all in the party Program. Workers' management also implies a degree of enterprise autonomy that hardly has a place in the Soviet command economy; it cannot come while management itself, for all its authority in the plant, has hardly any autonomy in relation to the environment.

---

[10] The Program aims at drawing an even higher percentage of women into gainful employment by means of expanded child-care facilities, shortcuts for housework, and higher minimum wages. The anti-parasite laws could presumably be employed to the same end. The drafters of the Program were probably aware that strong countertendencies may be appearing as the housing shortage is alleviated, real incomes of primary breadwinners rise, and the over-all sense of national or social urgency declines.

[11] With regard to this paragraph see particularly the following articles by Emily Clark Brown: "The Local Union in Soviet Industry: Its Relations with Members, Party, and Management," *Industrial and Labor Relations Review*, XIII, No. 2 (Jan., 1960), 192-215, and "A Note on Employment and Unemployment in the Soviet Union in the Light of Technical Progress," *Soviet Studies*, XII, No. 3, 231-40. On the recent wage reform see Walter Galenson, "The Soviet Wage Reform," *Proceedings of the Thirteenth Annual Meeting, Industrial Relations Research Association* (1961), pp. 250-65.

The party Program is concerned with something quite different, namely, the remaking of man into a "Communist man," that is, into a willing, eager, honest, and highly efficient worker. (Indeed, so eager and willing that the question of autonomy on any level would lose much of its meaning; and we are moreover told that the Communist society will retain the centralized guidance of production.) This is the Program's paramount goal, its center of gravity. In a sense, it is also its most conservative feature: it sets out to change man, not institutions, on the way to "communism." No one will say that the party has set itself an easy target.

IV

Money.—During the period of so-called War Communism, under the double impact of the direct emergency and a misguided doctrine, money lost virtually all its usual functions: as a medium of exchange, unit of account, and store of value. One could even say that it disappeared, were it not for its conspicuous presence in hyperinflated denominations. Under the impact of another dire emergency, and after a painful confrontation of doctrine with reality, its usual roles and functions were restored with the NEP. Then, roughly from 1929 on, as the market mechanism was squeezed out and the command principle enthroned in its place, the Soviet economy was again partially demonetized.

In what ways was the Soviet economy under Stalin partially demonetized? True, money retained the traditional functions cited above, but with many important exceptions. Because of the reliance placed on it for wage payment and consumer goods distribution (chiefly for labor-incentive purposes), money was most in its own in the relations between the state and the household sector and within the household sector itself. Yet even here there were important exceptions: distribution of income within the kolkhoz, most of which was in kind, the maintenance of forced labor, the rationing of urban housing at nominal rents, self-supply in housing and foodstuffs by both the agricultural and the nonagricultural populations, compulsory road labor by the peasantry, and so forth.

Money as a medium of exchange was also removed, or almost removed, from a considerable number of transactions in the production sector. Kolkhozy paid in kind for the services of MTS equipment, and more by way of tribute than by way of fee at that; the state purchased most foodstuffs from the kolkhozy and their members at "procurement prices" which were not far from zero; with insignificant exceptions,[12] nothing was paid by enterprises for the use of natural resources, or of

---

[12] For instance, the nominal rentals for urban sites and rather low stumpage fees in forestry.

fixed capital and a large part of working capital; the portion of working capital borrowed from the Bank carried only nominal interest rates; the "charter capital" extended by the state to its enterprises was not only interest-free, but was also nonrepayable; certain intangibles were not legally subject to sale or purchase, for example, patents, licenses (except for fiscal levies on some), "goodwill"; tangible capital assets were also generally not subject to sale after having become part of a state enterprise's "basic fund," and after 1941 even surplus equipment could not be easily disposed of. Finally, the use of money by enterprises was circumscribed in many ways (earmarking, rationing of producer goods) so as to minimize the chance of unauthorized claims against resources.

The function of money as a unit of account was equally seriously impaired. What could not be bought or sold generally carried no price at all (land, natural resources, intangibles, the services of capital as a factor of production in most cases), or was often accounted for at rather unrealistic prices (structures and installed equipment). The system of physical success indicators for management and of physical investment-choice indicators for planners, in itself partly a consequence of the demonetization, tended to reduce the role of money in accounting and calculation even further. The result was to render economic calculation often impossible or extremely difficult, quite apart from the rationality of such price parameters as existed. Agriculture, with its crazy quilt of prices and no prices, was only the most conspicuous example of a situation that cut across the whole economy. (Although the discussion in this and the preceding two paragraphs is in the past tense, much of what is said still applies at this writing.)

It would be difficult to assign a single explanation for the partial demonetization of the Soviet economy after 1929. Certainly ideological and doctrinal factors were quite important. Marxian economic analysis attributes more of a distributive than an allocative importance to "value categories" (price, wage, rent, interest), and with the distribution problem "solved" in the new order, there seemed to be little need for attention to them. This view still finds expression among those Soviet economists who see only a very limited connection between "the law of value" and resource allocation by the planning organs. Also, if certain things, such as land, are not for sale, why have prices for them? Why account for them? "Direct" calculation, that is, calculation in physical terms or in labor time, seemed to bring the economy closer to its ultimate goal of full communism—a tendency that was no doubt reinforced by the technocratic biases in Soviet planning.

Technocracy (though not necessarily under its own name) —whether in the earlier decades in the USSR, in the United States during the Great Depression, or in some underdeveloped countries today—is essentially a response to great economic need, to crisis, in the form of a revolt against conventional methods of problem-solving. It is another expression of the logic of haste. While the technocrat's dismissal of money is irrational, nonetheless long-range planning for a technological and economic revolution of the magnitude of that in the USSR in the thirties must rely a good deal on physical criteria, because value magnitudes become too unstable and unpredictable over time under such conditions.

Further, considerations of social control were doubtless also quite important. Money is a form of social power that may lead resources astray and is subject to only imperfect control by political authority. The considerable demonetization of agriculture under Stalin was thus a way of bringing this sector under the most direct political control for the extraction of its surplus. That this demonetization of agriculture, along with other measures applied to it, turned out to be disastrous for its long-run productivity is another matter. And, as we have already seen, the use of money funds by nonagricultural enterprises was also limited in many ways for control purposes.

The post-Stalin period saw a moderate but significant reversal in this regard, especially in agriculture, where relations between producers and the state were largely remonetized, mainly owing to the abolition of the MTS and the considerable reduction in the multiplicity of prices. Yet the kolkhoz's obligation to sell predetermined amounts of produce to the state remains. The relations between the kolkhoz and its members have also been considerably remonetized, chiefly by virtue of much higher farm prices, though payment in kind against labor days and self-supply are still important.

Outside agriculture the progress in remonetization has been less actual than by way of problem-setting and intellectual debate. The official position under Khrushchev has been the opposite of Stalin's—the role of "value categories" is to increase progressively, and the entry into moneyless communism is to be "dialectical" rather than gradual. (It is very convenient indeed to have both dialectical and smooth—*neuklonnyi*—progress in one's intellectual baggage!) The 1961 party Program reiterates this position, although one searches in vain in the literature of recent years for a clear explanation of just what the increased role of "value categories" is to represent henceforth. The answer is probably not yet available. We may note in passing, however, that questions of money, and gold,[13] still tend to be suffused with considerable mysticism in the Soviet economic mind.

One should take note, though, of the partial resolution along rationalist lines of such an important problem as that of "capital efficiency,"

---

[13] Note, for example, Khrushchev's point that the USSR might have to pay in gold for any food imports from "capitalist countries" (*Правда*, Dec. 16, 1961, p. 2).

that is, of allowing explicitly for the scarcity of capital. The resolution is partial because it only legalizes the use of a surrogate for the interest rate and legitimizes established practice; it fails to answer the crucial question of how such a charge is to be determined in fact. However, there are now those who advocate interest payments by enterprises on the capital invested in them by the state, and even repayment of such capital, various types of rent on natural resources, assignment of capital values to subsoil resources, relative valuation of different parcels of land, and even a consistent and integrated system of rational prices for all scarce goods and resources.[14] The fat is in the fire, but clearly major changes must take time. It seems that at this writing the 1962 reform of wholesale prices is to proceed according to rather conventional principles, that is, the principles that shaped such Soviet reforms from 1936 on.[15]

At stake is of course more than monetization; even more than economic calculation, rational prices, and allocative efficiency. At stake is the whole centralized structure of the Soviet economy, the command economy itself, and ultimately, the location and distribution of power in the society. This brings us to what is, with agriculture, one of the two most topical questions in the Soviet economy, the question of centralization-decentralization.

V

Over-all organization.—The Soviet press and economic literature may still eschew the word "decentralization," but they cannot avoid the thought. Many ideas on the subject are clearly abroad in the land. Managers, who often found the sovnarkhozy easier and faster to deal with than the old ministries and *glavki* but who have in fact gained hardly any additional powers since Stalin's death,[16] seem to be bringing their complaints more into the open again.[17] These are the traditional ones: delays in receiving plans, too many plan revisions, too many authorities, chronic supply difficulties, and—foremost—lack of power at the enterprise level and "petty tutelage" from above. The sovnarkhozy plead for more power as against their superiors, and republic authorities ask for more power vis-à-vis union authorities. Judging by the complaints, the situation has changed little on the whole since 1957, despite considerable optimism on this score at the time.

The complaints are perfectly understandable but should not be dismissed as mere ex parte pleas. The disinterested observer can see great

[14] See, for example, Robert W. Campbell, "Marx, Kantorovich, and Novozhilov: *Stoimost'* versus Reality," *Slavic Review*, XX, No. 3 (Oct., 1961), 402-18.

[15] *Экономическая газета*, Sept. 25, 1961, pp. 13-14.

[16] Reference is primarily to the decree of the Council of Ministers USSR, entitled "On Increasing the Rights of Enterprise Directors," dated August 9, 1955.

[17] E.g., *Экономическая газета*, Oct. 9, 1961, p. 23, and Dec. 18, 1961, pp. 8-12.

need for decentralization in the Soviet economy, and primarily to the following ends:

(1) To permit far greater modernization and innovation on the basis of dispersed initiative. At the moment such attempts run into serious obstacles not only because of management's conservatism but also because decision with regard to the necessary elements—finances, production of equipment, supply of materials, technological policy— is highly centralized, and co-ordination among them is poor and slow. A kind of "contradiction" has developed between the abundance of skill and talent on the spot and the organizational means for translating this creativity into reality. The much-publicized party and "public" supervisory committees, established mostly after the June, 1959, Plenum of the CC CPSU, can perhaps spur and goad allegedly conservative managers, but can they "fight city hall"?

(2) To permit a certain amount of local investment in response to local needs. The argument here is similar. Immediately after the 1957 reorganization there was apparently some thought even in the highest places of turning investment funds over to the sovnarkhozy in lump sums,[18] but manifestations of localism on their part led to progressive re- (not de-) centralization of this function.

(3) To permit greater lateral communication within the economy, a type of communication that necessarily suffers in a command economy. This refers to the sensitivity and responsiveness of production and distribution to demand (for both producer and consumer goods). It also refers to that specifically Soviet problem of trilateral communication between the designers, builders, and users of equipment and structures. The vertical communication that today largely substitutes for lateral communication is long and slow, passes through a large number of intermediate levels, and often involves decisions by a considerable number of authorities even at the highest levels. Better lateral connections would presumably also permit improvement in the success indicators for management.

(4) To alleviate the unfavorable trend of increasing complexity and burden of planning, checking on plan fulfillment, and collecting data. In the case of Soviet-type planning the main burden of the work (especially in production and supply planning) arises from the need to determine the *interrelations* between goods (factors, products, construction jobs) and between economic units (regions, enterprises). Thus, crudely speaking, the amount of planning work is proportional to the square of the product of the number of goods and the number of economic units. (Of course, in very many instances there are no interrelations between given goods or enterprises. This, however, does

---

[18] See especially Khrushchev's speech before a construction conference on April 12, 1958, printed (with considerable delay) in Строительная газета, July 2, 1958.

not affect our conclusion so long as the proportion of such empty cells in our notional matrix remains roughly constant.) It is clear, therefore, that in the absence of major methodological or organizational changes the burden of planning and related work in such a rapidly expanding economy as the Soviet must be growing very fast. Decentralization would seem to be one of the ways in which the burden of this work might be held down.

The "territorialization" of economic organization after the 1957 reform has by now resulted in a considerably more complicated structure than was probably originally intended. First, two additional territorial levels have been created: in mid-1960 republic sovnarkhozy in the three larger republics (RSFSR, Ukraine, Kazakhstan) to supervise the local sovnarkhozy; and in May, 1961, the so-called Councils for Co-ordination and Planning in seventeen newly-created "large economic regions," each embracing on the average about six of the original economic-administrative regions.[19] Secondly, by the end of 1961 there have been established eleven USSR State Commissions *(Komitety)* for individual branches of industry and for construction.[20] While the CCP's and the Commissions are presumably less concerned with day-to-day operations than with technological and investment policies, nonetheless the channels of communication within the economy must have been substantially lengthened and complicated.

The limits to decentralization in a command economy such as the Soviet, however, derive not only from the presumably considerable vested interests that might be arrayed against it. (In connection with the latter point, let us recall that the 1957 reorganization was carried out as part of a major power struggle in the Kremlin.) Such limits also stem from (a) the fact that the lower echelons' objectives do not always coincide with objectives at the top, and (b) from the lower echelons' incomplete information. That is to say, "centralism," to use the Soviet term, serves the crucial functions of safeguarding the regime's values and of assuring balance to the economy. The two have in common, *inter alia,* a certain dependence on the extent to which pressure is put on the economy's resources. The greater the haste and the less slack in the economy, the more the regime strives to prevent any unauthorized use (or non-use) of resources, and, at the same time, the sellers' market becomes more acute and the problem of balance arises more urgently. In short, given its political and economic realities,

---

[19] Экономическая газета, May 28, 1961, p. 2, and *Problems of Communism,* X, No. 5 (Sept.-Oct., 1961), 46-48.

[20] As of December, 1961, there exist the following "branch" State Commissions of the Council of Ministers USSR in industry and construction: automation and machine-building, aviation equipment, defense equipment, radio-electronics, electronic equipment, shipbuilding, chemical industry, ferrous and nonferrous metals, fuels, atomic energy, construction (Правда, Dec. 9, 1961, p. 2).

there is generally a substantial recentralizing tendency in the Soviet system, though it usually operates on a piecemeal basis as individual problems are faced and resolved by taking them away from the jurisdiction of lower authorities.[21]

Short of a renunciation of the command economy in favor of a radically different structure, what courses of action are open to reduce the costs of centralization or to decentralize without the disadvantages just mentioned? The one attracting high attention at the moment in the USSR (and, by reflection, abroad) is the use of mathematical techniques, primarily input-output matrices, in conjunction with modern computational equipment, to speed up the construction of plans and to permit the preparation of alternative plans. Academician V. S. Nemchinov, a leader in this new trend among Soviet economists, has propounded the more elaborate notion of "economic cybernetics" which would combine the high-speed plan-construction techniques with high-speed, continuous transmission of information to the planning center and of directives from it.[22] This is not the place to analyze at length the promise that input-output or economic cybernetics offer to the Soviet economy. It must be borne in mind, however, that the matrix would have to be very large to supplant the present set of material balances at the Gosplan USSR level alone; in planning for 1962, Gosplan USSR employed over 14,000 material balances. Even if a matrix of this size were constructed and successfully utilized, and if similar tables were employed at other levels, many of the present difficulties of the Soviet economy—sellers' market, faulty success indicators, faulty prices, and so forth—need not be completely remedied. Nor are the planners very like to automate entirely their delicate functions (and work themselves out of their own jobs besides).

Secondly, some sectors might be taken out of the command-economy structure and linked to the rest of the economy by means of a price nexus, as, for example, is already the case with the household sector. Steps in this direction have also been taken since Stalin's death (e.g., in 1955 and 1958) with regard to the collective farm sector. It was expected that collective farms would determine their production programs with reference to the prices posted by the state. But delivery quotas were never abolished, and because of the constant pressure from the top, the kolkhozy have been subjected to rather detailed control and guidance by local authorities.[23] Thus, the price mechanism has not been given a chance to be decisive. At any rate, agriculture can

---

[21] A noticeable recentralizing trend is proceeding at the time of this writing (end of 1961), affecting particularly "plan indicators," research, investment, and the construction industry. See, for example, *Правда*, Dec. 7, 1961, p. 4, and *Экономическая газета*, Oct. 9, 1961, p. 9, Nov. 27, 1961, p. 28, Dec. 18, 1961, pp. 4 and 7-8.

[22] *Экономическая газета*, Oct. 23, 1961, pp. 21-23.

[23] For recent confirmation see Khrushchev's speech, *Правда*, Dec. 25, 1961, p. 1.

be potentially so "separated out" because of its rather small use of current inputs from the rest of the economy. Where the flow of current inputs is much more important in relation to output, the given sector's reciprocal relation with the rest of the economy is greater, and therefore its "separation" by means of the price mechanism is not likely to be viewed with much favor so long as the command principle remains dominant.

Thirdly, a way of meeting some of the problems of the sellers' market is to merge enterprises with their suppliers, thus transforming the problems into intra-enterprise ones and thereby facilitating their solution, as was done in Czechoslovakia in 1958.[24] This was also done for years in the USSR in a relatively small number of conspicuous cases (the so-called *kombinaty*). Recently, a merger movement among industrial enterprises was started in the Ukraine.[25] The development bears watching, although the motives in this instance seem to be mixed: many of the mergers are horizontal, having been formed to amalgamate what are regarded to be uneconomically small units.

A more topical issue than greater enterprise self-sufficiency is regional autarky. There is a strong bias under Soviet conditions in this direction, for regional autarky may appeal both to the local interests, by easing supply problems, and to central authorities, by reducing planning complexities. In other words, it shortens the lines of communication, and over time may ease the problem of assuring balance. But of course in the short run it is likely to increase supply difficulties elsewhere, and in the long run may also amount to an uneconomic allocation of resources. An important reason for the creation of the "large economic regions" seems to be the countering of autarkic tendencies on the part of the local sovnarkhozy;[26] yet, autarkic development of the large economic regions may now be stimulated.

In sum, imbalance is avoided or reduced in the command economy through greater centralization or by permitting more regional or

OVERCENTRALIZATION

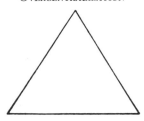
IMBALANCE   LOCAL AUTARKY

sectoral self-sufficiency. Overcentralization is avoided by risking imbalance or allowing autarky. And the suppression of autarky is bought at the cost of a high degree of centralization, or alternatively, of imbalance. We may therefore speak of the command economy's "triangle of hazards," the vertices of which are the three conditions named. (See Figure.) Moving away from one fault brings the

---

[24] See Jan M. Michal, *Central Planning in Czechoslovakia* (Stanford, 1960), pp. 53 ff.
[25] *Экономическая газета*, Dec. 4, 1961, p. 7.
[26] *Ibid.*, June 23, 1961, p. 2.

economy closer, though not necessarily in equal degree, to the other two.

The most recent recentralizing trend[27] is probably a response to a multiplicity of factors: the heightened pressure on resources[28] brought about by increased defense commitments, lags in construction of new capacity in a number of sectors, and the unsatisfactory performance of agriculture; autarkic moves by the sovnarkhozy; and lags in technological progress (in relation to intentions).

Neither the text of the party Program nor the speeches by Khrushchev and others at the 22nd Party Congress foreshadows any significant departure from the present system of planning and economic administration; on the contrary, they amount to its reaffirmation. And despite the traditional bows in the direction of "the role of local authorities" and "enterprise initiative," their general tenor suggests, if anything, stronger central controls for the balancing of plans and in investment and technological policy. Perhaps the only important contrary note was struck by Khrushchev when he said, "For the sake of better plan fulfillment it is necessary to give enterprises greater opportunities to dispose of their profits, and to use the latter more amply to stimulate better work by the enterprise's staff and for the enterprise's expansion."[29] It may be noted that this was the only point in the whole part of the speech dealing with planning and organization that elicited applause, according to the official transcript.

VI

The recovery of agricultural production stands out as one of the most noteworthy economic achievements of the regime since Stalin's death. It was brought about by a combination of measures, on the whole salutary both singly and in combination. One may mention among these the increased investment, the abolition of the MTS and acquisition of their equipment by the kolkhozy, much increased farm prices and the diminution in their multiplicity, certain tax concessions, the introduction of wage-like money pay in the better-to-do kolkhozy, and attempts at cost accounting. The length of this list, if nothing else, indicates determination and considerable flexibility in trying to solve the problem of agriculture. These measures jointly, plus of course the putting of some 100 million acres under the plow, have been instrumental in raising grain production by some 60 per cent, and gross

[27] See above, note 21.

[28] The budget for 1962 (*Правда*, Dec. 7, 1961) increases defense outlay to 13.4 billion rubles, or nearly 45 per cent above the amount originally budgeted for 1961. It is difficult at the moment to say to what extent this is a "real" increase. Note, however, that planned capital investments are to increase in 1962 by 8.1 per cent, against the 12-13 per cent planned for each of the two preceding years, while noncentralized investments are being reduced in absolute amount in comparison with 1961.

[29] *Правда*, Oct. 10, 1961, p. 6.

agricultural output by about 55 per cent, between 1953 and 1960. (These percentages are based on official data which may be appreciably exaggerated for a variety of reasons.) Yet per capita agricultural output is only moderately above the 1928 level and seems to have remained on a plateau since 1958.

Along with the salutary developments a good many doubtful practices have persisted: the imposition of pet projects from above, "campaigning," excessive targets, and, as we have already seen, little change in the authoritarian methods of planning agricultural output and procurements. Similarly, the trend toward kolkhoz "giantism" has continued. By the end of 1960, mostly through amalgamation, the number of kolkhozy was reduced to 44,000—only half as many as at the end of 1955—and the average kolkhoz came to contain nearly 3,000 hectares of plowed land and nearly 400 households.

The party Program in essence pledges to continue the salutary measures mentioned above. Increased money pay, some equalization of incomes among kolkhozy, increased social services to kolkhozniki—these and other policies, if continued, would tend to attenuate the differences between state and collective farms. Nevertheless, the collective farm system is to be retained, according to the Program, for another two decades (though probably progressively diminished in extent), and the private plot is to be similarly preserved. Judging by the Program's targets for agricultural output and productivity, the total agricultural population is to remain virtually stable in absolute numbers over the decade of the sixties, and to decline by 30 to 40 per cent in the succeeding decade. It would thus take considerable resources to raise kolkhoz incomes to sovkhoz levels. It would also be rather costly to abolish the private plot, nuisance though it be to the collective farm. As Newth has shown,[30] as late as 1959 the private sector (of which kolkhoz private plots made up nearly three-fourths the area) still produced about one-third of the total gross agricultural output and nearly one-half of the livestock products. Moreover, crop yields per hectare in the private sector have been 50 to 100 per cent higher than in the socialist (though here too there are questions of statistical reliability).

The agricultural production targets are however so high—2.5-fold increase in gross output by 1970, and 3.5 by 1980—that an aura of unreality surrounds everything the Program and Mr. Khrushchev say about agriculture. If the targets are taken even half seriously by the authorities, we may expect the pressure on the village to mount progressively to the point where the institutional and organizational prospects for agriculture outlined in the Program may well be re-exam-

---

[30] J. A. Newth, "Soviet Agriculture: The Private Sector, 1950-1959," *Soviet Studies,* XIII, No. 2 (Oct., 1961), 160-71.

ined. In fact, the implications are more profound. Success or failure in agriculture is bound to affect the pressure on resources in the economy as a whole, the fortunes of the consumer, the rate of urbanization and industrialization, the sense of haste, and the political climate in the country.[31] The gulf between the peasant's behavior and the regime's national and international aspirations may not be as deep as it was thirty or twenty-five years ago, nor do the peasants dominate the domestic picture as much, but the development and structure of the Soviet economy and the fortunes of the Soviet society have not yet cut themselves entirely loose from dependence on the peasant's will and whim. The reality of the whole Program in large measure depends on whether and how this chasm may be bridged.[32]

[31] Cf. Adam B. Ulam, "The New Face of Soviet Totalitarianism," *World Politics*, XII, No. 3 (April, 1960), 391-412.

[32] *Addendum in proof:* The March, 1962, Plenum of the Central Committee of the CPSU took place since these lines were written. Its proceedings serve to highlight several points made in the present article—among them, the tendency to centralize in response to mounting pressure on resources, a tendency that in this instance may eventually have significant impact beyond the bounds of agriculture itself.

Rationality in the Soviet Economy

HENRI CHAMBRE

The problems of the structure and organization of the Soviet economy
are especially relevant in the period that has followed the reform that
culminated in the creation of the administrative-economic regions and
the 104 *sovnarkhozy* in 1957, and the auxiliary arrangements that have
been made in the years since then. In March, 1961, a conference held
in Moscow and devoted to the planning process placed in the center
of its discussions the problems of division into economic regions. This
suffices to demonstrate the timeliness and great interest that G. Grossman's essay on the structure and organization of the Soviet economy
possesses.[1]

Grossman begins with the declaration that the section of the CPSU
program adopted in 1961 pertaining to the economy includes no concepts or objectives that are genuinely innovations in the realm of institutions, which is one of the essential elements in characterizing any
economy,[2] and he judges that the program ratifies the present situation
and contents itself with projecting it into the future. Moreover, he
adds, to a greater extent than with structural reforms the party today,
as yesterday, is preoccupied with building Communist man. This attitude of immobility, despite certain changes more superficial than real
in nature and only mildly inharmonious with policies in effect before
Stalin's death, is in his view explained by the fact that at the heart of
all the problems of today that the Soviet economy faces—not so different, moreover, from those confronted for the past thirty years—are to
be found the problems of the structure of that economy, or the localization and distribution of power in Soviet society. As for the contradictions in the economy between the era of Stalin and the era of
Khrushchev, they are due to the fact that the decision-makers of the

FATHER CHAMBRE *is director of studies at the École Pratique des Hautes Études
(Sorbonne) and the Institut de Science Économique Appliquée, Paris.*

[1] I have also profited from the early availability of the paper to me to devote to it a
session at the Seminar on the Economy of Slavic Countries of the École Pratique des
Hautes Études, so as to benefit the students, some of whom had visited the USSR for several months on one or more occasions in order to prepare theses or studies on this or that
aspect of the Soviet economy. Although I repeat some of the remarks suggested in the
course of this session, I take full responsibility for the reflections set forth here.

[2] Cf. François Perroux, *Le capitalisme*, "Que sais-je?" series (3rd ed.; Paris: Presses Universitaires de France, 1958), pp. 13-14.

Soviet economy have excessively reduced or suppressed the scope of the market, monetary exchange, and mobility of labor, thus resolving to place themselves outside economic rationality on the day when the command economy of the USSR becomes a more and more complex economy.

Without contesting the validity of an analysis that relies on solid studies, of which Grossman has given us numerous and pertinent examples, perhaps one may seek to offer some slight modifications of his judicious conclusions by way of a few marginal glosses concerning their exact scope.

Doubtless the essay, whose points that seem to us essential we have just recapitulated, does not *explicitly* embrace a comparison between American (or Western) economies and the Soviet economy. However, such a vantage point does not seem entirely absent; it is, I believe, *implicitly* contained in the analysis in question.

Now, in strict logic and to the extent that the question is not one of a comparison between economic *potentials,* it appears that it could only with difficulty be acceptable to compare even implicitly the American (or Western) economy of today and the Soviet economy of today. Despite the recent progress made by the latter, they are only partially comparable. In any analysis of this sort, it is useful to introduce the time factor. Indeed, if it is usual to emphasize that the ideological factor still plays a large role in the development of the Soviet economy,[3] it may be desirable to recall that this factor also played an important role in the industrial development of France in the mid-nineteenth century with St. Simonian doctrine, and that at least for close to a century in the development of the American economy the idea of the frontier, recently recalled to the voters by President Kennedy, and the myth of industrial progress have played a not less considerable role. Concerning this last proposition I wish here to cite as evidence (and I hope it will not appear too dubious to professional economists) only the descriptions of Sherwood Anderson in his fiction—particularly in his story *Poor White.*

In addition, concerning this particular factor, it may be well also to note that ideology has a greater importance and a greater power to induce changes in a country where it is guarded and carried by an organized party than it does in a country where it constitutes the common denominator of manufacturers or bankers—St. Simonians or not—but where it does not depend on any protective organism.

---

[3] Cf. J. Hersch, *Idéologie et réalités* (Paris: Plon, 1956), pp. 24 and 27. M. Rubel, "La croissance du capital en U.R.S.S. Essai de confrontation critique," *Économie Appliquée,* No. 2/3, 1957. Alexander Gerschenkron in *Continuity and Change in Russian and Soviet Thought,* ed. E. J. Simmons (Cambridge, Mass.: Harvard University Press, 1957), p. 107, and in *The Transformation of Russian Society,* ed. C. E. Black (Cambridge: Harvard University Press, 1960), p. 61.

In the thirty years of its swift industrialization, whose haste is well explained by the features of the structure and organization of its economy, as Grossman emphasizes, the USSR passed through a transformation which has taken about two centuries in the Western countries and the United States. What is more, the Soviet Union has been making the transition from a rural civilization to an urban and industrial civilization under the least favorable initial (and doubtless still existing) conditions, not only because of the failure of the agrarian reforms of 1861-1912 but also because of the impermeability to ideologies and of the homogeneity of the Russian peasantry—where the peasant is called *krest'ianin* (Christian)—which makes G. Gurvitch say that as a result, "it was concluded rather naturally that those who inhabited cities were not Christians, but were to a certain extent anti-Christian, representing Antichrist."[4]

Grossman justly remarks that the more or less conscious contempt of the factors of market, money, and mobility must lead to difficulties after the Soviet economy has reached the point of takeoff. But perhaps it would be well to modify this assertion to a slight extent when we are told that the "three M's" offer the largest field of operation and constitute the greatest stimulant of innovation, accumulation, and growth in a decentralized economy. Other factors have operated and are operating, which are far from being negligible and which it is well to consider in embarking on an analysis in depth of the mechanisms of a centralized economy. As François Perroux writes, *"force, power,* and *compulsion* are constitutionally foreign to the modern science of economics and the most recent developments in it have not succeeded in integrating them."[5] Nevertheless, no study of economic reality which endeavors to be concrete can dispense with the careful examination of the role of these factors. The historians of the great modern trusts or the biographers of the captains of industry of yesterday would suffice to call attention to them. It is the question of the rationality of economic activity that thus appears.

Doubtless one would agree with Grossman in pointing out that the criteria of economic rationality serve as the object of a strained discussion among Soviet economists,[6] of which this journal has taken note in a recent issue,[7] and that a Quarrel of Ancients and Moderns has appeared in Soviet economic circles. However, one may ask further

4 Cf. Georges Gurvitch, "Classes urbaines et classes rurales" in *Villes et campagnes,* collection published under the direction of G. Friedmann (Paris: A. Colin, 1953), p. 120.

5 F. Perroux, "Esquisse d'une théorie de l'économie dominante," *Économie Appliquée,* No. 2/3, 1948, p. 243.

6 Cf. "Rationalité et croissances économiques soviétiques," articles by Alec Nove, H. Chambre, *Cahiers de l'I.S.E.A.,* "Économie planifiée" series, No. 104 (August, 1960).

7 Cf. Robert W. Campbell, "Marx, Kantorovich, and Novozhilov: *Stoimost'* versus Reality," *Slavic Review,* XX, No. 3 (Oct., 1961).

if the pattern of Soviet economic behavior is of a sort so different from that of "capitalist" economic behavior—not that which is commonly described in the manuals and treatises on political economy but that which occurs *in reality* if we accept the analyses of François Perroux and Albert O. Hirschman.[8] From these indeed it appears that certain sectors of the economy or of industry are created or developed because they exercise "an exceptional de-stabilizing influence," because they are "a motor of development and not at all, without addition, a force of growth."[9]

It is a fact now well known that the successes of Soviet growth since 1930 do not depend on a property peculiar to long-term or current planning. They are linked with the allocation of investment to priority industrial sectors—yesterday the electrical, iron and steel, and coal industries, today chemical industries. They are linked with the creation of regions designed to stimulate and give an impulse to movement, poles of development or *bases* which play a role of movement, whose significance often appears long before their creation. Thus beginning in 1928/29 the First Five-Year Plan emphasized the importance that the creation of what became the Kuzbas[10] would have for the economic development of Western and Central Siberia. To these two primary factors must be added that of the considerable intellectual investments made by the USSR, even if their effects are not always well co-ordinated and directed. Finally, or more exactly at the same moment, there enter specific environmental factors: modification of psychological and social structures, stimulation and compulsion, which are too well known to require extended comment here.

In these conditions would it not be well to consider the economic systems under consideration as particular cases of that "generalized economy" that Maurice Merleau-Ponty[11] foresaw or that "fundamental economy" of which F. Perroux has spoken to us since 1943.[12] As H. Bartoli, professor at the Faculty of Law and Economic Sciences at the University of Paris, insists, "it is not at all a question of maintaining that social structures are analogous in different regimes or that systems must be reconciled in *a sort of syncretism wherein their strengths would weaken one another,* but of affirming that *in their struggles* these systems may reciprocally influence one another without the outcome's *being foreseeable or their contacts with underdeveloped coun-*

[8] Cf. F. Perroux, "L'univers économique et social," *Encyclopédie française,* Vol. IX (Paris, 1960). A. O. Hirschman, *The Strategy of Economic Development* (New Haven: Yale University Press, 1958). Alec Nove, *The Soviet Economy* (London: Allen & Unwin, 1961).

[9] F. Perroux, *La coexistence pacifique* (Paris: Presses Universitaires de France, 1958), II, 478.

[10] Cf. H. Chambre, "Le développement du bassin du Kuznetsk," *Cahiers de l'I.S.E.A.,* "Économie planifiée" series, No. 100 (April, 1960).

[11] Cf. M. Merleau-Ponty, *Les aventures de la dialectique* (Paris: Gallimard, 1955), p. 303.

[12] Cf. F. Perroux, *La valeur* (Paris: Presses Universitaires de France, 1943), p. 587.

tries requiring of either an excess of effort and inventiveness. The generalized economy is a restructuring of the concepts of science, responsive to massive and swift changes in the economic experiment that is under way. It is stimulated, attracted, compelled by a vision common to the Western societies, an economy without scarcity and a society without compulsion."[13]

Agreeing with Grossman in not believing that the Stalinian schema of development was an absolute necessity for the USSR for the period from 1930 to 1950, and emphasizing as he does the errors in method and the dilemmas to which it led, one would yet regard the slow changes in the economic policy of the USSR appearing thereafter, from the era of Stalin to the era of Khrushchev, not as a step backwards or a step towards the adoption of practices of the "capitalist" type, but as more or less fortunate attempts to improve, in a developing situation, an exact pattern of economic behavior, thanks to a more precise analysis of the economic functions in every industrial society.

Indeed, at the heart of all the more or less permanent problems encountered by the Soviet economy, there is that of communication—and this is found at every level of that economy. Moreover, Grossman also points this out in noting that the central question is that of the localization and distribution of power in the heart of society. It is true when one examines the motives that have led to the creation of the 104 economic *and* administrative regions in 1957 and to the imposition above certain of them of super-*sovnarkhozy* in 1961. It is true when one studies the manner in which the plans of production are prepared, the investments distributed, and the allocations of industrial goods made. It is still the case when one considers the changes carried out in agriculture or problems of industrial enterprise.

The solution of the problem of communication is linked with that of decentralization. Is it genuinely envisaged? One wonders, for in different sectors mentioned it is permissible to invoke the remark that a jurist made recently at the end of a careful study of the nature and function of collective agreements in the USSR: "The interventions of the law-maker have remained until now outside the wishes of the doctrine, and they are still too recent for it to be possible to appreciate his efforts."[14] But at the same time, one should note that, under the forms characteristic of each system, this problem of communication is relevant as much to the Western industrialized economies and societies as to the Soviet economy and society which is in the course of industrializing.

---

[13] H. Bartoli, in *Esprit*, No. 1, 1962, pp. 121-22.

[14] L. Greyffié de Bellecombe, *Les conventions collectives de travail en Union Soviétique*, in the collection "Études sur l'économie et la sociologie des pays slaves," École Pratique des Hautes Études (Paris: Mouton, 1958), p. 147.

Such are some of the remarks suggested by Grossman's essay, which the brevity of the time available to me prevents developing at greater length. I would repeat in closing that these marginal glosses should not conceal from the eyes of the reader the full importance of the paper here considered.

The More Answers, the More Questions

DAVID GRANICK

Economists, like other social scientists, usually find it easier to generalize boldly about their field in the absence of information than when data begin to multiply. The broad historical sweep of writers such as Ricardo and Marx cannot be found among economists of the twentieth century; when these wish to play the game of historical generalization, they are forced to do so within the very narrow confines of *caeteris paribus*. Progress in knowledge exacts its penalties.

Professor Grossman's paper is most interesting, particularly, in my opinion, in its treatment of demonetization in the Soviet economy. But what I should like to do here is to discuss not so much the paper itself as its underpinnings.

Grossman's paper, it seems to me, rests on a model of the Soviet economy which is best viewed as a guide to further research, which in turn may be expected to modify this model substantially. Considered as such, it seems to me to ask the proper questions and still today to be a useful guide in our present state of ignorance. But it would be presumptuous to treat the model as the only one that can properly be drawn from our current knowledge of the Soviet economy, and I fear that some incautious readers might give it this interpretation.

Let me present my understanding of Grossman's underlying picture of the Soviet economy, rounding out his presentation with much that I think is implicit. I hope that I am not reading too much into Grossman's article.

1. The production goals of the economy are centrally determined, and the important ones are fairly restricted in number at any period of time. It is the limitation on the number of such goals that creates the strong resemblance to a "war economy." In both cases, the objective is to maximize the production of a relatively small number of items subject to the constraint of producing a sufficient quantity of other goods and services (consumer goods and leisure in particular) to permit the continued functioning of the economy. The success of the economy is judged by its central planners in terms of its production of the few "important" goods, and by its production of sufficient items of other sorts to avoid prejudicing future growth in the output of the "priority" items.

MR. GRANICK *is professor of economics at the University of Wisconsin.*

2. In view of these social objectives of the economy, a "command economy" system of operations is employed. In this system, the central authorities spell out their production goals in physical terms and provide in physical units the various inputs needed to realize these targets. Integration of the economy is thus carried out centrally; there is no provision of, *and reliance upon,* a standard (such as money) which could provide a decisive guide to decentralized decision-making.

3. Although this command-economy system is not pure, it dominates the "important" segments of the economy. It determines what should be produced and how it should be produced. It effectively eliminates decentralized decision-making by executives of production units (e.g., heads of factories) as well as by the major owners of nonsocialized production inputs (namely, households which provide the labor for the economy). Only in such an unimportant area as the allocation of a predetermined volume and mix of consumers' goods among individual households is a market economy allowed to function; for central authorities renounce the command-economy tool of consumer rationing.

4. A command-economy system is inherently less efficient than a market economy. By "inefficiency" is meant the notion that at any moment of time, and with identical production inputs, the production-possibilities curve of a market economy would be beyond (i.e., to the right) of the production-possibilities curve of a command economy. In short, with a given amount of resources, a market economy can produce more goods and services owing to superior organization.

5. The high rate of growth of the Soviet economy, measured against that of market economies, is accounted for by the superior abilities of a command economy to mobilize resources for a restricted group of ends. In the Russian case, this has meant high investment in productive resources. (Here we set to one side all transitory factors such as the existence of a stock of social capital which could be exploited more intensively, the improvement of production techniques cheaply through use of technology already employed abroad, etc. These factors are a result of the stage of development rather than of the socio-economic system). This mobilization of resources for limited ends is simply a way of describing a process of exploitation of households, which are made to provide increased effort without a proper return in increased volume of consumer goods and services.

6. Since a command economy is less efficient than a market economy, the Soviet economy—if it is to grow at merely the same speed as a market economy would in the same environment—must engage in more such exploitation. Faster growth is attained only by still greater exploitation.

7. The Soviet leaders' current conservatism implies the continuation

of the "inefficient" co-ordinating mechanism of a command economy as contrasted with that of a market economy. Presumably, the justification for such conservatism is the continued desire to exploit the consumer in the interests of growth.

I find the above outline of the workings of the Soviet economy fairly persuasive. But it seems to me that there are some very difficult problems involved in evaluating it.

First of all, it must be recognized that Grossman is properly concerned in his model with those features which have been stable in the Soviet schema and which seem inherent to it, rather than with what has been transitory and an *ad hoc* response to outside events. Thus, in judging the model, we must distinguish between what is inherent and what has been accidental in Soviet reality. Such a distinction is far from simple, as I shall try to show with two examples.

Grossman treats Soviet direct controls over labor mobility and choice of occupation as one of the major features of the command economy. The evidence that direct controls over labor were important consists primarily of the two following groups of phenomena: forced labor for political prisoners, beginning on a large scale in the early 1930's and continuing through the mid-1950's; and general labor restrictions, which began at the end of 1938, were stiffened in mid-1940, and tailed off in the early 1950's. However, these two types of labor controls are subject to alternative interpretations.

Grossman's interpretation is that they are manifestations of a command economy, and inherent in the Soviet demonetization of the economy. By implication, the movement away from such controls in the mid-1950's is in the direction of a different type of economic system.[1]

Alternatively, such controls can be interpreted as purely transitory features of the Soviet economy. Forced labor can be considered not a desired means of placing labor in specific jobs and controlling its mobility, but a response to the aftermaths of collectivization and of Stalin's purges. Generalized labor controls can be treated as a means of war-preparedness, of fighting the war, and of recovery thereafter; in short, as a transitory phenomenon much like consumer rationing. In this interpretation, the second half of the 1950's represents a return to the Soviet "norm."

Grossman's treatment of agriculture contains the same difficulty of analysis. The Stalinist formula for industrialization had as one of its cornerstones, he tells us, collectivization. This was a kind of mass enserfment and "permitted a large unrequited extraction of agricul-

---

[1] Such an implication is in contradiction to Grossman's view of Soviet conservatism. But it is a radicalism of five to ten years ago rather than of the present.

tural surplus." Here is an orthodox view of the effect of collectivization, which seems to imply a decline in the peasant standard of living
—at least, relative to farm output.

In a sense, this is not a bad description. Collectivization certainly
accompanied, and probably made possible under the conditions of the
early 1930's, a sharp reduction in the proportion of agricultural produce consumed on the farm. It resulted in a wide dispersion of
incomes among collective farmers, depending on their principal crop
and on their closeness to urban centers, and it effectively prevented
them from moving to richer collective farms. It was an institutional
change which clearly was forced upon the peasantry rather than welcomed by it.

Yet there are other phenomena which blur the picture. According
to Professor Bergson, real income per worker on the collective farms
was—in 1937—much the same as real income per industrial worker.[2]
In this regard—and probably also with regard to per capita consumption—collective farmers on an average stood in a better relation to the
urban population than they had in 1928.[3] Although 1937 was an
excellent crop year, and this fact probably altered income distribution
in favor of the peasants as compared with earlier years of the 1930's,
Bergson's figures for the years after 1937 do not indicate any shift from
the 1937 relationship.[4]

"Enserfment" may have occurred in the sense of preventing movement to other farms. But, in the 1930's, peasants seem to have been
more or less free to decide whether or not to go to the city,[5] and
certainly the movement to urban areas was far more rapid than it had
been earlier. This urban movement seems to represent the same sort
of labor mobility which has occurred in market economies, and to be
the exact reverse of the "pigeon-holing" of the individual of which
Grossman writes.

Which are the relevant years to consider for this analysis? Is 1937
an anomalous year, and are the restraints on peasant income of the
early 1930's and of the 1940's the "typical" situation? Or is the 1937
pattern and the developments of the 1950's really "typical," with the
other years representing deviations from Soviet "normal"?

In trying to answer these questions, it seems to me that we cannot
get very far by looking at the Soviet economy alone. For we are not

---

[2] Abram Bergson, *The Real National Income of Soviet Russia Since 1928* (Cambridge,
Mass.: Harvard University Press, 1961), pp. 118-20. Throughout this paper I lean on
Bergson's results. It should be pointed out that other investigators, Dr. Naum Jasny in
particular, come to different conclusions. Bergson's book was probably not available in its
final form when Grossman wrote his article.

[3] *Ibid.*, pp. 256-57.

[4] *Ibid.*, pp. 255-57.

[5] *Ibid.*, p. 120.

asking historical questions about what actually happened, but rather we are trying to present a model of Soviet-type economies. Yet we are testing this model against the historical experience embodied in a single case study: that of the USSR. Naturally we cannot distinguish between the "accidental" and the "normal." There are no degrees of freedom in our test of the model.

Is the Soviet economy properly viewed as a "war economy," concentrating on a limited number of ends and, in particular, sacrificing consumption to growth in investment and military goods?

If we contrast the share of household consumption in Soviet "real" gross national product with that found in the United States[6] or in Western Europe, we can only agree. If we regard the slight increase in per capita consumption between 1928 and 1950—and the fact that in the latter year per capita consumption was still at about the 1913 level[7]—we must again agree.

But suppose that we take a different view. Suppose that we say that we should ignore the years between 1937 and the war, on the ground that their developments were determined by the "accidental" factors of the Purges and military preparation, and also the years of the war and postwar recovery. Then we compress together, as if they directly followed each other in time, the periods 1928-37 and 1949 to the present.[8] Even excluding communal services, 1937 per capita national consumption was between 3 per cent less and 22 per cent more than that of 1928—depending on whether we use 1937 or 1928 adjusted market prices. By 1955, per capita consumption in 1937 adjusted market prices was 60 per cent greater than in 1937,[9] and it has continued to rise since.

From this viewpoint, and using the 1937 adjusted market prices which are much less favorable to the Russians than the 1928 prices, one can conclude that the Russian experience is that of cutting per capita consumption for an initial period of eight years, and then commencing a rate of growth in per capita consumption faster than that experienced in the United States during any reasonably-long and sensibly-chosen historical period.[10] The Russian "model," stripped of extraneous years, here appears to be geared to rapid growth in all sectors of gross national product—including the consumption goods sector—after only a very brief period of "war economy" concentration needed to start the mechanism in motion. To quote Jasny, "If, already in 1937,

[6] *Ibid.*, Table 76, p. 277.
[7] *Ibid.*, pp. 7-8, 252-55.
[8] Admittedly, a treatment of the Purges as "accidental" is an extreme view. Bergson computes total 1949 consumption as roughly equal to the 1937 level. *Ibid.*, pp. 165 and 304.
[9] *Ibid.*, p. 252.
[10] Cf. *ibid.*, p. 284, for respective rates of growth.

consumers' incomes could have been . . . equal to those of 1928, sacrifices of the population for the great drive, if any, could have been only minor and very temporary."[11] Unless we give an enormous weight to the results of these first eight years, we can even go so far as to treat the Soviet economy as a consumer-oriented economy—even though certainly not one governed according to consumers' sovereignty.

What can be said about the efficiency of the Soviet "command economy"? Is Grossman correct in treating it as inherently less efficient than a market economy?

If we consider the growth in gross national product in the Soviet Union per employed worker—irrespective of whether he be urban or rural—as measured in Bergson's 1937 ruble factor costs, the 1928-40 rate of growth is a bare 1.0 per cent. But the 1950-55 growth rate is 6.1 per cent. In contrast, the American rate during selected periods since 1869 has varied between 1.6 and 1.9 per cent.[12] Even if we were to make allowances for the much faster rate of growth of capital goods in the USSR, efficiency (measured here as the output/input ratio) seems to have grown a good deal more rapidly in Russia during the 1950's than it has in America. Moreover, it can be argued that the decade of the 1950's is the relevant one for the Soviet Union, since the major growth in product of the 1930's was in the intangible products of a skilled and urbanized labor force and of the creation of institutions which made for observable, physical growth in later years.

As in all our other instances, however, a good case can be made for the opposite viewpoint. One may point to a host of special, transitory factors which permitted this rapid growth in Soviet efficiency during the 1950's—and so deny that such efficiency is "intrinsic" in the Soviet system. As indicated above, it seems to this writer that the nub of the problem is that we are dealing with a single case study—and that no conclusions are possible from it as to what is normal to the system.

Grossman points to a wide group of problems which have plagued the Soviet economy throughout the period of the Plans and which he considers—correctly, in my opinion—to be characteristic of a command economy. The failure of Soviet leaders to grasp the nettle of a shift to a market economy means, in his view, that these problems must continue.

Here, indeed, is conservatism on the part of the Soviet leaders. But the important question is whether it is "blind" or "sound" conservatism. Any system of operating an economy, or a smaller organization

---

[11] Naum Jasny, "On the Wrong Track," *Soviet Studies,* VIII, No. 1 (July, 1956), 50. Jasny made this statement as part of his complete denial that the 1937 data supported conclusions in any way resembling those of Bergson.

[12] Bergson, *op. cit.,* p. 271.

for that matter, has its inherent deficiencies. A policy of sound conservatism would appear to be that of recognizing this fact and of reconciling oneself to the ineradicable problems which develop out of what is considered to be a basically sound approach. Such acceptance might well be combined with a constant struggle against the difficulties which arise, not in the hope of eliminating them but rather with the objective of keeping abuses from rapidly spreading as they would otherwise tend to do.

A parallel may be sought in the American struggle against monopolization and the restraint of trade. Our antimonopoly efforts go back to 1890 and earlier; if anything, they have increased in intensity over time; yet one can claim little more for their results than that they have helped to prevent abuses from becoming more serious than they were originally. Following Grossman, we might then consider monopolization and restraint of trade as endemic in the American market economy. Would this view of the situation necessarily push us to opt for measures which may remove these inefficiencies—such as eliminating the market economy and private enterprise entirely, or alternatively breaking up all companies which attain more than a predetermined small share of the market for their products? Might we not be wiser to accept monopolization and restraint of trade as inevitable tendencies of the system, and to set the policy objective of merely holding their development in check? Clearly, our choice should depend upon what we think would be lost by a policy of attempting to reform the economic system in such a way as to eliminate these tendencies.

Actually, it seems to me that Grossman's dichotomy between a market economy and a command economy is one which must be used very carefully. This is because any modern industrial society operating under a market economy has major command-economy sectors within it. Individual companies, and often groups of companies under common control, usually comprise command economies. (Individual households are also command economies.) Issues of centralization versus decentralization in the administration of these companies are the same as those the Soviet leaders face: decentralization always threatens to lead to suboptimization at the expense of the best interests of the organization as a whole. The distinctive feature of a market economy is that these many "command economies" of individual corporations and households are linked together by the market instead of being made part of a single giant command economy.

Within major corporations in the United States, efforts at decentralization have usually revolved around attempts to partially change the administration of the corporation itself from the structure of a command economy to a market economy. But there has always been reluctance to push this too far—the same reluctance that one finds in the Soviet Union.[13] In recent years, the trend in American corporations is generally thought to be toward renewed centralization.

What seems distinctive about the Soviet Union, then, would appear to be the *size* of its command economy. If this is so, a small command-economy country such as Bulgaria is almost as *basically* different from the USSR as is a giant corporation run internally on command-economy lines but operating within a national market economy.

As Grossman correctly points out, the problems inherent in the command-economy organization of the USSR must inevitably increase rapidly as the economy grows, that is, as size increases. But the means at hand to wrestle with these problems are also improving. The use of computers—not so much today as, perhaps, in ten or twenty years—should make a truly revolutionary difference here.

In view of the current technological shift in man's ability to process information centrally, it seems to me clear that the ability of command economies of any given size to function relatively efficiently should improve rapidly. It is by no means clear whether this change will be more or less than sufficient to compensate for the growing complexity of the problem in an economy which is growing in size and complexity as rapidly as the USSR. Depending upon one's evaluation of the relative efficiency of the Soviet command economy at the present time as compared with what a market economy could do in the same circumstances—and, as I have argued, opinions may well differ sharply as to this—one might consider that the Soviet leaders would be well advised to place their bets and to concentrate their efforts on improving the functioning of their command economy rather than on shifting to a market-economy organization of their system.

In short, we—and doubtless the Soviet leaders as well—know too little about the workings of their command-economy system to be categorical as to the direction of change which is most likely to promote efficiency. In such a situation, economic conservatism is far from an irrational policy.

[13] Cf. the classic account of prewar decentralization within General Motors in Peter Drucker, *The Concept of the Corporation* (New York: John Day Co., 1946). Drucker reports that the decentralized divisions seemed to produce the best managers but that the centralized divisions were the most profitable.

Reply

GREGORY GROSSMAN

In his interesting and stimulating comment, Father Chambre addresses himself, with justice, to certain important points which were treated too tersely in my essay (for lack of space, I prefer to think). It is especially gratifying that he, the author of *Le Marxisme en Union Soviétique* (Paris, 1955), took this opportunity to re-emphasize the enormous importance of ideological factors in the shaping of the institutions of *both* the industrial West and the USSR, at the same time carefully pointing out the major difference between an ideology "guarded and carried [and, one might add, forcibly imposed—G.G.] by an organized party" and one that "does not depend on any protective organism." Chambre is also quite right, of course, in calling attention to the role of "force, power, and compulsion" and other factors that often fall outside the purview of conventional economic analysis. In varying extent and degree they have been present in all major industrializing experiences, whether enhancing or obstructing the extension of the market, the growth of labor mobility, and the intensification of the money economy. Moreover, the "three M's" have not of course been the prime movers of industrialization in some ultimate sense even in the West. Rather, they have been at once the concomitants of the industrializing process and the necessary conditions within which the creative and accumulating forces, rooted in some specific ideology, found their expression. Yet, in Stalinist industrialization, the elements of force and compulsion have been so conspicuous and comprehensive, and (as I tried to show) were, moreover, used deliberately to push back the scope of the "three M's," that we may be justified in speaking of a qualitatively different pattern in this regard.

Chambre's observation that Soviet economic growth has been not unlike "capitalist" growth, in the sense of an uneven advance of different industries and regions, is quite valid. In the Soviet instance we should, however, distinguish between the unequal priorities deliberately assigned to certain sectors and regions, and the equally real but unintended bottlenecks and "disproportions" that arise as a result of the superposition of rigid priorities and clumsy planning on generally overcommitted resources.[1] The former is an integral part of the Soviet

[1] For a closely related discussion of "tautness" in Soviet planning see Holland Hunter, "On Planning to Catch Up" in Reuben E. Slesinger, ed., *Trends in Economics* (Pittsburgh, 1960), pp. 1-19.

philosophy of industrialization; the latter is sternly disapproved by the governing doctrine, though a reality none the less. In Soviet theory, bottlenecks should not arise in a "correctly" planned and managed economy.

While granting that bottlenecks and uneven development may play a very positive role in spurring "capitalist" development, their salutary role in the Soviet case would seem to be less certain. We should distinguish here between the case where investment decisions are dispersed and may require "de-stabilizing influences" to respond amply, and the case (such as the Soviet) where investment planning is highly centralized, relies on a different "motor of development," and presumably contains the possibility, by virtue of concentrated information, of avoiding serious bottlenecks.

Professor Granick is quite right in stressing the very formidable uncertainties that beset one in any attempt to generalize Soviet experience, to distill, so to say, an ideal type out of the succession of emergencies and transitory events that link together to form the history of the Soviet economy. And yet, I would submit, the task is not so hopeless as might appear at first glance. First, Soviet institutions were transplanted more or less wholly to about a dozen countries in Europe and Asia after the last war. We can now discern regularities on an international plane, and they are quite pronounced. Further, the institutional differences that exist between these countries may be helpful as well as bothersome in this regard, for they subject the regularities to additional tests and heighten their significance where they stand out. Secondly, the same can be said of the Soviet economy itself in its various phases and at its various stages since 1929. In other words, we have perhaps more than just one case to generalize from. Taking both the international and the temporal dimensions into account, we may regard our sample as consisting of from a dozen to several dozen cases, depending on how we divide them up in time. Some phenomena appear wherever and whenever there exists anything like a "Soviet-type" economy; the sellers' market is a good example. Other phenomena, for example, extreme controls over nominally free labor such as those represented by the 1940 decrees, appear only at some times and places, and their relevance to the basic "model" or "system" is more difficult to define. Granick's questions on this very point are legitimate.

However, in my essay I attempted to deal more with the actual Soviet experience than with an ideal type. Granick grants me the scholar's compliment of reading a higher degree of abstraction and generalization into my remarks than I intended to convey. Thus, I would hesitate to maintain that "a command-economy system is inherently less efficient [in a static sense—G.G.] than a market economy." True, I should think that the Soviet economy scores very low on static efficiency (which is not at all incompatible with a high growth rate) and that many of its most bedeviling problems would all but vanish if a reasonably effective market mechanism were to take over. But the market mechanism would bring with it other difficulties, as the Yugoslavs have discovered. One may well doubt that *these* would be as detrimental to static efficiency as the present Soviet ones. Nonetheless, as every Western economist knows, the market mechanism does not per se assure a secure location on (or even reasonably close to) the production-possibility surface (translation for non-economists: most efficient utilization of the given resources and technology in the near term).[2]

Later Granick uses the notion of efficiency in the sense of the annual growth rate of the gross national product. But we might also think of "dynamic efficiency" as the relation between the growth rate and the resources contributing to the growth (rate of real saving, expenditure on education and training, percentage growth of the labor force, especially the nonagricultural labor force). Viewed from this angle, the dynamic efficiency of the Soviet economy would not seem to have been especially high even during the 1950's. Of course, the high growth rate as such has been chiefly a function of the large proportion of total resources devoted to growth (plus certain very distinct "advantages of backwardness"). If a high growth rate is indeed desirable, then the question boils down to whether a comparable pro- portion of resources cannot be mobilized by a politically authoritarian regime operating through a market economy rather than a command economy. The experience of other countries since the last war—Yugo- slavia, as well as a number of nonsocialist countries, some of which are not even authoritarian—would seem to indicate that this is not impossible.

There is no space here to comment adequately on Granick's discus- sion of the changes in per capita consumption since 1928.[3] (Nor am I sure that the actual record in this regard is crucial to the discussion in my article). I should merely like to mention that their precise inter- pretation is greatly complicated by the concurrent rapid urbanization of the population and commercialization of consumption. As we

---

[2] Incidentally, there seems' to be some terminological difference between us. For in- stance, I would hesitate to say (as does Granick in par. 3) that in the Soviet case "a market economy is allowed to function" because the "predetermined volume and mix of con- sumers' goods" is sold unrationed (and therefore presumably at more or less equilibrium prices). Following established usage, I should rather characterize this as a situation of free consumers' choice but not one in which the market mechanism operates decisively. I would also rather not associate myself with the phrase "exploitation of households" (par. 5, and cf. par. 7), the strictly economic meaning of which is not clear to me.

[3] Indeed, I did not yet have Bergson's valuable study of the Soviet real national income at my disposal when I was writing the article.

know, the proportion of urban population rose from 18 per cent in 1926 to 50 per cent in 1961.

Granick's last point I heartily endorse. For the Soviet leaders, economic conservatism is far from an irrational policy, in the sense in which conservatism is usually rational for the "ins."

THREE

The Development of Modern Russian Literature

HUGH McLEAN

Literature is clearly the messiest of the arts, the most protean, the most confused in its relation to "life." One envies the musicologist: except for vague references, in certain periods, to the emotions supposedly expressed by a given passage or work (especially when accompanied by a literary text), and perhaps an occasional cuckoo song, the musicologist can conveniently ignore the world outside his art. Music is an aesthetic organization of man-made sounds, and that is that. The student of the history of music, unless he is concerned with such things as composers' biographies, can afford to remain entirely within his medium, studying its structures and shapes, the succession and development of its styles.

But for the literary historian "life" is more complicated. To be sure, literature may be defined with similar neatness as an aesthetic organization of language, and it is certainly the responsibility of the literary historian—one too often neglected in some periods—to study rigorously the structures and development of these verbal organizations. But language, the medium of literature, has a dual nature not possessed by pure sound: it is referential, symbolic. A novel or poem is an aesthetic organization not only of words as things in themselves but through them of the referents of these words, which are usually phenomena connected with "life," the world of reality outside art. Thus a novel becomes an organization of something which stands for, or looks like, life—for instance, human characters and their fates.

The complex relationship between literature and life has been given a great variety of different interpretations in different literatures at different periods, not only by critics and aestheticians but by readers and writers themselves. Ideas on this subject are part of the ambiance of literature, its habitat, so to speak—the attitudes toward it and expectations from it of its producers and consumers. These in turn can hardly fail to affect the nature of the product.

MR. McLEAN is professor of Russian language and literature and chairman of the Department of Slavic Languages and Literatures at the University of Chicago.

It is not the epistemological problem—the degree of correspondence between the "reality" reflected in a work of literature and the reality outside—that has concerned most writers and readers, but rather the question of the function or use of literature in life. What is literature for? What, if any, are its proper uses in the life of the individual or of society? Answers to these questions have varied greatly but may be reduced to three general functions.

First, *aesthetic*. The function of literature is to provide its readers with aesthetic gratification. It has no other obligation, and questions of "truth" and effect on the world are irrelevant to it. Reality is a storehouse from which an author may draw "materials" which he then shapes to suit his artistic design, perhaps modifying them in the process. But the goal is the work of art itself, and there is no contrary line of force moving outward from art into life.

Second, *cognitive*. The work of literature embodies, reflects, and perhaps analyzes life, and through the work of art the reader derives knowledge of the world. The reader's purpose is not to experience or know the work of art itself but to know the world by means of it. In this case, of course, the epistemological question of the "truth" of art becomes crucial.

Third, *didactic*. Here a line of force radiates outward from the work of art into "life": its goal is to influence the reader, to change him, or through him to effect changes in the real world. The work of literature not only reflects or duplicates reality but judges it and seeks to amend it.

Obviously these categories are not mutually exclusive, and more than one function may be served by the same work. Furthermore, the aesthetic function is perhaps not quite of the same order as the other two. Every work of art by definition must serve an aesthetic function; the question is whether it fulfills, or is believed to fulfill, other "external" functions as well.

It seems to me that different periods in the history of Russian literature may be usefully characterized in terms of the prevalence of one or another of these functions, and that this prevalence may have something to do with the preponderance of certain genres and styles. Obviously I make no claim to originality either for the above categories or for their applications to Russian literature. I only hope that the following bird's-eye view may be illuminating.

Throughout most of the eighteenth century in Russia readers and especially writers placed enormous stress on the extra-aesthetic uses of literary art. This stress did not lead, however, as it did toward the middle of the nineteenth century, to any denial or minimization of the aesthetic or formal side of literature. Viewed retrospectively, the most notable literary achievement of the eighteenth century was undoubtedly the assimilation of all the major literary genres then current in the European tradition and the elaboration of a linguistic vehicle adequate to them. These were no mean achievements, and eighteenth-century writers deserve more credit for them than they often receive; few people realize how impossible the accomplishments of the nineteenth century would have been without the tremendous pioneering work that had gone before. In any case, such formal, "technical" questions as versification, the stylistic classification of the Slavo-Russian vocabulary, and the assignment of these classes to the appropriate genres were discussed publicly and without apology by writers in the eighteenth century. A century later they would become taboo.

But probably in the minds of eighteenth-century readers and writers too the external "uses" of literature loomed even larger than its formal organization. One might say that the historic "task" of the eighteenth century, as far as culture was concerned, was to accomplish the westernization of the Russian court and the Russian gentry. Literature was one of the principal tools for carrying out this task. It was an agent of civilization and enlightenment. The Russian rulers had to be taught European standards of manners and taste and European ideals of civic virtue, and the Russian *dvorianin* had to be taught what it meant to be a proper European gentleman.

Trediakovsky's choice for translation into dactylic hexameters of Fénélon's didactic novel *Télémaque* (itself written expressly for the purpose of inculcating ideas of civic virtue and responsibility in the young Duke of Burgundy) was indicative of the kind of influence he hoped to exert. To Trediakovsky, as to many of his contemporaries in Russia and the West, one of the great opportunities of literature was to administer "lessons to kings." Properly enlightened, the monarch could convert his kingdom to a realm of reason and virtue. It remained only to enlighten him. Lomonosov's innumerable odes written for various ceremonial occasions in the reign of Elizabeth were designed to impress upon her in as solemn a manner as possible both her responsibilities and her opportunities to emulate the great work begun by her father. Catherine II, herself a practitioner of the literary art, carried on the "lesson to kings" tradition with her fable of the "rose without prickles that stings not"—an emblem of the Virtue for which her grandson, the future Alexander I, was being taught to strive. Whether all these lessons penetrated is another matter, but throughout the eighteenth century the Russian rulers seem at least to have regarded literature as a necessary attribute of the dignity, prestige, and elegance of their court, and they were willing to grant it a good deal of patronage.

In the work of Sumarokov and his school the focus shifts from the tsars to the nobles, and the motto becomes rather *urok dvorianstvu*. The lesson to be taught was the lesson of *noblesse oblige,* that nobility of birth implied a civilizing responsibility toward society and was justified only if it was accompanied by nobility of character. The great comedies of Fonvizin provided vivid examples of nobles who fell short of this ideal, and much less vivid ones of the Dobroliubovs, Pravdins, and Starodums who lived up to it. Similar lessons, more explicit and less vivid, are to be found in the comedies and satires of Sumarokov himself, and in a host of others.

The cognitive role of eighteenth-century Russian literature is more difficult to assess. It was an age when the concrete-abstract dial was set very far in the direction of universal generalizations about human character without regard for time or place. This was a tendency of the period all over Europe, one intensified in Russia by excessive dependence on foreign models. Amid the abstractions and generalizations about love, duty, and civic virtue in eighteenth-century literature, Russian reality, especially social reality, appears only flickeringly. There are glimpses in the early satires of Kantemir, some vivid images here and there in the satirical journals, especially Novikov's, and big, juicy chunks in the comedies of Fonvizin. But by and large the "lessons" to be learned were moral rather than cognitive ones. Furthermore, comedy and satire ranked low in the hierarchy of genres. The great, grand, and prestige-laden forms were the tragedy, the epic, and the ode, and of these three the ode became, in Russia, *the* genre of the period. And the ode was a patterned, highly ritualistic recitation of known "truths" about the might and majesty of Russia and her monarchs, and it had little more cognitive value for its readers than the Lord's Prayer.

Toward the end of the eighteenth century the emphasis on didacticism begins to fade. Bogdanovich's *Dushen'ka* (1775) was probably the first work of stature that had no "ulterior" purpose at all, neither cognitive nor didactic value. It was a sparkling, light-hearted, graceful, mildly erotic verbal game engaged in purely for fun. Shortly thereafter, Derzhavin's *Felitsa* (1782) "exploded" the Lomonosovian ode, reducing it to an adroit, graceful, and amusing series of compliments to the Empress at the expense of some of her leading courtiers—a maneuver which notably succeeded in its extraliterary goal, that is, gaining some very tangible favors from the Empress for the poet.

The abandonment by literature of extra-aesthetic responsibilities was continued in the next generation. The chief modification introduced by the sentimentalist or pre-Romantic school was an expansion of the emotional range accessible for literary expression to include the tender melancholy so delighted in by Karamzin and Dmitriev and later the Gothic fantasies of death, ghosts, and the nether world which Zhukovsky imported from Germany and England. At the same time the rococo tradition of graceful erotic verse à la Parny was developed to a high peak of formal excellence by Batiushkov. Batiushkov passed it on to Pushkin, whose temperament it seemed to suit far more than the "night thoughts" of Zhukovsky. But in neither of these parallel traditions is the didactic or cognitive aspect of literature taken very seriously. For both Batiushkov and Zhukovsky literature is an enjoyable game, a display of verbal ingenuity, and a vehicle for emotional release.

In the Pushkinian age this attitude was still very much in the ascendant. *Ruslan and Ludmila* owes a great deal to the light, rococo tradition dating back to Bogdanovich and reinforced with playful eroticism directly from Parny; it includes a friendly parody of Zhukovsky's murky graveyard musings. There is as little cognitive or didactic content as a poem could possibly possess; its expressed "goal" is to attract the notice of the girls with a gay and slightly indecent story:

Счастлив уж я надеждой сладкой	Happy am I at the mere sweet hope
Что дева с трепетом любви	That some maiden with a quiver of love
Посмотрит, может быть украдкой	Will look, perhaps askance,
На песни грешные мои.	At these sinful songs of mine.

The same lack of ulterior purpose is apparent in all Pushkin's "Byronic" narrative poems, although in the last, *The Gypsies,* we do find the beginnings of an analytical (i.e., cognitive) portrait of the contemporary "hero of our time."

Evgenii Onegin, however, marks the beginning of a transition. This great progenitor of the Russian novel takes the Byronic hero and much to his discomfiture places him not amidst the awesome crags of the Caucasus or the voluptuous splendor of the harem of Bakhchisarai but in a contemporary Russian setting. Or rather in three of them: the classical, contrasting triangle made up of glittering, majestic Petersburg; easy-going, friendly old Moscow; and a lyrically beautiful countryside inhabited by quaint, old-fashioned gentlefolk. (The fourth classical Russian setting, the drab, unbearably backward provincial town was still lurking in the wings, to make a triumphal, if somewhat uncharacteristic, entry in Gogol's *Revizor.*)

Evgenii Onegin contains a great amount of apt social observation and commentary as well as psychological generalizations, which proved suggestive for generations to come. But in one vastly important respect *Evgenii Onegin* differs greatly from its latter-day descendants: it is in verse. This fact not only marks a significant distinction of form but also indicates a fundamental difference in artistic philosophy. Later in the nineteenth century it became one of the primary artistic aims of the great novelists to deny the artificiality of art, to erase the borderline between literature and life and create the illusion that reading a novel was equivalent to experiencing the events it describes. In this respect *Evgenii Onegin* is quite at the opposite pole. After all, everyone knows that verse is artificial; people do not speak in iambic tetrameter. One's admiration for a fantastic display of stylistic virtuosity is one of the pleasures to be derived from the poem. And the verse form of *Evgenii Onegin* is only the most obvious of many means by which Pushkin deliberately stresses the artificiality of his art. The toying with narrative planes, the play of digressions, taking the reader into the poetic workshop, "unfinished" and omitted stanzas, the abrupt ending—all are designed to create a free-and-easy intimacy between the reader and the work itself. It is almost as if we shared in its creation. And if cognitive values are present, they never obtrude upon the aesthetic integrity of the poem, which is an end and a delight in itself.

Although the years inclined him to humble prose, Pushkin's prose did not in fact show any tendency to subordinate the aesthetic to other functions of literature. In this respect Pushkin's prose is all immensely distant from Turgenev's, Tolstoy's, or Dostoevsky's. It is self-contained and self-sufficient: the material taken from reality has been fully integrated into the work of art. It does not seek to escape back into the world. The pleasure we derive, for example, from *The Queen of Spades* is in the skillful telling of an unusual and striking anecdote for which the characterizations are perfectly appropriate. It is a great work of art, but a work at rest. It has no function other than to be itself.

"The purpose of poetry is poetry," Pushkin once wrote in a letter to Zhukovsky, replying to a question about the "purpose" of *The Gypsies*.[1] By and large he maintained this view throughout his life. But that he should need to state it at all indicates that a contrary opinion had some currency; and, indeed, Pushkin mentions an example of it: "Ryleev's *Meditations* take aim, but they always miss" *(Dumy Ryleeva i tseliat, a vse nevpopad)*.

Ryleev had indeed revived the old eighteenth-century didactic strain (though in anything but an eighteenth-century style). But ideologically he stood it on its head. The duty of the citizen, according to Ryleev, was not to serve but to oppose the state:

Я ль буду в роковое время	At the fateful time will I
Позорить гражданина сан,	Besmirch the rank of Citizen
. . . .	. . . .
И изнывать кипящею душой	And with my seething heart pine away
Под тяжким игом самовластья?	Beneath the heavy yoke of tyranny?

This legacy left by the revolutionary martyr was to prove prophetic for the future of Russian literature.

But Pushkin, despite his own early "Ode to Liberty," basically disliked the "didactic fallacy" and never returned to it. People may

---

[1] "Ty sprashivaesh', kakaia tsel' u Tsyganov? Vot na! Tsel' poezii—poeziia—kak govorit Del'vig (esli ne ukral etogo). Dumy Ryleeva i tseliat, a vse nevpopad." «Письмо к В. А. Жуковскому от 20-ых чисел апреля 1825 г.,» А. С. Пушкин, *Полное собрание сочинений* (Moscow and Leningrad, 1949), X, 141.

choose to honor him for "praising freedom in a cruel age and begging mercy for the fallen"; but his real contribution lies elsewhere.

After Pushkin Russian literature begins in earnest to turn itself outward in the direction of "life." Gradually it undertakes to shoulder a burden of social, moral, and philosophical problems which would have seemed quite overpowering in Pushkin's day. It all seems to begin with Gogol and the "natural school," but the process is anything but a straightforward one, and it has been still further confused by divergent interpretations placed upon it later. In fact, the images of Gogol constructed by subsequent generations of Russian critics are so totally divergent that it is hard to believe they refer to the same man. For Belinsky, Chernyshevsky, and their *epigonoi,* Gogol was the great "poet of actuality" who sought to display Russian life and reality in their genuine truth. By this he gave literature an important significance in society, which through it acquired an understanding of "life." In other words, according to them, Gogol placed the cognitive function of literature foremost. On the other hand many twentieth-century critics, either formalistically or psychoanalytically oriented, have maintained that Gogol's work has less cognitive validity than that of almost any other writer you could name, that it consists almost entirely of exteriorizations of the author's own weird fantasies.[2]

Still another confusion arises with respect to the didactic function in Gogol, since there seems to be a total discrepancy between the author's intention (at least as retrospectively viewed) and his actual artistic performance. In his later life Gogol certainly cultivated a very exalted image of himself as a kind of divine instrument called upon to show Russia and the world the way to holiness. And this was not merely an aberration of his later years. His famous flight to Europe soon after the first performance of *Revizor* may not have been due, as is usually alleged, to his chagrin at the supposedly bad reception or inadequate performance of the play—actually the performance was reasonably good and the reception as warm as any playwright has a right to expect. As K. Mochulsky has suggested,[3] Gogol, like Novalis and Schlegel, believed in the miraculous power of art. His flight was from disappointment that his play had been received merely as a play; he wanted it to be a blinding vision in which all Russians would see their sins, fall on their knees, burst into tears, and be spiritually reborn. And of course much more obvious and better documented is the tragic struggle of Gogol's last years to turn *Dead Souls* into another transcendent morality play which would "burn the hearts of men" and transfigure them from within.

[2] E.g., И. Д. Ермаков, *Очерки по анализу творчества Н. В. Гоголя* (Moscow and Petrograd, 1924); Андрей Белый, *Мастерство Гоголя* (Moscow, 1934).

[3] К. Мочульскій, *Духовный путь Гоголя* (Paris, 1934).

But oddly enough, the sententious didacticism in Gogol's conception of his works does not appear in the works themselves, if we exclude a few chapters from the surviving portions of the second volume of *Dead Souls*. Didacticism was an aberration seen even by most of Gogol's contemporaries as something separate from and alien to his artistic works. It therefore had little effect on their literary repercussions and left no legacy for later Russian literature.

In its influence on later writers Gogol's artistic work did in fact bear more on the cognitive than the didactic function. Belinsky's extravagances apart, Gogol can be said to have legitimized new areas of reality for inclusion in literature. He showed that the ugly, the petty, the unseemly, and the grotesque can be materials for art of the highest order, and that characters with Lilliputian minds and dead souls can be made the heroes of major works of fiction.

But contemporary critics, especially Belinsky, went much further than this in their interpretation of Gogol. They discovered in him the unimpeachable source of knowledge about Russian life, and especially its evils, which their dissident hearts craved. Belinsky's rapturous statements about Gogol's dedication to Truth were not a valid description of the most fantastic and reality-distorting writer in all Russian literature, but rather a normative program for the future of Russian literature:

The perfect truth of life in Mr. Gogol's stories is closely bound up with the simplicity of his invention. He does not flatter life, nor does he slander it; he is glad to bring out everything that is beautiful and human in it, but at the same time he in no way conceals its ugliness. In both cases he is true to life to the last degree. He gives a real portrait of life in which everything is caught up in an amazing likeness, from the facial expression of the original to his freckles.[4]

One need only substitute the name "Tolstoy" for "Gogol" in this passage to accept it as a reasonable descriptive statement. It was Tolstoy, and not Gogol, who made the somewhat melodramatic claim, at the end of "Sevastopol in May," that the true hero of his story was Truth, "which I love with all the forces of my soul, which I tried to reproduce in all its beauty, and which was, is, and always will be beautiful." Belinsky's rhapsodies on Gogol may be taken as an expression of the *sotsial'nyi zakaz,* a desire of a group of Russian readers for what they mistakenly interpreted Gogol's work to be. And in Tolstoy and his cohorts the order was at last filled.

In one further respect Gogol stands quite apart from the later truth-worshipping tradition to which Belinsky hopefully assigned him, and adheres rather to the art-focused aestheticism of the Pushkin age.

---

[4] «О русской повести и повестях г. Гоголя» (1835). Cited from *Н. В. Гоголь в русской критике* (Moscow, 1953), p. 46.

Gogol, like Pushkin, never tries to make us forget that his works are the products of an artist's invention; on the contrary, he finds innumerable ways of stressing their artificiality—digressing, talking to the reader, going off into dazzling stylistic cadenzas, deliberately avoiding logical sequences, and whimsically toying with different narrative planes.

Gogol is thus a paradoxical, transitional figure. Although he intended to use his art to purify his readers' souls, his verbal feats were in fact as aesthetically focused and exhibitionistic as trapeze stunts; and yet eventually they did serve, partly through a critical misassessment of them, to move Russian literature further along the "road to life."

The next stage in the process takes place in the 1840's. First, the areas of life available for literary exploitation had to be still further expanded. Gogol's work, with an assist from Evgenii in *The Bronze Horseman,* had established the petty clerk as a mainstay of Russian literature; now all the "lower depths" were suddenly opened up. Russia was not alone in this. All over Europe "physiologies"—attempts to make literature see with the unflinching, dispassionate, analytical eye of the natural scientist—were much in vogue, exhibiting carefully dissected slices of the great European cities and titillating middle-class readers with lurid pictures of the vice and poverty of the slums. In 1845 Nekrasov edited a *Physiology of Petersburg,* and followed it with the *Petersburg Miscellany* containing Dostoevsky's *Poor Folk.*

But after all, urban scenes occupied a very small part of the Russian spiritual landscape. A far richer and more unexplored "depth" was the peasantry, and it was in the 1840's that the Russian muzhik marched into the foreground of literature for the first time, in the stories of Grigorovich and Dahl and most notably in the *Sportsman's Sketches* of Turgenev. Most educated Russians had been exposed to peasants off and on most of their lives; the majority of them spent at least part of the year in the country. But it took literature to open their eyes to what they saw there, to "strip off the wrappings," in Tolstoy's phrase, which prevented them from perceiving the individual personalities and lives that lay beneath the label. Through Turgenev's *Sketches* Russian readers learned, not so much that their peasants were poor and miserable, as that they were of the same order of being as themselves, with a comparable variety of characters, talents, and attainments. It was a genuine discovery.

However obvious, the moral conclusion to be drawn from this discovery was not so explicitly stated. Indeed, there is a curious paradox about the literature of this period, its relation to the didactic function. By implication, of course, the didactic intent is very strong. All the "peasant" books of the 1840's cry out from every page: what an unjust and inhuman society this is! But the cry had to be an implied cry; the moral could never be stated in so many words. Externally, this arose from the curious game Russian writers were obliged to play with the censors; according to its rules you could imply many things you could not state openly. But in this instance the censorship may have rendered an artistic service to Russian literature (I suspect there are others as well). In literature implied cries often sound louder than uttered ones. The power of the censor thus helped impose the logic of a new style.

The tendency of this new style was to let the facts speak for themselves. More and more, the commenting presence of the author came to be hidden from view. The conclusion was drawn that both the cognitive and didactic functions are better served if the reader feels that he has learned the lesson himself, as if directly from life, forgetting the intermediacy of art. For the artist there was a certain deprivation in this: he had to obliterate himself from his own work, to create the illusion of his own nonexistence. No more Gogolian verbal acrobatics, no bows to the audience; the author became a reporter without a by-line.

In Turgenev's *Sportsman's Sketches,* however, the stylistic logic of this development had not yet been carried to its full conclusion. Though no verbal acrobat, Turgenev was not quite ready to withdraw into the anonymity of high realism and deny the artificiality of his art. He still preserves, for instance, a relic of the multiple narrative planes of Pushkin or Gogol: the "sportsman" himself can turn to the reader with such bits of graceful *courtoisie* as "Give me your hand, dear reader, and come with me. The weather is beautiful; the May sky is a gentle blue . . ." ("Tat'iana Borisovna and Her Nephew") and at the same time serve as the observer of, and to some extent actor in, the events on the narrative plane. The sportsman is not fully characterized; we know almost nothing of his past or his inner life; nor does he moralize about the scenes he describes. He simply reports. But his style of reporting and his reactions to events are sufficient both to endow him with character and to give us the key to his unstated judgments. He is the Sensitive Young Man, morally alienated from his fellow landowners, whose pretensions, crassness, and cruelty he abhors, and of course socially alienated from the peasants, whom he observes sympathetically, but from a safe distance. Whatever his original prejudices, the reader, since he must see with the sportsman's eyes, is also pushed back to this double distance of class alienation and forced to see events with the sportsman's moral perspective. This was didacticism by remote control, and a very effective procedure it was.

The final stage in the retreat of art into anonymity came in the next two decades, the so-called Golden Age of Russian prose. This period is surely one of the most extraordinary and paradoxical epochs in the history of world literature. For creative power, scope, and sheer bigness it would be hard to find anywhere a literary quarter-century to surpass it. Superb fictional masterpieces were pouring off the presses almost every year, and sometimes more often. For the first time, Russia achieved recognition as one of the great literary powers of Europe. Yet at the same time, in the spirit of its literary life, this was undoubtedly one of the most antiartistic periods in the history of any literature.

On the one hand, literature certainly stood at the center of the nation's cultural life, and all eyes were focused upon it. It became everyone's beast of burden. People expected—and received—more from literature than ever before. Cognitively, it was supposed to provide them with a complete "encyclopedia of Russian life," a view into every nook and cranny of Russian society. And, although the demands for this were never so explicit, it was also to turn its explorer's gaze within, investigating the human heart with equal thoroughness and objectivity. Further, although the artistic convention required considerable restraint in direct moralizing, the artist was expected to provide by implication a clear-cut ethical system for judging the rights and wrongs of things. From their reading people were to go forth informed and uplifted, with a clear idea of how to live their own lives and a knowledge of how to right the wrongs they saw around them. Finally, writers were expected to grapple with the "accursed questions" of the ultimate meaning of human life and of man's destiny on earth, to answer the riddle of why we are here. In short, Russian literature was required to serve as the sociology, the psychology, the ethics, and the metaphysics of Russian man. It was quite a load for an art form to carry.

At the very time they were weighed down with all these extra-aesthetic responsibilities and yet somehow managing to turn out superlative works of art, Russian writers were subjected to unprecedentedly harsh and contemptuous treatment at the hands of the professional critics. Never, it would seem, was more scorn heaped upon literature generally, nor were people more eager to put literature in its place, to puncture its illusions, if not destroy it altogether. The period begins in 1855, with Chernyshevsky's famous master's thesis, in which he subordinates art to reality, not only causally (reality being the artist's source of materials) but qualitatively, quasi-aesthetically. Art is aesthetically never as "good" as the reality it copies; if you can see the Alps, you don't need a painting of them. Ten years later, Pisarev, in "The Destruction of Aesthetics," was ready to go a step further: all art is useless, if not harmful, and people ought to concern themselves with less trivial matters. There are more pressing things to be done than playing childish games with words. Belinsky had said that art should be a textbook of life; Chernyshevsky would make it a second-rate surrogate for reality; Pisarev would abolish it.

As has often been pointed out, these critical aberrations were partly due to the peculiar circumstances of Russian journalism. Russians knew that there were many things wrong with their society, such as serfdom, autocracy, bureaucratic corruption, economic distress, and so forth. But it was difficult and in many periods impossible to discuss these problems straightforwardly in print. Yet it was possible to publish a novel or play in which these problems were "reflected." Then, under the guise of literary criticism, the journalist could discuss what was reflected in the novel; but everyone knew that he was really discussing not the novel but the "real" social and ideological problems themselves. This was another game of substitutions, with rules established by the censors. Such games would have been fairly harmless, except that after a while people got used to them and came to believe that what Dobroliubov and his imitators wrote was really literary criticism, and even more, that since Dobroliubov was soon canonized as one of the intelligentsia's major saints, any other kind of literary criticism was frivolous, absurd, and silly, if not sacrilegious and wicked.

It has become customary for some time to inveigh against the anti-aesthetic extremes of the mid-nineteenth-century critics. But what is not so frequently pointed out is that in some ways these very extremes are merely the other side of a coin minted by the writers themselves, namely, "realism." As usually understood, both then and now, this term is taken to mean that realistic literature provides us with the "truth" about the world, that it reproduces reality accurately. This is the imperative that Chernyshevsky laid upon it, one which Tolstoy gallantly accepted. "Truth" thus became the basis for judging the quality of a work of art.

This judgment is an excessively difficult one, however, not only because of the permanent epistemological difficulty expressed by Pilate's great question but because of the further difficulty of measuring "truth" within a work of art. Yet people did, and do, try to measure it, and however difficult, the problem is a crucial one and cannot be shrugged off. Yet the difficulties may be partly avoided by looking at the problem another way. From the aesthetic rather than the epistemological point of view, "realism" would perhaps be better described as "illusionism." Illusionism is the burden of the stylistic development leading from Pushkin through Gogol and Turgenev to Tolstoy and Dostoevsky. The artist comes to strive deliberately, with all the techniques at his command, to rub out the boundary between literature and life, to give us the illusion as we read that we are experiencing life directly. Every effort is made to achieve stylistic transparency: the verbal texture must be as unobtrusive as a pane of glass. Without noticing the glass itself, we seem through it to perceive actual people living actual lives.

As practiced by such great artists, this illusionism was unbelievably successful. People really did come to equate literature with life. They really did look to literature for answers to the what's, the how's, and the why's of their own existence. And since these questions were serious ones, they did not like to be reminded that the novelist's art was a series of conjuror's tricks designed to make them believe in the reality of imaginary people and imaginary events. And the writers themselves were not loath to encourage this attitude. They wanted to be taken as seriously as they in fact were. While practicing their illusionistic magic, they willingly and eagerly shouldered the terrible burdens society asked them to bear. The cognitive and moral struggles of Tolstoy and Dostoevsky really do embody the cognitive and moral struggles of an entire generation. And if writers occasionally complained about the gaucheries of critics like Pisarev, they were perhaps not too angry about them after all. For a more aesthetically oriented criticism could only have opened up their bag of tricks and shown their secrets to the world. And what magician wants that?

However glorious, the great age could not last forever. The crisis came in the 1880's. The old sorcerers began to die off: Dostoevsky in 1881; Turgenev in 1883; Saltykov in 1889; Goncharov was mad and in retirement; Tolstoy grandly withdrew from literature, repudiating his earlier work. (Among other things, he was troubled by the dishonesty implied in illusionism and wanted to preach without wearing a mask.) And the sorcerers had no apprentices worthy of them. But the shadow they cast was a long one. People had forgotten that literature could be anything else than what the old wizards had made it. They waited for more *Annas* and *Brothers* to be born . . . and waited. By comparison, the short stories of Garshin or Korolenko seemed dwarfish and inconsequential. But the illusionist code lived on, with its cognitive and implied didactive demands upon literature. The revolutionaries who would set the dynamite to it had not yet appeared.

The greatest talent to emerge in the eighties was undoubtedly Chekhov, and though he shows some distant signs of approaching changes, he basically subscribes to the old system: illusionism, moral and cognitive responsibility, didactic implications. But there are differences in Chekhov. For one thing, he entered literature through the basement door; as a hack writer for cheap humor magazines, he could hardly affect the hieratic solemnity of his predecessors. But as he moves up into "high" literature, he tends to take up the old burdens once more. Yet his strength seems weaker—not his artistic powers, perhaps, but his self-assurance. Chekhov is of all things modest—something that could hardly be said of any of his predecessors. They had seemed more sure of themselves, firmer in their ideological convictions, more confident of their answers even to the "accursed" questions.

And we? We! We paint life as it is, and beyond that neither whoa! nor giddap! Whip us and we can't go a step farther. We have neither immediate nor distant aims, and our souls are as bare as a billiard table. We have no politics, we don't believe in revolution, there is no God, we are not afraid of ghosts, and I personally am not even afraid of death and blindness. A person who desires nothing, hopes for nothing, and fears nothing cannot be an artist.[5]

In this "failure of nerve" we may perhaps discern the first cracks in the foundation of the realist system. Its relation to life was becoming more passive, more indifferent, more purely reflective. But the old structure remained standing for many years, even after a new one, in quite a different architectural style, had been built alongside it. Many writers and readers continued to prefer its arrangements to anything more modern. And many years later its principles—or principles purporting to be derived from them—were enjoined upon Russian literature in the name of socialism.

The great revolt against nineteenth-century realism, with its concomitant principles of civic, ethical, and cognitive responsibility, begins in the 1890's. At first the realist citadel seemed unassailable, and the forces that undertook to storm it absurdly weak. Not only were all the leading writers, critics, and literary magazines solidly "realist" in orientation, but the public had long since forgotten that anything else was possible. Its only reaction to innovation was outrage or derision.

Furthermore, the attackers themselves were not only few in number but hardly giants in intellectual power, talent, or learning. The two "philosophers" of early symbolism, Flekser-Volynsky and Merezhkovsky, were both incorrigibly loose in their thinking and windy in their rhetoric, inconsistent, timid, and deficient in learning. The first of the Decadent poets, Balmont, though a man of notable talent, was incapable of rigorous thinking on any subject. For theorizing, the early Symbolists had to rely on Valerii Briusov, a man of infinitely greater intellectual prowess, though perhaps less poetic talent, than Balmont; but in 1895 Briusov was only barely out of the *gimnaziia* and at first seemed to have more taste for shocking the bourgeois than for serious literary work. His first undertaking was to make a splash as an *épater* poet, not to provide the theoretical underpinnings for a literary movement. It is an indication of how essentially weak the old structure was that it could be shaken by forces such as these. Yet in less than a decade the commanding heights of literature were almost all in Symbolist hands, and the whole atmosphere of Russian literature had been transformed.

[5] «Письмо к А. С. Суворину от 25-ого ноября 1892 г.,» А. П. Чехов, *Полное собрание сочинений и писем*, XV (Moscow, 1949), 446.

The initial revolt was directed not so much against the great realist tradition—that would have been too formidable a target to start off with—as against the smug and intolerant "positivism" espoused by the average Russian intellectual. Against it Volynsky raised the banner of philosophical "idealism," and however empty of content and poorly reasoned his system was, he succeeded not only in arousing the ire of Mikhailovsky but in raising doubts about the validity of some of the positivist premises. Perhaps things were not as simple or as settled as they had seemed. Merezhkovsky, in his famous article "On the Causes for the Decline and the New Currents in Contemporary Russian Literature,"[6] though his reasoning was as flimsy as Volynsky's, also scored some valid points. His most successful maneuver was to call attention to the anti-positivist sides of the great "realists" themselves—the interest of the older Turgenev in mysteries and ghosts, the great religious quest of Dostoevsky, the use of "symbols" in Goncharov. He saw in these elements the germ of "that ideal art which will come in Russia to replace vulgar utilitarian realism."[7]

There were also allies in the West. If Merezhkovsky had only a superficial acquaintance with them, Briusov was studying them hard, and it was through him that the impact of French symbolism was felt in Russia. Like it or not, he said to the Russian public, this *is* the new art, and you can't laugh it away. It was not so much a matter of theory. The theoretical revolt of the French Symbolists had been on much narrower and, characteristically, more purely literary grounds: rejection of the precision, elegance, and "scientific" emphasis of the Parnassians in favor of a more musical verse and more stress on nuances, dreams, and mysteries. Such a revolt had no meaning in Russia, where no Parnassian tradition existed. But the unashamed aestheticism of the French Symbolists was an asset to Briusov and his co-warriors, who had to fight a battle for the general autonomy of art, its freedom to pursue its own ends. And the desire to keep abreast of European culture, however unsympathetic some of its manifestations, was strong in the Russian educated public. Under Briusov's tutelage, it was forced to take cognizance of what was happening in Western art.

The Russian public was likewise obliged to take account of parallel developments in original Russian verse, not because of declarations or theories about it, but because of its sheer artistic magnetism. The success of the Symbolist movement was due far more to poetic practice than to theorizing. Balmont, though at first ridiculed, eventually

---

[6] Ably analyzed by Ralph Matlaw, "The Manifesto of Russian Symbolism," *Slavic and East European Journal*, XV (1957), 177-91.

[7] ". . . Novoe ideal'noe iskusstvo, griadushchee v Rossii na smenu utilitarnomu poshlomu realizmu." Д. С. Мережковскій, *Полное собраніе сочиненій*, XV (St. Petersburg and Moscow, 1914), 252.

enchanted readers with the sensuous musicality of his verse. This was an achievement in itself: it had been a long time in Russia since people had paid any attention to the form of poetry. The content of his poems was also a revelation: no Nadsonian civic sighs but an aggressive (if somewhat rhetorical) hedonistic egotism, a cult of the "moment," a cult of poetry for the sake of poetry, and even some gingerly toying with Nietzschean or Baudelairean amoralism. All that now seems obvious and trite in Balmont's poetry seemed startlingly daring and original in 1895. These were notes that had not been struck for many decades.

To Balmont's contribution Briusov added not only a much more coldly planned publicity-seeking series of shocks administered to the Russian public but also a thorough demonstration of hitherto unexplored formal and thematic possibilities of poetry, including a careful and systematic effort to duplicate in Russian the technical achievements of the French Symbolists. Moreover, he showed a keen and remarkably balanced critical sense and a vast scholarly knowledge of the literatures of the world; and he was totally dedicated to the cause of the new art. He was a formidable figure.

Essentially what the Balmont-Briusov team accomplished was to throw off the whole burden of responsibilities loaded onto literature by Belinsky and nobly borne for so many decades. Why should literature be required to face the painful problems of Russian society? What if it was more interested in exploring problems of versification? Why should literature undertake to teach people how to live? Poets are not their readers' keepers. And as for the "accursed" questions, Briusov, at least, was ready to stand the realist credo on its head: it may well be, he said, that the purpose of life is to provide experiences which can be transmuted into art. This was aestheticism with a vengeance.

In the generation of poets who emerge in the 1900's, however, and who are more properly called "symbolists," the cognitive function once again enters the arena of literature, though through a door boarded up for a long time, the door of direct revelation. With Blok, Belyi, and Viacheslav Ivanov the poet assumes a new responsibility. His poetic gift, they maintained, endows him with special cognitive powers not possessed by ordinary men. Through them he is able to perceive a higher, truer reality than the one accessible to our senses. To convey this reality he must resort to symbols. This was the true, the "Russian" meaning of "symbolism." Aesthetics, of course, was still of overwhelming importance for these poets, but the "poet as theurgist" was the ideal. To quote one of Blok's rare theoretical statements:

The symbolist is a theurgist, and has always been such: i.e., the possessor of secret knowledge, behind which stands secret activity; but he looks on this mystery, which only later proves to be a universal mystery, as something belonging to him alone. He sees in it a treasure above which blooms the flower of the fern on the June midnight; and he wants to pluck the blue flower on the blue midnight.[8]

This "revelationist" responsibility, however, soon proved too heavy even for Blok, and the new schools of poetry which appear in the decade after 1910, the Acmeists and Futurists, repudiated it. The Acmeists called for a return to a Parnassian clarity in representing the things of the real world, while the Futurists proclaimed the independence of the "self-sufficient word." The differences between them, however, were primarily stylistic, the Futurists being much more radical in their formal innovations; but they agreed in refusing to don the robes of the seer and visionary. One may also discern a difference between them in epistemological tendency. The Acmeist has a strong cognitive urge: he wishes to perceive and to know the real world. The Futurist, on the other hand, especially in his more extreme moments, wants to liberate poetry from all meaning, to create with a language free of referents, the so-called *zaumnyi iazyk*.

The Revolution of 1917 at first brought no fundamental changes to Russian literature. Writers, like other citizens, were forced to take sides, to assume some political posture. Some went one way, some another, but the decision seemed to have little to do with literature. Of the Symbolists, for example, Briusov became a Communist; Blok and Belyi "accepted" the Revolution, but on non-Communist terms; the Merezhkovskys, Balmont, and Viacheslav Ivanov rejected it entirely and emigrated; Sologub remained home in silent opposition. Of the Acmeists, Gumilev was shot as an anti-Soviet conspirator, Akhmatova and Mandelshtam remained detached and apolitical, but refused to emigrate; and Tikhonov became one of the mainstays of "Soviet" literature. Similar divisions took place in other schools.

The Revolution is an important biographical fact in the life of every writer, and it was soon to become a central theme in much of the literature written after 1917. But the Revolution did not at first have much effect on literature's philosophy or its conception of itself.

To be sure, there were rival groups of Marxist theoreticians wrangling over the application of their system to literature, a point rather neglected in the writing of the prophets. Some of them hunted eagerly for manifestations of the new "class essence" of the proletariat destined to appear in culture now that the bourgeoisie had been overthrown and hoped to discover untapped resources of literary talent among the

---

[8] «О современном состоянии русского символизма» (1910). А. Блок, *Сочинения в одном томе* (Moscow and Leningrad, 1946), p. 444.

factory workers. But the Proletkul't, however worthy as an enterprise in adult education, petered out in the early 1920's without having brought forth from its adepts anything very notable in the way of actual literature. Subsequent Marxist efforts came to center, characteristically, on two other questions. Literary "activists" devoted themselves to the "organizational" problems of Soviet literature, which meant controlling and manipulating the various writers' clubs, unions, and associations, whether "proletarian" or not, for party purposes. More contemplative souls tackled problems of Marxian criticism, which were more and more reduced to determining the "ideology" of a writer (or a work) and deciding how acceptable this ideology was in terms of the official orthodoxy.

As for the writers themselves, they were even less sure than the critics about the position of literature under the new regime. The tremendous experiences of the Revolution and Civil War cried out for literary exploitation; they were obviously a mine of literary material which would last for decades. But in their treatment of these themes Soviet writers did not at first return to the method of "classical" realism. First of all, stylistically they were mostly under the influence of the Symbolists' prose, particularly Belyi's, with its emphasis on ornamentalism, on ostentatious stylistic textures. This "opaque" prose of Pilniak, Babel, or the early Leonov was the very antithesis of the high-realist transparency. Artificiality or artfulness was one of its principal aesthetic dimensions.

Secondly, early Soviet writers on revolutionary and Civil War themes generally avoid the temptation to judge and moralize. A general ethical relativism seems to prevail. Previous events had been too cataclysmic for old moralities, and writers were hesitant to construct new ones. The exhibitions of human behavior under extreme stress which most of them had witnessed, either at the fronts or in the starving cities—the spectrum ranging from heroism through callous indifference to brutality—had revealed aspects of human nature to which old ethical systems seemed to have little relevance. Writers were at first content merely to describe, to state the facts.

Similarly, there was a widespread tendency in the early post-1917 years to avoid literary didacticism, even of a political rather than a moral sort. Most writers were reluctant to surrender the autonomy of literature that had been so hardly won in the battles of the previous decades. The Serapion Brothers, who included many of the most talented young writers on the scene, made autonomy one of the major tenets in their literary program:

We believe that literary chimeras are a special reality, and we will have none of utilitarianism. We do not write for propaganda. Art is real, like life itself. And, like life itself, it has neither goal nor meaning; it exists because it cannot help existing.[9]

Though admitting that cognitive content was present in the work of most of the "brothers," their manifesto (written by Lev Lunts) refuses to make "knowledge" a criterion for judging the value of literature. "We demand only one thing: that a work should be organic, real, should live its own life. *Its own life.* Not be a copy of nature, but live on a par with nature."

However admirable this declaration as a statement of aesthetic principles and courageous as a political act (even in 1922), its principles of stylistic diversity and cognitive and didactic autonomy were not destined to survive very long under conditions of Soviet life. The future lay in a different direction.

It was the fate of Mayakovsky's Futurism that pointed the way for Soviet literature far more than the manifesto of the Serapion Brothers. Before the Revolution this poet of formidable verbal talent had developed, partly from elements suggested by his master Khlebnikov, an original personal style with a diapason including both epic and lyric strains. After 1917 the epic side of his talent was enlisted in the service of the new regime; Mayakovsky became the most powerful poetic celebrant of communism. But, as Roman Jakobson has so brilliantly shown,[10] Mayakovsky only incorporated the Communist ideology as a component and not wholly assimilated part of a private and more transcendent "mythology" of his own, involving a veritable cosmic revolution against all the stagnation, stupidity, and vulgarity in the universe. And it was far from easy for Mayakovsky to maintain the buoyant optimism requisite for the Soviet epic. A tragic, lyric inspiration had to be suppressed, the inspiration which produced such wonderful poetry as *I Love* and *Concerning This:*

Но я	But I
себя	subdued
смирял,	myself
становясь	standing
на горло	On the throat
собственной песне.	of my own song.

But the official, public image of Mayakovsky, one assiduously cultivated since his death, is that of the *barabanshchik revoliutsii,* the uniformed poet marching in the service of Revolution and the state. Such an alliance between poetry and authority could hardly be said to have occurred in Russia since the eighteenth century. This official, didactic

---

[9] «Серапионовы братья о себе,» *Литературные записки,* No. 3 (1922), pp. 25-31. Cited from William Edgerton, "The Serapion Brothers: An Early Soviet Controversy," *American Slavic and East European Review,* VIII (1949), 51-52.

[10] «О поколении, растратившем своих поэтов,» *Смерть Владимира Маяковского* (Berlin, 1931).

aspect of Mayakovsky's work turned out to be the most prophetic side of his Futurism. But there is an essential difference between Mayakovsky's "service" and that of later Soviet writers. However difficult it may have been for him, Mayakovsky undertook his service voluntarily. Furthermore, he incorporated the official didactic function into his own poetic system without violating the latter's integrity. But this was not an example that every writer could follow.

Meanwhile, the Communist leaders debated what the official literary policy should be. Most of the original leaders of the Revolution, like Lenin, Trotsky, Bukharin, and Kamenev, had the Russian intellectual's traditional respect for culture, and although they had no hesitation about establishing a negative censorship over literature—you couldn't let the bourgeoisie engage in open propaganda among the Russian masses—they hesitated to make direct, positive prescriptions about the content of art.

Our Marxist conception of the objective social dependence and social utility of art [wrote Trotsky], when translated into the language of politics, does not at all mean a desire to dominate art by means of decrees and orders.[11]

The famous Central Committee resolution of 1925 seemed to guarantee at least a relative autonomy to art. But before long the leadership of the party passed into other, less refined hands, and the new bosses saw no reason why art should not be harnessed to their service like everything else. A new cultural revolution was in prospect, one ultimately more profound in its effects on literature than 1917: the "totalitarianization" of culture carried out between about 1928 and 1934.

Curiously enough, the original promoters of this revolution were the ultra-left Communist intellectuals, who were later almost to a man purged by the Stalinist leadership, either along with the Left Opposition (many of them shared Trotsky's political if not his literary ideas) or later on in the thirties. But during the 1920's they were the militant advocates of "proletarian" literature who kept beating the drums, in journals with such "militant" names as *On Guard, October, On Literary Guard,* for proletarian "hegemony" in art. At first this meant chiefly that "proletarian" (i.e., Communist) writers ought to be granted special privileges and encouraged in every way. But more and more it came to imply that "proletarian" critics ought to be given veto power over everything published in Russia and that the "fellow traveling" writers had better be made to toe the party line, or else. Organizationally, these militants sought control over all writers' associations, and in 1928-32 they in fact achieved it. Virtually all writers, whether "prole-

[11] Leon Trotsky, *Literature and Revolution,* trans. Rose Strunsky (New York, 1925), p. 170.

tarian" or not, were forced to join RAPP, where in fact they did receive "decrees and orders" from its "revolutionary" chieftain, Leopold Averbakh.

After four years of this "hegemony" its mission was accomplished: the writers had been softened up and were ready to become the docile servants the state wanted. They were frightened and demoralized and looked on liberation from the dictates of Averbakh as a liberalization of literary policy. This liberation did come in 1932, when Averbakh and his cohorts, having served their purpose, were cast into the ashcan of history. RAPP was abolished and an all-inclusive Union of Soviet Writers founded. How little this was a real liberalization has been effectively shown by Edward Brown: in the end it meant more complete control of literature by the party bosses.[12]

Two years later, at the first great Congress of the Writers' Union, the party announced that it had at last discovered the secret of applying Marxism to the actual production of literary art. This secret was the Method, and its name was socialist realism. Under the rule of the Method, Soviet literature since 1934 presents an essential unity and can be so treated. History, as it says in *1066,* has come to a . True, party pressures on literature have periodically been strengthened or relaxed; but essentially the situation has remained the same.

Under socialist realism the most important function of literature is the didactic one, and the rulers seem to take its powers very seriously. Literature is a tool for "engineering human souls," for constructing the new Soviet man. The choice of didactic ends, however, is not open for the writer to make on his own responsibility. This function has been assumed by the party. Party goals are obligatory for all Soviet citizens, and it is the writer's job to embed these purposes in the citizens' souls.

Cognition of reality is also officially part of the program of socialist realism. But this is an illusion. The party is not interested in acquiring new knowledge of reality: it knows everything already. According to the official gobbledegook, in socialist realism reality is to be shown in its "revolutionary development," and in such a way that only "typical" phenomena are brought out. "Translated into the language of politics," this in fact means that any "realities" the party does not wish portrayed in literature cannot be "typical" and are therefore, in effect, unreal. They are certainly not appropriate material for writers to discover. Once again, the decision as to what is "real" is not one for the writers themselves to make, although they may, especially during "liberal" periods, undertake to test just what the limits of the party's tolerance are. As for philosophy and the "accursed" questions, they too have faded out of Soviet literature. The party has answered them, and the answers are known: why should anyone look further?

12 Edward J. Brown, *The Proletarian Episode in Russian Literature* (New York, 1953).

Finally, the aesthetic function, though nominally present in Soviet literature, must always be kept subordinate to the didactic and pseudo-cognitive one. Moreover, too much attention to matters of artistic form is likely to lead to the heresy of "formalism," which means the use of techniques that might attract attention to themselves rather than to the party's message.

Thus literature in modern Russia has once again, as it was a hundred years ago, been subordinated to extra-aesthetic ends. But this time these ends are not determined by the intellect or conscience of the artist and freely chosen by him, but are dictated by the bureaucratic votaries of a rigid and Philistine orthodoxy. Under such conditions literature, if it can be said to exist at all, must lead a very feeble and truncated life, and it is difficult to foresee the circumstances under which it might be revived.

Russian Literature and the West

RUFUS W. MATHEWSON, JR.

Literature is indeed the "messiest" of disciplines, and any system of categories set up to contain it is certain to sag and to leak. It can be argued, for example, that *any* work of literature is some kind of report on experience—of the mind, the senses, the emotions, or the imagination (Blake *saw* his visions)—hence "cognitive" in some sense. But then, we have all been sternly lectured about the "intentional fallacy," and even if we know what the writer meant to pass on, how can we ever determine what arrives in the reader's mind at the other end of the aesthetic trans- action? It can be argued, too, that all art is either "didactic" or "aes- thetic" (is it art if it isn't?), or that the two categories implacably exclude each other. But it is not my intention to quarrel with Professor McLean's categories. If they are inexact, overlapping, nonexclusive (as he has acknowledged), I am convinced that no other kind would work any better, and can only express my admiration for the range, the accu- racy, and the coherence of the material he has conveyed to us in these leaky vessels.

He has told us the characterizing features of Russian literature at successive moments in its history, largely by describing the writers' dominant intention toward their readers in each period—to delight, to instruct, or to exhort. He has supplied relevant facts about style, form, theme, social background, individual biography as required to support his own intention. The picture is clear, correct, and persuasive, but the method has limitations. It is not just that writers are sometimes poor judges of what they have accomplished. Professor McLean has honored their intentions but has gone beyond them when he had to. It is rather a matter of perspective, of being held too close to the Russian tradition's version of itself while it was being formed. To put it another way, we are not taken far enough toward an understanding of what is unique and what is not in modern Russian literature. The rhythm discovered by Professor McLean (didactic-aesthetic-cognitive, etc.) differs only in particulars and in dates from a similar chart one could make for the development of literary sensibility in the West. (We must make an ex- ception for the Soviet regression since 1930, which is, after all, a political event.) Professor McLean brings us back to the familiar but mysterious

MR. MATHEWSON *is professor of Russian literature at Columbia University.*

pattern of correspondences between Russian and the parent culture but does not define the intricate connections between them. I do not mean that he should have tried to. It is another subject and one we know all too little about. But it is a dimension of the problem.

We have been badly served in this matter by modern Russian scholarship. Apart from Eikhenbaum's great pioneering studies of Lermontov and Tolstoy,[1] and a handful of other works by Soviet and Western scholars, concern with the action of European culture on Russian literature is discouraged or, in the worst phases of Stalinism, denounced as "cosmopolitanism." The Russian tradition is seen as largely self-sufficient, and as formed in some unexplainable way as a response to the rising movement of social protest. Thus the bulk of the best Russian writing is shown *to precede,* and, through ascending phases of "realism," to *lead up to* the Bolshevik Revolution and the highest form of art— socialist realism. By this intellectual sleight of hand Pushkin is made into a pillar of the Soviet regime. The thaw, it should be said, has produced a number of hopeful signs that this Stalinist version of the literary past is under attack. The publication of Tomashevsky's study of Pushkin and French culture and of the final volume of Eikhenbaum's epochal work on the formation of Tolstoy's mind tend to restore both writers to their original likeness.[2] Forthcoming studies of the Russian novel permit the hope that the special concerns, themes, forms, and techniques of the Russians will be set in relief against the broad tradition of which they form a part.

It is this question that concerns me here—the need to discover the exact combination of elements, to trace, over the years, the history of a literary form, first borrowed, then imitated, altered, transformed, and as sometimes happens, handed back to an astonished Europe, or in a given work, to discover the exact point of fusion, and the moment when the native genius transcends the model. There is space for only a few general observations on this dialogue with Europe, which I intend as supplementary to Professor McLean's presentation, as a sort of reconnaissance along its western frontier.

There are three stages in relations with the West, all of which have been repeated: self-sufficiency (the periods of Ivan IV and of Stalin), when Russian culture, unable to generate its own forms or traditions, is monumental, ornate, and sterile; apprenticeship (the eighteenth century), when imported forms are blindly imitated and much is learned

---

[1] Б. М. Эйхенбаум, *Лермонтов: Опыт историко-литературной оценки* (Leningrad, 1924); *Молодой Толстой* (Petersburg and Berlin: Z. I. Grzhebin, 1922); *Лев Толстой: Книга первая-пятидесятые годы* (Leningrad: Прибой, 1928); *Лев Толстой: Книга вторая-шестидесятые годы* (Moscow and Leningrad, 1931).

[2] Б. В. Томашевский, *Пушкин и Франция* (Leningrad, 1960); Б. М. Эйхенбаум, *Семидесятые годы* (Leningrad, 1960). A collection of Eikhenbaum's essays on Lermontov has also been published recently: *Статьи о Лермонтове* (Leningrad, 1960).

but little of value produced; independence (from 1830 to 1930), when Russia maintains full and nourishing contact with Europe but makes her own incomparable contribution to world culture. Sometimes, indeed, the European ingredient is negligible and the Russian tradition nourishes itself, but even then the two seem to move along parallel lines. Chekhov owes very little directly to the West, but we find him matching, or surpassing, de Maupassant in the designing of the modern short story. This and many similar instances suggest that there is a common logic of development, a shared process of evolution. And yet we would be compelled to conclude, I think, that the Russians had not invented a single new literary form or originated a new literary movement (let's forget the *agitprop* theater). The large groundswells that moved through Russia—romanticism, realism, symbolism, and so forth—had their origin in Europe's cultural storms. Although Russians have made startling innovations within the inherited forms, invention seems to require the richer, denser, more varied world of Europe. To anticipate a Soviet riposte, the new novel of socialist realism, is, in its essence, a familiar part of our sub-literature of *juvenilia* and moral uplift.

Russia's dependence on Europe and her continual effort to keep up have resulted in many strange paradoxes, exotic syntheses of borrowed forms, mysterious lags and spurts. In Catherine's time, who in Russia understood that the literati, led by the sovereign herself, were gobbling up two distinct and, in a sense, contradictory epochs of French civilization at the same time: the ordered symmetry of Boileau's definitions, foundation of a culture that adorned the realm of the absolute monarch, and the subversive critique of *les philosophes,* destined to bring the monarch down in ruins? A series of shocks—the savage rebellion of her own peasants, the collapse of the French monarchy—transformed Catherine from an Enlightened to a frightened despot, from a patron to a censor, and finally to a persecutor, of writers. She abandoned Montesquieu and Diderot, but some of her writers, Novikov and Radishchev, for example, schooled by now in a sterner mode of inquiry, could not limit their work to the graceful correction of manners. The literature designed "to delight," which Professor McLean noted at the end of the century, was no doubt a natural development, but the first collision between the state and the intelligentsia temporarily arrested another, perhaps more vital kind of growth, and formed patterns that dominated the century to follow. One thinks here of literature's "subversive" stance and of the enormous burden of social commentary and spiritual prophecy, first thrust upon literature by Catherine's sudden abdication as chief enlightener.

After a century of assimilation and experimentation, the Russian literary world had equipped itself by 1800 with a literary language, with up-to-date literary forms and with all the other paraphernalia of a modern literature—publishers, journals, critics, and a reading public. After this heroic achievement it was ready to give birth to Pushkin. There is no point in reanimating the vast argument about the nature and extent of his dependence on Europe. It is my own conviction that beneath the layers of patriotic legend, which make him into a Russian mixture of Victor Hugo and George Washington, one discovers not only an incomparable Russian poet but a European man of letters of great learning and flawless judgment who took exactly what he and Russia needed from Rousseau, Byron, Shakespeare, and all the others. Perhaps it does not need to be said here, but I want to emphasize that his practice of selecting, rejecting, combining, altering, and finally going beyond his models is one of his greatest gifts to the Russian tradition. One recalls Tolstoy's and Dostoevsky's vast labors to come to terms with European civilization—whether to accept it or reject it is not the point—and it is certain that Pushkin's own swift and surefooted passage through classicism, romanticism, and into realism could not have occurred without his exquisite knowledge of many literatures.

In a sense Pushkin overcame Russia's lag, depositing her, as it were, on the frontiers of contemporary literature. But Russians have never marched as obediently past the literary milestones as the French, for example. There are fewer formal literary battles, preceded by a fanfare of manifestoes, and followed by the new movement's domination of the cultural scene. New movements arrived in Russia, but the residues of old ones remained, providing a richer mixture of materials to choose from. In this sense Russia's cultural situation more nearly resembles America's than any other. We, too, were laggards and borrowers on the far fringes of Europe, just beginning to enter the main literary currents. Dostoevsky, to take one example, made brilliant use of the Byronic version of the Romantic personality in the 1860's and 1870's, long after it had lost its currency in Europe, and with it created a vision of life which joined Byron with Baudelaire and foretold Nietzsche, Kafka, Freud, and Camus. Herman Melville made the same brilliant use of his provincial vantage, creating out of Homer, the Bible, Shakespeare, and, like Dostoevsky, the clichés of an exhausted romanticism (Byronism, Gothic diabolism, transcendental vision) an aesthetic unity on a scale Europe's novelists never attempted.

Tolstoy defined himself and his art in a struggle *against* the Romantic conventions after Balzac, Stendhal, and, for that matter, Pushkin, had successfully worked their own way beyond them. And note that as Tolstoy found fresh ways of seeing and of telling what he saw and expanded the horizons of the novel to new limits, he found support in a rationalism that was still available to him because it had not been done to death in Russia by the Romantic assault on the eighteenth century. Tolstoy and Dostoevsky attacked the Napoleonic myth and Romantic egotism in the 1860's, and Mark Twain aimed to purge the American mind of all the falseness of romanticism when he wrecked the steamer *Walter Scott* on a Mississippi sand bar in 1884. And in these assaults on a tradition long dead in Europe, all three added new dimensions to the novel *(War and Peace, Crime and Punishment,* and *The Adventures of Huckleberry Finn).*

These observations, random and imprecise as they are, point to a significant freedom from the weight of tradition, the constrictions of militant literary schools, the very density of culture itself as it had grown layer upon layer in the European center. The Russian and the American writers were free of the pieties of the English novel (both could write about adultery, grand theme of the nineteenth-century novel) and of the oppressive skepticism and self-knowledge of the French (both could ask the most elementary questions about themselves, their countries, and their God, without embarrassment).

There is an element of provincial naïveté, perhaps, in the Russian writers' acceptance of their role as prophets, a function performed by philosophers, churchmen, or journalists in freer, more developed countries. Their willingness, in any case, accounts for the presence of that larger dimension, often called metaphysical, in the Russian novel. The Russians' initial concern was with society (as Professor McLean has observed), as it was for Dickens and Balzac. In addition, the Russians were held to their social responsibilities by an importunate school of "civic" criticism, steeped in the utilitarian views of French Romantic socialism. But they transcended both their models and their watchdogs by posing immense questions in their fiction or, as it sometimes seemed, by using the novel as an instrument to organize the whole of human experience.

These familiar ("cursed") questions are more concerned with a search for national identity, in Belinsky's sense that literature records the growth of national self-consciousness, than is sometimes recognized. They can be put in a slightly different form, I think, without altering their intent: Who am I (a Russian)? What is the meaning of life (in Russia)? What are my real relations (as a Russian) to God, morality, mankind, nature, history? These are questions that no nineteenth-century Frenchman or Englishman needed to ask, certainly not in so naked a form. But, again, the parallel with America is remarkable. Whitman, Thoreau, Melville, and Hawthorne, responding to similar pressures of conscience (slavery), similarly apprehensive about the new industrial society taking shape in Europe, asked similar questions about themselves and their countrymen. In both literatures, the search for answers, and sometimes the answers themselves, rise to a level of universal statement, of interest to all men. The two new nations on the wings of Europe paused, it would seem, at the same time, between 1840 and 1880, to ask who they were and where they belonged in the universe. The whole literate world has since become concerned with these inquiries.

Erich Auerbach has noted the presence of a Christian view of the human person as a distinguishing feature of Russian nineteenth-century prose.[3] This is another way to account for the amplitude, the energy, and the passion of the Russian writers' response to experience. The ultimate destiny of man was an urgent, even a practical, question. The drama of sin, guilt, and salvation ordered the sequence of events and shaped the artistic unity of the whole work. The traditional drama of the Christian soul was worked out in the idiom of "naturalistic" psychology. The same could be said of *The Scarlet Letter,* for example, and I would pause to note one more dramatic similarity between the Russian and the American experiences: the active presence of a religious "reality." One must distinguish between the American's reliance on the Old Testament and the Russians on the New—Adam's innocence as against Christ's—but in a certain sense it can be said that God and the Devil are "characters" in both literatures.

After 1880 in Russia the "unsophisticated" capacity for belief in absolute truths largely disappeared from literature as an era ended. It is exactly this element that is missing from the exact, particular studies of discrete situations that make up Chekhov's vision of experience. Moral concerns are present but they are implicit, transmitted through irony, seldom articulated by the characters or even visible to them. Above all, the separate insights in each work are not bound together in a system which touches the supernatural. The quality of the exchange between Europe and Russia changed too. In a sense, Russians became less dependent, but less demanding, too, and less ambitious in the use of what they imported. On the other hand, we cannot imagine *War and Peace* without the "library" of books Tolstoy read before he wrote it, nor any of the late Dostoevsky without the constant, often oppressive presence of European culture.

It is true, symbolism duplicated a familiar pattern: stimulus from abroad, import of ideas and techniques, native redefinitions and the subsequent generation of an authentic poetry. But the notion of parallel growth provides a more accurate perspective, I think. Symbolism touched off a chain reaction of poetic "revolutions" advancing in roughly the same direction, which in the West led to the brilliant epoch of modern poetry. By 1917 all the ingredients were present for an indefinite extension of the poetic renaissance in Russia, including the poets—Gumilev, Mandelshtam, Mayakovsky, Akhmatova, Pasternak, Tsvetaeva, Esenin, and others. But we have only fragments of it. The brutal war waged by Soviet Philistinism against these poets is one of the

3 Erich Auerbach, *Mimesis* (New York: Doubleday, 1957), pp. 459-63.

grimmest events in modern culture. (Only Pasternak can have come close to matching his potential.) The development of Russian verse has been arrested and the tradition broken off.

In prose Chekhov and others kept the realist strain alive, particularly in the smaller genres. Symbolists experimented with the language and the narrative mechanisms of traditional prose forms. One tendency, expressed most notably by Belyi, moved toward the narrative obliquity, the breakup of linear time schemes, the radically shifting point of view we have become accustomed to finding in different combinations in Proust, Joyce, and Faulkner. But the evolution of Russian prose has also been blocked by force. Only the remarkable work of Babel and Olesha and a few others who wrote in the 1920's indicates new directions it might have taken. Whatever else is memorable from the Soviet period echoes older forms, and promises nothing but stagnation for the future. The hard core of dogma in socialist realism has not only robbed the novel and short story of passion, energy, and suspense; it has also paralyzed the growth of the forms themselves.

Professor McLean has ended his account with a description of the Soviet scene in its bleakest aspect, without commenting on the literary ferment after Stalin's death. He is wise not to, perhaps, because any effort to categorize those confused impulses would constitute an act of prophecy. But there are, I would insist, encouraging signs that the genuine tradition has not been forgotten. Much of the prose of the thaw recalls the high-minded earnestness, even if it lacks the felicity, of the classical past. One feels again the action of individual consciences responding, however guardedly, to suffering and injustice. Denied the resources of a vital modern fiction, the writers have turned back to a loose-textured "Chekhovian" narrative or have just gone ahead, *faute de mieux,* with the plain, flat-footed style of socialist realism.

The young poets have expressed themselves on occasion with great vigor and, less often, with genuine artistry on many private and public matters they could not broach before Stalin died. Relations with the immediate past have been formally restored with the publication of works by Akhmatova, Pasternak, Tsvetaeva, and others from the lost generation of Russian verse. Scholars have proceeded cautiously but with determination to recover important areas of the literary past from the generalized fraudulence of Stalinist scholarship. There is in all domains of literature, too, a moderate but unmistakable opening to the West, reminding us again that however far it draws away or falls behind, Russian culture has no vital existence of its own apart from Europe. If it is able to re-establish the dialogue across the political abyss, we will all be the richer for it.

The Aesthetic Function in Russian Literature

GLEB STRUVE

I find very little to quarrel with in Professor McLean's skillfully fore-shortened picture of Russian literature before the present century, or in his over-all analysis of its various problems and aspects. His ingenious approach to it from the point of view of the three main functions of literature—the aesthetic, the cognitive, and the didactic—imparts clarity and incisiveness to his bird's-eye view of the period separating Lomonosov from the Symbolists. All one can do perhaps is to question here and there the relative emphasis laid on this or that function. Whatever may have been the eighteenth-century writers' own prevalent attitude, in retrospect one would be inclined to see both a greater concern with aesthetic values and a greater artistic achievement in the most valuable works of that century's literature (in Lomonosov as well as in Derzhavin, and even in Sumarokov; and not only in Bogdanovich). Similarly, when one looks in retrospect at the sum total of Turgenev's work, one must not forget that in spite of all its "cognitive" importance, especially as far as his novels are concerned (though the novels are not the most important part of Turgenev's literary legacy), Turgenev himself took trouble to stress, even with regard to his novels, that what mattered most in art was not *what* but *how*.[1] Turgenev's concern with questions of form and style cannot be doubted, even if his stylistic virtuosity, unlike that of Gogol's, is carefully concealed.

While it is true that in the post-Gogolian period we observe a gradual "self-effacement of the author" (in which one may be tempted, however, to see a reversion to one of the oldest traditions of Russian literature) and a "retreat of art into anonymity," this in itself does not imply that the writer was turning his back on aesthetic motivations and considerations: this was certainly not the case with Turgenev. The latter is, after all, closer to Pushkin than to Gogol, with his "verbal acrobatics." Professor McLean rightly describes Gogol as "a paradoxical, transitional figure," but he fails to explain, in terms of his general threefold scheme, how it happened that Gogol cut such a solitary figure in Russian literature, that he did not tread its *stolbovaia doroga*, and that his influence on his successors was largely due, as McLean rightly notes, to "a critical

MR. STRUVE is professor of Slavic languages and literatures at the University of California, Berkeley.

[1] *Собраніе сочиненій И. С. Тургенева въ 12 томахъ*, II (St. Petersburg, 1898), p. ix.

misassessment." It is interesting, however, to note that the late Konstantin Mochulsky, whom Professor McLean quotes in this connection, though proceeding from an entirely different standpoint, shared the view advanced by Belinsky and Chernyshevsky—namely, that Gogol had diverted Russian literature from the road indicated to it by Pushkin; in Mochulsky's view, Gogol switched Russian literature from aesthetics to religion, from Pushkin's path to Dostoevsky's.[2]

A tendency to generalize is always fraught with the danger of simplification. Professor McLean does not always avoid this pitfall, both on some general issues and with regard to some points of detail. As examples of such a simplification, I may quote his unequivocal statement that "in the spirit of its literary life, this [the Golden Age of Russian prose fiction] was undoubtedly one of the most antiartistic periods"; or—on the level of details—that the Russian muzhik "marched into the foreground of literature . . . most notably in the *Sportsman's Sketches* of Turgenev." The former statement is much too sweeping and unconvincing; the latter perpetuates the erroneous notion that Turgenev's famous book deals mostly with the peasants: there are quite a number of stories in it in which the muzhik plays no part whatever, and others in which he has a relatively small part.

As Professor McLean proceeds with his analysis, he becomes, handicapped as he is by space limitations, less and less specific and more and more inclined to overgeneralize; and there are some important lacunae in the picture he sees from his jetlike flight over the plains of Russian literature.

His equation of Russian nineteenth-century literary realism with "illusionism" is admirably formulated; but to say that Chekhov basically subscribed to the "old system"—even though Professor McLean does make certain reservations—seems to me to overlook some very important points. And we know how critical Chekhov was of some of the major writers among his immediate predecessors (Turgenev, Goncharov, Dostoevsky). It seems to me very significant that Boris Pasternak, through the mouth of Iurii Zhivago, pointed out the close affinity between Chekhov and Pushkin when he made the protagonist of his novel write in his diary:

What I have come to like best in the whole of Russian literature is the childlike Russian quality of Pushkin and Chekhov, their modest reticence in such high-sounding matters as the ultimate purpose of mankind or their own salvation. It isn't that they didn't think about these things, and to good effect, but to talk about such things seemed to them pretentious, presumptuous. Gogol, Tolstoy, Dostoievsky looked restlessly for the meaning of life, and prepared for death and drew conclusions. Pushkin and Chekhov, right up to the end of their lives, were absorbed in the current, specific tasks

---

[2] К. Мочульскій, *Духовный путь Гоголя* (Paris, 1934), p. 86.

imposed on them by their vocation as writers, and in the course of fulfilling these tasks they lived their lives quietly, treating both their lives and their work as private, individual matters, of no concern to anyone else. And these individual things have since become of concern to all, and their works, like apples picked while they are green, have ripened of themselves, mellowing gradually and growing richer in meaning.[3]

Apart from the somewhat snooty remarks about Volynsky and Merezhkovsky, both of whom are worth more than is implied in Professor McLean's characterization of them, is it fair to overlook, in speaking of the "revolt against realism," Vladimir Soloviev and Konstantin Leontiev? Professor McLean says that "the initial revolt was directed not so much against the great realist tradition—that would have been too formidable a target to start off with—as against the smug and intolerant 'positivism' espoused by the average Russian intellectual." This is, of course, true of Volynsky and Merezhkovsky; it is also true of Soloviev, who had, however, preceded them. But it is not so in the case of Leontiev and his remarkable essay on Tolstoy, with its underlying rejection of the whole of the Russian "realistic" school, its opposition of Pushkin to Tolstoy the novelist, and its welcome—on aesthetic grounds—of Tolstoy's new manner in his stories for the people, although Leontiev could have no sympathy with the ideas behind them. It is interesting that Leontiev agrees with Belinsky, with whom he had so little in common, in tracing Russian "realism" back to Gogol's influence—an influence which, in his eyes, however, was pernicious rather than beneficial.[4]

It seems to me a mistake to suggest that Briusov and Balmont were the most typical representatives of early Russian Modernism, and to ignore such writers as Fedor Sologub and Zinaida Gippius. On the other hand, to speak of the "Parnassian clarity" of the Acmeists is to overlook two important facts: one being that the Acmeists, even in their theoretical pronouncements (I have in mind the famous articles by Gumilev and Gorodetsky) did not proclaim the ideals of "Parnassism"; and the other, that none of them, except perhaps for Gumilev of *Chuzhoe nebo* (but this applies also to much of his *pre*-Acmeist poetry), could be described as true Parnassians in their poetic practice. It has always been my opinion that the only major Acmeist poet who lived up to the essentials of the Acmeist credo was Anna Akhmatova, and there is nothing Parnassian about her. The label fits Osip Mandelshtam even less (this is true even of *Kamen'*, his most Acmeist book); and there is not very much that is "Parnassian" in Gumilev's own late, mature poetry. Nor am I sure that one is justified in speaking of the "cognitive urge" as being characteristic of the Acmeists.

---

[3] Boris Pasternak, *Doctor Zhivago* (New York, 1958), p. 285.
[4] К. Н. Леонтьевъ, *О романахъ гр. Л. Н. Толстого: Анализъ, стиль и вѣяніе. Критическій этюдъ* (Moscow, 1911), *passim*.

When he comes to Soviet literature, Professor McLean sees in its initial phase a continuation of the "antirealist" trend of the preceding period. As an illustration of it he cites the "opaque" prose of Pilniak, Babel, early Leonov, and other writers representing what is usually designated as "ornamental prose"; they are, he says, "the antithesis of the high-realist transparency." Characterizing this early Soviet literature, he stresses that "artificiality or artfulness was one of its principal aesthetic dimensions." This is, of course, quite true. Equally true and pertinent is the observation about its "ethical relativism." But when he says that "it was the fate of Mayakovsky's Futurism that pointed the way for Soviet literature far more than the manifesto of the Serapion Brothers," adding that Mayakovsky was "the most powerful poetic celebrant of communism," his meaning is not quite clear to me. That the Serapion Brothers and their "manifesto" had little influence on the subsequent fortunes of Soviet literature, I agree. But then there was really no "manifesto"; there was only a provocative article by Lev Lunts, reflecting his personal (and perhaps Veniamin Kaverin's) view of literature and of its "stagnation" in Russia. The Serapions were not a literary school, not a homogeneous group, and perhaps Zamiatin was not so far off the mark when he said that they did not really exist, that they had been invented by him like Putois in Anatole France's well-known story.[5]

But in what way did the fate of Mayakovsky's Futurism point the way to Soviet literature? Or is the stress here on the word "fate"? This is not made quite clear. Mayakovsky "the most powerful poetic celebrant of communism" and Mayakovsky the Futurist should not be completely identified. One does not have to agree with Roman Jakobson (whose view of Mayakovsky is now being so violently attacked in the Soviet Union),[6] who sees an irreconcilable dichotomy between Mayakovsky the drummer of the Revolution and Mayakovsky the lyrical poet, to realize that Mayakovsky is one of the most tragic figures in Soviet literature, and that neither his poetry nor his personal fate in any sense "pointed the way to Soviet literature." Mayakovsky's identification with socialist realism is part of that Soviet myth-making which confuses so many issues. Without some further elucidation it is difficult to accept Professor McLean's statement that "this official, didactic aspect of Mayakovsky's work turned out to be the most prophetic side of his Futurism." Inasmuch as there was didacticism in Mayakovsky, it had little, if anything, to do with his Futurism or with Futurism *tout court*. In saying this I do not mean to come out as a champion of Futurism. All I mean to say is that it was only by renouncing the fundamental tenets of his own early Futurism that Mayakovsky was able to attempt even to adjust

---

[5] Е. Замятин, *Лица* (New York, 1955), p. 196.

[6] See З. Паперный, *Поэтический образ у Маяковского* (Moscow, 1961), pp. 18-21 and 422-26. On p. 19 will be found references to some other attacks on Jakobson.

himself to the demands that the party and the literary pundits were making on him and his art. Those attempts were not, and could never be, successful. Mayakovsky was bound to end as he did. Mayakovsky the harbinger of socialist realism is part of Soviet literary mythology.

Professor McLean gives a clear and succinct account of the "totalitarianization" of culture between 1928 and 1934. The pseudo-liberal nature of the 1932 literary "reform," which led to the setting up of a homogeneous and easily controlled and controllable Union of Soviet Writers, has long been clear to most people, although it did deceive many outside observers when it was first promulgated. I also agree with the statement that in the framework of socialist realism cognition of reality is a mere illusion, for any "realities" the party wishes out of the picture cannot be "typical" and are therefore "in effect, unreal." In other words, socialist realism boils down to the party view of the Soviet reality and, in the final analysis, to the current party line. This is what I said in the American edition of my book on Soviet literature,[7] and I see no reason to alter this diagnosis. In terms of his own tripartite scheme Professor McLean sees the aesthetic function in Soviet literature subordinated to the didactic and the pseudo-cognitive ones.

As he tries to peer into the future, Professor McLean says that it is difficult to foresee the circumstances under which true literature might be revived in Soviet Russia. Here, too, I agree with him, but I wish he had said more about some of the more recent developments. It is in this last part of his discussion that one particularly misses more specific references. I do not have so much in mind the so-called thaw—both its political significance and its impact on literature have always seemed to me to have been exaggerated out of all proportion, and I do not think it produced any work of true literary significance—but rather some of the goings-on in the last couple of years. Here one must distinguish between two different sets of phenomena.

One of them is represented by several recent utterances of Ilya Ehrenburg, who has been regarded, not without reason, as a sort of weathervane pointing the direction in which the literary-political winds in the Soviet Union are blowing. His article on Stendhal a few years ago, and even more so his "rehabilitation," in his memoirs now in progress, of a number of writers who cannot possibly be fitted into the socialist-realist scheme of things (they include Marina Tsvetaeva, Pasternak, Mandelshtam, Andrei Belyi, and Remizov),[8] are, to say the least, symptomatic. One can make all sorts of guesses, in terms of both personal and political

---

[7] Gleb Struve, *Soviet Russian Literature: 1917-1950* (Norman, Okla., 1951), pp. 368-72. See also my article "The Puzzling Theory of Socialist Realism" in *The Creative Artist in Communist Society*, ed. Henry W. Burke (Washington, D.C., 1959).

[8] И. Эренбург, «Люди, годы, жизнь: Книга третья,» *Новый мир*, Nos. 9, 10, and 11, 1961, *passim*.

psychology, to account for the candor with which Ehrenburg defends unpopular writers and unpopular approaches to art (among other things, he makes it quite clear, I think, that he prefers Pasternak and Mandelshtam to Mayakovsky). I have my own theory about it, but this is hardly the place to advance it. In any case, he is the first Soviet writer or critic in many years to pay such a fulsome tribute to the influence of Andrei Belyi and Remizov on Soviet literature, including some present-day writers who are not even aware of that influence, because it has reached them indirectly through others.[9]

But Ehrenburg is not alone. Recently several Soviet writers and critics have broached the subject of bringing "semi-forbidden literature" of the prerevolutionary period out of oblivion. Thus, last year the young poet Lev Ozerov published an article in *Literaturnaia gazeta,* in which he pointed out how much of the Russian poetic treasure (he obviously had in mind the poets of the prerevolutionary "modernist" period) still remained buried, and he urged Soviet editors (the article had specifically in mind the "Biblioteka poèta" series founded by Gorky) not to "abandon" some of those poets to the *émigrés* abroad.[10] More recently, two prominent Soviet critics have spoken in the same sense. Viktor Pertsov, who a few years ago tried to rescue from oblivion and neglect such writers as Andrei Belyi and Fedor Sologub, stressing the realistic aspect of some of their work, wrote in the same *Literaturnaia gazeta* about the "keen interest" *(obostrennoe vnimanie)* that some of the younger Soviet poets showed in such poets as Annensky, Mandelshtam, and Gumilev. After mentioning that these young enthusiasts of modern poetry had recently at last received a selection of Tsvetaeva's poetry, but omitting to recall that a volume of Annensky's complete poetry had already appeared in 1959, Pertsov made the reader feel that his article was a kind of *ballon d'essai,* that his unspoken thought was that it was now the turn of Mandelshtam and Gumilev to be published.[11] In fact, a volume of Mandelshtam's poems was also announced by "Biblioteka poèta" in 1959. It did not materialize then, and in the corresponding volume of the new edition of *Malaia Sovetskaia Entsiklopediia,* published in June, 1959, there was still no entry on Mandelshtam. But in the course of the last year there have been very persistent rumors about the forthcoming publication of his poetry. As for Gumilev, another Soviet critic, Kornelii Zelinsky, an ex-Constructivist, in an article written, it is true, for external consumption and so far apparently not mentioned in the Soviet press, not only called Gumilev an excellent poet but even compared his fate with that of André Chénier: both were

9 *Ibid.,* No. 9, pp. 106-8.

10 Лев Озеров, «Страна русской поэзии,» *Литературная газета,* March 28, 1961.

11 Виктор Перцов, «Поиски нового и великие традиции,» *Литературная газета,* February 27, 1962.

excellent poets and both paid with their lives for their counterrevolutionary activities. The implication was that there was no reason for not restoring Gumilev to literary life.[12] To mention but one other interesting fact of the same order, Sologub's novel *Melkii bes,* last reprinted in the 1930's, was reissued—somewhat inconspicuously—in 1958 by the Kemerovo Publishing House in the Kuzbas![13]

The other set of phenomena worthy of attention, which Professor McLean does not mention, is the steady stream of clandestine Soviet literature which, in the last few years, has been reaching the free world. This is something new. Some of it—and this was to be expected of underground literature in a totalitarian country—is of primarily ideological import and interest. But there is also in it the element of an aesthetic revolt against socialist realism. This applies in the first place to "Abram Tertz," his *Sud idet* (1959), his more recent *Fantastic Tales* (1961), and especially his brilliant essay on socialist realism, first published in French in February, 1959, in *l'Esprit.* I wonder whether Professor McLean doubts the authenticity of "Tertz": this is a point on which at present there can be no absolute certainty. That "Tertz" is a fake is naturally the theory advanced in the Soviet Union. For a long time there was a conspiracy of silence around him in the Soviet press (although the essay on socialist realism was once casually dismissed as a *fal'shivka*); but all recent reports from Moscow, whether printed or private, testify to a great interest aroused by his work and the ensuing speculation about his identity.[14] Although the authorship of some of the anonymous, clandestine poems published in *Harper's Magazine, Problems of Communism, Sovetskaia potaennaia muza* (Munich, 1961), and elsewhere, seems to be known, the identity of "Tertz" remains an intriguing mystery.[15]

It is difficult to assess the significance for Russian literature of these recent developments. Literature and politics are so closely interwoven in the Soviet Union that I, for one, would not be surprised if all these manifestations of unexpected literary "broadmindedness" and tolerance turned out to be part of Mr. Khrushchev's "cultural coexistence" policy, aimed at impressing and hoodwinking public opinion in the West. Lack of space prevents me from elaborating this point, but I would draw

[12] K. Zelinsky, "Russian Poetry Today," *Survey* (London), No. 40 (January, 1962), p. 51. Zelinsky's essay was written for an Italian survey of Modern European poetry, edited by Dr. Olga Muzio and to be published by the Casa Editrice Morcelliana.

[13] *Ежегодник Книги 1959: Систематический указатель,* I (Moscow, 1961), 420, No. 11980.

[14] See Alan Moray Williams, "Ces contes d'Abram Tertz sont-ils des faux ou de nouveaux 'Kafka'?" *Figaro littéraire,* April 7, 1962.

[15] Some interesting speculations about Tertz are found in Stefan Bergholz's introduction to the Polish edition of *Fantastic Tales—Opowieści fantastyczne* (Paris, 1961): "Czytając Terca (Zamiast przedmowy)," pp. 7-76. See also what is apparently a greatly abridged English version of it: "On Reading Tertz," *Survey,* No. 41 (April, 1962), pp. 145-50.

the reader's attention to a very perspicacious and suggestive article by Edmond Taylor in *The Reporter,* which can be easily supplemented by evidence from the area of arts and letters, pointing in the same direction.[16] But even if such be the case, this cultural reorientation on orders from above must meet with some spontaneous and genuine response on the part of Soviet writers. Though the aesthetic function of literature in Soviet Russia has been subordinated to the didactic and pseudo-cognitive ones, and ever since the advent of socialist realism all but suppressed, it has shown signs of breaking through whenever there was a chance. Leonov seems to me to be a good example of its vitality. Of course, in his later work, beginning with *Sot'* (though less completely so in his plays, even in the thirties), the element of "artificiality or artfulness," so strong in his early stories and even in *Vor,* is considerably minimized and carefully disguised, but it is never absent. And his revised version of *Vor,* published in 1960 and almost completely ignored by Soviet critics, is quite remarkable for the intensification of that "artificiality," for recourse to even more elaborate "formalistic tricks." It is this which makes this revision so different from other revisions of their earlier works by major Soviet writers, for example, Sholokhov or Slonimsky. I know that this opinion of mine is not shared by those outside the Soviet Union who have commented upon the revised version, but this is not the place to go into details.[17] It is interesting, however, that the Soviet author of the long introduction to the revised version of the novel even welcomed Leonov's experimentation with techniques and wrote:

. . . with his drafts, conjectures, setbacks, and tricks, the author now peers from behind the wings, now removes again all the scaffolding and rafters, captivating the reader by the spontaneity of feeling, and depth of thought, the sharpness of observation. And this very "game" fascinates and provides an aesthetic pleasure. . . . It shows that form is as much an active element of art as the idea.[18]

Lack of space allows me only a brief mention of what I consider the greatest lacuna in Professor McLean's otherwise illuminating survey and analysis. I mean his complete disregard of Russian literature outside Russia, that of the Russian *émigrés.* The fact that the Communist Revolution of 1917 divided the stream of Russian literature into two

---

[16] Edmond Taylor, "How the Russians Wage Political Warfare," *The Reporter,* May 10, 1962, pp. 16-20. On the other hand, Peter Viereck's reportage on Soviet literature today, published somewhat earlier in *The Reporter* ("The Split Personality of Soviet Literature," March 15, 1962, pp. 23-27), seems to me to err on the side of wishful political inferences and to draw some unjustified analogies.

[17] A year ago I read a paper on this subject at the Far Western Slavic Conference in San Francisco, and I hope one day to publish an extended version of it.

[18] Е. Старикова, «О романе Леонида Леонова,» in Леонид Леонов, *Вор: Роман* (Moscow, 1959), p. 33.

branches seems to me to be of paramount importance. Quite apart from the artistic superiority of much of *émigré* literature to the literature produced in Russia after 1930, the existence of this branch of Russian literature, free from outside pressures and extraliterary controls, may prove to be an important historical factor. While the older *émigré* writers carried on both the cognitive and the aesthetic traditions of the earlier periods, the younger ones profited by cross-fertilization from the West (it is enough to mention Vladimir Nabokov, who until 1940 was a Russian writer and whose Russian novels seem to me to be of more lasting interest and value than his recent American production).[19] The work of some of the outstanding *émigré* writers is now beginning to be rechanneled into the main stream of Russian literature. As a rule this happens posthumously; thus Bunin has been reinstated in the pantheon of Russian literary classics, although the subordination of Soviet literature to party guidance has resulted in some major expurgations. Not all of Bunin's works written in exile have been reissued in the Soviet Union. Of those that have, *Zhizn' Arsen'eva* (the first part of which was published in English under the title *The Well of Days*) has been subjected to severe and extensive cutting. It is significant, however, that in his introduction to the most recent one-volume Soviet edition of Bunin's selected prose works, Konstantin Paustovsky, himself one of the most attractive figures in present-day Soviet literature, speaks of *Zhizn' Arsen'eva* as *the* masterpiece of Bunin's works. This is in line with the opinion voiced by the present writer and many other *émigré* critics. Paustovsky even goes so far as to describe it as "one of the most remarkable phenomena in world literature," adding that it is "a great fortune" that "it belongs, in the first place, to Russian literature."[20] Paustovsky also speaks very highly of Bunin as a poet.

The way Ehrenburg has spoken of Remizov may be taken as heralding a similar posthumous reinstatement for him. If so, this will be of particular interest because with the return of Remizov to his native ground Russian literature will receive back one of its most "antirealistic" writers, one who had a decisive influence on the nonrealist period of Soviet literature, the period of its "opaque prose," to use Professor McLean's term. Nor can one disregard the nonfictional contribution of the Russian writers in exile—in literary criticism and scholarship, in philosophical essays, and so forth. If and when a literary revival at last

---

[19] Ehrenburg in his memoirs quotes Babel's opinion of Nabokov as a writer who "knows how to write but has nothing to write about"(*Новый мир*, No. 9, 1961, p. 147).

[20] И. А. Бунин, «Повести, рассказы, воспоминания,» *Московский рабочий*, 1961, p. 14. The text of Paustovsky's Introduction was also reproduced, as part of the forthcoming second volume of his *Золотая роза*, in *Тарусские страницы* (Kaluga, 1961); this collection of poems (including some unpublished ones by Marina Tsvetaeva and Nikolai Zabolotsky), stories (also one by Tsvetaeva), sketches, and essays, has been likened, for its unorthodox and independent spirit, to *Литературная Москва*, which was the literary sensation of 1956 and the high point of the so-called thaw.

comes, the achievements of Russian *émigré* writers, as well as their attitudes, will undoubtedly play a very important part in it. One of the encouraging signs of the changing intellectual and artistic climate in Russia, if one is to believe some recent testimony of numerous foreign visitors to Moscow and Leningrad, is the interest displayed there in *émigré* literary activities.

Reply

HUGH McLEAN

The two commentators have admirably complemented one another in extending and filling in the sketchy view of Russian literature I was able to provide. My "advent'rous song" turned out to have taken "middle flight" after all, despite the jetlike speed Mr. Struve credits me with. Mr. Mathewson, soaring far above me, has cast his eye over a vast vista of new territory, seeing Russian literary development in the perspective of Western culture as a whole. Mr. Struve, flying closer to the ground, has singled out with a sharp eye the many blurred and blank spots in the account I presented. The three of us together, let us hope, create a composite picture endowed with all the virtues of long-range vision, accuracy, and creative imagination.

Mr. Mathewson's vision is indeed a stimulating one and surely points the way to a promising avenue for future research. The whole subject of the relation of Russian to European culture, obvious and central as it may appear, has still been most inadequately explored, and Mr. Mathewson has shown us the kind of explorers we need, a kind largely lacking in the past. Too often parochialism, nationalist bias, and sheer ignorance on the part of critics and scholars—and not only Russian ones, may I add—have indeed led to an "isolationist" treatment of the development of Russian literature as something self-contained and self-sufficient, which it certainly was not, and to a vast overemphasis on the importance for the history of literature of the movements of social protest in nineteenth-century Russian society. My own presentation was to some extent guilty of the first, if not the second, of these distortions, and I am glad to have the focus re-established. On the other hand, most of the conventional "comparatist" approaches to the subject have been limited to the search for direct "influences" of one writer on another or to somewhat arbitrary juxtapositions of seemingly parallel figures in different countries, without any attempt to establish a genetic relation between them. However interesting the data unearthed in such quests, they do not help us much to get to the root of the matter. It is this root to which Mr. Mathewson directs us—the mysterious processes by which whole cultures interact with one another, and in particular, the curious position of Russia as a "backward" or peripheral country discovering herself by constant self-measuring against the more "established" countries to the west. I found Mr. Mathewson's observations on this subject fascinating, and especially his confrontation of Russia and America.

This approach need not be taken, as it has been and doubtless will be by oversensitive Russian patriots, as an attempt to belittle Russian artistic achievements or minimize their originality. Mr. Mathewson's point, with which I wholly agree, is that Russian literature could not have grown to the size and shape it did without the eternal shadow of Europe over it. The constant effort to find themselves in this shadow, to discover what it meant to be a Russian and a man, served as a powerful stimulus for the great Russian writers. It led them to plumb human depths and scale metaphysical heights no Western writer, whether satisfied with ready-made answers or more aware of the risks involved in seeking one's own, would have dared to attempt. It is one of the elements of Russian greatness.

With Mr. Struve's amendments and amplifications I am mostly in agreement; only a few require any rejoinder on my part. I should have made it clearer that the "retreat into anonymity" I ascribe to mid-nineteenth-century Russian literature did not imply that the writers had turned their backs on "aesthetic motivations"; on the contrary, their very anonymity was in part an aesthetic strategy which could be put into effect only with artistic skills of the highest order. My point was rather that extra-aesthetic considerations were overwhelmingly dominant in discussions and appraisals of literature by people other than writers, and that the writers themselves acquiesced in this situation, partly because they too were eager to see their art not only as an art, but as a vehicle for cosmological, sociological, and ethical truths. I also thought that in their anti-aesthetic extravagances the critics and common readers of the 1860's and 1870's inadvertently contributed to the illusionistic magic practiced by the writers; they naïvely proclaimed as dogma the very identification between literature and life which the writers wanted them to make. And I still maintain that for conscious, aggressive anti-aestheticism on the part of professional critics and the reading public at large it would be hard to find a more extreme period in the history of world literature than the Russian 1860's—though the period nevertheless was one of superlative artistic achievement.

My remarks on Mayakovsky were doubtless misleadingly formulated. Certainly, it was not Mayakovsky's Futurism as such which pointed the way for Soviet literature but rather his harnessing of poetry to the Communist ideology. Unlike many critics, I do not believe that—in Mayakovsky's peculiar case and for the limited time he used it—this harness really hampered his art or hurt its quality. On the contrary, communism may have represented a kind of poetic challenge for Mayakovsky: how could this exceptionally tough and flinty material be transmuted into poetry? And the very prosiness of Communist slogans fitted well into Mayakovsky's aesthetic system, one of the basic stratagems of which was the oxymoronic effect of placing extreme prosaisms in a lyrically charged context. But whether after 1930 Mayakovsky could have maintained his precarious balance, with all its moral ambiguities, is certainly problematical; and his was an utterly ruinous example for anyone else to follow. Mayakovsky managed to incorporate the official Communist ideology into his poetic system and essentially subordinate it to his own private "communism" (which included the ideological side of his Futurism, his dream of the *kommuna* as a place where the horrors of petty, grubby, self-seeking vulgarity would at last disappear). But in the case of his successors it was the poets who had to subordinate themselves to the ideology, rather than the other way around; the result was not a synthesis but a loss of artistic integrity, and with it, of real poetry.

Perhaps I should have said something about *émigré* literature. But I do not feel, by and large, that this literature has contained any notably new developments or can much affect the historical evolution of Russian literature. Freed from Communist censorship and pressures, the *émigré* writers could work out their own destinies within the limits imposed by a restricted market and isolation from much of their source material. But nearly all the major *émigré* writers had been fully formed before the Revolution; they went on writing much as they had before. Nabokov is the only second-generation *émigré* to achieve more than a local reputation, and Nabokov eventually found the *émigré* audience too restricted and became an English writer. It is true that for many years *émigré* literature preserved a level of literary culture which Soviet literature gradually lost, and that assimilation of the *émigré* experience might have helped Soviet literature regain the intellectual and aesthetic sophistication it so glaringly lacks. But I am afraid it is too late for any real reunion: the *émigré* literature is gradually dying out, and the reimportation of a dead tradition (very carefully selected, moreover) is not likely to exert any vital influence on Soviet literature. In short, *émigré* literature may be aesthetically valuable, but I do not consider it historically important, in the sense of its effect on the over-all development of Russian literature.

My colleagues are somewhat more optimistic than I about the future prospects of Russian literature. About the "thaw" of 1954-57 I agree with Mr. Struve: its *literary* significance has been exaggerated. As a manifestation of the long-suppressed sentiments of a part of Soviet society, as a contrast, a faint glimmer of human light after the dark night of Zhdanovism, it was of great interest. But it certainly produced no major works of literature. And I am afraid I cannot see any fundamental difference between the thaw of the mid-fifties and the situation today. The rehabilitation of officially "forgotten" writers began then, and it continues now. If this process does indeed go so far as to bring Gumilev, Mandelshtam, and Sologub back into the light of Soviet day, as Mr. Struve hopes it will, it will certainly be a step toward a restoration of historical justice. But whether these resurrections can bring about a revival of literary production of comparable quality is another matter.

After all, a living literature cannot be written by ghosts. To be sure, first-class literary ghosts are an enormous asset to a living literary tradition, and one of the many cultural crimes of the Soviet regime is that it impoverished Russian literature by suppressing dead writers as it oppressed living ones. One can only say that the revival of Russian literature, if it is to come, must be predicated on a reassimilation of these writers, and of much else, including most of what has happened in Western literature since the 1920's. But where are the present-day Gumilevs, Mandelshtams, and Sologubs? I cannot see them, not in such as Evtushenko certainly. However bold, admirable, or interesting as a symptom, Evtushenko illustrates very well the stylistic and cultural deficiencies which prevent Soviet writers from producing works of real artistic quality. There is something missing even in the best of these writers, whether it is lack of culture, lack of discipline, lack of striving for artistic excellence, or the old difficulties of censorship, prescribed Philistinism, and prohibitions against formal experimentation. Even the best present-day Soviet literature is somehow more deeply provincial, more limited, sentimental, and banal than the literature of thirty years ago, let alone earlier. Its worst feature is its *artistic* complacency. These occasional rumblings of moral and social doubt are not accompanied by comparable efforts in technique, or even by the recognition that such efforts are needed. Nor do I see "Tertz" as a harbinger of spring: for all his intellectual interest, he is certainly not much of an artist.

One explanation for the artistic doldrums in which Russian literature still flounders must lie, as Mr. Mathewson suggests at the very end of his essay, in the relations between Russian and European culture. If "Russian culture has no vital existence of its own apart from Europe," the Stalinist regime may have succeeded in breaking this connection more profoundly than is generally realized. For years the propaganda machine has assured Russians that they are the most advanced and progressive nation in the world and can have nothing further to learn from Europe or anywhere else. Such words are too humanly gratifying to be automatically rejected. The contemporary Western literature passed for importation into the USSR is carefully selected to protect socialist man against various noxious microbes of Western provenience. The result is a curiously spotty picture of Western literature. It is true that the older generation have never really lost touch with Europe: they carried their cultural lifeline inside them. But the younger generation have been successfully disoriented. Many of them suspect that there is something wrong, that they have missed something, that they must find the way to Europe again. But they no longer know the roads; they are bewildered and blind. For a really creative, dynamic, intellectually aware and sophisticated "dialogue with Europe" we must look not to Russia but to Poland. There the richness, subtlety, and profundity of intellectual and artistic life, particularly of the younger generation, far exceed anything present-day Russians have dreamed of.

If Russian literature is to be revived, the first requirement would be a recognition of the extent of its deterioration; and this, I suspect, is something few Russians are prepared to admit. If they see a problem at all, they see it in administrative terms: they may deplore the evils of the censorship and the screening system, berate the banalities of the officially approved literary style, and inveigh against the Philistine stupidity of party culture bosses. And certainly the removal of these ugly excrescences would seem to be a *sine qua non* of any literary renascence. But even if all the external obstacles were removed (which hardly seems likely), the whole process of education and self-discovery will virtually have to begin again. The Russians will have to go to school once again as they did in the eighteenth century, to find out what literature really is, and how you go about making it.

Part II

OLD RUSSIA

FOUR

The Problem of Old Russian Culture

GEORGES FLOROVSKY

Die wahre Kritik liegt im Verständnis.
Bachofen, ANTIQUARISCHE BRIEFE

I. THE PATTERN OF INTERPRETATION

There was, in Russian historiography of the last century, an established pattern of interpretation, and, to some extent, it is still commonly used. It was traditional to divide the history of Russia into two parts, and to divide it sharply and rigidly: the Old and the New, Ancient and Modern. The time of Peter the Great was regarded as the Great Divide, as the decisive turning point in the total process. Of course, it was much more than a chronological demarcation. Passionate value judgments were implied therein. Kliuchevsky has rightly stated: "The whole philosophy of our history was often reduced to the appraisal of Peter's reform; by a certain scholarly foreshortening, the whole problem of the meaning of Russian history was condensed into one single question—about the deed of Peter and the relation of his new reformed Russia to the old."[1] The Old Russia was regarded and evaluated in the perspective of the New, in the light of "the Reform." In fact, this approach was itself an integral part of the Reform, and its most ponderous legacy. This pattern of interpretation was first invented by the pioneers of the Reform in order to justify the break, which was intended to be radical and definitive, and then it was maintained in its defense. The story of Old Russia had to be presented in such a way as to show that the Reform was inevitable, necessary, and just. "The Old" meant in this connection the obsolete, sterile and stagnant, primitive and backward. And "the New" was depicted, by contrast, in the brightest colors as a great achievement and a glorious promise. The whole history of Old Russia, before Peter, was usually treated as a kind of prehistory—a dark background against which the whole splendor of the new cultural

FATHER FLOROVSKY is *professor of Eastern church history at Harvard Divinity School.*

[1] В. О. Ключевский, *Курс русской истории*, Part IV, lecture 68, in *Сочинения*, IV (Moscow, 1958), 201.

awakening could be spectacularly presented; or as a protracted period of infancy and immaturity, in which the normal growth of the nation was inhibited and arrested; or else as a lengthy preparation for that messianic age which had finally descended upon Russia, under Peter and by his sovereign will, from abroad if not from above. "History," in the proper sense of the word, was supposed to have begun in Russia only with Peter. It was assumed that only at his time did Russia enter the stage of history and civilization—indeed as a belated newcomer, sorely delayed in development, and thereby destined to tarry for a long time in the humble position of a learner, in the commonwealth of cultured nations.

There were manifold variations on this basic theme in Russian historiography. For our immediate purpose it would suffice to quote but one of them. Sergius M. Soloviëv had the reputation of a sober historian, and he well deserved the praise. His monumental *History of Russia from the Oldest Times* is still the most reliable survey of the subject, well documented and skillfully arranged. It is highly significant that Soloviëv simply loses his temper when he comes to the times of Peter, to the Reform. About Peter he writes in a very special style, passionate, nervous, and pathetic, at once elevated, ornate, and excited. It is the style of heroic legend. Indeed, for Soloviëv, Peter was *the* hero of Russian history, probably the only hero, and the last one. "Only Christian faith and the nearness in time saves us—and still incompletely —from the cult of this demigod and from the mythical conceptions about the exploits of this Hercules." Peter was almost a supernatural being. "The period of heroes comes to its end with the coming of civilization."[2] Peter concludes the epic period of Russian history and opens

---

[2] С. М. Соловьевъ, *Исторія Россіи съ древнѣйшихъ временъ*, XIV, chap. ii (St. Petersburg, n.d.: «Общественная Польза»), Book III, cols. 1057-58: "Obshchestvo iunoe, kipiashchee neustroennymi silami, proizvelo ispolina, kak iunaia zemlia v dopotopnoe vremia proizvodila gromadnyia sushchestva, skelety kotorykh privodiat v izumlenie nash melkii rod.... Devstvennaia strana predstavliala takoe obshirnoe poprishche dlia bogatyrei vsiakago roda"; cf. XXII, chap. v, Book V, col. 542: "Kto-to sil'nyi, neobyknovennyi iavilsia, proshel, ostavil neizgladimye sledy, porazil voobrazhenie, ovladel pamiat'iu naroda. Vsiudu dlia liudei chutkikh, ispolnennykh sily, slyshalis' slova: 'Idi za mnoi, vremia nastupilo'!" It must be noted, however, that in his *Public Lectures on Peter the Great* (1872) Soloviëv seems to be more cautious and reserved on this point. "Great men" should not be isolated from their environment, from the nation, and should not be regarded as miraculous or supernatural beings: they are children of their age and embody the hidden urges of the nation. Soloviëv then stresses the inevitability of historical development, the rhythm of history, the necessary stages of the process. Yet the general scheme of interpretation is still the same. There are two stages, or ages, of national life: in the first the life of the nation is dominated and guided by "feeling"—the period of youth, of strong passions and movements, the time of fire. And yet it is the time of immaturity, as vigorous as the energy may be. The nation must come of age, or perish. In the second stage its life is ruled by reason, or by thought. Everything is subjected to doubt. There are dangers in these awakenings, in the transition from superstition to unbelief. Nevertheless, it is a step forward. Western Europe passed into the mature age, the age of thought, at the time of the Renaissance. Russia did the same two centuries later. In fact,

the era of civilization for Russia. It means that for Soloviev there was no civilization in Russia before Peter, even if there was an enormous dynamic potential—in the state of chaotic fermentation. The change under Peter was most radical: from epic to history—from prehistory to history proper. Only since Peter has Russia become an "historic" nation.

There is in this interpretation a striking discrepancy between the political and the cultural course of the process. The political history of Russia was continuous from the very beginning, through the Reform— in spite of its cataclysmic character—up to the present. Old Russia was just a stage in the formation of the definitive Russian Empire. The unity of Russian history is seen precisely in the history of the Russian state. On the other hand, there is a radical discontinuity in the history of Russian culture. The culture of Old Russia has been simply dismissed, and it is assumed that it had to be dismissed and discarded, and replaced by another. It was not a link in the continuous chain. There was rather no such continuous chain at all. The true Russian culture had to be created afresh; actually, it had to be imported. As Soloviev phrased it himself, "It was the turn of the Russian people to serve a foreign principle."[3] The true history of Russian culture is, from this point of view, the history of Western culture in Russia. Old Russia was contrasted with the New as a "primitive society" with the "civilized." Many Russian historians of the last century were using these and similar phrases. Theodore I. Buslaev, one of the great founders of Russian historical philology, could not find in Old Russia any trace of genuine culture: no intellectual curiosity, no aesthetic vision, no literary skill. There was no dynamism, no advance whatever. In the same vein, A. N. Pypin would contend that actually there was almost no "chronology" in the history of Old Russian literature. For Buslaev the whole period of Russian history up to Peter could be characterized by two words: "primitivism" *(pervobytnost')* and "stagnation" *(velikoe kosnenie russkago naroda).*[4] From this point of view, Old Russian culture was to be studied by archaeologists, not by historians. Indeed, it was under the guise of "Russian antiquities" that the history of Old Russian culture was studied in the last century. The term "culture" is often used in a wider sense to include "primitive cultures." In that sense one could also speak of Old Russian culture, but only in that sense. It was a field for antiquaries, not for historians.

---

only at this point of transition does real history begin, although it is possible only on the basis of what had been accumulated or created in the age of feeling. There is, in Soloviev's vision of history, a peculiar blending of Hegelianism and the motives of the Enlightenment: belief in general laws of history and worship of knowledge and critical thinking. See «Публичныя чтенія о Петре Великомъ,» *Сочиненія Сергѣя Михайловича Соловьева* (St. Petersburg, 1882), pp. 88 ff.

[3] Соловьевъ, *op. cit.*, Book III, col. 1057: "Ochered' porabotat' chuzhomu nachalu."

[4] Ѳ. И. Буслаевъ, «Общія понятія о русской иконописи» (1866), *Сочиненія*, I (St. Petersburg, 1908), pp. 3-4, 21, 29, 32.

The line of Russian cultural development was not merely bent but really broken. The old order had passed away. Old Russia was a dead world. It had to be admitted, however, that the Reform, as radically as it had been conceived from the beginning, was not accomplished at once. The old world was terribly shaken, but it did not disappear. Much of the old order survived, but only beneath the level of "civilization" in those strata of the nation which resisted the Reform and attempted an escape. But these strata were, in a sense, outside history, and it had to be hoped that finally, with the spread of "enlightenment," they would also be dragged in. What remained from the old order was no more than "survivals." As Pypin said, "The life of the small civilized class was surrounded by the element of old custom." All survivals were actually in the realm of customs and routine, in that realm which is denoted by the untranslatable Russian word, *byt*.[5] But *byt*, at its best, is no more than a dead mask of culture. The Reform had split the nation into two parts: the civilized elite and the masses. It was in the masses that relics of Old Russia had been preserved. It was assumed that in good time they would be completely discarded.

It has been commonly assumed that culture had to be autonomous, that is, secular. The whole history of European civilization was usually presented in this way—as a story of progressive emancipation of culture from the stiffening control of the established religion, or of the Church. This scheme of interpretation was derived partly from the philosophy of the Enlightenment, partly from Positivism. It has been faithfully applied to Russian history also. By this criterion the whole history of Old Russia was summarily discredited in advance. Indeed, the major charge that has been raised against Old Russia is that its life was dominated by religion, enslaved in the dogmatic and ritual forms. There was little room in this old structure for criticism and free search. Very often "culture" was simply identified with "criticism." There was little understanding of its organic aspect. Only critical trends, within the established structure, could have had, from this point of view, any cultural significance. Accordingly, it was among the dissenters or nonconformists of various types that signs or tokens of potential cultural awakening were looked for, just as it was the fashion at one time to discover forerunners of modern times in the heretical and rebellious groups in the Middle Ages. Peter's Reform itself was warmly appraised as a deed of liberation from the control of religion. The concept of a "religious culture" was for the historians of the last century at least a paradox, and for most an obsolete dream and an ominous threat.

The vision of the contemporary historian has been drastically en-

---

[5] А. Н. Пыпинъ, «До-Петровское преданіе въ XVIII-м вѣке,» *Вѣстникъ Европы*, July, 1886, pp. 330 ff.; cf. Николай Трубицынъ, *О народной поэзіи въ общественномъ и литературномъ обиходѣ первой трети XIX вѣка* (St. Petersburg, 1912), chap. i, pp. 1-3.

larged in recent decades. The fiction of "unchanging Russia," ever the same for several centuries, in which many historians of older generations were still able to believe, has crumbled. One is bound to distinguish ages and stages. "Old Russia" appears to be an artificial and unhistorical concept. One must speak rather of various local cultures—of Ancient Kiev, of Novgorod, Tver, Moscow, and the like, and of Western Russia. These local cultures were, of course, interrelated and ultimately integrated into one great national culture. But first of all they must be understood in their distinctive characters. Some regional studies in the field of Old Russian culture were initiated already in the last century, and a number of provocative observations were accumulated. But much has been left undone. On the other hand, there was in these regional studies a tendency to overstress local distinctions. In any case, it is still too early to attempt a synthetic description of Old Russia as a whole. Obviously, there were deep internal tensions within the realm of Old Russian culture. The cultures of all societies are more or less stratified: there are always different levels, and high culture is always kept and promoted by a minority, the leading and creative elite. The problem is much more intricate and complex than was admitted by the historians of earlier generations.

The time has come when the story of Old Russia must be carefully revised and probably rewritten. This time it must be written as a history in its own right, and not just as a preamble to the history of New Russia. Of course, historical interpretation is inevitably retrospective—that is the very heart of the historical method. It was inevitable to look back at Old Russia. What was wrong in the traditional pattern was not the retrospection itself but the unfortunate selection of the observation point—and also the lack of congeniality with the subject of study.

The term "culture" is ambiguous; it is currently used in more than one sense. On the one hand, "culture" is a descriptive term. It denotes the structure of a particular society or of a particular group. Culture in this sense includes at once a certain set of aims and concerns and a complex of established habits. There is always an element of normative routine in any given culture, but culture is maintained only by exercise, by an active pursuit of certain goals. On the other hand, culture is a system of values. Of course, these values are produced and accumulated in the creative process of history in a particular environment and setting, and in this respect they are inevitably situation-conditioned. And yet they always tend to obtain a quasi-independent existence, that is, they become independent of that original historical context in which they came into being. Cultural values always claim universal recognition. Though they are rooted in their native soil, cultural values can be transplanted. This transfer of cultural systems is one of the major events of history. Cultures and societies are not identical. Societies may collapse and even disappear completely, but their cultures do not always perish with them. The most conspicuous example is ancient Greece. One can speak of its permanence in the life of other societies. Great creations of thought, charity, art, and letters may retain their intrinsic validity, even if there is nobody to appreciate them or if they are vigorously disavowed and repudiated in a particular group and at a particular time. There is always some prospect of recovery and revival. True values are perennial.

There are two different tasks for the historian of culture, although it is difficult to separate them in practice. On the one hand, there is a descriptive task. One has to establish an accurate inventory of those cultural values which are accepted and circulated in a given society at particular stages of its historical life. One must also find out in what particular manner they functioned in this society, and whether they were really living values and not just an external garb or a conventional decorative frame. It may happen that some of the accepted values are discredited in a particular society at a given date and cease to function. It may also happen that society itself degenerates and loses its cultural vitality. It may prosper; it may decay. And the historian must accurately record all the stages of the process. On the other hand, there is the task of interpretation. The complex of values can be studied as such. Thus we speak, for instance, of classical civilization. The fall of the classical world did not discredit classical civilization. One may speak at the same time of the corruption of imperial Rome and of the immortal glory of Roman law.

Let us return now to the problem of Old Russian culture. It may be true that Old Russia was not successful in her cultural endeavor, that her cultural effort resulted ultimately in a deadlock. Indeed, historians are never permitted to idealize the subject of their studies. Yet the historic collapse of Old Russia, accelerated by the intervention of new forces, does not by itself prove the inconsistency of that culture to which Russia was pledged and addicted. This culture must be examined in its inner structure, apart from its historic fate. These two different lines of research, in which different methods must be used, were unfortunately often confused by the historians.

II. THE WAYS OF OLD RUSSIA

Old Russia stood in a very definite cultural succession. She was in no sense isolated in the cultural world. She entered the commonwealth of civilized nations when she was christened by the Byzantine. She received then, together with the Christian faith, an impressive cultural dowry—a complex of cultural values, habits, and concerns. The Byzantine inheritance of ancient Kiev was conspicuous. The city itself was an important cultural center, a rival of Constantinople, an adornment of the empire. It was not the only center: Novgorod in any case must be mentioned. The literary production of the Kievan period was intense and diverse. Russian art was also taking shape. Behind the documents of the time we cannot fail to discern cultural activity, cultural forces. We discern groups and individuals eagerly committed to various cultural tasks. The movement of ideas has already begun.

The Kievan achievement must be regarded in a wider perspective. It was an integral part of the incipient Slavic culture. V. Jagić once suggested that in the tenth century there was a chance that Slavic civilization might have developed as a third cultural power, competing with the Latin and the Greek. The Bulgarian literature of the Simeonic age was already so rich and comprehensive as to stand comparison with the Byzantine.[6] Indeed, it was the same Byzantine literature, but already indigenized. This cultural promise was curtailed and frustrated. The great cultural impetus was checked. Yet the promise was real, and the actual achievement was by no means negligible. Of course, this incipient Slavic civilization was deeply rooted in the Byzantine tradition, just as Western culture was rooted in the traditions of the classical world. But it was more than a repetition or an imitation. It was an indigenous response to the cultural challenge. And it was mainly from Bulgaria that a rich supply of literary monuments was transferred to Kiev and other centers. Cultural taste and skill were formed. Cultural interests were aroused. Kievan Russia was not isolated from the rest of the Slavic world, as it was not separated from Byzantium and the West, or from the East. Kievan Russia was able to respond conscientiously to the cultural challenge. The ground was already prepared.

At this point certain doubts may be reasonably raised. First of all, the promise was actually frustrated, even if the measure of this frustration and lack of success should not be exaggerated. Was this due only to adverse conditions—the Germano-Latin pressure on the Western Slavs, the defeat of Bulgaria by the Greeks, the Mongolian conquest of Russia? Or was there an inherent weakness, a constitutional disease, that arrested the development both in Old Russia and in the Balkans? The adversity of external conditions was bound to have at least a psychological impact on the whole cultural situation, but further questions may be asked, and indeed have been asked, by modern scholars. Was the Byzantine inheritance a healthy one? Was the task undertaken by the Slavs sound and reasonable? Was their attempt to create a new national culture a sound enterprise? Or was it doomed to failure by its inner inconsistency? The questions were sharply put, and answers were often negative.

---

[6] V. Jagić, *Historija Književnosti Naroda Hrvatskoga i Srbskoga*, Vol. I.: *Staro doba* (Zagreb, 1867), pp. 52, 66.

It was inevitable that in the beginning the cultural elite should have been small, and the outreach of its activity rather limited. It was development at a normal pace. But was the Byzantine civilization really "received" in Old Russia? Golubinsky, for one, bluntly denied the fact. St. Vladimir wanted to transplant culture to his land, but his effort failed completely. Culture was brought in and offered but not taken, and, as Golubinsky added, "almost immediately after its introduction it disappeared without leaving any trace." Until Peter's time there was no civilization in Russia. There was no more than plain literacy, that is, the skill to read and to copy texts. Literacy, not literature, was the upper limit of Old Russia, according to Golubinsky. "Literacy, not culture—in these words is summarized all our history for the vast period from Vladimir to Peter the Great." Before Peter, Russians were, on the whole, quite indifferent to culture and enlightenment—*prosveshchenie* was Golubinsky's own term. Those few contradictory instances which he had to acknowledge, Golubinsky would hastily dismiss as incomprehensible riddles.[7] No contemporary historian would dare to endorse these sweeping generalizations of Golubinsky. But under some other guise they are still repeated. It must be noted that Golubinsky in no sense held the Greeks responsible for the Slavic failure. He never contested the value of Byzantine civilization. He only felt that probably the Byzantine offered too much at once, and also expected too much from the newly baptized nations. The fault was with the Russians themselves. Some others, however, would shift the blame to Byzantium. According to Jagić, the greatest misfortune of the Slavs was that they had to be reared in the school of senility: a young and vigorous nation was to be brought up on the decrepit culture of a moribund world that had already lost its vitality and creative power. Jagić was quite enthusiastic about the work of the Slavic Apostles. He had only praise for their endeavor to stimulate indigenous culture among the Slavs. But he had no appreciation for Byzantine civilization. This attitude was typical of his generation, and also of the next. The failure was then inevitable: one cannot build on a rotten foundation. There was no genuine vitality in the Old Slavic civilization, because there no longer was living water in the Byzantine springs. Seemingly there was a promise, but actually there was no hope.

The charge has been repeated recently in a new form. Quite recently the late Professor George Fedotov suggested that the cause of Old Russian backwardness, and indeed the tragedy of Russian culture at large, was precisely the attempt at indigenization. He had serious doubts about the benefits of the use of the Slavic vernacular. Having received the Bible and a vast amount of various religious writings in their own language, the Slavs had no incentive to learn Greek, for translations

---

[7] Е. Голубинскій, *Исторія русской церкви*, I/1 (2nd ed.; Moscow, 1901), pp. 701 ff., 720.

once made were sufficient for immediate practical needs. They were enclosed, therefore, within the narrow limits of an exclusively religious literature. They were never initiated into the great classical tradition of Hellenic antiquity. If only our ancestors had learned Greek, speculated Professor Fedotov, they could have read Homer, could have philosophized with Plato, could have reached finally the very springs of Greek inspiration. They would have possessed a golden key to classical treasures. But this never happened. Instead they received but *one* Book. While in Paris, a poor and dirty city as it was in the twelfth century, the Schoolmen were already discussing high matters, in the golden and beautiful Kiev there were but monks engaged in writing chronicles and lives of saints.[8] In other words, the weakness and backwardness of Old Russia depended upon that narrow foundation, exclusively religious, on which its culture had been built. The charge is by no means new. The lack of classical tradition was often emphasized as one of the peculiar and distinctive features of Old Russian culture. Fedotov's imaginary picture is pathetic, but is his argument fair and sound? The West seems to have had the golden key of Latin. How many in the West, however, were using that key for the purpose of which Fedotov speaks? And was the Latin known at that time sufficient for the task? Classical values were transmitted rather indirectly through Christian literature. Platonism was accessible through Augustine, Pseudo-Dionysius, Origen, and Gregory of Nyssa. It could be no less readily discovered in Byzantine ecclesiastical sources. The Christian Hellenism of Byzantium neither impresses nor attracts Fedotov. He has a twisted picture of Byzantium: Byzantine Christianity appears to him to be a "religion of fear," of *phobos;* human values were suppressed in it.[9] Anyhow, Fedotov contended that Kievan Russia never accepted this grim version of Christianity and developed its own conception: humanitarian and kenotic. And, in fact, that picture of Kievan Russia which Professor Fedotov himself has given us in his impressive book, *The Russian Religious Mind,* is bright and moving. Kievan Christianity, in his appraisal, has perennial value: "that of a standard, a golden measure, a royal way," in his own phrase. Indeed, we are given to understand that its attainments were so high because the Russians did not follow either the Byzantines or the Bulgarians, because they created their own Christian vision and way. In any case, it appears that Kievan Russia was vigorous and creative—at least in one field. What is more significant, basic human values were firmly established, high ethical standards acknowledged, and personal initiative disclosed and encouraged. There was strong human impetus in the Kievan culture. One

---

[8] Г. П. Федотов, «Трагедия интеллигенции» (1927), in *Новый град: Сборник статей* (New York, 1952), pp. 19-22.

[9] George P. Fedotov, *The Russian Religious Mind: Kievan Christianity* (Cambridge, Mass.: Harvard University Press, 1946), pp. 21-41.

has to assume, as was indeed Fedotov's own contention, that cultural
growth and advance were impeded at a later stage. The absence of the
classical tradition probably was not so tragic and fatal.

There is an increasing tendency in modern historiography to idealize
the Russian beginnings. The Kievan period is depicted as a kind of
golden age, a golden legend of Russia. Dark times came later—after the
Mongolian conquest. There was a visible decline in literary production, and there were no outstanding personalities in this field. A closer
scrutiny of extant sources, however, corrects this first impression.
Writers of that time, from the twelfth century to the fifteenth, are
aware of problems with which they are wrestling—the problems of the
artistic craft: problems of style and representation, problems of psychological analysis. There were in Russia at that time not only scribes and
nachetchiks, but true writers. There were not only skillful craftsmen
but real masters in art. The recent studies of D. S. Likhachev are very
suggestive, especially his analysis of the problem of man in the literature and art of Old Russia.[10] Behind the stylistic devices used by the
artists one can detect their spiritual vision, and this vision was the fruit
of reasoning and contemplation. The new wave of the "South Slavic"
impact did not mean just a transfer of new literary documents, mainly
translations, of spiritual and hagiographical content. It was a wave of
inspiration, a deep spiritual movement, stemming from the great Hesychast tradition, revived at that time both in Byzantium and in the restored Bulgarian kingdom. Both writers, chroniclers and hagiographers,
and painters, including the iconographers, were fully aware of the problem that they had to wrestle with—the presentation of human personality. It may be true that their concept of personality and character was
different from the modern view, and probably at this point their insight
was deeper. They did not depict fixed characters; they saw men in
process obsessed and confronted with problems, in the state of decision
and indecision. One may speak almost of their "existentialist" approach
to the problem of man. One may contend that psychology based on the
concept of temptation, inner struggle with the passions, conversion and
decision, was a deeper psychology than that which would deal with the
fixed character. In any case, it is more dynamic and less in danger of
falling into schematism of characteristic types. In the great Russian art
of the fourteenth and fifteenth centuries one discovers not only a high
level of artistic mastery but also deep insights into the mystery of man.
And this art was not only produced at that time but appreciated. Obviously, there was both a demand for this high art and an understanding
of it, in circles which could not have been very narrow. It would not be
an exaggeration to assume that the aesthetic culture of that time was

---

[10] Д. С. Лихачев, *Человек в литературе древней Руси* (Moscow-Leningrad, 1958); *Неко-
торые задачи изучения второго южнославянского влияния в России* (Moscow, 1958).

refined and profound. It was still a religious culture, but artistic methods were adequate to the problem of revealing and interpreting the ultimate mysteries of human existence in all its unruly and flexible complexity. The challenge probably came from outside—from Byzantium once more—but the response was spontaneous and creative. There was more than dependence or imitation. There was real response.[11]

One may be tempted to regard precisely this "dark" period, the period of intensive political and internecine strife, as the climax of Old Russian culture. Indeed, Russian art definitely declined in the fifteenth and especially in the sixteenth century and lost its originality and daring. The literary culture, however, was preserved on a high level till the Time of Troubles, and even later. The ideological content of literature became more comprehensive in the sixteenth century. There was an enormous synthetic effort in various fields of culture at that time. Strangely enough, it seems that precisely that synthetic effort, powerful and dynamic as it was, was the most conspicuous sign and symptom of decline, or at least of an internal crisis. The cultural inheritance of Moscow was rich and comprehensive enough to suggest the idea of systematization. The great national state, aware and conscious of its vocation or destiny, needed a culture of great style. But this culture had to be built up as a system. It was an ambitious and attractive task. The plan "to gather together all books available in Russia," which was undertaken under Metropolitan Macary in the middle of the sixteenth century, was probably a naïve and simplistic expression of a deeper conception. The plan itself was deeply rooted in the awakened consciousness of national greatness. But the vision was intrinsically static, and there was in it more than just a reflection of political ambition. There was a deeper urge for "establishment." The overarching idea was that of order. The danger to culture implied therein was probably felt in certain quarters. It has been usual to emphasize the importance of the conflict between the "possessors" and "nonpossessors" in the late decades of the fifteenth and the early decades of the sixteenth century. At one time the sympathy of the historian was rather on the side of St. Nilus of Sora and the Trans-Volga Elders. It seems that now the sympathy has been shifted to the other side. In any case, St. Joseph has won. And the idea of an established order was his greatest commitment. Indeed, he himself never speculated on the themes of culture. Nor, probably, did St. Nilus. But there is undoubtedly deep truth in the suggestion that it was in the tradition of St. Nilus that the only promise of cultural advance was available. Cultures are never built as systems, by orders or on purpose. They are born out of the spirit of creative initiative, out of intimate vision, out of spiritual commitment, and are only

---

[11] This theme must be elaborated in detail with reference to the modern study. It is enough to mention the recent works of Igor Grabar, V. N. Lazareff, M. Alpatov, etc.

maintained in freedom. It may be contended that Moscow missed its opportunity for cultural progress when it yielded to the temptation of building its culture on the social order of the day—*po sotsial'nomu zakazu,* as it were. The cultural capital of Moscow was not so meager and limited as has been often assumed. Even its technical equipment should not be minimized. The root of the cultural trouble and failure was in the pattern. One may use the word "utopia" in this connection. And one may specify this utopia as theocratic. But actually it was a kind of politico-cultural utopia, not in full conformity with the higher aspirations of the Christian man. Of course, the Christian conception is intrinsically bifocal: The community—the Church—is the form of Christian existence, but human personality is a supreme value. Man is a political being; but culture is built by creative individuals, and there is always the danger when it is oversystematized that it may degenerate into a routine. The weakness of the Moscow culture was not so much in the poverty of the content as in the failure of spirit.

The most disquieting question in the history of Old Russian culture is this: What was the reason for what can be described as its intellectual silence? There was a great art, and there was also an intensive creative activity in the political and social field, including ideological speculation. But surely nothing original and outstanding has been produced in the realm of ideas, theological or secular. It was easier to answer this question when it was assumed that Old Russia was simply primitive, slumbering and stagnant. But now we know that in many other respects Old Russia was able to attain a high level. Still one may be tempted by easy answers. It may be suggested, and actually has been suggested more than once, that the "Russian soul" was, by its inner constitution, rather speculative or intuitive than inquisitive, and that therefore the language of art was the only congenial idiom of self-expression. It may be suggested, on the other hand, that the "Russian soul" approached the mystery of Christian faith by way of charity and compassion and was therefore indifferent to the subtleties of theological speculation. It does not help very much if we try to collect scattered data indicating that a certain amount of philosophical information was available to people of Old Russia. A solid amount of patristic writings was indeed in circulation, but there is no proof that theological interest had been awakened. All easy formulas are but evasions. And the riddle remains. Moreover, all speculations that operate with the precarious concept of the "Russian soul" are utterly unsafe. Even if "national souls" do exist, they are made, shaped, and formed in history. For that reason they cannot serve as a principle of interpretation. Again, the character of the "Russian soul" has been so diversely described and defined as to require a thorough re-examination. It has been usual to emphasize the irrational aspect of Russian mentality and its constant lack of form. There is

enough evidence to the contrary. With adequate reason it has been contended that the "Russian soul" had always a strong feeling and understanding for order and form, and this specific insight was the root of its
great aesthetic achievements.[12] In its extreme expression it led to ritual-
ism, to the worship of external forms. Kliuchevsky had much to say
about the thrill of rite and habit when he attempted to explain the
genesis of the great Russian *raskol*.[13] And the same striving after order-
liness has created in Russia what we call *byt*. Of course, it may be
claimed that underneath the *byt* there was always chaos. Finally, we are
left with an antinomy, with an unresolved paradox.

In the total perspective of Russian historical development the paradox is even more spectacular. In the later period, after the Reform,
Russians have appeared to be probably one of the most intellectual
nations in Europe, inwardly troubled by all "damned problems" of religion and metaphysics. Exercise in philosophy, of various shapes and
shades, and commitment to theory and speculation were the distinctive
mark of the Russian mind in the last two centuries. This striking
phenomenon was usually explained by Western influence, direct and
indirect. It was suggested that dormant curiosity had been awakened
by the challenge of Western thought. One should ask at this point why
this intellectual curiosity was not awakened by the challenge of Byzantine civilization, which was renowned and notorious for its unquench-
able commitment to speculation, in a measure offensive for the sober
taste and mind of the West. Byzantium was not only dogmatic, but
ever searching and rather unquiet in its heart. Indeed, Byzantium knew
the mystery of harmony and cosmic order. But it also knew the thrill of
search and the "clouds of unknowing." But Byzantine challenge did
not awaken the alleged Russian soul.

The tragedy of Old Russia, which led to its inner split and impasse,
was not a tragedy of primitivism or ignorance, as has been contended
more than once. It was a tragedy of cultural aberration. The charge of
Golubinsky and of Fedotov is valid to some extent, but they were unable to phrase it properly. One may suggest that Byzantium had offered
too much at once—an enormous richness of cultural material, which
simply could not be absorbed at once. The charm of perfection was
tempting: should not the whole harmony be transplanted? The heritage was too heavy, and too perfect, and it was thrilling in its harmony,
in its accomplishment. Art also requires training, but in this case training is probably more formal—the acquisition of technical skill. In the
realm of the mind, training is indissolubly bound with the essence of

---

[12] See the penetrating essay of V. Shchepkin, "L'Ame du Peuple Russe dans l'Art Russe,"
in *Le Monde Slave*, May and June, 1928; the Russian text in *Воля России*, 1929, VIII-IX,
X-XI, XII.

[13] Ключевский, *Курс* ..., Vol. III, lectures 54 and 55; cf. «Западное вліяніе въ Россіи
XVII вѣка: Историко-психологическій очеркъ» (1897), in *Очерки и Рѣчи*, 1912.

the task. In this realm questions are no less important than answers, and unresolved problems, the "perennial questions," are the real stimulus and token of mental advance. Old Russia seems to have been charmed by the perfection, completeness, and harmony of Byzantine civilization, and paralyzed by this charm. Once more it must be stressed that Russian Byzantium was not just a servile repetition but a new and peculiar version of Byzantine culture, in which one can discern a true creative power. Some years ago I inscribed the chapter of my book, *The Ways of Russian Theology*, dealing with Old Russia: "The Crisis of Russian Byzantinism," and have rephrased it in the text: "The crisis of Byzantine culture in the Russian spirit."[14] The phrase was misunderstood by the critics and reviewers, or rather was not understood at all. I am willing to assume full responsibility for the vagueness: I should have explained my thought in a more explicit way. What I wanted to say then I am bound to repeat now. The crisis consisted in that the Byzantine achievement had been accepted, but Byzantine inquisitiveness had not. For that reason the achievement itself could not be kept alive.

The crisis became conspicuous in Moscow in the seventeenth century, in that great age of changes, shifts, and troubles in the Russian state and society. It was an age of great cultural confusion. Certain elements of Byzantine achievement were strongly challenged, including the traditional "symphony" of state and church. Moscow was moving hesitantly toward an increasing secularization of its political order. The impact of Western mentality was growing, first in the form of the new Kievan learning, which itself was an unfortunate hybrid of Polish and quasi-Byzantine factors. The spread of this pseudomorphic culture was felt at Moscow more as a shock or offense than as a challenge, and provoked only resistance along with blind imitation. There was a search, but it was a search for ready solutions. Probably it was a blind alley. And then came the Reform.

The ultimate tragedy was that the Reform itself was promoted in the same old manner. There was again the thrill of accomplishment or achievement. The spirit of the Reform was intrinsically utilitarian. There was again a charm—a charm of Western achievement, of Western habits and forms. Curiosity was aroused, but was it a sound and sober intellectual curiosity? The new civilization was accepted in its ready form, into which the life of the nation could not be fitted. There was an effect of astonishment, but no real awakening. The new culture was much less organic than the old one, and therefore even less spontaneous and creative. It is instructive that it was possible to present the whole history of Russian literature, including its ideological content, as a story of Western influence, as a story of consecutive waves of imported ideas and forms. Was the cultural initiative really awakened? One may have

---

[14] *Пути русскаго богословія* (Paris, 1937), pp. 1-2.

very grave doubts. It is not surprising that a paradoxical resistance to culture as such has been one of the vigorous trends in the new culture; though it was to some extent provoked also by the thought of a Westerner, Rousseau, it was deeply rooted in the psychology of "reformed" Russians. Was not the way of simplicity higher than the way of culture? Technical culture has indeed been transplanted. But did Reform promote any disinterested concern for higher culture? Was it a real advance in comparison with the culture of Old Russia? During the whole modern period complaints were loudly voiced on this theme: there was no genuine *will for culture,* although admiration and even respect for culture were rather widespread. The root of the trouble was still the same: Culture was still regarded as an order, as an achievement, as a system. For that reason one could propagate the acceptance of foreign forms; they were finished and ready to hand. Indeed, there was sometimes much vigor and also much obstinacy in this endeavor of adaptation, and it could instill vitality into the products. The thrill of the modern Russian culture is in its scattered explosions—the deeds of individuals. But there was no general culture. Moreover, the larger part of the nation was not yet involved in the process, and was much more outside the culture, and thus outside history, than it had been in the days of Old Russia. This was the sharpest objection against the new order in comparison with the old, as Kliuchevsky has so eloquently phrased it.

So much can be said about the old "society." Did this "unsuccess," to use the term of Wladimir Weidlé,[15] discredit that system of cultural values to which Old Russia was pledged and committed? Did this system crumble also? It is not for the historian to answer this question. It is a question for the philosopher. But the historian must insist that there are perennial achievements in the inventory of Old Russian culture. The greatness of the Old Russian religious art is in our day widely acknowledged, with understanding or simply by fashion. The vigor and freshness and the profundity of the Russian religious quest, although it seems to be often disguised by ritual formalism, is also increasingly recognized. There were profound human values in this old culture, as detached, as archaic, as exotic as it may appear to those trained in the Western ways. And it becomes more and more evident that Old Russian culture did, from its very inception, belong to the wider circle—to the circle of that civilization which had been built, on the composite basis of ancient classical culture, under the creative impact, and often under direct guidance and deep inspiration, of Christian faith and mission.

Old Russia, indeed, left a precious legacy, at least in the realm of art. At this point its "culture" survived its "paternal society," and must be studied as a perennial treasure in its own right.

15 Wladimir Weidlé, *Russia: Absent and Present* (New York, 1952), pp. 15 ff.

Pagan and Christian Elements in Old Russia

NIKOLAY ANDREYEV

The problems of vast compass raised in Professor Florovsky's erudite article can hardly hope to find a conclusive solution. Professor Florovsky, voicing his opinions with his customary brilliance, has presented us with a fascinating interpretation of civilization in pre-Petrine Russia. For my part, I should like to attempt to assess the abiding vitality of certain aspects of the pagan Slav civilization that formed the background of pre-Petrine Russia; and also to trace the gradual assimilation of Christianity by the Russian people as a whole, which led to the rise of a distinctive national medieval culture and the first belated signs of natural evolution towards a more secular and "modern" society during the dawn of the modern age—before the numbing onset of "revolutionary" change effected by Peter the Great once again drove a deep rift between the educated minority and the mass of the people.

THE HERITAGE OF PRE-CHRISTIAN RUSSIA

The absence of native, contemporary documentary evidence on the Slavs of pre-Christian Russia makes it necessary to exercise great caution in seeking to establish the character of this indigenous, organic, primitive, yet tenacious and distinctive, civilization. Its representatives were Slavonic tribes that in the course of centuries had spread gradually— usually following the course of rivers but in a generally eastward direction—across the great East European plain. From the scanty information available about these people, it may be assumed that they were of hardy stock, capable of great feats of endurance, notably hospitable, emotional, and, in time of war, cruel.

It is noteworthy that this pre-Christian Slavic Russia was known to the Scandinavians as the "land of towns" and that the anonymous Bavarian Geographer (866-890) also referred to the large number of "towns."[1] Some information about the characteristics of this civilization is provided by the Russian Chronicles. Traces of pagan influence are to be found in decorative folk art; in some cases motifs and patterns of the most ancient origin have persisted into the twentieth century.

MR. ANDREYEV *is lecturer in Slavonic studies at Cambridge University.*

[1] Of course, the term "town" must not be understood in its present connotation; what is meant here is more probably *gorodishchi*, i.e., more or less fortified centers, usually enclosed by wooden stockades; it may sometimes refer to mere villages. Cf. М. Н. Тихомиров, *Древне-русские города* (Moscow, 1956), pp. 9 ff.

Today, archaeological research has given us a picture of the tastes of the early Slavs, examples of their handicrafts and of the kind and quantity of their material possessions. Unfortunately, the wooden architecture of the time has not been preserved; the tragedy of all Old Russian architecture was its vulnerability to that scourge of medieval Russia—frequent and destructive fires. It may be assumed, however, that the architecture of that period with its decorative carving, its *gornitsy* or upper rooms, its porches, and the variety of form shown in the roofing of buildings often attained real aesthetic merit.[2]

The text of the treaties signed with Byzantium by Oleg (911) and Igor (944) bears witness to the existence of a distinctive social system, and it has been suggested that they indicate certain aspects of the Slav's "customary law."[3] As early as the seventh century Byzantine authors noted, not without surprise, that the Slavs and Antes "are not governed by one man but from ancient times have lived in democracy: they discuss together what is good or harmful for them." The Byzantines, accustomed to autocratic government, considered this "disorder and anarchy."[4] There can be no doubt that the *veche* was already an important institution in the social structure of pre-Christian Russia and had its roots in the distant past of the Slav peoples.

The most striking witness to the existence of civilization among the Russian Slavs is found in their religious beliefs, which were inspired by nature: they had a faith in magic powers that was closely connected with the cult of "Moist Mother Earth." Reflected most vividly in Russian folklore, these beliefs proved exceptionally tenacious and vigorous. *The Lay of the Host of Igor,* in which the writer refers to the Russian people collectively as the "grandson of Dazhbog,"[5] is rich in references to heathen deities and is inspired throughout by an essentially pantheistic conception of the world, of nature, and of poetry. Since this poem is perhaps the most brilliant expression of the persistence of the old pagan tradition, it is scarcely surprising that the ecclesiastical copyists were not particularly concerned with preserving it.

Thanks to the pertinacity of pagan beliefs among the masses of the people, there arose the phenomenon of *dvoeverie* (ditheism), whose existence is confirmed by historians of all schools; this belief is still alive in some places today.[6] Kievan and Muscovite history is rich in examples of the perpetual struggle waged by the Church to put down

---

[2] Б. А. Рыбаков, «Искусство древних славян,» *История русского искусства*, I (Moscow, 1953), pp. 39-92. Б. А. Рыбаков, *Ремесло древней Руси* (Moscow, 1948), pp. 35-119.

[3] *Памятники русского права*, ed. А. А. Зимин (Moscow, 1952), pp. 4 ff.

[4] *Прокопий (из Кесарии): Война с готами* (Moscow, 1950), p. 297.

[5] *Слово о полку Игореве*, ed. В. П. Адрианова-Перетц (Moscow-Leningrad, 1950), p. 16.

[6] During the author's archaeological and archaeographic expeditions to Petserimaa in Estonia in 1937 and 1938 on behalf of the Kondakov Institute in Prague, he witnessed striking examples of the persistence of this *dvoeverie* in the Pskov-Petseri Monastery itself: devout local women would bring "offerings" of country produce (butter, eggs, and cream)

pagan survivals. It also seems probable that, to a certain extent, ecclesiastical suppression of the popular Russian theater (the *skomorokhi*) was inspired by the same fear of the non-Christian moods induced by these singers of "diabolic songs," these demonstrators of "unhallowed" customs and "satanic" rites. A recently discovered wall painting in Melyotovo dating from 1465 shows a remarkable image on the west wall of the church representing Antichrist in the guise of a wandering player:[7] a unique apotheosis of the Church's condemnation of that "devil's brood," the *skomorokhi*. Obviously, too, as in Western countries, certain attributes of the pagan deities were passed on to Christian saints.[8]

All these examples (which could be multiplied many times) are presented here only as reminders of the very considerable vigor and longevity of Russia's pagan heritage. Christianity in Russia was not transplanted into an uncultured soil, into a wild desert, but into a powerful community which, though scattered and illiterate, had its own customs, art, and religion and which, in some sectors, had long maintained contacts with other civilizations.[9] Although certain influential groups and even, perhaps, whole centers such as Tmutorokan had previously accepted Christianity, its subsequent introduction as the official religion of the state was conditioned by the predominantly political motives of St. Vladimir.[10]

The new official religion, if the Korsun version of the conversion is to be believed, was brought into Russia much like any other trophy of a successful campaign. Paganism had a considerable hold on the population; a few years before the conversion, Vladimir had attempted to erect a pagan Pantheon in Kiev to strengthen the ideological unity of the state. Not surprisingly, there was considerable resistance to the new faith—in some districts right up to the twelfth century (the rising of the *volkhvy* [pagan priests] and other incidents). Naturally, the Grand Dukes and the Christianized upper stratum of the society of that time were anxious to transform "the Greek faith" into a national

---

to lay before a wooden statue of St. Nicholas the Miracle-Worker—gifts which were subsequently collected by the monks for the use of the abbot.

[7] Iu. N. Dmitriev, who published this painting, «Мелетовские фрески и их значение для истории древне-русской культуры,» *Труды отдела древне-русской литературы*, VIII (1951), 403-12, failed to understand the significance of this unique fresco and gave a wrong reading of the word *Антъ* (p. 410).

[8] On pagan traditions in ancient Russian culture, cf. Е. В. Аничковъ, *Язычество и древняя Русь* (St. Petersburg, 1914) and Н. Галковскій, *Борьба христіанства съ остатками язычества въ древней Руси*, I, II (Moscow, 1913). The best account in English is to be found in George Vernadsky's *Origins of Russia* (Oxford: Clarendon Press, 1959), pp. 108-73.

[9] Cf., for example, M. I. Rostovtsev, *The Origin of the Russian State on the Dnieper*, in the Annual Report of the American Historical Association for 1920 (Washington, D.C., 1925).

[10] George Vernadsky, *Kievan Russia* (New Haven, 1948), p. 71.

religion as quickly as possible. Certain events of the reign of Yaroslav the Wise—the appointment of a Russian as Metropolitan of Kiev; the cult of Vladimir, who was pronounced "the equal of the apostles," the true teacher of the newly-converted country, and a saint (Constantinople opposed his canonization for a long time)—prove that the Russians did not wish to be "led" by the Greeks but claimed the right to choose what suited them from the "Byzantine heritage." Such traces of cultural indocility are even apparent in the hagiography of the period. Thus the first Russian saints, Boris and Gleb, died not for the sake of Christ but in the name of obedience to their elder brother, laying the foundations, as it were, for the essentially Russian idea of nonresistance to evil. Their canonization also called forth opposition on the part of the Greeks, who generally were not inclined to encourage religious nationalism among newly converted peoples.[11] It may be that it was in this early period of Russia's struggles for some autonomy in her ecclesiastical existence that there first sprouted the seeds of Grecophobia, which was to become traditional in Old Russia and was to combine curiously with an ill-defined nostalgia for the old pagan world. This inherent resistance to Byzantium was to manifest itself more than once—though later, after the people had fully assimilated Christianity, it was to take the form of the defense of the purity of Orthodox faith: in the vexing question of the appointment of the metropolitans at Vladimir-on-the-Klyazma; in the attitude Russia assumed towards the Florentine Union; in her reaction to the fall of Constantinople; and in the formulation of the famous theory of the Third Rome. This tendency reached its culmination in the seventeenth century when the Old Believers, in a kind of reprise of the themes of the first expositor of Russian Grecophobia, Hilarion of Berestov, did not grudge even their lives in the struggle against the enunciation of principle of the Patriarch Nikon: "I am Russian, but my faith is Greek." In many ways the violence of their opposition to this principle was not so irrational as is usually believed.[12]

Indisputably, Byzantine influence after the introduction of Christianity gave both form and content to Russian culture, but the pagan foundation acted as a counterbalance which prevented the full and unquestioning absorption of the Byzantine heritage.

MEDIÈVAL CULTURE AND ITS DECLINE

Christianity was at first largely confined to the towns; it was not by chance that during the first centuries most monasteries were founded either in or near towns. The spread of enlightenment was carried out

---

[11] Г. П. Федотов, *Святые древней Руси* (Paris, 1931), p. 20.

[12] А. В. Карташев, *Очерки по истории русской церкви*, I and II (Paris, 1959). Cf. II, pp. 121-230 for Nikon's reforms.

intensively throughout the first hundred years after the conversion, but it was directed chiefly at serving the aims and purposes of the dynasty and the Church itself. The process took a long time. It needed the Mongol invasion, which laid waste to all the large towns (the centers of the new learning) except Novgorod and Galich, and the almost simultaneous encroachments of the Teutonic knights on the Western borders, which marked the beginning of the *Drang nach Osten,* before Christianity (albeit still tinged with survivals of paganism) became thoroughly assimilated by the masses of the people. The Church became the focus of all hope, not only celestial but also terrestrial, and came to be identified with the spirit of Russia itself. The alien world revealed to the Russians at the time of the conversion—a monotheistic, hierarchic world of contradictory values and the consciousness of sin —at last took on a specifically national form and was accepted by the people as their own. St. Sergius of Radonezh, equally sensitive to all aspects of his complex heritage, embodies the supremely harmonious national ideal of this period. He is at once monk and nature lover, gentle with his spiritual children and a lover of toil; he is a hermit but is able to direct a monastic community; he is the teacher and the inspiration of a whole pleiad of Russian ecclesiastical figures of the fourteenth and fifteenth centuries; but he is also the servant of the rising realm of Muscovy and takes his stand above the pettiness of local interests. He is simple and wise, a man of action and a mystic. He is a bright light for the Church, for the state, and for the illiterate peasant.[13] He is very close in spirit to another great luminary of medieval Russia, the incomparable genius of religious art, Andrei Rublev. Both are distinguished by a harmonious combination of the purest Christian outlook and a remarkably loving regard for man—who is in fact the object of the Christian message in general and of the Orthodox interpretation of Christianity in particular. These two men stand out as supreme representatives of the cultural achievement of Old Russia and are not unworthy to take their place among the best exemplars of medieval Christendom. The over-all quickening of cultural activity in the fourteenth and fifteenth centuries, without which these two figures could not have flourished, appears to many historians as the highest point achieved by the civilization of pre-Petrine Russia; certainly in the field of painting, the art of Andrei Rublev and of his school is recognized both by his contemporaries and by modern historians of art as the culmination of this achievement.[14]

At this moment in time it would seem quite logical to expect a further flowering of art and thought in a Russian Renaissance. But this

---

[13] I. Smolitsch, *Russisches Mönchtum* (Würzburg, 1953), cf. chapter on St. Sergius of Radonezh. G. Fedotov, *A Treasury of Russian Spirituality* (London, 1952), pp. 50-83.

[14] В. Н. Лазарев, *Андрей Рублев* (Moscow, 1960). М. Алпатов, *Андрей Рублев* (Moscow, 1959).

did not happen. The reason for this was not the "backwardness of Russia" but simply that as a mere province of the Mongol empire, the country had been cut off from Western Europe since the thirteenth century. But Moscow had been learning "imperialism" from the Mongols and became so proficient that finally, in the 1460's under Vasilii the Dark, she was able to disregard the remaining purely nominal restrictions of "the Tartar yoke."[15] Moscow, as the new center of power, had to fight for its political existence "against the steppe," conducting a hard struggle for the internal unity of its new-forged state, and inaugurating the long battle for an outlet on the sea, which was not concluded until two hundred years later when Peter the Great finally hacked out his "window onto Europe."

Humanism, the first stirrings of a scientific approach to the surrounding world, and thoughtful criticism of established ideas and practices were appearing in the West, but they had no place in the beleaguered Russia of that time. Nevertheless, the first stirrings of a similar impulse are to be found in the religious heresies of the fifteenth and sixteenth centuries and in the various utterances of individual freethinkers; these tendencies were of course rigorously suppressed by the "Church Militant," which had entered into a marriage of convenience with the lay authorities as represented by the Grand Dukes and later Tsars.[16] As Professor Florovsky rightly points out, the very extensive work on the propagation of knowledge undertaken by Metropolitan Macary in the sixteenth century was really an attempt to canalize and organize learning rather than a genuine work of creation: it was, in fact, purely "educational," and was devoted to the collecting and codifying of information rather than to original thought.

This period, however, was not one of complete stagnation in the world of ideas. Strangely enough, the innovations of the time found expression within the Church itself and, under the protection of militant orthodoxy, in the spheres of church architecture and of religious painting. The Muscovite period is marked by many completely new developments in architecture. It is significant that even when foreign architects were called in (as, for example, during the building of the Moscow Kremlin in the fifteenth century), they did not reproduce Western models but apparently worked under definite directions from their Muscovite patrons and in styles that corresponded to Russian aesthetic canons. Buildings constructed between the fifteenth and seventeenth centuries—stone cathedrals, palaces, the great houses of indi-

---

[15] George Vernadsky, *Mongols and Russia* (New Haven, 1953), pp. 325-30.
[16] Some interesting and new ideas on this subject have appeared in Н. А. Казакова and Я. С. Лурье, *Антифеодальные еретические движения на Руси* (Moscow-Leningrad, 1955); Я. С. Лурье, *Идеологическая борьба в русской публицистике* (Moscow-Leningrad, 1960); А. А. Зимин, *И. С. Пересветов и его современники* (Moscow, 1958); А. И. Клибанов, *Реформационные движения в России* (Moscow, 1960).

vidual magnates, fortifications, the walls and gateways of monasteries and wooden churches—are all distinguished by innovations in style and by excellent technical workmanship.[17] In the Muscovite, as in the Kievan period, architecture remained one of the highest creative achievements of Russian civilization.

The impact of new ideas was expressed in the sphere of icon painting by innovations in composition[18] in the so-called mystico-didactic style, the introduction of which was in part the direct result of Western (Roman Catholic) influence.[19] Previously, religious art had been almost exclusively confined to simple subjects: "portraits" of Christ, the Blessed Virgin, the apostles and saints, or scenes from the Gospels. But in the fifteenth century artists began to launch into "theological philosophizing"; some compositions were so complex that they required an explanatory commentary and caused considerable intellectual fermentation.[20] Artists developed liturgical themes and created entirely original cycles of frescoes, new in content, in color distribution, and in the actual technique of painting.[21] In reply to a question about one of these icons the leading authority of the period, Maxim the Greek, replied that such icons "are not painted anywhere but in Russia."[22] Now he has been proved right: at the end of the fifteenth century and during the sixteenth century, Russian icon painting was indeed uniquely innovatory in content and made interesting and important advances in the technique necessary to deal with more complex and more detailed, frequently multifigured, compositions. This is a new chapter not only in the history of Russian religious art but also in the history of thought in Muscovite Russia, in which a new and more speculative frame of mind struggles for expression in the new compositions and techniques. These lead away from the clarity and harmonious insight of Rublev, but they create a new "language," at once more complex and more esoteric, adapted to the treatment of mystical and didactic themes.

The first signs of disintegration in the sphere of icon painting do not appear until the seventeenth century, after the Time of Troubles, when features of poorly understood naturalism begin to penetrate the work

---

[17] Cf. *История русского искусства*, III (Moscow, 1955) and IV (Moscow, 1959); also G. H. Hamilton, *The Art and Architecture of Russia* (London, 1954), pp. 115-43.

[18] Н. П. Кондаков, *Русская икона*, IV (Prague, 1933), pp. 268-98.

[19] Л. Мацулевич, «Хронология рельефов Дмитровского собора во Владимире Залеском,» *Ежегодник Российского Института Истории Искусств* (Petersburg and Moscow, 1922), I, 2.

[20] Н. Андреев, «О деле дяка Висковатого,» *Seminarium Kondakovianum*, V (Prague, 1932), 191-242; *idem,* «Иоанн Грозный и иконопись XVI века,» *ibid.,* X (1938), chap. iv, pp. 195-98.

[21] J. Myslivec, "Liturgické hymny jako náměty ruských ikon," *Byzantinoslavica*, III, No. 2 (1931).

[22] Н. Андреев, «Инок Зиновий Отенский об иконопочитании и иконописании,» *Seminarium Kondakovianum*, VIII (Prague, 1936), pp. 272-73.

of the craftsmen who painted icons, in part as a result of the influence of West European pictures. The famous objections of Patriarch Nikon and of Protopop Avvakum were directed against this wave of naturalism.[23]   Nevertheless, even the lofty icon painting of Simeon Ushakov and other real masters of the seventeenth century is subject to the new tendencies towards the secularization of Russian culture. This process of secularization continued throughout the seventeenth century, gaining particular impetus from the beginning of the schism which foreshadowed the end of that unity of outlook conditioned by the Orthodox Christian interpretation of the world, which for seven centuries had been so carefully nurtured by Church and state. Secularization penetrated literature, education, and methods of recording history;[24] the reforms of Peter the Great were already ripening within a Russia that was growing out of its medieval ideals. The trenchancy of Nikon and, later, of Peter caused profound schisms where there might have been evolution. As in Vladimir's time, "revolutionary methods" were preferred to "evolution." It is interesting that the common people, in the seventeenth as in the tenth century, remained either passively submissive or actively hostile to the "reformers." This second cultural schism was still unhealed at the time of the 1917 Revolution.

[23] This subject is often misinterpreted. N. Andreyev, "Nikon and Avvakum on Icon Painting," *Revue des études slaves*, XXXVIII, Mélanges Pierre Pascal (Paris, 1961), has attempted to reconstruct the true history of this ideological struggle against innovations.

[24] Cf. the very important observations of Д. С. Лихачев, *Человек в литературе древней Руси* (Moscow-Leningrad, 1958), pp. 7-26, 119-67. Cf. also D. Čiževskiy, *History of Russian Literature* (The Hague, 1960), pp. 320 ff.

Images of Muscovy

JAMES H. BILLINGTON

In this essay Professor Florovsky brings a rare combination of sympathetic understanding and restless questioning to the study of Russian culture. Cutting through a century of scholarly clichés about "Old Russia," he finds inadequate not only the cultural provincialism of erudite liberals like A. Pypin and S. Soloviëv, whose real interests lay in post-Petrine Russia, but also the simplified explanations of Old Russian cultural development presented by church historians like Golubinsky and sympathetic students like Buslaev and Fedotov.[1] As in his penetrating *Ways of Russian Theology,* he quietly draws attention away from easy answers to difficult but important questions. It would be presumptuous for anyone—let alone a non-Slav far inferior in age and wisdom to Father Florovsky—to pretend to answer them, but one can at least gain valuable guidance for a fresh appraisal of old Russia by facing up to four major tasks that his discussion sets before us: (1) distinguishing different periods and regions within pre-Petrine Russian culture, (2) accounting for its "intellectual silence," (3) analyzing its inner structure, and (4) appraising separately its historical fate and its intrinsic worth.

(1) Any consideration of Old Russian culture invites one major division—which is both chronological and regional—between Kiev and Muscovy. There is, to be sure, a bridge between them through Vladimir-Suzdal; but the cosmopolitan, urban culture of the former centered on the Dnepr and the southwestern steppe is clearly distinct from the more monolithic and monastic culture of the latter centered on the Volga and the northeastern forests. The culture of Kievan Russia has been, as Professor Florovsky points out, exhaustively studied and somewhat idealized in recent years; but the impression has been created of a kind of cultural vacuum between the fall of Kiev and the rise of Petersburg.[2]

MR. BILLINGTON *is associate professor of history at Princeton University.*

[1] To this list one could add many Western admirers whose image of Old Russia has often been largely a function of their discontent with new Europe. See, for example, Alfred Rambaud's revealing exclamation in the introduction to *La Russie Epique* (Paris, 1876): "Nous sommes devenus d'abord tellement Gallo-Romains, puis tellement Français, que nous avons cessé d'être des Gaulois. Ah! si nous possédions sur nos origines celtiques tout ce que possèdent les Russes sur leur origines slaves!"

[2] The Soviet glorification of Kievan culture has led to a diminution of serious scholarly work on the later period. Though there has been more done recently, there is still no popular volume for the Muscovite period comparable to Grekov's often republished *The Culture of Kievan Rus* (Moscow, 1947); no broad study of secular town culture of the

A case could be made, however, for the contention that the Kievan period really belongs to the "ancient history" of Russia: a period in which the Eastern Slavs were drawn into Mediterranean civilization by Byzantium but which is related to subsequent Russian history only in the rather remote sense that Roman and Merovingian Gaul is related to modern France: as the source of its religious orientation and linguistic and artistic forms. Just as French history really begins later in a new cultural and political center (Paris) within a new area (the Île de France) with a monastic revival (in Cluny and Cîteau) and a soaring new architecture (the Gothic); so does Russian history in many ways really begin with the rise of Moscow within the region known in the early chronicles as the *Zalesk* (the forested Volga-Oka region), and with the monastic revival begun by St. Sergius and the new architecture of tent roofs and onion domes.[3]

The distinctiveness of Moscow from Kievan Russia is illustrated by the fact that the city is not even mentioned in the chronicles until the middle of the twelfth century,[4] did not have its own permanent prince until the early fourteenth, and possessed none of the great monuments of Byzantine architecture to be found in nearby Vladimir or Suzdal. The political accomplishments of its grand princes were aided by their special links with the Mongols, but its material and spiritual culture

---

fourteenth–seventeenth century period comparable to Tikhomirov's *The Towns of Ancient Russia* (Moscow, 1959) for the earlier period; no continuation beyond the Kievan period of the projected history of Russian culture by Н. Каргер and Н. Воронин, *История культуры древней Руси, домонгольский период* (2 vols.; Moscow-Leningrad, 1948-51). There is probably as much written on the *Lay of the Host of Igor* as on the entire literature of any subsequent century of Old Russia. Western scholars have only partially redressed the predictable Soviet neglect of the religious factor, and the best Western scholars often concentrate on the Kievan period. G. Fedotov's *The Russian Religious Mind* (Cambridge, Mass.: Harvard University Press, 1946) deals only with this period; his useful, but less scholarly, *Treasury of Russian Spirituality* (New York, 1948) extends, however, almost to the present. F. Dvornik's exaggerated characterization of Kievan Russia as "a center of culture far ahead of anything similar in the latin West" *(The Making of Central and Eastern Europe* [London, 1949], p. 240) leads him to exaggerate the "darkness" and "obscurity" of the Muscovite period, *ibid.*, pp. 260-61.

[3] Among the many works pointing from different perspectives to the existence of an original Muscovite culture linked with the North and distinct from Byzantine and even Kievan civilization are И. Забелинъ, *Черты самобытности въ древне-русскаго зодчествѣ* (Moscow, 1900); А. Некрасов, *Возникновение московского искусства* (Moscow, 1929); И. Евдокимов, *Север в истории русского искусства* (Vologda, 1920); И. Некрасовъ, *Зарожденіе національной литературы въ сѣверной Руси* (2 vols.; Odessa, 1870); А. Кизеветтер, *Русский север: Роль северного края европейской России в истории русского государства* (Vologda, 1919); С. Платонов, *Прошлое русского севера* (Berlin, 1924); and М. Тихомиров, «Москва и культурное развитие русского народа XIV-XVII вв.,» *Вопросы истории,* No. 9, 1947, pp. 3-18. See also, however, Н. Воронин, «Владимиро-суздальское наследие в русском зодчестве,» *Архитектура СССР,* No. 2, 1940.

[4] *Лѣтопись по ипатьевскому списку* (St. Petersburg, 1871), p. 240. Tikhomirov (*Towns* ..., pp. 432-34) undermines the theories based on overenthusiastic readings of recent Soviet archaeological findings that Moscow was in fact much older than its first mention of 1147 in the Chronicles.

was almost entirely the product of the monastic revival that began with the founding of the monastery of the Holy Trinity in 1337 in the woods northeast of Moscow. In one of the most remarkable missionary movements in Christian history, faith and culture were soon taken 750 miles due east to the foothills of the Urals by Sergius' disciple, Stephen of Perm. By 1397, the year after Stephen's death, the movement had penetrated three hundred miles due north when another disciple, St. Cyril, founded his famous monastery on the White Lake; and forty years later it carried yet another three hundred miles north with the founding of the great Solovetsk Monastery on a bleak archipelago in the White Sea. In northeast Russia alone some eighty monasteries were founded in the fourteenth century (nearly as many as had existed up to that time in all of Russia); and some seventy more were added in the first half of the fifteenth.[5] These cloisters remained the center of the culture that developed and spread on to the Pacific in a second wave of eastward expansion in the late sixteenth and early seventeenth century.

The monasteries were often military and economic as well as religious centers, and the culture that developed in them reflected both the harsh material conditions and the fundamentalist faith of a frontier people. Religion was essentially practical. Even in Kievan times theology had been historical rather than rational; and for Muscovy religion meant victory in battle, deliverance from the plague. Men were—for practical reasons—more literate than is often thought, but they were less literary than many writers about "old Russian literature" would have one believe.[6] They worshiped with sounds, images, and incense rather than words and ideas. Thanks to God was expressed in such communal rites as the building of *obydennye tserkvi,* wooden temples that were fashioned out of the virgin forest between sundown of one

---

[5] Estimate of В. Иконниковъ, *Опытъ изслѣдованія культурнаго значенія византіи въ русской исторіи* (Kiev, 1870), p. 119; accepted by М. Левченко, *Очерки по истории русско-византийских отношений* (Moscow, 1956), p. 531. B. H. Sumner, *Survey of Russian History* (2nd ed.; London, 1947), p. 182, estimates that 150 cloisters were founded in Russia as a whole between 1340 and 1440; M.-J. Rouët de Journel, *Monachisme et Monastères Russes* (Paris, 1952), pp. 39, 43, estimates 180 from the early fourteenth century to the beginning of the fifteenth and 300 for the fifteenth and sixteenth centuries as a whole; Igor Smolitsch, *Russisches Mönchtum* (Würzburg, 1953), pp. 81-82, n. 2, follows Kliuchevsky in citing figures that suggest slightly smaller over-all totals.

The old but still valuable history of monasticism by П. Казанскій, *Исторія русскаго монашества до основанія Троице-Сергіевой Лавры* (Moscow, 1855), pp. 9-10, makes it clear that the period prior to the foundation of the Monastery of St. Sergius is only a kind of prehistory of Russian monasticism, and that subsequent monasticism was a distinct and more important development. For this development, see materials listed in Smolitsch, *op. cit.,* pp. 14-27; and В. Соколовскій, *Участіе русскаго духовенства и монашества въ развитіи единодержавія и самодержавія въ московскомъ государствѣ въ концѣ XV и первой половинѣ XVI вв.* (Kiev, 1902).

[6] The extent of basic pre-Petrine literacy and education is underestimated even in such balanced discussions of Russian culture as that of П. Милюковъ, *Очерки по исторіи русской культуры* (Paris, 1931), II, Part II, 687-731. For details on the early period see Ѳ. Успенскій, *Очерки по исторіи византійской образованности на Руси* (St. Petersburg,

day and sundown of the next, while the women sang hymns of praise and burned candles before icons.[7] Indeed this culture expressed itself best in practical construction—of wooden churches and buildings, which have almost totally disappeared, and of great stone churches and monasteries, which still exist in various stages of neglect throughout the USSR. The latter are no less remarkable than the transplanted Byzantine splendors of early Kiev and Novgorod and reflect the fruitful addition of wooden construction forms and of foreign techniques: Italian in the rebuilt Kremlin of the late fifteenth century, oriental in the sixteenth-century St. Basil's Cathedral in Red Square, Persian and Dutch in the great seventeenth-century cathedrals of Yaroslavl.[8] Some idea of the richness and variety of Muscovite architecture can be gained by looking at two of its last and greatest monuments: the massive, yet simple and beautifully balanced ensemble of the Kremlin in Great Rostov; and the soaring and exotic lonely wooden church of the Transfiguration at Kizhi, with its twenty-two ascending barrel vaults *(bochki)* and superimposed, onion-shaped cupolas.

(2) Part of the answer to the "intellectual silence" of Old Russia lies in the harsh frontier conditions of Muscovy. Part also lies in the de-

---

1892) and В. Перетцъ, «Образованность въ кіевской Руси,» in М. Довнаръ-Запольскій, ed., *Книга для чтенія по русской исторіи* (Moscow, 1904), I; for the later period, А. Соболевскій, *Образованность московской Руси XV-XVII вв.* (St. Petersburg, 1892); А. Архангельскій, *Образованіе и литература въ московскомъ государствѣ конца XV-XVII вв.* (3 vols.; Kazan, 1898-1901); and *Очерки исторіи СССР XVII в.* (Moscow, 1955), pp. 554-67. А. Галкинъ, *Академія въ Москвѣ въ XVII ст.* (Moscow, 1913), especially pp. 5-6, n. 1, is more skeptical. Some measure of the extent of the loosely organized but effective primary education in high Muscovy is shown by the fact that more than 300,000 alphabet primers were printed in the Moscow printing office during the second half of the seventeenth century (figure cited from an unpublished dissertation in *Очерки ...*, pp. 558-59)—compared with 33,237 in Lvov (one of the most active of the West Russian printing centers) for the entire period 1582-1722. See Е. Медынский, *Братские школы украины и белоруссии в XVI-XVIII вв.* (Moscow, 1954), p. 52. In addition to this type of primer *(bukvar')*, the dictionary of foreign terms *(azbukovnik)* became a virtual encyclopedia, and an important media of popular education, beginning in the mid-sixteenth century. See А. Карповъ, *Азбуковники или Алфавиты иностранныхъ речей по спискамъ соловетской библіотеки* (Kazan, 1877), especially pp. 23 ff. and bibliography, p. 3, n. 1.

This popular literacy, however, contributed little to, and gained little from, the written literary culture of the monasteries. See A. Poppé, "Dans la Russie médiévale, Xe-XIIIe siècles: Écriture et culture," *Annales Economies Sociétés Civilizations,* January-February, 1961, pp. 12-35. The separation of monastic from popular culture became more acute in many respects after the fourteenth century, following the introduction of complex cursive writing *(skoropis')* and South Slavic stylistic embellishments and archaisms. Popular secular literature—epics, tales, etc.—thus tended to be transmitted in oral rather than written form. Even in the monasteries much of the instruction was oral—a novice being known by the term "obedient listener" *(poslushnik).*

[7] See the account of building such a church in Vologda at the time of the plague of 1653-54 in *Чтенія въ обществѣ исторіи и древностей при московскомъ университетѣ,* III (1893), especially pp. 13-16.

[8] In addition to basic Russian and Western works on these churches cited in George Hamilton, *The Art and Architecture of Russia* (London, 1954), p. 278, see materials in И. Грабар, ed., *Исторія русскаго искусства* (Moscow, 1959), IV, 650-58.

cisiveness and brutality of the Muscovite subjugation of a third distinct cultural entity within "old" Russia: the politically sophisticated culture of westward-looking Novgorod and Pskov (the golden age of which lies in the period between the decline of Kiev and the full victory of Moscow).[9] But why the continued silence of the great monasteries and prosperous trading centers even in the later period, when Novgorod and Pskov had been absorbed and contacts with the West were manifold? Why the Muscovite preference for rhetoric rather than reason, the "golden-tongued" Chrysostom rather than the "cursed logic" of the early Greeks? Why was the ordering of knowledge seen as the "swaggering" of heretical "almanach mongers," and theological disputation as irreverent "comedies and masquerades before the portals of our Lord"?[10]

The oft-quoted statement of Pushkin that the Mongols, unlike the Moors, did not bring Aristotle with them is more an alibi than an explanation,[11] since there were older Greek texts available and newer Jewish and Arab ones filtering in through Novgorod and other centers. More important is the general lack of a classical heritage—a factor that Professor Florovsky has tended to play down. All of Kievan as well as Muscovite Russia lay well beyond the political borders (if not the economic orbit) of the Hellenistic and Roman empires. Partly as a result, Old Russia never acquired (at least until the seventeenth century) a clear diocesan structure and episcopal order for its church, any uniformly recognized body of canon law, or any clear distinction between law and morality in the civil sphere.[12] Russia also had the misfortune

[9] For a brief but perceptive and up-to-date effort to characterize the distinctive culture of Novgorod, see М. Тихомиров, «Великий Новгород в истории мировой культуры,» *Вопросы истории,* No. 1, 1960, pp. 42-52. Regional peculiarities and loyalties are, of course, generally played down (if not suppressed altogether from the record) by Soviet scholars.

[10] Citations from Avvakum and the influential late sixteenth-century Ukrainian elder from Mount Athos, Ivan Vyshensky, referenced and shown to be typical by A. Florovsky (brother of Professor Florovsky), *Le conflit de deux generations—la latine et la byzantine—dans la vie intellectuelle de l'Europe orientale aux XVI-XVII siècles* (Prague, 1937), pp. 8-10, 16.

[11] Particularly as cited by Grekov at the conclusion of his *Culture . . .*, p. 144. For Tatar influence—most marked in administrative, military, and ceremonial matters—Н. Веселовскій, *Татарское вліяніе на посольскій церемоніалъ въ московскій періодъ русской исторіи* (St. Petersburg, 1911) supplements the discussion and material in George Vernadsky, *The Mongols and Russia* (New Haven, 1953), pp. 333-90, and M. Cherniavsky, "Khan or Basileus," *Journal of the History of Ideas,* Oct.-Dec., 1959, pp. 459-76.

[12] On the lack of any distinct legal vocabulary in Muscovy, see articles by Boris Unbegaun in *Revue des études slaves,* XXXIV (1957), 129-35; and XXXVI (1959), 47-58. Although hierarchical authority and precedence had been established earlier and canon law extensively used in both the ecclesiastical and civil spheres, there was considerable confusion and local variation prior to the establishment of a central bureaucracy under Patriarch Filaret (1619-33) and the first publication of the basic "Pilot Book" in 1650 and 1653. See Николай Ярушевичъ, *Церковный судъ въ Россіи до изданія Соборнаго Уложенія Алексѣя Михайловича* (Petrograd, 1917)—doctoral thesis of the recently deceased Metropolitan of Moscow—and other material referenced in *Библиографія по исторіи народовъ СССР* (Moscow-Leningrad, 1932), Part II, pp. 71-73, and in М. Горчаковъ,

to be cut off from the West at the very time when Greek logic and the main corpus of Roman law were being rediscovered in the high medieval West. Fanaticism and anti-intellectualism tend to be greatest in harsh material conditions; and in Kievan Russia more than in Byzantium, in Muscovite Russia more than in Kievan, faith and fighting, war and worship became closely intertwined. The tenacious qualities needed for survival—*dolgoterpenie* (long-suffering) and *blagochestie* (ardent devotion)—were hailed alike by chroniclers and hagiographers as supreme virtues.

Perhaps the most important explanation for the intellectual silence lies in the nature of the Byzantine impact on Russia; for Byzantium was no more a monolith than Old Russia, and its influence on the latter was concentrated in two very distinct periods, and exercised in each case largely through the intermediacy of Balkan Slavs.[13] The first wave of South Slav influence (which brought Christianity and the main features of Byzantine culture to Kievan Russia) occurred at a time when the great doctrinal controversies of the Eastern Church had been settled and its energies newly engaged in the artistic creativity that followed the defeat of the iconoclasts. Thus, the almost fundamentalist attachment to inherited forms and formulas and the bias toward an aesthetic rather than a philosophic culture—already noticeable in Kievan times— merely reflect the exultation of new converts over the general Byzantine "victory of Orthodoxy" and the return of the icons. The second wave of South Slav influence brought a more specifically antirationalist bias, bearing the decisive imprint of the antischolastic Hesychast mysticism of fourteenth-century Byzantium.[14] The Hesychast belief that ascetic discipline, inner calm *(hesychia)*, and unceasing prayers of the spirit would prepare man for divine illumination was the major spiritual force behind the proliferation of monasteries and smaller spiritual communities *(skity)* in fourteenth- and fifteenth-century Muscovy. Hesy-

---

«Кормчая книга,» in *Энциклопедическій словарь*, XVI, No. 31 (St. Petersburg, 1895), 292-94.

[13] For the South Slav influence on Old Russia see two basic surveys of the entire subject with documentation of the Russian and South Slav materials respectively: М. Тихомиров, «Исторические связи русского народа с южными славянами с древнейших времен до половины XVII века,» *Славянский сборник* (Moscow, 1947), pp. 125-201; and V. Мошин, "O periodizaciji rusko-južneslavenskih književnih veza," *Slovo* (No. 11?, 1961?—copy consulted in manuscript by courtesy of the editor, Professor Hamm of Vienna). For the "first wave," see also В. Николаев, *Славянобългарският фактор в християнизацията на Киевска Русия* (Sofia, 1949); for the second, А. Соболевскій, *Южно-славянское вліяніе на русскую письменность въ XIV-XV вѣкахъ* (St. Petersburg, 1894), and H. Schaeder, *Moskau das Dritte Rom* (2nd ed.; Darmstadt, 1957), pp. 1-12; Г. Винокур, *Избранные работы по русскому языку* (Moscow, 1959), pp. 59-62; and titles listed in Sumner, *Survey* . . . , p. 471, n. 179, second paragraph.

[14] On the Hesychast tradition and its transmission to Russia, see I. Smolitsch, *Leben und Lehre der Starzen* (Cologne, 1952), pp. 23-63, with valuable references pp. 234-39, and in his *Mönchtum*, pp. 107-8. See, in addition, Jean Meyendorff, *St. Grégoire Palamas et la mystique orthodoxe* (Paris, 1959).

chasm helped impart to the quickening spiritual life of Muscovy its suspicion of "Latin" definitions and sacramentalism; and the South Slav chroniclers' inclination toward apocalypticism—in the face of the Turkish conquest of Serbia, Bulgaria, and then Constantinople itself in the late fourteenth and mid-fifteenth century—was echoed in the north in the early sixteenth century at the time of the fall of Pskov, and magnified in the seventeenth when the latinized Poles overran Muscovy itself.[15] The nervous religiosity and prophetic intensity of Muscovy provided the raw energy and sense of destiny that enabled Russia to become a great power in the course of the struggle with Poland in the seventeenth century; but these qualities also left a fateful legacy of irrational, anarchistic, and even masochistic impulses.

(3) There was a structure to the civilization of Muscovy; but it is to be sought not in the words of a *Codex Justinianus* or a *Summa Theologica* but in the forms of the iconostasis, the wall of holy pictures that separated the altar sanctuary from the rest of a Muscovite church. In Byzantium and Kievan Russia icons had often adorned the central or "royal" doors leading through this partition, and even the low screen or arcaded barrier itself. But it is in Muscovy that one first finds the ordered, many-tiered screen of icons often extending up to the ceiling: a pictorial encyclopedia of the Christian faith and a graphic expression of a hierarchical and ritualized religious society. Already in the earliest surviving iconostasis (the three-tiered screen painted in the late fourteenth century for the Archangel Cathedral in the Moscow Kremlin by several monastic artists including Rublev) one sees a richness of color and grace of composition equal to anything in Christian art; and one sees how functions once borne by mosaic and fresco art were being taken over by the icon in the wooden world of Muscovy.[16]

The development of the icon and the iconostasis represented, both aesthetically and theologically, a humanization of the Christian message: a material link between the often remote God of Orthodoxy and the simple hopes and fears of an awakening people. The screen lay along the "boundary between heaven and earth,"[17] where this prophetic, pilgrim civilization felt itself to lie; and the forms upon it were the human ones that God had assumed in coming out from his holy

---

[15] In addition to Schaeder and other discussions of the "Third Rome" theory referenced Архангельскій, *Очерки изъ исторіи западно-русской литературы XVI-XVII вв. Борьба* in R. Wolff, "The Three Romes," *Daedalus*, Spring, 1959, p. 309, nn. 1, 2, see А. *съ католичествомъ и западно-русская литература* (Moscow, 1888), I, especially pp. 81-84, 111-19, 133-36 and notes; and С. Белокуровъ, *Арсеній Сухановъ* (Moscow, 1891), I, especially pp. 166 ff.

[16] Н. Машковцев, ed., *Исторія русскаго искусства* (Moscow, 1957), I, 83-91; L. Uspensky and V. Lossky, *The Meaning of Icons* (Boston, 1952), especially pp. 59, 68; Hamilton, *op. cit.*, pp. 66-69.

[17] Uspensky and Lossky, *op. cit.*, p. 59. Old Russian civilization, in the words of V. Zenkovsky, viewed itself as "moving toward the transformation of earthly dominion into ecclesiastical dominion." *A History of Russian Philosophy* (New York, 1953), I, 37.

place in the sanctuary to his chosen but still unsanctified people. Each icon provided a means of grace and hope of glory; each was a "meditation in color," a reminder of God's concrete involvement in human history, and at the same time an "external expression of the transfigured state of man."[18] The candles lit before these icons were small symbols of hope in a world where both light and heat were scarce; reminders of the other forms within the "holy and life-giving Trinity" which God himself had assumed in coming directly to the apostolic founders of his Church: the dazzling light that revealed Christ transfigured before them on Mount Tabor and the fiery tongues of the Holy Spirit that came to them at Pentecost after Christ's final ascension.[19]

As an ensemble, the iconostasis provided (like the elaborate chronicles and genealogies of the Muscovite period) a continuing record of sacred history, moving from the Old Testament patriarchs and prophets in the highest row to the local saints in the lowest. The central panels moved down to man—as had God himself—through the Virgin to Christ, who stood at the center of the main row of panels and immediately over the royal doors. Modeled on the *pantokrator* that had stared down in lonely splendor from the central dome of earlier, Byzantine cathedrals, the figure of "Christ enthroned" acquired on the iconostasis a less severe expression and an entourage of holy figures deployed on either side and inclined towards him in adoration. He now had a gospel in his hand opened to the text: "Come unto me, all ye that travail and are heavy laden, and I will refresh you."[20]

Amidst this sea of pictures, Muscovite thought tended to crystallize in images. The popular term for saint was *prepodobnyi* or "very like" the holy images, and the reverence for these images helped doom the rationalistic movements that came in from Novgorod and then from the Protestant tradesmen of Northern Europe. The political ideology of Muscovy has been well described as a belief that "the Tsar is the living icon of God, just as the whole Orthodox Empire is the icon of the

---

[18] Uspensky and Lossky, *op. cit.*, p. 39. The defeat of the iconoclasts just before Russia's conversion was a kind of pictorial vindication of the Christology of the creed, "a second victory for the human image of Christ exalted over the image of salvation through the transformation of humanity into something wholly different, implied in most of the older oriental heresies." George Every, *The Byzantine Patriarchate 451-1204* (London, 1947), p. 111. Uspensky and Lossky justly remark (*op. cit.*, p. 46) that "if Byzantium was preeminent in giving the world theology expressed in words, theology expressed in images was given preeminently by Russia." Josef Myslivec, *Ikona* (Prague, 1947), p. 47, refers to the icon as the "everlasting memorial of the victory of Orthodoxy and of Platonic idealism" in the East; Eugene Trubetskoi refers to the icon in the title of his book as an *Умозрѣнie въ Краскахъ* (Moscow, 1916). For a basic history, see N. Kondakov, *The Russian Icon* (Oxford, 1927); for an analysis and glossary of terms, see L. Réau, *L'Art Russe des origines à Pierre le Grand* (Paris, 1921); for critical discussion of other monographs and reproductions, see Hamilton, *op. cit.*, pp. 272-76.

[19] Mark 9:2-8; or, more vividly, Matthew 17:1-9; and Acts 2:1-4. These scenes are, of course, favorite subjects of icons.

[20] Matthew 11:28.

heavenly world."[21] Like the citizens of Muscovy the figures on the
screen had their own *mestnichestvo* or prescribed order of rank. Each
panel bore a fixed relationship to the central figures of the Virgin and
Christ; all were in a sense mysteriously equidistant from God himself.
The term *chin* used to designate this prescribed order on the screen
(and particularly the central *deisusnyi* or "prayer" row centered on the
panel of Christ enthroned) became the general term for rank and order
of all sorts; and its verbal form *uchiniti* the main term for all forms of
command and direction.[22]

The artistic decline of the icon in the sixteenth and seventeenth centuries graphically illustrates the ossification of forms and loss of spiritual feeling that marked the decline of Muscovite culture. After Peter,
icon screens in the synodal church became increasingly burdened with
the rococo decor placed between the pictures and the lacquer and metal
placed over them. The prophetic Old Believers continued to build
iconostases of the old sort—but without an altar or sanctuary (and thus
without any sense of God's real presence) behind them. In the new
empire, the authority of the *chin* gave way to that of the *chinovnik*—
and thence to the Bolsheviks, whose pictures atop the mausoleum display all the ritual arrangement and stereotyped facial expressions of a
chin on the iconostasis emptied of all transcendent meaning and aesthetic grace.

Even the most casual visitor to a Soviet art museum cannot help
being struck by the disparity between the beauty of the older icons—the
most majestic of which have usually been taken from dismantled iconostases—and the barren naturalism of subsequent Russian painting. The
brief moments of fresh achievement in Russian painting during the last
seventy years—in the work of such men as Vriubel, Kandinsky, and
Filonov—have drawn (like so much of the creative accomplishment of
the late imperial period) on the forms, if not the faith, of Russia's older
religious culture. Indeed, that which separates all of early Russian culture from that which followed Peter (or more properly, Catherine) is
not just the difference between religious and secular culture, but the
gulf between an aesthetic and a moralistic outlook on life. In some
ways the secularized literary culture of aristocratic St. Petersburg and

[21] Fedotov, *Russian Religious Mind*, p. 208.

[22] For Ivan IV's fascination with the concept of *chin* and its application to musical ceremony, see К. Кузнецов, «Из музыкального прошлого Москвы,» *Советская музыка*, No. 5,
1947, especially pp. 37-38; for Alexis Mikhailovich's later fixation on the idea see the article
by С. Платоновъ, in *Историческій вѣстникъ*, XXIV (1887), pp. 267-69, and also Alexis'
famous *chin* for his falcons reprinted in П. Бартеневъ, *Собраніе писемъ Царя Алексѣя
Михайловича* (Moscow, 1856), pp. 87-146. See also *ibid.*, pp. 125-26, n. 16, for the significance of *chin* and other etymologically related terms; V. Du Feu, "Some Features of the
Vocabulary of Russian Royal Letters (1613-38)," *Oxford Slavonic Papers*, III (1958), 160-61,
for the uses of *uchiniti;* and В. Ключевскій, *Исторія сословій в Россіи* (3rd ed.; Petrograd, 1918), for the actual status and history of *chiny* within the society.

the restless reformatorial spirit that it engendered can be seen as a kind of fascinating but unreal interlude—beautiful and transitory as the white nights of the northern summer—between the Moscow of the Third Rome and that of the Third International.[23]

(4) Far from diminishing the importance of Old Russian culture (as Professor Florovsky's article might be taken to imply), consideration of its historical fate apart from its inner structure makes it seem even more deserving of serious study. For this "old" culture—its ritualized Orthodox worship, its animistic popular cosmology, and its heroic oral epics—remained the dominant one for most Russians down to at least the mid-nineteenth century. The ordinary muzhik continued to view as something alien to him both the Swedo-Prussian rule of the Petersburg bureaucracy and the patina of Polish and then French culture adopted by the ruling aristocracy. The continuing hold of Old Russian culture is demonstrated in three concrete and far-reaching developments in post-Petrine Russia: (a) the virtual secession from participation in the political and cultural life of the empire by the Old Believers (who regulated most of the internal commerce and much of the manufacturing of early modern Russia); (b) the violent and recurring peasant rebellions with their idealization of the past and belief in the return of a "true Tsar"; and (c) the revival and expansion of the Hesychast tradition of monastic elders and inner piety in the late eighteenth and early nineteenth century.

As to the intrinsic worth of this culture, one is impressed with Father Florovsky's modest and heartfelt conclusion, and conscious of the outsider's responsibility to avoid being either romantic or patronizing. Aesthetically, there seems little doubt that the icons, bells, and incense of Old Russia are preferable to the lithographs of Lenin, humming machines, and cheap perfume of the USSR; that the iconostasis is preferable to the subway mosaic, and the contours of a Muscovite church to the *sovnovrok* ("new Soviet rococo") of an Intourist hotel. There is attractiveness also to the cultural ideal of a "shining city of Kitezh" or a Kiev "glistening with the light of holy icons, fragrant with incense, ringing with praise and sacred, heavenly songs."[24] There is, however, a kind of utopian fanaticism about any belief in a "New Jerusalem" or "Third Rome," and the cruelty, violence, and vulgarity of Muscovy

[23] This idea is present not only in Oswald Spengler, *Decline of the West* (New York, 1928), II, p. 435, and in apocalyptically inclined Russian historians and novelists of the late imperial period, but even at the beginning of the semi-official novelistic portrayal of the Bolshevik take-over: Alexis Tolstoy's *Road to Calvary* (New York, 1946), pp. 1-3.

[24] From the "Sermon on Law and Grace," by Ilarion of Kiev, the first native Metropolitan of Kiev, in Н. Гудзий, *Хрестоматия по древней русской литературе XI-XVII веков* (Moscow, 1938), p. 60. The idea of a "new Jerusalem"—at Constantinople, Kiev, Moscow, or at Patriarch Nikon's monastic retreat of that name—was at times even more important than that of a "new Rome" in the Christian East. See D. Stremooukhoff, "Moscow the Third Rome: Sources of the Doctrine," *Speculum*, Jan., 1953, pp. 84-86; R. Stupperich,

tended to grow along with its prophetic pretensions. Indeed, the monastic epistle first setting forth the theory of Moscow as the "Third Rome" also discusses at length the problem of sodomy.[25]

In the world of religious experience—the fairest testing ground for such a culture—it might be that modern man could find in the mystical theology of the Eastern Church perspectives more relevant to his present condition than those offered by many more familiar theologies. In any event the Christian culture of Old Russia was built on praise rather than definition, a sense both of God's awesome remoteness and of his all-permeating "energies," calls for repentance paired with premonitions of apocalypse, and, above all, an undaunted belief in the possibility of transfiguration in this life and resurrection in the next. Its great festival was Easter—celebrated with particular intensity in the Muscovite north, where it ended a dark winter as well as a long fast. The joyful greeting "Christ is risen!" was always answered by "In truth, risen!" which seemed to apply to all of creation. All that had passed away were only "asleep until the common rising of all,"[26] when "the goodness hidden in the hearts of the holy shall be revealed in their risen bodies" just as trees long veiled in snow and darkness "put out their leaves in the spring."[27]

Thus, to the believer, there is always the consolation that "except a grain of wheat fall into the ground and die, it abideth alone"[28] and the hope that, dying, it may in some mysterious way bring forth the fruit promised by the evangelist. But to the historian, Old Russian culture may appear only as a long since harvested and burnt-out field in which only a few splendid husks remain.

"Kiev—das zweite Jerusalem," *Zeitschrift für slavische Philologie*, XII (1935), pp. 332-54; and Белокуровъ, *op. cit.*, pp. 173-75, 187-88, 214-15. On the popular Kitezh legend, whereby God allegedly preserved this faithful city from Batu Khan, placing it in a lake beyond the Volga (or, in some versions, on a mountain), see В. Комарович, *Китежская легенда* (Moscow-Leningrad, 1936).

[25] See text in В. Малининъ, *Старецъ Елеазарова монастыря филоөей и его посланіе* (Kiev, 1901), pp. 49-56.

[26] Ilarion of Kiev in Гудзий, *Хрестоматия . . .*, p. 59.

[27] Tikhon Zadonsky as cited in N. Gorodetsky, *Tikhon Zadonsky* (London, 1952), p. 163.

[28] John 12:24. Dostoevsky placed this passage at the beginning of *The Brothers Karamazov*.

Reply

GEORGES FLOROVSKY

I am most grateful to my commentators for their candid remarks and suggestions. Indeed, the main purpose of my original essay was precisely to provoke discussion. It was a query, not a summary and not a digest. Problems must be first sharply focused and carefully identified before they can be taken up profitably and eventually solved. On many points raised in my paper I have no solution to offer. I am only asking questions. Yet it is important to ask proper questions.

Now, in reply, I have to stress once more the basic plurality in the historical approach itself. "Societies" and "cultures" cannot be unconditionally identified, although cultures have *historical* significance only in so far as they are embodied in certain particular societies, which serve as their bearers, and are cultivated and propagated in these societies. Yet, on the other hand, different societies may share the same culture, and the continuous existence and growth of a culture may be effected in a sequence or succession of different societies. Professor Billington seems to ignore this crucial distinction. He tends to dissociate Moscow and Kiev. He goes so far as to suggest that "Russian history in many ways really begins with the rise of Moscow." The Kievan period then becomes a kind of isolated episode, unrelated to the later formation of Russia, an archaic phenomenon. Indeed, the ancient Kievan state and Muscovy are two different "societies," of different social structures and in quite different situations, with different territorial bases and different international settings. And yet there was still an obvious and unbroken "succession" and unity: Kievan inheritance was an integral part of the Muscovite cultural tradition, though it was, of course, reinterpreted and reassessed.

In spite of all regional shifts and changes, "Russian culture" was one and continuous from the archaic Kievan times to the most modern times of the new Russian Empire. One cannot subtract *historically* the "Kievan inheritance" from the general economy of that complex and comprehensive bloc that we call "Russian culture." And this continuity is not just an artifact of modern historiographical interpretation. This continuity was reflected in the very process of cultural formation and can be traced on several levels. Probably the most conspicuous instance is in the history of Russian epics. The merry Prince Vladimir is the key figure in the Russian *byliny*, which assumed their final shape in the creative memory of the Russian North. Ancient Kiev, as unhistorically (that is, in the perspective of another development) as it may be pictured in the *byliny,* is an integral and pivotal part of the Russian total epic memory and tradition. Kiev was never forgotten in the North. The other instance is the complex history of old Russian *letopisanie.* All later chronicles and chronographs compiled in various centers of the North—Vladimir, Novgorod, Tver, or Moscow itself—usually included the old Kievan material and were permeated with a strong feeling and conviction of uninterrupted cultural succession. There was, through the centuries, a persistent vision of an overarching "national" unity, or of the unity of the "Russian Land," a vision of "all Russia," of a continuous Russia, even on the political level, and it was much more and much deeper than just an "imperialistic" pretense. It was, indeed, a search for the political unity of a nation. In any case, ecclesiastical unity was always strongly maintained and defended well into the fifteenth century in spite of strong claims for regional autonomy both in the West and in the North (Novgorod), and although Metropolitans of "all Russia" moved to the North, to Vladimir first and then to Moscow, they retained their old and original title of Kiev while vigorously claiming authority and jurisdiction over the whole of Russia. It is significant that it was a man of Volynian descent, St. Peter, who decided to settle in Moscow. Again, strong emphasis on continuity is obvious in the development of Novgorod, an integral part of the ancient state organization and also an integral part of the later national unity under Moscow domination.

The whole problem of historic continuity between Kiev and Moscow must be investigated cautiously and judiciously. It is an intricate and delicate problem.[1] Actually, it is the crucial problem of pattern and scope of Russian history. Is Moscow a true and legitimate successor of ancient Kiev, or is it a new beginning altogether and a separate formation? Or did ancient Kiev find its organic continuation rather in the Galician kingdom of Daniel, and later in the Lithuanian state? This is a commonplace of Polish and Ukrainian historiography, and for that reason it requires a cautious re-examination. Now, apart from all political considerations, one is able to discern a cultural unity of "all Russia" grounded in common faith and in common national memories. Once more we have to emphasize the basic difference between "culture" and "society." Of course, Moscow society was a distinctive formation, very different from that of ancient Kiev, and the Moscow culture of the fourteenth and later centuries was, in many respects, a new development. In a wider perspective, however, Kiev and Moscow did belong

---

[1] See, for instance, А. Н. Насонов, «*Русская земля*» *и образование территорий великорусского государства* (Moscow, 1951), also the collective work, *Вопросы формирования русской народности и нации* (Moscow and Leningrad, 1958); cf. Alexandre V. Soloviev, *Le Nom Byzantine de la Russie* (The Hague: Mouton & Co., 1957), and his earlier studies quoted in this essay. I have no intention of giving here a complete bibliography on the subject.

together, as also did Moscow and St. Petersburg. The Kievan period was an organic stage in the formation of Russian culture, and not just an archaic prelude. Russian culture is larger and more comprehensive than just its Muscovite component. The conventional scheme of Russian cultural history, in all its branches—history of literature, history of art, and the like—can be impartially vindicated: one must begin at the Kiev of St. Vladimir and Iaroslav, and pass through Moscow, in order to arrive at the great national culture of the last century. And it is so in spite of all shifts and rifts, of all changes and transformations. There is an enormous field for research.[2] One final remark should be added at this point. We are accustomed to speak of European culture (or civilization) and to stress its unity, although, historically speaking, this culture actually existed only in various local and regional embodiments, even in the Middle Ages, before the national consciousness in the West had been awakened and articulated. There were always several regional societies, often in sharp and bitter tension, and yet it is quite proper to speak of one continuous cultural process. It seems that a similar criterion should be used by the historians of Russia: there was one comprehensive Russian culture in the process of formation in spite of the diversity of regional societies with their distinctive marks and peculiar contributions.

Let us turn now to the problem of Russian beginnings. Dr. Andreyev's reminder of the pre-Christian heritage of Russia is certainly relevant and welcome. Indeed, the very reception of the Byzantine Christian heritage was possible only because the ground had been already well prepared. For that reason the reception of the Byzantine heritage was more than imitation or just repetition; it was rather a creative response or recreation of imported cultural values and ideas. The fact remains, however, that the only Russian culture we know, that is, the culture that was embodied and reflected in literature and art, was built on a Byzantine foundation and was a direct continuation of the Byzantine cultural endeavor and effort. Even the *Tale of the Host of Igor* reflected the patterns of Byzantine rhetoric. Of course, foreign traditions were superbly indigenized, and it is easy to detect manifold national motives. But the bases, and probably the driving power also, were mainly Byzantine. D. S. Likhachev, in his recent general survey of *The Culture of the Russian People from the Tenth to the Seventeenth Century*, rightly stresses this point. Christianity was a religion with a highly developed literature, which Russian paganism lacked. Accordingly, Russian literature stemmed from the Christian Byzantine

---

[2] On the distinction between "societies" and "cultures" see the valuable suggestions of Pitirim A. Sorokin, *Social Philosophies of an Age of Crisis* (Boston, 1951), pp. 205 ff.; cf. also his article "Toynbee's Philosophy of History," in *The Pattern of the Past: Can We Determine It?* (Boston, 1949), pp. 127 ff.

spring.[3] Dr. Andreyev identifies many national motives as "pagan," and as such they had to remain alien to the total structure of the cultural whole. More important was, of course, the national tension between the Greeks and the Slavs. I would prefer complete caution at this point. We should not read too much of later Grecophobia into the texts of the pre-Mongolian times. At that time, it seems, the spirit of political and canonical independence did not yet control the inner life of culture. Metropolitan Hilarion himself was deeply Byzantine in his style and ethos, as were Cyril of Turov and Clement of Smolensk. Indeed, Tsar Simeon of Bulgaria was as king and politician a staunch enemy of Byzantium, and yet culturally he was profoundly Greek—an accomplished Byzantine literate. The Slavs at that time were sensible enough to recognize the universal value of that Christian culture which had been offered to them in Greek garb and shape and in the context of Byzantine political expansion. Indeed, this universality was implied in the initiative of SS. Cyril and Methodius themselves. The *cultural* Grecophobia in Russia was a much later development, and its growth— in Muscovite times—has hardly strengthened Russian culture. Culture, in its deepest sense, can never simply emerge out of "national spirit." It is always initiated by "reception," by inheriting accumulated traditions, by assessing the universal stock of higher values. In this sense true culture is itself universal and supranational. And even the formal strength of any particular culture is first expressed in the scope and span of its synthetic power. True culture is always catholic, in the Socratic sense of the word.

At this point I want to stress once more the basic duality of our total approach to the phenomena and problems of culture. I am afraid my commentators did not pay enough attention to this crucial distinction. Professor Billington seems to suggest that I am inclined to diminish the historical importance of Old Russian culture. In fact, no less than Professor Billington am I responsive to the thrill of Old Russian religious culture in its manifold branches, and my personal estimate of it is on the whole appreciative, positive, and rather high. My doubts refer only to its *historical function,* or significance, in the total and actual destiny of Russian society. Culture is *for the historian* first of all a concrete historic phenomenon which must be visualized in the total perspective of the formation of that particular society in which this concrete culture has originated and to which it primarily belongs. In this connection, the significance of particular cultural phenomena and of each particular culture taken en bloc is to be determined primarily by their *function* and their *impact,* negative or positive, destructive or constructive. On the other hand, however, culture is a complex, code, congery, or system

---

[3] Д. С. Лихачев, *Культура русского народа, X-XVII вв.* (Moscow and Leningrad, 1961), p. 16.

of certain values and treasures, which must obviously be described and evaluated in their own terms, regardless and even in spite of their historical significance or function. Indeed, in both cases we would be involved in the process of evaluation, but the methods and criteria used are, and must be, different. For instance, literary critics, on the one side, and historians of literature, on the other, differently assess and apprehend the same phenomena. Their conclusions may in certain cases converge or even coincide. But quite often they will sharply diverge. Poor or bad novels may be historically significant and important as typical and influential phenomena, as symptoms and vehicles of drives and ideas. It is enough to mention Chernyshevsky's *What Is To Be Done?* From the literary point of view, it was a poor thing. And yet historically it was the pseudo-gospel of several generations, important as a confession and as a prophetic program. Of course, historians may try to explain why poor art or literature commanded attention, sympathy, and acceptance in a particular age or in a particular social group by referring to a decay in taste and understanding or to a particular psychological condition, and in doing so they may go beyond the limits of their historical competence and make judgments as critics of art and letters. It may happen that great creations of art or letters pass unnoticed or are deliberately ignored or rejected in their immediate environment. Historically they will be insignificant, that is, without influence or response, and will be described by historians as peculiar and marginal phenomena. Not all of them will be rediscovered and reappraised in any manner at any time. And yet their value is intrinsic. In brief, cultural appraisal and historical evaluation do not necessarily coincide. We must distinguish clearly these two dimensions of interpretation. We may highly cherish the legacy of Old Russian culture, and yet as historians we must take seriously the fact of its *historic "unsuccess,"* of its internal crisis, of its tragic dissolution and collapse. This is the primary question for the historian. And he must try to find an *historical* answer to the problem.

Professor Fedotov inscribed one of the chapters of his admirable book, *The Saints of Ancient Russia,* "The Tragedy of Russian Holiness." The term "tragedy" does not belong to the regular vocabulary of historians; it is rather a religious or philosophical term. But the fact which Fedotov pointed out requires the full attention of historians. As great and holy as St. Sergius of Radonezh undoubtedly was, his deepest spiritual legacy was somehow lost in the cultural life of Muscovy. One may admit the partial truth of that "social monasticism" which was promoted by St. Joseph Volotsky, and yet, historically speaking, the victory of the Josephites was in the general economy of the Muscovite culture rather destructive. No need to multiply instances.

The major riddle of Old Russian culture was, of course, its "intellectual silence," or rather, dumbness. Professor Billington tends to explain it by external factors, such as "the harsh frontier conditions of Muscovy." I would not claim to have a satisfactory answer to the riddle, but I would look for it in the inner structure of the Muscovite spiritual world. The "harsh frontier conditions" did not prevent or impede the flowering of art, that is, the awakening and maturing of the aesthetic insight. Why should they, by themselves, impede the intellectual awakening? In fact, there was enough intellectual curiosity in Moscow society, but there was no genuine intellectual drive. The lack was especially conspicuous in the seventeenth century. What was the reason? Once more, I do not pretend to have an adequate answer to this crucial question. But I do still feel that my provisional hypothesis of a "charm of accomplishment" deserves further exploration, especially because it applies both to the Muscovite culture and to the westernizing endeavors of the eighteenth century, and even, probably, to the various utilitarian and moralistic trends of the nineteenth century. I do not suggest, as has been done more than once, that anti-intellectualism, or indifference to abstract problems and speculation, is an essential characteristic of the "Russian soul," the alleged *âme russe*. I do not believe in the existence of any such "collective soul." National characters, if such do exist, are being made in history, and change. Yet, there is still some continuity of basic attitudes, although radical anti-intellectualism developed in Russia under foreign influence and at a comparatively late date. In any case, the structure of the "Russian soul," as can be observed in its cultural expressions, is rather antinomical and cannot be reduced to any simple formula. The "thrill of accomplishment" has a utopian tenor; it implies the expectation that the ideal may be adequately and definitively realized or incarnated. The dynamism of search is subdued to the static pattern of accomplishment.

Professor Billington invokes also another external factor: the brutal subjugation of the westward-looking Novgorod and Pskov. The annexation of these two republics was rather harsh and brutal—so much must be conceded. But it is hardly historically fair to idealize the constitution and policy of these two republics. Historically speaking, one may contend that this annexation was a progressive endeavor and was justified by the general logic of national development and integration.[4] What is much more important, from the cultural point of view, is that all basic achievements of Novgorod and Pskov were actually included in the Moscow "gathering of culture" in the sixteenth century, so that this Moscow synthesis was almost entirely composed of Novgorod material. Whatever may be said about the political aspect of the annexation, little if anything has been lost of the Novgorod cultural heritage. And it

[4] Cf. В. Н. Бернадский, *Новгород и Новгородская земля в XV веке* (Moscow and Leningrad, 1961).

is still uncertain whether the westward orientation of the two northern republics was a real asset and a token of advance and not an entanglement in antiquated social and economic policies of the Hanseatic League.

Indeed, Professor Billington mentions a number of other factors: the lack of classical heritage, the laxity of diocesan structure in the Church, the lack of a commonly accepted body of canon law and of any clear distinction between law and morality. All these topics must be discussed and examined in detail. Only, it seems, they are rather symptoms than factors. Did I play down the impact of the lack of classical heritage? In fact, it must be shown in what manner this lack actually impeded intellectual growth in Russia. I dare only to contend that there was enough stimulating challenge in that theological inheritance which was received from Byzantium and appropriated in Russian culture. But the challenge was not responded to in the sphere of intellect as it was responded to creatively in the realm of art. This is what I have labeled "intellectual silence." Was the reason for this phenomenon already given in the very nature of the Byzantine impact on Russia—that is, in the nature of the Byzantine inheritance itself—or was it rooted in the manner and character of the response? This is the crucial question.[5] Where was rooted the bias toward an aesthetic rather than a philosophical culture? In the Byzantine heritage itself, or in the attitude of the Russians? In Byzantium, in any case, the period of iconoclasm and the one immediately after was characterized not only by an activity in the realm of art but also by a strong philosophical revival. Nor is it fair to overstress the anti-intellectual bias of the Hesychast movement, which stood rather in the mainstream of the Greek intellectual tradition. The Byzantine defense of holy icons was not primarily a vindication of art or ritual but basically a dogmatic endeavor—the defense of the crucial and ultimate reality of Incarnation. This theological, that is, "intellectual," aspect was gradually lost in the disproportionate growth of ritual, as splendid as its artistic achievement and as moving as its emotional appeal might have been. Now, St. Sergius himself did not care at all for splendid temples or for gorgeous rites and robes, and it was just in the spirit and the temper of St. John Chrysostom. But the thrill of splendor finally prevailed. It was not St. Sergius' legacy or tradition. And, in fact, "splendor" itself rapidly degenerated into decoration and ornamentation, on the Russian soil, and not without a Novgorod impact. To sum up, it is difficult to explain *historically* both the general "unsuccess" of Old Russian culture and, in particular, its "intellectual silence," simply by certain external circumstances and conditions, or

[5] Cf. Dmitri Obolensky, "Russia's Byzantine Heritage," in *Oxford Slavonic Papers*, Vol. I (Oxford, 1950); reprinted in *Selection*, ed. Cecily Hastings and Donald Nicholl, II (London: Sheed and Ward, 1954), 87-123.

by the deficiencies of the Byzantine inheritance. There were also some deeper internal causes. In spite of its strength and richness, the Muscovite culture failed to accomplish its purpose and collapsed. Of course—and it must be repeated emphatically—this "historic unsuccess" by itself does not negate the intrinsic value of the doomed culture, just as an historic success by itself does not exonerate internal poverty and primitivism in victorious systems. We are returning again to the initial duality: culture as *a function of society* and culture as a complex of values. Christianity is the Divine Truth, but Christian societies fail and collapse.

In this brief response to the challenge of my gracious commentators, I cannot attempt any systematic re-examination of all important issues they have raised or stressed. The purpose of this exchange of views was rather to initiate discussion. But what we actually need most urgently is not a general discussion of certain basic topics, but rather a patient re-study of sources, critically evaluated and impartially assessed. General discussion is fruitful only in so far as it helps to discern problems, to dismiss prejudices of all sorts, to dispel gratuitous assumptions. The time for a new historical synthesis probably has not yet come. What we really need most is monographic research. This is the most valuable part of the current historiography in the field of Russian culture, old and new.

Further Remarks on the Problem of Old Russian Culture

D. S. LIKHACHEV

The discussion on the problems of Old Russian culture in the journal *Slavic Review* (March, 1962, pp. 1-42) appears to me in the highest degree interesting and important. Not a single culture has evoked or to this day is evoking such contradictory evaluations as the culture of Old Rus.

In a short essay I can focus only on certain of the most important questions.

ON CONTINUITY IN THE DEVELOPMENT OF RUSSIAN CULTURE

The attempt of certain scholars to differentiate sharply between "Muscovite Rus" and "Kievan Rus," and to see in them two distinct cultures with only tenuous historical and geographical connections with each other seems to me unjustified. Professor G. Florovsky already gave an answer on the essence of this problem; however, I should like to strengthen the decisiveness of his objections and somewhat supplement them.

It is inaccurate to see a territorial break between Muscovite and Kievan Rus. "Kievan Rus" is a conventional designation. Kievan Rus was not limited to Kiev and its immediate surroundings. The great political and cultural role of Novgorod, first in Kievan Rus and later in Muscovite Rus, is well known. In the twelfth century the Vladimir-Suzdalian land—the land in which Moscow developed—acquired outstanding importance in Kievan Rus. The architecture of Vladimir-Suzdal was perhaps the best in Kievan Rus, and the literature, composition of chronicles, and painting of Vladimir in the twelfth and thirteenth centuries were not inferior to that of Kiev proper. Despite political fragmentation, in the realm of culture Kievan Rus constituted

MR. LIKHACHEV *is Corresponding Member, Academy of Sciences, USSR, and professor at Leningrad University.*

an amazing cultural unity—from Ladoga in the north to Tmutorokan in the south, from Yaroslavl in the east to Galich and Polotsk in the west. The majority of literary works were produced in the most remote parts of this broad territory. Nikon the Great wrote his chronicle in Kiev and in Tmutorokan. The *Kievo-Pecherskii Paterik* was produced in Kiev and in Vladimir. Serapion of Vladimir wrote in Kiev and in Vladimir. The entire composition of the Russian chronicles was based on the exchange of chronicle evidence among the different regions. Cases are known in which manuscripts written in Novgorod were bound in Kiev.

The "intelligentsia" of Kievan Rus possessed very great mobility, and constantly traveled from principality to principality. Bands of builders, fresco-painters, and churchmen were continually moving from one principality to another, even in the years immediately following the Tatar-Mongol invasion. The cultural ties Alexander Nevsky had with Galician-Volynian Rus are known.[1] Moscow grew up on the territory of the Vladimir-Suzdalian principality, which was culturally one with Kiev; it arose on the territory of Kievan Rus. Gradually including in its domains Rostov, Tver, Yaroslavl, Novgorod, Pskov, and so forth, it all the more broadly embraced domains with the rich cultural tradition of Kievan Rus. Thus it is clear that Moscow Rus was territorially linked with Kievan Rus.

But did not Moscow Rus perhaps forget the cultural traditions of its own land, breaking with them and striking out on its own path? Of course, history does not remain fixed on the same spot; the life of society develops, and culture also develops. However, in regard to Moscow Rus it must be said that in it there existed a quite distinct version of the traditions of Kievan Rus. The proverbial Muscovite conservatism of the sixteenth and seventeenth centuries, the effort to judge everything "according to antiquity and duty" (according to the customs of olden times) arose on the basis of the peculiar revival of Kievan antiquity in all realms of cultural life in the fourteenth and fifteenth centuries.

It is noteworthy that at the time of the struggle for national independence in the fourteenth and fifteenth centuries, the Russians turned to their own national past. The heightened interest of Muscovite Rus in old Kiev, old Vladimir, old Novgorod can be observed in ecclesiastical and political life. It was expressed in intensified effort in historical thought, in the compilation of numerous and extensive collections of chronicles, of historical works, in increased attention to the works of the eleventh to the beginning of the thirteenth centuries: the *Discourse on Law and Grace* by Metropolitan Hilarion of Kiev, the *Tale of Bygone Years*, the *Tale of the Host of Igor*, the *Kievo-Pecherskii Paterik*. They were copied and imitated. The restoration of pre-Mongol build-

---

[1] For details see Д. Лихачев, «Галицкая литературная традиция в житии Александра Невского,» *Труды Отдела древнерусской литературы*, Vol. V (1947).

ings and frescoes was being carried on in Vladimir and Novgorod. The Muscovite princes were tracing their genealogies to the "old prince Vladimir," and Russian *byliny* were being unified into a single Kievan cycle. It is clear that Muscovite Rus did not simply follow Kievan traditions, but consciously cultivated them.[2] The struggle for the Kievan heritage—territorial, political, and cultural—inspired Moscow in the course of three whole centuries. Kievan Rus played the role of "its own" ancient times, in the cultural revival after the Tatar-Mongol invasion. The Ukraine and Belorussia in the same period also continued Kievan traditions, but being included in the make-up of foreign states they were not in this period capable of reviving Kievan traditions on such a large scale.

The question of the links of post-Petrine culture with the culture of Old Rus is more complex. In contrast to the effort of Muscovite Rus to emphasize its continuity with Kievan Rus and to revive the traditions of the epoch of independence, Petrine Russia consciously broke the links with Old Rus and "broke through a window onto Europe." This conscious endeavor at rupture with tradition, however, ought not to confuse us. The more we study concretely the history of Russian art, Russian literature, and Russian science in the seventeenth to the nineteenth centuries, the clearer it becomes that the rupture was more external than internal. The flowering of Russian literature, music, and architecture in the later period has deep roots in the millennium-long development of Russian culture. In Russian literature and social thought one may observe a striking continuity of themes, models, and ideas. The whole of Russian literature, both old and new, from the eleventh to the twentieth century, is filled with civic pathos, the effort at education—in which moral themes play a role of first importance. This may be said in general; as for the particulars, take for example the work of genius, the *Tale of Woe and Misfortune,* and you will be convinced that in it there is much that gives rise to the heritage of the humanist themes of Russian literature of the nineteenth century.

The principles of design of Russian architecture of the seventeenth century were expressed in the planning of Petrine Petersburg. The ensembles of the Russian kremlins and monasteries were reflected in the architecture of the eighteenth and the beginning of the nineteenth century (compare the building of the Zakharov Admiralty in Leningrad). The palette of Russian icon painting was repeated in individual pictures of the eighteenth century and inspired the Russian painting of the beginning of the twentieth century. The tormented themes of the social thought of the sixteenth and seventeenth centuries in a new fashion but within the boundaries of continuity agitated the Russian social thought of the nineteenth century.

[2] For details on the turning to the time of national independence see my book, *Национальное самосознание древней Руси* (Moscow and Leningrad, 1945), pp. 68-81.

All of this, of course, requires much study and research. I am sure that research will demonstrate the presence of links rather than their absence.

On the "Intellectual Silence" of Old Rus

The discovery, at the beginning of the twentieth century, of the aesthetic value of the Old Russian icons occurred simultaneously with the discovery of the culture of Old Rus. For a long time the icons were its most notable representatives. They spoke the voiceless language of color and line, but they were in consequence no less intellectual. The speculative side of the icon was as astonishing as its aesthetic side.

After the icon, Old Russian architecture was discovered. I remember that the remarkable scholar to whom the honor of discovering the icon fundamentally belongs, Igor Grabar, who had been a not less remarkable painter, assigned first place not to the painting but to the architecture of Old Rus. I. Grabar wrote, "Summarizing everything that Russia achieved in the realm of art, one comes to the conclusion that she was above all a nation of architects. A flair for proportions, an understanding of outline, a decorative instinct, an inventiveness with forms—in a word, all the architectural virtues are encountered so constantly and universally in the course of Russian history that they lead to the idea of the absolutely exceptional architectural gifts of the Russian people."[3]

Of course, architecture was also a "silent" art, but no less intellectual than icon painting. If the medieval Gothic cathedrals of Western Europe may be termed philosophical and historical encyclopedias in stone, then Russian churches with their complex systems of fresco paintings deserve this characterization no less. Those who speak of the "intellectual silence" of Old Rus evidently leave completely out of the reckoning the literature of Old Rus. By its very nature literary art is not silent in its message. Consequently, Old Russian literature seems to them unworthy of attention.

Old Russian literature indeed is little known and as yet is far from completely evaluated from the aesthetic standpoint. Often one hears reproaches of Old Russian literature for having no Dante or Shakespeare! However, Dante and Shakespeare cannot serve as measures for the literature of Old Rus. It was a literature of a folkloristic type, and not at all of a personal sort. We cannot demand of an embroideress of the people that she with her threads should create a picture that would raise her name to the level of that of the genius Rembrandt. In Old Russian literature one finds another kind of art, high and one which delights us, but not one of a personal type. Old Russian composers of

---

[3] И. Грабарь, *История русского искусства*, I (Moscow, 1910), 4.

books (I refrain from calling them "writers") engaged in "the embroidery of words," combined verbal stitches and popular themes, and created productions of astonishing verbal richness and refinement. I refer merely to the writings of Epiphanius the Wise, to his golden art of weaving words, his art of "wickerwork of the word." The great themes that excited the Old Russian composers of books for the most part were not worked out by them in writing, but were only transferred to writing out of the life of society. The productions of Old Russian literature must be compared not with the works of Dante or Shakespeare, but with the great epic poems of the past, with the *byliny,* the lyrics of folklore, the ritual poetry of the people. When in the seventeenth century the literary art began to change its folkloristic character, there appeared works of a new type: the *Life of Avvakum,* the *Life of Epiphanius,* in part the *Tale of Woe and Misfortune,* and many others.

In the culture of Old Rus there are many other peculiarities of its intellectual type. In Old Rus theological thought was little developed, but to make up for it publicistics and especially historical thought attained a broad and deep development. The interest in history permeated all sides of the culture of Old Rus. Thousands of manuscripts of chronicles, chronographies, "books of degrees," historical tales and legends, have been preserved. Each principality, each episcopate, sometimes municipal chancelleries, monasteries, individual churches carried on their own writing of chronicles, in which local events are set in the framework of the events of general Russian history and at times world history. Historical argumentation predominated in Old Russian diplomacy, publicistics, the deciding of juridical disputes, and so forth. The whole of Russian life was filled with the spirit of history. I remember, for example, that Russian churches of the eleventh to seventeenth centuries were often erected in commemoration of one historical event or other. Saint Sophia in Kiev was built on the spot of the victory of Yaroslav the Wise over the Pechenegs. The Uspensky Cathedral in Kolomna is a monument to the victory of the Russians at Kulikovo. The Church of the Ascension in Kolomenskoe was built in honor of the birth of Ivan IV. The Church of Basil the Blessed is a monument to the annexation of the state of Kazan. The cathedral of the Novodevichi monastery in Moscow was founded in remembrance of the liberation of Smolensk, and its paintings are devoted to the glory of Russian arms and of the Russian state. Very much could be written on the historicism of Old Russian culture; this topic is one of the most interesting.

Finally, one last remark. In Old Russian culture the aesthetic moment notably predominated. The philosophical and social thought for the most part was clothed in artistic form. In some measure this continued to be true in the nineteenth century; the unaccustomed artistic form prevents one from noticing the existence of great Russian philosophy. The reproach to Russian culture in the nineteenth century for an absence of philosophy has now ceased; it is time also to cease to reproach Old Russian culture for its alleged "intellectual silence," which is directed at it only because its world view was clothed in the form of art and not in the form of scientific treatises.

FIVE

The Nature of Imperial Russian Society

I

How does one go about describing briefly a large and complex society in the process of rapid change? The problems involved are not only of space but also of conceptualization. To be comprehensive yet succinct one must fall back on generalizations, which always run the danger of concealing the very nuances that make up the richness and diversity of a culture. Moreover, the nature and direction of change in modern societies is a matter of continuing controversy, and a common basis of theory and terminology cannot be taken for granted. No society in modern times has been more subject to conflicting assumptions and interpretations than that of Russia. Under these circumstances, perhaps the best solution is to adopt an approach sufficiently general to do justice to the complexities involved and at the same time definite enough in its point of view to offer a consistent interpretation—as well as a reasonably clear basis for controversy.

The interpretation suggested here is one which sees the world as composed of well over one hundred politically organized societies, each with its own deep-seated traditional institutions, undergoing at different stages a process of change which has certain universally common features. This process of change, which can be traced to the revolutionary expansion of knowledge originating in Western Europe in the Middle Ages, tends to affect in one degree or another all aspects of human activity. It seems likely to result eventually in a world of modern societies which will be essentially similar in function but which will retain for the foreseeable future significant features of their diverse traditional structures of institutions and values. There is no set pattern which guides the interaction of the modern and the traditional, and indeed in any society there are innumerable ways in which traditional institutions can be adapted to modern functions. The course of change therefore depends to a considerable degree on the nature of leadership, and in practice an important element in the history of a society consists of

MR. BLACK *is professor of history at Princeton University.*

arguments, conflicts, rivalries, and struggles among individual leaders and groups of leaders representing a wide variety of points of view and interests. Chance, in the form of the presence or absence of far-sighted and effective leaders at critical moments, has an important share in this process.

Russia is one of these societies, differing from others in her traditional culture as others differ from each other, but also undergoing like them the characteristic interaction of the traditional and the modern. It is not possible in brief scope—if it is possible at all—to describe the intricacies of this subtle and many-faceted process of change. What will be attempted here is something much more limited: a brief description of certain distinctive features of traditional Russian society as it existed in the eighteenth and early nineteenth centuries, an indication of the principal ways in which that society was changing under the impact of modern ideas and institutions, and finally some suggestions as to the significance of this interaction of the traditional and the modern. It is scarcely feasible to document these observations in any detail, for there is an enormous body of literature which deals with this period, but a few references will be made when they seem to be called for in regard to specific matters of interpretation.

II

A brief statement of the features that distinguished Russian imperial society must of necessity be highly selective and impressionistic, and it is proposed here to touch on only five characteristics: the physical setting, the autocratic state, the system of social stratification, the agrarian economy, and the multinational structure.[1]

The most significant features of the physical setting of imperial Russia were its size, its location, and its poverty. The conquest of Siberia in the sixteenth and seventeenth centuries resulted in a vast increase in the territory under the rule of Moscow. This large territory inherited by Peter nevertheless lacked either well-defined frontiers or suitable maritime outlets for commerce, and at the same time was subject to many pressures on the long frontier with Europe and Western Asia. In the course of the many wars of the eighteenth and nineteenth centuries the frontiers of the empire were further extended, and indeed throughout this period Russia was by all odds the largest country in the world in terms of territory. At the same time the number of inhabitants grew from 14 to 170 million, with the result that Russia was by 1917 inferior in population only to China and India. As significant as its

---

[1] Boris Brutzkus, "Die historischen Eigentümlichkeiten der wirtschaftlichen und sozialen Entwicklung Russlands," *Jahrbücher für Kultur und Geschichte der Slaven*, X (1934), 62-99, and Rushton Coulborn, "Der europäisch-russische Gegensatz," *Die politische Meinung*, II (February, 1957), 13-26, offer suggestive interpretations of imperial Russian society.

size was its location, bordering as it did on Europe and on the broad sweep of Asia stretching from the Bosporus to the Kuril Islands. In earlier centuries Byzantine influences, and to a much lesser extent Mongol and Ottoman, had played a vital role in the culture of Muscovite Russia. To this extent Russia, like Byzantium itself, could be said to have cultural roots in both Europe and Asia. In the period of the empire, which was one of almost exclusively European influences, the principal significance of geographical location lay in the realm of foreign policy. In an age in which Europe was embracing the world, a country of Russia's size and position could not well avoid being drawn into the affairs of the many countries on its borders and beyond.[2]

Economic poverty was also an important element in the Russian setting. The vast size of the country was to a considerable degree illusory, since only a small part of it was suitable for agriculture, and much of that had a poor soil or climate. It is now known to be rich in natural resources, but before the First World War only its petroleum and a few other minerals had been adequately developed. In per capita terms Russia was very poor by the standards of the European countries which were her principal competitors. Perhaps the best way of expressing the problem confronting the statesmen of the empire was that they had to find a means of converting her rather meager and scattered resources into effective national power. This is no doubt a rather abstract formulation, yet Peter the Great must have looked at things somewhat in this fashion when he undertook to strengthen the administrative apparatus of a state which already had a claim to autocratic power well established in theory if not in practice.

It would probably not be going too far to say that in no other major society in the eighteenth and nineteenth centuries did the sovereign and the state play as great a role as they did in Russia. Prussia in the eighteenth century and China and Turkey in earlier times are among the first examples that come to mind of centralized political systems which had a comparable role in the life of the country. In the nineteenth century, at any rate, the Russian empire stood alone as a society in which a great many aspects of human activity were to a large extent administered or at least regulated by the state. The Russian government was formally an autocracy in the sense that all political authority was vested in the autocrat. The theory of autocracy came from Byzantine political thought and, modified by adaptations from Tatar and Ottoman administrative practices, it became a reality in the course of the fifteenth and sixteenth centuries as the princes of Moscow succeeded

[2] George Vernadsky, "The Expansion of Russia," *Transactions of the Connecticut Academy of Arts and Sciences*, XXXI (July, 1933), 391-425, provides a succinct account. The very extensive development of the lands beyond the Urals after 1861 is described in Donald W. Treadgold, *The Great Siberian Migration: Government and Peasant in Resettlement from Emancipation to the First World War* (Princeton, 1957).

in consolidating the political power which had been shared since the thirteenth century by the various principalities of northeastern Russia and their Tatar overlords. What was in theory an autocracy was often for all practical purposes an oligarchy, however, for the princes of Moscow had great difficulty in establishing effective and orderly control over the ruling families whose lands they successively incorporated into the new state. The reigns of the principal architects of the Muscovite political system—Vasilii II the Blind, Ivan III the Great, and Ivan IV the Terrible—were marked by continual internecine strife culminating in the Time of Troubles. After the establishment of the Romanov dynasty in 1613 it was half a century or more before the central administrative system was sufficiently effective to permit the sovereign to free himself from the assembly of notables which had established the dynasty and guided its early fortunes. It was this system which Peter the Great reshaped and rationalized on the basis of Swedish and other European models to form the "regulated state" which, with significant changes to be sure, lasted until 1917.[3]

Under the system established by Peter the emperor was more of an autocrat than the tsars had ever been, yet the oligarchy composed of high civilian and military officials and leading families of noble landowners continued to play an independent role throughout the eighteenth century during the reigns of eight rulers who were relatively weak for reasons of youth, sex, or mental disability. Paul, the last of these rulers, is generally portrayed as mad—but there was a method in his madness. He took the first measures in the direction of reaffirming the authority of the autocrat, and this authority was further consolidated by his successors.[4] Despite the many political changes which occurred during the last century of the empire, the sovereign remained an autocrat in theory and to a considerable extent in practice, although only in the reign of Nicholas I did he in fact approximate the theoretical model.[5]

A more fundamental question than the relationship of the autocrat to the oligarchy is that of the role of the state in society. No less than two-fifths of the forty million peasants in European Russia were directly administered by the state before emancipation, as were many economic enterprises as well. Through its administration of the Holy Synod, the Academy of Sciences, all higher education, and most primary and

---

[3] Б. И. Сыромятников, «*Регулярное» государство Петра Первого и его идеология* (Moscow, 1943) offers what is probably the most perceptive discussion of Peter's reforms.

[4] М. В. Клочковъ, *Очерки правительственной деятельности времени императора Павла I* (Petrograd, 1916) develops this theme.

[5] Nicholas V. Riasanovsky, *Nicholas I and Official Nationality in Russia, 1825-1855* (Berkeley, 1959), and Sidney Monas, *The Third Section: Police and Society in Russia under Nicholas I* (Cambridge, Mass., 1961) present in graphic detail the theory and practice of autocracy in the reign of Nicholas I, and offer a valuable guide to the large literature on this subject.

secondary education, and through the censorship, the state had a direct and permeating influence on the intellectual life of the country. The rapid economic and social changes which occurred after the emancipation of the serfs did not have the effect of reducing the role of the state. On the contrary, the state played a leading role in this process. There were few phases of Russian life in which it was not directly interested, and over many of the most important it had a virtual monopoly through direct administration and a decisive influence in policy-making.

One of the most significant consequences of the "omnicompetence" of the Russian state, to borrow Sumner's felicitous term,[6] was its influence on the position of social strata. It was as though the autocrat could imagine no other way to assure the state of the support of its leading citizens and a regular income from the rather backward agrarian economy than by binding all individuals to its service. In a purely formal sense, all citizens of the empire were divided into three general categories: natives, non-natives, and Finns (who were a separate category by virtue of inhabiting an autonomous Grand Duchy). The native citizens in turn were divided by statute into four estates or strata—nobility, clergy, townsmen, and peasants—but these categories were not very meaningful. There were important differences between hereditary and personal nobles; townsmen were separated into four quite distinct categories—notable citizens, merchants, tradesmen, and artisans; the clergy were an occupational group rather than a social stratum, for both those who left the clergy and children of clergymen in general were legally regarded as townsmen of the rank of notable citizens; moreover a nobleman could also be a member of the clergy. Perhaps only the peasants were a legally homogeneous class, although there were significant differences between state peasants and serfs as well as those imposed by the widely varying customs of the diverse regions of Russia.[7]

More fundamental than these formal distinctions was that which prevailed substantially until the revolution of 1905 between the privileged and the unprivileged. The privileged were not subject to direct taxes or corporal punishment and could travel freely within the country. Only the nobles and townsmen of the rank of notable citizens, totaling between 1 and 2 per cent of the population, enjoyed these privileges. The nobles also had the privilege until 1861 of owning serfs. Moreover, the privileged had access to political power, if they did not actually share it, while the unprivileged bore the burden of supporting the privileged as well as the heavy superstructure of the state. The unprivileged were subjected to severe restrictions as to movement, along

[6] Benedict H. Sumner, *A Short History of Russia* (New York, 1943), pp. 84-85.

[7] Н. М. Коркуновъ, *Русское государственное право* (2 vols.; St. Petersburg, 1913), I, 274-368, provides the best analysis of the formal system of stratification; the historical background is discussed in В. О. Ключевский, *История сословий в России* (3rd ed.; Petrograd, 1918).

with other forms of personal and social discipline, and had virtually no access to the ranks of the privileged before the middle of the nineteenth century. Indeed the gap between the two groups tended to widen during much of this period, as the privileged gained in education and influence while the position of the peasants in particular became more depressed. These hardships weighed even more heavily on the non-natives—the Jews, the Moslems, and the various indigenous peoples of Siberia. The grosser inequities were relaxed in the latter part of the nineteenth century and were largely removed after 1905, but the government yielded reluctantly and only under great pressure. The growth of civil liberties in the last decades of the empire thus released accumulated tensions which could be contained only by a political system whose authority was not weakened by economic distress or foreign defeats.[8]

The system of social stratification also had the effect of inhibiting the development of a sense of political responsibility. This was in part the result of the corporative organization of the social strata, which tended to isolate them from each other. Thus the hereditary nobles, three categories of townsmen (the merchants, the tradesmen, and the artisans), and the peasants were organized in corporative associations by province, town, or village. These associations were collectively responsible for the conduct of their members, and in the case of the townsmen and the peasants had important fiscal and disciplinary functions. This form of social organization encouraged these groups, which formed the bulk of the population, to negotiate directly with the government rather than to seek common cause against it. This attitude was further encouraged by contradictory prevailing trends of political thought which maintained either that the autocratic state was good, or that it must be eliminated, or that it should be ignored as a necessary evil. It was not until the end of the nineteenth century that the possibility of effective political action against the state within the framework of the empire was widely accepted.[9]

The system under which the peasants were bound to the soil and to the noble landowner is known as serfdom, and it existed in its most rigorous form between 1649 and 1861. Russian serfdom must be distinguished from feudalism as it existed in Western Europe. Feudalism was a political system characterized by a contractual relationship between lord and vassal, whereas in serfdom the relationship was primarily

---

[8] The structure and functioning of the stratification system are discussed in К. Коча-ровский, *Социальный строй России* (Prague, 1926); Г. Б. Слиозбергъ, *Дореволюціонный строй Россіи* (Paris, 1933), pp. 78-108, 258-79; Robert A. Feldmesser, "Social Classes and Political Structure," *The Transformation of Russian Society: Aspects of Social Change Since 1861*, ed. Cyril E. Black (Cambridge, Mass., 1960), pp. 235-52 (hereafter cited as *Transformation of Russian Society*); and Robert C. Tucker, "The Image of Dual Russia," *Transformation of Russian Society*, pp. 587-605.

[9] Leopold H. Haimson, "The Parties and the State: The Evolution of Political Attitudes," *Transformation of Russian Society*, pp. 110-45.

economic and was based not on contract but on the edict of the sovereign. There had been elements of the lord-vassal relationship earlier in Russian history, but these had disappeared with the rise of serfdom.[10] The state created serfdom as a means of assuring itself of a reliable source of revenue in a situation in which land was plentiful but labor was scarce, and agriculture was the principal source of income. The conditions of peasant life were so hard in Russia in the fifteenth and sixteenth centuries, because of the endemic civil strife and the increasing need of the state for revenue to meet the requirements of national defense, that the peasants tended constantly to escape to the south or east to avoid oppression. Various efforts were made to restrict the freedom of movement of the peasants, and these finally culminated in the middle of the seventeenth century in the imposition of a form of serfdom noted for its oppressiveness.[11]

There were numerous and large-scale peasant revolts both before and after the imposition of serfdom, but in every case they were repressed. In the course of the two centuries during which serfdom was in force, the machinery of government underwent a fundamental transformation, the noble landowners won a substantial relaxation of their obligations to the state, and modest beginnings were made in the development of an industrial system. There was no comparable improvement in the status of the peasants, whether under the state, the crown, or the landlords, however, and in the case of the latter it tended to become more oppressive. This is not to say that the nobles benefited by the system either, for most of them were persons of limited means and they were increasingly going into debt during the first half of the nineteenth century.

Serfdom had been established principally for the benefit of the state, and no doubt it provided the basis for a type of stable administrative and fiscal control over the peoples and the resources of the country which could not readily be achieved by other means. Stability was achieved at the price of stagnation, however, for there was no Russian counterpart of the rapid economic and social change which the societies of Western and Central Europe experienced during the period in which serfdom prevailed in Russia. Serfdom tended to discourage initiative on the part of peasant and noble landowner alike, and in a variety of ways inhibited the growth of industry. It may be argued that the real

10 For a discussion of this important question see Marc Szeftel, "Aspects of Feudalism in Russian History," *Feudalism in History*, ed. Rushton Coulborn (Princeton, 1956), pp. 167-82; and Rushton Coulborn, "Russia and Byzantium," *ibid.*, pp. 344-63. The extensive controversy in Russian historiography on this issue is reviewed by Marc Szeftel in *ibid.*, pp. 413-19. A similar conclusion is reached in George Vernadsky, "Feudalism in Russia," *Speculum*, XIV (July, 1939), 300-323.

11 Jerome Blum, *Lord and Peasant in Russia from the Ninth to the Nineteenth Century* (Princeton, 1961), provides a comprehensive account of the origins and development of serfdom.

obstacle to social and economic change in Russia was in the minds of its leaders, and that much could have been done even within the framework of serfdom to stimulate technological improvements in agriculture and to encourage industry. In any event, as the conception of a modern society began to gain adherents among Russian leaders, a process in which the defeat in the Crimea appears to have had a large influence, serfdom was the first institution which they undertook to reform.[12]

The attempt to present a brief characterization of a complex society runs a particular danger in the case of Russia, since only 43.3 per cent of the population was Great Russian at the end of the nineteenth century, and the many minority peoples enjoyed a wide diversity of traditional institutions. What has been said about the decisively centralizing character of the administration must be modified to the extent that the Ukraine, the Baltic provinces, and Congress Poland all enjoyed a degree of autonomy during parts of the period under consideration, and the Grand Duchy of Finland had substantial privileges except for the short period between 1903 and 1905. Similarly as regards social stratification and the agrarian system, there were many differences in the position of the various minority peoples. Indeed, it was long the practice of the imperial government to respect the diverse institutions of the peoples annexed in the course of the expansion of the empire, and it was only toward the end of the nineteenth century that a rigorous policy of administrative and cultural Russification was attempted.[13]

The multinational character of imperial Russian society also had grave consequences in the realm of foreign policy. The chief concern of Russia in annexing these peoples, located almost entirely on her borders with Europe and Western and Central Asia, was for her own security. The territories they inhabited either blocked Russian access to the Baltic and Black seas; or, as was the case with Poland and Central Asia, might have come under the rule of other great powers to the detriment of Russia's interests; or again, as was the case with the Ukraine and Georgia, actually sought Russian protection against neighbors they feared more. It would doubtless be going too far to say that Russia had no imperialist ambitions, for numerous proposals for annexing noncontiguous territories can be found in her diplomatic records. The ambitions of Russia's statesmen were nevertheless limited, by the standards of the time, and were concerned principally with adjacent territories of strategic significance for commerce or defense. In this sense Russian statesmen favored a continental policy, resembling perhaps that of China in earlier times and of the United States in the

---

12 G. Pavlovsky, *Agricultural Russia on the Eve of the Revolution* (London, 1930), and Geroid T. Robinson, *Rural Russia Under the Old Regime* (New York, 1932).

13 These developments are reviewed in L. I. Strakhovsky, "Constitutional Aspects of the Imperial Russian Government's Policy Toward National Minorities," *Journal of Modern History*, XIII (December, 1941), 467-92.

nineteenth century, and did not undertake to create an extensive overseas empire such as those carved out by the seafaring societies of Western Europe.

III

It has already been noted that the institutions of imperial Russian society underwent many changes in the course of two centuries, and indeed the history of this period is punctuated with numerous reforms, revolts, assassinations, wars, territorial issues, and social conflicts reflecting the continuing readjustments in the structure of Russian society as well as the idiosyncrasies of its leaders. At the same time it was undergoing a more fundamental transformation, which was stimulated primarily by the example of the societies of Western and Central Europe. These societies were in the forefront of a revolutionary process intellectual in its origins and political in its initial impact, accompanied by economic growth and social change of unprecedented proportions. The levels of achievement attained in the course of this revolutionary transformation, which may be referred to in general terms as "modern" or at least "modernizing," were the prototypes of those which were eventually to become the goal of virtually all societies.

The initial reaction of Russia's political leaders to this momentous development was to adopt, or at least adapt, those modern institutions which seemed best suited to preserving the traditional Russian society from the increasingly threatening competition of its neighbors. This reaction is represented typically by the reforms of Peter the Great, which rationalized the civil and military structure of the central government and tightened the control of the state over the noble landowners and the townsmen, and of the landowners over the peasants. No attempt was made, however, to adapt to Russian society the economic and social institutions which were being developed in the more modern societies. Peter's reforms were explicitly defensive in their motivation and implications, and they were successful in preserving the traditional social structure of the country with relatively few changes for a century and a half. In the course of time the gap between a relatively static Russia and an increasingly dynamic West grew to a point where it could not fail to cause concern to Russian leaders, and during the reigns of Alexander I and Nicholas I many plans and proposals for reform were considered and some actually undertaken. Nevertheless, human nature being what it is, they preferred the certainty of problems which they understood and felt confident in handling to the uncertainties of a thoroughgoing social transformation. It took the defeat in the Crimea to shift the balance of official opinion in favor of reform, and it has become customary to regard the emancipation of the serfs in 1861 as the turning point between the passive and the active phases of the attitude of Russia's political leaders towards modern ideas and institutions. It will of course be recognized that 1861 is in most respects simply a symbolic date, since some segments of Russian society felt the breath of reform a generation or more earlier, while others were relatively unaffected until a good deal later. Indeed, it was not until the end of the nineteenth century that Russian society as a whole was gripped by thoroughgoing change.

It has already been noted that the modern revolution was intellectual in its origins, resting as it did on the phenomenal expansion of knowledge which had its roots in the Middle Ages, and its initial impact on Russia was similarly intellectual. This impact may be traced back to the movements favoring the revision of religious texts and doctrine in the fifteenth and sixteenth centuries, and to the appearance in the seventeenth century of isolated nobles with a Western outlook.[14] It was nevertheless not until the eighteenth century that there was a general turning to the West on the part of the state and the nobility, and only in the nineteenth century did the problem of "Russia and Europe" come to absorb the full attention of Russian intellectuals. The diversity and brilliance of Russian political and literary thought concerning the relationship of traditional to modern values and institutions is probably matched only by that of China and Japan among non-European peoples. It produced a wide spectrum of interpretations, ranging from the strongest reaffirmation of the rightness and sanctity of the Russian way of doing things to the view that the imperial state was a form of "oriental despotism" which must be destroyed to make way for the socialist society toward which mankind was alleged to be moving ineluctably.

This rich body of thought moved in two currents, which were continually intermingling but which remained reasonably distinct. The first was represented by the political leaders and high officials, starting with Peter the Great and ending with Witte and Stolypin, who sought to adapt imperial Russian society in one degree or another to the requirements of the modern world. Their views were set forth in speeches, reports, memoranda, and statutes, and perhaps in deeds more than in words. The second source of intellectual activity was that represented by the intelligentsia, who almost by definition were disassociated and not infrequently alienated from the governing circles. The intelligentsia left a fascinating heritage of speculation and interpretation which reflected a broad understanding of European society and a deep concern for the destiny of the Russian people. They had a profound influence on the development of Russian society during the

---

[14] Dmitrij Čiževskij, *History of Russian Literature from the Eleventh Century to the End of the Baroque* (The Hague, 1960), chaps. vi and vii, provides a valuable discussion of early European influences.

period of the empire, since their works were read and discussed by all educated people. They nevertheless remained until the end alienated from official Russia, which bore the burden of responsibility and deserves much of the credit for the extent to which Russian society was transformed by the time of the First World War. The intelligentsia as a group did not gain access to political power until the fall of the empire, and this access was terminated for all but a few when the Bolsheviks began to suppress deviations from orthodoxy in the early 1920's. In the realm of scholarship Russia joined the world of modern knowledge in the course of the eighteenth and nineteenth centuries and made distinguished original contributions.

The history of Russian thought in the nineteenth century as a general phenomenon has yet to be written. Much able work has been done on individual writers and on the leading intellectual movements, such as the Decembrists, the Slavophiles, the Populists, and the Marxists. The thought of the reforming officials has not, however, received comparable attention. Neither the prerevolutionary intelligentsia nor the writers of the Soviet Union have been attracted to this subject, for reasons which are not hard to find, and Western scholars are only now beginning to explore it. Interest in intellectual history seems to have been concerned principally with a desire to study the background of the political revolution of 1917, and this has resulted in a serious neglect of the fundamental process of political, economic, and social change as a central issue in Russian thought.[15]

In the political sphere the adoption of modern institutions in Russia can be seen in the many reforms which had the purpose of rationalizing the system of law and administration, integrating the various territories and social strata, and establishing a closer rapport between state and society to the end that political decisions could be effectively formulated, communicated, and implemented. The reforms of the eighteenth century had performed a similar function for the state itself, and it was now a question of extending this process to the entire society. The codification of the laws by Speransky was the first significant step in this second phase, and it was followed in the 1860's by an extensive reform of the judiciary and local government and of the administrative system of the central government. As late as 1905, however, the state had relatively few direct administrative contacts with the peasants except for a rather scanty police force and the land captains established in 1889. Peasant affairs were handled largely by the peasants themselves. The administration of the Stolypin land settlement required the government

15 The literature on this subject is virtually inexhaustible. Among recent American contributions, Theodore H. Von Laue, "The Industrialization of Russia in the Writings of Sergej Witte," *American Slavic and East European Review,* X (October, 1951), 177-90, and Marc Raeff, *Michael Speransky: Statesman of Imperial Russia, 1772-1839* (The Hague, 1957), are examples of a renewed interest in the thought of reforming bureaucrats.

for the first time in its history to establish organs for administering directly at the local level policies ultimately affecting a large proportion of the population and involving the co-ordination of several ministries.[16] This was a very late development, however, and the weakness of the imperial bureaucracy was soon revealed in the harsh test of war.

The effort to transform the political system of imperial Russia along the lines pioneered by the societies of Western Europe provoked a struggle among several trends of thought. One was that of the supporters of the traditional system as it had been consolidated in the eighteenth and early nineteenth centuries. This was the view of the imperial family and its immediate entourage, and it had strong support in the army and bureaucracy and in the cabinet, even when that body was headed by a reforming minister. The reforms of the 1860's had indeed been launched by the emperor himself, but more in the Petrine spirit of trying to achieve a new conservative stability than with a view to a thoroughgoing social reconstruction. This approach continued to have strong official support until the end, and one may well attribute the catastrophic character of the fall of the empire to the stubbornness with which one group of its leaders resisted change.

Another main trend was the very large one represented by those both in the government and among the intelligentsia who favored fundamental change by evolutionary means and looked to models ranging from England and France to Prussia and Japan. The diversities of their various programs make it difficult to contain these many groups in a single category, but the Fundamental Laws of 1906 provided them with a more or less acceptable basis for action and there was a significant degree of continuity from the four successive Dumas to the Provisional Government. Included also in this category were the leaders of the national minorities who demanded a degree of self-government. Only the Poles insisted unconditionally on independence. This issue has been beclouded by war, revolution, and civil war, but it appears that under "normal" circumstances the leaders of the other minority peoples would in all likelihood have been satisfied on the eve of the First World War with some form of federalism.

A third trend was composed of those who had no faith in evolutionary changes within the framework of the empire. This was the view of the Bolsheviks and many Socialist Revolutionaries, who saw their political role principally as a destructive one so long as the empire survived. The final arbiter among these various approaches, as it turned out, was the First World War. The strains of the conflict eroded the political structure of the empire, and in so doing undermined the prospects for evolutionary change within its framework. The collapse of the empire

---

[16] This subject has been studied recently in George L. Yaney, "The Imperial Russian Government and the Stolypin Land Reform," unpubl. Ph.D. diss. (Princeton, 1961).

opened the way for a revolutionary approach, and the revolutionaries were much more at home than the liberals in the ensuing chaos.[17]

Among the changes which occurred during the last half-century of the empire, those in the intellectual and political realm have attracted the most attention, but the remarkable economic growth in its later decades deserves equal emphasis. Agricultural production, which had not been able to keep up with the growth of the population during the first half of the century, increased much more rapidly, especially after the 1880's. Not only did agricultural production surpass the rate at which the population was growing, but it was also significantly diversified to include industrial crops and potatoes. The expansion of industrial production was of course much more rapid, with an annual average rate of growth of somewhat over 5 per cent for the period 1885-1913. The rate for the 1890's, the period of most rapid growth, was surpassed only by that of Japan, the United States, and Sweden. Underlying the increased rates of growth in agriculture and industry was the construction of an extensive railroad network, which grew from 1,000 miles in 1860 to 40,000 miles at the time of the First World War. In terms of national income, the Russian rate of growth for the period as a whole was higher than that of the United Kingdom, France, and Italy, somewhat below that of Germany, and considerably below that of the United States and Japan. On a per capita basis Russia's position was of course less favorable, owing to the rapid growth of her population. By the time of the First World War real income per capita was about the same as that of Italy, which means that it was still a great deal lower than that of the advanced industrial societies.[18]

Although Russia had thus in no sense attained a leading position as an industrial society at the time of the First World War, what is significant is that by the 1880's it was launched on a pattern of economic growth comparable in rate and dimensions to that of the more advanced societies. It should also be noted that this was very largely the achievement of the imperial government, which took the initiative and bore the main burden of building railroads and supplying capital to industry, and also provided the principal market for the output of heavy industry. No doubt the sovereign and the conservative-minded courtiers and ministers, like Peter the Great in his day, still thought of industrialization principally as a means of bolstering the autocratic system.

---

[17] The adaptation of Marxism to the Russian environment is a matter of particular interest. See especially Adam Ulam, "The Historical Role of Marxism and the Soviet System," *World Politics*, VIII (October, 1955), 371-401; and Karl A. Wittfogel, "The Marxist View of Russian Society and Revolution," *World Politics*, XII (July, 1960), 487-508.

[18] Alexander Gerschenkron, "The Rate of Industrial Growth of Russia Since 1885," *Journal of Economic History*, VII, Supplement (1947), 144-74; and Raymond W. Goldsmith, "The Economic Growth of Tsarist Russia, 1860-1913," *Economic Development and Cultural Change*, IX (April, 1961), 441-75.

The leading cabinet members and high officials, however, had a vision of a Russia transformed into a modern industrial society. Their goal may be said to have been of a West European character, but their methods were quite different. Little attention was devoted to agriculture, and such income as it normally provided was channeled into industry. Railroads and heavy industry were favored as against consumer goods. Modern technology was imported from the West to make up for deficiencies in skilled labor, and economies were made in management and supervision by concentrating production in large plants. A not inconsiderable role in this growth was played by private entrepreneurs and small businessmen, but the pace was set by the government and by the large enterprises which it controlled or patronized. Indeed, it was the role of the government as planner, investor, entrepreneur, and consumer which distinguished economic growth in Russia from that in the societies which started earlier.[19]

This economic growth was accomplished by fundamental social changes. The urban population grew from 7 to 20 million during the last fifty years of the empire, the rigid system of social stratification disintegrated rapidly, and the foundations were laid for a new stratum of professional people, businessmen, and officials. This "middle class" was drawn from all of the traditional strata. The nobles, clergy, and townsmen were naturally the principal sources of recruitment for this new stratum at the start, but the peasantry and workers were gradually drawn into it and represented in the long run its principal reserve of manpower. The nobles lost much of their distinctive position in the last decades of the empire and, with the exception of the relatively few families of great wealth, did not gain much advantage from their remaining formal privileges in the evolving industrial society. At the same time the industrial working class grew apace, and numbered some 3.5 million at the end of this period. In 1913, according to the official classification, 70.2 per cent of the population were farmers, 16.7 per cent were wage and salary workers, 7.2 per cent were craftsmen, 3.6 per cent were self-employed townsmen, and 2.3 per cent were military and others.[20]

The institutions of higher education were the chief training ground for this new class, and their enrollment in proportion to the population

---

[19] See Alexander Gerschenkron, "Problems and Patterns of Russian Economic Development," *Transformation of Russian Society*, esp. pp. 42-61, for a discussion of the underlying economic policies of the imperial government.

[20] Warren W. Eason, "Population Changes," *Transformation of Russian Society*, pp. 72-90, summarizes and interprets Russian statistical materials; Valentine T. Bill, *The Forgotten Class: The Russian Bourgeoisie from the Earliest Beginnings to 1900* (New York, 1959) has performed a useful service in calling attention to the role of the entrepreneur; Gaston V. Rimlinger, "Autocracy and the Factory Order in Early Russian Industrialization," *Journal of Economic History*, XX (March, 1960), 67-92, discusses the status of the workers in the last decades of the empire.

increased more than nine times between 1885 and 1914. The increase in secondary-school enrollment was even greater, and by the time of the First World War Russia had made substantial progress toward a system of universal elementary education. The social mobility accompanying the growth in higher education is reflected in the fact that the proportion of children of peasants, craftsmen, and workers enrolled in the universities grew from 15.7 per cent in 1880 to 38.8 per cent in 1914, and in the higher technical institutes was 54 per cent in the latter year.[21] The officer corps was no doubt the most conservative branch of the bureaucracy, but it appears that by the end of the empire a majority of the new officers came from non-noble families as did some of the leading generals in the First World War.[22] In recording these changes it should be noted that this rapid growth in educational opportunities and social mobility was not achieved without a momentous struggle. In the central government the reformers waged a constant battle with the traditionalists, and were strongly aided by the increasingly effective support which they received from the local government institutions, the municipalities, and the Duma. At the time of the First World War, Russia was still a country where 78 per cent of the population was agricultural and rural illiteracy was high. The changes of the last half century had been so rapid, however, that contemporary reforming statesmen could look forward with confidence to the day when the empire would attain the level of achievement of Western societies.

Something should also be said about the personality changes which may have accompanied this general process. National character in the sense that it is used by the social psychologists is a controversial concept which is still in an early stage of formulation, and one hesitates to venture into a territory so ridden with pitfalls. Yet it is clear that the personality of the individual reflects the character of his upbringing in the family setting, which in turn depends on the larger social context. When the latter undergoes the drastic changes represented by urbanization, one would expect the family and its individual members to be vitally affected. In the case of the Great Russian people, for example, it has been maintained that the characteristically patriarchal peasant family tended to produce a personality which was markedly ambivalent. This is to say that the Great Russian personality contained simultaneously elements of great vitality and serious depression, which may be explained as resulting from a family setting in which an awesome father was both feared and resisted. As a peasant society with these characteristics is urbanized, with the mother as an urban worker gaining a posi-

[21] Nicholas Hans, *History of Russian Educational Policy (1701-1917)* (London, 1931), pp. 229-42, provides a convenient summary of educational statistics.

[22] Raymond L. Garthoff, "The Military as a Social Force," *Transformation of Russian Society*, pp. 326-27, reviews the available evidence on the changing social status of the officer corps.

tion of authority more nearly equal to that of the father, an altered family setting is produced in which the children are exposed to somewhat different influences and will develop correspondingly different personalities. This example suggests what is meant by the effects of social change on personality, and it also reveals the difficulties which confront one in trying to deal with Russia in these terms. Russia was a vastly complex empire with many traditional cultures, of which the Great Russian was only one. Moreover, the available studies deal principally with the Soviet period, and there is little factual data from earlier decades to draw on. One may argue that Chekhov, Gorky, and their literary colleagues did a pretty good job of reporting social change at the family level without benefit of professional training in the behavioral sciences, but it is difficult for a historian to generalize on the basis of their findings. It is also clear that the impact of social change on personality was at its very earliest stages in the last decades of the empire, and that one would not expect to find general manifestations of a transformation of national character in Russia until well into the twentieth century. Under the circumstances the best one can do is to call attention to this important aspect of social history and to regret that one cannot do it justice.[23]

IV

The interaction of traditional and modern institutions and values in imperial Russian society should be considered in terms both of its general implications and of its particular significance for the crisis provoked by the collapse of the empire in the First World War.

The prevailing Western approach between the two world wars to Russian developments was to assume that the institutions characteristic of the more advanced societies of the West represented the model which other societies were destined to follow. There was therefore a tendency to judge the empire as well as its successors by the extent to which they adopted the Western pattern in such matters as civil liberties, representative government, education, and the role of the state in economic growth. By this standard the empire was reactionary, the Provisional Government had liberal aspirations, and the Soviet Union represented a bewildering combination of modern and traditional elements. In the course of the past quarter of a century many other societies have entered and some have completed the experimental phase of adapting the tra-

---

[23] A valuable introduction to this subject will be found in Clyde Kluckhohn, "Recent Studies of the National Character of Great Russians," *Human Development Bulletin* (February 5, 1955), pp. 39-60; Henry V. Dicks, "Some Notes on the Russian National Character," *Transformation of Russian Society*, pp. 636-52; and Alex Inkeles and Daniel J. Levinson, "National Character: The Study of Modal Personality and Socio-cultural Systems," *Handbook of Social Psychology*, ed. Gardner Lindzey (2 vols.; Cambridge, Mass., 1954), II, 977-1020.

ditional to the modern, and the process of transformation can now be seen as a much more complex matter than one of simply duplicating Western institutions. It seems clear that there are certain functions which all modern societies must perform—political decision-making effective for the entire population, sufficient savings to permit a reasonable rate of economic growth, education, social mobility, and so on—and perhaps most important of all, a value system compatible with the necessary institutional changes. It is also clear, however, that there is a wide degree of variety in the extent to which the diverse traditional institutional systems are adaptable to the functions of modern societies. No society can avoid very profound changes as it modernizes, but some traditional institutions are much more adaptable than others.

What is significant in the case of Russia is that its traditional institutional system was different from those of the societies of Western Europe, as indeed it was from those of non-European societies as well. In Western Europe modern political institutions, for example, evolved from those of feudalism into a characteristic form of liberal government in which political power was shared by elected representatives and a permanent civil service. In Russia, by contrast, the starting point was not a feudal system but an autocratic state which had characteristically exercised very extensive political functions. It was not difficult for this state, in the generation after the defeat in the Crimea, to initiate a very fundamental reorientation of national life. Between 1861 and 1917 the autocracy in Russia put into effect a series of reforms which resemble in many respects those achieved by very different methods in France between 1789 and 1848—if one may risk an historical analogy.[24] To extend the analogy a step further, one may suggest that the autocratic state in Russia played a role similar not only to that of the middle class and the Napoleonic empire in France but also to that of the samurai in Japan, the Young Turks in the Ottoman Empire, the army officers in Egypt, and the European-educated politicians in Africa today. Modernizing political leadership may take many forms, and the alternatives available to political leaders cannot fail to be profoundly affected by the traditional political institutions which a society has inherited from earlier centuries. This is not to assert an institutional or a cultural determinism. It is rather to suggest that, however similar the ultimate functional goals, political leaders in different societies are likely to proceed by different routes.

It would be outside the limits set for this paper to venture beyond the fall of the empire in February/March, 1917, but it is relevant to

[24] Theodore H. Von Laue, "Die Revolution von aussen als erste Phase der russischen Revolution 1917," *Jahrbücher für Geschichte Osteuropas*, IV (1956), 138-58, stresses the differences between the Russian and French revolutions, in contrast to Isaac Deutscher, "The French Revolution and the Russian Revolution: Some Suggestive Analogies," *World Politics*, IV (April, 1952), 469-81.

discuss the bearing on subsequent developments of the changes which the empire was undergoing in its final decades. It is well enough to attribute the fall of the empire to the strains of the First World War, for the connection between the two is clear, but it is also necessary to note that the crisis was not so great that a more effective government might not have been able to cope with it. The vital struggle in the last decades of the empire was that which was going on within the government between those who supported the traditional autocracy to the bitter end, and those who favored the transformation of Russia into a modern bureaucratic and constitutional state. The Wittes and Stolypins were still separated by a wide gap from the liberals, but the gap was perhaps no wider than that which separated them from the emperor. The lines dividing the various conservative and liberal conceptions of an evolutionary constitutionalism were becoming increasingly blurred in the last years of the empire, and much would have depended on the leadership which might have emerged.

The war came at a time when these conflicts between the emperor and his critics within the government were still unresolved, and in fact it only served to make them more bitter. The fragmentation of Russian politics at this stage was such that the collapse of the autocracy in 1917 resulted in a situation in which no alternative had any wide support. There was of course a significant group of leaders favoring parliamentary democracy who had gained political experience in the Duma and in local government, but the political methods which they favored were not generally understood or accepted. Where parliamentary democracy has been successful it has in fact been a value system widely supported by many elements of a society rather than one reflecting the interests of a particular social stratum. The vast majority of Russians—whether peasants, workers, bureaucrats, officers, or professional people—were not generally familiar with the values and techniques of parliamentary democracy. To this extent the task of leaders favoring parliamentary methods in 1917 was infinitely more difficult than that of those prepared to rely on force. This does not necessarily mean that the empire might not under other circumstances have developed into a political democracy of the type familiar in the West, or even that something resembling such a system may not yet develop in Russia at some future time. It means only that, at the time the empire collapsed, the balance of domestic political experience weighed heavily in favor of those leaders who were prepared to employ authoritarian methods.

Russia and Modernization

HUGH SETON-WATSON

My own approach to this subject is very much the same as Professor Black's. Imperial Russia, it seems to me, was the prototype of the "underdeveloped society" whose problems are so familiar a theme in our own age. The study of nineteenth-century Russia is the study of a society in process of modernization, and probably the most useful service which non-Russian historians can render is to try to regard this process as a whole, and particularly to differentiate between those aspects of Russia's modernization process which are common to several known historical cases and those which are peculiar to Russia. The following comments on Professor Black's article are offered from this point of view.

The physical setting, rightly stressed by Professor Black at the outset, may be regarded as a peculiarly Russian aspect. Here human and physical geography are closely interrelated. Other nations besides the Russians have lived in forest areas where it was desperately hard to make a living. Some similarities could probably be found with the earlier history of the Germans, Poles, and Swedes, though the still greater severity of the Russian climate should be taken into account. But surely the case of the south Russian steppes is unique. Here is much of the most fertile grain land in the world, which for centuries was barely cultivated, being in fact *Durchmarschgebiet* for successive waves of nomadic invaders. Indeed it was only after the final subjugation of the Crimean Tatars by Russia in the late eighteenth century that its agricultural wealth began for the first time in history to be systematically exploited. In the previous centuries, Russia south of the forest zone had two "open frontiers," to the west and to the southeast. But whereas the "open frontier" in North America was a factor of opportunity, and so of liberty, in Russia it was a factor of insecurity, and so of despotism. The constant need of Russia for protection against enemies held back by no natural frontier—no Pyrenees, no English Channel—is surely a major factor in the development of autocracy. A strong central military command was indispensable. In fact Russian society as a whole became so militarized that—paradoxically—army officers as a separate category never acquired a special status, though the profession of arms of course had high prestige. It is true that the "open frontier" did offer oppor-

MR. SETON-WATSON *is professor of Russian history at the School of Slavonic and East European Studies, University of London.*

tunities to enterprising individuals, especially in Siberia. But the autocratic state caught up with them in time. Unlike the American pioneers, they had no ocean between them and their monarch. To sum up, the vastness, the absence of naturally defensible frontiers, and the vulnerability to incursions from west, east, and south for more than a thousand years constitute an exceptional, if not unique, environment.

Another factor, also to some extent peculiar to Russia, has barely been mentioned by Professor Black. This is the Orthodox Church. Orthodoxy came late to Russia, but Russia is the only Great Power since the great age of Byzantium which has been Orthodox. It is true that under the Tatar yoke the Church suffered indirectly from the restrictions placed on the sovereignty of the Russian princes. But these were at no time comparable with the destruction of independent rulers in the Balkan Christian countries by the Ottoman Turks. (Incidentally, a comparison of the status of the Orthodox Church under the Tatars and the Turks, based on a detailed study of both with the use of Moslem documents, would be a task of great value.) In the period following the removal of the Tatar yoke the Church of course became extremely powerful, while from Peter the Great onwards it declined. Nevertheless, it seems to me that the role of the Orthodox Church even in nineteenth-century Russia has hitherto been grossly underrated. There is surely more to be said of it than is found in that fine example of anticlerical rhetoric, Belinsky's *Letter to Gogol*. One may sympathize with Belinsky in his particular argument with Gogol, and admit that the picture of obscurantism and superstition which he paints is an important part of reality. But it is only a part. Religion cannot be simply dismissed from modern Russian history, as has been the fashion for the last hundred years. This is true not only of Bolshevik historians, but of the radical *bien pensants* who dominated Russian historical literature long before 1917.

It seems to me that Professor Black somewhat overrates the power of the oligarchy, and underestimates that of the autocracy, in the period following the death of Peter the Great. It is true that the following rulers were weak. But the astonishing fact remains that none of the disputed successions, or reigns of foreign women, were used to establish any institutions that would give the nobility a regular share in central government. The failure of Golitsyn's project at the accession of Anna Ivanovna is the most striking example. The Guards officers objected to particular claimants to the throne, and particular favorites, but they never sought to limit the power of the autocracy as such. The tsars continued to wield arbitrary powers, though of course their practical ability to put them into practice depended on the strength of their characters and the ability of their advisers. The nobility were "independent" in the sense that they controlled the lives of their serfs. They were themselves pocket autocrats on their estates. But they left central power to the monarch. This situation is surely basically different from that in Europe. European "absolute monarchies" had arisen in the course of centuries of struggle between the monarchs and the nobility, which had its own corporate institutions and its own corporate consciousness. Even Louis XIV ruled through the regular channels. This was also the case in Prussia. It was not so in Russia. Surely this is what Speransky meant when he said that "monarchical government" did not exist in Russia.

I am also unable to agree with Professor Black's implication that there is any sense whatever in which Russian expansion was "less imperialistic" than that of any other Power. What is "imperialism" anyhow? Were the Arabs imperialists when they conquered Spain from the Visigoths, who had themselves conquered it from Rome three centuries earlier? Or the Christian princes when they drove the Arabs out of Toledo and Cordoba? Or the Tatars when they conquered southern Russia, or the Russians when they captured Kazan? The Volga is *russkaia reka* in the song, but from the early Middle Ages until the eighteenth century it was a Turkic river, and largely remained so even until the 1920's. Acquisition of border territories in the interest of security is how virtually all empires have arisen. British traders in India seized land in order to ensure their right to trade. They had got there in the first instance in the pursuit of trade, not conquest. Much the same is true of Russian-protected Tatar traders in Central Asia and the conquest of Turkistan in the 1860's. Russian expansion seems to me to have exact parallels in the history of other nations, being morally neither better nor worse. It differs only in that it combines many different forms, roughly comparable with the expansion of the Île-de-France, the Spanish *reconquista,* French acquisition of Burgundy, North American conquest and extermination of the Red Indians, and British occupation of continental India.

The last problem raised by Professor Black which I should like to discuss, and at greatest length, is the problem of the middle classes. Here I do not think that I significantly disagree with Professor Black, but I should like to urge that definitions should be further developed, and to emphasize the complexity of the subject.

It seems to me that it is a mistake, in discussing nineteenth-century Russia, to speak of "a middle class." In Russia there were three separate "middle classes"—the businessmen, the government servants, and the intellectual elite. These three categories exist to some extent in almost any organized society. In traditional societies of course the intellectual elite is provided by a priesthood, while the category of government servants is not very well developed, and the businessmen are merchants with rather small capital. Modernization increases the importance of all three groups. This is characteristic of all underdeveloped societies, including post-Petrine Russia. What is not characteristic of all is a tendency for the three groups to become fused into a single "middle class," unified by a common ethos. This did in fact happen in post-Reformation Europe, and the process was accelerated by the industrial revolution. In the period after the Reformation the "bourgeois ethos"— individualism, in matters of religion, of business enterprise, and later also of political opinion—became widespread. It was this bourgeoisie—a social and cultural category rather than an economic one—which carried out the industrial revolution. This bourgeoisie was especially strong in the Protestant countries—England, Scotland, Holland, and then the United States of America—but it was also to be found in France, northern Italy, western and southwestern Germany. In Russia, however, it did not exist. Russia had capitalists and bureaucrats (including professional army officers), and from the 1830's or so it acquired also a secular intellectual elite, the intelligentsia. But these categories remained clearly distinct from each other, and certainly none of the three had anything which can remotely be described as a bourgeois ethos. In all this, however, Russia was not exceptional but typical. This difference between three middle classes, and this absence of a bourgeois ethos—and so, of a bourgeoisie—is typical of all the underdeveloped societies which have been modernized since the mid-nineteenth century in many parts of the world. It is northwest Europe and North America which have been exceptional.

The role of the intelligentsia in Russian political history is of course very well known. Even so, too little attention has been paid to the intelligentsia as a social group. Historians, whether Soviet or pre-Soviet, Russian or foreign, have studied their ideas in meticulous detail, but have on the whole neglected their emergence as a specific social group. Should one dare to brave Marxist and quasi-Marxist wrath by describing them as a "class"? Historians have also made too little effort to distinguish the general from the peculiarly Russian features of the intelligentsia. There is indeed a widespread tendency to consider the great political role of the intelligentsia as a peculiarly Russian phenomenon. Yet it is nothing of the sort. The national and social revolutionary movements of the Christian peoples of the Ottoman Empire were created and led essentially by intelligentsia. So also have been and are the similar movements in Asia and Africa. President Nasser is an example of this category (intelligentsia-in-uniform, as were the Russian Decembrists, but none the less intelligentsia for that). Again, though the intellectual qualities of the two men, if measured by traditional academic standards, are clearly very diverse, both Léopold Senghor and Patrice Lumumba must be regarded as examples of intelligentsia.

Even the "populist outlook"—the determination to "serve the people," to pay one's debt by devoting one's special skills and knowledge not to enriching oneself but to raising the masses up out of squalor and poverty—is not coi fined to Russian history. This outlook (as opposed to the particular political ideologies or political tactics adopted at particular periods in the face of particular needs) is shared, to take only some examples at random, by the Yugoslav Marxist students of the 1930's, the Rumanian Iron Guardist students of the same period, the early pioneers of *Aprismo* in Peru, and the early followers of Sun Yat-sen. The difference between the Russian intelligentsia and these later examples is a matter rather of nuance than of clear distinction. It seems to me that the Russian revolutionary intelligentsia, at least in the second half of the nineteenth century, was marked by an exceptional spirit of selfless devotion to the cause and of indifference to its own interests. Revolutionary fervor and heroism are of course to be found in all such movements, but the Russians had, I think, an overdose of idealism above and beyond the normal ration. It would be interesting to explore this question. I suspect that the explanation might be found in the direct and indirect influence of Orthodox Christianity on Russian thinking. The disproportionate number of *popovichi* among early Russian revolutionaries has often been noted. This was probably due to the fact that children of priests, being able to get a rudimentary education in seminaries, were more favorably placed for developing what talents they had than were other *raznochintsy*. But the *popovichi* may have introduced into the growing intellectual elite a peculiarly religious way of thinking. It would be interesting to know to what extent *popovichi* predominated among the Balkan revolutionaries. Professor Black, with his thorough knowledge of modern Bulgarian history, would be well placed to investigate, and draw conclusions from, this matter.

Modernization in Western Europe was a more or less spontaneous process, resulting from social development. It was accelerated or retarded by individual monarchs or cardinals, but it was not deliberately initiated by them. Modernization in Russia, Asia, and Africa has been deliberately initiated. Every government which sets out forcibly to modernize has to create a modern secular intellectual elite. It has to create a system of modern education. In the early stage of modernization, there is bound to be a profound gulf between the new intellectual elite and the majority of the nation. This "cultural gap" is inevitably a cause of frustration to the elite and a source of weakness to the state. This dangerous period of transition cannot be avoided unless the government and the society are willing to accept stagnation, leading to conquest by more progressive nations.

But if the problem of the "cultural gap" is common to all societies in which modernization is deliberately adopted and artificially pursued, the ways of handling the problem may and do vary. And here again there is an undoubted element of the unique in the Russian story.

Alexander I intended to create a system of education which would give every able child the chance to improve himself and to rise. But the absence of schools and teachers, and the poverty of the Russian state, greatly increased by the burden of the wars against Napoleon, prevented the achievement of his aims. In the following reign, under Count S. S. Uvarov, educational policy acquired a definite class bias. It was intended that higher education should be available only to the upper classes. However, the resources available were still so small, and the desire for education still comparatively so restricted, that even without Uvarov's class bias, it is clear that those who would have benefited from education would have been overwhelmingly the children of nobles and rich merchants. In fact the reign of Nicholas I was in a sense a period of genuine educational progress. The disastrous trend came in the second half of the century. The famous circular from the Minister of Education, recommending that children of "cooks, washerwomen, coachmen and suchlike people" should not be given an education above their station, was issued in 1887—nearly a century after Alexander I had created the Ministry of Education. Thus in Russia the "cultural gap" was kept artificially wide for an inordinately long time, in the belief that to educate the people was dangerous. The classical example of a contrary course is Japan, whose reformers decided that an educated people would be stronger than an uneducated people, and that mass education would not weaken but strengthen the regime. They accomplished their task in about thirty years, and the results justified their expectations. It is true that Japanese boys and girls were not brought up to be liberal democrats. But the "cultural gap" in Japan was narrowed, and this contributed enormously to the brilliant successes of Japan in the first four decades of the twentieth century. In Russia, on the other hand, the gap remained wide open, and contributed greatly to the continued alienation, not only of the intelligentsia in the narrower sense, but of the whole public (*obshchestvo*) from the regime, and so to the breakdown not only of tsardom but of the Russian state.

No other modernizing state has ever made such a bad job of national education as Imperial Russia, nor such a good job as Japan. Their examples are still far too little known by the "educationalists" of the West or of the Asian and African nations, who are lavish in the use of rhetoric about education but might well find that study of Russian and Japanese experience would be more beneficial to them than the ritual invocation of "Asianism" or *négritude*.

These scattered comments were intended as a contribution to discussion on a number of interesting problems and as a tribute to Professor Black's admirable and stimulating survey of this great subject.

The Russian Empire as an Underdeveloped Country

NICHOLAS V. RIASANOVSKY

Professor Black's analysis of imperial Russian society places him un-
mistakably with those scholars who treat Russia essentially as an underdeveloped country and its modern history as an attempt, successful or
tragic, to catch up with the West, or, in any case, to "develop." To use
the author's own words:

> The interpretation suggested here is one which sees the world as composed
> of well over one hundred politically organized societies, each with its own
> deep-seated traditional institutions, undergoing at different stages a process
> of change which has certain universally common features. This process of
> change, which can be traced to the revolutionary expansion of knowledge
> originating in Western Europe in the Middle Ages, tends to affect in one
> degree or another all aspects of human activity. . . .
>
> Russia is one of these societies, differing from others in her traditional
> culture as others differ from each other, but also undergoing like them the
> characteristic interaction of the traditional and the modern.

This view of Russia as a backward country in the process of modernization,[1] or rather versions of this view, inspired the Westernizers—in an
inverted form the Slavophiles as well—the Russian intelligentsia as a
whole, and most schools of Russian historiography. Yet its restatement
and development since the Second World War has been much more
than a matter of repetition. Contemporary writers, such as H. Seton-
Watson and Von Laue among historians, as well as numerous economists and other specialists, have profited by advances in the social sciences, by a better understanding of the complexity and interdependence
of factors involved in the process of modernization, and perhaps especially by a new perspective. Where once in the old-fashioned perception
Russia and its peculiar problem of "Russia and the West" stood alone,
the contemporary view sees dozens of countries in Europe, Asia, Latin
America, and even Africa, sharing the Russian predicament and problem. Westernization or "development" has become the key to modern,
particularly recent, history. Black's "over one hundred politically organized societies" all follow the same path. Needless to say, this approach
fits well the political and cultural outlook of our day.

MR. RIASANOVSKY *is professor of history at the University of California, Berkeley.*

[1] Possibly, Professor Black's understanding of his ubiquitous "change" varies significantly from the widespread concept of "modernization," but he nowhere makes that clear.
His analysis concentrates on such actual points as industrialization, the advent of capitalism, and the increase in social mobility.

Professor Black's variant of the popular thesis has, in my opinion, two uncommon features: an emphasis on leadership and an emphasis on ideas. The stress on the importance of leadership is powerful and explicit. To quote the most significant instance:

There is no set pattern which guides the interaction of the modern and the traditional, and indeed in any society there are innumerable ways in which traditional institutions can be adapted to modern functions. The course of change therefore depends to a considerable degree on the nature of leadership, and in practice an important element in the history of a society consists of arguments, conflicts, rivalries, and struggles among individual leaders and groups of leaders representing a wide variety of points of view and interests. Chance, in the form of the presence or absence of far-sighted and effective leaders at critical moments, has an important share in this process.

The role of ideas appears implicitly more than overtly, and in fact it certainly needs further elaboration. Still, it is "views" as well as "interests" that leaders represent. Indeed, the entire all-important process of change "can be traced to the revolutionary expansion of knowledge originating in Western Europe in the Middle Ages"—a most controversial point, if one stops to think about it.[2] Ideas, thus, seem to be important and even determining components in Professor Black's view of social change.

To digress and speculate for a moment, leadership and ideas occur naturally to students of the Russian empire. Leadership, it would seem, appears crucial in every reign, both when it succeeded, as in the time of Peter the Great—the main subject of Professor Black's historical studies in recent years—and when it failed, as under Nicholas II. The significance of ideas needs more elaboration. The imperial Russian government was not on the whole well served by theoreticians. The entire Russian Right has been considered a failure intellectually. Characteristically, within the last few weeks I have been asked to read a manuscript which emphasizes the failure and decomposition of the ideology of the Russian Right and to participate in the session on "The Conservative Tradition in Modern Russian History" at the forthcoming American Historical Association meeting, where one paper will deal with "an analysis of the weaknesses of Russian conservative thought in the nineteenth century" and another with the Black Hundreds.[3] While I see no basic objections to this standard approach to the Russian Right, it bears repeating that the Right ruled the empire. Naziism has taught us how tremendously effective and important even a most repulsive and

[2] And even more sharply: "the modern revolution was intellectual in its origins."

[3] The relative theoretical poverty of the Russian Right did not, of course, preclude some valuable contributions. See, for example, Richard Pipes, *Karamzin's Memoir on Ancient and Modern Russia: A Translation and Analysis* (Cambridge, Mass., 1959). For an extremely inclusive and therefore richer view of Russian conservatism see Marc Raeff, *Michael Speransky, Statesman of Imperial Russia, 1772-1839* (The Hague, 1957).

irrational ideology can be, provided it is held with deep conviction by those who have power. The Russian *ancien régime,* to be sure, produced no naziism. Yet it, too, had its creed, its "official nationality," to which it adhered with remarkable persistence. Failures, to repeat, could be quite as significant as successes. If Nicholas I could not mold the country to his own liking, he did much to block its political, social, and economic evolution, to "freeze" everything for thirty years. Leadership, after all, remains inseparable from its purpose.

Professor Black, then, allows generously for leadership and ideas in his scheme of things. He operates within a richer and more varied historical framework than, for example, the Marxists, or, to use a closer comparison, Professor Von Laue.[4] Yet he suffers from his very virtues. Modernization has been an effective thesis in explaining recent history largely because of its close link to technology and economics and the accompanying assertion, or at least suggestion, of inner logic and determinism. If leadership is decisive, the system flies open at one end. If ideas ultimately determine events—and there is no parallel explanation of the origin of ideas—the system has no secure foundation. There is a story that shortly after the opening of the St. Petersburg-Moscow railroad two ladies who had boarded the train at an intermediate station marveled over that great new scientific invention, which was carrying one of them to Moscow and the other to St. Petersburg while they sat side by side. My point is not to be facetious, but to indicate that Professor Black might have too much of a good thing. Moreover, the elements in his presentation which I like especially well are precisely the ones that vitiate systems.

Professor Black's analysis raises other problems, too. On the one hand, he stresses the originality, separateness, and, so to speak, equality of his "well over one hundred" societies. Yet, on the other hand, their modernization, their entire historic evolution is measured by their adoption and adaptation of the forms of life which originated and developed in Western Europe. Obviously, in this Westernizer framework some societies become much more equal than others. In regard to Russia, the author's approach eliminates the misleading dichotomy between the empire of the tsars and the rest of Europe, understood as an organic and monolithic West. But it leaves open the issue of the actual relationship of Russia to leading Western societies. Professor Black does little to elucidate this connection, except to indicate his awareness of the rich common heritage of Russia and other European countries and at the same time to point out what appears to him to be a radically different nature of Russian autocratic government and

---

4 My knowledge of Professor Theodore Von Laue's views is based not only on his many published articles but also on numerous personal talks and on partial acquaintance with his forthcoming book on Witte and the industrialization of Russia.

society compared with those in the West. A further study of these issues appears in order, whether from Professor Black's point of view or otherwise.

The scheme tends to equate traditional with static and modern with dynamic. Possibly for this reason, the reader at times cannot pin down to a definite period the author's discussion of such subjects as serfdom or the weakness of the Russian gentry. Professor Black, of course, needs no reminding that traditional Russian society also evolved. But he might be interested in one reader's impression that the abstract quality of his exposition of pre-modern Russia results in part from his frame of reference and not entirely from inadequate space.

Professor Black's five distinguishing features of Russian imperial society, which "must of necessity be highly selective and impressionistic," consist of the physical setting, the autocratic state, the system of social stratification, the agrarian economy, and the multinational structure. They suggest a geographic, economic, and social emphasis, if not necessarily determinism. Only the multinational structure is unusual on such a list, and Professor Black does little with it. Omissions may be more significant. Strikingly, the list includes no ideological or cultural factors, although, as already mentioned, ideas are assigned much importance elsewhere. By contrast, even Sumner—a great admirer of Soloviëv, Kliuchevsky, and the geographic and sociological schools of Russian historians—selected "the Church" as one of the seven elements that made Russia and Russian history.[5]

Professor Black's ensuing discussion of his five factors, and of the evolution of Russia, is stimulating and pointed, although of necessity brief and oversimplified. The author, however, appears to overstate the significance of the autocratic state in Russia, enormous as that significance undoubtedly was. Thus—as he knows well—his assertion that "serfdom had been established principally for the benefit of the state" represents at best one view of the matter. Professor Black even writes:

It was not difficult for this state, in the generation after the defeat in the Crimea, to initiate a very fundamental reorientation of national life. Between 1861 and 1917 the autocracy in Russia put into effect a series of reforms which resemble in many respects those achieved by very different methods in France between 1789 and 1848—if one may risk an historical analogy. To extend the analogy a step further, one may suggest that the autocratic state in Russia played a role similar not only to that of the middle class and the Napoleonic empire in France but also to that of the samurai in Japan, the Young Turks in the Ottoman Empire, the army officers in Egypt, and the European-educated politicians in Africa today.

Similarly, the author tends to overemphasize the significance of the state

[5] Benedict H. Sumner, *A Short History of Russia* (New York, 1943).

in the industrialization of Russia. Many readers will also challenge Professor Black's estimate of the intentions of Russian autocrats, together with the results which they achieved. To quote a particularly controversial instance: "Peter's reforms were explicitly defensive in their motivation and implications, and they were successful in preserving the traditional social structure of the country with relatively few changes for a century and a half."

One more point should be made. Although classifying Russia as a backward country and ranging it on a scale with other underdeveloped nations in the process of modernization can serve and has served useful purposes, there are, it is important to emphasize, many other ways of looking at it and comparing it with other societies. For example, whereas the usual rating based on economic development and modernization would place imperial Russia and the United States pretty much at opposite extremes, at least among "Western" states, other approaches may bring the two much closer together. Thus a student of intellectual and cultural history can profitably look at the Russians and the Americans as living on the periphery of a cultural world centered in Great Britain, France, and Germany. Indeed, the insistence on "culture" in certain American academic, intellectual, and social circles, the culture represented by Paris and Oxford, probably gives a better insight into the attitude of the educated Russians towards "the West" than many a learned analysis of the matter. *Letters of a Russian Traveler* reads like letters of my college friends on their first trip to Western Europe—I suppose, like my own letters as well—except that Karamzin wrote with remarkable fluency and grace. Or, to mention a more common area of comparison of the two gigantic countries: the Western expansion of the United States has often been likened to the Russian advance into Siberia and Central Asia, and the two did have much in common. Thus Professor Treadgold, among others, found the Turner hypothesis fruitful for his study of the Russian migration to Siberia in the last decades of tsarism.[6] Time does not have to be an insuperable barrier for understanding and insights. I was repeatedly surprised by the marvelous penetration of a friend of mine into some aspects of Nicholas I's rule of Russia. His field is the Roman empire.

To conclude, Professor Black deserves our gratitude for his important and able presentation of the nature of imperial Russian society. As usual, it is much easier to criticize than to affirm. Moreover, the approach to recent history, Russian history included, through the process of modernization is useful, stimulating, comprehensive, and very much in keeping with the orientation and interests of our age. It is to be hoped that it will be applied by many scholars in painstaking detail to various aspects of modern Russian history.

[6] Donald W. Treadgold, *The Great Siberian Migration* (Princeton, 1957).

Reply

CYRIL E. BLACK

I

It is important to combine specialized and detailed scholarship with broad interpretations permitting comparisons, analogies, and generalizations embracing several societies, even though such interpretations risk many pitfalls unknown to conventional scholarship. Such exercises are particularly important in regard to Russia because of the strategic position that it has occupied in time, place, and influence in the spread of modern ideas and institutions from Western Europe to the rest of the world. There is a long Anglo-American tradition of applying to Russian society the conceptual framework developed for the study of Western Europe, and this approach still has its adherents. The Eurasian school in Paris between the wars had some interesting new things to say on this question, but its position was never fully formulated. The Soviet Marxists for their part have succeeded in fitting everything into place, but they have done this at the price of ignoring some very important distinctions. One cannot interpret Russian developments without some general conception of what is universal and what is particular in the evolution of societies, and in a rapidly changing world this matter must be constantly reconsidered. To the extent that Professors Seton-Watson and Riasanovsky find the main propositions in my paper acceptable, there may possibly be a growing consensus among a new generation of historians whose point of view differs a good deal from that of the generation writing between the two world wars. At the same time, their emendations and amplifications reveal significant areas of controversy, and these deserve further consideration.

II

Professor Seton-Watson's comments are concerned in particular with the role of the Orthodox Church, the nature of the autocracy, the Russian form of imperialism, and the composition of the middle class. His comments also have some implications of a general theoretical character about which I would like to make some remarks.

As concerns the Orthodox Church, what strikes me as being of relatively little importance in imperial Russia, by contrast with the Muscovite period, is its formal theology, structure, and political role. The church was thoroughly subordinated to the state in an administrative sense, and in its official capacity it was not a particularly fertile source of ideas or inspiration. What seems to me of much greater importance

202

is what might be called the value system or "ideology"—to use a much abused term—of the Orthodox faith. This was no doubt only a part of a more general value system characteristic of imperial Russian society which included important secular elements, but Orthodoxy probably accounted for some of its most significant features. This unofficial Orthodoxy was expressed at a sophisticated level by leading thinkers such as Soloviëv, Dostoevsky, and Berdiaev, among others. At a more popular level it took the form of the beliefs and attitudes of the common people, for whom religion provided much of the vocabulary and symbolism for the expression of thought. It is a difficult matter, however, to define just what these values were. It may well be, as is often asserted, that this value system stressed otherworldliness, encouraged passivity in regard to the political authorities, emphasized the importance of the group at the expense of the individual, deprecated the accumulation of private property, and advanced the view that the Russians are the only "God-bearing" people. To the extent that one can see important reflections of such attitudes in contemporary Soviet society, it may well be that these were in fact important elements of the prerevolutionary value system and that they have now assumed a Marxist aspect. My own feeling is that not enough is known about the value system of imperial Russia or about its Orthodox component, and that this is among the significant questions that deserve further study.

As regards the autocracy and the oligarchy, there may have been some misunderstanding of the way in which I used the terms. I defined the oligarchy to include the "higher civilian and military officials and leading families of noble landowners," and thought of the autocracy much more narrowly as the autocrat himself. For Professor Seton-Watson the autocracy comprises the autocrat together with the bureaucratic apparatus, and the oligarchy consist of the leading noble families and the Guards officers who led their regiments into action at critical moments. His definitions may well correspond more accurately to current usage, and in that event I am inclined to agree with the substance of his remarks. I have been impressed by the fact that more often than not between 1725 and 1917 the initiative in the great decisions of state came not from the autocrat but from the leading bureaucrats. This is particularly true of the dramatic reforms in the reign of Alexander II. The circumstance that all decrees were issued in the name of the emperor obscures this somewhat, but the fact remains that Peter alone among the rulers of the empire had the ability and imagination to offer outstanding personal leadership.

It seems that the problem of Russian expansionism offers a more lively source of controversy, although here again it may be more a question of terminology than a fundamental difference in interpretation. On rereading my remarks on this subject I was relieved to find that the "less imperialistic" which Professor Seton-Watson puts in quotation marks does not come from my paper, although my use of the term "imperialist" was perhaps ambiguous. The distinction I had in mind was between a continental and an overseas expansionism. In this case it amounts also to a distinction between a policy inspired by a bureaucratic government and one inspired by chartered trading companies, or between motives of security and of commerce. Apart from nebulous schemes involving India and parts of Africa, and rather minor financial investments and technical assistance missions in Persia and Mongolia, characteristically commercial expansionism in the period of the empire was limited essentially to Alaska and Manchuria. As an exporter almost exclusively of agricultural products and natural resources, Russian commerce was with the developed societies rather than with the undeveloped, with countries where the flag could not follow trade. The sale of Alaska after the discovery of gold is a classic example of a government sacrificing economic gains in the interest of security. In the case of Manchuria and the associated treaty ports, the reverse was true. The distinction between continental and overseas expansionism strikes me as particularly important in the modern age, when political leaders are confronted by the powerful but antagonistic trends favoring administrative and economic integration on the one hand and nationalistic separatism on the other. In the case of an overseas empire, which characteristically embraces a wide diversity of cultures, the nationalist trend tends to gain the upper hand. In a continental empire, on the other hand, administrative and economic integration have a good chance of success if the nationalities problem can be worked out. In any event, it does not seem to me that moral judgments are involved in this distinction. Morality in these matters concerns the way peoples are ruled rather than the motives underlying the creation of an empire.

I find Professor Seton-Watson's comments about the middle class particularly valuable. The sources and character of the modernizing leadership are perhaps the key to an understanding of the process of change characteristic of the modern age, and scholars trained in the Western tradition have to be constantly on guard against applying concepts valid in their own culture—and the "middle class" is typical of such concepts—to societies with a somewhat different background. I would not go so far as Professor Seton-Watson, however, in his use of the term "intelligentsia" to describe a variety of modernizing leaders around the world. In Russia the intelligentsia certainly formed an important group, distinct both from the bureaucrats—many of whom were well-educated intellectuals—and from the merchants. What is significant about the Russian situation, however, is less the distinction and influence of this group than the fact that so many able and well-educated individuals should have been alienated from public service to the extent that their principal contribution was one of comment and criticism. The difference between the Russian intelligentsia and the leaders of the new states in Asia and Africa seems to be more than a nuance, as Professor Seton-Watson asserts. Sun Yat-sen and Fidel Castro may perhaps be considered as members of an intelligentsia in the Russian sense, but Kemal in Turkey, Chiang in China, and Nasser in Egypt were military bureaucrats well along in their professional careers before they seized power, and the leaders of modern Japan were likewise predominantly bureaucrats. If one is going to make a distinction between an intelligentsia and a bureaucracy, I would hazard a guess that persons trained for the civilian and military bureaucracy have contributed more modernizing leaders in the new states than have members of an intelligentsia. As I suggested in my paper, I believe that the role of the modernizing bureaucrats in imperial Russia also has been greatly underrated.

The comparative study of modernizing leadership is related to a question of a more general theoretical character which seems to me relevant at this point. In his opening paragraph Professor Seton-Watson refers to imperial Russia as "the prototype of 'the underdeveloped society' whose problems are so familiar a theme in our own age." Later on, in discussing the question of the middle class, he appears to regard imperial Russia and all of the underdeveloped societies as a single general category distinct from the societies of "northwest Europe and North America." This strikes me as much too sweeping a generalization, and one that tends to blur the distinctive character of the various societies concerned. I would prefer an approach that places greater emphasis on the diversities among the traditional societies that form the base from which modernization has proceeded. One example from Professor Seton-Watson's argument will illustrate my point. He compares the educational policies of Russia and Japan in the nineteenth century, much to the advantage of the latter. I take no exception to what he says in this regard, but he neglects to point out the very significant difference in their point of departure. By the end of the seventeenth century Japan had a relatively high rate of literacy. Not only were bureaucrats, merchants, and townspeople in general comparatively well educated, but there was also a significant degree of literacy in the villages and a brisk trade in books in the market places. In seventeenth-century Russia, by contrast, literacy was very limited even in the towns. I do not know what difference this made in the educational policies of these countries a century or two later, but I suspect that it was considerable. In brief, I do not think that Russia in the sixteenth, seventeenth, and eighteenth centuries was particularly typical of traditional societies in general—whether the comparison is with a contemporary African society, or with China, Japan, or India two or three centuries ago, or with

England and France in the later Middle Ages. I would be inclined to emphasize not only the fundamental diversities among traditional societies but also the essentially different institutional structures that modern societies are likely to possess even when they perform essentially similar functions. Consequently, I am more impressed with the uniqueness of Russian institutions than with the features it shares in common with other developing societies. There are "many roads to modernization," to paraphrase Khrushchev, and that of imperial Russia is only one of them.

III

Professor Riasanovsky's comments raise issues of a different order, for he is somewhat more inclined than Professor Seton-Watson to probe the usefulness of interpretations of imperial Russian society based on the concept of modernization. I will therefore discuss these issues under four headings: modernization as a framework of interpretation, the role of ideas, the role of leadership, and the comparison of modernizing societies.

It is perhaps a virtue of the term "modernization" that it is at the same time broad enough to embrace a wide variety of phenomena and new enough to be relatively free from the accretions of usage and meaning that have rendered such terms as "nationalism," "liberalism," "conservatism," and "socialism" virtually useless. Yet modernization itself is not a useful concept unless it is employed in a reasonably systematic fashion, although an adequate exposition would take more space than I have been allotted here. Perhaps it will suffice for the purposes of this discussion to say that I use it to describe the impact on the totality of human activity of the rapid expansion of knowledge that has taken place since the Middle Ages. If one grants that innovation in some form has characterized civilized societies throughout history, modernization refers to the distinctive features of this process in modern times. As a means of handling this totality of human activity in a reasonably expeditious fashion, I have found it convenient to think of it in terms of five aspects: intellectual, political, economic, social, and personal or psychological. This is no doubt an arbitrary and oversimplified division, but it has been useful for my purposes. Several fundamental questions, which I will not attempt to answer here, are raised by this approach: What is modernity? How do the traditional and the modern interact? How can one describe and compare the transition from traditionalism to modernity in a wide variety of societies at different stages of development?

My paper on the nature of imperial Russian society was no doubt too brief and fragmentary to serve as a very satisfactory example of this approach, but it will have to do for the moment. What is significant, in any event, is that this is supposed to be an "approach" rather than a "system," if by the latter term one means some sort of closed system with a built-in determinism which claims to hold the key to the past, present, and future. I am therefore not particularly concerned when Professor Riasanovsky suggests that the emphasis on ideas and leadership leaves things somewhat open-ended, for that seems to me the way they are. Historians can describe the problems confronting a society and the alternatives available to it, but they cannot foresee how these will be perceived by a diversity of leaders or which solutions will finally be adopted. I would be inclined to stress the interaction of the five aspects of modernization rather than the determinism of any one of them, except insofar as all phenomena must be filtered through the human brain, whether consciously or unconsciously, before they can be historically significant. This approach has a number of advantages, even if it does not offer a closed system. In emphasizing the totality of human activity, it encourages a multidisciplinary approach to history without denying the significance of the traditional political emphasis in historical writing. In viewing each society as one of many in a pluralistic world, it stresses the value of comparing societies—with due regard for different stages of development—as a means of understanding both their similarities and their differences. Perhaps most important of all, this approach directs attention to the universal process of change which is the most prominent feature of our age, and thus helps the scholars and their readers to get away from the many forms of traditionalism and provincialism characteristic of historical writing.

Professor Riasanovsky makes his most telling point when he notes that I have not emphasized ideological or cultural factors in the second section of my paper, in which I describe the distinguishing features of imperial Russian society. The third section, on the transformation of that society, is organized on the basis of the various aspects of modernization, and there the intellectual aspect receives the consideration that it deserves. I am inclined to agree, however, that even at the risk of some repetition more attention should have been given to the traditional ideology or value system of the empire. In a treatment not limited to the empire, this would come more properly under the discussion of the Muscovite period. Any discussion of the traditional ideology should certainly include, as I have already noted in my reply to the comments of Professor Seton-Watson, due recognition of the role of religion and of the church.

In stressing leadership, which is of particular concern to the political aspect of modernization, I am referring not just to the "great men and women" of history but to the relatively few thousands in any field of activity who are the most skillful and exert the greatest influence. Professor Riasanovsky is inclined to feel that I overstate the leadership role of the autocratic state in Russia, but I am not willing to concede this point. Perhaps he is thinking in absolute terms whereas I am thinking in relative terms, but it seems to me that in the nineteenth century Russia was the most state-directed of all the major societies. In any event, I did not mean to imply that either the state or traditional Russia as a whole was in any sense static. It does seem to me, however, that until 1861 the empire did not face up to the problem of changing the agrarian system within which at least four-fifths of the population lived. Indeed, the reforms of Peter and his successors tended to strengthen serfdom and in that sense were "defensive." I would say the same of the reforms carried out by the French government in the century or two before 1789. It seems to me that the various trends in Russian thought can best be understood in terms of their perception of the changing world around them. If one thinks of Witte and Stolypin as conservatives, whatever their differences in outlook, then some of Russia's most vigorous modernizers have been conservatives. To put it differently, I think it is more significant to know whether Russia's leaders were traditionalists or modernizers than whether they were liberal or conservative, especially since the latter terms tend to be used in ways more relevant to Western European societies than to Russia.

I would be inclined to agree with Professor Riasanovsky that there are many ways of comparing societies, but all of them seem to me to be relevant to the way in which they modernize. Perhaps the key to our difference on this issue is that I do not regard modernization simply as a "Westernizer framework," or as the "adoption and adaptation of the forms of life which originated and developed in Western Europe," to use Professor Riasanovsky's terminology. To my mind modernity consists of a body of scientifically verifiable knowledge and the impact of this knowledge on a wide variety of institutions; and the forms that this takes will tend to differ from one society to another depending on the character of the traditional institutions and the way in which leaders decide to do the job. For example, the political structure and legal institutions of the United Kingdom, the United States, the Soviet Union, and Japan differ considerably, although they face very similar administrative problems as societies at roughly the same stage of development. It is thus more a question of adaptation than of adoption, and of substance rather than of form. Scientifically verifiable knowledge has universal validity, but the way it affects diverse traditional ideas and institutions is a relative matter. No doubt imperial Russian society was "backward" in relation to the societies of Western Europe, but once this was generally recognized the question of whether to modernize was no longer so controversial. Certainly after 1861 the vital question was how to modernize, and on this issue there is still plenty of room for controversy in Russia as elsewhere.

Part III

RUSSIA'S WESTERN BORDERLANDS

SIX

The Role of the Ukraine in Modern Society

IVAN L. RUDNYTSKY

MR. RUDNYTSKY *is associate professor of history at La Salle College.*

THE SETTING OF THE PROBLEM

A striking difference between the historical development of the countries of Western Europe and that of those of the eastern half of the continent has been often observed. The former, particularly France and England, have enjoyed, in spite of some periods of revolutionary upheaval, a millennium of continuous growth. Germany's fate has been much less favorable, and farther to the east it is impossible to find any country which has not experienced, at one time or another, a tragic breakdown and an epoch of a national *capitis deminutio,* sometimes extending for centuries. Here one will think of the subjugation of the Balkanic peoples and Hungary by the Turks, of the crushing of Bohemia by Habsburg absolutism, of the partitions of Poland.

The Ukraine is a typically East European nation in that its history is marked by a high degree of discontinuity. The country suffered two major eclipses in the course of its development. The medieval Rus' received a crippling blow from the hands of the Mongols, was subsequently absorbed by Lithuania, and finally annexed to Poland. In the middle of the seventeenth century the Ukraine rose against Polish domination, and a new body politic, the Cossack State, came into existence. By the second half of the eighteenth century, however, the autonomy of the Cossack Ukraine was destroyed by the Russian Empire. A new upward cycle started in the nineteenth century. The movement of national regeneration culminated in the 1917 Revolution, when a Ukrainian independent state emerged, to succumb soon to Communist Russian control. This third, last great division of Ukrainian history, which lasts from the 1780's to the Revolution, and in a sense even to the present, forms what may be defined as "modern Ukrainian history."

When nationalist movements got under way in nineteenth-century Eastern Europe, they were of two different types. In one, the leadership remained with the traditional upper class (nobility), into which newcomers of plebeian background were infused only gradually. Their programs were characterized by a historical legitimism: their aim was the restoration of the nation's old state within its ancient boundaries. In the movements of the second type, leadership had to be created anew, and the efforts were directed toward the raising of a "natural," ethnic community to a politically conscious nationhood. These latter movements had a slower start than the former, but they drew strength from their identification with the strivings of the masses, and they were able to profit from the inevitable democratization of the social structure. When the territorial claims of nations of the two types clashed, as happened frequently, those of the second category usually prevailed in the long run. The two categories are referred to as the "historical" and the "nonhistorical" nations respectively. If these concepts are to serve as useful tools of historical understanding, the following things are to be kept in mind. "Nonhistoricity," in this meaning, does not necessarily imply that a given country is lacking a historical past, even a rich and distinguished past; it simply indicates a rupture in historical continuity through the loss of the traditional representative class. Second, the radical opposition that appears between these two types when they are conceived as sociological models by no means precludes the existence in historical reality of borderline cases, as for instance the Czechs.

Prima facie evidence assigns the Ukraine to the category of the "nonhistorical" nations. The modern Ukrainian nation is not simply a continuation or restoration of the Cossack Ukraine of the seventeenth and eighteenth centuries, or, of course, even less of the Kievan and Galician Rus'.[1] On the other hand, one must not overlook the links that connected the nineteenth-century national *risorgimento* with the Cossack epoch. The modern nationalist movement started in those areas of the Ukraine where the Cossack traditions were the strongest, and originally most of the leaders came from the descendants of the former Cossack officers *(starshyny)* class. Symbols and ideas derived from the Cossack tradition played an important role even as late as the 1917 Revolution.[2]

Ukrainian history of the nineteenth century may mean two different things: a history of the nationalist movement on the one hand, and a

[1] It is significant that the Third Universal (Manifesto) of the revolutionary Ukrainian parliament, the Central Rada, which proclaimed the formation of the Ukrainian People's Republic (November 20, 1917), and the Fourth Universal, which declared the Ukraine a sovereign state completely separate from Russia (January 22, 1918), avoided any reference to historical rights and were completely based on the principle of democratic self-determination. Since the president of the Rada and the originator of these two acts was the dean of Ukrainian historians, Mykhailo Hrushevsky, this omission was not fortuitous. It reflected an essential trait of the ideology of the Ukrainian movement.

[2] A parallel situation may be found at the transition from the first to the second epoch of Ukrainian history. The Cossack State was not a direct continuation of the Kievan State, but neither was it without connections with this predecessor. The Ukrainian ("Ruthenian," in the nomenclature of the time) gentry, burghers, and clergy, among whom the traditions

history of the country and the people on the other hand. The two are closely interrelated, but they do not coincide.

Beginning with the 1840's and until the 1917 Revolution, there was an uninterrupted chain of groups and organizations, formal and informal, that were committed to the idea of the Ukraine's cultural and political regeneration as a separate nation. Combated and persecuted by tsarist authorities, the movement was irrepressible. At times it demonstrated a great vitality (as in the 1870's); at other times it seemed to have gone into hibernation (as in the 1880's). It would be a fruitful task, which has not yet been fully accomplished by historical scholarship, to trace the course of the Ukrainian nationalist movement, somewhat as the course of the Russian revolutionary movements has been traced by Jan Kucharzewski and Franco Venturi.

It is clear, however, that until the eve of the 1917 Revolution, Ukrainian nationalism retained the character of a minority movement. (This refers to the Russian Ukraine only; the situation was different in Austrian Galicia.) The peasant masses were, until 1905, little touched by the nationalist movement. Thoroughly Ukrainian in all their objective, ethnic traits, they had not yet adopted a modern national consciousness, and generally remained politically amorphous. The members of the upper classes were mostly Russified and, except for those engaged in the Ukrainian movement, regarded themselves as belonging to the Russian nation. The question arises whether under such circumstances the student is entitled to include in "Ukrainian history" everything that happened on Ukrainian soil.

A memoirist has noted the following observation. If the train from Kiev to Poltava which carried delegates for the unveiling of the monument to the poet Kotliarevsky in 1903 had crashed, this would have meant, it was said jokingly, the end of the Ukrainian movement for a long time; nearly all the leading personalities of the movement traveled in two cars of that train.[3] But how is one to explain a movement that at the turn of the century had only a few thousands of self-professed adherents, by 1905 began to assume a mass character, and after another twelve years erupted, in 1917, as a nascent nation of over thirty million? The answer can be only this: there were at work among the population of the Ukraine other forces which, without being identical with the nationalist movement, were pointed in the same direction, and finally, as if drawn by an irresistible attraction, merged with it. The nationalist movement played the role of the catalyst, and in this sense it was extremely important. But we cannot historically explain the origins of

---

of the Kievan Rus' remained alive even under Polish domination, provided the Cossack military organization with a religious-political program, and partly also with a leading personnel, which lifted the anti-Polish revolt of 1648 to the level of a war of national liberation. This is the point in which the Ukrainian Cossacks radically differed from similar Russian communities of frontiersmen, the Don and Iaik (Ural) Cossacks.

[3] Євген Чикаленко, *Спогади (1861-1907)* (New York, 1955), p. 337.

the modern Ukrainian nation if we concentrate on the nationalist movement alone. We must take into account also various other forces: for instance, the activities of the Ukrainian zemstvo or those of the Ukrainian branches of "All-Russian" revolutionary organizations, from the Decembrists, through the Populists, to the Marxist and labor groups at the turn of the century.[4] All of them made their contributions to the formation of the modern Ukraine. Moreover, a closer scrutiny shows that these movements, though not endowed with a fully crystallized Ukrainian national awareness, usually possessed it in an embryonic stage in the form of a "South Russian" sectionalism, or "territorial patriotism."

Thus it may be stated that the central problem of modern Ukrainian history is that of the emergence of a nation: the transformation of an ethnic-linguistic community into a self-conscious political and cultural community. A comprehensive study of this subject would have to include an investigation into the factors that shaped the nation-making process, either by furthering or by impeding it. The interrelation with all the other forces, active on the wider East European scene, would have to be taken into account.

The character of modern Ukrainian history changes definitely after 1917. The making of the nation was basically completed during the revolutionary years 1917-20.[5] For the last four decades the central issue of Ukrainian history was the nation's struggle for survival under foreign rule and for the restoration of its liberty and independence. The struggle was—and is to the present day—primarily directed against Soviet Russia. But in the interwar period it was, in the western portion of the Ukraine's territory, directed also against Poland, and during the years of World War II against Nazi Germany as well.

METHODOLOGICAL APPROACHES

In studying Ukrainian prerevolutionary history, stress ought to be placed primarily on social-economic developments and on the evolution of social thought; a politically oriented historical investigation would be relatively unproductive.

Not having an independent state nor even such a semi-independent autonomous body politic as, for instance, the Poles possessed in the

[4] Limitations of space do not permit bolstering these statements with proper references. Two short examples must suffice: the memoirs of V. Debagorii-Mokrievich and the first part of those of I. Petrunkevich, the former for a presentation of revolutionary Populism, and the latter for one of zemstvo liberalism, in the Ukraine of the 1870's. Both men were of Ukrainian descent, but regarded themselves as members of the Russian nation, and wrote in Russian. Nevertheless, they were quite aware that the people among whom they were working differed in many essential respects from the Great Russians and had to be approached in a different way. An unmistakable Ukrainian aura pervades these reminiscences.

[5] Only in some backward areas, such as the Carpatho-Ukraine (Sub-Carpathian Ruthenia), was the crystallization of a modern national consciousness delayed until the 1930's.

"Congress" Kingdom, the Ukrainians were unable to participate in politics on a governmental level: they were not directly connected with the great world of diplomacy and military affairs. The international order established in Ukrainian lands in the last third of the eighteenth century by the Russian annexation of the Black Sea coastal areas as well as of the "Right Bank" (i.e., of the territories west of the Dnieper), and by the annexation of Galicia by the Austrian Empire, remained basically unchanged until 1914. This long period of stability made any idea of international change seem remote and unrealistic to contemporaries.[6]

Conditions in the Russian Empire were such that an overt political life on a nongovernmental level was also impossible, at least until 1905. In this respect, the Ukrainians in Austria had a great advantage over the majority of their compatriots, who lived under Russian rule. After the 1848 Revolution, Galician Ukrainians took part in elections, possessed a parliamentary representation, a political press, parties, and civic organizations. In the Russian Ukraine political strivings could be expressed only through illegal channels, namely, through underground groups, whose activities were necessarily of limited scope. In the long run it was, however, inevitable that changes of social structure and intellectual trends were to have political effects.

The two great stages in the prerevolutionary Ukraine's social development were the abolition of serfdom in 1861 and the rise of modern industrialism toward the end of the century. Neither movement was limited to the Ukraine but rather was common to the Russian Empire as a whole. Still, the Ukrainian lands possessed certain social-economic peculiarities of their own, and the idea, generally held by Western scholars, of the Ukraine's complete integration in the economic fabric of the empire, "like Pennsylvania's in the United States," is incorrect. The Ukrainian peasantry had never known the system of the "repartitional commune," and they were undoubtedly more individualistically minded than the Great Russian muzhiks. Ukrainian agriculture was connected through the Black Sea ports with the world market; most of Russia's agricultural exports came from the Ukraine. The rapid development of Ukrainian mining and heavy industries was due to a massive influx of foreign investments. The economic connections of the Ukraine were in many respects closer to the outside world than to Central Russia.[7]

---

[6] It is, however, to be noted that each of the major international conflicts in which the Russian Empire was involved—the Napoleonic, Crimean, Balkanic, and Japanese wars—had definite repercussions in the Ukraine. In each case movements arose which attempted to take advantage of Russia's predicament for the betterment of the Ukraine's position.

[7] An early Ukrainian Marxist, Iulian Bachynsky, developed in his essay *Ukraina irredenta* (1895) the thesis that while the industries of Congress Poland were working for and dependent on the Russian market, Ukrainian industry was rather competitive with that of Central Russia. From this he drew the prognosis that the Ukraine was more likely than Poland to secede from Russia. This reveals the shortcomings of a purely economic interpretation of historical events, and for this Bachynsky was criticized by such outstanding

Agrarian overpopulation and the harsh lot of industrial workers led to a sharpening of social tensions in the Ukraine. A characteristic of the Ukrainian scene, a phenomenon to be found also in other "non-historical" countries, was the overlapping of social and national conflicts. The great landowners, capitalists, and industrial entrepreneurs were predominantly members of the local Russian, Polish, and Jewish minorities, or foreigners. Thus the coming revolution was to be simultaneously a social and a national one. The Ukrainian national movement was not limited to any single social class. It had individual supporters among the members of the upper classes, and it reached into the class of industrial workers. Still, it found the strongest response among the middle strata: the prosperous peasantry, the rural intelligentsia and semi-intelligentsia, the emerging native petty bourgeoisie of the towns. Close links existed between Ukrainian nationalism and the cooperative movement, which was growing at great speed in the years preceding World War I. The larger cities retained a predominantly Russian character, and this was to be a great handicap to the Ukraine during the Revolution. But, judging by the example of other countries with a similar social structure, the "Ukrainization" of the urban centers would have been a question of time.[8]

The impact of the economic policies of the Russian government on the Ukraine must also be considered. Some economic historians active during the early Soviet period (M. Slabchenko, M. Iavorsky, O. Ohloblyn, M. Volobuev) used the term "colonialism" to define the Ukraine's position in relation to the former empire. This concept, borrowed from the Marxist arsenal, was not altogether well chosen. Tsarist Russia possessed genuine colonies, such as Transcaucasia and Turkestan, but the Ukraine could not be counted among them. The administration looked rather on the Ukraine as belonging to the core of the "home provinces" of European Russia. The economic progress of the Ukraine ("South Russia") was in many respects faster than that of the Great Russian center. Nevertheless, the economic policies of the government were mostly adverse to Ukrainian interests. The Ukraine, for instance, carried an excessive load of taxation, since the revenues collected in the Ukraine did not return to the country but were spent in other parts of the empire. The construction of railroad lines, which was dominated by strategic considerations, as well as the existing system of freight rates and customs duties, failed to take Ukrainian needs into account. Contemporaries were well aware of the issue. It is noteworthy that the industrial groups of the "South"—who were of non-Ukrainian background and had no connections with the nationalist movement—

---

contemporaries as M. Drahomanov and I. Franko. Still, the facts pointed out by Bachynsky were certainly significant.

[8] One may recall that Prague and Riga preserved well into the nineteenth century a predominantly German outlook.

tended to form regional syndicates and associations for the defense of the area's economic interests, neglected by the government of St. Petersburg.[9]

The other major field of prerevolutionary Ukrainian history was social thought. It is a well-attested historical rule that in countries that lack political liberty there exists a tendency toward an "ideologization" of politics and, simultaneously, toward a politicization of cultural and intellectual life. Where civic strivings cannot be expressed through overt, practical activities, they are diverted toward the realm of theoretical programs and ideologies. Under such circumstances, creators and carriers of cultural values tend to develop a strong feeling of civic vocation. This applies to both the Russian and Ukrainian nineteenth-century societies, but there was an important difference between the two. The Russians, as members of an independent and powerful nation, even if subordinated to a despotic regime, had few grievances of a specifically national nature. Thus the mental energies of Russian intellectuals were mostly concentrated on the construction of social or theocratic utopias. Ukrainian intellectuals, on the other hand, were bound to vindicate the claims of their country as a separate national entity.

The magnitude of the task facing Ukrainian intellectuals can hardly be exaggerated. The consistent policy of the tsarist government—which, in this respect, found full support from Russian public opinion, including its left wing—was to deny the very existence of a Ukrainian nationality. Those elements of the Ukrainian heritage which could be assimilated were declared to belong to the "All-Russian" nation, of which the "Little Russians" were a tribal branch; the other elements of the Ukrainian heritage, which were unfit for such an expropriation, were systematically suppressed and obliterated. For instance, determined to relegate the Ukrainian language to the level of a peasant dialect, the Russian government imposed in 1876 a general prohibition of all publications in Ukrainian. Against these tremendous pressures, Ukrainian linguists and ethnographers defended the idea of a Ukrainian ethnic individuality on an equal footing with the other national groups of the Slavic family; Ukrainian historians, from Kostomarov to Hrushevsky, demonstrated the continuity of their country's past development from prehistoric times to the present.

[9] The greatest wrong which tsarist Russia committed against the Ukrainian people in the field of social-economic policies was the introduction of serfdom in 1783. As long as the Cossack officers showed an inclination toward political separatism, the tsarist policy was to pretend the role of "defender" of the common people against the local upper class. Later, when the danger of separatism had diminished, the interests of the peasantry were sacrificed, in order to reconcile the Ukrainian gentry with the loss of their country's political autonomy. Russian-style serfdom was introduced in the Ukraine at a time when it was already on the way toward extinction in other parts of Eastern Europe, and when even in Galicia it was being restricted by the policies of Austrian "enlightened despots," Maria Theresa and Joseph II.

A national consciousness implies not only a system of ideas of a more or less rational, cognitive nature but also an emotional commitment, which is more likely to be stimulated by poets and writers than by scholars. It is not fortuitous that the representative hero of the nineteenth-century Ukraine was not a statesman or a soldier, but a poet—Taras Shevchenko. His historical significance is not to be measured by purely literary standards. The Ukrainian community saw and continues to see in him a prophetic figure, whose inspired word touches and transforms the very hearts of his people.

As far as the Ukrainian political program is concerned, its foundations were laid in 1846-47 by a circle of young intellectuals in Kiev, known under the name of the "Cyril and Methodius Society." Gradually revised and elaborated, it remained the platform of the Ukrainian movement until the Revolution. Its classical exposition is to be found in the writings of the outstanding Ukrainian thinker of the second half of the nineteenth century, Mykhailo Drahomanov. Divergencies of views between individuals and groups were inevitable, but there was in the Ukrainian movement a far-reaching consent on essentials. These included: a strong insistence on radical social reform but without the spirit of fierceness and exclusiveness of many Russian revolutionaries; emphasis on political liberty and Western-style constitutionalism; a program of federalistic reconstruction of the empire as a means of satisfying Ukrainian national aspirations without necessitating a complete break with Russia. However, from the 1890's on, there existed an alternative program of separatism and state sovereignty of the Ukraine. It gained the acceptance of the Galician Ukrainian community, but in the Russian Ukraine the majority of the spokesmen remained faithful to the traditional federalistic program. They depended on the hope that a future democratic Russia would be able to divest itself of the tsarist traditions of imperialism, centralism, and national oppression. The final conversion to the idea of the Ukraine's independent statehood was effected in 1917, under the impact of experiences with Russian "revolutionary democracy." The evolution of Ukrainian political thought from federalism to separatism resembles the development of the Czech national program from Palacký to Masaryk.

It is important to take notice of the ideological terms in which Ukrainian thinkers defined their nation's opposition to the Russian Empire. The first to formulate the issue was the former leader of the Cyril and Methodius Society, M. Kostomarov: he contrasted the Kievan tradition of liberty and individualism with the Moscow tradition of authoritarianism and of the subordination of the individual under the collective.[10] Stripped of Kostomarov's romantic terminology, the problem was repeatedly restated by later Ukrainian publicists and

[10] Cf. Kostomarov's essay «Двѣ русскія народности,» originally published in the journal *Основа* (St. Petersburg), No. 3, 1861.

political theorists. They saw the Ukraine, because of its deeply in-
grained libertarian attitude, as an organic part of the European community of nations, of which despotic Muscovy-Russia had never been a
true and legitimate member. "Most of the national differences between
the Ukraine and Muscovy can be explained by the fact that until the
eighteenth century [i.e., until the establishment of Russian rule] the
Ukraine was linked to Western Europe. In spite of the handicaps
caused by the Tatar invasions the Ukraine participated in Europe's
social and cultural progress."[11] These words of Drahomanov, a left-
wing liberal and socialist, are paralleled by those of a conservative
thinker, V. Lypynsky: "The basic difference between the Ukraine and
Moscow does not consist in the language, race or religion, . . . but in a
different, age-old political structure, a different method of the organization of the *élite,* in a different relationship between the upper and the
lower social classes, between the state and society."[12] Ukrainian thinkers believed that the emancipation of their country, whether through
federalism or separatism, would accelerate the liberalization of Eastern
Europe as a whole. According to their conviction, the centralistic
structure of the empire was the base on which tsarist despotism rested.
The break-up of this monolithic unity, whose maintenance required a
system of universal oppression, would release the creative, libertarian
forces of all peoples, not excepting the Russians.

An investigation of Ukrainian prerevolutionary intellectual history
should not omit those scholars of Ukrainian origin who worked at
Russian universities, published their works in Russian, and who are
therefore usually regarded as Russian. Let us name but a few of these
men: the philosophers P. Iurkevich and V. Lesevich; the economists
N. Ziber, N. Iasnopolsky, and M. Tugan-Baranovsky; the sociologist
M. Kovalevsky; the jurist B. Kistiakovsky; the linguist A. Potebnia; the
literary scholar D. Ovsianiko-Kulikovsky; the military theorist M. Dra-
gomirov. The list could easily be expanded. The question arises: with
what right can these "luminaries of Russian science" be claimed for the
Ukrainian intellectual tradition? In studying the lives of these men we
find that while skirting an overt identification with the Ukrainian
cause, which would have been catastrophic for their careers, they remained in touch with the nationalist movement, as its "secret disciples."
If that were all, their Ukrainian connection would be of only a biographical relevance. More important is the fact that the structure of
thought of these scholars betrays their Ukrainian bias, although it is
often expressed in a subtle way, not immediately perceptible to an
outsider. One example, which illustrates the point, must here suffice.
It refers to F. Mishchenko (1848-1906), the brilliant student of ancient

---

[11] М. Драгоманов, *Вибрані твори,* I (Prague, 1937), p. 70. The passage quoted is from
the Autobiography, originally published posthumously in 1896.
[12] Вячеслав Липинський, *Листи до братів-хліборобів* (Vienna, 1926), p. xxv.

history who was particularly concerned with the questions of Greek communal self-government and federalism. According to a recent Soviet study, "in this stubborn insistence on the federalist principle we can detect the influence of the ideas of Ukrainian bourgeois nationalism."[13]

The emergence of the modern Ukrainian nation may be understood as the outcome of an interaction of social forces and ideas. The social transformation taking place in Ukrainian lands in the course of the nineteenth century prepared the people for the acceptance of the nationalist ideology elaborated by several generations of intellectuals. The policy of tsarist Russia consisted in containing the activities of the intellectual circles while upholding a system of paternalistic supervision over the masses, which was to protect them from "contamination" and to keep them in a state of perpetual civic infancy. This policy was relatively successful in that the formation of the modern Ukrainian nation was delayed for decades. But it could not be prevented, as the emergence of an independent republic in 1917 was to prove.

REGIONAL VARIATIONS

The prerevolutionary Ukraine did not possess territorial unity. In each of the two great empires, Russia and Austria-Hungary, several Ukrainian lands with strongly developed sectional traits may be distinguished. An historical investigation into the origins of the modern Ukrainian nation must take these regional variations into account.

We may differentiate between those principal Ukrainian lands in which the nationalist movement had taken root in the prerevolutionary era, and those which were passive in the process of nation-making. We shall call the latter category marginal Ukrainian lands. The difference between the two was not determined by the size, as some of the principal territories (e.g., Bukovina) were smaller than some of the marginal group.

Limitations of space do not permit a discussion of the marginal lands, which included the Kuban territory of Northern Caucasia, the Kholm (Polish: Chełm) area in the Congress Kingdom of Poland, and Sub-Carpathian Ruthenia (the Carpatho-Ukraine) in Hungary. There are the following principal Ukrainian territories; in Russia, the Left Bank, the *Slobids'ka*, the Southern, and the Right Bank Ukraine; in Austria, Galicia and Bukovina. Since Ukrainian history is so often approached from a centralistic Moscow–St. Petersburg perspective, an attempt will be made to give special attention to those Ukrainian lands which do not fit into the framework of Russian history and which for this reason are often overlooked by Western scholars.

The Left Bank Ukraine (i.e., the Ukrainian territory east of the

[13] М. В. Нечкина, ed., *Очерки истории исторической науки в СССР*, II (Moscow, 1960), 307

Dnieper) corresponded with the area of the former autonomous Cossack State, the so-called hetmanate. Vestiges of the old institutions survived here until the reign of Nicholas I: the governor-generalship of Little Russia was dissolved in 1835, and the traditional Ukrainian civil law abolished in 1842; the self-government of the towns, based on the Magdeburg Law, had been suppressed in 1831. The Left Bank nobility, descendants of the Cossack officer class, repeatedly attempted to revive the autonomous order. The Napoleonic invasion of 1812 and the Polish insurrection of 1830 offered opportunities, and these autonomist strivings survived until the 1840's. However, in contrast with Poland and Hungary, historical legitimism was not to remain the platform of Ukrainian nationalism. The Left Bank nobility did not possess enough strength and solidarity to determine the course of the nation's renaissance. As a corporate entity the class loses importance after the middle of the century. Ukrainian nationalism took shape, ideologically and organizationally, under the auspices not of historical legitimism but of Populism. Nevertheless, the Left Bank provinces of Poltava and Chernyhiv (Chernigov) continued to be the geographical core of the Ukrainian movement. No other section of the Ukraine provided such a large proportion of nationalist leaders, and here the movement had succeeded in making considerable headway among the masses some years before the outbreak of World War I.

The Ukrainian cultural revival found its first important center further to the east, in the *Slobids'ka* Ukraine *(Slobozhanshchyna)*. In the seventeenth century this territory belonged to Muscovy, but was largely uninhabited. It was settled by refugees from the Dnieper Ukraine, who brought with them the Cossack system. The Cossack regiments of the *Slobozhanshchyna* remained under the direct control of the central government, and did not share in the turbulent political history of the hetmanate. But Kharkov, the capital of the *Slobozhanshchyna,* was to become in 1805 the seat of the first modern university in Ukrainian lands. This was achieved with contributions from the local gentry and burghers.[14] In the 1820's and 1830's, a group of writers and scholars connected with the Kharkov University laid the foundations of Ukrainian vernacular literature and of Ukrainian ethnographic and folkloristic studies. The motive was nonpolitical, but the enthusiasm for the "folk," inspired by the Romantic School of Kharkov, was to become a constituent element of modern Ukrainian nationalism, one of an importance hardly inferior to the traditions of political autonomy which originated in the Left Bank.

The Southern Ukraine (the steppes) consisted of the former territory of the Zaporozhian Sich and the possessions of the Crimean Tatars and Turkey. In the eighteenth century this was still largely an uninhabited

---

[14] The founders of the Kharkov University came from a circle influenced by the ideas and the example of the philosopher and spiritual reformer Hryhoryi Skovoroda (1722-94).

"no man's land," and until well into the nineteenth century the territory preserved the character of a frontier country. Besides Ukrainians,
the territory attracted numerous other settlers: Russians, Germans,
Greeks, Bulgarians. No other section of the Ukraine had so many
ethnic minorities as the South. The Ukrainians of the steppes and of
the Black Sea coast, most of whom had never known serfdom, displayed
a spirit of self-reliance and enterprise. It was no accident that during
the Civil War peasant anarchism, represented by Nestor Makhno,
found many supporters in the South. The South's participation in the
nationalist movement was relatively small; its contribution to the
making of the modern Ukraine was predominantly economic. Under
the Old Regime the Right Bank was economically, as well as politically,
connected with Poland, while the Left Bank and the *Slobids'ka* Ukraine
were turned toward Muscovy. The frontier on the Dnieper separated
the western and the eastern half of the Ukrainian ethnic area. This
changed with the opening of the Black Sea ports. Now the trade of both
the Right and the Left Banks became oriented toward the South. This
was a decisive step toward an economic integration of Ukrainian lands
and toward the formation of a unified Ukrainian national economy.
The South also became, from the 1880's on, the scene of a mighty development of mining and heavy industry in the Donets and Krivoi Rog
basins, which induced some writers to call that territory—with some
exaggeration—a "Ukrainian America." The South became the economic center of gravity of the modern Ukraine.

The historic individuality of the Right Bank (territory west of the
Dnieper) was determined by the fact that even after the Russian annexation of 1793 the Polish nobility remained the socially dominant element in the land, and to a large extent preserved this position until
1917. Indeed, the landowners as a class rather profited by the change
of the regime, since their domination over the peasantry was more
effectively backed by the police and army of an absolute monarchy than
by the inefficient administration of the late Commonwealth. The magnates, masters of huge latifundia, adopted an attitude of loyalty toward
the empire. The middle and petty gentry, on the other hand, did not
abandon hopes for the restoration of the Polish State, stretching to its
historical frontier on the Dnieper. The two insurrections of 1830 and
1863, which originated in Congress Poland, spilled over to the Right
Bank Ukraine. The local Polish conspirators made attempts to win the
Ukrainian peasants to this cause, using the Ukrainian language in their
proclamations and promising that in the future reborn Poland the
Ukraine-Rus' would form an autonomous body. This agitation met no
favorable response. The memories of old Poland were hateful to the
Ukrainian masses, who had not forgotten the Cossack wars and to
whom the very word "Poland" was a symbol of oppression. The spokesmen of the young Ukrainian nationalist movement consistently rejected

Polish claims to the Right Bank, as this implied a partition of the Ukraine between Russia and Poland. This may be regarded as a striking example of the incompatibility of "historical" and "ethnic" nationalism. The inability of the Poles and the Ukrainians to compose their differences and to evolve a common policy toward Russia fatefully determined the further development of both nations.[15] In spite of this failure the Polish-Ukrainian entanglement in the Right Bank had some positive aspects from the point of view of the progress of the Ukraine toward nationhood. Polish influence in nearly half of the Ukrainian ethnic territory served as a counterbalance to Russian domination. Through the nineteenth century the western part of the Ukraine remained a zone of tension, where Russian and Polish forces competed for supremacy. In the long run, this strengthened Ukrainian self-awareness as a nation distinct from either Poland or Russia. The Polish nobility of the Right Bank consisted in a large measure of the Polonized descendants of the old Ukrainian aristocracy; and even the originally Polish families had, in the course of generations, become acclimatized to the Ukrainian environment and felt strong "territorial patriotism." For instance, Polish writers from that area used local motives and formed a "Ukrainian school" in Polish literature; some of them were bilingual and belonged as much to Ukrainian as to Polish literature. Polish-Ukrainian scholars made valuable contributions to the study of the country's history and ethnography. The Ukrainian community definitely rejected the program of a "Jagiellonian federation," dear to the hearts of the Polish-Ukrainian minority; still, certain concepts formulated by the publicists of the Right Bank had an impact on the growth of Ukrainian political ideologies.[16] Some members of the Polish minority in the Ukraine, "not wishing to be alien colonists in their native land" (to use an expression of one of them), crossed the borderline separating the two nationalities and identified themselves fully with the Ukrainian cause. They were few, but from their number came some of the outstanding leaders of modern Ukrainian nationalism. Being thoroughly Western in their cultural background, they led the Ukrainian movement away from the Russian connection.[17]

[15] The case of Finland might be used here as an illuminating contrast. The upper classes of Finland were Swedish. But they did not try to bring the country back, in the name of "historical rights," under the rule of Sweden. Rather they united their forces with those of the native Finnish majority for the common defense of the liberty of the homeland. This cooperation was to be eminently beneficial to both Finland and Sweden, and to the Swedish-Finnish minority as well.

[16] An example of this is the idea of a Polish-Ukrainian political writer, F. Duchiński, according to whom the Russians were not really a Slavic people, since they were of Ugro-Finnic stock, which had become linguistically Slavicized; this implied a deeper ethnic difference between the Russians and the Ukrainians than the close affinity of the two East Slavic languages would suggest. This conception, whatever its scholarly merits, enjoyed a considerable popularity in Ukrainian circles.

[17] Three men merit mention in this context: Volodymyr Antonovych (1834-1908), historian and archaeologist, the founder of the "Kievan historical school," the leader of the

In turning to the Ukrainian territories of the Habsburg Empire, we shall first mention Bukovina. This small land, acquired from Moldavia by Austria in 1774, had a diversified population. The Ukrainians predominated in the north, the Rumanians in the south; there were also numerous Germans and Jews and a sprinkling of Armenians and Gypsies. German served as a lingua franca among Bukovina's motley inhabitants. The easternmost university with German as a language of instruction was at Chernovtsy, the capital of Bukovina; the city itself seemed a cultural outpost of Vienna. Some local Ukrainian writers started their literary careers in German. On the eve of World War I the Ukrainians of Bukovina enjoyed more favorable conditions of national development than those of any other territory: they had achieved a share in the province's government proportionate to their numbers.

Perhaps the most striking feature in the rebirth of the Galician Ukraine was the unique role played by the Greek Catholic (Uniat) Church. "This is the only national church which is not a state church, the only one which, while a branch of the Church Universal, is, at the same time, entirely national. . . . Even unbelievers love the national church which they regard as a vehicle of incomparable efficacy in the political struggle."[18] The Eastern Rite drew a clear-cut demarcation line that separated its adherents from the Poles, and the allegiance to Rome was a bulwark against Russian influence.[19] At the beginning of the nationalistic movement, the clergy provided a ready-made leadership for the Ukrainian community. This was clearly displayed during the 1848 Revolution, when the Galician Ukrainians ("Ruthenians," in the terminology of that time), guided by their bishops and priests, made their political debut. Of utmost sociological importance was the fact that the Greek Catholic clergymen were married, and formed a quasi-hereditary class; in their style of living they resembled a lesser gentry.[20] In later times, toward the end of the century, this ecclesiastical hegemony was felt to be inadequate to the needs of a modern society, and was

---

secret organization *Hromada* and of the Ukrainian movement in Russia during the most difficult period of reaction in the 1880's and 1890's; Viacheslav Lypynsky (1882-1931), eminent historian, political philosopher, and conservative leader; and the Metropolitan Andrii Sheptytsky (1865-1944), for forty-four years the head of the Greek Catholic Church in Galicia and the outstanding Ukrainian ecclesiastical figure of the century.

[18] Stanislas Smolka, *Les Ruthènes et les problèmes religieux du monde russien* (Berne, 1917), pp. 225 and 228.

[19] The Uniat (Greek Catholic) Church had been suppressed in the Right Bank Ukraine by the Russian government in 1839. Tsarist Russia at all times showed an implacable hostility to Ukrainian Catholicism of the Eastern Rite, and this attitude has been inherited by Soviet Russia.

[20] In works of fiction dealing with the Anglican clerical milieu, for instance, in Oliver Goldsmith's *The Vicar of Wakefield*, one encounters an atmosphere strikingly similar to that which used to prevail in the patriarchal homes of the Galician priests. There was, however, one major difference: the clergymen of the Church of England were the social allies of the English aristocracy, while those of the Greek Catholic Church stood in a radical opposition to Galicia's Polish aristocracy.

increasingly resented; this led to a strong anticlerical, secularist trend. But the lay intelligentsia, who gradually assumed the leadership of the nationalist cause, were largely sons of clerical families. A handicap of the Ukrainian movement in Galicia was the poverty and economic backwardness of the land, and even more crippling was the circumstance that political power had rested, since the 1860's, in Polish hands. In a settlement comparable to the Austro-Hungarian Compromise, the Viennese government turned over the administration of Galicia to the Polish ruling class, sacrificing the interests of the Ukrainian nationality.[21] The Poles used their dominant position to block, by all possible means, the progress of the Ukrainian community. For instance, Polish resistance prevented the creation of a separate Ukrainian university, although at the University of Lviv (Lemberg) there were several Ukrainian chairs. Still, Austria was a constitutional state, and this enabled the Galician Ukrainians to apply civic self-help. In this they achieved signal successes. The country was covered with a dense and ever-expanding network of economic, educational, and gymnastic associations, branching out to every village. The peasant masses, who owed to this work not only an improvement of their living conditions, but also a new feeling of human dignity and civic pride, became deeply imbued with the nationalist spirit. The discipline and the militancy of the movement were hardened through a stubborn, protracted political warfare against the dominant Polish administration. Gradually, the balance of forces between the two communities began to shift. A turning point was the introduction of universal manhood suffrage by the Austrian electoral reform of 1907; a large Ukrainian representation appeared for the first time in the Vienna Parliament, and the central government was forced to adopt a new policy toward the Polish-Ukrainian dispute. Polish control over the Ukrainian majority in eastern Galicia could no longer be maintained, short of physical violence, and the reform of the province's constitution appeared to be only a question of time.[22] In contrast with the Russian Ukraine, where the nationalist movement, although advancing quickly, had not yet succeeded in encompassing the whole people, the Galician Ukrainians were already, before 1914, a fully crystallized national community.

---

21 The crownland "Kingdom of Galicia and Lodomeria" also included, besides the territory of the Old Rus' principality of Halych (from which its name was derived), an ethnically Polish area, west of the river San. In the Ukrainian, eastern part of Galicia there existed, as in the Right Bank Ukraine, a socially privileged Polish minority of landowners and town dwellers. In the province as a whole the numerical strength of the Polish and the Ukrainian groups was approximately equal, but the aristocratic character of the Austrian constitution and Vienna's policy favored the Polish element. From 1848, and to the last days of the monarchy, the Ukrainians strove for a partition of the province on ethnic lines, but in vain.

22 A new electoral law for the Galician Diet was adopted early in 1914, but the outbreak of the war prevented its implementation. The Ukrainians were to receive some 30 per cent of the seats in the Diet, and a share in the autonomous provincial administration. This

The fact that the nineteenth-century Ukraine lacked territorial integration was a sure sign that a Ukrainian nation, in the full meaning of the word, did not exist at that time. But there were many symptoms indicating that the historical trends of the various sections were converging.

All parts of the Ukraine (excepting the "marginal" lands) passed through the same stages of growth, which might be labeled the "Age of Nobility," the "Populist Age," and the "Modernist Age." No full presentation of this periodization scheme will be attempted here.[23] But one or two points might be stressed. During the first epoch, which lasted approximately to the middle of the century, the leadership of the society rested with the nobility of Cossack descent in the Left Bank and the *Slobids'ka* Ukraine; with the Polish-Ukrainian nobility in the Right Bank; and with the Greek Catholic clergy, who also formed a sort of a hereditary gentry, in Galicia. Populism was strongest in the Ukrainian lands east of the Dnieper, where it partly overlapped with Russian revolutionary Populism; but analogous currents existed also among the Polish-Ukrainian society of the Right Bank, in the shape of the "Peasant Lovers" *(khlopomany)* movement, and in Galicia, where its first wave was represented by the *narodovtsi* ("People's Nationalists") of the 1860's and 1870's, and the second by the Radicals of the 1880's and 1890's.

As time went on, cooperation among various Ukrainian lands increased steadily. The foundation of the first modern nationalist organization, the Cyril and Methodius Society, in 1846 was the result of an interpenetration of the autonomist tradition of the Left Bank with the *Slobids'ka* Ukraine's cultural revival. The integrating economic function of the South has been mentioned. By the turn of the century, the old sectional differences among the Ukrainian lands in the Russian Empire had either disappeared or lost most of their importance.

Differences remained between Galicia and the Dnieper (Russian) Ukraine as a whole, and they were deep enough to create considerable political friction during the Revolution. Nevertheless, the relations between the Dnieper Ukraine and Galicia offer eminent examples of interregional cooperation. Galicia was intellectually rather arid. The ideas which inspired the Ukrainian rebirth in Galicia came almost without exception from the Dnieper Ukraine. The work of outstanding leaders of East Ukrainian origin, such as M. Drahomanov and M. Hrushevsky, was closely associated with Galicia and had profound, durable impact there. On the other hand, after the ukase of 1876,

still fell short of what the Ukrainians demanded on the basis of their numerical strength, but the Polish monopoly of power was at last broken.

[23] The writer has tried to do this in the article "The Intellectual Origins of Modern Ukraine," *Annals of the Ukrainian Academy of Arts and Sciences in the U.S.*, Vol. VI (1958), No. 3-4.

which suppressed all overt Ukrainian activities in the Russian Empire, Galicia became the sanctuary of the entire Ukrainian nationalist movement. Works of East Ukrainian writers were published in Galicia and smuggled into the Russian Ukraine. Tangible nationalist achievements in Galicia served as an encouragement and model to Ukrainian patriots under Russian rule. Galician Ukrainians, while fighting for an equality of rights with the Poles, were thinking not only of themselves: they believed that their homeland was destined to become the "Piedmont" of a future independent Ukraine.

One final comment. No issue facing the Ukrainian people in the nineteenth century was more portentous than the dilemma of choosing between assimilation in an All-Russian nation or assertion of separate national individuality. The far-reaching Russification of the Ukraine was an obvious fact, and it could not be explained entirely by the repressive measures of the tsarist government. Russia radiated the tremendous prestige of a great power and of a brilliant imperial civilization. Many Ukrainians, dazzled by this glory, were eager to participate in it. How humble and pitiful appeared what the Ukrainian patriots dared offer in opposition to the splendid Juggernaut! How preposterous was the disproportion of forces between those which stood at the disposal of a huge and despotic state and those of a handful of dreamers, armed with nothing but faith! Little wonder that the spokesmen of the Ukrainian movement instinctively adopted a protective coloring and tried to appear as harmless as possible. They often presented their cause as a nonpolitical, cultural regionalism, comparable with the Provençal *Félibrige*. When formulating a political program, they did not go beyond the demand of a federalistic reorganization of the Russian Empire, which, after all, might have been acceptable to some Russians. Ukrainian patriots were, certainly, sincere in these protestations of political innocence. But the tsarist administration saw the situation in a different light: firmly convinced that the rebirth of the Ukraine presented a deadly threat to the future of Russia as a great power in Europe, they waged a war of annihilation against even the most innocuous expressions of Ukrainian nationalism, while at the same time offering to "loyal Little Russians" tempting opportunities of career, recognition, and material rewards. The spell of Russia reached those Ukrainians living outside the frontiers of the empire. In Galicia there existed, in the second half of the nineteenth century, a pro-Russian current. The Galician Russophiles (called "Muscophiles" by contemporaries) favored the adoption of Russian as the language of literature.[24] At one time the majority of the land's intelligentsia seemed to lean to

[24] The Russophile movement emerged, in the 1860's, as a reaction to the hegemony which the Poles had achieved in the province. It was also fed by conservative sentiments which saw a special value in the traits of the cultural heritage, common to all Eastern Slavs: the Slavonic liturgy, Cyrillic script, Julian calendar, and the traditional name of Rus', which could be easily identified with Russia.

the Russophile side. The contest between the Russophiles and the nationalists dealt with apparently trivial questions of language, grammar, and orthography, but in truth the entire future of the Ukrainian cause hinged on the outcome. Galicia was the proving ground, where the partisans of the national abdication and of the national self-assertion measured their strength. The issue was of course relevant to the whole Ukrainian people, but only outside Russia could the contest be waged overtly, and by means of persuasion, without the tsarist police officer appearing on the scene. To both Galician currents came aid from beyond the frontier: the Russophiles received subsidies from St. Petersburg, while the nationalists had the moral support of the Dnieper Ukraine. In a slow, tenacious effort the Russophile group was pushed back, gradually reduced to an impotent faction, and at last completely absorbed by the growing nationalist movement. This was a turning point in the history of Russo-Ukrainian relations, and the effects were soon felt also in the Dnieper Ukraine. The trend toward Russification was reversed. By 1917 the entire Ukraine was swept by the torrent of a national revolution.

The Awakening of the Ukraine

ARTHUR E. ADAMS

For one who has too often clashed with Ukrainian nationalist scholars over the question of the role of the Ukraine in modern history, Professor Rudnytsky's study is both refreshing and encouraging. I am sincerely grateful for his objective analysis of a subject so fraught with nationalist passions that rational discussion is frequently impossible.

Above all, Professor Rudnytsky must be applauded for his courageous assessment of the insignificance of the Ukraine as a political entity prior to 1917. By emphasizing the discontinuity of its political history, its lack of territorial integration, the conditions which made overt political activity impossible before 1905 (except for Galicia), he has performed a valuable service, for this clears the air of a certain amount of nationalistic dross that has long hampered effective investigation in this area. As he puts it: "The fact that the nineteenth-century Ukraine lacked territorial integration was a sure sign that a Ukrainian nation, in the full meaning of the word, did not exist at the time." I am in complete agreement with this conclusion and consider it the necessary starting point of any rational effort to understand the role of the Ukraine in modern history.

I also agree with Professor Rudnytsky's identification of the "central problem of modern Ukrainian history" as that of "the emergence of a nation: the transformation of an ethnic-linguistic community into a self-conscious political and cultural community." Since there is no meaningful political history of the Ukraine as a whole prior to 1917, those who wish to examine prerevolutionary history, as Professor Rudnytsky points out, must study social-economic developments (or more specifically, the effects of the abolition of serfdom in 1861 and the rise of modern industrialization late in the nineteenth century) and the evolution of social thought (in particular, the development of the nationalist movement in the several regions of the Ukraine). Taken by itself, this definition of the area of fruitful study is somewhat narrow. The roots of Ukrainian thought and action run far deeper than the nineteenth century and far wider than the boundaries of the Ukraine, as the author duly recognizes in other passages of his paper.

A basic disagreement lies in our approaches to the revolutionary era following 1917. Essentially this concerns a question of periodization, which, to my mind, has great significance. Although Professor Rudnyt-

MR. ADAMS is professor of Russian history at Michigan State University.

sky says at one point that "the making of the nation was basically completed during the revolutionary years 1917-20," he clearly treats 1917
as the cut-off date, the climax of the national awakening. It seems
obvious to me that the more active period of the "raising of a 'natural,'
ethnic community to a politically conscious nationhood" only began in
1917. The following years, 1918-20, completed the process and were
indeed the most crucial in the whole history of the Ukrainian national
movement.

Professor Rudnytsky also attributes greater significance to the nationalist movement as a factor in bringing the Ukraine to an awareness of
itself as a nation than I believe it actually deserves. While it was undoubtedly important, I do not agree that it was the magnetic center
toward which all other forces in the Ukraine "pointed in the same
direction" were pulled, "as if drawn by an irresistible attraction," until
they "merged with it." Certainly the nationalist movement had little
influence on the great majority of people living in the Ukrainian lands
during the nineteenth century and the first sixteen years of the twentieth. Professor Rudnytsky appears to be of two minds on this topic.
"It is clear," he says at one point, "that until the eve of the 1917 Revolution, Ukrainian nationalism retained the character of a minority
movement. (This refers to the Russian Ukraine only; the situation was
different in Austrian Galicia.) The peasant masses were, until 1905,
little touched by the nationalist movement." They were "politically
amorphous." This is correct. Equally correct is his statement that the
upper classes of the Ukraine "were mostly Russified and, except for
those engaged in the Ukrainian movement, regarded themselves as belonging to the Russian nation." I would emphasize that the main cities
and the growing class of urban workers also considered themselves to be
Russian. Despite his acknowledgment of these facts and of the territorial disunity of the Ukrainian lands, Professor Rudnytsky believes
that the nationalist movement "erupted, in 1917, as a nascent nation of
over thirty million." And in the last line of his article, he concludes:
"By 1917 the entire Ukraine was swept by the torrent of a national
revolution."

It is my belief that while Ukrainian nationalist groups did help to
bring about a national awakening, the nationalist movement itself was
but one component of a complex process involving other forces, events,
and ideas of equal, or perhaps greater, significance. Moreover, I would
contend that the awakening itself began on a limited scale in 1917 and
became an almost universal phenomenon only in the next two years.
The following examination of developments during and after 1917
indicates the nature and operation of several of the above-mentioned
"other forces, events, and ideas" and demonstrates the limited role of
the national movement.

With the collapse of imperial power in St. Petersburg and the establishment of a provisional government in Russia's capital, a tiny and isolated group of nationalist intellectuals proclaimed the Rada (council) Government at Kiev. This organization thereafter spent some eight difficult months bickering with St. Petersburg for limited Ukrainian autonomy within a federation of Russian states. While the Rada was a daring and noble experiment, it neither inflamed the imaginations nor captured the loyalties of the people of the Ukraine. Nor was it vigorous enough to introduce an effective central and provincial administrative system. When the Bolsheviks came to power at St. Petersburg in November, the Rada was too weak to halt the Red Guard units sent to remove it. To secure their government against the Bolsheviks' incursion, Rada representatives signed a treaty with Germany early in 1918, and soon thereafter, at the Rada's invitation, German military forces occupied the Ukraine. This sealed the Rada's doom, for the occupation authorities demanded great mountains of food supplies for the German homeland. Unable to fulfill its procurement quotas, the Rada in April lost its power to Hetman Paul Skoropadsky, a puppet of the Germans, who devised harsh and effective measures for separating the Ukraine's peasants from their produce.

If anything served to arouse in the Ukrainian people a genuine awareness that they represented a nation, it was the German occupation and Skoropadsky's officious regime. The "nationalism" that flared up in the Ukraine in the summer of 1918 had little in common with the literary nationalism of the intellectuals. Angry peasant *haidamaky* attacked Germans with age-old partisan methods, fired by hatred of the "foreign robbers" and the hetmanate. This was a nationalism of xenophobia, of local patriotism, of men desperate for farm lands they considered their own, and of families forced to fight to stay alive in the face of enemy depredations. In mid-1918 this movement was chaotic, disunited, led by many centers and parties, both Ukrainian and Russian. It is at least arguable that emotions—hatred of the unbearable tyranny of foreigners and a lust for land—not the influence of nationalist intellectuals and their ideas, were the predominant motivating factors. I should emphasize here that it is not my intention falsely to minimize the role of the nationalist movement. Members of the village intelligentsia who were dedicated to the national movement often led local partisan bands and zealously propagated the nationalists' ideas and ideals; yet, it must be remembered, other groups found themselves under such widely diversified leaders as ignorant peasants, reactionary officers, ex-soldiers, Jew haters, and representatives of the Russian Menshevik, Bolshevik, and Social Revolutionary parties.

In the latter months of 1918 the process of "raising a 'natural,' ethnic community to a politically conscious nationhood" through internecine strife continued. After the German war effort collapsed in early November, Skoropadsky wavered toward federation with Bolshevik Russia. The Germans permitted Volodymyr Vynnychenko's Ukrainian National Union to launch an insurrection which established the Directory, piloted by Vynnychenko and Symon Petliura, as the executive organ of a new Ukrainian republic. Space does not permit extensive description of this government, nor does the full story of its brief tenure need recounting here. The most pertinent facts for the present discussion are these: In mid-November Petliura summoned "all Ukrainian soldiers and Cossacks to fight for the independence of the Ukraine against the traitor, the former tsarist servant, General Skoropadsky," and his appeal was enthusiastically answered by thousands of peasants and Cossacks. Within weeks he possessed an army of over 100,000 men, led by Cossack atamany, peasant rebels, Skoropadsky's former officers, and disciplined nationalists from Galicia.

This fervent taking up of arms appears to have been a magnificent display of a people uniting behind a government it recognized as its legitimate national center. The angry men who flocked to Petliura's colors perceived in the Directory's first Universals their own objectives: land, vengeance upon the big landowners who had been protected by Skoropadsky, and a chance to shoot at the hated Germans. But, tragically, the nationalist leaders failed to implement their promises, and the Ukrainian people separated from the Directory almost at once.

Within the space of the first month of 1919, Petliura's great armies dwindled until barely 20,000 men remained. A convergence of many factors hastened this nationalist disaster. Cruel, reactionary, and uncontrollable officers like Ataman Peter Balbachan, who commanded the Left Bank for Petliura, quickly disillusioned the peasant-soldiers. Military pressures from the Bolsheviks and internal political dissent so harassed and paralyzed the republic's embryo government that it could neither gather strength nor make bold decisions. With the Germans fleeing and the Directory's promises going sour, Petliura's "nationalist" squadrons simply melted away. Many, hearkening to the Communists' siren song of equality, self-government, and radical social reform, went over to the Bolsheviks. Others, mainly bold Cossack leaders or peasants like Nestor Makhno, taking advantage of the Directory's weakness and the Bolsheviks' chaos, harassed German stragglers and local authorities. By the time the Bolshevik army reached Kiev in the first days of February, its ranks largely composed of deserters from Petliura, the Directory was helpless. It withdrew westward.

Petliura was able to keep some forces moving in the western Ukraine and even to occupy Kiev again for a day in August, 1919, after the White General, Anton Denikin, had driven out the Bolsheviks. But the cause of the nationalist intellectuals was lost in February, 1919, primarily because they had failed to satisfy the demands of the Ukrainian people for national leadership and radical social reform. Lest this be taken as a condemnation of the nationalists, it should be noted that the Directory was born in a period of chaos. It held Kiev only six weeks, during which time it suffered Bolshevik invasion as well as Allied intervention. It was unable to secure strong allies, and the complicated political and social problems it faced defied rapid solution. The fact remains that the nationalist movement did not so strongly attract the unleashed social forces of the Ukraine that they merged with it. Rather, most of the people of the Ukraine, borrowing some ideas from the movement, passed on in search of objectives which chaos and conflict were making imperative.

An account of the transformation of the people and the lands of the Ukraine into a self-conscious nation cannot be halted with the departure of Vynnychenko and Petliura from Kiev. The process was to continue all through 1919. Just as German occupation and plundering and Skoropadsky's hateful land policies served to stimulate Ukrainian self-awareness, so did the coming of the Bolsheviks in the early weeks of 1919. And just as peasants, Cossacks, and townfolk had deserted the Directory when it failed to live up to their needs, so from March to August, 1919, they abandoned the Bolsheviks, repudiating the Communist autocracy and such institutions as the Cheka and the agricultural commune. Almost immediately after the Bolshevik, Vladimir Antonov-Ovseenko, and the Aleksandriia Cossack, Ataman Grigorev, had driven the French from Odessa, desertions and rebellions within the Red Army of the Ukraine rose to such heights that the Bolsheviks' strength was dangerously weakened. Soon after Grigorev's rebellion and Makhno's dismissal from the Red Army (May and June), General Denikin's White Army forces advanced through the Ukraine, driving the Bolsheviks before them, repelling some native groups and attracting others. One might almost picture the actions of the peoples of the Ukraine during this period as those of a blind but purposeful mass seeking a leader, following one, then another, but soon pushing on because no major political party would accept the popular goals. Certainly this process was neither conscious nor planned; yet the pattern is there.

The thrust and counterthrust of opposing armies continued into early 1920. By that time the Ukraine had become a nation in fact as well as in the minds of its people. The years of revolution and civil war had united the ideas of a wide variety of political and intellectual movements with the aroused xenophobic passions and patriotic pride of the masses. Among the most important components in the cauldron that brewed the Ukraine's awareness of itself as a nation were the peasants' desire for land and the urban workers' thirst for social justice and self-government. The final product, a widespread belief that the Ukraine was a unique political and cultural nation, was so powerful that the Bolsheviks themselves were compelled to come to terms with it.

In the process of national awakening described above, a number of important influences should be singled out for special emphasis. Of these the roles played by non-Ukrainian political parties deserve much more attention than they have been given in the past. The Bolshevik wing of the Social Democrats might be mentioned here, because the Bolsheviks' positive influence is so seldom acknowledged and because even the devil should be given his due. It is evident that many Bolsheviks who worked in the Ukraine during the years of revolution and civil war quickly recognized the Ukraine's need for special treatment. This appears to have occurred not so much because they were exposed to the Ukrainian nationalist ideology as because experience persuaded them that the Russian Communist Party's ideas and practices had to be adjusted to suit the Ukrainian environment if Bolshevism was to succeed. To mention only a few examples, there were men like Vladimir Zatonsky and Iurii Piatakov, who helped to establish the Communist Party of the Ukraine (KP[b]U), only halfheartedly supported by Lenin, and proceeded to struggle against Lenin's declared wishes for the right to make independent decisions. While these two lost their fight early, others carried it further. Even Leon Trotsky, working in the Ukraine in mid-1919, saw the sense of such an attitude; and the Old Bolshevik, G. Lapchinsky, after the victory of Denikin in late 1919, bravely declared the need for a reconstituted Ukrainian Communist party that would be independent of the Russian party.

Impressed by defeat and the exhortations of his lieutenants, Lenin, in December, 1919, and January, 1920, issued detailed instructions to Bolsheviks working in the Ukraine to encourage the use of the Ukrainian language and to make every effort to avoid offending the Ukrainian *amour-propre*. Obviously he introduced these changes, hoping they would ease the work of regaining power in the Ukraine; nevertheless, such decrees, along with the widely propagated principle of the right of every nation to self-determination, were instrumental in persuading many Ukrainians that they should control their own destinies.

Another contributing influence should be heavily underlined. Identifying certain social forces which were of special significance, Professor Rudnytsky includes "symbols and ideas derived from the Cossack tradition," which, he declares, "played an important role even as late as the 1917 Revolution." Once again I would agree with his thought, but would go further both in time and emphasis. In 1918 and 1919 men calling themselves Cossack atamany seemed to spring up everywhere. Cossack captains, crafty illiterate rascals, or cool and well-trained officers called out the local villagers, adopted the title "ataman of this or that," wrote stirring appeals for action based upon references to the traditions of the Zaporozhian Sich, and fell to fighting. Such men compounded homespun political philosophies of varying portions of Cossack lore, Social Democratic or Social Revolutionary ideas, anarchism, and so forth. Above all they saw themselves as Cossacks of the seventeenth century fighting for freedom. These chieftains ruled much of the countryside and led the military forces, personifying in word and deed the Cossack ideals. Because such leaders exercised direct and important influence upon men and events, the impact of the Cossack tradition upon the final stages of the development of Ukrainian political consciousness was immense.

Finally, the action of yet another social force demands special emphasis. This is the Ukrainian peasant. Professor Rudnytsky has mentioned the "self-reliance and enterprise" of the peasants of the southern steppes. During the revolutionary years, when the bars of effective civil and military authority were down, the peasant displayed all the courage and anarchic willfulness of the fabled hero Il'ia Muromets. The prideful intransigence of Nestor Makhno and his followers is but one symbol of this character. While Makhno himself gained his anarchist ideas in a Moscow prison, the uneducated steppe dwellers who fought for him were moved by their own elemental, anarchic love of liberty. In his heart and mind the Ukrainian peasant bore memories of the murderous, rampaging *haidamaky* who had been his ancestors; he held a grudging respect for the Cossack traditions of his neighbors; above all he was driven by a towering hatred of outsiders and tyrants and by the desire for land.

The bloody rebellions against Germans and their puppets, against Petliura and the Bolsheviks, and the brutal pogroms—all testify to the irrational fury of the peasants' demands. One is tempted to suggest that the nationalist intellectuals and Russian political leaders did not so much teach the peasant as flee before him. At least in part, the final years of the awakening of the Ukraine should be viewed as a history of a peasant *jacquerie* that crushed all lesser forces beneath its boots, until, at last, peasants and land were so exhausted that Bolshevism's patient workers were able to slip into power almost unchallenged.

It has been the destiny of the awakened nation to remain a "captive" of Moscow for over forty years.

The Ukraine and the Dialectics of Nation-Building

OMELJAN PRITSAK and JOHN S. RESHETAR, JR.

EAST OR WEST?

One of the merits of Professor Rudnytsky's article is his recognition of the need for particular methodological approaches to the study of the Ukrainian past. However, in his opinion the Ukraine is a typical East European nation in that its history has been "marked by a high degree of discontinuity" in contrast with such Western nations as England and France which "have enjoyed, in spite of some periods of revolutionary upheaval, a millennium of continuous growth." In addition, the Ukraine is supposedly a "nonhistorical" nation, by which Rudnytsky does not mean that it has lacked a historical past but only that it has suffered "discontinuity" as a result of having lost the "traditional representative class." Consequently, the Ukrainian national movement in the nineteenth century was not in the hands of the traditional gentry and was supposedly not characterized by historical legitimacy. The Ukrainian leading stratum had, according to Rudnytsky, to be "created anew" in order to direct the " 'natural,' ethnic community to a politically conscious nationhood."

In spite of their originality and attractiveness, these theoretical formulations of the author cannot be accepted without reservation. The loss of statehood as well as the unification of ethnographically homogeneous territory in a single state cannot be regarded as sufficiently characteristic to provide criteria for the division of Europe. Such "Western" states (in Rudnytsky's terminology) as Italy and Norway have also suffered decline or discontinuity at times. In employing the terms "East" and "West" with respect to Europe one cannot rely on geographical location or on the current political situation and include Poland, Hungary, or the Czech territories in "Eastern" Europe. Although Rudnytsky has defined what he means by the "East," we regard it as necessary to discuss this methodological problem in some detail, bearing in mind that the terms "East" and "West" are so specific and meaningful that it would be unwise to introduce new concepts even as working hypotheses.

In the late eleventh century two opposing cultural spheres emerged

MR. PRITSAK is professor of Far Eastern and Slavic languages and literature at the University of Washington. MR. RESHETAR is professor of political science at the University of Washington.

in Europe: the Western-Catholic-Roman and the Eastern-Orthodox-Byzantine. Only the former provided the basis for a culture character-ized by a degree of universality—that of Western Europe. A people converted to Catholicism became an equal member of a large family united by a common cultural language and an understanding of the need to learn from the works of the ancient Greeks and Romans. Each people had an opportunity to learn from the ancient model and to make its own contribution to the development of this common culture. Originally the leadership was exercised by the clergy, which was inter-ested in learning and was motivated by the idea of *ora et labora*; this brought the church closer to the people and raised their cultural level. The acceptance of Roman Law and the rise of autonomous cities (for example, the Magdeburg Law) created the basis for coexistence and the later emergence of the third estate in addition to the clergy and nobility. Concessions obtained by the nobility led ultimately to the development of the constitutional order. The wars of investiture, on the one hand, preserved the independence of the church from the state and, on the other hand, led to the churches' acquiring a national character. Hu-manism and the Reformation secularized culture and promoted the development of popular literary languages along with the progress in the exact sciences and geographical discoveries. These developments in their ultimate form came to constitute Western culture, which is based upon individual freedom.

Byzantium knew but one universality: the idea of a single ruler of the Rhomaioi and of all Christians—the Byzantine emperor. It viewed the world as divided into Rhomaioi and "barbarians." The Orthodox Church, being dependent upon secular authority, concerned itself with the salvation of individual souls; *ora et labora* was replaced by the anchorite and hermit. The monastic communities did not become centers of learning in the full sense. The Slavs who accepted Christian-ity from Byzantium never participated fully in the high Byzantine culture, for they were regarded as inferior and their cultural develop-ment was largely limited to the sphere of the monastic communities. For the Slavs there was prepared a translation of selected religious texts in the Slavic ("Church-Slavonic") language—a language not possessing a literary tradition and often not capable of conveying the subtleties of higher learning and secular culture.[1]

Although the classical Greek traditions persisted in Byzantium, the Slavs, especially the Eastern Slavs, derived little benefit from this fact for the reasons discussed above. As the Eastern Slavic languages devel-oped, Church Slavonic—the sole source of culture—became less and less comprehensible. The Reformation—as a reaction—was possible only in a Catholic milieu; conditions in the Orthodox world were not condu-

[1] For example, see the viewpoint of G. P. Fedotov as described by Georges Florovsky in "The Problem of Old Russian Culture," *Slavic Review,* XXI (March, 1962), 9.

cive to the secularization of culture. Thus it is not surprising that Marxism remained a body of social and political theory in the West, while in Russian Leninism it assumed the form of a quasi religion.

Does the Ukraine belong to the East or the West? At the time of the emergence of Western culture, between the thirteenth and seventeenth centuries, the Ukraine, though of the Orthodox faith,[2] constituted a component of states of the West European type. The Galician-Volhynian King Danylo sought a union of the two churches and received his crown from a papal legate in 1253. Earlier, in 1245, the Kiev metropolitan, Peter Akerovych, went to Lyons and concluded a Union with the Church of Rome. The Galician-Volhynian state employed Latin in its official documents. With the demise of the dynasty (1340) part of the Ukrainian lands came under the Hungarian state and later under the Polish state; part joined the Lithuanian state, which originally (1386) entered into a real union with Poland, which later (1569) became a personal union.

The various cultural achievements of the West did reach the Ukraine, though with some delay or without the possibility of full development. Humanism, the Reformation, and the Counter Reformation all left their mark in the Ukraine. Thus the Reformationist Mykhailo Vasylevych (1556-61) and the Unitarians Symeon Budny (1562) and Vasyl Tiapynsky translated parts of the Scriptures into the living Ukrainian language of their time.[3] That Church Slavonic was not replaced by the Ukrainian language for another two centuries was due in no small part to the authority of the apologist for Orthodoxy, the anchorite from Athos, Ivan Vyshensky.[4] It is well known that the

[2] In this context mention should be made of the cult of St. Clement, Pope of Rome, in Kiev. He was the patron of the Kiev Cathedral, the Tithe Church of the Virgin, built by Volodymyr the Great. In his honor there was compiled a book of miracles, *Чудо* (two known versions date from the twelfth century). Михайло Грушевський, *Історія українсь-кої літератури*, III (Kiev and Lviv, 1923), 105-9. When in 1147, as a result of political tension between Kiev and Byzantium, the question arose as to how to obtain a new metropolitan, the Bishop of Chernyhiv, Onufrii, offered an interesting solution. He proved that just as the patriarch of Constantinople in consecration employs the sacred relic of the hand of St. John, so in Kiev a metropolitan could be consecrated with the reliquary of Pope Clement. It is significant that when this method was approved by all six bishops of Southern Rus' (the present Ukrainian territory) the Kiev Orthodox Metropolitan Klym Smoliatych («книжникъ и философъ, так якоже в Руськой земли не бяшетъ»—Hypatian Chronicle, s.a. 1147) was consecrated by means of the pope's reliquary. The bishops of Northern Rus', under the leadership of Nifont (who effected the Novgorod separatism discussed elsewhere) refused to recognize the validity of this method.

[3] Михайло Грушевський, *Культурно-національний рух на Україні в XVI-XVII віці* (2nd ed.; n.p., 1919), pp. 46-57. Also see Грушевський, *Історія української літератури*, V (Kiev, 1926), Part I, and the preface by D. Čiževsky in the *Annals of the Ukrainian Academy of Arts and Sciences in the U.S.*, III, No. 1 (1953), 485-87.

[4] Indicative of Vyshensky's quaint and intolerant attitude is the following statement (1599-1600): «Евангелиа и Апостола в церкви на литургии простым языком не выворочайте. По литургии ж для зрозуменя людского попросту толкуйте и выкладайте. Книги церковные всѣ и уставы словенским языком друкуйте. Скажую бо вам тайну великую: як диавол толикую зависть имает на словенский язык, же ледве жив от гнѣва; рад бы его до щеты погубил и всю борбу свою на тое двигнул, да его обмерзит и во огиду и ненавист

Kiev metropolitan, Peter Mohyla (1596-1647), introduced the study of Latin in the College founded by him as a means of combating the Jesuit Counter Reformation. The distinctive Ukrainian baroque in architecture, literature, and the arts also testifies to a unity with the West.[5]

The tragedy of the Ukrainians is that since the fifteenth century their territory has been a "borderland" between East and West, incapable of committing itself entirely to either side and denied a free choice because it has been coveted by both.[6] Yet, if the Ukrainian nation exists to this day, it is not only because of the linguistic differences between Russian and Ukrainian but mainly because of a distinctive cultural tradition.

"Nonhistorical" or "Incomplete" Nationhood?

Rudnytsky's use of the term "nonhistorical" with reference to the Ukrainian nation in the nineteenth century is not entirely accurate. The Ukrainian national rebirth began in the latter part of the eighteenth century among the Left Bank gentry descended from the officer class of the former hetmanate. It is from this milieu that the *Istoriia Rusov* emerged to demonstrate that the rupture in historical continuity was far from complete. The Ukrainian national movement in the nineteenth century, instead of being "nonhistorical," can be said to have been "incomplete"[7] in terms of the hetmanate state form following the fall of Mazepa (1709).

The Ukrainian Cossacks, both the Zaporozhian Host and the "town Cossacks," acquired significance in the second half of the sixteenth century. Originally this was a social or corporate movement without political or religious overtones. The Host acquired a national character during the second decade of the seventeenth century when it intervened, under the leadership of Hetman Peter Sahaidachny (1616-22), in the struggle of the Orthodox Rus' against Catholicism and Church Union in the Polish state. Their crowning achievement in this sphere was the re-establishment in 1620 of the Ukrainian Orthodox ecclesiastical jurisdiction, under the Host's military protection, in the persons of

---

приведет.» Иван Вишенский, *Сочинения* (Moscow and Leningrad, 1955), p. 23. Significantly, the language used by Vyshensky was far from being Church Slavonic; it was rather the Ukrainian language of that time. As a product of Humanism and the Reformation, philological studies emerged in the Ukraine of the late sixteenth century. Two of the most important works should be mentioned here: The *Slavenorosskii* (Church Slavonic–Ukrainian) dictionary by Pamvo Berynda (Kiev, 1627) and the first grammar ever written of the Church Slavonic language, by Meletius Smotrytsky (Eviu, 1619).

[5] Дмитро Чижевський, *Історія української літератури: Від початків до доби реалізму* (New York, 1956) provides a discussion of the baroque in Ukrainian literature, pp. 248-317. A separate province of Ukrainian literature from the sixteenth to the eighteenth century consists of that written in Latin. For a brief characterization of this literature see *ibid.,* pp. 318-20.

[6] This problem is discussed at length in Eduard Winter, *Byzanz und Rom im Kampf um die Ukraine, 955-1939* (Leipzig, 1942).

[7] The definition of "incomplete" nationhood as applied to eighteenth-century literature is discussed in Чижевський, *op. cit.,* pp. 322-23.

a metropolitan and five bishops consecrated by Patriarch Theophanes of Jerusalem.[8]

Ecclesiastical circles soon appreciated the worth of this new ally and began to see in the Host not only defenders of the Orthodox Church but also the direct descendants of the Princely Rus'. However, when the Orthodox hierarchy, under the leadership of Metropolitan Job Boretsky (1620-31), began to develop a plan for an alliance of Orthodox rulers ostensibly directed against the Ottoman Empire but in fact against Poland, they relied not on the strength of the Zaporozhian Host but on the more effective power of an Orthodox ruler—the Muscovite Orthodox tsar. However, the Kiev clergy viewed the tsar from a distance in highly idealized terms.

The Orthodox College established in Kiev in 1632 by Metropolitan Peter Mohyla (later known as the Mohyla-Mazepa Academy) played an important role in raising the educational level, but its membership, with certain exceptions, regarded the issue of Ukrainian statehood with equanimity, once serious political difficulties arose. Like the socialists in the nineteenth century, the Ukrainian elite of the Orthodox Church in the seventeenth and eighteenth centuries were interested not in local but in "universal" problems. In order to attract the support of the most powerful Orthodox ruler, the Muscovite tsar, the Kievan Orthodox Church elite manufactured—or at least gave their approval to[9]—the historic conception of the "transfer" of the princely seats: Kiev–Vladimir-on-the-Kliazma–Muscovy. This concept was most precisely formulated in the *Synopsis*, which was first published in 1670 or 1674 and was reissued in approximately thirty editions and used as a history textbook until the mid-nineteenth century. In this first textbook on East European history no mention was made of the Zaporozhian Host, although the author or authors of the *Synopsis* had lived under the protection of the Cossack State. It was only in 1904, 230 years later, that the Kiev historian Mykhailo Hrushevsky demonstrated the unscholarly and harmful effect which this artificial scheme of lineage had upon both Russian and Ukrainian historiography.[10]

---

[8] After the annexation of Kiev by Lithuania the Grand Prince Olgerd re-established the Kiev metropolitanate in ca. 1354. However, until 1448 the Moscow and Kiev metropolitanates were often occupied by the same person, who was usually of Greek origin. From the Union of Brest (1596) until 1620 the Kiev metropolitanate was Uniat.

[9] Two recent studies on the *Synopsis* are: И. П. Еремин, «К истории общественной мысли на Украине второй половины XVII в.,» *Труды Отдела древнерусской литературы*, X (Moscow and Leningrad, 1954), 212-22, and С. Л. Пештич, «'Синопсис' как историческое произведение,» *ibid.*, XV (Moscow and Leningrad, 1958), 284-98. According to data cited by Peshtich the 1674 edition was not the original. There are indications that two other editions, of 1670 and 1672, existed, which unfortunately have not been investigated. Peshtich also demonstrated that the *Synopsis*, before being printed in Kiev, was subjected to Muscovite censorship. Not having the text of the original uncensored version, we are not in a position to determine what additions or deletions in the text resulted from censorship.

[10] See Hrushevsky, "The Traditional Scheme of 'Russian' History...," *Annals of the Ukrainian Academy of Arts and Sciences in the U.S.*, II, No. 4 (1952), 355-64.

Despite its generally apolitical attitude, the Kiev clergy actively collaborated with the revolution led by Hetman Bohdan Khmelnytsky which began in 1648. Its success confronted the hetman with numerous problems. Beginning as a Zaporozhian military dictatorship, the enlarged new state required a broader form of government. At this time the representatives of the old elite of Rus' and Lithuania-Rus', the magnates and gentry (both Orthodox and Catholic), came in great numbers to serve the new state.[11] Thus emerged the concept of a tradition-based complete state—of the type of a hereditary Rus' principality—with religious tolerance and cooperation between social classes. The nature of this state—unique for its time—was most fully reflected in the Swedish-Ukrainian treaty of 1657 and in related documents.[12]

However, Khmelnytsky was unable to consummate this effort. During the limited tenure of his rule (1648-57) numerous wars on various fronts compelled the hetman to conclude treaties with his neighbors. One of these treaties, that with Muscovy concluded at Pereiaslav in 1654, proved to be a heavy burden impeding the development of the Cossack State. The Muscovite tsar Alexei Mikhailovich, finding it easier to extend his domain by means of direct negotiations with Poland than by waging war, quickly forgot about the terms of the Pereiaslav Treaty and hastened to conclude a profitable settlement at Vilna (1656), ignoring the Ukrainians and their interests. This occurred because the tsar chose to interpret the quasi-protectorate relationship between himself and Khmelnytsky (stipulated in the text of the Pereiaslav Treaty) as an act of submission by the hetman (see note 34).

After Khmelnytsky's death, Muscovy succeeded in inflaming class and religious differences within the Hetman State and, employing the so-called *chern'* and part of the Orthodox clergy, provoked a civil conflict—the so-called Ruina (Ruin) between 1663 and 1674. As a result, the aristocracy and gentry, the bearers of the concept of the complete state, were physically liquidated. The re-emergence of a gentry-officer class under Hetman Ivan Samoilovych (1672-87) led to the renewal of the idea of a Rus' principality during the hetmanate of Ivan Mazepa (1687-1709) and to his treaty with Charles XII of Sweden. The defeat at Poltava in 1709 destroyed forever the idea of a Rus' principality.[13] The repressive measures of Peter I led to the decline of all independent political thought. There emerged the notion of a *modus vivendi* in

[11] See W. Lipiński, *Z dziejów Ukrainy* (Kiev, 1912) and also Вячеслав Липинський, *Україна на переломі, 1657-1659* (Vienna, 1920).

[12] *Архивъ Юго-Западной Россіи*, Part III, Vol. VI (Kiev, 1908), 332-37; Липинський, *op. cit.*, pp. 48-49; 282, n. 185; and Михайло Грушевський, *Історія України-Руси*, IX (Kiev, 1931), Part II, pp. 1392-97; X (Kiev, 1937), 64-69.

[13] On Ukrainian political thought during the Cossack State see Олександер Оглоблін, «До історії української політичної думки на початку XVIII віку,» *Записки історично-філологічного відділу У.А.Н.*, XIX (1928), 231-41.

which an incomplete "Little Russian" state would exist as an autonomous part of the Russian Empire.

The plight of the Ukraine lay not so much in the fact of the destruction of the Hetmanate State and the Zaporozhian order (historical discontinuity) as in the fact that after 1709 the use of harsh and repressive measures by Peter I and the emergence of Russian imperialist centralism caused the concept of a *complete* Ukrainian Cossack State to be replaced by a Cossack class autonomy which could be defined as an *incomplete* state.   Under these circumstances the granting to the Ukrainian Cossack officer class of rights equal to those of the "All-Russian nobility" in 1835 was a way of satisfying, to a certain degree, the needs of this "incomplete" nation.

The ideas of romanticism, democracy, and socialism reached the Ukraine and influenced the gentry youth. However, not having inherited from their parents the national and political ideas of a "complete nation," they limited their efforts to enlightening the local peasants or were attracted to democratic or socialist movements on the imperial level. The so-called Ukrainophiles and *khlopomany* are of particular interest. They viewed the nationality question in class terms, identifying their gentry status with the Russian (or Polish) nation; by associating themselves with the serfs they were severing their old ties as identified in terms of class and nation. However, their ideal was not nationalization of the gentry but their own individual "democratization."[14] Despite their dedication and their love for the Ukrainian people, the "Ukrainophiles" perpetuated the concept of the "incomplete" Ukrainian nation. During the second half of the nineteenth century the Ukrainian populist movement was taken over from the gentry by persons from other classes, the intellectuals or so-called "conscious Ukrainians." However, this group unconsciously followed in the footsteps of the gentry and also preserved the "incomplete" nation. The socialist element devoted its energies to opposing the Ukrainization of the nobility and the emerging bourgeoisie and in this way hindered the process of advancing the Ukrainian nation to a state of "completeness."

SEPARATISM

The term "separatism" in the sense of a cultural-political secession of a part of the territory of ancient Rus' is frequently associated by publicists and even by specialists in East European history with the Ukrainian movement of the nineteenth century. In actual fact separatism in Eastern Europe commenced much earlier—and in the north.

Great Novgorod and Vladimir-on-the-Kliazma departed from the Kievan model to such a degree that they can be said to have set a sep-

[14] Typical of this approach is В. Антонович, «Моя исповѣдь,» in *Основа*, Vol. I, 1862, pp. 83-96. An interesting characterization and criticism of the so-called "conscious Ukrainians" is provided by Вячеслав Липинський, *Листи до братів-хліборобів* (Vienna, ca. 1926), pp. 1-62.

arate course for themselves early in the twelfth century. Novgorod became wealthy as a result of its intermediary role in east-west trade and soon found a common language with the other centers of Baltic commerce. The German Hansa, which was emerging at this time, was closer to Novgorod than was "continental" Kiev after the decline of the trade route "from the Varangians to the Greeks." In 1136 Novgorod— under the ideological leadership of Bishop Nifont (1130-56)—dethroned Prince Vsevolod Mstislavich, sent from Kiev, and laid the groundwork for the unique (in Eastern Europe) republican system of "Great Lord Novgorod" and of "Saint Sophia." Authority now reposed in the representatives of the commercial aristocracy, in the *veche*. The *veche* elected the bishop *(vladyka)*, who, as head of the "Council of Lords," became the *de facto* head of the state; it also elected the executive in the persons of the mayor *(posadnik)*, the head of the town militia *(tysiatsky)*, and the prince, who was now in fact only a military commander. Great Novgorod demonstrated its independence by establishing its own *svod* or revised collection of chronicles, the *Sofiiskii vremennik*. The other attribute of independence in the Rus' of that time—a separate metropolitanate—was not acquired, but the *vladyka* did obtain the title of Archbishop in 1165.[15]

As a result of being located very advantageously on trade routes far removed from the chronic danger presented by Turkic nomads, the colonial part of ancient Rus'—the Vladimir-Suzdal territory—flourished during the second half of the eleventh and first half of the twelfth century. The cities and population grew, and the conditions of a colonial way of life were conducive to the strengthening of princely authority. In place of the Kievan system of a *veche* and a class of boyars, there arose a system of rule based upon a military service class derived from various lands and classes and loyal to the prince.

It was Andrei Bogoliubsky (1157-74) who effected the separatism of the Vladimir-Suzdal territories. Andrei's father, Iurii Monomakhovich, still recognized the primacy of Kiev in Rus'; and when, after various attempts in 1149 and 1150, he finally obtained the throne of Kiev in 1155, Andrei as his son obtained the Kievan Vyshhorod in accordance with the traditional system. However, Andrei fled from Vyshhorod to the North that same year, without his father's knowledge, in order to take over the Vladimir-Suzdal territories within two years. After the death of the father, Andrei refused to reign in Kiev. This demonstrative act was the first manifestation of a reappraisal of values in Kievan Rus'[16] and was soon to be reinforced by another act. The Polovetsian

15 See Д. С. Лихачев, «'Софийский Временник' и новгородский политический переворот 1136 года,» *Исторические записки*, XXV (1948), 240-65. Also see *Очерки истории СССР, IX-XIII вв.* (Moscow, 1953), pp. 334-57.
16 Andrei's refusal to accept the Kiev throne is regarded by the Russian historian S. Soloviev as a "sobytie povorotnoe." С. М. Соловьев, *История России с древнейших времен* (Moscow, 1959), I, 529-34.

hatred for Kiev and its cultural worth prompted Andrei-Kitai (Andrei Bogoliubsky's mother was a Polovetsian, and in addition to his Christian name of Andrei he had the Polovetsian name of Kitai)[17] to plunder and ruin Kiev in 1169, employing these barbarous means to cause this older center to lose its attraction. *Thus, the Vladimir-Muscovy period of East European history began not with the acceptance of the Kiev tradition but with its negation and destruction.* In order to separate his territories from Kiev Andrei attempted to obtain from Byzantium approval for the establishment of a separate metropolitanate in Vladimir, but these efforts met with failure.

However, the other attribute of sovereignty—a separate *svod* of chronicles—was achieved by Andrei's successor, Vsevolod (1176-1212) in 1177. In this revised chronicle, preserved in the Laurentian Chronicle of 1377, the Kievan tradition is accepted only up to the time of Vladimir Monomakh (1113), that is, up to this formative period of the Vladimir-Suzdal dynasty.[18] The northern chronicles came to reflect a declining interest in southern affairs, and after the ruination of Kiev by the Tatars in 1240 the fate of the southern Rus', especially the Galician-Volhynian state, receives no mention. This silence was all the more remarkable in view of the fact that the northern Rus' and southern Rus' remained within the same ecclesiastical jurisdiction, that of the metropolitan of "Kiev and all Rus' " and, in addition, were subordinated to the same political order—that of the Golden Horde, which had a highly developed postal system.

Thus, it was not Mongol domination which separated the northern Rus' from the southern Rus' but rather the lack of any sense of community and the absence of mutual attraction and interest. The attempt to lay claim to the Kiev tradition manifested itself in Muscovy only in modern times under the influence of the imperialist political design.

In contrast, it should be noted that the attitude in the southern Rus' toward Kiev and its tradition was very different. When Roman of Volhynia acquired Galicia in 1199 he became the most powerful ruler in southern Rus', and it is not without reason that the contemporary chronicler termed him the "autocrat of all Rus'." However, neither Roman nor his successors inflicted ruination upon Kiev. Roman accepted the entire Kiev tradition. The Hypatian Chronicle, which transmitted the Galician-Volhynian *svody* (the last of which was edited in 1289), preserved in its entirety the Kiev *svod* of the twelfth century (to 1198).

The entire question of the relations between the northern and south-

[17] Andrei «иже прежде крещенія нарицашеся Китай, а потомъ отъ великіе ревности к вседушныя любве своея к Богу, прозванъ бысть Боголюбскій.» *Синопсис* (5th ed.; St Petersburg, 1762), p. 107. Cf. Д. С. Лихачев, *Повесть временныхъ лет* (Moscow and Leningrad, 1955), II, 432: "Syn polovchanki Andrei Fogoliubskii imel polovetskoe imia Kitai."
[18] М. Д. Приселков, *История русского летописания XI-XV вв.* (Leningrad, 1940), pp 64-78.

ern Rus' might be better understood in terms of a geographic analogy and a historical model. Let us assume for a moment that the southern mother Rus' territory (the present Ukrainian territory) was divided from the northern colonial territory of Rus' (the present Russian territory) by a sea in the same way that the mother country England was divided from the colony of New England by the Atlantic Ocean. Let us further assume that George Washington, after having proclaimed the independence of the colonies, had plundered and ruined London (as Andrei Bogoliubsky had sacked Kiev in 1169), and that five centuries later the head of the renewed state of the mother country had concluded a quasi-protectorate agreement with the head of the United States government. Let us also assume that the United States interpreted this quasi protectorate as an act of submission and as a perpetual union of the two "English" countries in a manner analogous to that which occurred in Eastern Europe after the Pereiaslav Treaty of 1654. Let us in addition assume that the Americans now imposed an official politico-historical concept regarding the transfer of the state center in accordance with the scheme: London–Boston–Philadelphia–Washington, D.C. (in a manner analogous to the official Russian scheme: Kiev–Vladimir-on-the-Kliazma–Moscow–St. Petersburg). Let us in conclusion assume that, relying on the fact that English colonists came and settled in the United States before and after it declared its independence, American political leaders officially proclaimed the entire culture and history of England prior to American independence to be the first period of American history and culture; Englishmen in the mother country are permitted to begin their history and culture approximately two centuries after the proclamation of American independence.[19] Under these hypothetical but analogous circumstances if English historians (England has now become Britain just as southern Rus' has become *Ukraina*) were bold enough to treat the history of England-Britain as a single whole commencing with the beginnings of English history and culture (Beowulf, Chaucer, Shakespeare)—which the Americans had now appropriated—such historians would be officially branded as "nationalists"[20] and would be imprisoned or exiled. To complete the

[19] According to official Soviet historiography the Ukrainian nation and its culture are said to have begun in the fourteenth and fifteenth centuries. Prerevolutionary Russian historiography was based firmly on the assumption of the transfer of centers, and consequently had no place for the history of the Ukraine except to associate it with separatism in the modern period. Beginning with the *Замечания по поводу конспекта учебника по истории СССР И. Сталина, А. Жданова и С. Кирова* (Moscow, 1937) the following scheme has been dominant: prior to the thirteenth century there existed a common Old-Russian nation *(sic)*, which during the fourteenth and fifteenth centuries developed into three East European nations—the Russian, Ukrainian, and Belorussian—but for the period prior to the fourteenth century the terms "Old Russian" or "Russian" are used interchangeably, and this period is in fact appropriated for the Russian nation by official Soviet historiography. Research on this early period is centered in Moscow and Leningrad. Studies published in the Ukraine are permitted to deal with this early period only in a cursory manner.

[20] A curious practice is occasionally encountered in the works of certain American

analogy, any political movement which would attempt to liberate Britain from foreign occupation would be denounced as "separatist."

REUNION?

Histories of Eastern Europe have reflected a particular methodology. The linguistic term "Old (or "common") Russian language" (*drevne-russkii iazyk*, used for "Old Eastern Slavonic")—which is as much of a linguistic abstraction as a "common West Slavic language," a "common Indo-European language," and the like—has frequently been adopted by historians as a historical datum for the purpose of defining the first stage of the so-called "Old Russian nationality" (*drevnerusskaia narod-nost'*).[21]

By way of contrast, no historian of Poland or of the Czech lands commences his history with the period of "common West Slavic linguistic unity." Nor do these historians write of a common culture of a hypothetical "common West Slavic nationality" but rather of separate Polish and Czech cultures. However, the term "Old (or "common") Russian culture" is used in spite of the fact that the cultural "unity" of the Russian and Ukrainian lands between the eleventh and thirteenth centuries was not different from that of the Poland and Bohemia (Czech lands) of that period. This cultural "unity" was based on the fact that the Ukraine (in its modern sense), like Bohemia, was the donor, while Muscovy, like Poland, was the recipient. Poland received Christianity from Bohemia just as the Kiev missionary, Saint Kuksha, was converting the Viatichi—ancestors of the present Russians—in the second half of the eleventh century and was martyred by them.[22] The eastern counter-

---

specialists on the history of Eastern Europe. In bibliographic annotations a double standard is sometimes evident: tendentious works of Russian and other historians are frequently cited without any qualifying adjectives, while Hrushevsky is referred to as a "nationalist" because he dared to demonstrate the incorrectness of the concept of the "transfer" of centers. In actual fact Hrushevsky was, in his politics, not a "nationalist" but a socialist and a leader of the Ukrainian Social Revolutionary Party. Clearly, if the adjective "nationalist" is to be employed it should be on the basis of the same standard. In accepting unquestionably the terminology of official Soviet Russian historiography, American scholars should know that the Soviet use of the epithet "nationalist" does not correspond to the Western meaning of the same term, since a former member of the Central Committee of the CPSU can also be branded as a "nationalist" if his viewpoint should conflict with the current general line of the party.

[21] See, for example, the chapter on the emergence of the "Old Russian nationality" in *Очерки истории СССР: Период феодализма IX-XV вв.*, I (Moscow, 1953), 251-58. It is worth noting that in this chapter, as in other works of this character, the terms "Old Russian" (meaning "Old Rus'") and "Russian" are used synonymously. In this context one is prompted to ask if it is not time that American historians of Eastern Europe abandon the terminology used by Russians (for reasons of their own) and employ one that is strictly objective. For example, the term "Kievan Russia" connotes a nonexistent relationship of Kiev with a Russia which emerged several centuries later; obviously the accurate term is "Kievan Rus'," since *Rus'* is not identical with *Russia*.

[22] An account of Saint Kuksha is to be found in the Kievan *Patericon*. For a Russian translation see *Художественная проза киевской Руси XI-XIII вв.* (Moscow, 1957), pp. 158-59.

part of Latin as the cultural (foreign) language of the Western Slavs was the alien Church Slavonic language. Similarly, the ancient Russian literary language of Muscovy and its literature developed under the influence of the literary language and literature of the Ukrainian lands (Kiev, Chernyhiv, Halych) in the same way that the Polish literary language emerged as a result of Czech influence. The East Slavic–West Slavic parallel should be qualified to the extent that in the Ukrainian and Russian lands there were two branches of a single dynasty, while Bohemia and Poland had their own dynasties—although at times these dynasties were united in marriage. Thus on occasion both countries were ruled by the same king (for example, Boleslaw I of Poland, Wenceslaus II of Bohemia). Poland also acquired its own archbishopric in the year 1000, just as the Vladimir-Suzdal lands, after their separation, endeavored to obtain their own metropolitanate (which occurred only at the end of the thirteenth century).

It is generally accepted that the Viatichi provided the basis for the Muscovites (later the Russians), while the Poliane were the ancestors of the Rus' (later Ukrainians).[23] The Kiev Chronicler Nestor, author of the *Povest' vremennykh let* (written approximately in 1113, or fifty-six years prior to Andrei Bogoliubsky's separatism) did not express any sense of unity with the Viatichi. Nestor constantly emphasized that the Poliane existed apart *(osobo)*; he did not regard the Viatichi as an Eastern Slavic tribe but as having emerged from the Western Slavic *Liakhi*. While the Poliane, according to Nestor, had civilized customs and laws and knew the institution of marriage, the Viatichi "lived in the forests like beasts, ate unclean food, employed foul language in the presence of their fathers and [*de facto*] daughters-in-law, did not practice marriage...."[24] Since in Nestor's time Vladimir Monomakh (1055-1125) waged war against the Viatichi, their chief Khodota and his clan, and since Christianity came to the Viatichi only in the second half of the eleventh century or in the first half of the twelfth century, it is clear that in the eleventh and twelfth centuries there was no sense of oneness

---

23 On the Viatichi as the basis of the later Muscovite or Russian literary language (*akan'e*, etc.) see the various works by A. A. Shakhmatov, for example: А. А. Шахматовъ, *Введеніе въ курсъ исторіи русскаго языка* (Petrograd, 1916); *Очеркъ древнѣйшаго періода исторіи русскаго языка* (Petrograd, 1915); *Древнѣйшія судьбы русскаго племени* (Petrograd, 1919). See also П. Н. Третьяков, *Восточнославянские племена* (2nd ed.; Moscow, 1953), pp. 221, 238-41.

A lengthy polemic on the character of the language of the Poliane and the Old Kievan language resulted in acceptance of its Ukrainian character. See Л. А. Булаховський, *Питання походження української мови* (Kiev, 1956), pp. 104-24.

It is known that the Russian philologists N. P. Pogodin and A. I. Sobolevsky propounded the thesis that the inhabitants of Old Kiev were Great Russians who migrated to the north after Kiev was seized by the Mongols in 1240. Bulakhovsky has cast doubt upon this hypothesis in the following terms: "The linguistic facts do not support the hypothesis of Pogodin and Sobolevsky regarding the 'Great Russian' population of Old Kiev and the Kievan Principality (Kyiivshchyna)"; *ibid.*, p. 217.

24 *Повесть временных лет*, edited by Д. С. Лихачев, I (Moscow and Leningrad, 1950), 14-15.

which could have later served as the basis for the emergence of an "old (or "common") Russian nationality." Similarly, if the nations of Western Europe had not yet emerged in the eleventh and twelfth centuries, why should an "old (or "common") Russian nationality" have existed at that time? Indeed, is it not, at long last, time to identify this anachronism as the legend that it is and lay it to rest?

During the course of more than four centuries from 1240 to 1654, the ancestors of the Russians and Ukrainians lived in different states and in entirely different cultural spheres. Before 1620 there were no significant regular contacts between cultural representatives of the two peoples.[25] In 1954, as part of the Soviet tercentenary of the Pereiaslav Treaty, there occurred in the Soviet Union a reaffirmation of the political thesis regarding the "eternal oneness" of the Russian and Ukrainian peoples based on the legendary common "Old Russian nationality" of the eleventh and twelfth centuries discussed above.[26] Thus the 1654 treaty was interpreted as a "reunion" of the Ukrainian and Russian "fraternal peoples" by applying to an event of the seventeenth century populist ideas which emerged under the influence of nineteenth-century romanticism. In actual fact the Pereiaslav Treaty, like all other treaties of that time, was between two rulers or two states and not between two peoples. It is evident that "reunion" in 1654 would have had to be preceded by a previous act of union of which, as we have indicated, there is no record.

Let us turn to this meeting of Russians and Ukrainians in 1654.[27] Let us commence with the alleged feeling of oneness. For the Russians of that time the Ukrainians were foreigners or *inozemtsy* (I, 318), "Cherkas-foreigners" (I, 463), "foreigners of the Lithuanian lands" or

[25] It is for this reason that in the Pereiaslav Tercentenary edition of selected documents none is dated prior to 1620. See note 27.

[26] It is significant that both nations, the Muscovites and the Ukrainians, developed different messianic concepts: while in Muscovy the political "Third Rome" concept emerged, one finds in the Ukraine the Kiev religious concept viewing that city as the "Second Jerusalem." See R. Stupperich, "Kiev—das Zweite Jerusalem," in *Zeitschrift für slavische Philologie*, XII, No. 3-4 (1935), 332-54.

[27] The collection of selected documents on the "reunion" is: *Воссоединение Украины с Россией: Документы и материалы в трех томах* (Moscow, 1953); Vol. I (1620-47), 585 pp.; Vol. II (1648-51), 559 pp.; Vol. III (1651-54), 645 pp.

In our discussion of the differences between Muscovy and the Ukraine in the mid-seventeenth century we have relied almost exclusively upon this official Soviet selection of documents designed to demonstrate the thesis of "reunion." The representative quotations from these documents included in our discussion are not footnoted separately; reference is made in parentheses in the text to specific citations from these volumes. (The title of this collection is hardly accurate in view of the fact that prior to 1654 the term *Rosiia* was applied to the Ukraine and not to Muscovy, for which the term *Rusiia* or "Muscovite state" was used.)

The accounts of foreigners who visited the Ukraine and Muscovy in the sixteenth and seventeenth centuries and who were impressed with the many basic differences between the two nations can be found in В. Січинський, *Чужинці про Україну* (Lviv, 1938), pp. 36-135. An English translation is available: V. Sichynsky, *Ukraine in Foreign Comments and Descriptions* (New York, 1953), pp. 39-138.

inozemtsy litovskoi zemli (I, 258), "Lithuanians" or *litvin* (I, 252), "Cherkasy of the Lithuanian people" or *iz litovskikh liudei cherkasy* (I, 260). The Russians always distinguished between themselves and these "Lithuanians" or "Cherkasy" (for example, II, 244; III, 532). At the time of the Ukrainian Cossack uprising led by Khmelnytsky in 1648 the tsarist government ordered a reinforcement of the frontiers for defense "against the Cherkasy and Tatar advance" (II, 51). The Ukraine was, for the Russians, either the "Lithuanian land" (I, 252) or "White Rus' " (II, 152, 303), while the Russians referred to their country as the "Muscovite state" or *Moskovskoe gosudarstvo* (II, 280, 281). The Ukrainians sharply distinguished themselves from the Russians, calling the latter *Moskali* (III, 88) or as *narodu moskovskoho liude* (III, 215). The Ukrainians, using the old terminology, referred to themselves as (singular) *Rusyn* (III, 344) or (plural) *Rus'* (II, 66, 255; III, 264) and their land as either *Rosiia* (III, 157, 215) or *Ukraina* (II, 379). Thus Khmelnytsky refers to the Muscovite tsar as *tsaru moskovskii* (II, 35), and only after being instructed by the Muscovite envoy Unkovsky (March 13, 1649—II, 144) does he commence to address the tsar by the official title of *vseia Rusii samoderzhets* (II, 132).

The differences between the Ukrainian and Russian languages were sufficiently great to require that documents written in Ukrainian *(beloruskim pis'mom)* be translated into Russian (see *"perevod s lista z beloruskogo pis'ma"*—II, 350, 370; III, 128, 277, 354). The negotiations had to be conducted with the aid of interpreters. Thus the Muscovite delegation headed by Buturlin in December, 1653, included two Ukrainian language interpreters (III, 417)—Bilial Baitsyn (probably a Tatar) and Stepan Kolchitsky (a Galician trained in the Kiev Mohyla College). The Ukrainian delegation headed by Bohdanovych and Teteria (March, 1654) included an interpreter for Russian, Iakov Ivanovich *("tolmach' voiskovyi")*.[28] Illustrative of the linguistic relationship of the time was the account of the Muscovite diplomat-monk Arsenii Sukhanov of 1649. Khmelnytsky had granted refuge to a pretender to the Muscovite throne, Timoshka Akundinov, who claimed to be Ivan Shuisky, grandson of Tsar Vasilii Shuisky (1606-10). Sukhanov attempted in vain to persuade the Ukrainian government to extradite the pretender and endeavored to use the influence of the Patriarch of Jerusalem, Paisius, with whom he was traveling in the Ukraine. He asked the Patriarch to write to Khmelnytsky; the Patriarch consented but asked Sukhanov to prepare a draft of the letter to be sent. Sukhanov states that he "wrote in Russian and the Russian was translated into Greek and the Patriarch ordered a translation into Latin for the Hetman [Khmelnytsky]" (II, 184). It is clear that Khmelnytsky knew Russian only poorly and required a letter in Russian to be translated

---

[28] *Акты, относящіеся къ исторіи Южной и Западной Россіи*, X (St. Petersburg, 1878), 427.

into Latin, a language of which he had a good knowledge. In addition, Latin was widely used in the Cossack State of that time.

It is common knowledge among specialists that literary intercourse between the Ukraine and Muscovy in the seventeenth century was that of two peoples totally foreign in language and in spirit. Muscovy's low cultural level at that time led to the persecution of Ukrainian literature and its authors.[29]

Ukrainian and foreign ecclesiastics as well as the Ukrainian administration in the 1649-54 period regarded the Cossack State as an independent political unit, the equal of the Muscovite State. Thus Sukhanov reported to the tsar on May 9, 1649, that the visiting Orthodox high clergy, the metropolitans of Corinth and Nazareth, "in the prayers for long life and in the litanies pray for the Hetman as Sovereign and as the Hetman of Great Rosiia" (II, 187). In correspondence between Ukrainian and Russian authorities in the 1649-53 period it is clear that the Ukrainians assumed complete equality between Muscovy and the Ukraine. Thus the form of titling the hetman was the same as that of titling the Muscovite tsar—both were referred to as "By the Grace of God Great Sovereign."[30] Trade between Muscovy and the Ukraine was attributed to the fact of consent by both rulers—"your tsar and our Bohdan Khmelnytsky Hetman of the Zaporozhian Host."[31] When the Muscovite frontier authorities in 1651 addressed correspondence to Polish officials in the Ukraine in accordance with previous practice, they were informed that the Polish officials had fled three years before and that correspondence should be addressed to the Ukrainian authorities if they wished to have friendly relations (III, 25-26). In dealing with frontier incidents the Ukrainian local governor refused to act except upon an order from the hetman.[32]

The uprising led by Khmelnytsky occurred at a time when the idea

---

[29] See, for example, В. Эйнгорнъ, *Сношенія малороссійскаго духовенства съ московскимъ правительствомъ въ царствованіе Алексѣя Михайловича* (Moscow, 1894-99); И. П. Еремин, «К истории русско-украинских литературных связей в XVII веке,» in *Труды Отдела древнерусской литературы АН СССР*, IX (1953), 291-96. See also А. Н. Пыпинъ, *Исторія русской литературы* (4th ed.; St. Petersburg, 1911), Vol. II.

[30] See the *intitulatio* in the letter of the *sotnyk* of Hlukhiv S. Veichik to the Muscovite *voevoda* of Sevsk Prince T. I. Shcherbatov (April 22, 1651; III, 25): «Божию милостию великого государя нашего пана Богда[на] Хмельницкого, пана гетмана всего Войска Запорозкого.... Божию милостию великого государя царя і великого князя Алексія Михайловича, всея Русії самодержца....» The letter also contained the following Ukrainian admonition: «Теди живіт з нами подрузкий і знайте як писат.»

[31] Cf. the Russian translation from Ukrainian (*perevod zhe z beloruskogo pis'ma*) of the letter of the *sotnyk* of Kotel'nytsia H. Tripolev to the Muscovite *voevoda* of Vol'noe V. Novosiltsev of March 2, 1653 (III, 254).

[32] Cf. a letter of the *polkovnyk* of Poltava M. Pushkar to the *voevoda* of Belgorod Prince I. P. Pronsky of June 5, 1650: «Прислал ти ко мні воєвода в Плотаву станічнова голову Єпіфана с товарищи для сиску москаля Мишкі, што збежал з Білагорода, воровство зділавши. Єст у нас тот москал Мишко; але я не могу без росказаня єго милости пана гетмана видат, єстлі грамота от єго милости пана гетмана до мене будет, і я єго зараз видам . . .»

of dynastic legitimacy was dominant in Europe. Since Khmelnytsky was from the gentry but was not a member of a ruling dynasty, his sole means of obtaining support was to enter into a treaty with a sovereign on the basis of a quasi-protectorate, protectorate, or vassal relationship. In order to launch the uprising Khmelnytsky required the military support of the Crimean khan, a vassal of the Ottoman Porte (in the Ottoman Empire the system of vassalage was highly developed and widely used), and thus himself became in 1648 a quasi-protected ruler under the Ottoman Porte. This relationship was never annulled by either side. Two years after the Pereiaslav Treaty, Khmelnytsky decided to participate in an anti-Polish coalition of states led by Sweden (including Prussia, Transylvania, Moldavia, Walachia, and Lithuania), and he concluded a treaty with Sweden which established a quasi-protectorate relationship with the Swedish king.

Although Sweden was in conflict with Muscovy, the Muscovite tsar did not protest categorically against the Ukrainian ties with Sweden, and Khmelnytsky did not regard his accepting a Swedish protectorate as being incompatible with a continuation of the tie with Muscovy. Thus, after the Pereiaslav Treaty Khmelnytsky continued to conduct his own foreign policy, which was based on the establishment of good relations with all neighboring states except Poland. This meant that he had to enter into a (quasi-) protectorate relationship with each of these neighboring rulers. At the end of his life Khmelnytsky was simultaneously a quasi-protected ruler of three sovereigns—the Ottoman Porte, Muscovy, and Sweden—who were engaged in mutual conflict.[33]

Khmelnytsky was reared in the Polish-Lithuanian gentry-democracy in which the bilateral acts of ruler and subjects and such political institutions as the personal and real union, protectorate, and the like were rooted in tradition; he also knew, through personal experience, the political practices of the Ottoman Porte. When in 1653 Khmelnytsky required Muscovite military aid, he decided to submit to the "high hand of the Orthodox tsar" of Muscovy.[34] However, despotic Muscovy, representing a very different tradition, could not comprehend any con-

---

[33] In June, 1657, Hetman Khmelnytsky insisted upon maintaining the tie with Sweden, in a statement made to the Muscovite envoy Buturlin, in the following terms: "I will never sever my ties with the Swedish king because our alliance, friendship, and understanding are of long duration having commenced more than six years ago before our subjection to the high hand of the tsar"; *Акты, относящіеся къ исторіи Южной и Западной Россіи*, III (St. Petersburg, 1861), 568.

In April, 1657, the Ukrainian envoy to the Ottoman Porte, Lavryn Kapusta, presented a diplomatic note in which the sultan was addressed as "our highest lord" *(dominum nostrum supremum)* and in which emphasis was placed on "testifying to our old friendship, sincere fidelity and service" *(ut nostram antiquam imicitiam ac sinceram fidelitatem ac servitia erga eandem Portam declararemus) Архивъ Юго-Западной Россіи*, Part III, Vol. VI (Kiev, 1908), 216-17.

[34] There is a vast literature dealing with the nature of the Pereiaslav Treaty, discussed in Грушевський, *Історія України-Руси*, IX, Part II (Kiev, 1931), 865-69; H. Fleischhacker, "Aleksej Michajlovič und Bogdan Chmel'nickij," in *Jahrbücher für Kultur und Geschichte*

tractual relationship between the tsar and his subjects.[35] Muscovy knew only a unilateral submission to the tsar, and Khmelnytsky could not conceive of such a relationship. For this reason the ceremonial aspects of the establishment of this treaty relationship commenced very dramatically on January 8, 1654. Khmelnytsky was dumfounded by the statement of the Muscovite envoy Buturlin, who refused to take the oath on behalf of the tsar and declared that in Muscovite practice it was unthinkable that a subject could demand an oath from the tsar. Khmelnytsky refused to take the oath and walked out of the church in Pereiaslav in which the ceremony was to take place (III, 464-66, and note 38 *infra*).

---

der Slaven, N.F., XI, No. 1 (1935), 11-52; А. Яковлів, *Договір Богдана Хмельницького з московським царем Олексієм Михайловичем 1654 р.* (New York, 1954), pp. 64-69.

Various interpretations have been offered: personal union, real union, protectorate, quasi protectorate, vassalage, military alliance, autonomy, incorporation. In our opinion the Pereiaslav Treaty, which was a result of lengthy negotiations between two signatories having different systems, cannot be subsumed under a single category. In view of our discussion it is reasonable to conclude that in substance, from Khmelnytsky's point of view, it was a military alliance (Hetman Orlyk termed the Pereiaslav Treaty implicitly "le Traité d'Alliance," see the end of this note) like others he had with the Ottoman sultan and the king of Sweden. In a formal sense the Pereiaslav Treaty had as well elements of a personal union and of a quasi protectorate. It can be regarded as a personal union, since the treaty had been concluded with the tsar (and there were no common institutions apart from the person of the tsar) and because of the preservation of a separate Cossack State and its continuing to be a subject of international law capable of imposing tariffs.

There is also a basis for regarding the Pereiaslav Treaty as a quasi protectorate in view of the following considerations: Since the tsar as an absolute monarch identified his person with the state, the Pereiaslav Treaty was not only an agreement between two rulers but was also a treaty between two states. This is also evident in the fact that in addition to Khmelnytsky, the Zaporozhian Host appeared as an official treaty partner whom Hetman Orlyk described as "les États de l'Ukraine" (see end of note). If it were only a personal union there would have been no place for a hetman and the tsar could have assumed the title of hetman. Instead, Khmelnytsky remained as hetman and was empowered to conduct foreign relations (having full competence with certain precisely defined limitations); had Pereiaslav established a complete protectorate (as contrasted with a quasi protectorate), the hetman would not have had the right to conduct foreign relations. In addition, the Ukraine preserved her full state apparatus after 1654, and the Muscovite troops stationed in the Ukraine were circumscribed in their rights in the same way that American troops stationed in Western Europe under NATO have been forbidden to intervene in the internal affairs of the host country.

The duration of the treaty had been determined as *voveki*; in the Russian language of the seventeenth century this word did not have the meaning "eternity" but "perpetual" in the sense "for life," for example, in a document of 1641 the word *voveki* is explained by means of *do smerti zhivota svoego* ("to the end of his life"; I, 318). Therefore, each of Khmelnytsky's successors was supposed to renew the treaty.

Hetman P. Orlyk gives in 1712 the following definition of the Pereiaslav Treaty: "Mais l'argument et la preuve la plus forte et la plus invincible de la Souveraineté de l'Ukraine est le Traité d'Alliance solennel conclu entre le Czar Alexei Mikailovstch et le Duc Chmielnicki et les Etats de l'Ukraine. Ce Traité fut arrêté en 1654 et signé par les Plenipotentionaires nommez de part et d'autre pour cet effet. Un Traité si solennel et si précis qui étoit appelé Traité Perpétuel..." Philippe Orlik, *Deduction des droits de l'Ukraine: D'apres un manuscrit, conservé dans les archives du chateau de Dinteville avec une introduction et des notes* (Lviv: publié par I. Bortchak, 1925), p. 9.

[35] See, for example, H. Fleischhacker, *Die Staats- und völkerrechtlichen Grundlagen der moskauischen Aussenpolitik (14.-17. Jahrhundert)* (2nd ed.; Darmstadt, 1959), pp. 168-69.

After the conclusion of the treaty, on March 21-27, 1654, a joint military campaign was undertaken against Poland. Both armies operated in White Ruthenia but independently of each other. Thus began the strange phenomenon of "a battle of two Rus' for the third."[36] The Ukrainian Cossack Army, in response to the request of the local population of White Ruthenia, introduced the Cossack system establishing a White Ruthenian military-governmental region *(polk)*. The Ukrainian army attempted to outmaneuver the Muscovite army in taking White Ruthenian territory under its protection, and this even led to armed clashes between the two "allies."

All of the documentary evidence makes it perfectly clear that Khmelnytsky's relations with Muscovy were rationalized not by any sense of common national, linguistic, or other ties but only by the fact of a common religious faith. Nowhere in the Pereiaslav documents is there any reference to "reunion" or to dynastic claims of the Muscovite tsars to the Ukrainian lands. It should also be borne in mind that the various Eastern Slavic branches of the Orthodox Church of that time had developed their distinctive characteristics, even though all, including the non-Slavic Rumanian principalities of Moldavia and Walachia, used the Church Slavonic language. As a result, the dialectic manifested itself here as well: thus the Kiev Orthodox ecclesiastical leadership, which between 1620 and 1648 had been interested in obtaining support from the Muscovite Orthodox tsar for an Orthodox alliance, categorically refused—in the person of the Kiev metropolitan, Sylvester Kosov —to take an oath to the tsar apart from that of Khmelnytsky (III, 481-82). Nor did the Kiev clergy wish to leave the jurisdiction of the patriarch of Constantinople and accept that of the Moscow patriarchate.[37]

[36] В. Липинський, *Україна на переломі*, I (Vienna, 1920), 35-39; Fleischhacker, *Die Staats-und völkerrechtlichen Grundlagen . . .*, pp. 176-90. See the decree *(universal)* of Khmelnytsky of February 2, 1656, appointing Ivan Nechai as governor *(polkovnyk)* of White Ruthenia in the collection of Khmelnytsky's documents published in 1961 by I. Krypiakevych and I. Butych (cited in note 37), pp. 470-71.

[37] Metropolitan Sylvester Kosov, speaking through his representative, Innokentius Gizel, in July, 1654, based his refusal to submit the Ukrainian Church to the jurisdiction of the patriarch of Muscovy on the following considerations: Kiev's ties with Byzantium were said to date from the times of the Apostle Andrew (the old Kievan legend of the Princely Period); only a decision of an Ecumenical Council could determine a change in the jurisdiction of a metropolitanate. *Акты, относящіеся къ исторіи Южной и Западной Россіи*, X (St. Petersburg, 1878), 751-54.
The frequently expressed view that the existence of a common religious faith between Muscovy and the Ukraine was a determining factor in bringing about the Pereiaslav Treaty must not be accepted without question. Indeed, before 1685 Ukrainian religious ties were with the Constantinople patriarchate and not with the patriarch of Moscow. A revealing letter sent to the Sultan Mehmet IV by Khmelnytsky on December 7, 1651, gives evidence of this: "Since all Greece accepts the suzerainty of Your Imperial Majesty, my gracious Lord, all Rus' [Ukrainians] which are of the same faith as the Greeks and having their [religious] origins with them, wish each day to be under the rule of Your Imperial Majesty, my Gracious Lord." *Документи Богдана Хмельницького*, edited by I. Крип'якевич and I. Бутич (Kiev, 1961), p. 233. Thus it is clear that in emphasizing religious ties Khmelnytsky was simply employing a stylistic element of his political lexicon.

The Ukrainians understood the Pereiaslav Treaty as obligating both signatories[38] and as a military alliance in the form of a personal union and (quasi) protectorate. For the Muscovites the treaty was simply the first step toward the military occupation of the Ukrainian Cossack State. Conflict was inevitable. Within four years, in 1658, Ivan Vyhovsky, Khmelnytsky's successor (who had been chancellor at the time of the Pereiaslav Treaty), directed a manifesto in Latin to the rulers of Europe (*Regibus, Electoribus, Principis, Marchionibus, Rebus Publicis*) in which he explained what had prompted his decision to oppose Muscovy:

We, All of the Zaporozhian Host, do declare and testify (*Nos Universus Exercitus Zaporovianus notum testatumque facimus*) before God and the entire world. . . . Our Host, having received promises and obligations from the Grand Prince of Muscovy and having expected—because of a common religion and having voluntarily accepted protection—that the Grand Prince would be just, sympathetic and generous towards us; that he would act honestly, that he would not persist in the destruction of our liberties but would actually enhance them in accordance with his promises. But our hopes were not to be fulfilled. . . . In Kiev, our capital (*in civitate nostra principali Kioviensi*), this was not the case even during Polish rule—a fortress has been built and a Muscovite garrison stationed there in order to place us in bondage. We have seen examples of such bondage in White Ruthenia where two hundred gentry families—though sympathetic to them [the Muscovites]—were forcibly deported to Muscovy; 12,000 free men from the Mohyliv and other parts of White Ruthenia were deported to the forests of Muscovy and in their places were brought Muscovite colonists. . . . Following the death of Bohdan Khmelnytsky of eternal memory, Muscovy determined to ruin the entire Little and White Rus'. Upon the election of Hetman Ivan Vyhovsky Muscovy introduced dissension among us, planting rumors that the Hetman is a Pole and favors Poland more than the Zaporozhian Host. . . . The [Muscovite] commander Romodanovsky, under the pretext of maintaining order, intervened in our internal affairs: he had the audacity to distribute the Hetman's titles and insignia, replacing [Ukrainian] military governors, instigating subjects against the Hetman and destroying cities which supported their own Hetman. . . . In this way there has been revealed the cunning and deception of those who—first with the aid of our civil war (*nostro interno et civili bello*) and later openly turning their weapons against us (without any provocation on our part)—are preparing

---

[38] Although the text of Buturlin's account to the tsar (in the form in which it is available) does not refer to any official promises made to Khmelnytsky on behalf of the tsar in place of the oath which the hetman wanted Buturlin to take, it is apparent that such promises were made. Gizel's petition addressed to the tsar in connection with the Pereiaslav Treaty, written but six months after the conclusion of the treaty, emphasizes in two separate passages official promises made to Khmelnytsky by Buturlin on behalf of the tsar. «О семъ прежде въ Переяславлѣ гетману вашего царского величества запорожскому бояринъ твой Василей Васильевичъ Бутурлинъ извѣщал и имянемъ вашего царского величества обѣщалъ, яко не токмо войску Запорожскому, но и всѣмъ намъ духовнымъ права и волности ваше царское величество потвердити изволитъ. . . . По обѣщанью Василья Васильевича Бутурлина, именемъ вашего царского величества . . .» (*Акты ЮЗР*, X, 751-54). It is impossible to question the accuracy of this source.

for us the yoke of bondage. Declaring our innocence and invoking Divine succor, we are compelled in order to preserve our liberties to have recourse to a just defense and seek the aid of our neighbors so as to throw off this yoke. Thus it is not we who are responsible for the war with Muscovy which is everywhere becoming inflamed."[39]

The first actual meeting of Russians and Ukrainians in 1654 was a meeting of two different worlds, which, in spite of the superficial aspects of a common Orthodox faith, led not to "union" (let alone "reunion") but to chronic misunderstanding and mutual conflict.[40]

Rus', Malorossiia ("Little Russia"), Ukraina

The term *Rus'* (from a grammatical point of view a Slavic collective noun derived from *rus*; the singular form being *rus-in*) is derived from the name of the Norman Varangians, who in the middle of the ninth century became soldiers of fortune and, later, rulers of all Eastern Europe. Kiev became the center of their rule, and the Kiev territory came to represent the land of Rus' par excellence. The princes of Rus' in the broadest sense included all lines of the Rus' dynasty (the Riurikovichi), their retinues *(druzhina)* and territories. After the acceptance of Christianity, the metropolitanate which united all of Western Europe in a single ecclesiastical jurisdiction was termed "of all Rus'" (πάσης 'Ρωσίας). Since the metropolitan was usually a Byzantine Greek, an agent and guardian of the idea of the universal rule of the Byzantine emperor and his interests, the political concept of a single *complete* Rus' state did not emerge in the Kiev period.[41] The sole unity which Rus' possessed at that time was limited to the metropolitanate "of Kiev and of all Rus'."

---

[39] *Архивъ Юго-Западной Россіи*, Part III, Vol. VI (Kiev, 1908), 362-69. See also the statement made by Hetman I. Mazepa (1708) in which he announced his decision to annul the treaty with Peter I (as is known, in the Muscovite-Russian interpretation this act of annulment was regarded as "treason"—*izmena*): "I had decided to write a letter of thanks to his tsarist highness (Peter I) for the *protection* [*protektsiu*], and to list in it all the insults to us, past and present, the loss of rights and liberties, the ultimate ruin and destruction being prepared for the whole nation, and, finally, to state that we had bowed under the high hand of his tsarist highness as a *free people for the sake of the one Eastern Orthodox Faith*. Now, *being a free people, we are freely departing*, and we thank his tsarist highness for this protection. We do not want to extend our hand and spill Christian blood, but we will await our complete liberation under the *protection* of the Swedish King." «Письмо Орлика къ Ст. Яворскому» in *Основа*, Листопадъ, 1862, p. 15.

[40] A similar conclusion has been drawn by Kliuchevsky: "Not comprehending each other and not trusting each other, both sides in their mutual relationship did not say what they thought and did what they did not wish to do.... Therefore, the Little Russian [Ukrainian] question, so falsely posed by both [Russian and Ukrainian] sides, encumbered and corrupted Moscow's foreign policy for several decades...." В. О. Ключевскій, *Сочиненія*, III: *Курс русской исторіи*, Part III (Moscow, 1957), 118-19.

[41] М. Дьяконов, *Очерки общественнаго и государственнаго строя древней Руси* (4th ed.; St. Petersburg, 1912), p. 388. Ф. И. Леонтовичъ, «Національний вопросъ въ древней Россіи,» *Варшавскія университетскія извѣстія* (1894), IX, 1-16, (1895) I, 17-65. С. В. Бахрушин, «Держава Рюриковичей,» *Вѣстник древней исторіи* (1938), No. 2 (3), pp. 88-98.

The process of creating a political concept of the state related to the name Rus' began only in the thirteenth and fourteenth centuries when on the peripheries of the Rus' territories there emerged two states: the *Regnum (Ducatus) Russiae* (the Galician-Volhynian State) and the Great Muscovite Principality. The rulers of the latter, beginning with Ivan Kalita (1325-41), titled themselves Princes "of all Rus' " (since Ivan the Terrible: *vseia Rusii* "of all Rusiia") imitating the metropolitan's title. Before the reign of Peter I both in the East and in the West the term "Rus' " (Russi, Rutheni; Russia, Ruthenia, ar-Rūs, etc.) was customarily applied to the present Ukrainian territory and its inhabitants; for what is today known as the center of Russia proper the term "Muscovy" was employed.

The term *Malorossiia* ("Little Russia") was of Greek origin (ἡ μικρὰ 'Ρωσία; in Latin, *Russia Mynor*). The term was employed by the Byzantine Patriarch to identify the second Rus' metropolitanate established in 1303 at the insistence of the Galician-Volhynian rulers in response to the decision of the then metropolitan of Kiev "and of all Rus'," the Greek Maxim, to take up residence in Vladimir-on-the-Kliazma in 1299. In adopting the title of metropolitan, the rulers of the Galician-Volhynian State called themselves the rulers of "all Minor Rus' " as, for example, Boleslav-Iurii II: "Dei gracia natus dux tocius Russie Mynoris";[42] in the same way the princes of Muscovy claimed to be rulers "of all Rus'."

It is important to note that this assumption of the title of the metropolitanate testifies to the fact that sovereignty in Eastern Europe until the fifteenth century (Ivan III) was closely related to the metropolitanate.[43]

The Byzantine concept which lay behind the use of the terms Major Rus' and Minor Rus' is a matter of conjecture. It is known that amongst the Greeks the *metropolis* or mother *polis* was denoted with the adjective μικρός ("minor") in contradistinction to the *colonies* which were termed μέγας ("major," "great"), as, for example, "Magna Graecia" in reference to the Greek colonies in Southern Italy. An analogous situation exists with reference to the term "Asia Minor." This interpretation is also supported by the fact that the Lithuanian Prince Olgerd in 1354 referred to Kiev as "Mala Rus'."[44]

Under the influence of humanism the Greek term 'Ρωσία (adopted by

---

[42] See photo plate IX in the symposium *Волеслав-Юрій II: Князь всей Малой Руси* (St. Petersburg, 1907).

[43] The Fathers of the Synod of the Church of Constantinople in 1389 declared: "Since it was impossible to concentrate secular authority in Rus' in one person, the Holy Fathers of the Synod established a single spiritual authority." *Acta patriarchatus Constantinopolitani*, ed. F. Miklosich and I. Müller (Vienna, 1860), I, 520. A monastic rule of the late fifteenth and early sixteenth century prescribes that prayers shall be offered on behalf of «князей нашихъ, а не царя, зане нѣсть царствія здѣ, въ нашей Руси.» В. Иконниковъ, *Опытъ русской историографіи*, II, Part II (Kiev, 1908), 1085.

[44] Грушевськиŭ, *Історія України-Руси*, V (Lviv, 1905), 389.

Muscovy as a result of its interpretation of the Pereiaslav Treaty of 1654) came to be used among Kiev clergy in the fifteenth century and became prevalent in the Mohyla College in Kiev during the seventeenth century.[45] The ancient name *Roxolania* also was used at that time with reference to the Ukrainian territories.[46] There then developed the concept of three Rosiia's: the Major Rosiia, the Minor Rosiia, and the White Rosiia (as in the *Synopsis*). Under the influence of these ideas of the Mohyla College the Muscovite tsar Alexei Mikhailovich, after the conclusion of the Pereiaslav Treaty of 1654, changed his official title from tsar "of all Rusiia" *(vseia Rusii)* to "of all Great and Little and White Rosiia" *(vseia Velikiia i Malyia i Belyia Rosii)*.[47] This change, effected in 1655, elicited considerable opposition in European diplomatic circles at the time.[48]

The hetmans of the Ukrainian Cossack State prior to 1709 did at times designate the people of their territory—which they commonly called *Ukraina*—as *malorossiiskii*, as Mazepa did in 1707.[49] In 1713 Peter I by means of a decree established the practice of referring to the old Muscovite State as *Rossiia* and using the term *Malorossiia* instead of *Ukraina*.[50] Prior to this the term *Ros(s)iia* had been used only in the tsar's title and not with reference to the Muscovite state. The association of the term *Malorossiia* with the incomplete nature of Zaporozhian Cossack statehood, as a result of the repressive measures employed by Peter I and his successors, caused the term to become unpopular among

---

[45] П. Житецький, *Нарис літературної історії української мови в XVII віці* (Lviv, 1941), p. 5.

[46] Chancellor Vyhovsky insisted during negotiations with Sweden in 1657 that the basis of the treaty should be "das Jus totius Ukrainae antiquae vel Roxolaniam, da der Griechiesche Glaube gewesen und die Sprache noch ist, biss an die Weixel . . ." Липинський, *Україна на переломі*, p. 282, n. 185.

[47] In the middle of the seventeenth century in the Ukraine the term *Rosiia* was employed, while in Muscovy the term *Rusiia* was used. The Kiev Metropolitan Sylvester Kosov bore the title "Mytropolyt Kyievskyi, Halytskyi i vseia Rosii" (III, 215) or "vseia Malyia Rosii" (III, 157). The title of the tsar of Muscovy was "vseia Rusii" (III, 7, 60, 372). Also in the documents relating to the Pereiaslav Treaty the tsar called himself "vseia Velikiia i Malyia Rus(s)ii Samoderzhets"; *Полное собрание законов Российской Империи* (1830), I, doc. no. 119, p. 325. After May 8, 1654, the tsar completed the title as follows "vseia Velikiia i Malyia i Belyia Rossii Samoderzhets"; *ibid.*, p. 338.

[48] See Грушевський, *Історія України-Руси* (Kiev, 1931), IX, Part II, p. 1396; cf. p. 1113. As a result of the unhappy experience after the Pereiaslav Treaty, the hetmans endeavored to guard against the usurpation of the Ukrainian name in a foreign monarch's title. In the treaty between Mazepa and Charles XII there was a special provision dealing with this matter: "5. L'on n'innovera 'rien à ce qui a été observé jusques à présent au sujet des Armes et du Titre de Prince de l'Ukraine. S.M.R. ne pourra jamais s'arroger ce Titre ni les Armes." Philippe Orlik, *Deduction des droits de l'Ukraine* (see note 34), p. 11.

[49] See «Письмо Орлика Стефану Яворскому,» *Основа*, Листопадъ, 1862, pp. 13-14.

[50] В. Січинський, *Назва України* (Augsburg, 1948), p. 22. It was only after the uprising led by Mazepa that Peter I changed the title of "vseia Velikiia Malyia i Belyia Rossii Samoderzhets" (quoted for the last time in a document on Nov. 1, 1708, in *Полное собрание законов Российской Империи* (1830), IV, 424, to the new form of "samoderzhets Vserossiiskii," which was used for the first time in the *Gramota malorossiiskomu narodu* of Nov. 9, 1708. *Ibid.*, IV, 426.

Ukrainians. *Malorossiia* when employed by the Russians, especially in the nineteenth century, was felt by the Ukrainians to be derogatory.

The term *Ukraina* in the Kiev (twelfth century) and Galician-Volhynian (thirteenth century) Chronicles is used in a general sense to refer to "country" or "borderlands" (1187, 1189, 1213, 1268, 1280, 1282). In the sixteenth century *Ukraina* was used as a more specialized geographic term to refer to the Middle Dnieper region; accounts of the period refer to the inhabitants of the territory as "Ukrainians." The prominent polemicist Meletius Smotrytsky (1587-1633) in enumerating in his *Verificacia* the various Rus' (Ukrainian and White Ruthenian) "tribes" in the Polish State mentions the Volhynians, Podolians, Ukrainians, and others.

Since the Middle Dnieper region became at that time the center of Ukrainian Cossackdom (the town Cossacks as distinct from the Zaporozhians) they came to be called "Ukrainian" in a manner comparable to the Russian practice of calling both the urban and Zaporozhian Cossacks *Cherkasy* after the city of the same name. The term *Ukraina* became intimately associated with the Ukrainian Cossacks. They began calling the Ukraine their "mother" and "fatherland," and some of the hetmans and even colonels of the Zaporozhian Host even used the term in their titles.[51]

As the Cossack movement broadened, the term *Ukraina* was extended to all lands embraced by the movement. *Ukraina quae est terra Cosaccorum* or *l'Ukraine ou Pays de Cosaques* of the Western authors of the seventeenth and eighteenth centuries is not only the name of the territory but designates the relation of the land to the people inhabiting it.[52] This meaning of the term "Ukraine" penetrated the masses.

The population of the Ukrainian lands did not experience any general emotional uplift either in the Kiev Rus' or in the Galician-Volhynian Rus'. The wars with the Polovtsy never had an "all-national" character. In addition, the Polovtsy, like the Poles and Magyars and other peoples, were an inseparable part of the princely Rus'; war was waged against them one day, and the following day they became allies in a military campaign of one Rus' prince against another.

The Khmelnytsky Era elicited an emotional upheaval of a kind never before experienced by the Ukrainian masses; this elemental force, misled by demagogues in foreign service after Khmelnytsky's death, was more destructive than creative (especially during the *Ruina*, 1663-74), but it aroused an individual and collective feeling which was to leave an indelible mark. The Ukrainian masses idealized Khmelnytsky's

[51] See Грушевський, *Історія України-Руси* (2nd ed.; Kiev and Lviv, 1922), VIII, Part I, p. 263.

[52] See the numerous maps by de Beauplan, Homann, and others. For a recent account in English which surveys this cartographic documentation see Bohdan Krawciw, "Ukraine in Western Cartography and Science in the Seventeenth and Eighteenth Centuries," *The Ukrainian Quarterly*, XVIII (Spring, 1962), 24-39.

struggle against the "Polish lords" and yearned for this "Ukraine"—a utopian state of ideal Cossack freedom. Hence it is not surprising that after the term *Malorossiia* became discredited (because it had become a symbol of the colonial policies of the Russian state after 1709), the son of the people, Taras Shevchenko, associated his great talent not with the name *Malorossiia* but with *Ukraina* and thus resolved the question of what his people should be called.

STAGES AND THE DIALECTIC

The process by which the Ukrainian national movement acquired a political character can be understood more readily in terms of certain aspects of the dialectic. Its emergence occurred in spite of its having been consigned (prematurely) to the historical archives and written off as a "lost cause." What began as an apolitical and cultural movement was transformed into a political phenomenon, although few of its earlier nineteenth-century proponents had this as their professed goal. The movement developed in a series of stages, each of which often gave the appearance of being self-contained and inconsequential but actually contained the seeds of further development and provided the basis for the following stage. A series of official policies designed to keep the Ukrainian masses helpless, voiceless, and submerged gave the appearance of being very effective in the nineteenth century but in the end bred the very forces which these harsh measures were designed to eliminate entirely or render impotent.

If, as Rudnytsky suggests, the Ukrainian peasant masses were barely touched politically by the national movement prior to 1905, it is hardly surprising in view of their inertia and benighted condition as serfs prior to 1861—thanks to Catherine II. In the period between the emancipation of the serfs and the 1905 Revolution, any political activity under the conditions of an autocratic monarchy could only be conspiratorial. The peasantry, in spite of its willingness to rebel sporadically, was hardly qualified for sustained political activity. Indeed, it is surprising that some of them were able to participate in the First and Second Dumas and defend Ukrainian rights in spite of Russian efforts to destroy Ukrainian national identity in the name of an artificial "All-Russian" nation.[53] This vain effort embraced a wide range of policies and techniques.

The attempts to outlaw the use of the Ukrainian language in print began as early as 1720, when Peter I forbade publication of all books except those dealing with religious matters, and these had to be verified with the Russian texts.[54] The need for more effective measures led to

---

[53] J. S. Reshetar, Jr., *The Ukrainian Revolution 1917-1920* (Princeton, N.J., 1952), pp. 34-36, 40.

[54] П. Пекарскій, *Наука и литература при Петрѣ Великомъ* (St. Petersburg, 1862), II,

Interior Minister Peter Valuev's secret circular of July 20, 1863, pro-
hibiting publication of Ukrainian scholarly and popular books except
for belles-lettres. The Ems Decree of Alexander II (May 18, 1876) forbade the importation of Ukrainian publications from the Western
Ukraine, which was under Austrian rule, and permitted only historical
works and belles-lettres to be published by Ukrainians living under
Russian rule (on the condition that Russian orthography be used) and
forbade theatrical productions and publication of Ukrainian folk songs
and lyrics. Other techniques for denationalizing Ukrainians included
the development and propagation of a distorted "All-Russian" historiography centered on Muscovy and claiming the Kiev Principality as
the cradle of the Russian state. The official use of the term "Little
Russian" served to create an invidious effect. The absence of public
Ukrainian-language schools retarded the emergence of a national intelligentsia, although it could not deprive the Ukrainian masses of their
native tongue in daily life.

A most damaging technique, though one which failed in the end,
was that of corrupting the Ukrainian upper classes with titles, rewards,
estates, and serfs in return for their joining the ranks of the "All-
Russian" nation. This process resulted in formidable losses for the
Ukrainians and gains for the Russians. Thus the composers Maxim
Berezovsky and D. S. Bortniansky were appropriated by Russian music;
Bortniansky was taken from the Ukraine in 1759 at the age of eight to
sing in the choir of the royal court. Feofan Prokopovich and Stefan
Iavorsky, alumni of the Kiev Mohyla-Mazepa Academy, were induced
by Peter I to come to Russia and aid in implementing his reforms;
these two Ukrainians, whose names symbolize this phenomenon, made
their not inconsiderable talents available to the monarch and in return
received high ecclesiastical office.[55] This willingness to serve resulted,
in part, from the fact that Muscovy in 1685 had succeeded in obtaining
the approval of the patriarch of Constantinople for its annexation of
the Kiev metropolitanate, which had been within the Constantinople
jurisdiction before that time.

The Petrine practice of recruiting talented foreign personnel wherever it could be found was a vital aspect of the creation of an "imperial
culture" embracing various nationalities. For those recruited to serve
this empire it was easy to identify with a larger integrating unit—one
which enjoyed success and which, to its instruments, represented a new
and "higher" development. If certain of the Ukrainian higher clergy
played a role here, it was because they had been educated abroad and
were indispensable to Peter I in his efforts to Europeanize Muscovy at
a time when the less educated Russian clergy were resisting reform. The
Ukrainian higher clergy were also attracted to this service early in the

[55] See К. Харламповичъ, *Малороссійское вліяніе на великорусскую церковную жизнь*
(Kazan, 1914).

eighteenth century by the prospect of enjoying the support of a very firm political authority—something which was lacking in the Ukraine at times.

Rudnytsky's tripartite periodization of the development of the Ukrainian national movement (in terms of the ages represented by the nobility, populism, and modernism) is useful, but it does not reveal fully the range of contradictory forces which shaped the movement. To appreciate the distinctiveness of each and to understand their mutual relationship it is necessary to distinguish between at least five stages.

The *first stage* might be called the Novhorod-Siversk stage, after the region in the northern part of the Left Bank in which the *Istoriia Rusov* was apparently written. The author of this unique work cannot be identified with absolute certainty, but it is clear that he was a member of the Ukrainian gentry, a man of considerable erudition who wrote with wit and sarcasm.[56] The *Istoriia Rusov,* a historico-political tract disguised as a chronicle, was written in the late eighteenth or very early nineteenth century in a language close to the literary Russian of the time but abounding in purely Ukrainian expressions and proverbs.[57] The work first circulated in manuscript form among the Left Bank gentry and was not published until 1846. It traces Ukrainian history back to the princely period and stresses the earlier ties with Lithuania and Poland but deals primarily with the Ukrainian Cossack State and with Khmelnytsky and Mazepa. The author is very critical of the Muscovites and their mistreatment of the Ukrainians. He has Mazepa, in a speech, declare that Muscovy appropriated from the Ukrainians their ancient name of Rus'.[58] In a speech attributed to Hetman Pavlo Polubotok, Peter I is referred to as a hangman and "Asiatic tyrant."[59] *Istoriia Rusov,* in lamenting the fate of the Ukrainians, implied the right of each people to self-development free from foreign domination, but it also conveyed a certain feeling of resignation. *Istoriia Rusov* was far removed from the arid *Synopsis* of 1674 (earlier attributed to Innokentius Gizel). Thanks to its colorful style and its emphasis on the Cossack State, *Istoriia Rusov* was to have an influence far beyond the narrow circle within which it first circulated.

The *second or Kharkov stage,* originally centered on the Left Bank in the Poltava region, is characterized by the development of modern Ukrainian literature. Representatives of the gentry or persons associated with them decided to write in Ukrainian rather than in Russian.

[56] For data regarding the controversy over the authorship of *Istoriia Rusov* see Andriy Yakovliv, "*Istoriya Rusov* and its Author," and Olexander Ohloblyn, "Where Was *Istoriya Rusov* Written?" in *Annals of the Ukrainian Academy of Arts and Sciences in the U.S.,* III, No. 2 (1953), 620-95. Also see Elie Borschak, *La légende historique de l'Ukraine: Istorija Rusov* (Paris, 1949). For a general work on the Novhorod-Siversk stage see Олександер Оглоблин, *Люди старої України* (Munich, 1959).

[57] Чижевський, *Історія української літератури,* pp. 304-5.

[58] *Історія Русів,* ed. O. Ohloblyn and trans. V. Davydenko (New York, 1956), p. 275.

[59] *Ibid.,* pp. 308-9.

These included Peter Hulak-Artemovsky, Hryhoryi Kvitka-Osnovia-nenko, and, above all, Ivan Kotliarevsky. Thus Kotliarevsky, like the other Ukrainian authors of the late eighteenth century, wrote as the representative of an "incomplete" literature wishing to complement the new complete Imperial Russian literature. His travesty on the *Aeneid* became an epopee of Ukrainian Cossackdom and breached the confines of the "incomplete" literature; this made him, in retrospect, the father of an independent modern Ukrainian literature. While these belle-lettrists were apolitical and did not challenge Russian rule, the fact that they wrote in Ukrainian—whatever their motives—was of great conse-quence. In the end it overcame the pessimism expressed by Alexander Pavlovsky, the compiler of the first Ukrainian grammar in 1818, who regarded Ukrainian as a "disappearing idiom."[60]

The 1840's witnessed the emergence of the *third or Kiev (Right Bank) stage,* which saw the Ukrainian movement begin to assume a political form and acquire its most eloquent literary spokesman. The impetus provided by the originally apolitical Left Bank gentry and by *Istoriia Rusov* led to the formation, early in 1846, of the secret Saints Cyril and Methodius Society *(Bratstvo).*[61] Rudnytsky's discussion of this first consequential Ukrainian political group, which had no more than a hundred members, correctly stresses its political nature. Several distinctive but neglected aspects of its program merit attention. The Society was Christian in its outlook as reflected in its program, Kosto-marov's *Books of Genesis of the Ukrainian People.* In addition to the basic freedoms and republican government, it advocated the absolute equality and fraternal union of all Slavic peoples, but it also glorified the Ukrainian past, especially the Cossack State, and was critical of Muscovy and its tsars.[62] The emphasis on Slavic unity based on genuine

[60] М. Грушевскій, *Очеркъ исторіи украинскаго народа* (St. Petersburg, 1906), p. 411.

[61] An early secret political group among the Left Bank gentry in the Poltava region at the time of the Decembrist movement was the Lukashevych Circle, whose members were said to have advocated an independent Ukraine. See Юліян Охримович, *Розвиток української національно-політичної думки: Від початку XIX століття до Михайла Драгоманова* (2nd ed.; Lviv, 1922), pp. 7-8, and Д. Дорошенко, *Нарис історії України* (Warsaw, 1933), II, 289.

[62] Thus in verse 84, in discussing Khmelnytsky's Pereiaslav Treaty with Tsar Alexei Mikhailovich: "Ukraine soon perceived that she had fallen into captivity because in her simplicity she did not realize what the Muscovite tsar signifies, and the Muscovite tsar meant the same as an idol and persecutor." Regarding Peter I and Catherine II the *Books of Genesis* had this to say: "the last tsar of Muscovy and the first [St.] Petersburg emperor [Peter I] destroyed hundreds of thousands [of Ukrainian Cossacks] in ditches and built for himself a capital on their bones." "And the German tsarina Catherine [II], a universal debauchee, atheist, husband slayer, ended the [Zaporozhian] Cossack Host and freedom because having selected those who were the *starshiny* [elected elders] in Ukraine, she allotted them nobility and lands and she gave them the free brethren in yoke, she made some masters and others slaves." Микола Костомаров, *Книги битія українського народу* (Augsburg, 1947), pp. 20-21, 22. For an English translation see *Kostomarov's "Books of Genesis of the Ukrainian People"* with a commentary by B. Yanivs'kyi [Volodymyr Mija-kovs'kyj] (New York: Research Program on the U.S.S.R. Mimeographed Series, No. 60, 1954).

national equality should not obscure the Society's insistence (in verse 104—or 109 in the later enumeration) that "Ukraine will be an independent Republic *(Rich Pospolita)*." Quite clearly, the failure to achieve complete national equality would imply a solution outside a Slavic union. The arrangement advocated was not federalist in fact (though called that), because it did not provide for a Slavic central government but was more in the nature of a loose confederation. However, Kostomarov's *Books of Genesis* depicted the Ukrainians as willing to forgive Muscovy and Poland their depredations. Indeed, the Cyril and Methodians preached a benign kind of Ukrainian messianism with which the *Books of Genesis* concluded: "Then all peoples, pointing to the place on the map where the Ukraine will be delineated, will say: Behold the stone which the builders rejected has become the cornerstone."[63] Thus the Ukrainians were to play a leading role in the projected Slavic union, since they were the least corrupted and most democratic Slavic people as a result of not having their own gentry (apart from those who were Russified or Polonized) and of having suffered national oppression and foreign rule.

The suppression of the Cyril and Methodius Society in March, 1847, and the arrest of its members constituted an important turning point. Some, like Kostomarov, were frightened into conformity. The impact which this experience had on Taras Shevchenko was profound, and, as Rudnytsky points out, the poet's role as national prophet had consequences which were to be felt long after his death in 1861. In the mid-nineteenth century the Ukrainian movement was at a crucial juncture. Shevchenko's decision to write in the Ukrainian language and to combat tsarist Russian rule rather than accommodate himself to it meant that Ukrainian was to develop fully as a literary language and that the banner of national liberation was to have a worthy bearer.

Cultural Russification had by now become a very real threat. This had not been the case in the eighteenth century, because culturally the Russians had little to offer the Ukrainians at that time. The works of Kotliarevsky and Lomonosov could compete as exponents, respectively, of the Ukrainian and Russian languages, and Lomonosov even studied in Kiev. However, with the appearance of Pushkin and the full and rapid development of the Russian literary language the balance shifted in the nineteenth century to the detriment of Ukrainian. This is well illustrated in the case of Nikolai Gogol, who wrote in Russian as the leading representative of the "Ukrainian School" of Russian literature; however, his father, Vasyl Hohol'-Ianovsky (1780-1825), wrote in Ukrainian. Shevchenko's decision to devote his great talent to the preservation and enrichment of the Ukrainian language made possible the course of events which followed.

If there may be some uncertainty regarding where a dialect ends and

[63] Костомаров, *op. cit.,* p. 24.

an independent language commences, it is an indisputable fact that an independent literary language is not so much a linguistic as a cultural phenomenon. A prerequisite for an independent literary language is the creativity of a poet of genius who shapes the raw linguistic material into an instrument capable of conveying the most sensitive feelings and abstract ideas. This poet of genius who assured the existence of an independent Ukrainian literary language was—in the spirit of dialectical development—not a member of the gentry with a university education but the self-taught, redeemed serf, Taras Shevchenko. However, Shevchenko's role was not confined to literature. Relying upon the heritage of the three preceding stages (as exemplified in *Istoriia Rusov,* Kotliarevsky, and the Cyril and Methodius Society) and also upon the popular tradition and interpretation of the Ukrainian Cossack revolution, Shevchenko created in fully developed poetic form not only the vision of an independent Ukraine (separate from Catholic Poland and Orthodox Russia) but also the idea of an armed struggle for its attainment.[64]

If prophets are not theologians, poets of genius are not political ideologists. Shevchenko's visions, which transcended the limited horizons of his contemporaries, could influence Ukrainian political thought only with the passage of time and the advent of appropriate conditions. The second half of the nineteenth century saw the Ukrainian movement limited to an apparently apolitical cultural Ukrainophilism. The *Hromada* (community) movement grew, emphasizing education in the Ukrainian language and love of the Ukrainian past and of the peasantry. The first such *Hromada,* formed among Ukrainians in St. Petersburg, published the journal *Osnova* in 1861-62 with the financial support of the Ukrainian gentry. The *Hromada* movement quickly spread to the Ukrainian cities and led to the *fourth or Geneva stage,* in which the Ukrainian movement acquired a clearly political character. This occurred as a result of the removal by Alexander II of Mykhailo Drahomanov from his professorship at the University of Kiev. Drahomanov went to Switzerland in 1876 and with the financial support of the Kiev Community began to publish *Hromada,* the first Ukrainian political journal, as well as brochures designed to develop Ukrainian political thought and to inform Europeans of Ukrainian problems and of the plight of his countrymen under Russian rule.[65] He was the first to appreciate the true content and the political essence of Shevchenko's works and took the first steps to realize in political practice Shevchenko's poetic visions. Drahomanov's contribution was to insist that

---

[64] Shevchenko's attitude towards Russian rule and the misbehavior of Russians in the Ukraine is especially evident in the poems «Кавказ,» «Великий льох,» «Катерина,» «Іржавець,» «Суботів,» «Розрита могила,» and «Сон» (1844). It is also significant that Shevchenko consistently referred to the Russians as *"Moskali."*

[65] On the Ukrainian publishing house in Geneva see Євген Бачинський, «Українська друкарня в Женеві,» *Науковий збірник,* II (New York, 1953), 58-104.

the Ukrainian movement could not remain apolitical and purely cultural, that all political movements in the Ukraine had to have a Ukrainian national character, and that the Ukrainian nation had a right to complete equality.[66]

Drahomanov's work bore fruit in the form of the *fifth or Galician stage*, in which, as a result of his influence, the first Ukrainian political party was formed in 1890. The Galician Radical Party took an important step forward and laid the groundwork for the demand for independent statehood, although Drahomanov personally favored a genuine East European federalism based on national equality. In 1895 this demand was expressed by Iulian Bachynsky in his *Ukraina irredenta*, whose Marxist conclusions and naïveté Rudnytsky criticizes without recognizing the significance of his having advocated Ukrainian political independence as a goal.[67] The circle is closed with the advent of Ukrainian political groupings within the Russian Empire, beginning in 1900 with the founding of the Revolutionary Ukrainian Party (RUP) by a group of students in Kharkov. Significantly, the founder of this political party, Dmytro Antonovych, was the son of the typical apolitical Ukrainophile, Volodymyr Antonovych (see note 14). Although RUP was to split over the issue of whether it should be socialist, its beginnings reflect the close contacts which had developed between the two parts of the Ukraine under Russian and Austrian rule. These had begun several decades earlier, as, for example, when Elisabeth Miloradovych of the East Ukrainian gentry financed the purchase of a printing press for the scholarly publications of the Shevchenko Scientific Society, which had been founded in Lviv in 1873. As a result of Hrushevsky's endeavors, the Shevchenko Society soon acquired the status of a national academy of sciences.[68] The development of Ukrainehood now reached a new stage at which Shevchenko's poetic vision began to approach realization.

The fact that the Ukrainian movement developed in spite—and in part because—of the existence of the Austro-Russian political frontier which divided the Ukrainian territories reflects an important aspect of this broad topic which Rudnytsky has avoided. Thus he has chosen to define the Ukraine's role in modern history in terms of the origins of its struggle for self-determination and the background of its efforts to extricate itself from the toils of Russia's empire. However, he has eschewed consideration of the implications which any significant change

---

[66] See *Mykhailo Drahomanov: A Symposium and Selected Writings*, Vol. II, No. 1 (1952), of *The Annals of the Ukrainian Academy of Arts and Sciences in the U.S.* Also see Охримович, *op. cit.*, pp. 89 and 111.

[67] Юліян Бачинський, *Україна Irredenta* (Lviv, 1895), pp. 74, 131-32. Also see Yaroslav Bilinsky, "Drahomanov, Franko and Relations between the Dnieper Ukraine and Galicia," *Annals of the Ukrainian Academy of Arts and Sciences in the U.S.*, VII (1959), 1542-66.

[68] See the discussion in Dmytro Doroshenko, "A Survey of Ukrainian Historiography," in *Annals of the Ukrainian Academy of Arts and Sciences in the U.S.*, V-VI (1957), 261-75.

in the status of the Ukrainians has for an understanding of the international relations of East Central Europe.[69]

Rudnytsky has also exercised the historian's prerogative of confining his treatment to the events preceding 1917. This has enabled him to offer some important guideposts to an understanding of the origins and nature of Ukrainian claims, but has obscured somewhat the interplay of conflicting forces which has been at the heart of Ukrainian development. It is in the understanding of this contradictory process that the dialectic can be of use.

In addition to being characterized by struggle and the conflict of opposites, the Ukrainian movement has time and again led to the emergence of forces quite the opposite of those intended either by the movement's supporters or detractors. Thus the literati who wrote in Ukrainian early in the nineteenth century were loyal subjects of the tsar but unknowingly made possible the later political manifestations of nationalism. It was among the largely Russified Left Bank gentry that the movement had its modern origins; yet a class which gave every appearance of having been bought off by the Russian regime actually served an opposite purpose. Another example is provided by the Orthodox theological seminaries, which, though designed to serve as instruments of Russification, produced some of the leading exponents of Ukrainian nationalism as well as the clergy who affirmed the autocephaly of the Ukrainian Orthodox Church in 1921. The Union of Brest (1596), unlike preceding efforts to this end, was brought about by Polish pressure on the Ukrainians, but the Ukrainian Catholic Church which resulted from it became an important means for preserving the nation and resisting Polish (and Russian) encroachments.

Nor has the post-1917 period been exempt from this dialectical process. The anti-Communist Ukrainian People's Republic (UNR), led by Symon Petliura, was supposedly defeated, though it won a victory in compelling the Russians to abandon the practice of calling Ukrainians by the pejorative term "Little Russians" and to concede, at least in theory, that the Ukrainian SSR was "sovereign." The Ukrainian SSR, the UNR's most bitter antagonist, soon found itself compelled to defend Ukrainian rights. Khristian Rakovsky, who helped destroy Ukrainian sovereignty in 1919-20, became its advocate in 1922-23. Mykola Skrypnyk, Mykola Khvylovy, and other enemies of the UNR found it impossible to be loyal executors of policies made in Moscow.

There are numerous paradoxes and contradictions, not the least of which is that in spite of frequent Russian collective expressions of antipathy to manifestations of Ukrainian self-reliance, there have been individual Russians who have devoted themselves to the Ukrainian cause. Thus the historian Mme Efimenko was of Russian descent but

[69] See, for example, Leon Wasilewski, *Kwestja-Ukraińska jako zagadnienie międzynarodowe* (Warsaw, 1934).

identified herself with Ukrainians. Kostomarov was partly of Russian descent. The Russian philologists Shakhmatov and Korsh, along with others, were instrumental in obtaining recognition for Ukrainian as a Slavic language distinct from Russian. Herzen and Bakunin expressed sympathy for the Ukrainians. Brullev was responsible for obtaining Shevchenko's redemption from serfdom, and the governor-general Nikolai Repnin encouraged the poet in his career and treated him as an equal.

A dialectical approach also recognizes the need to avoid being misled by appearances. Thus an ethnography and a "Southwestern Geographical Society," which on the surface appeared to be harmless and apolitical, led to a greater appreciation of Ukrainian distinctiveness. Galicia remained under Polish rule for centuries but became at one time the indispensable center of Ukrainian nationalism. The Russian monarchy appeared to have reduced the Ukraine to the status of a province, but subsequent events were to confirm the prognosis offered in Kostomarov's *Books of Genesis:* "And the Ukraine was destroyed [by Catherine II]. But it only appears to be so."[70] If the larger Ukrainian cities have contained substantial numbers of Russians in spite of Stalin's promise of March 10, 1921, that they would "inevitably be Ukrainized,"[71] one cannot judge Ukrainian developments exclusively in terms of superficial aspects of urban life.

The struggle for and against Ukrainian national identity, in addition to being fierce, is taking place on many levels and is assuming varied forms, although it is often not recorded directly. Yet it is no less meaningful for that fact. It would be naïve to underestimate the modern counterpart of the "splendid Juggernaut" and its willingness to employ any and all means to stunt Ukrainian cultural development and render the nation "incomplete." Yet 37,000,000 Ukrainians chose to declare their nationality in the 1959 Soviet census, and who can say with certainty that the Ukrainian cause may not receive new form and meaning from quarters from which such aid would appear least likely to come? May not Ukrainian membership in the United Nations and in other international bodies also, in the long run, have objective results different from those intended by Stalin in 1945? The role of the Ukraine is fraught with imponderables and even risks—as it has been in the past— but it is also the embodiment of promise. Such a nation as the Ukraine has had to be both refractory and resilient in order to survive, and in surviving it makes possible the ultimate fulfillment of its hopes.

[70] Костомаров, *op. cit.,* p. 24.
[71] И. В. Сталин, *Сочинения* (Moscow, 1952), V, 49.

Reply

IVAN L. RUDNYTSKY

I am grateful to the commentators for their thoughtful consideration. Professor Adams compliments me for my "courageous assessment of the insignificance of the Ukraine as a political entity prior to 1917." I am appreciative of the compliment, but I am sorry to say that it is based on a misapprehension of my point of view. As the problem is a historically important one, I will try to restate my argument.

The strength of a political movement must be measured in relative terms, taking into account specific circumstances. If one uses Western standards, all nongovernmental, societal political forces in nineteenth-century Russia may easily give the impression of being "insignificant." This refers not only to Ukrainian nationalism but also to Russian revolutionary and oppositionist movements, all of which had a narrow stratum of active supporters. This was the outcome of a system in which a despotic, hypertrophic state faced an atrophied, politically inarticulate, and cowed society. The outward expressions of the pre-1917 Ukrainian national movement may have been modest, and the number of persons actively engaged in it limited. Still, its strength should not be underestimated by a historian. Its vitality was proven by the fact that it survived systematic repression by a powerful state; and it always bore within itself the potential for a radical transformation of the political structure of Eastern Europe as a whole.

Perceptive contemporary observers were able to assess the political significance of the Ukrainian problem. Here are the comments of a German traveler, Johann Georg Kohl, who visited the Ukraine in the 1830's:

Such is the aversion of the people of Little to those of Great Russia that it may fairly be described as a national hatred, and the feeling has rather strengthened than diminished since the seventeenth century, when the country was annexed to the Moscovite empire. . . . Before their subjection, all the Malorossians were freemen, and serfdom, they maintain, had never been known among them. It was the Russians, they say, that reduced one-half of the people to slavery. During the first century after the union, Little Russia continued to have her own hetmans, and retained much of her ancient constitution and privileges, but all these have been swept away by the retrograde reforms of the last and present century. . . . To this day, the battle of Poltava is remembered throughout Little Russia with feelings similar to those with which the battle of the White Mountain is remembered in Bohemia. . . . Should the colossal empire of Russia one day fall to pieces, there is little doubt but the Malorossians will form a separate state. They have their own language, their own historical recollections, seldom mingle with their Moscovite rulers, and are in number already more than 10,000,000.[1]

It is noteworthy that these striking observations and predictions were made before the emergence of modern Ukrainian nationalism as an organized movement. The following excerpts are from a report which the Austrian consul in Kiev, Eduard Sedlaczek, submitted to the Ministry of Foreign Affairs in Vienna in 1893:

The Little Russian national movement continues to grow, although the greatest caution is being observed. . . . I know personally many a civil servant and teacher whose attitude in office is regarded as blameless who, however, in an intimate circle betrays a frame of mind far from friendly toward the government. . . . The present time is characterized by a substantial increase in studies on Little Russian history and ethnography, published in Russian. This is the natural outcome of censorship, which deals severely with Little Russian publications. . . . These [informal] groups, which are spread throughout the entire country, have a purely literary and scholarly outlook, and so offer nothing palpable to the police, but in fact they serve to strengthen the Little Russian patriotic awareness.[2]

This report illustrates the condition of the Ukrainian movement during the era of reaction. To obtain a notion of the impressive progress it was able to achieve in the subsequent twenty years, there is no better witness than S. N. Shchegolev, a member of the Russian Black Hundred. He was the author of a thick work on Ukrainian nationalism, published in 1912, which has been called "a handbook for the police."[3] Regardless of the author's tendency and purpose, the book is rich in factual information drawn from the contemporary press. The reader gets the distinct impression that all of "South Russia" was, on the eve of the First World War, honeycombed by the activities, overt or covert, of the Ukrainian national movement. The study of Shchegolev's work reveals the deep roots out of which blossomed the Ukrainian "miracle" of 1917; it also shows the erroneousness of the view of Professor Adams, according to whom the Ukrainian revolutionary parliament, the Central Rada, was "a tiny and isolated group of nationalist intellectuals." In reality the Rada was the crest of a powerful mass

---

[1] J. G. Kohl, *Russia: St. Petersburg, Moscow, Kharkoff, Riga, Odessa, the German Provinces of the Baltic, the Steppes, the Crimea, and the Interior of the Empire* (London, 1844), pp. 527-29.

[2] The report of Eduard Sedlaczek, drawn from the archives of the Ministry of Foreign Affairs in Vienna, has been published by Dmytro Doroshenko. See Дмитро Дорошенко, «Український рух 1890-их рр. в освітленні австрійського консула в Київі,» *З минулого: Збірник, т. I* (Праці Українського Наукового Інституту, т. 48) (Warsaw, 1938), pp. 59-70. The passages quoted are on pp. 63-65.

[3] С. Н. Щеголевъ, *Украинское движеніе какъ современный этапъ южнорусскаго сепаратизма* (Kiev, 1912).

movement.[4] The Rada's main problem and difficulty was not lack of popular support, as Professor Adams implies, but, quite to the contrary, the inadequacy of leadership: the national elite was neither numerous enough nor sufficiently experienced politically to master the spontaneous rising of the masses and to grasp power firmly in a large country under complicated and trying internal and international conditions.

In writing my paper, I deliberately limited myself to the prerevolutionary epoch. Professor Adams' contribution, however, is mainly devoted to the Revolution of 1917-21. This puts me in an awkward position. I lack space to offer a concerted discussion of the history of the Ukrainian Revolution, while, at the same time, I cannot leave some of Professor Adams' statements unchallenged.

Professor Adams' conception of the Ukrainian Revolution is basically one of a wild and chaotic peasant revolt, of a *jacquerie*. This picture, which may have been induced by his scholarly interest in the Makhno movement of the Southern Ukraine, is an extremely one-sided one, almost to the point of caricature. I do not think of denying the existence of those "anarchistic" features, but they were not the dominant ones in the history of the Ukrainian Revolution.

Let us, for instance, refer to the conservative regime of 1918, headed by Hetman Paul Skoropadsky. According to Professor Adams, Skoropadsky was simply a "puppet of the Germans." I contend that this view is a gross oversimplification. General Skoropadsky, a scion of a family distinguished in Ukrainian annals, returned during the Revolution to the service of his homeland, in very much the same manner as his former comrade-in-arms, General Mannerheim, returned to the service of Finland. Skoropadsky played an important role in the events of 1917 in the Ukraine, long before the coming of the Germans. It is true that the hetmanate of 1918 needed German protection for its survival, but it also found support among the conservative and moderate Ukrainians.[5]

---

[4] A test of strength of the Ukrainian movement was the election to the Russian Constituent Assembly in the late fall of 1917. "The five million votes obtained in the clear by the various Ukrainian lists constitute an impressive showing from any point of view, and must be augmented by at least another half million votes as the Ukrainian share of the joint lists agreed upon with other parties. . . . In the face of such a clear-cut demonstration of strength, it is simply not possible to contend that the Ukrainian movement was a weak and artificial thing, concocted by a group of hyper-nationalistic intellectuals." Oliver Henry Radkey, *The Election to the Russian Constituent Assembly of 1917* (Cambridge, Mass.: Harvard University Press, 1950), pp. 18 and 30. The validity of this test has been explicitly recognized by Lenin himself. Rosa Luxemburg, like Professor Adams, believed that the Central Rada was without a mass basis, and she criticized Lenin for the "coddling" of Ukrainian nationalism. In justifying his policy Lenin referred to the results of the election to the Constituent Assembly as a proof that the Ukrainian movement was a force to be reckoned with. It is to be noted that in the eight provinces of the Ukraine the Bolsheviks obtained only 10 per cent of votes. Cf. Jurij Borys, *The Russian Communist Party and the Sovietization of Ukraine* (Stockholm, 1960), pp. 159-60.

[5] The background of the Skoropadsky coup has been recently studied by Oleh S. Fedyshyn from German archival sources. It appears that Skoropadsky was not hand-picked

During its short duration, the hetmanate could show a number of creditable achievements, including the foundation of two Ukrainian-language universities, in Kiev and Kamenets-Podolsk, and of an Academy of Sciences, of which the present Academy of Sciences of the Ukrainian SSR is a lineal continuation. Skoropadsky's political life did not end with the fall of the hetmanate. Actually, he gained moral stature during the years of exile, and a considerable segment of the Ukrainian community outside the borders of the USSR continued to look upon him, during the interwar period, as the legitimate pretender to the Ukraine's throne. All this is not intended as an apologia for Skoropadsky or the regime headed by him in 1918, but is meant as a warning against simplistic clichés in the treatment of the history of the Ukrainian Revolution.

The failure of the Ukrainian Revolution is obvious: it did not succeed in giving permanence to an independent, democratic national state. A perceptive student, however, whose vision is not limited to success and failure, might feel the obligation to weigh the causes of this failure and to try to discern what, in spite of defeat, the permanent achievements of the Ukrainian Revolution have been.

Among the new nations emerging in Eastern Europe at the end of World War I none had greater handicaps than the Ukraine. The country's normal development had been warped and retarded by the dead hand of Russian tsarism. There was, in 1917, a staggering backlog of unfulfilled tasks, which had to be shouldered all at once, whereas other stateless nations had been able to solve these preliminary problems gradually, over decades. For instance, there did not exist in old Russia one single school with Ukrainian as the language of instruction. The Ukraine was faced simultaneously with the task of creating a network of elementary schools and of forming an independent government, an army, and a diplomatic service. One may also add that imperial Russia, in whose shadow the majority of the Ukrainian people had lived for such a long time, was a very poor training place for self-government and civic maturity. There was a standing joke in Ukrainian circles: "Why won't Britain annex us as a colony? Then we would be ready for independence in ten years." The social tensions in the country were acute. In the Ukraine, in contrast with Great Russia, the movement of social protest did not flow in orthodox Bolshevik channels; still, it offered a favorable ground for subversive propaganda coming from Moscow, and it impeded the consolidation of the democratic Ukrainian People's Republic.

---

by the Germans. The right-wing conspiracy against the socialistic Rada government was formed by Skoropadsky on his own initiative. German military authorities arrived independently at a decision to get rid of the "uncooperative" Central Rada. The two parties reached an agreement only a few days before the coup of April 29, 1918. See Oleh S. Fedyshyn, "German Plans and Policies in the Ukraine, 1917-1918" (unpubl. doctoral dissertation, Columbia University, 1962).

Internationally, the Ukraine had first to shoulder, in 1917, the un-welcome heritage of the war against the Central Powers, then, in 1918, the burden of the German occupation, and finally, in 1919, to face the lack of recognition and the political hostility of the victorious Entente. Isolated and deprived of any outside support, the Ukraine had to sus-tain a war on three fronts: against Soviet Russia, against the White Army of General Denikin, and against Poland. The Polish-Ukrainian struggle merits a special mention, as it is usually overlooked by Western historians, who approach the Ukrainian Revolution as a part of the Russian Civil War. The Polish-Ukrainian conflict was by no means a local affair affecting Galicia only; it exercised a fateful impact on the whole development of the Ukrainian cause. Galicia was the section of the Ukraine with the highest level of national consciousness. In civic discipline and public order the territory compared favorably with all the other East European countries of that time, and the population was impervious to Communist propaganda. It was the intention of the Ukrainian leaders to use Galicia as the stronghold and the base in the struggle against Soviet Russia. This was prevented by the Polish attack, which diverted the best Ukrainian forces from the anti-Bolshevik front in the critical months of the winter and spring of 1919. On the other hand, the political obtuseness and rigid centralism of the White Army prevented the coalition of all anti-Communist forces. Despite these tragic circumstances, the Ukraine offered a stubborn, protracted resist-ance and kept on fighting. Viewed in this light, even "peasant anarch-ism," by which Professor Adams has been so impressed, may be under-stood as an elemental groping of the Ukrainian masses after liberty, independence, and a just social order.

Professor Adams is right in stressing that Ukrainian patriots also worked in the Soviet camp. Nevertheless, the Soviet regime occupies a very different place in Russian and Ukrainian history. In Russia, the victory of the Bolsheviks was over their internal opponents; Soviet Russia is, for better or worse, the legitimate heir of the traditional Russian state. The position of the Ukraine is, in this respect, analogous rather with that of the "people's democracies" established after World War II. The Soviet regime was imposed on the country from the out-side; the weak local Communists (among whom ethnic Ukrainians formed only a minority) would never have been able to secure power in the Ukraine without outside intervention. The "Ukrainian Soviet So-cialist Republic" represents a compromise between the fact of Russian domination and those conquests of the Ukrainian Revolution which could no longer be obliterated. It speaks for the farsightedness and political flexibility of Lenin that he, modifying his original centralistic program, perceived the necessity of neutralizing the forces of Ukrainian nationalism by appropriate concessions.

The permanent achievements of the Ukrainian Revolution were, first, a profound "mutation" of the collective mind of the Ukrainian people, their crystallization into a modern nation, and, second, a shift in the international power structure of the eastern half of the continent. "The East European upheavals of 1917-20 have led to three great results: the victory of Bolshevism, which entered into the historical inheritance of Muscovy-Russia, the re-establishment of Poland, and the re-emergence of the Ukraine as the third great force of the East European area, alongside Great Russia and Poland."[6] It is noteworthy, for instance, that the changes which took place in Eastern Europe after the Second World War represent not only an expansion of Moscow's imperial sphere, but also the fulfillment of the territorial program which the Ukrainian movement advocated for generations: the consolidation of all lands of Ukrainian speech in one Ukrainian body politic. This, in turn, has brought a shift in the balance of forces between the Ukraine and Russia, whose full impact only the future will be able to tell.

Professor Adams informs us that he has "often clashed with Ukrainian nationalist scholars," and he complains that "nationalistic dross has long hampered effective investigation in this area" of modern Ukrainian history. Professor Adams graciously exempts me from this criticism, but I cannot help feeling that his complaints are out of place. Ukrainian scholars in Western lands are few, and there is little danger that they will be able to "brainwash" anyone. As far as modern Ukrainian history is concerned, it is difficult to see what "nationalistic dross" has impeded its study. Is it not rather true that Ukrainian history, modern or old, has not yet been discovered as a separate area of studies by Western scholars, and is treated, if at all, only incidentally, on the margin of Russian history? The expression "nationalist scholars," as used by Professor Adams, implies a judgment of value. I have not heard that a historian of Russian background, working in the United States, has been ever labeled "nationalistic," even if he displays obvious symptoms of Russian patriotic fervor. Why this difference in treatment? The answer, I think, is that views and interpretations traditionally expounded by Russian scholarship have received wide currency and are given credence, without questioning of their premises. Conceptions which run counter to this orthodoxy are not weighed for their scholarly validity but are automatically ruled out of court as allegedly biased and "nationalistic." I do not, of course, expect that views defended by Ukrainian historiography should be accepted uncritically; but they merit a proper hearing.

A great Russian statesman, Sergius Witte, once said:

We have not yet fully realized that since the times of Peter the Great and Catherine the Great there has been no Russia, but a Russian Empire. If some 35 per cent of the population are ethnic minorities, and the Russians

---

[6] W. Kutschabsky, *Die Westukraine im Kampfe mit Polen und dem Bolschewismus in den Jahren 1918-1923* (Berlin, 1934), p. 1.

are divided into Great Russians, Little Russians, and Belorussians, it is impossible to conduct in the nineteenth and twentieth centuries a policy which disregards this historical fact of capital importance, which disregards the national traits of the other nationalities, composing the Russian Empire, their religion, language, etc.[7]

The "historical fact of capital importance" stressed by Witte nearly half a century ago has even now not been fully digested by many American scholars in the field of East European and Slavic studies. The history of "Russia" is usually approached as one of an essentially homogeneous area rather than one of a multinational empire, comparable, in this respect, to the former Ottoman and Austrian empires. This results, I believe, in a one-sided and inadequate understanding of the East European historical process. To correct this would require a profound revision of the traditional historical perspectives, and this is opposed by the great force of intellectual inertia. "Nationalist historians," of whom Professor Adams complains, may be given credit for performing a useful function—that of gadflies, who awaken sluggish thought from its dogmatic slumber.

The commentary of Professors Pritsak and Reshetar raises many questions, particularly that of the classification of the Ukraine as Eastern or Western, and that of historicity and nonhistoricity. On the first point, I am inclined to agree with Oscar Halecki that the Ukraine is Eastern *and* European; the second question was treated in the article. These, and other issues raised by Professors Pritsak and Reshetar, are worth substantial debate at some time, but further comment does not seem appropriate in an article on the modern Ukraine. The reader of the commentary will see that there are many interesting topics for discussion in the field of Ukrainian history, and I am appreciative of Professors Pritsak and Reshetar's intensive study.

[7] С. Ю. Витте, *Воспоминания*, III (Moscow, 1960), 274.

SEVEN

The Problem of Unity in the Polish-Lithuanian State

OSWALD P. BACKUS III

When we look at the Polish-Lithuanian state from the Union of Krewo in the late fourteenth century, through the period of its greatness in the sixteenth century, to its demise in 1795, we are moved to wonder why this state disintegrated before the machinations of the great powers. The contrast between the glory of its greatness and the futility of its end seems incomprehensible. Scholars who have centered their attention on the *liberum veto* have not managed adequately to explain the state's decline. They contend in effect that the nobility by its selfish exercise of the *liberum veto*—that is, the right of a single noble to veto any legislation proposed in the parliament—reduced Poland-Lithuania to nought. To be sure, the selfishness of these nobles was increased by the machinations of outside powers, the real devils. By their bribes, by their armies, by various forms of interference they weakened and ultimately suppressed a state which nonetheless had shown an enormous ability to maintain itself and had contributed through its great men and great institutions to the culture of the world.[1]

Regrettably, despite a large amount of careful research, a thorough analysis of the political, economic, cultural, ethnic, and other factors bearing on the failure of Poland-Lithuania has never been made. It is not my purpose here to attempt such a thorough analysis but merely to sketch a few issues that I believe to be of major importance. I shall raise these issues in the chronological order in which I believe they became crucial: they concern two related aspects of the problem of unity. (1) To what extent was unity realized, and (2) what undermined the union which had been created? It is my view that the achievement

MR. BACKUS *is professor of history at the University of Kansas.*

[1] Many Polish scholars have looked beyond the *liberum veto* for a complex of internal factors, e.g., see the brilliant essay by Oswald M. Balzer, *Konstytucya Trzeciego Maja: Reformy społeczne i polityczne ustawy rządowej z r. 1791* (3rd ed.; Krakow, 1922), and Stanisław Kutrzeba, *Historia ustroju Polski w zarysie: Korona* (8th ed., rev. by Adam Vetulani; Warsaw, 1949), pp. 338-41. A typical view is expressed by Georg Manteuffel-Szoege, *Geschichte des polnischen Volkes während seiner Unfreiheit, 1772-1914* (Berlin, 1950), pp. 5-6.

of Polish-Lithuanian unity was impeded from 1385 through the sixteenth century by various forms of political competition, by the failure to establish a strong monarchy, and by some of the differences in culture between the constituent lands. In the sixteenth century the Reformation gave a new dimension to existing difficulties, besides adding new stresses. Later, though political competition and cultural diversity became in general less troublesome, economic strains, the Ukrainian problem, the selfish obstructionism of the nobles, and intervention from the outside were major causes of weakness. At the risk of oversimplifying, I would argue that real unity did not exist in the era of the Jagellonian dynasty, and that no sooner was a modest degree of unity achieved than it began to be undermined. The problem of unity has a related aspect, less emphasized by historians—the viability of a multinational federation. Such viability has been assumed by many Polish scholars—an assumption which has encouraged them to treat the Jagellonian federation as an extraordinary political phenomenon of the late medieval or early modern age which at its height linked effectively, albeit loosely, such disparate peoples as Hungarians, Czechs, Poles, Lithuanians, Ukrainians, Belorussians, and Russians.[2]

POLITICAL COMPETITION

One might question the extent to which real unity existed at any time in the history of Poland-Lithuania. As I have suggested above, I am willing to argue that in the late fourteenth, the fifteenth, and the sixteenth centuries there never was any real unity in the state. The major cause was the political competition between Lithuania and Poland; it should be borne in mind that Lithuania was a separate political entity. To be sure the original Union of Krewo opened the possibility that Lithuania and Poland would be one. It was intended that Jagailo, the great prince of Lithuania, would become the king of Poland; no doubt no one ever imagined that Jagailo would, either in effect or in fact, lose his position as great prince of Lithuania. However, the ambitions of his cousin Vitovt and the desire of many nobles to retain a degree of autonomy made it impossible for Jagailo to retain the great principality of Lithuania. Instead, after a few years of struggle with Vitovt he was compelled to recognize Vitovt first as his viceroy in Lithuania and, in 1401, as a virtually independent great prince of Lithuania. Whatever the legal fictions may have been by which Jagailo saved face, the facts of the matter were that Vitovt really ruled Lithuania. It is true that some scholars have emphasized the technical legal position of Jagailo, tending thereby to minimize the reality of Vitovt's strength and the reality of Vitovt's independent exercise of power.[3] That the

[2] The outstanding protagonist of the Jagellonian federation is Oscar Halecki. See especially his *Dzieje Unii Jagiellońskiej* (2 vols.; Krakow, 1919-20).

[3] Anatol Lewicki, "Über das staatsrechtliche Verhältnis Litauens zu Polen unter Jagiell

death of Vitovt in 1430 did not bring Lithuania back into the fold of the united Polish-Lithuanian state is perhaps the clearest evidence of the reality of Vitovt's power. Instead of turning to Jagailo, the Lithuanians elected Svidrigailo, a younger brother of Jagailo, as great prince of Lithuania, rather obviously desiring to continue Lithuania's independence. To be sure, not all of the nobles seem to have shared in this desire: many of them rose up partly on the grounds of friendliness to Poland and supported Sigismund, who was pro-Polish. It is dangerous, however, to overemphasize pro-Polish sentiment. One must consider the uprising evidence of Sigismund's personal disappointment that he, Vitovt's brother, had not succeeded to Vitovt's position and that instead Svidrigailo, a brother of the former opponent of his brother Vitovt, had obtained the prize. Furthermore, it would appear that some of the dissatisfaction of the nobles who supported Sigismund resulted from the fact that they were Catholic, since, as Catholics, they may very well have feared Svidrigailo's pro-Orthodox views.[4]

Political competition between Poland and Lithuania was heightened by Poland's attempted seizure of Volhynia in 1431 and the long-standing Polish-Lithuanian dispute over Podolia. Casimir, the successor both of Sigismund as great prince of Lithuania and of Ladislas as king of Poland, weakened his own position in Lithuania to some degree by failing to combat the Polish control over much of Podolia. Ownership of Podolia remained a major issue throughout the sixteenth century. Although Casimir's ability to make concessions and compromises helped to make a partial success of the Polish-Lithuanian union, one must recognize that he was unable to weld the two states into one.

Poland's desire for territorial gains was inextricably linked to the desire of Polish nobles to dominate Lithuania or parts thereof. One may, if one wishes, regard the grant in the Horodlo union of 1413 to Lithuanian nobles of numerous rights already enjoyed by Polish nobles as evidence of the sort of cooperation which tended to support union. The rigid exclusion of Orthodox nobles from the grant is not consonant with that view and may be reasonably considered an expres-

---

und Witold," *Altpreussische Monatsschrift,* XXXI (1894), No. 1-2. Josef Pfitzner, *Grossfürst Witold von Litauen als Staatsmann,* "Schriften der Philosophischen Fakultät der Deutschen Universität in Prag," No. 6 (Brno, 1930), pp. 105-13, stresses that Vitovt did not enjoy full autonomy in the years immediately following 1392. Balzer makes it quite clear that in the period 1386-1398/1401 the great prince exercised strong control in the patrimonium of the great prince, from which military and court services were extracted, but less control in the appanages of the princes—a situation that had existed in Poland prior to 1385. Oswald M. Balzer, "Istota prawna zależności książąt litewsko-ruskich w dobie 1386-1398/1401," *Sprawozdania Towarzystwa Naukowego we Lwowie* (Lwow, 1922), I, 196-204.

[4] Матвей К. Любавскій, *Очеркъ исторіи литовско-русскаго государства* (Moscow, 1910), pp. 61 ff. Antoni Prochaska, *Król Władysław Jagiełło* (Krakow, 1908), II, 254-86. Svidrigailo, in his policy of supporting the struggle for an Orthodox metropolitanate in Lithuania, was continuing the policy of Vitovt and thus was not merely pro-Orthodox in his own right. Михайло С. Грушевський, *Історія України-Руси,* V (Lvov, 1905), Part II, 398-404.

sion of a desire to dominate. There was certainly such a desire among Poles. For example, in the late fourteenth century a Polish noble, Pan Spytko Melsztynski, sought and obtained control of Podolia, a sizable province of Lithuania. Despite the reversion of Podolia to the Lithuanian crown after Melsztynski's death, other Polish nobles subsequently secured positions in the same province. Furthermore, Polish interest in union was not so great that Poland refrained from exploiting, supporting, or at least applauding separatist movements inside Lithuania which might improve Poland's chances for making territorial gains at Lithuania's expense.[5]

Another major factor in the perpetuation of political competition was the emergence of advisory and parliamentary institutions both in Poland and in Lithuania which involved nobles in the making of decisions at the level of the central government in a more consistent and regular fashion than had previously prevailed. There has been substantial debate whether the larger parliamentary body, the *seim,* existed in Lithuania before the beginnnig of the fifteenth century, and whether the Lithuanian council, the *rada,* had any significance before the middle of that century.[6] Nonetheless, such institutions emerged in both countries and by their existence afforded the nobility of each country more opportunity to advocate local interest and thereby to impede effective union. Successive kings of Poland and great princes of Lithuania, such as Casimir, Alexander, Sigismund, and Sigismund Augustus, all had to deal with separate parliaments in both Poland and Lithuania. The strength of these separate parliaments may be gauged by the fact that even the Union of Lublin of 1569 was unable to effect a merger of the parliamentary institutions; it was compelled to recognize the stability of the parliaments and to provide for their continued existence in the resultant, somewhat more closely united federal union.[7]

Lithuanian-Polish competition was further complicated by separatist tendencies within the various provinces of Lithuania. One of these, Samogitia, was a lodestone for the Teutonic Order of Knights in East Prussia, who managed from time to time to obtain control of it. In consequence, Samogitia made use of its special position to get special privileges from Casimir around 1440, when he came to the throne of

---

[5] The desire of Polish nobles to dominate is a theme of Өедоръ Еленевъ, *Польская цивилизація и ея вліяніе на западную Русь* (St. Petersburg, 1863), p. 20. He blames the Poles for starting serfdom in Volhynia and Podolia.

[6] М. К. Любавскій, «Литовско-русскій сеймъ: Опытъ по исторіи учрежденія въ связи съ внутреннимъ строемъ и внѣшнею жизнью государства,» *Чтенія въ императорскомъ обществъ исторіи и древностей россійскихъ при московскомъ университетъ,* CXCV (1900), 30, labels the Lithuanian seim of 1401 as the first. His view was challenged by both M. V. Dovnar-Zapolsky and N. A. Maksimeiko. For a brief statement of the dispute see М. К. Любавскій, «Новые труды по исторіи литовско-русскаго сейма,» *Журналъ министерства народнаго просвѣщенія,* CCCXXXXV (1903), 137.

[7] George Vernadsky, *Russia at the Dawn of the Modern Age* (New Haven and London, 1959), pp. 247-48.

Lithuania. The Samogitian nobility always resisted full domination by the central government of Lithuania. Separatism also existed in such provinces as Kiev, Smolensk, and Polotsk, and to a perhaps even greater degree among the nobles in the lands about the upper Oka River. Many of these nobles were only partly under Lithuanian domination, and they often followed policies more in their own interest than in that of any united Polish-Lithuanian state. Their separatist tendencies compelled the central government of Lithuania to pay particular attention to its outlying areas and to its relations with the adjacent Russian principalities, particularly the great principality of Muscovy. In sum, separatism increased the tendency of Poland and Lithuania to follow often conflicting and competing foreign policies.

Clearly such separatism had bases in law. Thus, as Iasinsky has stated, the charters of the different provinces and areas of Lithuania show that they lived under different laws. Iasinsky also asserted that there was no all-Lithuanian statute until 1529. That point has been disputed by those who have emphasized the importance of the union of Poland and Lithuania; they may be quite right in asserting that the Privilege of 1447 or even that of 1434 had the force of law in all the provinces of Lithuania. However, such a dispute partly misses the point. How much force did local law retain? Was local custom still important? Is it probable that local law and custom strengthened separatism and prevented any effective union?[8]

The issue of Lithuanian-Polish political competition was reduced in importance only after Lithuania had become more Polonized and had decided that competition with Poland was a luxury she must forgo in view of the rise of Muscovy. Ivan the Terrible made many successful attacks on Lithuania. It was during the blood bath, called the *Oprichnina,* by which Ivan attempted to stamp out insubordination among the nobles that the Union of Lublin of 1569, perhaps significantly, occurred. The Lithuanian decision to cooperate with Poland more effectively may have been linked with the sentiments expressed by Prince Kurbsky, a Muscovite defector, that nobles had the right to enjoy certain traditional privileges which contributed to their status.[9] The extent to which the Lithuanian nobles accepted the views of Kurbsky can never be known. It is significant, however, that whereas before the reign of Ivan the Terrible, Lithuanian nobles deserted

---

[8] М. Н. Ясинскій, *Уставныя земскія грамоты литовско-русскаго государства* (Kiev, 1889), Part I, pp. 3, 73-74. At one point Fedor I. Leontovich went further than Iasinsky and stated that the first confirmation of privileges applying to the whole of Lithuania occurred in 1547. See his «Правоспособность литовско-русской шляхти,» *Журналъ министерства народнаго просвѣщенія* (new series), Part XX (1909), sec. 2, p. 81. It seems more likely that the Privilege of 1434 was the first to apply to all of Lithuania. Oscar Halecki, "Litwa, Ruś i Żmudź, jako części składowo Wielkiego Księstwa Litewskiego," *Rozprawy Akademii Umiejętnosci: Wydział historyczno-filozoficzny,* LIX, 232-34.

[9] J. L. I. Fennell, ed. and trans., *The Correspondence between Prince A. M. Kurbsky and Tsar Ivan IV of Russia, 1564-1579* (Cambridge, Eng., 1955), pp. 204-17.

Lithuania for Muscovy, during his reign such desertions markedly decreased and after his reign were very rare. No longer were Lithuanian political aspirations to represent a significant obstacle to cooperation with Poland.

In fairness, I feel compelled to stress the tendency of some of the Polish and Lithuanian nobles to make common cause; one significant example was the cooperation against the Teutonic Knights, of which the Battle of Grunwald is a symbol.[10] There was even some cooperation against the rising Muscovite state long before the reign of Ivan the Terrible. There were also cooperative aspects, as mentioned above, in the grant of 1413 to the Lithuanians of the right to bear the arms of the Polish nobles. And one must remember that Polish and Lithuanian nobles often elected a man as their common ruler, even before 1569, and on significant occasions took the necessary steps to make possible the raising of armies in defense of the Polish-Lithuanian union. Thus, for example, in the Livonian campaign during the late sixteenth century there is clear evidence of Lithuanian-Polish cooperation. Such efforts toward military cooperation may have influenced the drive toward judicial reform which resulted in the reform of the lower courts in 1578. To be sure, sometimes this cooperation was directed against the power of the Polish and Lithuanian rulers and can therefore be said to represent an undermining of the union. However, such efforts do have their cohesive aspects in that they represent cooperation among nobles. In fine, despite these evidences of cooperation, I maintain that competition was the dominant tendency.

In view of my assertion that Lithuanian-Polish political competition represented a real obstacle to union, one may wonder why this issue has not heretofore received greater stress in the scholarly literature. I believe that this comparative inattention is in part a result of the conception of the importance of the Jagellonian federation which has become common more recently in Polish historiography. Oscar Halecki has been the major protagonist of the view. The union is now viewed as an early example of an international political ideal of the twentieth century, as expressed in the League of Nations and in the United Nations. One of the things that Halecki found great about the Jagellonian federation was that it allowed so much autonomy to the constituent parts of the federation. Autonomy thereby became in his mind a virtue—the very autonomy which, I would maintain, lay at the basis of Lithuanian-Polish political competition.[11] Although not all historians have followed in the footsteps of Halecki, many have

[10] Lithuanian and Russian cooperation in the Battle of Grunwald (Tannenberg) of 1410 is clearly delineated by Stefan M. Kuczyński, *Wielka wojna z zakonem kryzyżackim w latach, 1409-1411* (Warsaw, 1960), e.g., pp. 233-42, despite his underlying thesis that the Poles played the most significant role.

[11] I should stress the existence of scholarly literature which disputes the organic incorporation of Lithuania into Poland, particularly in respect to law and culture. See particu-

affirmed the view that the Polish monarchy was weakened by the extinction of the Jagellonian dynasty. They have seen its demise, just three short years after the Union of Lublin of 1569, as a great misfortune, because they have repeatedly maintained, albeit with increasing reservations, that Poland was strengthened by her possession of a prince from Lithuania whose position was virtually inherited and who, because of his substantial power within Lithuania, was able to maintain a higher degree of control over Poland than subsequent rulers could. The rise of the *liberum veto* in the seventeenth century has therefore been seen as a direct, though not a necessary, consequence of the end of the Jagellonian dynasty.[12] I believe one may disagree.

The Failure to Establish a New Monarchy

I come now to a second cause of the weakening of Poland and of the difficulties encountered by the Polish-Lithuanian union. In an age when monarchs like Henry VIII, Francis I, and others were strengthening their control over their countries—creating what some authorities have chosen to term the new monarchies—the rulers of Poland-Lithuania were losing many of their powers. They lost them in fact before rather than after the end of the Jagellonian dynasty. I believe such a formulation to reflect more nearly accurately the views of the time itself than would the assertion, perhaps a rationalization, that ruler and nobles were working out a balance of powers, an experiment in government which might well have succeeded.

In 1425 the nobles of Poland attempted to check their king at Brest by a charter of liberties containing a proviso that unless Jagailo's son confirmed those liberties, the nobles would be free not to adhere to him. Jagailo did not grant this charter, but the Polish nobles continued to press their case, hopeful that they might be able to gain greater power.

Casimir IV made concessions in privileges to the nobles of Lithuania and Poland in 1447 and 1454; yet he was a centralizer who attempted to strengthen the monarchy in a way which enables us to regard him as a parallel, although an incomplete one, to the New Monarchs of Western Europe. His policy of centralization was by no means abandoned by his successors, who nonetheless did substantially strengthen the positions of the rada in Poland and in Lithuania. In Poland, particularly through the statute of *nihil novi* of the Constitution of Radom of 1505, and in Lithuania, through a parallel provision of the privileges of 1506, the nobles procured that no new law could be introduced by the ruler without the approval of the rada, that is, without the approval of

---

larly the outstanding essay, all too infrequently noted, И. И. Лаппо, «Литовско-русское государство в составе Речи Посполитой,» *Vědecké Práce Ruské Lidové University v Praze*, II (Prague, 1929), 63-76.

[12] See Halecki's careful formulation, *A History of Poland* (New York, 1943), pp. 131-33. Cf. Kutrzeba, *Historia ustroju Polski ...*, pp. 261-70.

those nobles within the rada, and, in the case of Poland, without the approval, as well, of the district deputies.[13] Thus, not only were separatist tendencies given a more effective forum, as has been indicated above, but also the power of the nobles vis-à-vis the ruler was strengthened.

Despite these concessions to the nobility, the late fifteenth and early sixteenth centuries witnessed the desertion of Lithuania by substantial numbers of outlying nobles. Among their important reasons were probably their loss of land and, even more important, their loss of positions in local government to persons from Lithuania proper and to representatives of the central government of Lithuania. In effect the desertions were in part a protest against the efforts by the Lithuanian government to strengthen its control over the outlying regions.[14] It is hardly surprising, then, that during the sixteenth century the rulers of Lithuania found it difficult to establish firm control over either the state or the nobility. Their policies seem indeed to have been shaped by the interrelated necessities of diminishing the suspicions of their intentions among the nobles and of making concessions to them. In Poland-Lithuania we witness little of that cooperation between crown and lower gentry which was characteristic of the rising national monarchies. For example, Sigismund II Augustus did not establish a strong state on a constitutional basis in cooperation with the lower gentry of Poland, although at the time many ambitious representatives of great noble families advanced their own fortunes. Ultimately in 1572 the dissatisfaction of the lesser Polish nobles moved them, under the leadership of Zamoyski, to establish the principle that each noble might vote on succession to throne. This blow against the greater magnates focused the attention of the lesser nobles, not on cooperation with the king of Poland and the great prince of Lithuania, but on strengthening the position of the lesser nobles vis-à-vis the greater nobles, even at the expense of the king.

Despite the capacity of such later rulers as Stephen Bathory and Jan Sobieski, a new monarchy was never established in Poland. Instead,

[13] It is clear that the rada gained and that the nobles were the chief beneficiaries of that gain. Karol Górski, "Rządy wewnętrzne Kazimierza Jagiellończyka w koronie," *Kwartalnik historyczny,* LXVI (1959), 726-59. Górski, nonetheless, terms the reign of Casimir in Poland as absolutistic or proto-absolutist. See also Любавскій, «Литовско-русскій сеймъ,» *op. cit.,* pp. 367-74, who saw the Lithuanian rada gaining in power. Fryderyk Papée, *Polska i Litwa na Przełomie Wieków średnich,* I (Krakow, 1904), 29, sees Casimir as a centralizer but concedes that "centralization was not allowed to be realized as absolutely as elsewhere." There is evidence of tendencies developing in early sixteenth-century Lithuania which point in the direction of the dynastic state, i.e., centralization. See O. P. Backus, "The Problem of Feudalism in Lithuania, 1506-1548," *Slavic Review,* XXI (1962), 657-58. Although the nobles followed their own interests, they did sometimes think in terms of strengthening the state. Anna Dembińska, *Zygmunt I zarys dziejów wewnętrzno-politycznych w latach, 1540-1548* (Poznan, 1948).

[14] Oswald P. Backus, *Motives of West Russian Nobles in Deserting Lithuania for Moscow, 1377-1514* (Lawrence, 1957), p. 98.

the power of the ruler was ultimately subordinated to that of the nobility. The act of 1572, because it so greatly increased the power of the lesser nobles, played an important role in undermining the Polish-Lithuanian union.

CULTURAL DIVERSITY

A third important cause of the difficulty in establishing Polish-Lithuanian unity in the fourteenth through sixteenth centuries was the very real difference in culture between Poland and Lithuania. Poland was a Catholic state which contained many institutions more nearly analogous to those in the West than were the institutions of Lithuania—which, in my opinion, has properly been considered by H. Jablonowski as "a land of transition."[15] To be sure, one might argue that from some points of view all of East Central Europe should be regarded as an area of transition; so much depends upon the perspective which one adopts. One may look upon France and Russia as the two countries that must be compared, and see everything in between as variants on Western or Eastern themes. In any case, the day is long past when one may safely identify Poland very simply with Western Europe. On the other hand, even such scholars as Halecki, in his emphasis on the unity of Western Christendom, have tended to draw a line, albeit a shifting one, of demarcation between Poland and Eastern Europe.[16] Likewise a more recent authority, G. Rhode, while proceeding with caution, has nonetheless through his examination of the outlook of the Poles, come to the conclusion that in the late fourteenth century they regarded themselves as the rampart of Western Christendom.[17] All such scholarly explanations seem, in my opinion, to have an unfortunate tendency to encourage less scholarly attempts to draw clear-cut lines between the cultures of Eastern and Western Europe. Furthermore, I must express disapproval of the related popular tendency to project back into the past the present division between East and West. I am compelled to emphasize that the position adopted by Jablonowski is more convincing; that any attempt to understand the problems encountered by the Polish-Lithuanian state must start from the premises of cultural differentiation between Lithuania and Poland and the absence of any sharp dividing line between East and West. Perhaps one should first ask, to clarify the issue of cultural diversity, what is a culture?

Borrowing from Feliks Koneczny, I would suggest that a culture can most easily be defined by reference to the ways in which it differs from

[15] Horst Jablonowski, *Westrussland zwischen Wilna und Moskau: Die politische Stellung und die politischen Tendenzen der russischen Bevölkerung des Grossfürstentums Litauen im 15. Jh.* (Leiden, 1955), p. 155.

[16] Oscar Halecki, *The Limits and Divisions of European History* (New York, 1950), pp. 105-22.

[17] Gotthold Rhode, *Die Ostgrenze Polens: Politische Entwicklung, kulturelle Bedeutung und geistige Auswirkung*, Vol. I.: *Im Mittelalter bis zum Jahre 1401* (Cologne and Graz, 1955), pp. 242-93, see especially pp. 246-53, 259.

another culture or cultures, and that law offers some of the clearest clues to cultural differentiation. Law embodies the purposes and goals that the lawmakers are striving to execute and achieve. One of the most important purposes is the maintenance and extension of values, particularly the moral values advocated by religion.[18]

The simple application of Koneczny's technique, an examination of law, especially family law, property law, and the law of inheritance (which he regarded as crucial), involves a great risk, namely, that one may fail to ask some fundamental and highly significant questions. Was the written law enforced? Was custom, which had the force of law, in conflict with written law, and did it reduce the effective enforcement of the written law? Were there competing and conflicting systems of written (or even customary) law at the central and local levels? Answers to these questions must be sought, if we are to determine what purposes were really dominant and, therefore, how extensive cultural differentiation actually was.

Such questions are especially important in any examination of Polish-Lithuanian unity. Obviously, an examination of the laws establishing and reinforcing union and the many laws of the central governments of Poland and of Lithuania, so full of parallel provisions, may lead directly to the conclusions that Poland and Lithuania were fast becoming one and that they agreed on an underlying religious ethic.[19] Such conclusions, however, should be challenged. First, as has already been indicated, there were local laws in Lithuania which helped to strengthen separatist tendencies. Second, though there are as yet no detailed studies to help us to understand local differences in family law and in the law of inheritance, and little work has been done which clarifies local property law, it does appear that at the local level and even on the central governmental level, Lithuanian law shows a marked influence of Kievan, that is, early Russian law, and differs in significant respects from Polish law. Since, regrettably, there has been insufficient attention in published studies to the purposes of law and to the effectiveness of enforcement, much more research is needed before one may rely heavily on legal differences as a key to Polish-Lithuanian cultural diversity.

Nonetheless, there are adequate grounds for rejecting the proposition that there was any full agreement by Poland and Lithuania on an underlying religious ethic. We do know that there was religious dispute within Lithuania itself. In the late fourteenth century, paganism

---

[18] See the article by Anton Hilckman, "Feliks Koneczny und die Vergleichende Kulturwissenschaft," *Saeculum,* III (1952), 571-602.

[19] See Stanisław Kutrzeba and Władysław Semkowicz, eds., *Akta unji Polski z Litwą* (Krakow, 1932). See also Leon Rzyszczewski and Antoni Muczkowski, eds., *Codex diplomaticus Poloniae quo continentur Privilegia Regum Poloniae, Magnorum Ducum Lithaniae, Bullae Pontificium nec non jura a privatis data illustrandis domesticis rebus gestis inservitura* (2 vols.; Warsaw, 1847-52).

was rampant there, and at that time Orthodoxy flowed in with greater force than Catholicism. Orthodoxy was establishing itself in Lithuania; in contrast, the Hussite heresy flourished in Poland for a few decades until it was destroyed in 1439. To be sure, the Krewo union of 1385 with Poland and the Lithuanian Privilege of 1387 established one of the major features of Lithuanian religious policy, namely, support of the Catholic Church. A consequence of such support was an opportunity for Catholic prelates to advise the great princes of Lithuania. Nonetheless, the Lithuanian state found it necessary to respect the rights of the Orthodox. Thus in 1430 Vitovt affirmed the rights of the Orthodox in Belsk. Jagailo promoted the rights of the Orthodox in Lutsk and then in Lithuania generally, probably in support of the campaign of Sigismund Keistutovich to oust Svidrigailo from his position as great prince of Lithuania. Tolerance of Orthodox tendencies did not, however, mean religious tolerance of non-Catholic sects in Poland proper, for at the very time that rights were being extended to the Orthodox in Lithuania, even by the king of Poland, pressure was being exerted upon the Hussites within Poland. During the later fifteenth century the Lithuanian government tended to support the conversion of Orthodox persons to the Catholic Church or, when this plan appeared unfeasible, to give modest encouragement to the Orthodox Church. Ultimately, in the early sixteenth century, in Lithuania, encouragement of the Orthodox Church became more noticeable, despite intervening moments when the idea of religious union between the Orthodox and the Catholic churches was actively advanced by the rulers of the Lithuanian state in collaboration with the Papacy. Tolerance of the Orthodox and a general policy of religious toleration prevailed in sixteenth-century Poland.

In the present context, the question whether there was or was not tolerance at a given moment is less important than the fact that there was an issue of religious differentiation within Lithuania and much less of an issue of religious differentiation in Poland. Thus the average Lithuanian had more difficulty in identifying himself with a united Polish-Lithuanian state, especially if he was Orthodox.[20]

Although religion was an important issue in cultural differentiation, it was not the only one. One must look at language too, although it can be argued that in some societies language has not proved to be the crucial indication of cultural differentiation, since law and religion

---

[20] Religious difference is revealed in Грушевський, *Історія України-Руси*, IV, V, Part II. It is particularly stressed in Д. М. Бантышъ-Каменскій, *Исторія Малой Россіи отъ водворенія Славянъ въ сей стране до уничтоженія гетманства* (4th ed.; Kiev, 1903). Yet Ludwik Kolankowski, *Dzieje Wielkiego Księstwa Litewskiego za Jagiellonów*, Vol. I: *1377-1499* (Warsaw, 1930), 401-2, even fails to consider the position of the Orthodox Church when discussing the Lithuanian Privilege of 1492. That religious difference remained a problem in the eighteenth century is evident from such sources as Władysław Konopczyński, ed., *Dyaryusz Sejmu z r. 1746*, Vol. II of *Dyaryusze Sejmowe z Wieku XVIII* (Warsaw, 1912), p. 299.

reveal much more. In the fourteenth and fifteenth centuries we know that the court documents of Lithuania were generally written in Russian. The Russian used was not the Russian of the official court documents of Muscovy, but an ancestor of modern Belorussian. Nonetheless, it bore similarities to the various kinds of Russian used in the documents of the many principalities of Russia. The use of Russian in Lithuanian court documents reflects the predominance of the Russian-speaking population (i.e., the early Belorussians) within the Lithuanian state; they probably formed some 75 per cent of the whole.

Russian was not the only language used. Latin was common in documents of the late fourteenth and fifteenth centuries, particularly in documents relating to relations with Poland, such as those about union. This use was doubtless a reflection of Latin's role as the language of international diplomacy during the Middle Ages and the early modern period. It was used in many documents in Poland, but Polish was coming into use as well. It was not until the sixteenth century that Lithuanian documents began to appear in Polish, and only after the Union of Lublin was the use of Polish in them truly common. Only by the time, late in the seventeenth century, when most documents of the Lithuanian government appeared in Polish, may Polish be considered the official language of the united Lithuanian-Polish federation. Although Polish was not the language of the majority of the people, it became increasingly the language of the elite, the nobility, whose actions largely determined whether or not union would be successful. It must be remembered that there is little evidence of popular leadership in opposition to the Polish-Lithuanian union. The question of cultural identity or cultural differentiation has then more significance in connection with the elite than with the mass of the people, at least so far as the problem of Polish-Lithuanian unity is concerned.

In the discussion above, there is a possible logical hiatus: no attention has been given to the issue of whether one may properly speak of a Lithuanian culture. The hiatus might provoke the view that, in the absence of any distinct Lithuanian culture, questions of cultural differentiation are indeed nugatory. In that case one might counter with the assertion that the concept of "a land of transition" implies that the crucial cultural difference was between Poland and Russia, rather than between Lithuania and Poland. In fact, there is little doubt that Lithuania lacked a single, unified culture. The Lithuanians, the Russians, and the ancestors of the modern-day Belorussians and Ukrainians, not to mention such minorities as Tatars, Karaites, Armenians, and Jews, represented diversity; the Lithuanians with their pagan background tended most strongly to come under Polish influence, whereas the Ukrainians and even some Belorussians with their Orthodox background, under the impact of Polish influence, tended to reject it and increasingly to develop along distinct and independent cultural lines.

If, as has been suggested, Lithuania was a land of transition and was not culturally integrated with Poland, then it would seem quite logical that the Lithuanians may have had no sense of identification with the Jagellonian federation during the period of the Jagellonian dynasty. In other words, much more research on cultural differences is needed before we may obtain a clear view of the issue of Lithuanian-Polish unity.

THE REFORMATION

Political competition and cultural diversity within the Polish-Lithuanian union were complicated by the Reformation. Of course, many Poles remained Catholic and many Lithuanians remained Orthodox. A large group of noble families from Great Poland and from East Prussia came out in support of Lutheranism in the twenties of the sixteenth century. One of the by-products of that development was the secularization of the Teutonic Order of East Prussia and the establishment of the former Grand Master as Duke of Prussia and a vassal of the king of Poland. In Lithuania many noble families came out in support of Calvinism. Lutheran Poles often had closer connections with Germans than with the Calvinist Lithuanians. As Calvinism and Lutheranism flourished, the concern of Sigismund I and his successor Sigismund II Augustus mounted. The latter sometimes shied away from legal reform (which might well have strengthened the monarchy), because such reform might entail the adoption of some of the points of view of the Protestant nobles. One should not forget that the ambitions of noblemen (discussed in the first section) were often bound up with their religious convictions. The reluctance of certain nobles to supply money for campaigns stemmed not only from their fear of undermining their own position vis-à-vis the ruler but also from a fear of strengthening Catholicism to the disadvantage of Protestantism. It is perhaps in this context that one can understand the difficulties of Stephen Bathory in securing money to fight in Livonia and the dissatisfaction of the nobles with the costs of the Livonian war. Sigismund III Vasa was perhaps among all the Polish rulers the most intolerant in his attitude toward the Protestants, although the degree of his intolerance is a matter of some debate.[21] Be that as it may, his reign saw a reduc-

---

21 The high degree of religious tolerance in sixteenth-century Poland-Lithuania has been stressed by Oscar Halecki, *From Florence to Brest* (Rome and New York, 1958), pp. 142-44. For an emphasis on religious intolerance see Бантышъ-Каменскій, *Исторія Малой Россіи* . . . , pp. 115-16. Anti-Orthodox activity in the Ukraine and the flowering of the Orthodox Church there are both mentioned by George Vernadsky, *Bohdan: Hetman of Ukraine* (New Haven, 1941), p. 21. Anti-Protestant polemics are discussed by Ludolf Müller, "Die Kritik des Protestantismus in der russischen Theologie vom 16. biz zum 18. Jahrhundert," in *Akademie der Wissenschaften und der Literatur Abhandlungen der Geistes- und Sozialwissenschaftlichen Klasse*, No. 1, 1951, pp. 34-35, 46-51. That Orthodoxy did flourish in the late sixteenth century and early seventeenth century is evident from К. В. Харламповичъ, *Западнорусскіе православные школы XVI и начала XVII в.* (Kazan, 1898).

tion in the importance of Lutheranism and Calvinism within Poland proper; Calvinism continued to be active somewhat longer within Lithuania. This divergence may have perpetuated a sense of different loyalties, evident in the unwillingness of the Lithuanian Protestants to fight aggressively against Sweden in the early seventeenth century. Nonetheless, the Counter Reformation ultimately succeeded in Lithuania in overcoming Protestantism and in strengthening Catholicism at the expense of Orthodoxy in Poland-Lithuania. An important step was the acceptance of the Uniat Church at the Union of Brest in 1596, which brought many Orthodox into the Catholic fold. It is not demonstrable that the Uniat Church was accepted by a majority of the Orthodox within Poland-Lithuania, and it is evident that the Uniat Church was a cause of unrest in the eastern provinces. It must nonetheless be admitted that insofar as the coming of the Uniat Church helped to rally the nobility behind the Pope in some sort of common religious cause, it contributed to unity.[22] Religious differences between Poland and Lithuania became a less important factor in weakening the union, although they remained acute in some parts of the Ukraine.

It is regrettable that more work has not been done on the history of Protestantism in Lithuania and Poland and on its impact on the union. This can be explained by the fact that the history of this area has been written largely by scholars of Catholic or Orthodox persuasion who were convinced that Protestantism should be regarded negatively, and who at the same time tended to argue that there was a reasonable degree of tolerance of religious differences by their respective churches.

Economic Difficulties

Another factor deserves particular attention, namely, economics. Unfortunately we know too little about the economic developments in the area to be able to decide to what extent they tended to draw Poland-Lithuania apart or to hold it together. We have some very useful descriptions of economic developments which tell us a great deal, but they fail to answer several crucial questions.

We can say with confidence that from the late sixteenth century on, the Polish-Lithuanian state experienced economic difficulties. These may be considered a consequence of the impact of the well-known price revolution in the West together with a gradual loss of trade. Indeed, a glance at general European history shows us that Poland-Lithuania underwent what many a central European state experienced at the time; namely, the adverse consequences of the shift of the center

---

[22] Halecki, *From Florence to Brest*, p. 419, asserts that a majority of the inhabitants of eastern Lithuania and eastern Poland joined the Uniat Church, thereby making possible "a common way of life under the same federal constitution and in friendly contact with Western culture."

of commercial and economic activity from the Mediterranean and central continental Europe to the Atlantic seaboard, resulting from the enormous expansion of trade in metal and goods with the Americas and India. Economic developments of the late sixteenth century and the seventeenth century, especially the decline in production caused by the devastation of war, pressed upon the nobility and may well have sharpened their struggle to preserve their own rights. It was a factor, therefore, in the pressures to preserve the noble and aristocratic republic of Poland, to develop the *liberum veto,* and to prevent the emergence of a strong absolutist state.

Earlier economic developments, however, deserve to be mentioned. We might ask, how important was the decline in eastern trade in the late fifteenth century? We know very well that the fall of Constantinople and in particular the subordination of the Khanate of the Crimea to Turkey in 1475, the fall of important trade centers in the Dnieper area, and the loss to Poland-Lithuania of the Black Sea littoral together brought to a virtual end a rather flourishing trade which Poland and Lithuania had formerly conducted with the East. The local consequences of this in such a city as Lwow are well known. On the other hand, this decline seems, in general, to have been offset by an expansion of trade through Danzig and other Baltic towns. Indeed, one has the general impression of an over-all increase in commercial activity during the sixteenth century.[23]

One might also ask: How important was the price revolution in the sixteenth and seventeenth centuries so far as the Polish and Lithuanian nobles were concerned? It is clear that the Polish nobleman was eager to obtain a larger cash income. This is clear, above all, from the intensification of agriculture which produced for the nobles many more agricultural products in larger quantities to sell on the open market. This intensification was in part the consequence of the conversion of dues in kind into fixed cash payments, together with the decline in the real value of the cash payments. It may have had cultural roots as well: the nobility may have come to know and thus have been impelled to seek a higher standard of living. The possibility seems quite reasonable when one considers the cultural flowering in Poland-Lithuania during the sixteenth century.

Be that as it may, the sixteenth century was also clearly a period in which the nobles began to feel economic pressures. Did economic pressures, whether the consequence of cultural or other causes, combined with a rise in religious consciousness or with a rise in the identification of persons with specific religious groups, lead toward hostility against minorities? Jews, Armenians, and Germans were among those particularly involved in commerce, that is, in buying the products of

[23] Jan Rutkowski, *Historia gospodarcza Polski* (3rd expanded ed.; Poznan, 1947), pp. 83-88.

the soil from the nobles and in lending nobles money; and Jews, Armenians, and Germans were increasingly disliked.

In any consideration of the dates and consequences of the economic difficulties, two issues suggest themselves for immediate examination in more detail. One concerns the actual extent and significance of the price revolution in Poland. Many documents and materials are available from which the course of prices could be charted; indeed, much work has already been done on prices in major cities; but a thorough coverage of all Poland-Lithuania is necessary.[24] The second issue concerns the development of the legal device of the mortgage to facilitate borrowing. How extensive were mortgages, and what interest rates were charged? There is evidence that there was a general decline in interest rates; but high rates prevailed when persons attempted to borrow money without mortgages. The mortgage can be regarded, I believe, as a clue to the extent of commercialization. Behind it lies a change from the concept of land as an inalienable object adhering to the family, indeed, to the very way of life of the possessor, to the concept of land as an object of trade. In the shift from the medieval to the modern economic outlook, attitudes toward land have been crucial, and in the shaping of those attitudes the role of the mortgage has probably been quite important. As Polish and Lithuanian nobles yielded to pressure were they in fact contributing to an undermining of their own status? One might make contrasting studies on the basis of available documents, for example, contrasting the situations in Lithuania proper with those in Volhynia and in parts of greater and little Poland. Such studies, as well as detailed studies on economic developments and difficulties, especially at the local level, would help to clarify the relative importance of economic factors in the problem of the unity of Poland-Lithuania.[25]

THE UKRAINE

Another element of considerable importance in the history of Poland-Lithuania is the rise of the Ukraine and its struggle against Poland-Lithuania. The crux of that rise was the development of Cossack power and the desire of the Cossacks to expand and maintain a high degree of independence. Stephen Bathory and Sigismund had conceded the Cossacks considerable power in order to gain their help in the subordination of Muscovy, in the late sixteenth and early seventeenth centuries. This concession may well have led the Cossacks to

---

[24] Andrzej Wycański, "W sprawie kryzysu XVII stulecia," *Kwartalnik historyczny,* LXIX (1962), 657-59.

[25] The need for more detailed local studies as a basis for more nearly accurate broad appraisals of economic developments was a motive for the recent study by Józef Mitkowski, "Uście Zielone: Miasteczko prywatne ze szczególnym uwzględnieniem stanu w XVIII wieku," *Zeszyty Naukowe Uniwersytetu Jagiellońskiego* (Krakow, 1956), pp. 113-63.

think of themselves as free. Such a sense of freedom, however, probably had its roots in the earlier government and society of the Cossacks.
They lived in *volosti* and focused their attention in the summer on
fishing, hunting, salt distillation, and trading. Grouped in military
units, with a few thousand men in each regiment, they developed the
practice of electing their own chief officer, the hetman, and by such
processes created a somewhat democratic society within a society. The
Union of Brest led to a war between the Cossacks and Poland in 1596.
The major point at issue was whether all Orthodox should join the
Uniat Church, which maintained that it was the sole representative of
the Ukrainians. Despite the slaughter of Cossacks by Żółkiewski,
Kishka was able to convince his people that advantages could be
derived from collaboration with Poland. By such collaboration they
played a role in support of Poland in the struggle over Moldavia and
Walachia, in the war between Sweden and Poland over Livonia, and in
the Polish attempt to take over Russia during the Time of Troubles.
When, however, the Time of Troubles had passed, and Poland had
failed to maintain its position in Muscovy, the main thrust of Polish
policy seems to have been in the direction of dominating the Cossacks
rather than of seeking their cooperation, to Poland's advantage. In
1614 the Poles threatened war, and beginning in 1617 the Poles laid
particular stress on their right to appoint the hetman. Nonetheless,
Sahaidachny, the hetman, supported Poland and was able to extract
from her a promise to recognize the Orthodox Church in return for
Cossack help in Moldavia. The vacillations in Polish policy between
support of the Cossacks and cooperation with them on one hand and
attacks against the Cossacks on the other hand, suggest a lack of any
clearly formulated policy.

The Cossacks were not the only influence upon the development of
a Ukrainian self-consciousness in the seventeenth century. Indeed,
were it not that some of the issues which excited the Cossacks began to
excite the whole Ukrainian population, it is doubtful whether the
Ukrainian problem would have become so crucial in the history of
Poland-Lithuania. One basis of the development of self-consciousness
was religious. More and more, after the Uniat Church had been effectively established at the Union of Brest, the gentry were either Catholic
or pro-Catholic, depending upon whether they were Polish or native
Uniat. The people, on the other hand, oppressed by the gentry in
economic matters and pressed to enter the Uniat fold, began to identify
themselves with the Cossacks. In this way, popular bases of revolt
against the central government of Poland-Lithuania gained in importance. One must recognize, however, that the people had little power
to influence the making of decisions at this time. This was recognized
generally then and should not be lost sight of today, even though we
are sometimes inclined to lay special stress upon the mass of the people

because they play a role in decision-making in some societies of the twentieth century.[26] At the time, events were much more strongly influenced by certain dominant personalities who emerged in the Ukraine and who, by their dynamism, were able to invigorate the movement toward Ukrainian independence. Bohdan Khmelnytsky was one major figure of this type. He gathered together in his hands the leadership of the forces arising from the dissatisfaction of the Cossacks and from the dissatisfaction of the broad mass of the people of the Ukraine. Unfortunately for Poland-Lithuania, adequate compromises with Bohdan's position were either not made or made too late. One may argue that the failure to make timely compromises was one of the significant failures of the Jagellonian federation. Such a line of reasoning suggests that the Jagellonian federation did not emphasize local autonomy so strongly as it is asserted to have done by some of its admirers. The reasoning recalls the desire of the Poles to dominate, which has already been discussed. Contrariwise, one might argue that Poland-Lithuania failed to follow a forceful enough policy; that more force, rather than compromise, was needed. To be sure, the Ukraine failed in its attempt to gain freedom. Instead, because of its incapacity, unhelped, to overthrow Polish domination, it was compelled to turn to Moscow—a step that paved the way for Muscovite domination of the eastern Ukraine and its integration into the expanding Russian empire.[27]

There is a variety of opinion about Polish behavior and influence in the Ukraine. Ukrainian and Russian nationalists are inclined to emphasize the evil of Polish domination, and Polish historians are inclined to emphasize the comparative kindness of the Poles. According to the latter, in her failure in the Ukraine, Poland was largely the victim of her own political naïveté rather than of her own cruelty. The extent to which Polish Catholic nobles abused Orthodox peasants is a matter of considerable dispute.[28] There is some unresolved speculation about the extent to which some Poles who went east mingled with the Cossacks and brought with them patterns of Czech or other western military organization present in Poland which would have influenced

[26] Without minimizing the importance of popular disturbances in causing the Ukraine to revolt against Poland-Lithuania in the seventeenth century, even a recent Soviet historian has made it clear that Bohdan Khmelnytsky, the main leader of that revolt, believed that despite the desirability of the support of the common people, their views counted little in the eventual outcome. Л. С. Абецедарский, «Борьба белорусского народа за воссоединение Белоруссии с Россией в середине 17 в.,» *Воссоединение Украины с Россией 1654-1954: Сборник статей* (Moscow, 1954), p. 201.

[27] For a discussion of the eastern Ukraine's incorporation into Muscovy see Mikhail S. Hrushevsky, *A History of the Ukraine*, ed. O. J. Fredriksen (New Haven, 1941), pp. 319-46.

[28] Vernadsky, *Bohdan: Hetman of Ukraine*, while recognizing the importance of other issues, lays greatest stress on the activities of Bohdan in bringing about the loss of the Ukraine. Бантышъ-Каменскій, *Исторія Малой Россіи* ..., emphasizes anti-Orthodox activities of the Poles.

the organization and the tactics of the Cossacks. In other words, some Poles may, paradoxically, by their active participation in the Cossack host, have directly contributed to the strengthening of separatist tendencies in the Ukraine and thus to the undermining of the Polish-Lithuanian state—or at least to the reduction of its power.

One can hardly disagree with the statement that the loss of the eastern Ukraine was a major indication of the failure of the Polish-Lithuanian union. One wonders what motives—the desire for economic advantage, the will to proselytize, fear of the Cossacks—impelled the Poles to behave as they did and to follow the policy which they did. One may of course argue that the behavior of the Poles was not crucial, that the existence of cultural diversity and political competition was of far greater importance. Nonetheless, no one can deny that a truly successful union might well have avoided the loss of the eastern Ukraine.

EIGHTEENTH-CENTURY DEVELOPMENTS

By the eighteenth century the unity of Poland-Lithuania was in many respects more of a reality than before. Despite the continued presence of Orthodox in eastern provinces, there was in Poland-Lithuania a higher degree of cultural identity than before and a marked diminution in political competition between the constituent members of the union. Unfortunately, while unity had been strengthened, the union itself was declining.

Any examination of factors contributing to that decline naturally focuses attention on outside intervention and on the role of the nobility and the *liberum veto*. These issues have been so fully discussed that it seems inappropriate within an essay of this type to consider them in detail. Suffice it to say, that at least from the time of Sigismund III Vasa in the late sixteenth century to the time of the partitions, one ruler after another, far too frequently for the well-being of Poland-Lithuania, attended to external interests, even at the expense of internal affairs.[29] And if some of them, as, for example, Jan Sobieski, were quite aware of the importance of internal issues, the need of fighting

---

[29] See W. F. Reddaway *et al.*, eds., *The Cambridge History of Poland* (2 vols.; Cambridge, 1950-51), Chapters 1-4. Jean Fabre, *Stanislas-Auguste Poniatowski et l'Europe des lumières* (Paris, 1952), pp. 21-43. A clear statement of French interference is Emanuel Rostworowski, *O Polska Kôrone Polityka Francji w latach, 1725-1733* (Wroclaw and Krakow, 1958). The theme of foreign interference and the intrigues of nobles is stressed in Otto Forst-Battaglia, *Eine unbekannte Kandidatur auf dem polnischen Thron: Landgraf Friedrich von Hessen-Kassel und die Konföderation von Bar* (Bonn and Leipzig, 1922). On the second partition see Tadeusz Soplica (Adam Wolański), *Wojna Polsko-Rosyjska 1792 r.* (2 vols.; Poznan, 1922-24). Related to the issue of the selfishness of the nobility is the question of the moral state of Poland. N. I. Kostomarov has treated, among others, gluttony and drunkenness, *Послѣдніе годы Рѣчи-Посполитой* (3rd ed.; St. Petersburg, 1886), I, 29-89. Although it is currently unfashionable to consider such matters, they may help to explain the demise of Poland-Lithuania.

the Turks and the force of French interference prevented any effective moves to strengthen the monarchy and thereby to strengthen the Polish-Lithuanian union. I flatly assert that it was Poland-Lithuania's misfortune not to have developed an absolutist monarchy, strongly in control of the land, because the lack of such a monarchy seems, in truth, to have been the precondition to foreign intervention, which, in turn, ultimately caused the disintegration of that state.

Of course, it is also necessary to view the disappearance of Poland-Lithuania in a larger perspective. The strengthening of the Habsburg Empire (in part a reflection of the weakening of the Ottoman Empire) and the rise of Russia and Prussia—these developments constituted an historical conjunction, unfortunate in the extreme for the future of the Polish-Lithuanian union, for these states were the powers which erased Poland-Lithuania from the map of Europe by the partitions of 1772, 1793, and 1795.

CONCLUSIONS

I have stressed throughout this essay those developments which impeded the unity of Poland-Lithuania and contributed to its downfall. I have done so both because of personal conviction and because of the need of a corrective to the views of earlier historians who, by starting from the premise that a rather successful union was achieved, have made the end of Poland-Lithuania harder to comprehend.

While admitting the existence of unifying factors, I maintain that at the present stage of historical research one should emphasize the failure of the Jagellonian dynasty to establish effective unity. It could not overcome political competition and cultural diversity and was therefore unable to create an absolute monarchy. The Reformation made more certain this failure of the dynasty. Subsequently, economic developments and the loss of the Ukraine, both major complications, may well have decisively undermined the Polish-Lithuanian union. The paralysis in political decision-making, caused by the *liberum veto,* and foreign intervention administered the *coup de grâce* to the union: they did not destroy an otherwise healthy union.

It seems to me that any more thorough probing of the history of the Polish-Lithuanian state must proceed by a greater concentration on local history. The historiography of the Polish-Lithuanian union has been studded with examples of Polish, Lithuanian, Ukrainian, or Russian nationalism; none of these vantage points is now adequate. We must attempt to see what were the motivations in various specific localities, because the Polish-Lithuanian union embraced numerous peoples in various transitional cultural areas, and we may hope thereby to develop a clearer image of the institutional structure. We must penetrate beneath the nationalist conventions of the nineteenth and twentieth centuries to the local issues, which were probably far more important in the fifteenth through eighteenth centuries. Only then can we obtain a clearer image of the extent of political competition and cultural diversity, of the obstacles to absolutism, and of possible alternative sources of strength. Only then may we better define the impact of the Reformation, of economic developments, and of the loss of the eastern Ukraine. Only then may we arrive at any better understanding of the real issues underlying the history of the union and comprehend the tragedy of its failure.

Why Was Poland Partitioned?

OSCAR HALECKI

The interesting essay of Professor Backus raises once more the old question why the Polish-Lithuanian state disintegrated in 1795. Looking back as far as 1385; calling the commonwealth (this is the only correct translation of the official name *Rzeczpospolita*) the "Polish-Lithuanian state" (a name which corresponds to its dualistic character but never appears in the sources), while even the partitioning powers simply called it Poland; and speaking of its "disintegration" instead of its partition, the author reveals in advance the opinions which he clearly formulates in his conclusions.

He thinks that in spite of periods of apparent greatness, for example, in the sixteenth century, Poland was doomed from the time of the Union of Krewo, in 1385, four hundred years before the partitions, because of "the failure of the Jagellonian dynasty to establish effective unity" and because it "was unable to create an absolute monarchy." According to Professor Backus it is not enough to blame the *liberum veto* and the selfishness of the nobles. In his opinion "foreign intervention"—a strange understatement indeed—only contributed to administer "the *coup de grâce*" to a state which far from being "an otherwise healthy union" had never shown that "enormous ability to maintain itself" stressed by those who consider outside powers "the real devils."

Rejecting such views of the "protagonists of the Jagellonian federation" (including that of the present writer[1]), Professor Backus regrets that "a thorough analysis of the political, economic, cultural, ethnic, and other factors bearing on the failure of Poland-Lithuania has never been made." As a matter of fact, no other problem of Polish history has received more attention in either Polish or in foreign historiography, and no further research, desirable as it is, will ever remove the opposition between two conflicting interpretations. The school which considers Poland a failure and her partitions a natural consequence has received the support of Professor Backus "because of personal conviction" and because he wanted to make "the end of Poland-Lithuania" easier to understand. He has indeed raised important issues which

MR. HALECKI *is professor emeritus of Eastern European history at Fordham University.*

[1] I regret that on one occasion, summarizing views very different from my own, Professor Backus referred (in his note 12) to their "careful formulation" in my *History of Poland*

though not entirely new, have never been discussed before in a spirit so definitely unfavorable to Poland, notwithstanding some occasional qualifications.

It is understandable that German and Russian historiography used to be particularly critical of the commonwealth in order to justify its partition. Today, however, some German historians are making a serious effort to study Poland's past more objectively,[2] and even Soviet scholars, though obviously severely critical of "the Poland of the nobles," consider the partitions, in agreement with Lenin, a typical case of imperialism. It is therefore surprising and regrettable that in America, where the fall of Poland deeply shocked contemporary public opinion and where an outstanding historian, Robert H. Lord,[3] produced in 1915, after painstaking research, the standard work on the second, the decisive, partition, proving the joint responsibility of Russia and Prussia, there now seems to be a turn toward an approach which would confirm the negative interpretation of Poland's past.[4] This is one more reason for discussing the latest and most far-reaching expression of such views.

Before entering into any details regarding the problem of unity, which for Professor Backus is decisive, two different meanings of the word "unity" must be distinguished. If by unity we mean uniformity in a centralized state under absolute government, without any regional autonomy and competition, and without cultural pluralism, then it must be admitted that such a unity never existed either under the Jagellonians or later in the commonwealth. But has really only such a body politic a chance and a right to survive? Professor Backus added in that connection the specific question of "the viability of a multi-national federation." For American historians it would seem particularly difficult to give to all such questions a negative answer.

Furthermore, is it really impossible to reconcile an organic, freely accepted unity—in the second meaning of the word—with a constructive, freely recognized diversity? Must a long-lasting effort in that direction, even if not completely successful, be condemned because it was

---

[2] One of them, Gotthold Rhode, is criticized by Professor Backus (note 17) for not having rejected altogether and in advance the conception of Poland as the rampart of Christendom, when starting his thorough study of her eastern frontiers.

[3] Professor Backus, mentioning (note 29) the second partition, referred the reader not to Lord's comprehensive work (*The Second Partition of Poland: A Study in Diplomatic History*, Cambridge, Mass., 1915) but to a description of the Polish-Russian war of 1792 in a rather unimportant Polish monograph.

[4] It is a matter of particular regret that a scholar of Professor Francis Dvornik's distinction, who has made most valuable and highly objective contributions to a better understanding of early Polish history, in his latest, otherwise very remarkable book *The Slavs in European History and Civilization* (New Brunswick: Rutgers University Press, 1962) blames the whole constitutional development of Poland, supports the views of Russian historiography on Poland's eastern policy, and joining the usual condemnation of the *szlachta*, singles out the selfishness of that leading part of the nation as the cause of the partitions.

impeded and undermined by various factors which in the case of Poland have been examined by Professor Backus in chronological order?

In that order the obstacles created by what he calls "political competition" came, of course, first. It is only natural that after centuries of Polish-Lithuanian antagonism, the Union of Krewo did not eliminate at once any competition between the contracting parties, and that the legal interpretation of the agreement of 1385 was controversial, as it continues to be in historiography. But that rather vague agreement was soon replaced by a long series of charters[5]—a real mine of information for any student of federalism—which in a process lasting from 1401 to 1569 gradually recognized the full equality of the grand duchy of Lithuania with the kingdom of Poland, an equality which was confirmed in 1791 on the eve of their common ordeal. The political conꓥpetition which at first opposed Jagello (in Lithuanian, not Jagailo but Jogaila) and Vitold (in Lithuanian, not Vitovt but Vytautas) rather than Poles and Lithuanians, did not entirely disappear in the relations between the two nations. But it was mainly because of foreign interference by Sigismund of Luxemburg and the Teutonic Knights, and in connection with continued rivalries among the members of the dynasty, that after Vitold's death a civil war interrupted for several years the peaceful evolution of the union.

This was too bad but happened also in the development of the most successful federations as late as the nineteenth century. In the middle of the fifteenth century, Polish-Lithuanian relations were appeased by the wise policy of Jagello's son, Casimir. He isolated both those Polish leaders who really wanted to dominate Lithuania,[6] considering it an autonomous part of the *Corona regni Poloniae,* and those Lithuanian magnates who challenged his own authority. They did it not because he left most of Podolia to the Poles (contrary to the Polish claims, he also left most of Volhynia to the Lithuanians)—a question which already in the later fifteenth century ceased to be "a major issue"[7]— but in connection with "the emergence of advisory and parliamentary institutions" which Professor Backus considers a "major factor in the perpetuation of political competition."

As a matter of fact, emerging almost simultaneously in both states— a first evidence that they were successfully assimilated without any necessity "to weld the two states into one"—these institutions made political competition a normal, peaceful process, since the representa-

---

[5] They are available in an excellent edition, which is quoted by Professor Backus (note 19), but only in order to warn the reader that such "laws" do not justify the conclusion "that Poland and Lithuania were fast becoming one and that they agreed on an underlying religious ethic."

[6] In order to support his charge that the Polish nobles wanted to dominate Lithuania, Professor Backus (note 5) quotes an obscure Russian pamphlet published in 1863, the year of the Polish uprising.

[7] See O. Halecki, *Ostatnie lata Świdrygiełły i sprawa wołyńska za Kazimierza Jagiellończyka* (Krakow, 1915).

tion of each country now had indeed "more opportunity to advocate local interests." This, far from impeding effective union, if by union we do not mean enforced uniformity but a pliable and therefore sound federal system, was a school of free discussion and the best chance for closer cooperation. The only difference and source of trouble was that the Polish *sejm* included from the middle of the fifteenth century, besides the royal council, freely elected deputies of the provincial dietines, whereas in the grand duchy the *rada* remained supreme for another one hundred years and the role of the boyars, the lesser nobles, very limited. This difficulty was eventually overcome in 1569, by the Union of Lublin, which contrary to the assertion of Professor Backus did succeed in merging the two separate parliaments in one common diet with equal opportunities for all nobles of both states. That reform, which greatly contributed to the unity of the commonwealth, had been requested seven years before by an extraordinary *sejm* of the grand duchy in the name of all its constituent parts, from purely Lithuanian Samogitia in the north to Ruthenian Volhynia in the south.[8]

This leads to another factor which according to Professor Backus complicated Lithuanian-Polish competition. He greatly overestimates the separatist tendencies in the various provinces of the grand duchy, especially that in Samogitia, which was completely satisfied by the special privilege received soon after Casimir's election in 1440 in the midst of an exceptional crisis when he was a boy of thirteen years. After that crisis a real separatism existed only in the upper Oka River region, a remote area, the only one where Lithuania's expansion temporarily penetrated into Great Russian territory[9] and where petty princes remained in power, vacillating between Lithuania and Muscovy.

In all other provinces the so-called centralization under Casimir's rule, started already under Vitold, was eminently successful. Members of his own dynasty, who wanted to create hereditary duchies, were replaced by governors appointed by the grand duke, who, however, was wise enough to respect the *starina* and to confirm that local tradition in provincial charters. Their provisions were not at all in contradiction with those of the general privileges which long before the all-Lithuanian law code of 1529 were granted to the grand duchy as a whole. The recognition of local laws and customs, far from strengthening separatism, made effective union easily acceptable.

[8] That long petition, which I discovered fifty years ago in the Czartoryski Archives, is summarized in my article "Sejm obozowy szlachty litewskiej pod Witebskiem w r. 1562 i jego petycja o unię z Polską," *Przegląd historyczny*, XVIII (1914), 320-52. Not denying at all that the Union of Lublin created a common Polish-Lithuanian diet, recent Russian historiography (G. Vernadsky, quoted by Professor Backus in note 7, quotes himself I. I. Lappo) has only added some information on separate Lithuanian conventions which in the first decades after 1569 were occasionally held in preparation for the general diets.

[9] What Professor Backus writes about "Russians," the "Russian" language, etc., in the other parts of the Polish-Lithuanian state, refers to the other two East Slavic nations, today called the Ukraine and Belorussia.

The grand duchy was anxious to safeguard its separate statehood, and each of its provinces wanted to retain its self-government. But in spite of occasional political competition with Poland, both the general and the provincial charters included, at the request of those concerned, new rights and liberties on the Polish pattern. Professor Backus admits that competition with Poland was reduced and cooperation with her developed when the grand duchy was threatened by the rise of Muscovy, especially at the time of Ivan the Terrible. He thinks, however, that it can never be known to what extent the Lithuanian nobles accepted the views expressed by Prince Kurbsky in his correspondence with the tsar. Actually, we know this very well.[10] Even those of them who were of Orthodox faith and Ruthenian origin defended their "dear country," as they called the grand duchy, against Muscovite aggression. Even before the Livonian campaign they requested the help of the Poles, and they were opposed to Moscow's system of government even before the famous Russian prince defected from his country to Lithuania.[11]

This explains the great constitutional reform in the grand duchy which in the years from 1564 to 1566 prepared the Union of Lublin and which Professor Backus has overlooked. He mentions only the additional decisions of 1578, which created in Lithuania as in Poland a supreme court of appeal, although the reform of the lower courts was part of the basic changes of 1564-66, along with the revision of the Lithuanian Statute and the creation of local dietines for the election of the deputies to the diet, as in Poland.

All this contributed not only to the unity of the commonwealth, which thus could pass the test of the three interregna after the end of the Jagellonian dynasty in 1572, but also to the development of civic liberties and to the limitation of the power of the common ruler. It therefore leads to the second part of Professor Backus' paper, in which he attempts to explain the lack of unity in the Polish-Lithuanian state by "the failure to establish a new monarchy," that is, an absolute form of government.

He is right in recalling that the rulers of both the Polish and the Lithuanian state were already losing many of their powers before the end of the Jagellonian dynasty, whose founder rejected in 1425 the draft of a charter making the Polish throne elective but granted such a charter five years later—a rather important detail which has been omitted. It was the "centralizer" Casimir who started that cooperation with the lower gentry which was characteristic, not of the rising national monarchies in the West, but precisely of Poland and Lithuania,

---

[10] See their statements quoted by K. Chodynicki, *Kościół prawosławny i Rzeczpospolita Polska do r. 1632* (Warsaw, 1934), pp. 106-7.

[11] As to the earlier defections of "West Russian nobles" from Lithuania to Moscow, studied by Professor Backus in the book quoted in his note 14, see my comments in the *American Historical Review*, LXIII (1958), 1037-38.

particularly in the later Jagellonian period. Even King Alexander, who at first cooperated with the senate, confirmed in 1505 the equal legislative power of the house of deputies. And Sigismund Augustus, after initial troubles with the diets, decided in 1562 to cooperate with the lower gentry both in Poland and in Lithuania. Professor Backus points out that he failed to establish through such a cooperation "a strong state on a constitutional basis." The king simply realized that an absolute monarchy had always been impossible in Poland, had become impossible also in Lithuania, and far from promoting the effective union of both states, which he so much desired, would make that union impossible too. In the days of Zamoyski, a statesman trained in the political school of the last Jagellonian, it became equally evident that the principle that each noble could vote at the election of the common ruler, far from undermining the Polish-Lithuanian union, would protect it against the possible intrigues of ambitious magnates.

Strangely enough, the same historians who are rightly critical of absolutism, for instance, of that of the Habsburgs from which the constitutional rights of Bohemia and of Hungary had to suffer, blame the Poles for having feared the destruction of their own constitution under an absolute form of government. And the same historians who criticize the influence of a so-called aristocratic oligarchy in Poland—not without a great deal of exaggeration, at least as far as the sixteenth century is concerned—blame those Poles who by extending political rights and liberties to a large part of the nation, checked for a long time the power of the magnates, whose rivalries endangered the unity of the commonwealth. These attitudes, which have also influenced the interpretations of Professor Backus, have never been explained.

Much longer is the next part of his essay, where he discusses the most interesting problem of cultural diversity. No further research is needed to realize that when the Poles, Lithuanians, and Ruthenians (the Belorussians and Ukrainians of today) were politically united, they were culturally very different and that this created serious difficulties. But this difficulty was overcome through a gradual process of assimilation, in which the Lithuanian and Ruthenian upper classes spontaneously accepted the Western culture of the Poles, the magnates being the first to do so even before they accepted political integration; whereas the masses of the non-Polish peoples, although they also came under Western influence, were left undisturbed in their native culture until they achieved full national development in our democratic age. The whole old grand duchy of Lithuania, which was indeed a "land of transition" and which at the end of the fourteenth century had to decide whether it should join the West or the East, by uniting with Poland in a federal system or submitting to Moscow,[12] turned toward

12 We now know that there was an alternative plan of a marriage of Jagello not with the queen of Poland but with a daughter of the grand prince of Moscow, Dmitrii Donskoi.

the West, and in spite of a cultural diversity which never disappeared in the commonwealth but soon ceased to be a threat to its unity, that trend toward integration with the West survived in the whole area even after the partitions of Poland.

All this is most definitely denied by Professor Backus, who raised in that connection important issues going beyond the scope of his topic. He not only warns against drawing "clear-cut lines between the cultures of Eastern and Western Europe," but sees even in any historical "demarcation" between these parts of the continent a "tendency to project back into the past the present division between East and West." Disagreeing with those who emphasize "the unity of Western Christendom," he himself speaks of a Western Europe, but only in order to exclude Poland from the real West. Wondering "whether one may properly speak of a Lithuanian culture," which is hardly fair, whatever definition of culture may be used, he reduces the "crucial" issue to the cultural differentiation between Poland and Russia. There was indeed a profound contrast between those two; but precisely because there was no such contrast between the Poles and their immediate eastern neighbors, the unquestionable cultural diversity which seemed to separate them could become a diversity in unity, in the true spirit of federalism.

In the case of the Lithuanians this was facilitated by the fact that from their original paganism they were at once converted to Latin Catholicism. But even the Orthodox faith of the Ruthenians did not at all exclude the community of what Professor Backus calls "an underlying religious ethic." He feels the necessity of describing in some more detail the relations between Orthodox and Catholics under the Jagellonians, but is not quite clear in doing so. Vitold not only affirmed the rights of the Orthodox in special cases, but respected these rights always and everywhere. During the civil war after his death, Jagello himself not only promoted the rights of the Orthodox, but as early as 1432 planned to extend to the Orthodox of the grand duchy the rights enjoyed by the Catholics. With his agreement, this was actually done in the privilege which Sigismund granted to that state two years later, the first charter which made no discrimination between Catholic Lithuanians and Orthodox Ruthenians.[13]

Professor Backus returns to the religious obstacles to unity in his brief discussion of the Reformation which, in his opinion, was a significant complication of the problem of unity of the Polish-Lithuanian state. It was just the contrary. Though the Reformation temporarily endangered religious unity in both Poland and Lithuania, the very fact

---

This would have meant an early absorption by Moscow not only of all eastern Slavs but of the Lithuanians as well, and possibly a partition of Poland already at the end of the fourteenth century, when it was first planned by her western neighbors.

[13] This is well explained, against the whole background of the position of the Orthodox Church in the commonwealth, in Chodynicki's excellent book, cited above (note 10).

that this crisis started, developed, and ended simultaneously and similarly in each of the two states was a new evidence of the high degree of cultural unity which had been achieved in their relations. In both countries the movement started with a penetration of Lutheranism; in both of them the nobles, the main supporters of the Reformation, disliking the German origin of Lutheranism, soon turned to Calvinism which in turn was undermined in both countries by the Anti-Trinitarians; the peaceful triumph of the Catholic Counter Reformation was again the same in the kingdom and in the grand duchy, leaving in each state a small Protestant minority of various denominations.

All this is well known, because the history of Protestantism in Lithuania as well as in Poland has not been written "largely by scholars of Catholic or Orthodox persuasion," but mostly by Protestants, many of them Germans,[14] and by Catholic Poles regarding Protestantism positively and with sympathetic understanding, considering it even an important element of Lithuania's westernization.[15]

The Reformation also contributed to the westernization of the Ruthenians, many of whom, after a Protestant interlude, did not return to Orthodoxy, but became Catholics of the Latin Rite. Whether those of the Orthodox who accepted the Union of Brest were a majority, is indeed "not demonstrable." However, it can be demonstrated that the union was concluded on the initiative of the Ruthenian hierarchy, secretly approved by the Greek patriarch of Constantinople,[16] and ratified at the synod of 1596 by six members of that hierarchy, including the metropolitan of Kiev and the archbishop of Polotsk, while only a minority of two bishops rejected it under the influence of Prince Constantine Ostrogski, a Polonized magnate who was himself under strong Calvinist and even Anti-Trinitarian influence.

To what extent, why, and when the Uniat Church became a source of unrest in the eastern provinces of the commonwealth will always remain controversial questions, connected with the problem of the Ukraine and the Ukrainian Cossacks, which Professor Backus studies separately.[17] In this case he is right in speaking not only of a cause of weakness but of a threat to the unity of the commonwealth, especially

---

[14] See the chapter on the Reformation in the highly objective *Kirchengeschichte Polens* (Berlin, 1930) by the Protestant theologian Karl Völker, particularly his exhaustive bibliographies, including, e.g., the numerous, less objective but very informative works of the Lutheran pastor T. Wotschke on the Reformation in Poland and Lithuania.

[15] This is the opinion of the leading Polish specialist in the field, Professor Stanisław Kot, who is a Catholic but whose attitude toward the Reformation is absolutely positive. See his essay *La Réforme dans le Grand Duché de Lithuanie: Facteur d'occidentalisation culturelle* (Brussels, 1953).

[16] This results from a document I discovered in 1962, which will be printed and discussed in the 1963 volume of the (Ukrainian) *Analecta Ordinis S. Basilii M.*, published in Rome.

[17] The "economic difficulties" which Professor Backus studied before turning to the Ukrainian problem are not discussed in this commentary, because he feels himself unable to say "to what extent they tended to draw Poland-Lithuania apart or hold it together."

since the border region where Cossack power developed had never been fully integrated with either the Lithuanian or the Polish state. He repeats, however, the old error that it was the Union of Brest which led to the first serious uprising of the Cossacks. That rebellion started and was crushed in the summer of 1596, before the Synod of Brest even met, and the quarter of a century following that religious union, in which the Cossacks were for a long time not interested at all, was precisely the period of their closest cooperation with the Poles, including their outstanding participation in the defense against the Turks (not merely in the Moldavian question) in 1621.

It was only one year earlier that under foreign influence coming from Moscow and from Constantinople, particularly from the violently anti-Polish patriarch Cyril Lucaris, that the use of Cossacks against the Uniat Church was begun. But even when in 1632 the restored Orthodox hierarchy was recognized by the new king, Ladislas IV (this had been Sahaidachny's main request), troubles with the Cossacks continued, mainly on social grounds. In that respect unquestionable and regrettable mistakes were made by the Poles; but only after the initial success of the uprising of 1648, which, like that of 1596, was motivated also by Cossack disappointment that a planned war against the Turks was given up, did the movement turn into clear separatism. In the Hadiach agreement of 1658, ratified by the diet of 1659, the Poles were ready to grant to the Ukraine more than local autonomy: the dualistic commonwealth was to receive a trialistic structure, a "Ruthenian duchy" under Cossack leadership being placed as an equal partner beside the Polish kingdom and the Lithuanian grand duchy. But the Cossacks were already divided between those who favored a reconciliation with Poland and those who preferred submission to Moscow, if not to Turkey. The result was a partition of the Ukraine between Poland and Muscovite Russia,[18] a great setback for the future of the Ukrainian national movement, a great success for Moscow, and for the commonwealth a great "reduction of its power," as Professor Backus rightly says.

However, far from "undermining the Polish-Lithuanian state," the loss of the eastern Ukraine contributed to its coherence and to the fact that from the turn of the seventeenth century there was in the commonwealth "a higher degree of cultural identity than before and a marked diminution in political competition between the constituent members of the union." Professor Backus admits this, but fails to draw the only logical conclusion when briefly discussing the eighteenth-century developments. If during the century which preceded the partitions, there was more unity in the Polish-Lithuanian state than ever before, then it was not the lack of unity which "contributed to its

[18] See Z. Wójcik, *Traktat Andruszowski 1667 r. i jego geneza* (Warsaw, 1959), where the whole background is very objectively discussed in the light of unpublished sources.

downfall." Nor has "the premise [or rather the evidence] that a rather successful union was achieved" made "the end of Poland-Lithuania harder to comprehend."

That end is not difficult to understand at all. The commonwealth had been so weakened through invasions of almost all its neighbors (except Austria) in the seventeenth and early eighteenth century, and its constitutional reform had been delayed so long by interventions and pressures of Russia and Prussia,[19] that even if the *szlachta* had been less selfish than privileged classes usually are, the aggression of those two, now overwhelmingly stronger powers, which Austria joined contrary to her own real interest, simply could not be successfully resisted. But even the powers which wiped Poland off the map, when trying to justify the partitions by the most incredible arguments (including the "Jacobinism" of the Poles), never claimed that their victim was not really a union: the artificial boundaries which they drafted after much bargaining disregarded both the administrative divisions and the ethnic frontiers within the commonwealth.

Therefore, even a greater concentration on local history, interesting as such and never neglected in Polish historiography,[20] would not shed new light on the question why Poland was partitioned.[21] What needs to be explained—and this will be the positive conclusion of an unfortunately negative commentary—is the problem how the Polish nation survived in spite of the destruction of the Polish state. This ought to be done not only by continuing the study of Polish history from 1795 to 1918, with due attention to the no less tragic destiny of the partners of the Poles in the old commonwealth, but also by doing justice to the achievements of the preceding eight centuries and to the heritage which that commonwealth has left behind, including the contributions of its non-Polish parts.

---

[19] French interference, which tried in vain to strengthen the monarchy in Poland, cannot be compared to Russian and Prussian interference, which worked in the opposite direction. The French policy in the years 1725-33, studied in the valuable monograph of E. Rostworowski (quoted by Professor Backus in his note 29), could have saved Poland, had it been more consistent and energetic at the time of the election of 1733.

[20] The series *Źródła dziejowe* was dedicated from 1883 (Vol. XII) to the systematic study of Poland's individual provinces at the turn of the sixteenth century, mainly from the economic and social point of view. The best volumes (XVIII to XXII), dealing with the Ruthenian lands, have been edited by Aleksander Jabłonowski, who studied also the cultural and ethnic background in a highly objective spirit. And soon after the reopening of the Polish University of Wilno in 1919, that center started publication of the *Ateneum Wileńskie* (a regional review dedicated to the history of the grand duchy of Lithuania and its various provinces) which continued until another partition of Poland, in 1939.

[21] In his last footnote Professor Backus also recommends for study "the moral state of Poland." This could indeed contribute to a better understanding of the partitions, but on two conditions. Not only the Poles but also their enemies should be submitted to that test of morality. And statements of Kostomarov on the "gluttony and drunkenness" of the Poles should not serve as an inspiring starting point for such a study. They do not deserve any comment.

How Firm Was the Polish-Lithuanian Federation?

JOSEPH JAKSTAS

There is abundant literature in historical writings treating the disintegration and downfall of the Polish-Lithuanian republic *(Rzeczpospolita)*. Since the impressive book of Michał Bobrzyński, *Dzieje Polski w zarysie* (1879), the manifold aspects of the internal life of the republic have been repeatedly revealed and presented as causes of its ruin. In the meantime the origin, development, and achievement of the Polish-Lithuanian union have attracted the attention of most Polish historians. The subject matter has been for the most part treated in a positive sense, with stress on the political, the social, and especially the cultural results of the union. Professor Oscar Halecki with his *Dzieje Unii Jagiellońskiej* (1919) is the leading Polish authority in exalting the union.

The disintegration and fall of the Polish-Lithuanian federation, on the one hand, and the union on the other were supposed to be two entirely different things, and it seemed that they should be treated separately. But Professor O. P. Backus in his essay "The Problem of Unity in the Polish-Lithuanian State" has brought these two historical events together in order to show their interdependence. Consequently, the essay can be regarded as a new view of the fateful events in the history of the Polish-Lithuanian state and deserves the most careful consideration.

Professor Backus also touches on the inner causes of the downfall of the republic as described in historical literature, but he finds the exposition not thorough enough. In his brief essay he avoids going into this highly complicated problem and confines his exposition to the Polish-Lithuanian union. He sees in the incompleteness of the union one of the main causes leading to the decadence of the federation.

The first of the three headings under which the author treats his thesis—namely, the political competition, deserves the most attention. It was, as a matter of fact, sometimes noted in Lithuanian historiography, and was regarded as separatism of the grand duchy. The separatism accompanied the union from its beginning and precluded the fulfillment of the stipulations set by Jogaila at Krewo. Professor Backus rightly stresses the decisive role played by Vytautas (Vitovt) and his

MR. JAKSTAS *received his doctorate at the University of Kaunas, Lithuania, and taught history there and at the University of Vilnius before coming to the United States.*

worthy successor Svidrigaila in the opposition to the union. The Polish penetration into Podolia, as noted by Professor Backus, might also have been one of the stimuli of the Lithuanian opposition to the union.

It would have been desirable if Professor Backus had outlined the protracted rivalry of Poland and Lithuania for Podolia and Volhynia. The struggle began after the extinction of the Rurikids who ruled those provinces, and continued for many years (1340-80) before the Union of Krewo. The possibility that the aspirations of the Polish nobles, especially those of Little Poland, led them to seek the union with the grand duchy cannot be denied. After the union, the Poles took the opportunity to extend their domination over Podolia and Volhynia when King Jogaila and the Grand Duke Sigismund Kiejstuto-vicz concluded the treaty at Vilnius (Wilno) in 1432. Sigismund had just been elevated to his new position by the support of the Poles, and sought their help against Svidrigaila. Therefore, he had to satisfy the Polish demand in the aforementioned treaty.[1]

But the Lithuanian nobles, it seems, did not easily yield the terri-tories to Poland and sought to retain them. The ousted and defeated Svidrigaila resided in Podolia and at his death (1452) bequeathed the province to Lithuania.

The dispute over Podolia and Volhynia erupted anew under Casimir Jogaila, who was elected grand duke of Lithuania in 1440. When Casi-mir, after seven years of independent rule in the grand duchy, became king of Poland, he issued the famous privilege for the Lithuanian nobles and declared that he would safeguard the grand duchy within the limits held by his predecessors. The Lithuanian nobles had de-manded such a declaration, obviously in view of the continual dispute with Poland over Podolia and Volhynia. The dispute over the two lands lasted several years and culminated in the Seim of Parchovo (1452). Here arose the threat of war between the two federated states, and some Lithuanian nobles returned to the Poles the coats of arms they had received in Horodlo. Professor Backus quite correctly states in his paper, "Poland's desire for territorial gains was inextricably linked to the desire of Polish nobles to dominate Lithuania or parts thereof." The fateful Union of Lublin (1569) obviously testified to this Polish intent.

It is well known that the so-called real union was forced upon the Lithuanians by the imminent danger from Muscovy. They sought the help of Poland because they were not able to withstand the increasing Russian pressure and for that reason were willing to negotiate a closer union. But the Poles exploited the union to annex Podolia and Vol-hynia and, in addition, the Kievan Ukraine to the Dnieper and the territory of Siversk beyond this river. Thus practically the whole

---

[1] Władysław Wielhorski, *Polska a Litwa: Stosunki wzajemne w biegu dziejów* (London, 1947), p. 117.

southern part of the grand duchy came under Polish rule. In view of the loss of the vast territories seized by Moscow during the sixteenth century, one can really speak of the first partition of the grand duchy. It is strange indeed that one of the partitioners was at the same time the partner of the union which had created "the Commonwealth of both peoples."[2]

The Polish nobility flooded into the annexed Ukraine, which was partly devastated by the raids of the Crimean Tatars, and acquired huge estates granted by the privileges of the kings. They enslaved the masses of the Ukrainian population by introducing the first regular corvée. "The Ukraine at the beginning of the seventeenth century was the home of an oppressed and exasperated people."[3]

The oppression resulted in a general revolt of the Cossacks and Ukrainian population under the leadership of Bohdan Khmelnytsky. It was a revolution of the orthodox "Byzantinian" people against the Polish magnates and their associates in the exploitation—namely, the Jews. Terrible plunderings and massacres of the Poles and Jews accompanied the uprising.[4] As a consequence of the revolt, the Ukraine on the left bank of the Dnieper, including Kiev, came under Moscow; and some southern parts of the Ukraine came under the Turks.

The events concerning the Ukraine weakened rather than strengthened the Polish-Lithuanian federation. It is noteworthy that the case of the Ukraine introduced for the first time in parliamentary procedure the famous *liberum veto*. Professor Backus repeatedly mentions the *liberum veto* and says that the parliaments or seims in both states impeded the union. But separate parliaments existed only until the Union of Lublin. After the union, the common seim, as well as the common king, represented the real union. Nevertheless, Lithuanian separatism and a form of resistance against the union appeared in the common seim, as, for instance, in 1652, when for the first time the *liberum veto* was used.

The late Polish historian, S. Koscialkowski, who last treated the *liberum veto*,[5] rightly saw its roots in the old federalism of the Polish state. From this federalism originated the customary rule of *unanimitas,* required for legislative decisions of the seim, which was a congress of delegates from the independent districts, lands, palatinates, and other units. The delegates had merely to transmit the requirements of their mandators to the seim and were not bound by the decision of the majority. Thus the *liberum veto* was inherent many years in the federative Polish state before it was voiced by the Lithuanian delegate.

[2] S. Koscialkowski, *Dzieje Ziem Wielkiego Księstwa Litewskiego* (London, 1953), p. 68.

[3] George Vernadsky, *Bohdan: Hetman of Ukraine* (New Haven, 1941), p. 12.

[4] S. M. Dubnow, *History of the Jews in Russia and Poland* (New York, 1946), I, 14. Paul Goodman, *History of the Jews* (New York, 1953), p. 153.

[5] S. Koscialkowski, *"Liberum veto": W trzechsetną rocznicę sejmu z r. 1652. Studia i szkice przygodne* (London, 1956).

The delegate was Vladislaus Sicinski, the envoy of the district Upyte. According to Koscialkowski, he acted under the instigation of the Lithuanian great hetman, Janusz Radziwill, who, one year earlier, had commanded the Lithuanian troops on the march against the Cossacks and had captured Kiev. Probably he disagreed with the Poles concerning the treaty of Bila Tserkva, concluded with the Cossacks, and therefore incited his delegate, Sicinski, to protest against its acceptance by the seim. In connection with this, it may be of interest to mention that the same great hetman was the leader of the Lithuanian gentry that concluded the union with Sweden at Kedainiai in 1655 and disrupted the union with Poland.

Be that as it may, the *liberum veto* was used repeatedly in the common seim after 1652, and was mostly voiced by the envoys of the grand duchy and of the Russian provinces. Maybe the *liberum veto* meant an indirect protest against the union and the predominance of the Poles. The separatistic tendencies in the provinces of Lithuania and the different laws could hardly have had a direct influence upon the union, because diversity in laws and in political status was characteristic of medieval states. There was a *sui generis* unity in diversity.

The grand duchy of Lithuania, which had its beginning in the small territory around Vilnius and developed into a huge political body, embraced different Slavic lands. Those lands were already political units formed earlier in the centuries following the founding of Kievan Russia. The Lithuanian rulers had no wish to change the customs, laws, and political status of these lands but, on the contrary, were anxious to preserve them, and in the privileges asserted to honor the *starina*. Thus, the numerous Slavic lands of the grand duchy lived under their own laws.

The most evident example of the particularism in the grand duchy was the land of Samogitia. It had been an autonomous province since the beginning of the state in the thirteenth century and had preserved its autonomy throughout the ages. Then the nucleus of Lithuania was the territory called "The Upper Land" *(Aukštaičiai)*, where the first rulers had feudal domains and from where they extended their domination. Vilnius became the central place of their rule in the beginning of the fourteenth century—or perhaps even earlier—and rose to become the capital of the grand duchy. Samogitia remained outside the developing state and leaned toward it merely because of the unceasing raids of the Teutonic Order. As Professor Backus says, Samogitia was the · lodestone for the Teutonic Knights and therefore required protection from the Lithuanian state. But the Samogitians safeguarded their particularism and even rebelled against Vytautas in 1418, when he sought to infringe upon their liberties. Later, in 1441, they acquired a special privilege from Casimir, as mentioned by Professor Backus, which was confirmed by his successor Alexander. Consequently, Samogitia developed into a semi-independent territory and was sometimes even called a princedom.

Thus, federalism prevailed in the grand duchy and in Poland as well, and could hardly impede the union. On the contrary, the federalism or semi-independence of some Russian provinces, especially those of the Oka River, challenged the Lithuanian leaders to establish a closer union with Poland. At that time, the growing Moscow state tried first to attract the autonomous Russian provinces and then started to invade them. Not separatism but cooperation prevailed between the two federated states in the presence of the Moscow danger. Quite rightly Professor Backus asserts in his paper, "There was even some cooperation against the rising Muscovite state long before the reign of Ivan the Terrible."

The Muscovite danger, as was noted above, caused the Lithuanian gentry to approach Poland with the proposal of a closer union, which was completed in Lublin in 1569. As the Muscovite danger induced both states toward cooperation in the sixteenth century, so in the fourteenth century the danger of aggression from the Teutonic Order had forced them toward the union formed in Krewo in 1385. This union was of great importance for both states because it enabled them to win the decisive victory at Tannenberg and to bring the Teutonic Order to the edge of destruction.

The failure to establish a new monarchy was another cause for the decadence of the Polish-Lithuanian state. Its position among the growing monarchies was noticeably weakened by the absence of a more or less centralized monarchy and the retention of the medieval gentry republic. A course that was really against the general trend of the time was taken when, after the successful attempt of Casimir Jogaila to strengthen the monarchy, his successors granted privileges to the gentry. In this way the gentry republic arose and produced its deplorable consequences.

The cultural diversity in the Polish-Lithuanian relationship, as treated in Professor Backus' essay, is of a very crucial nature. The author here raises the concepts of West and East, touches on the particular theory of F. Koneczny about cultural differentiation, and accepts the opinion of Jablonowski, who regarded Lithuania as a land of transition. Consequently, Lithuania was neither a West nor an East European country. It was from the beginning a borderland for both of them, and corresponded more or less to what today is called Central Europe.

Professor Backus states the legal differences between Poland and Lithuania without going into detail for lack of appropriate research. He takes up religious differences as one of the keys to the Polish-Lithuanian cultural diversity. Lithuanian paganism and Orthodoxy, and Polish Catholicism with a slight admixture of Hussitism made both countries culturally different. However, the remark that "paganism was rampant" in Lithuania can hardly be supported. On the contrary, the Lithuanian paganism of the fourteenth century was a pure anachronism, and such rulers as Gediminas (Gedymin) and his successors, Algirdas (Olgerd) and Kestutis (Keistut), favored the acceptance of the Western creed. But the Teutonic Order involuntarily prevented the conversion of Lithuania by its unceasing attempts to subjugate her.

It must be noted that the Orthodox Church gained no converts among the Lithuanians (except for those dignitaries, even some members of the ruling dynasty, who, either through marriage or office, intermingled with the Russians and accepted Orthodoxy). This fact can be considered evidence that the Orthodox-Russian element had only a very weak cultural influence on heathen Lithuania.

But what about the Slavic language (or Russian, as the author calls it) in which the court documents were written? In fact, the official Slavic language did not reflect a numerical predominance of the Russian-speaking population, as Professor Backus says. As a matter of fact, the Slavic language was accepted for court documents because it was the only written language in the grand duchy. The pagan Lithuanians could not elevate their native language to a written form, and the international Western language, Latin, was unknown in Lithuania. The estimate of Professor Backus that 75 per cent of the whole population within the Lithuanian state spoke Russian is too high. More acceptable is the estimate of W. Wielhorski, who followed the well-known research of J. Jakubowski and corrected it, and concluded that the population of Lithuania proper before the Union of Lublin was about half the total population of the grand duchy.[6] In connection with the language the author notes the gradual Polonization of Lithuania, principally of the nobility. According to his opinion, Polonization had worked toward strengthening the union since the sixteenth century. Here seems to be the proper place to explain the role of the Catholic Church in the process of Polonization.

At that time the Christianization of Lithuania and the organization of its church proceeded in close collaboration with the Polish Church. Many priests and several bishops were Poles or had been educated in Poland. Consequently, Catholicism and, in its wake, Western culture were first implanted in Lithuania by way of Poland. The conversion of Lithuania meant her westernization, and its concomitant was Polonization. We have here a historical development similar to what had gone on in the preceding centuries between the Germans and Western Slavs. The Christianization of the Slavs by German missionaries and the church also brought about in varying degrees their Germanization. But Lithuania was less open to Polonization than the Western Slavs were to Germanization, because she was already an established state. Polonization did not immediately penetrate the masses of the people.

6 Wielhorski, *op. cit.,* p. 67.

It gradually affected the nobility from the sixteenth century onward, and with some of them the Polish language replaced their native Lithuanian or Russian.

An evident act of the westernization of the grand duchy was the famous Union of Brest (1596), which attempted to bring the Orthodox Church into the fold of Rome. Professor O. Halecki, not without reason, says that the Union of Brest completed the political Union of Lublin.[7] Both helped to bring the grand duchy closer to the civilization of the West. The comparatively easy spread of Calvinism in Lithuania also testifies to the affinity of the nobles with the West.

Calvinism in Lithuania was much stronger and lasted longer than in Poland and consequently could have weakened the union if it had prevailed. Perhaps the unwillingness of the Lithuanian Calvinists to fight aggressively against Sweden, as noted by Backus, resulted from their religious sentiments. But the renascent Catholicism, acting mainly through the Jesuit Order, stamped out Calvinism and some separatistic tendencies. The restrengthening of Catholicism contributed to the consolidation of the union, as Backus remarks. The *aperçu*, sketched in quite general terms about economic difficulties, does not contribute much to the problem of the Polish-Lithuanian unity. As the author says, more detailed studies, especially on the local level, would help to clarify the economic factors in the problem of the union. The lack of such studies prevents the author from drawing any conclusions.

The short discussion of the Ukraine focuses on the rise of the Cossacks. It is of some importance to mention in this connection the Crimean Tatars and their terrible raids in the fifteenth and sixteenth centuries. The Cossack community, a certain kind of military order after the Western pattern, was formed to meet the urgent need of resisting the assaults and pillages of the Tatars and to take revenge. The Cossacks developed a spirit of independence and liberty, and rose against the Poles when they attempted to hamper their freedom.

The whole effect of the case of the Ukraine and of the revolt on the union constitutes a subject for some special investigation. In this connection it would be important to investigate the policy of the Lithuanian great hetman, Janusz Radziwill. As was already mentioned, he participated in the war against the Cossacks in 1651 and, one year later, incited Sicinski to voice a veto in the seim against the treaty of the Poles and the Cossacks. Three years later he headed the Lithuanian nobles in concluding the union with Sweden in Kedainiai that disrupted the union with Poland. It is not impossible that dissension concerning the union dictated his policy and that he sought ways and means to avoid it. Professor Backus remarks, "One can hardly disagree with the statement that the loss of the eastern Ukraine was a major indication of the failure of the Polish-Lithuanian union."

[7] Oscar Halecki, *A History of Poland* (2nd ed.; New York, 1956), p. 139.

The last section, "Eighteenth-Century Developments," deals with the fall of the Polish-Lithuanian state. The assertion of Professor Backus that the elective rulers tended to put interests outside Poland above interests inside Poland is especially applicable to the Saxon dynasty, whose kings ruled in the republic throughout almost all of the eighteenth century (1697-1763). They preferred their old adopted Saxony to the elective Poland-Lithuania, and sought to enrich the former by the means extracted from the latter. The republic was dragged into the Great Northern War which caused the invasion of the two powers, Sweden and Russia. The vast destruction and complete ruin of the country was the sad result. The unfortunate elective kings paved the way to the intervention of the foreign powers and to the three partitions that followed.

In his concluding remarks, Professor Backus returns to the introductory statement about the internal causes of the fall of the republic. The failure of the union was one of the main causes and deserves careful consideration. Nevertheless, his expounded opinion about the *coup de grâce* dealt the union by foreign intervention is hardly acceptable. The highly creative reform under the last king, Stanislas Poniatowski, aimed at restraining the selfish nobility and putting the state on a new foundation. But the foreign interventions, particularly that of Russia, disrupted the useful reforms and destroyed the state. What the foreign powers administered was not the *coup de grâce* but the mortal blow to the union.

Gratifying is the effort of Professor Backus to discard the nationalistic considerations of the last two centuries and to give more attention to the local developments in the fifteenth through the eighteenth centuries. The people of the respective times should be shown as they appear in the historical sources and in accordance with the prevailing ideas of the age. Certain supranationalistic considerations must replace the nationalistic point of view in all investigations concerning East Central Europe, where so many people and languages are mingled. The paper of Professor Backus is a noteworthy example of impartial exposition in every respect.

Reply

OSWALD P. BACKUS III

The commentaries of my colleagues, Professor Halecki and Dr. Jakstas, which make contributions both of fact and of judgment, represent diverse reactions to my paper. Indeed, at times, my colleagues advance opinions diametrically opposed. The very diversity of their reactions moves me to re-emphasize my view that additional research into many aspects of the subject is needed.

On the issue of the extent of separatism, Professor Halecki asserts that I "greatly overestimated the separatist tendencies in the various provinces of the grand duchy, especially that in Samogitia, which was completely satisfied by the special privilege received soon after Casimir's election in 1440...." Dr. Jakstas, on the other hand, when writing of the subsequent period, asserts that "Samogitia developed into a semi-independent territory and was sometimes even called a princedom." Commenting on the Reformation, Halecki denies that this was a complication and asserts, "the very fact that this crisis started, developed, and ended simultaneously in each of the two states was a new evidence of the high degree of cultural unity which had been achieved in their relations." Dr. Jakstas counters with the affirmation, "Calvinism in Lithuania was much stronger and lasted longer than in Poland and consequently could have weakened the union if it [Calvinism] had prevailed." While Professor Halecki minimizes the Polish desire to dominate Lithuania, Dr. Jakstas emphasizes it and writes with regret, "It would have been desirable if Professor Backus had outlined the protracted rivalry of Poland and Lithuania for Podolia and Volhynia." Professor Halecki emphasizes cooperation between Poland and Lithuania, but Dr. Jakstas, while affirming the reality of such cooperation, asserts, "it is well known that the so-called real union was forced upon the Lithuanians by the imminent danger from Muscovy."

The identification of issues worthy of particular research is impeded by the mode of Professor Halecki's response. First of all, Professor Halecki argues about issues slightly different from those I raised and thus creates at times unwarranted impressions that I am inaccurate. For example, he asserts that the failure of Poland-Lithuania has received an enormous amount of attention. But that does not directly answer my statement that there exists no "thorough analysis of the political, economic, cultural, ethnic, and other factors bearing on the failure of Poland-Lithuania...." Furthermore, he asserts that local history was "never neglected in Polish historiography." That does not answer my contention that "a greater concentration on local history" is needed. Moreover, he asserts that it is wrong to desire a new monarchy or absolutism. Yet I have made no moral judgment on absolutism; I have never said that I liked it. I have written only that, in a world of absolute monarchies, Poland-Lithuania as a result of its evolution was not in a position to preserve itself.

Secondly, Professor Halecki answers an overstatement of mine with another overstatement. In connection with Podolia I asserted, "Ownership of Podolia remained a major issue throughout the sixteenth century." He answered that it "already in the later fifteenth century [had] ceased to be a 'major issue'." From evidence presently available to me, I believe that Halecki is right in this implication that it was not "a major issue" in the late fifteenth century. I believe, however, that he is wrong in using the word "ceased"; or if it may be said to have ceased, it must also be said to have revived again in the succeeding century. Poles in western Podolia committed depredations on Lithuania and eastern Podolia in the 1540's and 1550's. With Polish claims to eastern Podolia advanced in 1563 and subsequently and with the resultant incorporation into Poland of eastern Podolia along with Volhynia and Podliashe, Lithuanian tempers rose. These events might well have prevented the union of 1569 had Lithuania not feared war with Muscovy.[1]

Thirdly, Professor Halecki counters a statement of mine with a flat general contradiction. I assert that cultural diversity led to difficulties, and that these difficulties had significant consequences. Halecki, while admitting certain difficulties, asserts, "this difficulty was overcome through a gradual process of assimilation . . . [of the] upper classes . . . whereas the masses . . . although they also came under Western influence, were left undisturbed in their native culture until they achieved full national development in our democratic age."

Fourthly, Professor Halecki, on occasion, implies that I have said more than I have said. For example, the statement "All this is most definitely denied by Professor Backus . . ." implies that I have denied the entire contents of the preceding paragraph of his commentary. In fact, while treating cultural diversity as an impediment, I have affirmed rather than denied one important point in that paragraph of his, namely, that there was a process of assimilation going on. Our difference lies not over whether there was any assimilation but over its consequences. Furthermore, when he objects to the fairness of wondering about the existence of a Lithuanian culture, he implies that I denied its

---

[1] Professor Halecki himself has written a monograph on the union of former Lithuanian lands with Poland, *Przyłaczenie Podlasia Wołynia i Kijowszczyzny do Korony w roku 1569* (Krakow, 1915). It contains a chapter entitled "The Extension of the Incorporation to the Kiev Land and the Last Protests of Lithuania."

existence. I have stated, "In fact, there is little doubt that Lithuania lacked a single, unified culture." Obviously, in the context I was dealing with the issue of cultural diversity inside Lithuania, a land of many peoples; I was not denying that Lithuanians in the narrow sense, that is, those whose language was Lithuanian, had a culture of their own.

Fifthly, Professor Halecki repeats an exaggeration which tends to make cooperation between Poland and Lithuania appear a greater reality than it actually was, that is, that there was an effective merger of the seims of Poland and Lithuania in 1569. This I must deny. It is, in my opinion, tendentious to assert or to imply that there was an effective merger. An effective merger means a merger that produced certain desired results. The views of Professor Halecki (and even to some degree of Dr. Jakstas) are based on the assumption that a merger of the seims was sought which might produce certain results, specifically the existence of a common seim or diet to act as a legislature for the commonwealth together with the disappearance of separate seims. If in fact such a merger was sought, then the merger accomplished was clearly ineffective: Lithuanians met after the union of 1569 in a chief seim *(golovnoi seim)*, which at times even ruled the country; minutes of meetings of that seim have been preserved. It should be noted in this connection that the Lithuanian legal code, the Lithuanian Statute of 1588, contains no mention of the union of 1569 and does not reflect an effort to adjust Lithuanian law to Polish law in conformity with the words of the union of 1569. In the face of the evidence above, certainly one cannot argue that the merger was effective.[2]

I must admit, however, that there is room to argue that the merger was effective if one postulates that the intended merger was somewhat different from what Professor Halecki and Dr. Jakstas assume it to have been. The drafters of the acts of union of 1569 may have been prepared to settle for a joint diet that would deliberate only on joint problems, and to allow traditional institutions to continue, that is, to allow separate seims to meet of their own volition to solve problems which were not joint problems.[3] If that is so, I must concede that one can argue that the merger was effective in terms of its objectives, that is, that it pursued more limited goals with greater success.

As to the Cossacks, I should in fairness, at this point, acknowledge that I have made what Professor Halecki has graciously termed an "old error." I said that the Cossack uprising resulted from the Union of Brest in 1596. He is quite right in criticizing that statement, for the uprising occurred before the Synod of Brest met; however, he is unjustified in implying that the Cossacks were unaffected by efforts to

[2] See George Vernadsky, *Russia at the Dawn of the Modern Age* (New Haven, 1959), pp. 246-48.

[3] Kutrzeba and Semkowicz, eds., *Akta unji Polski z Litwą*, pp. 344-45, 359-60, 368-69 (Arts. 8 and 16).

impose religious unity. This he does by remaining silent about the fact that the Cossack uprising attained a very significant anti-Uniat dimension, that the organization of the Uniat Church and agitation for it had started before the Synod of Brest, which finally accepted it, and that the Cossacks attacked the pro-Uniat Orthodox, to whose defense the Poles then came successfully. In this case, it appears to me that Professor Halecki's concentration upon a factual error may have the unfortunate effect of inducing the reader improperly to disregard the underlying causation.

As to court reforms, I should have written reforms of the "upper" rather than the "lower" courts in 1578. The later reforms, it is my opinion, better illustrate reforms which may have been the result of military cooperation. It seems to me that there was much too much disagreement between Poles and Lithuanians over the questions of union and military strategy for one to be able to see in the Lithuanian seim's judicial reforms of the sixties evidence of the influence of military cooperation. Indeed for a substantial period of time Lithuanians found themselves alone on battlefields in opposition to Muscovite Russians. It strikes me that Professor Halecki might well have recognized the irrelevance of the reforms of the sixties in the context of military cooperation as a source of broader cooperation. Incidentally, both Professor Halecki and I have erred in writing of judicial reforms of 1578. We should have written of reforms of 1578-81, since Lithuania received her reforms of the upper courts later than Poland. Parenthetically, I might note that the difference in the time of issuance of these reforms points up the tendency to regard Poland and Lithuania as retaining their separate identities.

Sixthly, Professor Halecki's questionable use of labels in discussing a rather significant development may tend to confuse the reader. He states: "It was only one year earlier [1620] that under foreign influence coming from Moscow and from Constantinople, particularly from the violently anti-Polish patriarch Cyril Lucaris, that the use of Cossacks against the Uniat Church was begun." If the label "foreign" is applicable to influences from Constantinople at a time when the Orthodox Church in the Ukraine and Belorussia was organized as a diocese under the patriarch of Constantinople, then influences from Rome must also be labeled foreign, when the Catholic Church in Poland-Lithuania was organized in dioceses under the Pope. But should one look on such religious influences as foreign? Is that not anachronistic, to say the least? The phrase "foreign influence coming from Moscow" tends to obscure the fact that Kievan clerics and Cossacks themselves often wrote to the tsar. Professor Halecki's choice of words and his attack on Patriarch Cyril Lucaris obscure the facts that the Orthodox hierarchy was restored by Patriarch Theophanes of Jerusalem (Cyril Lucaris became patriarch only in 1621) and that the Cossacks, far from being "used," themselves requested that restoration. Finally, by labeling the sometimes pro-Protestant Cyril "violently anti-Polish," Professor Halecki makes "foreign" anti-Polish sentiment seem to be the real cause of the restoration of the Orthodox hierarchy.

Lastly, I should note that Professor Halecki's repeated reference to a virtually irrelevant issue adds to the difficulty of identifying questions worthy of investigation. Professor Halecki directs the attention of American historians to the possibility of a parallel between Poland-Lithuania and the United States. His implication seems to be that in my search for an explanation of the failure of the Polish-Lithuanian commonwealth, I am implying that in the American Civil War or the War between the States, the United States had no right to survive. Interestingly, when he connects American history with that of Poland-Lithuania, he is, by implication, indeed by the very juxtaposition of his words, asserting that the history of the United States is in essence the question of "the viability of a multinational federation." Anyone conversant with American history can hardly view *ante bellum* Georgia and Maine, despite certain differences in culture, indeed despite possible cultural conflicts, as members of a multinational confederation in the sense that Lithuania and Poland were.

I have tried in the foregoing discussion to indicate some of the impediments to the identification of issues which result from the mode of Professor Halecki's response. I have tried incidentally to indicate all instances in which I believe that Professor Halecki has properly detected overstatements or misstatements on my part. Lack of space compels me to remain silent on many other issues on which Professor Halecki has directly or indirectly challenged both my interpretations and my data.

There are criticisms which my critics have not chosen to make. (1) Can it not be argued that I have underestimated social conflicts? Recent Soviet historiography may have overemphasized the importance of peasant rebellions, yet social conflict may properly be singled out for attention in the relations between peasants and lords, between simple Cossacks and highly placed Poles. Social conflict may be regarded as an ultimate cause of the Ukraine's "incapacity" to overthrow Polish domination. (2) Can it not be argued that I have glossed over the loss of rights sustained by Ukrainians and Belorussians in 1569? The transfer of most of the Ukraine to Poland may be viewed as a violation of the rights of those people who had previously come to enjoy virtual legal parity with the Lithuanians within the grand duchy. One may conclude that the revival of the concept of equality of rights in the Treaty of Hadiach of 1658 in a somewhat reduced form was implicit recognition of that violation.[4] (3) Can it not be argued that I have, by impli-

---

[4] See Грушевський, *Історія України-Руси*, X, 331-45, for texts of the Treaty of Hadiach of 1658.

cation, asserted that the coming of Catholicism and the Uniat Church was a truly effective force for unity earlier than it was? One can hardly imagine that the seizure of Orthodox churches and monasteries by the Polish government and their transfer to the Uniat Church during the years 1596 to 1620, when the Orthodox Church was not recognized, helped to instill a sense of community between the despoiled and the despoilers. (4) Can it not be argued that by de-emphasizing the role of the people in making decisions, I have improperly detracted from the greater opportunity among the Cossacks for people to play such a role? These are some criticisms of my presentation which could properly be made and which may help to throw more light on the conflicts in interpretation.

Despite my objections, I believe that this exchange has been worth while. Certain issues emerge as demanding more detailed consideration. Dr. Jakstas' analysis focuses rightly on my conception of the interdependence of the union and the fall of the Polish-Lithuanian federation. Despite Professor Halecki's rejection of this issue, and indeed because of the mode of his rejection, I believe most strongly in the necessity of further, more detailed examination of the reality of that interdependence and its role in the eventual disappearance of Poland-Lithuania from the map of Europe. Furthermore, it seems to me that much more research needs to be done regarding some commonly accepted assumptions. Our disagreement over the effectiveness of the merger of the seims in 1569 is merely one case in point.

The dispassionate tones of Dr. Jakstas' critique, even when he is in disagreement, and his willingness to deal directly with the issues I have raised, should be singled out for special attention. His attitude contributes to the establishment of an atmosphere free from nationalistic considerations, one which can facilitate efforts to discuss and investigate issues as objectively as possible.

And finally I am happy to echo Professor Halecki's call for an explanation of "how the Polish nation survived in spite of the destruction of the Polish state."

EIGHT

Russia and the East: A Comparison and Contrast

I

Among the phenomena of modern history, few equal in importance the victory of the Bolsheviks in 1917 and the rise of the Soviet Union. And among the problems posed by this development, few equal in importance the question of Russia's institutional heritage. The USSR represents an extraordinary concentration of state power, and its ruling class is a managerial bureaucracy. Did these traits play a significant role in tsarist Russia? If so, did they derive from an agrarian order similar to that which produced the modern private-property-based industrial societies of the West? Or did they have a non-Western—perhaps an Oriental—root?

The state of tsarist Russia came into being in the fifteenth and sixteenth centuries under the hegemony of the Muscovite great dukes, who from 1547 onward officially called themselves tsars. It persisted with significant modifications in the Petrinian and post-Petrinian periods. And although its power structure was shaken in the middle of the nineteenth century and seriously undermined by the 1905 revolution, it endured until 1917.

According to Kliuchevsky, in the fifteenth century the Muscovite rulers pursued a policy of subduing the territorial princes that was "not a manifestation of feudal fragmentation" but a device for the national concentration of power.[1] This policy resulted in the emergence of state servants whose maintenance was secured through the assignment of service land. In the sixteenth century these men, as *oprichniki*, overwhelmed the independent forces of the land (the *zemshchina*); and in 1611 they arrogantly proclaimed that they were *the* country.[2] Some decades after the establishment of the Romanov dynasty they became known as the *dvorianstvo*—a service nobility. They were, in fact, "a

MR. WITTFOGEL *is professor of Chinese history at the University of Washington.*

[1] В. О. Ключевский, *Сочинения* (Moscow, 1956-59), I, 362 (*Курс русской истории*, lecture 20).

[2] *Ibid.*, IV, 71 (lecture 62).

new ruling class"[3] that drew its strength essentially from its relation to the autocratic state; and this remained the case until the middle of the nineteenth century, when "Russia came to be controlled neither by an aristocracy nor by a democracy, but by a bureaucracy, that is, an agglomeration of individuals of diverse origin, functioning outside of society, devoid of any particular social identity, and united only through their promotion to *chinovnik* rank."[4]

II

Medieval Europe was characterized by a feudal fragmentation of power. The sovereign was not the master *(dominus, despotes)* of his vassals; he was the first among equals. In the ceremony of investiture, which had a contractual quality, he gave them land (a "fief"), and in return they rendered him certain *conditional and limited services*. In contrast, the Muscovite ruler stood above his serving men as their *master*. Their land (the *pomestie*) was remuneration for *unconditional and unlimited services*.

Virtually all serious scholars have stressed the peculiarity of the Muscovite service land system. Kliuchevsky pointed to the possible Oriental roots—the Byzantine and the Mongol. He expressly rejected the former and by implication accepted Gradovsky's view on this matter: "The concept of the prince as the supreme landowner arose only in the Mongol period. . . . Later the Russian princes inherited for their own full use these state rights from the Khan, and this legacy shattered the emergence of private property."[5] Thus, although in another and much more elaborate argument Kliuchevsky explained the rise of Russia's autocracy as resulting from the "frontier" situation of the sixteenth century,[6] he indicated, by citing the Gradovsky passage, his awareness of the Oriental background of the Muscovite service land system.

Kliuchevsky insisted that in Muscovy the people were not really free and that there were no independent classes (the contrast to Kievan Russia and the feudal West is obvious); but he did not consider the Muscovite state an Oriental despotism. And this is his reasoning: In the Muscovite Empire "there existed neither free persons possessing full rights nor free and autonomous classes. However, society was not an undifferentiated mass, as in the case of Oriental despotisms. . . ." Under the pre-Muscovite system of appanages (hereditary domains of princes and boyars), the classes were separated by economic and occupational differences. In Muscovy, there were "not classes [*sosloviia*], but simply

---

[3] *Ibid.*, III, 7 (lecture 41).

[4] *Ibid.*, p. 9.

[5] *Ibid.*, II, 217 (lecture 32).

[6] *Ibid.*, p. 208 (lecture 31). For a critical appraisal of Kliuchevsky's frontier argument see Karl A. Wittfogel, *Oriental Despotism: A Comparative Study of Total Power* (New Haven and London: Yale University Press, 1963; paperbound ed.), pp. 22 ff.

service grades," their services being "not identical for all, since service alone gave the classes which were subject to it greater or lesser powers to make decisions and issue orders, and to other classes their service left only the obligations of obedience, of execution. On one class was placed the obligation to govern; other classes served either as the instruments of the supreme administration or material for military conscription; while yet other classes bore different tax burdens. . . . Needless to say, the lower *strata,* on which the upper rested, had to bear the heaviest burdens; and of course were oppressed by them. Yet even the highest governing class, upon which state service conferred the power of commanding the rest, did not have direct legislative sanction of its political privileges."[7]

It is clear from this argument why Kliuchevsky did not equate the Muscovite state and Oriental despotism, although he recognized important similarities between them. In both cases, the population was unfree; and Muscovy's system of service land apparently had an Eastern root. But although in Russia the all-demanding state ruled over several classes that differed in their services and social position, he believed that comparable gradations were lacking in the East.

Kliuchevsky's view of Oriental despotism as the rule over an undifferentiated mass of people who were equally without rights closely resembles Montesquieu's image of the despotic governments which, he noted, flourished essentially in Asia[8] and which made all men in their nothingness equal.[9] However, this image does not jibe with the historical facts, which show that, except for some extremely simple cases, stratification in occupation, property, and social status characterized virtually all types of "Oriental" societies in the Old World and pre-Spanish America. Such stratification can be documented for the "simple" Oriental societies of the Pharaohs and the Incas, where private-property-based independent artisans and traders played little or no role but where officials, priests, and commoners were clearly distinguished. It can be documented for the "semi-complex" Oriental societies of the Western hemisphere (the Maya and Aztec), the Near East, and India, where the distinctions between the rulers, priests, commoners, and an underprivileged bottom stratum were modified in form, but only in form, when Muslim rule supplanted Hindu rule. And it can be documented for such "complex" Oriental societies as China, where an early stratification (scholar-officials, peasants, artisans, merchants)

---

[7] Ключевский, *Сочинения,* III, 54-55 (*Курс* . . . , lecture 43).

[8] Baron de Montesquieu, *The Spirit of the Laws,* trans. Thomas Nugent (New York, 1949), pp. 269; see also pp. 68, 213, and 266.

[9] *Ibid.,* pp. 25 and 74. Montesquieu asserted that despotism was mitigated by such factors as the care for waterworks in China and Egypt (p. 274)—or through the good intentions of the government in Russia (p. 59). But he discussed the Russian state as an instance of despotic rule, and hinted at the persistence of "particular causes" that might again involve the Russians "in the very misery which they now endeavor to avoid" (p. 59).

was complicated by the general extension of private property to land and by the periodic duplication of class structure through conquest.[10]

Obviously then, the diversities of class and the limited privileges that Kliuchevsky considered a peculiarity of tsarist Russia were present in virtually all agrarian societies of the Oriental type. And, like tsarist Russia, these societies also were characterized by urban centers, professional crafts and trades, and—under certain circumstances—private land-ownership. But although Kliuchevsky's understanding of Oriental despotism was inadequate, his historical account leads to the conclusion that the society of tsarist Russia was a variant of the non-Western order which traditionally had been called "Oriental" or "Asiatic" society and which, for reasons of institutional identification, may be designated as "agromanagerial" society.

III

Many who have referred to the tsarist regime as an Oriental despotism have done so without giving much consideration to the nonpolitical aspects of the great civilizations of the East: India, China, Egypt, and so forth. And many who studied these civilizations have failed to recognize that they and tsarist Russia have a common institutional denominator.

One of the pioneers in the comparative study of governments, Bodin, claimed that many countries in Asia, certain countries in Africa (primarily Egypt and Ethiopia), and Muscovy and Turkey in Europe were "seigneurial" states; and he contrasted them with the "royal" and "lawful" monarchies of Europe's rising absolutism.[11] But while he viewed the rulers of the Eastern countries as the masters of their subjects' persons and property, he did not specify their socio-economic setting.

Chaadaev was essentially interested in the relation of state power and religion when he associated tsarist Russia and the Orientally despotic Eastern Roman empire of Diocletian and Constantine, and when he called the Russian state that blocked Protestantism "an oriental despotism supported by an oriental cult." In dealing with the problem of Protestantism, Chaadaev noted that Russia's "temporal" (Orientally despotic) power was "founded in the Mongol school."[12] Kovalevsky, the economic historian, stressed the existence of a system of military service land "in the entire Mohammedan world and especially among the

---

[10] Concerning simple, semi-complex, and complex subtypes of Oriental society and the effects of conquest on indigenous stratifications, see Wittfogel, *Oriental Despotism*, pp. 230 ff. and 324 ff.

[11] Jean Bodin, *The Six Bookes of a Commonweale*, ed. Kenneth Douglas McRae (Cambridge, Mass., 1962), pp. 201 ff.

[12] *Вѣстникъ Европы*, Apr., 1906, p. 568, and А. С. Хомяковъ, *Полное собраніе сочиненій*, II (Moscow, 1911), 510; cited in Richard Hare, *Pioneers of Russian Social Thought* (London and New York, 1951), pp. 18-19.

Tatars for centuries before it appeared in Moscow," adding that the Russians introduced it "through the imitation of the Tatar Khanates."[13] Kovalevsky was, of course, correct when he noted that the Muslim rulers employed this system before Muscovy did, but he oversimplified the issue by ascribing it essentially to the Muslims. Actually the service land system was used by the Mongols whether or not they professed Islam.[14] And by focusing on the political institutions of tsarist Russia and the Islamic world, Kovalevsky overlooked the fact that the hydraulic institutions that characterized many areas of the latter realm played no role at all in the former. Miliukov, who recognized that the Muscovite state followed an Oriental model and that its service land system derived, not from Western feudalism, but from Eastern institutions,[15] also failed to raise the hydraulic problem.

IV

Comments on other than the political institutions of the Orient have been made over the centuries, usually with reference to the strong despotic states of the East. But it was only in the course of the development of political economy that serious attention was given to economic conditions and, especially, to state-managed waterworks for the purposes of irrigation and communication.

The classical economists initiated what may be called the "hydraulic" approach to Oriental society. From 1853 this approach was employed by Marx, who underlined the peculiarity of Asiatic economy by speaking of an "Asiatic mode of production,"[16] and, fifty years later, by Max Weber, who underlined the hydraulic core function of Oriental officialdom by calling it a hydraulic ("Wasserbau-") bureaucracy.[17]

Marx associated Oriental despotism with the waterwork societies of Asia and with nonhydraulic Russia. Despite serious deficiencies, this insight was a major contribution to the comparative study of power and to the multilinear theory of societal development. It surely deserves better treatment than it receives at the hands of the Communists.[18]

[13] Maxime Kovalewsky, *Institutions politiques de la Russie,* trans. from the English by Mme Derocquigny (Paris, 1903), p. 43.

[14] According to Dr. Spuler, the Mongols gave land as salary to government officials, generals, and soldiers "according to the sources in most, perhaps in all parts of the empire"; and he notes the occurrence of service land grants in Asia Minor, Armenia, Georgia, Sirwan, Mesopotamia, Qazwin, Sustar, and Horasan. Bertold Spuler, *Die Mongolen in Iran* (Berlin, 1955), p. 329.

[15] Paul Miliukov, *Russia and Its Crisis* (New York, 1962), pp. 117-20.

[16] For references see Wittfogel, *Oriental Despotism,* Chap. 9, and *idem,* "The Marxist View of China," *China Quarterly,* Nos. 11 and 12 (July-Sept. and Oct.-Dec.), 1962.

[17] Max Weber, *Wirtschaft und Gesellschaft: Grundriss der Sozialökonomik,* Part III (Tübingen, 1921-22), p. 117; cf. also Max Weber, *Gesammelte Aufsätze zur Religionssoziologie* (3 vols.; Tübingen, 1922), I, 319, and *Wirtschaftsgeschichte von Max Weber* (Munich and Leipzig, 1923), p. 275.

[18] See Karl A. Wittfogel, "The Marxist View of Russian Society and Revolution," *World Politics,* XII, No. 4 (July, 1960), 504, and *Oriental Despotism,* pp. 398 ff.

Marx held that two "circumstances" were specific for Asiatic society: (1) government "care of the great public works, the prime condition of . . . agriculture and commerce," and (2) the mass of the producers spread out in self-contained villages.[19] Tsarist Russia was characterized only by the second circumstance, but Marx and Engels considered this sufficient to maintain an Orientally despotic state. Classing the *mir* as a variant of the dispersed Oriental village communities, they called tsarist Russia "semi-Asiatic" and the tsarist regime, unqualifiedly, an "Oriental despotism."[20]

Marx's discussion of tsarist Russia was as inadequate as his—and the classical economists'—discussion of India and other countries in which both Oriental "circumstances" were present. Neither Adam Smith, James Mill, Richard Jones, John Stuart Mill, nor Marx and Engels specified the managerial tasks performed by representatives of the Orientally despotic state.

V

This omission is crucial. In the course of history many attempts have been made to exert total power, and among those who made them not a few, to strengthen their position, used all organizational means at their disposal. However, the persistence of total power depended not only on the will and ingenuity of the rulers but also, and decisively, on the character and range of their managerial activities.

In countries with substantial hydraulic tasks, managerial activities include: (1) various types of *construction:* canals, dikes, defense works, state highways, monumental palaces, temples and tombs, and certain supplementary industrial installations, including quarries and mines; (2) various types of *organization:* the registration of persons and land, the servicing of some of the big constructions (waterworks, long walls, and roads), the establishing and directing of coordinated and standardized armies, quick communication through a state post, and so forth; (3) various types of *acquisition:* mass employment of commandeered labor to till the "public fields" for the maintenance of the court, officials, army, and temples, and/or the collection of a general tax, and confiscation or other means for reducing and weakening private property.

It goes without saying that several of these operations interlock and that the hydraulic regimes are not the only agrarian governments that engage in managerial activities. The city states of classical Greece and Rome undertook public works—the building of roads, aqueducts, and drainage systems—but their management did not require the services of

[19] Karl Marx in *New York Daily Tribune,* June 25, 1853.

[20] For Marx's and Engels' statements on this point see Wittfogel, *Oriental Despotism,* pp. 375-76; *idem,* "The Marxist View of Russian Society and Revolution," *op. cit.,* pp. 490 ff.

a permanent directing bureaucracy. Feudal rulers also engaged in numerous managerial activities—but their efforts were confined to their personal domains, and the power of the managerial bureaucracy was limited not only by this circumstance but also by the prominence of the military, whose activities involved little administrative organization. In both instances the managerial activities might be significant, but even when they were, they did not lead to the creation of an agro-despotic state and a polarized society headed by a managerial monopoly bureaucracy.

This, however, was exactly what happened in countries that engaged in substantial hydraulic activities. The governments of hydraulic states carried out managerial tasks that, in terms of human control, were of primary importance. To be sure, the hydraulic states of the past are not identical with the modern *total* managerial Communist regimes (comparatively speaking, they were only *semi*-managerial), but their managerial activities were sufficiently comprehensive to concentrate all political power in the bureaucratic top of the society and to keep the nonbureaucratic elements fragmented and powerless. The result was the rise of the most enduring (and oldest) type of single-centered society.

VI

The historical evidence shows all this. And it does more. It shows that in a number of countries located at the periphery or in the interstices of the hydraulic world, the government carried out few or no hydraulic tasks but many managerial nonhydraulic functions of a kind that had no counterpart in the multicentered agrarian civilizations of classical antiquity, feudal Europe, or Japan. Certain territorial states of pre-imperial China, the Byzantine Empire after the loss of its hydraulic provinces, and the pre-Spanish Maya governments belong here. The managerial activities of these regimes were less comprehensive than those of the hydraulic governments, but they too made the rulers strong enough to exert total power over the mass of the people. They represent a nonhydraulic subtype of agromanagerial society.

Tsarist Russia is clearly another variant of this nonhydraulic subtype. Another variant. Dissimilar to early ideas of Oriental society, which were built on oversimplified concepts, the present analysis, following the empirical data now at hand, recognizes several subtypes and within them a distinguishing diversity in ideas, technology, and institutions.

VII

The Russian variant of nonhydraulic agromanagerial society had several noteworthy peculiarities. It was strongly and differently influenced by two "Oriental" forces—Byzantium and the Mongols. The Byzantines profoundly affected the cultural (religious, artistic, and legal) life of the Russians; but they never defeated the Russians militarily, and they did not Orientalize their patterns of state and society. The Mongols defeated Russia militarily, but, unlike the Moors in Spain, they did not occupy the newly subdued land. From about 1240 to 1480[21] they controlled and exploited Russia through a network of on-the-spot representatives, whose authority was bulwarked by an ever-present threat of renewed military invasion. But they did not substantially alter the civilization of their Russian subjects, who in large degree preserved the Byzantine heritage.

Remote political control exercised by a pastoral people, with a fixed capital, who employed devices of Oriental statecraft, was a peculiar constellation, but it was not a unique one. Similar methods were used by pastoral conquerors before the Mongols invaded Russia and by the Mongols over others besides the Russians. The masters of the Liao Empire ruled Northeast China and the sedentary Pohai of Manchuria from a supreme capital in the steppe and a number of lesser capitals, located for the most part in the agricultural regions they subdued.[22] The tribal Qara-Khitay (Kara-Khitans) dominated Turkestan, including Bukhara and Samarkand, from a tent city.[23] The Mongols of the Golden Horde dominated Russia and other subdued agricultural lands from the steppe area of the Lower Volga, the Qypchaq (Kypchak), where those tribesmen who remained cattlebreeders grazed their numerous herds,[24] while others in quickly increasing numbers[25] lived together with non-Mongol groups in towns.[26]

Dr. Arnold Toynbee considers it a "very far-fetched piece of speculation" to assume that the Mongols of the Golden Horde learned "the tricks of the 'hydraulic agromanagerial' trade from brother Tatars who had ridden off in the opposite direction to conquer 'hydraulic agromanagerial' China."[27] Actually, the relation between the Mongols who "had ridden off" to conquer China and the Mongols of the Golden Horde is no matter of speculation; it is a fact established by solid historical evidence.

The Mongols conquered China north of the Yellow River in 1211/12, Turkestan in 1219/20, and the whole of North China in 1234; and they began employing the agromanagerial methods of administration immediately after seizing these territories. They ran a state post and were familiar with Oriental methods of census-taking, taxation, and corvée

[21] Kliuchevsky stated that the Mongol yoke had been "lying heavily on North-Eastern Russia for two and a half centuries (1238-1480)." Ключевский, *Сочинения*, II, 122 (*Курс* ..., lecture 26).

[22] Karl A. Wittfogel and Fêng Chia-shêng, *History of Chinese Society, Liao*, American Philosophical Society, *Transactions*, XXXVI (Philadelphia, 1949), pp. 61 ff. and 367 ff.

[23] *Ibid.*, p. 659.

[24] Bertold Spuler, *Die Goldene Horde* (Leipzig, 1943), p. 423.

[25] *Ibid.*, p. 296.

[26] *Ibid.*, p. 268.

[27] Arnold J. Toynbee, review of *Oriental Despotism* by Karl A. Wittfogel, *American Political Science Review*, LII (Mar., 1958), 197.

labor[28] when, in 1237, the great khan, Ogadai—not as "brother" but as the supreme ruler of the Mongol Empire—dispatched his nephew Batu to take Russia and other Western lands. And during the next two decades when the Mongols of the Golden Horde were consolidating their system of control in Russia, they continued to acknowledge the authority of the great khan, who was residing, surrounded by his secretarial staff, in his steppe capital, Qara Qorum (Karakorum),[29] while Batu and his successors were administering Russia and other conquered territories from the steppe area of the Lower Volga.

The first fixed capital of the Golden Horde, Sarai, was built before 1254[30] but probably after 1242.[31] The second capital, New Sarai, whose date of origin is uncertain, came into its own probably a few generations later.[32] Literary and archaeological evidence testify to the character and dimension of this urban center of the Mongol masters of Russia. The khan's large palace was surrounded by the residences of high dignitaries. Special quarters were provided for such artisans as metal workers and potters, and there were installations for conducting water to the workshops. By 1333, when Ibn Batuta was a visitor, the city "possessed beautiful bazaars and broad streets, thirteen mosques, baths, and other public facilities,"[33] and was said to have more than 200,000 inhabitants.[34] At the close of the Mongol period, when Russia had recovered from the devastations of the conquest, Moscow may have had about 94,000 inhabitants.[35]

The Mongol's remote control over Russia poses many problems that require further investigation. The same is true of another peculiarity of the Mongol-Russian relation, namely the slow growth of agromanagerial statecraft in Russia despite the fact that the Mongols applied it there. To be sure, the slow transformation of a multicentered agrarian society into a single-centered agromanagerial order is not unique. In Rome this process probably began in 211 B.C., when the Romans decided to perpetuate the Hellenistic version of an Oriental despotism they had found in the kingdom of Syracuse; it advanced substantially

[28] For the administrative practices of the masters of the Mongol Empire at that time see Erich Haenisch, *Die Geheime Geschichte der Mongolen* (Leipzig, 1948), pp. 145 ff.; *Yüan Shih*, Po-na ed. (Shanghai), Chap. 2, pp. 1b ff.; Chap. 121, p. 9a; Chap. 191, p. 2a.

[29] *The Journey of William of Rubruck to the Eastern Parts of the World, 1255-56, as Narrated by Himself, with Two Accounts of the Earlier Journey of John of Pian de Carpini*, trans. from the Latin and ed. William Woodville Rockhill (London, 1900), pp. 221 and 226.

[30] Pelliot states that Sarai was founded in 1254 (Paul Pelliot, *Notes sur l'Histoire de la Horde d'or*, Paris, 1950, p. 142), but Rubruck referred to Sarai as an established fact, not a city that had been created only a few months before he visited the region in the fall of 1254 (*The Journey of William of Rubruck . . .*, pp. 258 ff).

[31] Spuler, *Die Goldene Horde*, p. 267.

[32] *Ibid.*

[33] *Ibid.*, pp. 268-69, 416.

[34] *Ibid.*, p. 267.

[35] J. C. Russell, *Late Ancient and Medieval Population*, American Philosophical Society, *Transactions*, XLVIII, Part 3 (1958), 129.

when they applied similar policies in other conquered areas that previously had non-Eastern forms of government; and it came to a climax in the first century B.C. when victorious Roman generals employed in their Italian homeland the methods of total power then prevailing in the provinces.[36]

In Russia the slowness of the transformation was due to entirely different causes, and among them the Mongol policy of remote control was outstanding. Whether the centrifugal political order of Kievan Russia[37]—which at best possessed some quasi-feudal aspects[38]—accelerated or retarded the process is a moot question. There is no doubt, however, that the Mongol conquerors of Russia weakened the forces that until 1237 had limited the power of the princes, that they employed Oriental methods of government to keep Russia prostrated and exploited, and that they did not intend to create a strong—and politically challenging—agrodespotic state. Hence the germs of the system of total power they planted could bear fruit only after the end of the Mongol period. Dr. Vernadsky has called the effect of the Mongol pattern on Muscovy "influence through delayed action."[39] In the same vein it may be said that an institutional time bomb exploded when the Mongol control collapsed.

A third peculiarity was the impact of Europe's commercial and industrial revolution on Russia, and in this respect Russia's proximity to the West became enormously important. Since the dawn of Greek history agromanagerial states had existed alongside or near a variety of pluralistic Western societies, but these societies were not then engaged in a technical, economic, and military revolution that would make industrialization a life-and-death question for an Eastern neighbor. In the eighteenth and nineteenth centuries Ottoman Turkey was faced with just this question, but internal disintegration and external encroachment prevented a successful industrial and military adjustment. Russia, however, was sufficiently independent to meet the new threat. Peter I's modernization took a primarily technical form. The Napoleonic War, which brought Russia still closer to the West, was followed by a veritable revolution of ideas. And the defeat in the Crimean War initiated profound changes that loosened the despotic power structure—without, however, causing its disintegration. At the close of the nineteenth century and during the first fourteen years of the twentieth cen-

---

[36] Wittfogel, *Oriental Despotism,* pp. 208 ff.

[37] For a stimulating reinterpretation of the character of Russia's pre-Kievan and Kievan society, see Imre Boba, "Nomads in the Formation of the Kievan State" (unpubl. doctoral diss., University of Washington, 1962).

[38] Most scholars agree that, measured by the key criterion of a contractual lord-vassal relationship, Russia's pre-Mongol society was not feudal, although certain of its features may be considered quasi feudal or marginally feudal. For a survey of the various attempts to define these conditions see Marc Szeftel, "Aspects of Feudalism in Russian History," in *Feudalism in History,* ed. Rushton Coulborn (Princeton, 1956), p. 181.

[39] George Vernadsky, *The Mongols and Russia* (New Haven, 1953), p. 335.

tury, Russia's industrial capitalism grew spectacularly. Although still predominantly agrarian, tsarist Russia developed an industrial sector unmatched by any other Oriental society in transition.

Thus agromanagerial methods of government were introduced into Russia by conquerors who, for more than two centuries, dominated the country by a system of remote control. They took shape during a long "incubation period."[40] And the resulting Orientally despotic regime, from the eighteenth century onward, promoted industry in a way that gave the final loosening-up—and the year 1917—a quality completely its own.

These are some of tsarist Russia's most conspicuous peculiarities. Others appear in the various aspects of the regime's agromanagerial activities, to which we shall now turn our attention.

VIII

When the Mongols conquered Russia, they brought their new subjects "neither algebra nor Aristotle." Pushkin might have added: They did not make the Russians great builders either. In other parts of their realm, the Mongols engaged in some construction; they built new irrigation works in Mesopotamia and Persia;[41] they created and maintained some hydraulic installations in and around New Sarai;[42] they rebuilt some of the cities they had destroyed and they founded others.[43] But they do not seem to have employed the constructional methods of Oriental statecraft in their Russian *ulus*.

Nevertheless, after 1480, the Muscovite rulers, who were quickly gaining control over the labor power of all of Russia, built large-scale constructions of a certain type. They soon had fortified lines of defense against the Tatars: "Such lines, *cherty*, as they were then called, consisted of chains of towns, forts, and watchtowers which were enclosed by log palisades, or a stockade, standing, of pointed stakes, with ditches, ramparts, wooden *abatis*, and obstacles of tree trunks in the forest reserves." The oldest line, relatively close to Moscow, was four hundred versts long. A second line stretched from Alatyr to the Sura River; it was strengthened by a subsidiary line of minor fortifications. A third set of fortifications consisted of several groups of towns that faced the steppe. It was established at the close of the sixteenth century.[44]

If the Mongols did little to instruct the Russians in the realm of large-scale nonhydraulic construction, they taught them crucially im-

[40] *Ibid.*, p. 372.

[41] Spuler, *Die Mongolen in Iran*, pp. 319-20.

[42] Spuler, *Die Goldene Horde*, p. 420. Irrigation works that in part had a Turkestan background and that may have been in existence before the arrival of the Mongols made it possible to grow vegetables, fruits, and some millet near the capital.

[43] *Ibid.*, pp. 296-97, 426-27, and 430; *Die Mongolen in Iran*, pp. 448-49.

[44] Ключевский, *Сочинения*, II, 211-12 (*Курс . . .*, lecture 31).

portant devices of organization and acquisition. And they suggested others. Through practice and imitation the Muscovite princes were able to employ these devices to consolidate and develop their autocratic government.

A few years after the conquest of Russia was completed, the masters of the Golden Horde carried out a preliminary census that Carpini observed,[45] and the great khan, Mongka (Mangu), shortly after his enthronement (1251/52) ordered that a census be taken throughout the whole Mongol Empire.[46] According to the dynastic history of the Mongol dynasty, in 1253 a Mongol, Pieh-erh-ke, was selected to direct the work in Russia.[47] According to a Russian chronicle, one of the two Mongol officials who organized the census in Russia in 1257 bore the name Berkai.[48] Bretschneider is convinced that the Chinese and Russian sources are referring to the same Mongol official.[49] Pelliot refines the argument linguistically and suggests the possibility that the word in question *(bärgä* or *bärkä)* may connote a title rather than a personal name, but by implication he accepts Bretschneider's conclusion that the words Pieh-erh-ke and Berkai refer to the same fiscal functionary.[50] The census of 1257—and another in 1275—served as the basis for taxation and military conscription. The population was divided into tens and multiples of ten,[51] a system that had been employed for many centuries in China and was adopted by such Inner Asian invaders of China as the Huns, the Ch'i-tan founders of the Liao Empire,[52] and the Mongols.[53]

After 1480 the Muscovite rulers continued census-taking, that is, they pursued a policy that the sovereigns of feudal nations could not enforce at all[54] and that their postfeudal successors could employ only during the later phase of absolutism. Kliuchevsky points to a state register dated 1500 covering part of the old territory of Novgorod.[55] The first European visitor who gave a detailed account of post-Mongol Russia, the German ambassador, Baron von Herberstein, reported on the basis of his two sojourns in 1518 and 1526 that "every second or third year

[45] *The Journey of William of Rubruck . . .*, p. 94, n. 1.
[46] Spuler, *Die Goldene Horde*, p. 31.
[47] *Yüan Shih*, Chap. 3, p. 4b.
[48] Nikon Chronicle, Полное собраніе русскихъ лѣтописей (St. Petersburg, 1841-1949), X, p. 142; Spuler, *Die Goldene Horde*, p. 333; cf. also M. Karamsin, *Histoire de l'empire de Russie*, trans. St. Thomas and Jauffret (11 vols.; Paris, 1819-26), IV, 91 and 94.
[49] E. Bretschneider, *Mediaeval Researches from Eastern Asiatic Sources* (2 vols.; London, 1910), II, 80.
[50] Pelliot, *op. cit.*, p. 49.
[51] Nikon Chronicle, ПСРЛ, X, 141. Vernadsky, *op. cit.*, p. 150, n. 40.
[52] Wittfogel and Fêng, *op. cit.*, p. 530.
[53] Haenisch, *op. cit.*, pp. 77-78. The Mongols learned the fundamentals of Chinese statecraft mainly from a sinicized Ch'i-tan, Yeh-lü Ch'u-ts'ai (see his biography in the *Yüan Shih*, Chap. 146).
[54] The seeming exception, the Domesday Book, probably was inspired by Byzantine and Saracen administrative practices inherited and transmitted by the Norman conquerors of Sicily (Wittfogel, *Oriental Despotism*, pp. 213-14).
[55] Ключевский, *Сочиненія*, II, 221 (*Курс . . .*, lecture 32).

the prince holds a census through the provinces."[56] Under Ivan IV the
registers of land and people had become highly intricate; recent students of Muscovy's administration have called the Muscovite cadastre
an outstanding bureaucratic achievement.[57] A hundred years later, in
1662, Petty tried to persuade his English readers that the taking of a
cadastre would do the privileged estates "no harm."[58] In 1753 a bill
proposing the annual counting of the population was opposed as being
"subversive of the last remains of English liberty." It was defeated.
The first English census was taken only in 1801.[59] Most countries of
Europe introduced the system in the eighteenth century.[60]

Different also from feudal Europe and Japan, the Muscovite rulers
did not depend on loose agglomerations of fighting men who served the
sovereign conditionally and for a limited time. Following the Mongol
pattern, their armies were government-controlled centralized bodies,[61]
and their fighters served, of course, unconditionally.

The Muscovite rulers furthermore followed the Mongol pattern in
maintaining a state post for communication and intelligence. The
Mongols called the post stations *yam*,[62] and the Muscovite princes continued to use this designation for the postal system which they set up
soon after the collapse of the Mongol yoke. Herberstein summarized
the situation thus: "The prince has post stations in all parts of his
dominions with a regular number of horses at the different places, so
that when the royal courier is sent anywhere he may immediately have
a horse without delay." And not only official couriers. Distinguished
foreign travelers, whose horses were tired, also could change them
"on reaching another inn on the road (they call their inns *jama*)" and
"the post-master . . . in their language is called *jamshnick* [sic!]." Using
post horses (and there might be from thirty to fifty at a single station)
one of Herberstein's servants covered the six hundred versts from Nov-

---

[56] Sigismund von Herberstein, *Notes upon Russia: Being a Translation of the Earliest
Account of That Country Entitled Rerum Moscoviticarum Commentarii*, trans. and ed.
R. H. Major (2 vols.; London, 1851-52), I, 95.

[57] See references to Gautier, Lappo-Danilevsky, *et al.* in Epstein's notes to Heinrich von
Staden, *Aufzeichungen über den Moskauer Staat*, ed. Fritz Epstein (Hamburg, 1930), p. 57.

[58] *The Economic Writings of Sir William Petty*, ed. Charles Henry Hull (Cambridge,
Eng., 1899), I, 15; cf. pp. 34, 53.

[59] Sir Jervoise Athelstane Baines, "Census," *Encyclopaedia Britannica* (11th ed.; 1910-
11), V, 663.

[60] Karl A. Wittfogel, "General Introduction," *History of Chinese Society, Liao*, p. 31.

[61] The Muscovite armies were centrally located and systematically organized bodies of
fighters, each major detachment having a right wing, advanced and rear guard, and a left
wing; Ключевский, *Сочинения*, II, 149 (*Курс* . . . , lecture 27). Fletcher was impressed
neither by the order nor the valor of these forces (Giles Fletcher, "Of the Russe Common
Wealth or Manner of Government by the Russe Emperour . . . ," in *Russia at the Close of
the Sixteenth Century*, London, 1856, p. 77). Similar criticism has been directed at the
Byzantine armies, often without recognition of the fact that, despite their deficiencies,
they often constituted a very effective military instrument because of their state-imposed
cohesion (see Wittfogel and Fêng, *op. cit.*, pp. 536-37).

[62] Spuler, *Die Goldene Horde*, pp. 412-13, and *Die Mongolen in Iran*, pp. 422-23; cf.
Vernadsky, *op. cit.*, pp. 127-28.

gorod to Moscow in seventy-two hours.[63] At the time of Ivan IV the state post was very elaborate and very expensive.[64] Kliuchevsky devotes several pages to descriptions of the institution given by foreign visitors to Russia in the sixteenth and seventeenth centuries.[65]

Another important managerial activity of the tsarist regime was both organizational and acquisitive—the handling of the quickly growing service land, whose possessors, besides rendering military and other services, had to collect a tax from "their" peasants, part of which they handed over to the crown.[66]

The conversion of service land into privately-owned land in 1762 removed one important managerial task from the government roster. But, as noted above, before this occurred the regime had taken on another—the running or supervising of the new (particularly the heavy) industry. By the end of the eighteenth century, state enterprises employed almost two-thirds of all industrial labor.[67] And although in the nineteenth century the private sector expanded conspicuously, until the Emancipation large numbers of laborers continued to work in state enterprises, especially in the Ural Mountains, where they were engaged in "mining, iron-smelting and other mechanical industries."[68] By 1900 the government still controlled either directly or by means of licensing about 45 per cent of all large modern enterprises of industrial production and communication.[69]

These activities of the regime were highly significant both because of their dimension (in Western countries the sector of state-controlled enterprises was much smaller) and because they expressed the will of the government to continue performing crucial managerial activities in the growing sphere of modern economy. This will asserted itself also in the matters of credit control. The Soviet economic historian, Liashchenko, recognized that "from the standpoint of organization, the Russian banking system differed materially from the banking system of the Western capitalist countries." Indeed, "the state bank was the

[63] Herberstein, *op. cit.*, I, 108-9; cf. Ключевский, *Сочинения*, II, 343 (*Курс* ..., lecture 38).

[64] Staden, who served Ivan IV from 1564 to 1573, had ample opportunity to observe its operations: "There are also postal stations definitely throughout the length and width [of the land] in which lived volunteers (*freiwillige Leute*) with very good horses so that one could come in six days from Moscow to any surrounding border or from the border to Moscow. One jamme or postal yard is separated from another by 20, 30, 40, 50 versts. The Jammen and postal stations annually cost the great duke quite a lot for maintenance ...." Staden, *op. cit.*, p. 59; see also pp. 13, 35, 75, 104, 107, 111, and 182.

[65] В. О. Ключевский, *Сказания иностранцев о московском государстве* (Petrograd, 1918), pp. 262 ff.

[66] See Staden, *op. cit.*, pp. 9 ff. and 56 ff.; cf. Epstein's notes, pp. 221 ff. and 228 ff.

[67] See James Mavor, *An Economic History of Russia* (2nd ed., 2 vols.; New York, 1925), I, 368, 441, and 493.

[68] *Ibid.*, II, 368.

[69] The estimate rests on statistical data given in Sergei Prokopowitsch, "Über die Bedingungen der industriellen Entwicklung Russlands," *Archiv für Sozialwissenschaft und Sozialpolitik*, Suppl. X (1913), pp. 16 ff. and 22.

central bank of the entire Russian credit system" and "the director of the Credit Department . . . controlled the entire financial apparatus of the country."[70] We need not share Lenin's view that whoever controls the credit system of a country controls its entire modern economy to recognize that the tsarist regime's control over Russia's credit system was of the greatest socio-political importance.

IX

As noted above, the power of the regime derived from a close linkage of its organizational and acquisitive activities. The registration of the population was largely for fiscal purposes. Many peasants paid their tax in labor and/or kind or cash either directly to the government or to the *pomeshchiki* who acted as tax collectors for the government. The Oriental quality of this revenue pattern is easily apparent if we compare tsarist Russia with the Greek and Roman city states (where free men paid virtually no taxes), with feudal society (where the sovereign depended essentially on revenues from his personal domain), and with feudalism-rooted absolutism (where the sovereign collected few or no taxes from the land of the privileged estates).

When its rationality level was low, an Orientally despotic regime relied heavily on arbitrary confiscation, and when this level was high— usually when private property, trade, and commerce were well developed—this method of exploitation was less frequently used (cf. ancient Babylonia and imperial China). During the Muscovite period arbitrary confiscation flourished,[71] and the methods employed were similar to those customary in other "semi-complex" agromanagerial societies.[72] But from the eighteenth century on, the regime concentrated on more rational ways of weakening private property. In the decades following the Emancipation the tax imposed on the upper classes rose from 17.5 per cent to 44 per cent of the entire national tax;[73] and by the close of the nineteenth century the peasants were contributing about 50 per cent of their income to the tsarist regime.[74]

Another standard device of Oriental statecraft that kept private property weak was the fragmentative law of inheritance. The tsarist rulers applied this device also to service land; and Peter's attempt to introduce the single-heir principle failed because Russia lacked the corporate (feudal) gentry which in the West, by the system of entail, was able to maintain its group interest against internal and external pressures. In

[70] Peter I. Lyashchenko, *History of the National Economy of Russia to the 1917 Revolution*, trans. L. M. Herman (New York, 1949), pp. 701-2 and 706.

[71] For the mid-sixteenth century see Staden, *op. cit.*, pp. 11 ff.; for the close of that century see Fletcher, *op. cit.*, pp. 61 ff.

[72] See Wittfogel, *Oriental Despotism*, pp. 75 ff.

[73] П. Милюковъ, *Очерки по исторіи русской культуры* (St. Petersburg, 1900), I, 157-58.

[74] See Nicolai-on, *Die Volkswirtschaft in Russland*, trans. Georg Polonsky (Munich, 1899), pp. 142 ff.

1741 the fragmentative system was restored, and it persisted after the *pomestiia* were converted into private property. Haxthausen was struck by the peculiar character of the Russian nobles—men who were little interested in agriculture, who lived mostly in cities, and who were always eager to enter government service. Manifestly, Haxthausen was unfamiliar with Oriental patterns of land tenure and inheritance; but he found the Russian nobility "no aristocracy in the European sense of the term" and landed property decidedly unstable. As the first reason for this condition he mentioned "the equal division [of the estate] among all sons," a feature that seriously "splits the property." In Russia "a large fortune rarely reaches the third heir."[75] Dr. Blum in his scholarly study of the Russian peasantry views the landed nobility as a class that was increasingly able to oppose the tsarist government. Yet he too recognizes "the inevitable result of splintering patrimonies with each successive generation." In the nineteenth century "as in earlier centuries, once wealthy families were reduced to poverty in as few as three generations."[76]

X

Our survey of the managerial activities of the tsarist regime, although necessarily incomplete, draws attention to some highly significant facts. It shows, among other things, that in contrast to the Byzantine Empire, which fulfilled more constructional tasks at the beginning of its non-hydraulic period than later, the tsarist regime, which originally executed major constructions only with regard to defense from the time of Peter I, began increasingly to create and operate industrial installations (including mines and smelteries). As these installations multiplied, the organizational and operational functions multiplied also. And while the growth of all these functions was accompanied by the growth of the private economy, they remained sufficiently weighty to counterbalance, to a very considerable degree, the greater freedoms enjoyed by the representatives of private property and enterprise. This continued to be the case even after the Crimean War, when the regime reluctantly encouraged the evolution of economic and social forces actively antagonistic to the old order.

The simultaneous development of these two trends still left the Orientally despotic state in total control of the politically pulverized population. At the close of the nineteenth century, the nonsocialist Miliukov recognized this situation when he called the tsarist autocracy

[75] August von Haxthausen, *Studien über die innern Zustände, das Volksleben und insbesondere die ländlichen Einrichtungen Russlands* (3 vols.; Hannover and Berlin, 1847-52), III, 46-48.

[76] Jerome Blum, *Lord and Peasant in Russia from the Ninth to the Nineteenth Century* (Princeton, 1961), p. 376. Cf. the Chinese notion that a wealthy family may become poor in three generations and wealthy again in another three—this last, it should be added, if a lucrative government position is attained.

"a state stronger than society."[77] The socialist Lenin expressed a similar view when at the turn of the century he commented that the Russian people, like the Chinese people, were being ruled by an oppressive "Asiatic government."[78] But the anti-autocratic trend, which was strong even before 1904, became formidable after Russia was defeated by Japan. The revolution of 1905, the political response to this military disaster, did not achieve its ultimate goal, but it compelled the autocracy officially to tolerate a variety of groups and parties dedicated to the creation of a representative government and a pluralistic society. In 1911 Lenin described Tolstoy's world outlook as "the ideology of Oriental, Asiatic society"—a society that was characterized by stagnation and one that prevailed in Russia until 1905. "The year 1905 was the beginning of the end of 'Oriental' stagnation."[79]

Miliukov's and Lenin's statements—and many more could be cited—indicate, from two widely separated points of view, the nature and dimension of the historical process that unfolded in Russia in the later part of the nineteenth century and at the beginning of the twentieth. Non-Communist Russian writers who after 1917—first inside the Soviet Union and later outside its borders—have been emphasizing the strength of the democratic ("Western") forces in pre-October Russia do honor to these forces and help the comparative analyst to identify them. But the difficulties the Russian partisans of democracy encountered and the institutional meaning of their dramatic rise and fall after the February Revolution can be clearly understood only if we recognize the nature of the enemy they had been combating for decades and that in 1917 they briefly overcame.

Our study of these events acquires a new socio-historical reality if we realize that among the many recent attempts to transform a single-centered into a multicentered society, the attempt made in Russia went far indeed, but that there, as in other agromanagerial societies in transition, those who spearheaded the struggle were faced with a singularly grave obstacle—a state that for centuries was stronger than society.

[77] Милюковъ, *op. cit.,* p. 126.
[78] В. И. Ленин, *Полное собрание сочинений* (Moscow, 1958——), IV, 383.
[79] *Ibid.,* XX, 101 ff.

"Oriental Despotism" and Russia

NICHOLAS RIASANOVSKY

Having recently put out a history of Russia, I have been the recipient of many comments on my book. One professor wrote to the publishers: "This is O.K. but doesn't seem to add very much. . . . The point of view seems standard-Western." Apparently he had found nothing more stimulating, for he added generously that he might want to use my history as a text. Well, Professor Karl A. Wittfogel's point of view is neither standard nor "Western." Moreover, as we all know, his judgment of Russia forms but a very small part of a total system which emerged out of China to sweep across the face of the earth and establish itself in strength in such remote places as pre-Columbian America. Indeed, as I read Wittfogel's critique of Toynbee's critique of Wittfogel's views, I was forcefully reminded of a fascinating confrontation I once witnessed between Toynbee and Sorokin. For it is already clear that Wittfogel belongs with Sorokin and Toynbee rather than with the more pedestrian contributors to the *Slavic Review*. To be sure, questions have been raised whether what these remarkable men write is of relevance to historians. I would answer these questions emphatically in the affirmative. Unfortunately, I am much less certain exactly what to do when confronted with a magisterial and soaring piece by Wittfogel, which is to be analyzed in a few pages. To add to my difficulties, I am supposed to say something not only on Professor Wittfogel's treatment of his subject but also on the subject itself.

Under the circumstances, I shall limit myself to selective and sometimes random comments both on Wittfogel's views and on Russia in its relationship to Asia. I must admit in advance the charge that the very nature of the discussion is bound to be unfair to Professor Wittfogel, whose earlier outline of his system required some five hundred pages. My only weak defense is that the entire procedure is also quite unfair to a commentator.

Professor Wittfogel believes that what he calls "Oriental despotism" originated through the need for large-scale, centrally-directed hydraulic works. A despotic state based on an agromanagerial bureaucracy arose essentially to construct and maintain such works. Prepared to build canals and dikes, it could easily erect huge walls or pyramids. With its

MR. RIASANOVSKY *is professor of history at the University of California, Berkeley.*

population counted, organized, and controlled by bureaucrats, it found itself in a position to mobilize mass armies or engage in sweeping economic undertakings. Although the exact economic, social, and political structure varied from case to case, each Oriental despotism displayed a hypertrophy of the power and role of the state and, the reverse side of this, a weak society. Once established, Oriental despotisms proved to be remarkably durable. Moreover, the system could spread rapidly through borrowing—"infection" might be a better word here—by other peoples or societies that did not themselves have to be hydraulic or entirely agrarian. Thus, hydraulic China established a classic Oriental despotism, which the Mongol conquerors borrowed from it and which in turn came from the Mongols to Russia and proceeded to determine Russian history from the thirteenth century to the present.[1]

Professor Wittfogel annexes in this manner Russian history as one of the battlefields in the age-old struggle between Oriental despotism and free society—one could almost write between evil and good, darkness and light, Ahriman and Ormazd. Yet the annexation remains precarious. Whereas China possessed a hydraulic society, and the Mongols at least established a dynasty in China as well as states in certain other hydraulic areas, the Russians had no massive hydraulic works and no Chinese example but only limited and often distant contacts with their Mongol overlords to transform themselves according to the Mongol image which had become the image of Oriental despotism. Moreover, the transformation occurred not during the time of the contacts, but later. There was an "incubation period." "An institutional time bomb exploded when the Mongol control collapsed"—whatever that means. It should be added, a point not mentioned by Professor Wittfogel, that the transformation was, apparently, also unconscious: consciously the Russians invariably likened the Mongols to the plague, to a "scourge of God" to be more exact, while they tried to model their thought, institutions, and activities on their own concept of themselves, on their past, and on Byzantium. Professor Wittfogel, of course, recognizes the marginal or "peripheral" status of Russia as an Oriental despotism, and peripheral in more ways than one. Kievan Russia, he thinks, was a polycentric society, which belonged therefore in terms of his dichotomy to the free world. He continues his analysis to point out that Russia never entirely succumbed to Oriental despotism, that society persisted in its struggle against the state to the extent of winning a stunning, if short-lived, victory in the spring and summer of 1917. Still, the real issue is not whether Russia was a peripheral Oriental despotism but whether it was an Oriental despotism at all.

[1] Additionally, according to Wittfogel, Russia was affected, presumably from the tenth century, by another Oriental despotism, the Byzantine. I am not, however, going to discuss the extremely important subject of Russo-Byzantine relations for at least three reasons: in general, it is not considered a part of the topic of Russia and Asia; while Wittfogel does include it in his scheme, he devotes very little attention to it; and, finally, I lack space.

The impression that Russia does not fit the pattern of Oriental despotism deepens as one studies specific evidence. Not only did the Russians fail to construct hydraulic works, but in general they would not engage in the massive building characteristic of Oriental despotism. To quote Wittfogel, the Mongols "did not make the Russians great builders." The only exception to this generalization which he cites is the complex line of defenses which the Russians finally erected against the Mongols, and the like of which the Golden Horde itself never possessed! There are, needless to say, different kinds of influence. In this instance it might be worth spelling out, however, that aspirin is not borrowed from a headache.

Oriental despotisms are characterized by the weak development of private property and by its fragmentation. In Russia private property of various kinds went very far back and achieved a remarkable growth and differentiation. True, it could be considered fragmented in that, as a rule, fathers divided their possessions among their children with the result that property, in particular landed estates, quickly became split and scattered. This pattern of inheritance, however, dated from the earliest period of Russian history, and in part it would seem prehistory, preceding by centuries the Mongol conquest. What the regime described by Wittfogel as Oriental despotism tried to do in Russia was to reverse the process and to keep the estates together by making each estate the inherited property of one son only. Professor Wittfogel notes Peter the Great's legislation to that effect and its dismal failure, but does not focus attention on the fact that such legislation is the very opposite of what an Oriental despotism can be expected to promulgate.

The economic policies of imperial Russia appear also to have been the opposite of those of an Oriental despotism as defined by Wittfogel. The modern Russian state did play a major role in the economic life of the country, although Wittfogel somewhat exaggerates this role. But, a point to be kept in mind, it made strenuous efforts from the time of Peter the Great onward to promote private enterprise. In fact, the acme of the state direction of economic life, the period of the 1890's, when Sergius Witte was the imperial minister of finance, remains most notable for the very rapid and impressive rise of a privately owned and operated heavy industry. One does not have to be a Soviet historian to recognize that, at least as far as these new businessmen and their associates were concerned, the role of the state could not be adequately described as that of a juggernaut crushing society.

Examples could be multiplied to show that Russia does not fit the concept of Oriental despotism. But in a brief commentary I must move to a still more important consideration: it is that the concept of Oriental despotism does not fit Russia and Russian history. What Professor Wittfogel's view of the evolution of Russia manages almost entirely to omit is Russian history itself, with its centuries and centuries of continuous economic, social, and political development, its internal crises and intrinsic problems. Instead we are offered the Mongol bacillus of Oriental despotism. The subject that interests Professor Wittfogel so much, that of the development of Russian institutions, in particular the emergence of an autocratic and despotic Muscovite state and its transformation into a westernized empire, has been studied by generations of Russian historians. Unfortunately, there is very little evidence of their work in Professor Wittfogel's essay. Judging both by his text and his footnotes, he relies almost exclusively on the 5 per cent of Russian historical sources and studies that happen to have been translated into, or written in, Western languages. What he needs is the 95 per cent that have not been so translated or written. Of a staggering amount of scholarly writing trying to interpret the evolution of Muscovite and imperial Russia in terms of geography, the Russian past, the Byzantine heritage, outside pressure, Western influence, or class struggle—to mention only a few of the more obvious approaches—Professor Wittfogel seems to be aware only of Kliuchevsky's frontier theory. He disapproves of the frontier theory and therefore substitutes the Mongol bacillus. *Quod erat demonstrandum.*

To belabor the obvious, no single factor is at all likely to have accounted for the main course of Russian history, nor are these factors distinct and unchangeable entities. The sheer size of the country cannot be excluded as an influence for autocracy in Russia because it proved to be an influence for democracy in the United States. Nor is class struggle *ipso facto* a bad explanation for much that transpired in Russia on the ground that it led to quite different results in England. It is the unique combination of extremely complex circumstances evolving through time that accounts for the development of a country. There is no substitute for studying Russian history as such.[2]

Because Professor Wittfogel views his subject, Russia and Asia, from the standpoint of his theory of Oriental despotism, not from the standpoint of Russian history, his approach remains extrinsic throughout. Not only does he attach more weight to the Mongol impact than to the frontier conditions of life, or, in the case of the origin of *pomestiia,* to possible Mongol analogues than to the situation and needs in Russia— or, for that matter, than to Western analogues stressed by Pavlov-Silvansky and others. He continues this line of interpretation when dealing with the better-charted developments of modern times. In particular, Professor Wittfogel appears to present the important role of the imperial Russian government in the economic modernization of the country as a function of the Orientally despotic nature of the govern-

[2] I realize, of course, that what Professor Wittfogel has to contribute to Russian history is not in the nature of a detailed investigation of facts. And, to repeat, I welcome his contribution. Indeed, it is impossible for a Toynbee or a Wittfogel to specialize in the history of every country which he discusses or classifies. Regretfully, it is usually equally impossible for specialists to agree with these master builders.

ment, and even as the particular form that Oriental despotism took in Russia. He does not mention alternate, and intrinsic, explanations, such as the argument that a late industrialization of a nation necessitates massive government participation.[3] Wittfogel's suppositions of Mongol influence and origin are time and again supported largely by the fact that things developed differently in the West. To extend the methodology—not quite fairly, I grant—one might argue that the Russian language must be really Mongolian because it certainly is not French.

Oriental despotism aside, what was the influence of the Mongols on Russia? Part of the answer lies in the evidence of Mongol practices and terminology in such spheres of Muscovite activity as administration and finance. Census-taking, certain forms of taxation, road building, and the postal service in Russia have been linked to the Mongols. To be sure, the Mongol influence should not be exaggerated even in this restricted area. For example, Mongol financial policies often failed in Russia. Thus, the invaders replaced the old "smoke" and "plow" taxes with the cruder and simpler head tax, which did not at all take into account one's ability to pay. But this innovation disappeared when Russian princes, as intermediaries, took over from the Mongol tax collectors. And even the postal system in Russia dated back to Kievan times, although the Mongols did enlarge and improve it. What is more, many historians would deny even the possibility of a major direct influence of the Mongol state and society on their Russian counterparts on the grounds that the Mongols and the Russians generally kept far apart and especially that Mongol society, law, and institutions were much more primitive than the Russian. How could a nomadic people in a clan stage of development influence profoundly the successors to the highly advanced Kievan state? Here, however, caution may be in order, although the burden of proof must surely rest on those who assert the great significance of the few Russian borrowings from the Mongols. Perhaps Professor Wittfogel's vision of the surpassing importance of such items as the census and the postal service will inspire fruitful research.

Professor George Vernadsky and certain other specialists excepted, the historiographical issue of the Mongol impact on Russia has had little to do with direct borrowing. Rather, historians have generally adhered to one of two main points of view: the first denied all long-range significance to the Mongol conquest of Russia, the second considered it lastingly important in terms of its destruction, burden, and pressure. Scholars of the second school emphasized the weight of the yoke itself and of the subsequent quasi-permanent hostilities with the successor states to the Golden Horde in the rise of such fundamental

[3] See especially Alexander Gerschenkron, *Economic Backwardness in Historical Perspective: A Book of Essays* (Cambridge, Mass., 1962).

Russian institutions as the service gentry system and serfdom. Or they pointed to a certain intellectual and cultural retardation and even regression as attributable in part to the Mongol devastation and exactions. It would seem that it is along such lines that the best case for a profound Mongol influence on Russia can be made, although this case will have little in common with either the Eurasian glorification of Mongol statehood or Wittfogel's condemnation of it as an instance of Oriental despotism, that crucial infectious disease of history.

In concluding, I want to express my appreciation of Professor Wittfogel's original and stimulating effort. As I had occasion to write earlier in the pages of this periodical, it is much easier to criticize than to affirm. This is especially true when the affirmation encompasses in effect all of human history. Professor Wittfogel may even deserve the rank of prophet, especially if his original Oriental despotism, the Chinese, prevails in the world.

Russia and Islam

BERTOLD SPULER

Professor Wittfogel is doubtless right when he designates the autocratic regime in Russia in tsarist times as a variant of "Oriental despotism" and when he indicates the great influence of the Mongols of the Golden Horde and their linguistically Turkicized descendants, the Tatars, on the Russian system of government. A discussion on this issue is today scarcely necessary any longer.

One may indeed ask whether the root of this development may be designated simply as "Oriental." That would mean—apart from the problem of the Byzantine heritage in the Russian conception of the state (to be discussed later)—that the word "Oriental" refers to a unitary set of facts. If I here leave aside the societies of East and South Asia, which I am unable to appraise on the basis of knowledge of the sources, it seems to me in any case necessary to make distinctions for the Islamic area. Thus the original form of the Islamic state under the prophet Mohammed himself and his first successors, the "correctly guided caliphs" (632-61), and also under the Omayyads (until 750) cannot be spoken of as despotism; and naturally not as democracy either, as the modern Muslims are eager to do in order to gain contemporary advantages. The fundamental elements of democracy, such as free, equal, and secret elections, separation of powers, constitutional guarantees of the rights of individuals and of the organs of state, an independent judiciary, and so forth, are absent from early Islam.

If the period before 750 is especially stressed, it follows of itself that thereafter a swift and fundamental change took place, starting with the takeover of the government by the Abbasids. Here are to be found, as is known, many of the essential marks of an Eastern despotism: the concentration of the powers of government in the hands of a monarch and in the metropolis (in this case Baghdad), the development of a hierarchically organized officialdom responsible only to him, judicial arbitrariness, and frequent seizure of private property. The aristocratic constitution of the Omayyad state, with the participation of hereditary princes and nobles in the government, was succeeded by "orientalization" under the Abbasids, a development of which the Muslims of that time were thoroughly aware. They correctly saw in the governmental methods of the pre-Islamic Persian sovereigns, especially the Sassanids,

MR. SPULER *is professor of Islamic studies at the University of Hamburg.*

the prototype of the Abbasid administration; the caliphs referred to it as their model without reserve, indeed with pride.[1] (One might moreover cite parallel developments in Western Europe, perhaps Spain under the Habsburgs or France under Louis XIV and Louis XV, in order to appraise with fundamental skepticism the claim of the West never to have experienced the same thing.)

In this "orientalized" form Islam then further developed in the eastern part of the Islamic area up to the threshold of the present and also at the same time forced the religion into many adaptations, concerning which there is no need to speak in detail here.[2] In any case one may thus employ the expression "Oriental" or "despotic" in relation to the form of government prevailing in Islamic regions only when one clearly distinguishes it from that of early Islam. To characterize the difference between it and modern despotisms, we must add that even this "Oriental despotism" was no ideological dictatorship. Islam left to the individual world views that then expressed themselves almost exclusively in different religions, the most far-reaching kind of free hand; it resorted only in certain periods (to some extent against Manichaeism and Hinduism) to repressive measures. Naturally, Professor Wittfogel, for the time he deals with, has had this image of later Islam in mind. Thus the foregoing may be regarded only as a contribution to terminological precision.

However, the pre-Islamic Iranian culture (that in its turn had undergone a development) did not belong to the great river valley (hydraulic) cultures of mankind. The regulation of great rivers played no role in the Iranian highland, though there was the irrigation system of underground canals, the *qānāt,* which was carried out by individuals and small, self-sustaining groups. Since in that period Mesopotamia was repeatedly under Iranian rule, it may be observed that the irrigation there was undertaken by a population that during the whole period was not Iranized but was Aramaic or Aramaicized; it thus contributed nothing to the formation of the Persian system of government.

The Turks and also the Mongols living in western Asia (who soon became linguistically Turkicized and religiously Islamized) were decisively influenced by the Islamic-Iranian culture. In the beginning they were not bearers of a river valley culture either. That is true also of the Fergana Basin in the Middle Ages and in modern times, where from the outset there was no single great river with periodic flooding to regulate, but the water of numerous mountain streams that had to be used, and indeed by individuals or manageable groups,[3] as with the

---

[1] For details see Bertold Spuler, "Iran: The Persistent Heritage," in *Unity and Variety in Muslim Civilization,* ed. Gustave E. Von Grunebaum (Chicago, 1955), pp. 167-82.

[2] See Bertold Spuler, "Iran and Islam," in *Studies in Islamic Cultural History,* ed. Gustave E. Von Grunebaum (Menasha, Wis., 1955), pp. 47-56.

[3] Василій В. Бартольдъ, *Къ исторіи орошенія Туркестана* (St. Petersburg, 1914).

qānāt in Iran. The teachers of the Turks were in this respect Iranian border peoples outside the Persian realm of the Arsacids and Sassanids, who (as, for example, the Tadzhiks) have in part preserved their Iranian language up to the present day, insofar as the Fergana Turks are not merely linguistically Turkicized Iranians. This feature of the Turkish and also of the Mongolian culture explains why, despite occasional individual measures such as Wittfogel mentions, the irrigation system of Mesopotamia was destroyed precisely in Mongol times. If the Tatars built and made use of irrigation works on the Volga, I would, in this respect following Toynbee, not ascribe it to a Mongol root or to influences out of Mongolian China; the connections in question were very early cut off by the Golden Horde.[4] Rather I would see in this the early effects of the brisk intercourse between the Golden Horde and Egypt, a country with a typical river valley (hydraulic) culture. Indeed, all sorts of Egyptians came to the Volga.[5] Thus the Tatars on the Volga, deeply hostile to their ethnic brethren in China and Iran (both countries of old cultures subjected to the Mongols), were much more exposed to influences from Egypt and Asia Minor; moreover, their conversion to (Sunnite) Islam is to be traced to stimuli from this quarter. In view of all this I cannot, in spite of certain kinds of hydraulic technical works in Sarai, consider the Golden Horde as belonging to the "hydraulic civilizations." Oriental despotism has also been able to rise on foundations other than those of a river valley culture, as we saw, for example, in Iran.

Next to the Orient stands Byzantium as a source of the Russian conception of the state, administration, and culture. Reference was made to this model as willingly and unreservedly as the caliphs had done with Iran. Professor Wittfogel appears to be convinced that the system of military fiefs in Russia in essence goes back to Mongol and other Oriental (Islamic) models. The differences between a "fief" in the Western sense, with its ethical obligations and in many respects also its system of inheritance, and the *iqtā'* of Islam cannot be examined here;[6] in comparison the character of the Russian service fief *(pomestie)* would have to be discussed in detail. (That might moreover be true also of the question of the models of the land tax in Russia.) On the contrary, the question of how far the kind of "tenure" also present in Byzantium *(pronoia)*, including its influence on the Ottoman *tīmār* system, is relevant, seems to me also of great importance. The state of research on the Byzantine *pronoia* is in its details unfamiliar to me; I thus cannot clarify the relative influences of Asia Minor and the Mongols—also as

---

[4] Bertold Spuler, *Die Goldene Horde* (Leipzig, 1943; Wiesbaden, 1964), pp. 38-43.
[5] *Ibid.*, pp. 399 and 435.
[6] See, e.g., Claude Cahen, "L'évolution de l'iqta' du IXe au XIIIe siècle: Contribution à une histoire comparée des sociétés médiévales," in *Annales: Économies, Sociétés, Civilisations*, VIII, No. 1 (1953), 25-52.

regards their ethical side—in this respect. Professor Wittfogel has in any case not mentioned this point.

I fully agree with Professor Wittfogel's arguments concerning the domination of a settled civilized people by nomadic border peoples; but I might mention in addition that the conversion of the Tatars of the Golden Horde to (Sunnite) Islam hindered their amalgamation with the mass of the Eastern Slavs (they thus did not suffer the fate of the Normans/Varangians). The acceptance of this religion linked them with a cultural realm in which religion played an absolutely decisive role in the political, social, and legal aspects of life. Islam, as is known, appeared in a region without a fully developed state organization. It was not that it (like Christianity, or indeed Buddhism) had to adapt itself to already existing state forms.[7] Rather, Islamic theocracy was developed on the basis of an existing form of belief, which rapidly matured into a world religion. As a result, Islam as a religion guaranteed its believers, even under despotisms, certain fundamental rights. Other religions of course did the same, but Islam, which penetrated political life far more deeply than Christianity did, went (and goes), in my opinion, because of its origin, farther than other religions in this respect. No Muslim sovereign or despot could (up to the threshold of the present, when secularization has made great strides in Islamic regions, as elsewhere) infringe fundamental rights. He could interfere neither with worship services nor the Muslim form of marriage law and inheritance. Above all, Islam protected private property and the use of the profits of "religious foundations" (*waqfs*) for their owners as stipulated by the founders; it also restricted the serfdom of the peasants (so that the Volga Tatars were personally free farmers when they came under Russian sovereignty).[8] It promoted commerce and labor on an individual basis; it sanctioned the inviolability of the home; it recognized the difference between rich and poor as willed by God and as a result of the development of individual classes and strata, like every high culture.[9] In addition, the structure of Sunnite Islam did much to prevent bloody religious struggles within an Islamic state or charges of heresy against individual Muslims with all the consequences that follow therefrom. Cer-

[7] On this question see Bertold Spuler, "Der Islam," in *Die grossen Religionen*, ed. Gerhard Günther (Göttingen, 1961), pp. 77-91.

[8] Bertold Spuler, "Die Wolga-Tataren und Baschkiren unter russischer Herrschaft," in *Der Islam*, XXIX, No. 2 (1949), 145.

[9] On this problem, which was misunderstood by Kliuchevsky, I may for the sake of simplicity refer to the following works: Claude Cahen, "Die islamische Stadt," in *Saeculum*, IX, No. 1 (1958), pp. 759-76; Claude Cahen, *Mouvements populaires et autonomisme urbain dans l'Asie musulmane du Moyen-Age* (Leiden, 1959); Gustave E. Von Grunebaum, "The Structure of the Muslim Town," in *Islam: Studies in the Nature and Growth of a Cultural Tradition* (London, 1955); Solomon Dov Goitein, "The Rise of the Near-Eastern Bourgeoisie in Early Islamic Times," in *Cahiers d'histoire mondiale*, III, No. 3 (1957), 583-604; Louis Gardet, *La cité musulmane* (Paris, 1954).

In all these works there are also to be found further references dealing with conditions outside of the city (whose role in Islamic areas is a leading one).

tainly the lack of almost all the sources from Tatar pens impedes our understanding of the history of the Golden Horde and imposes on us a certain restraint in analyzing the situation. Yet we may assuredly say that we know nothing (aside from insurrections and the ensuing civil strife) of any bloody excesses resulting from the pure caprice of a sovereign among the Tatars of the Volga. Even Timur (and to some extent Genghis Khan) raged not against his own people, as Ivan IV did, but only against subject peoples or prisoners.

If the structure of an Islamic state was as just described, it possessed, especially in its always well organized theologians who would not have borne encroachments on these "fundamental rights" patiently, formidable counterforces against a development that would have left a "state stronger than society." Thus I would not in any event characterize it as "Oriental despotism." If however one is to do so, I would—with full recognition of far-reaching Tatar influences on many branches of administration, the military, traffic, and so forth, in Russia—trace the enormous power of the Russian state vis-à-vis society back not to "Oriental" but rather to Byzantine models and (partly unconscious) East Roman roots. In Constantinople the church was close to being an organ of the state, and in many ways became a kind of duplicate of it. Certainly it also protected a series of fundamental rights and in certain spheres confined despotism within limits. Seen as a whole, however, the church proved weaker in relation to the state than Islam, which, as had been said, never had had to adapt to a state, which, on the contrary, had clearly indicated the difference between the political and the religious and human spheres (in spite of the theocracy) and strongly underlined it. The few Islamic sovereigns who sought to control the development of dogma by state interference always paid dearly for such attempts. Not one case of a Photius or Nikon (in his struggle against the Old Believers), no establishment of a Most Holy Governing Synod, is to be found in a (Sunnite) Islamic state. In this respect, Orthodoxy, with a structure so sharply different from that of Western Christendom, paved the way for the state to become all-powerful in relation to society and (in this respect the Moscow Patriarchate of today, following old tradition, behaves similarly) to remain so. In the relationship between state and society, state and subjects, I thus see Byzantium, not "the Orient" or in particular Islam, at work—the Orient in any event only insofar as one classifies Byzantium as belonging to it. But that is a question I do not wish to explore here.

In treating such an important and difficult problem as that of the Tatar and Byzantine heritage in the Russian state, we are all in the awkward situation that really none of us commands in equal measure all relevant components in their antecedents and consequences: the Old Slavic, the Norman/Varangian, the Byzantine-Orthodox, the Mongol-Tatar, the Islamic, and in increasing measure also the Western. Thus remarks such as the foregoing naturally remain partial and one-sided. They can be most useful within the framework of a scholarly discussion among specialists, of the kind that has been so successfully introduced in the pages of this journal.

Reply

KARL A. WITTFOGEL

1. The question the editor of the *Slavic Review* invited us to discuss was Russia and the East. Being an institutional historian, I suggested in the introductory article that we focus our attention on the socio-political key issue: the relation of "Oriental" despotism and society to Russian history. And the arguments of Professors Spuler and Riasanovsky as well as my own have indeed been mainly directed to this issue.

The basic prerequisite for the success of our venture was, of course, a positive attitude on the part of the participants toward the feasibility of cooperation between representatives of various disciplines. Professor Spuler welcomes such a procedure. I myself have practiced it for a long time. Professor Riasanovsky, despite some affirmative gestures, takes an essentially negative position. His procedure underlines the methodological problems raised by our topic.

2. Professor Riasanovsky implies that he has read more books on Russian history than I, and particularly sources that have not been translated. I am sure he has. But what is the significance of this for our issue? The Russian historian who wishes to make a scholarly inquiry into Russia's relations to the East will either have to master the major languages and sources of the Orient, or, if he cannot do this, he will have to rely on a division of labor, which in scholarly matters has been practiced since Aristotle made his comparative study of Greek and non-Greek countries and since the classical geographers described foreign lands whose language they did not know. That is, he will have to utilize studies made by persons familiar with the language and conditions of the areas in question.

Nor is this all. The Russian historian who wishes to make a scholarly inquiry into Russia's relation to Oriental despotism will either have to make a comparative study of total and nontotal systems of power, or, if he cannot do this, he will have, again, to rely on a scholarly division of labor; that is, he will have to utilize studies made by social scientists who have specialized in this field.

3. The two Oriental nations that especially affected the history of Russia prior to recent times were Byzantium and the Mongols of the Golden Horde. It is generally agreed that during the Kievan period, when Byzantine influence was very great, Russian society was pluralistic (multicentered) and that its political order was not absolutistic,

352

whereas, at the end of the Mongol (Tatar) period there emerged in Muscovite Russia a single-centered society dominated by an autocratic state that exerted great power. The historical evidence suggests that this state fulfilled a number of managerial functions which in this form —and/or dimension—were not fulfilled by the states of late feudal and post-feudal Europe. It suggests on the other hand that in the Orient many states fulfilled such functions. To determine whether the Mongol conquerors of Russia did engage in such activities, it would seem necessary to identify the institutional peculiarity of the masters of the Golden Horde. How does Professor Riasanovsky approach this task?

In the first paragraph of his comment Professor Riasanovsky refers to his recent *History of Russia.* I am glad in my reply to consider also this book which presents his ideas on the role of the Gorden Horde and Byzantium and other pertinent issues in greater detail than his comment does. In his *History* Professor Riasanovsky asserts that the Mongols, after the conquest of Russia, "remained nomads in the clan stage of development. Their institutions and laws could in no wise be adopted by a much more complex agricultural society."[1] In this argument Professor Riasanovsky bases his rejection of the possibility of the transfer of Mongol institutions to Russia on his image of the character of Mongol society. What is his evidence? Did he, before reaching his negative conclusion, consult the pertinent Oriental sources? Did he utilize studies made by specialists familiar with these sources? He did neither. Professor Riasanovsky might have consulted a recent study of Turkestan which shows that pastoralists with a fixed center ruled a highly complex (hydraulic) agricultural society on the eve of the Mongol conquest.[2] He might have consulted Professor Spuler's *Die Mongolen in Iran,*[3] which shows how the Mongol conquerors administered this highly complex hydraulic society. And he certainly should have consulted the outstanding modern study of the Mongol rulers of Russia —Professor Spuler's *Die Goldene Horde.*

Professor Pelliot, until his death in 1945 the world's leading expert in the field of Asian languages and cultural history, described this book as the first major study of the Horde since Hammer-Purgstall's daring— and unavoidably premature—attempt in 1835. "Benefiting from the recent work of the philologists, archaeologists, and numismatists," and "directly using the Russian, Turkish, Arabic, and Persian texts," Professor Spuler demonstrated that the task, though enormously difficult, can be carried out successfully.[4] If Professor Riasanovsky had consulted this study, he would have found that the masters of the Golden Horde were not, as he asserts, just "nomads," but pastoralists who ruled their

[1] Nicholas V. Riasanovsky, *A History of Russia* (New York, 1963), p. 81.
[2] See "Qarā-Khitāy" by Karl A. Wittfogel and Fêng Chia-shêng, with the assistance of Karl H. Menges, Appendix V to *History of Chinese Society, Liao,* pp. 619 ff.
[3] Spuler, *Die Mongolen in Iran.*
[4] Pelliot, *Notes sur l'Histoire de la Horde d'or,* pp. 7-8.

subjects from a strong urban center in accordance with patterns of settlement and power that had existed in Inner Asia since the time of the Huns.

Professor Riasanovsky obviously was unaware of these facts when, in his *History,* he presented his unrealistic picture of the masters of the Golden Horde. However, this was no longer the case when he wrote his critical comment on my introductory article. As the reader will recall, my article indicates the ways in which Inner Asian semipastoralist conquerors controlled complex agricultural civilizations, and it refers specifically to the Golden Horde (and its large and splendid capital) with exact documentation from Professor Spuler's *Die Goldene Horde.* Without a word of explanation Professor Riasanovsky repeats his earlier characterization of the Mongols of the Golden Horde as "a nomadic people in a clan stage of development," exclaiming: "How could a nomadic people . . . influence profoundly the successors to the highly advanced Kievan state?" True, he does respond to some of my data on the organizational and acquisitive activities of the Mongols by recommending "caution"; and he calls my "vision" regarding the significance of the census and the postal system conducive to "fruitful research." But research in this field can scarcely be very rewarding if it starts with a false idea of the Mongols and an equally false idea concerning the relation between the Inner Asian (semi-) pastoralists and the agricultural peoples they subjugated.

Professor Riasanovsky might have been expected to act with less restraint in the matter of Russia's relation to Byzantium. In his *History* he contrasted the attitude of the Russians toward the Mongols ("a scourge of God") with their attitude toward the Byzantines: "When the Muscovite state emerged, its leaders looked to Byzantium for their high model."[5] And in his comment he again speaks of the Russo-Byzantine relations as an "extremely important subject." But he abstains from discussing this relation (1) because "in general, it is not considered a part of the topic of Russia and Asia"; (2) Wittfogel, although including it in his scheme, "devotes very little attention to it"; and (3) because of considerations of space.

Regarding point 1: Chaadaev, Miliukov, and others classed the Byzantine influence on Russia as Oriental. Regarding point 2: In my article I not only listed Byzantium as a subtype of Oriental despotism; I also repeated the gist of the conclusion I reached in *Oriental Despotism* from a twofold (institutional and historical) treatment of Russo-Byzantine relations—namely that the Byzantines "profoundly affected the cultural . . . life of the Russians," but, not having subdued them militarily, "did not Orientalize their patterns of state and society." Regarding point 3: No reasons of space should have kept him from restating his "high model" argument, which certainly requires further elaboration.

[5] Riasanovsky, *op. cit.,* p. 82.

In view of the importance Professor Riasanovsky ascribes to the Byzantine issue, it is unfortunate that even in his *History* he did not give his readers a documented comparison of the major institutions of the Byzantine Empire and tsarist Russia,[6] and that, in addition, he failed to inform them of Kliuchevsky's explicit rejection of Byzantium as the root of one of the key institutions of tsarist autocracy, the *pomestie:* "Neither the term nor the concept of the Russian *pomestie* can well have been an imitation of any word or institution of Byzantine state law."[7]

But let us for the sake of argument assume that the political institutions of tsarist Russia not only resembled those of Byzantium but were actually derived from them. What follows with regard to the over-all interpretation of Russia? If the Byzantine Empire was a variant of a multicentered society of the medieval Western type, then, of course, this would be very basic to our argument—but also very puzzling, since tsarist Russia, in contrast to the West, constituted (as generally agreed) a single-centered society. And if the Byzantine Empire was a variant of an Oriental despotism (as comparative institutional analysis suggests), then the establishment of Byzantium as Muscovy's "high model" only replaces an ugly Tatar picture by a culturally attractive picture of an Orientally despotic ancestor. In either case the question concerning the institutional character of the root (or "model") can be adequately answered only if we tackle it by recourse to the social sciences—ultimately by recourse to a comparative study of political power, total or otherwise. That is, the interarea approach ought to be combined with the interdisciplinary approach. Professor Riasanovsky seems reluctant to employ either.

4. "There is no substitute for the study of Russian history itself." None indeed. For an account of certain cultural features that are not institutionally determined, concentration on a country's general history may be extremely fruitful—as Professor Riasanovsky's survey of various aspects of Russia's cultural history shows. But there is no substitute either for the study of institutional history when a clarification of sociopolitical conditions is required. With a polite bow, Professor Riasanovsky dissociates himself from what he calls the "master builders'" treatment of Russian history. In view of the significance of the issue, we wish he had specified his objections. Does his designation "master builders" refer to those who impose arbitrarily created general concepts on the socio-historical process? If so, no realistic social scientist would disagree with him. If, however, his designation mirrors his disbelief in the existence of recognizable socio-historical regularities (small and

---

[6] For a documented comparison of the peculiarities and historical changes of some major aspects of Byzantine institutions, including the *pronoia,* with tsarist Russia, see Wittfogel, *Oriental Despotism,* pp. 120, 129, 147, 174 ff., 178, 187, and 276-77.

[7] Ключевский, *Сочинения,* II, 217 (*Курс русской истории,* lecture 32).

large) and his unwillingness to use concepts identifying these regularities, then he is refusing to use tools that are essential for the adequate treatment of the institutional history of Russia or, for that matter, of any country. The harmful effect of this attitude is easily apparent. By disregarding the historical depth of the concept of Oriental despotism, Professor Riasanovsky is blind to the treatment of Russia's Orientally despotic features by distinguished historians of Russia. In his *History* some are not even mentioned (e.g., Tugan-Baranovsky, Mavor, and Kulischer); others, who are mentioned, are cited without reference to their contributions in this field (e.g., Karamzin, Kovalevsky,[8] Kliuchevsky, Miliukov, and Sumner[9]).

And by disregarding the differentiations in the concept of Oriental despotism, Professor Riasanovsky deprives himself of a conceptual tool for identifying the variety of socio-political features that are, or are not, essential and specific for all forms, or for some forms, of Oriental despotism. His arguments on certain features and changes in managerial state power, land tenure, property, and industrial development are inevitably hampered by his failure to recognize (1) the peculiar conditions of the slow growth of the tsarist power structure (especially the peculiar interrelation between the decay of such balancing old forces as the *veche* and the growth of Moscow's new managerial functions), (2) the significant institutional changes that generally occur within the established agrarian managerial order (including changes in the form of state services, remunerations, and patterns of inheritance, and (3) the disintegration of the despotic order (a period during which the government increasingly engaged in new managerial activities in the spheres of industrialization and credit control while permitting greater leeway to the private sector).

5. My response to Professor Spuler's comment can be relatively brief. I am naturally pleased to learn that he considers tsarist Russia a variant of Oriental despotism and that he acknowledges the great influence of the Golden Horde on the Russian system of government. His remarks about the diversities of Orientally despotic governments point to problems that deserve the serious attention of the area specialists and, of course, of comparative students of political and other institutions. The diversities in the relation between state and religion are indeed many; the picture becomes still richer if we include the agromanagerial societies of pre-Spanish America.[10] There are also many identifiable diversi-

---

[8] In addition to the evidence given in my introductory article and *Oriental Despotism*, see Kovalevsky's statement that Russia possessed "an Oriental and despotic state"; Maxime Kovalewsky, *Institutions politiques de la Russie*, p. iii.

[9] Cf. Sumner's statement that tsarism was rooted in the "ideas and ritual" of Byzantium and "the fact and practice of the Tatar Khans"; B. H. Sumner, *A Short History of Russia* (rev. ed.; New York, 1949), pp. 82-83.

[10] See Wittfogel, *Oriental Despotism*, pp. 86-100; also pp. 190-91, 274, 181 ff., 284-85, 318-19, 346-47, and 362.

ties in the patterns of organized water control: government-managed macro-hydraulic systems, certain meso-hydraulic systems, also government-managed; and smaller (hydro-agricultural) units managed by non-governmental agencies, either with or without state supervision.[11]

The peculiarities of "compact," "loose," and "managerial" hydraulic configurations present a fascinating research target. The hydraulic and hydro-agricultural developments in the Fergana Basin and Iran are certainly cases in point. Greek evidence suggests government-controlled water works under the Achaemenids; and Arab sources document similar developments for the time of the Abbasids. Preserved records speak of powerful hydraulic officials assisted by ten thousand underlings in East Persia, and of hierarchies of hydraulic officials in tenth- and sixteenth-century Persia.[12] In these, as in other instances, conceptual clarity and institutional specification will help us to decide whether we are faced with hydraulic conditions, and if so, whether the administrative arrangements involve massive hydraulic tasks (which are easily recognized) or meso-hydraulic tasks (which often are difficult to identify).

6. Professor Spuler asks whether the institutional complex we are discussing is suitably designated as "Oriental." I understand his concern and, in considerable degree, I share it. The traditional terms— "Oriental" or "Asiatic" society and despotism—are narrowly geographical. They disregard the institutional aspect of the matter. And they obscure the fact that the conditions under contemplation have been found in four out of the five continents (Australia being the exception). For these reasons I have suggested calling this order "agromanagerial" and "agrodespotic," and the function of large-scale government-managed water control "hydraulic." These terms fit not only the Orient proper but also the higher civilizations of ancient Meso- and South America and the Pueblo Indians of the American Southwest, certain irrigation tribes in East Africa, and the peoples of some Pacific islands, especially ancient Hawaii.

But having said this, we must add that the largest, most populous, and most enduring agromanagerial societies were indeed located to the east of the European scholars who developed the concept of a peculiar "Oriental" power structure and society. We recognize this geohistorical fact when we use the old geographical nomenclatures interchangeably with the new institutional terms.

---

[11] In 1931 I outlined these diversities and their ecological foundations with regard to traditional China in *Wirtschaft und Gesellschaft Chinas, Erster Teil, Produktivkräfte, Produktions- und Zirkulationsprozess* (Leipzig, 1931), pp. 61-93, 187-300, 410-56. Despite the growing interest in the hydraulic problem, comparatively little has been done since to enlarge our knowledge of this vital aspect of the various hydraulic civilizations.

[12] Wittfogel, *Oriental Despotism*, p. 53. For a summary of recent studies of Iranian waterworks (including ancient dams and reservoirs and complex systems of *qānāts* administered by *mīrābs*) see Henri Goblot, "Dans l'ancien Iran, les techniques de l'eau et la grande histoire," *Annales: Économies, Sociétés, Civilisations*, XVIII, No. 4 (May-June, 1963), 499-520.

The preservation of the designations "Oriental" and "Asiatic" despotism is desirable also from the standpoint of Russian history, since a number of outstanding historians discussed the history of tsarist autocracy with this concept in mind and not infrequently with express reference to the term. It is desirable, and perhaps even more so, from the standpoint of the history of modern Russian thought.

In this history the ideas of Marx and the Russian Marxists have played a considerable role; and while Marx's and Engels' interpretation of tsarist Russia as an Oriental despotism is easily accessible to readers familiar with German and other Western languages, many writings of the Russian Marxists have not been translated; and it is in these writings (and, of course, also in the translated works of Plekhanov and others) that we find Marx's Oriental theories repeated and applied—with increasing stress on the disintegration of the old order, but with arguments that are meaningful only if Marx's basic frame of reference is known. Professor Riasanovsky, who in his *History* devotes a good deal of space to other aspects of Russian Marxist thought, would certainly have deepened his readers' insights by bringing this matter to their attention; but his self-imposed conceptual black-out prevented him from doing so. His attitude underlines once more the need of conceptual clarity for the attainment of historical accuracy. And it strongly underlines the need for the historians of modern Russia to point to the fact that Marx, Engels, and Plekhanov, and, following them, the great majority of all Russian Marxists until 1917 viewed contemporary Russia as having emerged, not from a feudal or postfeudal order, but from a "semi-Asiatic" society headed by an "Oriental" despotism.

NINE

Russia and the West: A Comparison and Contrast

HENRY L. ROBERTS

Comparisons of Russia with the "West" have been a staple of historians and of contemporary observers for a very long time, and no end is in sight. A recent appraisal of Soviet developments in the decade after the death of Stalin was devoted in part to a consideration of the prospects for "a gradual convergence of the social and/or political systems of the West and the Soviet Union."[1] The variety of the contributors' responses—"very likely," "necessarily uncertain," "unlikely any meaningful convergence," "highly improbable," "depends on what is meant by 'gradual' "—suggests an ample range of disagreement, both in expectations for the future and in the characterization of the contrasts underlying these expectations.

The Russians themselves have, of course, been perennially preoccupied with this act of comparison. As Sir Isaiah Berlin has observed, in speaking of the nineteenth century: "Russian publicists, historians, political theorists, writers on social topics, literary critics, philosophers, theologians, poets, first and last, all without exception and at enormous length, discuss such issues as what it is to be a Russian; the virtues, vices and destiny of the Russian individual and society; but above all the historic role of Russia among the nations; or, in particular, whether its social structure—say, the relation of intellectuals to the masses, or of industry to agriculture—is *sui generis*, or whether, on the contrary, it is similar to that of other countries, or, perhaps, an anomalous, or stunted, or an abortive example of some superior Western model."[2]

Such concerns are not uniquely Russian. Americans and Canadians, colonial offspring of European culture, have spent a great deal of time meditating on their relations to the Old World; the inhabitants of the

MR. ROBERTS *is professor of history and director of the Program on East Central Europe at Columbia University.*

[1] *Survey: A Journal of Soviet and East European Studies,* No. 47 (Apr., 1963), pp. 37-42.
[2] Isaiah Berlin, "The Silence in Russian Culture," in *The Soviet Union, 1922-1962: A Foreign Affairs Reader,* ed. Philip E. Mosely (New York: Praeger, for the Council on Foreign Relations, 1963), p. 337.

British Isles continue to have ambivalent feelings about the Continent; the Germans, though situated in Central Europe, have written at length about the significance of Germany's Eastern and Western "faces"; in Italy they say that Europe stops somewhere south of Rome; indeed, of the major European nations only the French seem not to have been much bothered by this particular problem of identification. Still, the relative intensity and persistence of the preoccupation in the Russian case, the fact that at times it has loomed as *the* question in discussions of Russian society and culture, would indicate a somewhat special problem.

It should be noted at the outset that what is involved here is not simply a nation-to-nation comparison but rather the relationship of one country, Russia,[3] to a more complex entity, the "West," by which is usually meant Western Europe. This latter entity, though comprising a number of nations, is assumed to have a degree of unity, the possession by its members of common features, against which Russia can be compared and contrasted. In other words, the question really means: does Russia belong to the West or not, is it a part of the West or is it somehow alien from that cluster of nations? Historically it is clear that the pathos and passion this question has aroused derive from the issue of participation or nonparticipation. And while, as we shall see presently, the historian might prefer to deal with it in different terms, this issue still lies at the heart of most discussions of Russia and the West.

We can take, as an example, two articles appearing recently in this journal. The one presented Russia as belonging to an East European cultural sphere quite sharply differentiated from, and opposed to, that of Western Europe: Eastern-Orthodox-Byzantine as against Western-Catholic-Roman. It urged, moreover, that the terms "East" and "West" in this setting "are so specific and meaningful that it would be unwise to introduce new concepts even as working hypotheses."[4] The second article, in contrast, was inclined to argue that while there have been periods, usually sterile ones, of Russian self-sufficiency and isolation, Russia and the West have "a common logic of development, a shared process of evolution. . . . Russian culture has no vital existence of its own apart from Europe."[5] Although the authors are addressing different themes, the trend of their thought is clear: one sees Russia as essentially distinct from the West, the other as linked to and dependent on it.

---

[3] "Russia," of course, comprised numerous nationalities, and the term has occasioned much debate. In this piece, however, I shall not attempt to deal with this problem. By Russia I mean the Russian state or the culture and society of its Great Russian inhabitants only.

[4] Omeljan Pritsak and John S. Reshetar, Jr., "The Ukraine and the Dialectics of Nation-Building," *Slavic Review*, XXII, No. 2 (June, 1963), 224-26.

[5] Rufus W. Mathewson, Jr., "Russian Literature and the West," *Slavic Review*, XXI, No. 3 (Sept., 1962), 413 and 417.

The disconcerting feature of this divergence—and both positions have respectable ancestries—is not simply their apparent incompatibility but their plausibility and persuasiveness when presented in the course of the authors' argument. From these, and other examples, we must suppose that in considering Russia's relation to the West we are not dealing with a simple question of fact—otherwise it would have been settled long since—but with a more subtle and troubling problem.

In the face of conflicting interpretations which do not appear to arise from crude errors of fact, one can explore at least three possible avenues of explanation: (1) One may look for the warping presence of animus or prejudice as the source of trouble; (2) one may attempt to achieve a more satisfactory "perspective" that can somehow encompass or reconcile the conflicting interpretations; or (3) one may conclude that each interpretation is substantially correct in its own context but together they are not reconcilable because they are answering quite different questions and intentions and are, in fact, operating on different planes of thought. We shall look at each of these possibilities in turn.

That an enormous amount of passion and animus has entered into comparisons of Russia and the West is perfectly obvious. One thinks, for example, of Dostoevsky's painful encounter with Turgenev in Baden in 1867. According to Dostoevsky, Turgenev "abused Russia and the Russians vilely and terribly," and told him that the fundamental point of his (Turgenev's) book *Smoke* lay in the sentence, "If Russia were to perish, it would cause neither loss nor distress to mankind."[6] In his account of the meeting, Turgenev, while denying that he would have expressed his intimate convictions to Dostoevsky, allowed that the latter had "relieved his feelings by violent abuse of the Germans, myself and my latest book."[7] We cannot go into the roots of this particular clash, but the passion evoked here by the Russia-West controversy is intense and unmistakable.

When Poles or Rumanians, despite the presence of linguistic or religious ties with the Russians and a fair measure of common if hardly joyful history, argue that Russia is not of the West, whereas their own nations most emphatically are, one feels that this is more than an academic classification, that it is an argument born of fear or desperation, and that the extrusion of Russia from the "West" is at the same time a call for support and assistance on the part of the Western nations. When a German author contends that the Russians, from the very beginning of their history, have been quite incapable of scientific and technological advance and have had to borrow and steal such knowledge from the West, which they hoped to overrun, one can agree

---

[6] Jessie Coulson, *Dostoevsky: A Self-Portrait* (London: Oxford University Press, 1962), p. 163.

[7] *Ibid.*, p. 165.

with his enthusiastic translator that "this book is part of the Cold War."[8]

Undoubtedly the advent of the Soviet regime has greatly intensified passion and prejudice by placing Russia in the most violent possible antithesis to the rest of Europe: Communist Russia versus the Imperialist West. Moreover, the search for communism's Russian roots or antecedents, a natural and perfectly proper inquiry, has led to heightened and perhaps inappropriate emphasis on those features of the Russian past that would seem to mark it off most sharply from Western Europe: the prominence that has been given in recent years to Ivan the Terrible's *Oprichnina*, the Marquis de Custine's animadversions, and the murky character of Nechaev is surely in good part a reflection of present concerns.

And yet, while we may grant that when passions are strong the door is opened to the tendentious selection and misuse of evidence, we may doubt whether this can be defined as the major source of our difficulty. For one thing, the presence of passion or prejudice itself requires explanation, and that may lead us back, in circular fashion, to tensions inherent in the Russia-West comparison. For surely the fact that Dostoevsky and Turgenev, whatever their personal differences, should have clashed so violently on this subject does point to a peculiar quality in the Russian society of the time that should have made such great artists so painfully self-conscious about the national identity. One might have reservations about certain Polish or Rumanian views of Russian-Western relations, but it remains true that these nations have had long and intimate exposure to Russia: their fear of Russia as an alien intruder is at least derived from immediate experience. As a Rumanian writer remarked not long ago, with some acerbity: "There are some who feel that personal experience of the things described, or the fact that the writer has personally witnessed the events discussed, throws a suspicion of bias upon the author. A writer, in other words, is suspect precisely because he has too great and too close a knowledge of his subject. For our part, we feel that ignorance is not a guarantee of objectivity."[9]

So while we may strongly suspect that when we run across that tired phrase "Scratch a Russian and find a Tartar" we are not likely to get much enlightenment about either Russians or Tartars, it does not follow that no problem exists.[10] More than that, when we ask such a question as whether the 1917 Revolution brought Russian history

[8] Werner Keller, *East Minus West = Zero: Russia's Debt to the Western World, 862-1962*, trans. Constantine Fitzgibbon (New York: Putnam, 1962), p. 7.

[9] Constantin Visoianu, in the introduction to *Captive Rumania*, ed. Alexandre Cretzianu (New York: Praeger, 1956), p. xvi.

[10] Happily, the question of what the Russians *are* if they are not Western is beyond the scope of this paper. I am informed that a discussion of Russia and the East has been prepared for the preceding issue of this journal.

closer to that of the West by placing it in the sequence of the other great "modernizing" revolutions of the last three centuries, or whether, on the contrary, it increased the distance by destroying, or disrupting, some potentially important convergent lines of development, we find ourselves faced with a real and quite intricate problem of historical interpretation, one that is not reducible to animus or partisanship.

Turning now from the role of animus, which while making the subject more prickly does seem to be marginal rather than central, we may consider some of the efforts that have been made to overcome, modulate, or get around the antithetical "either-or" of the Russian-Western relationship. It is my impression that these efforts have been quite fruitful in new insights, although, as we shall see, they tend to blur the Russia-West comparison or at least remove it from the center of the stage.

The most obvious approach is to replace the Russia-West polarity (with its overtones of an even more extreme Orient-Occident opposition) by the conception of a European "spectrum" ranging clear across the Continent, with changes occurring by degrees and shadings. This conception has the distinct advantage of calling in question the picture of the "West" as a homogeneous unit, which comparisons of Russia with the West so frequently posit. For example, the much vexed question of the existence of East European "feudalism" is cast in a rather different light when we are told that "the existence of a hierarchy is no longer thought to be a prerequisite to feudalism in the West, largely because the neat hierarchy assumed to have existed in the West is found to have been virtually a phantom."[11] Once this simple unity of the West is dissolved and the tremendous variety of its historical experience and its institutional and cultural forms is taken to heart, then the way is open to a much more flexible and subtle series of comparisons: within and between regions of Europe, and on different levels—religious, social, institutional, and the like. Moreover, if Europe is seen as a spectrum, one can then attempt to locate the smaller nations of Eastern Europe in a more relaxed fashion; when the West, or Western Europe, is presented as a sharply identifiable unit then there always is the painful scramble to determine who will be permitted to slip in under the tent.

I have the impression that there is much to gain through comparative studies in this vein—studies that would include Russia in the spectrum. For one example, recent investigations comparing the recruitment and social composition of the higher bureaucracy in the Habsburg and Hohenzollern monarchies[12] could profitably be extended

[11] Oswald P. Backus III, "The Problem of Feudalism in Lithuania, 1506-1548," *Slavic Review*, XXI, No. 4 (Dec., 1962), 650.

[12] For example, Nikolaus von Preradovich, *Die Führungsschichten in Österreich und Preussen (1804-1918)* (Wiesbaden: Steiner, 1955).

to include imperial Russia. For another, I should like to see a close historical study of the correlation, if any, between certain patterns of landholding and leasing and peasant unrest from France and western Germany eastward to Russia.

It must be admitted, however, that this picture of Europe as a spectrum, with Russia, say, at the red end, does not take care of several important problems. It does not overcome the subjective sense of sharp contrast and opposition, which, as we have seen, has played such a significant role in the making of Russia-West comparisons. Moreover, the existence of sovereign states, of political boundaries, does mark real breaks in the spectrum, which is not a continuum, as anyone who has crossed a frontier post in Eastern Europe well knows. Finally, the fact that in the important realm of power politics Russia is usually set off, not against its immediate smaller neighbors, but against great powers farther to the West has certainly had a polarizing effect, of which the Iron Curtain division of Europe after 1945 is only the most recent and violent example. The impact of this effect upon other spheres of life and politics is very great indeed, as is illustrated by the sad history of countries and individuals that at times have sought to play the role of "bridge" between East and West. Still, for the student of history or comparative politics the "spectrum" approach does have real attractions, not least in helping do justice to the enormous richness and multiplicity of the European scene.

A second device for tackling the Russia-West comparison has been that of the "time lag." For those inclined to seek similarities rather than contrasts the time lag is very convenient: features in the Russian scene that seem different from the West are shown to be the same, but corresponding to an earlier date in the West; opposing trends turn out to be merely tangents drawn at different points along the same curve. Thus, it is thought enlightening to say that the style of Soviet life today is Victorian or at the latest Edwardian. (Such resemblances or echoes do not, of course, necessarily imply a time lag. On a fresco from the Palace of Knossos there is a charming Cretan lady whom the archaeologists call La Parisienne: presumably the parallel, though attractive, is fortuitous.) The use of the time lag is valid only if a more or less identifiable sequence of stages is occurring and if more than one nation or culture has come to participate in this sequence, usually by borrowing and adaptation. W. W. Rostow in his study of the stages of economic growth provides an analytical framework for the succession of stages and then places the different modernizing countries in their rank in this procession. Within such a defined setting he does show that Russia experienced a time lag vis-à-vis Western Europe in achieving the famous "take-off" and in reaching "maturity." At the same time the burden of his message is the general similarity of these stages: "In its broad shape and timing, then, there is nothing about the Russian sequence of preconditions, take-off, and drive to technological maturity that does not fall within the general pattern; although like all other national stories it has unique features."[13]

The time lag has its problems, however. As Thorstein Veblen pointed out some decades ago,[14] the latecomer to a historical sequence does not simply duplicate earlier performances; there is usually a foreshortening of the stages, a leaping over of certain steps, and a lumpy mingling of the old and the new. Among the Russian Marxists Trotsky had perhaps the best sense of this feature of the time lag; indeed it underlay his thesis of permanent revolution. Despite the Marxist predilection for a unilinear view of history and its stages, Trotsky was able to observe: "The indubitable and irrefutable belatedness of Russia's development under influence and pressure of the higher culture from the West results not in a simple repetition of the West European historic process, but in the creation of profound *peculiarities* demanding independent study."[15] In other words, the conception of the time lag, although serving to increase the comparability of nations by putting them on the same track, may actually, when refined, reinforce the appearance of individuality and uniqueness.

A study of the mingling of the foreign and the indigenous, for which the term "symbiosis" can sometimes be used appropriately, affords a third approach to the comparative study of Russia and the West. In my judgment this is probably the most fruitful of all, since it corresponds to the common-sense observation that, in modern times at least, all nations are increasingly taking over or being bombarded by external influences which they must digest, naturalize, or otherwise cope with as best they can.

Two examples can illustrate the utility of this approach to a comparative study of Russia and the West. It is certainly to the Slavophiles that we owe part of our sense of Russia's difference and uniqueness. Not only were they intent upon stressing the differences, but the way they wrote and the features of the Russian scene they chose to emphasize strike the Western reader as peculiarly Russian. And yet, as we know from their education and the intellectual currents that influenced them, the conceptual apparatus of the Slavophiles was borrowed directly from German idealism and romanticism.[16] Paradoxically, increased access to "Western" ideas was to sharpen the picture of a Russia-West antithesis.

Or, to take an instance from the eighteenth century, a recent essay

[13] W. W. Rostow, *The Stages of Economic Growth* (London and New York: Cambridge University Press, 1960), p. 67.

[14] In his *Imperial Germany and the Industrial Revolution*.

[15] Leon Trotsky, *The History of the Russian Revolution*, trans. Max Eastman (3 vols.; Ann Arbor: University of Michigan Press, 1960), I, 464.

[16] See Nicholas V. Riasanovsky, *Russia and the West in the Teaching of the Slavophiles* (Cambridge: Harvard University Press, 1952).

on the education and upbringing of the Russian nobleman[17] first brings
out certain "Russian" features in his childhood experience: "The Russian nobleman of the 18th century normally lacked strong roots in any
particular area and had no real feeling of attachment to a specific
locality and to a family estate on which his ancestors had lived for
generations. . . . There is little evidence of the attachment to and the
ties with the ancestral home which characterised the mentality of the
western noblemen." The child was under the supervision of serf nurse-
maids and tutors who had no rights and very rarely any powers of
discipline. From this very "Russian" setting the young nobleman was
sent to a school, where he received "a completely western education
which had practically submerged the Muscovite traditions of learning
and education by the middle of the 18th century." The author suggests
that the effect of the somewhat abstract Enlightenment education upon
children with this particular background was to produce a distinct cast
of mind, exceptionally rationalistic and didactic, that was to have
important consequences for Russia in the next century. For our present
purposes the most interesting feature of this analysis is the way in which
Russian and Western influences are seen to combine to produce a
personality that is neither the traditional Muscovite nor the French
man of the Enlightenment but rather the forerunner of the nineteenth-
century *intelligent*.

Such an approach to the historical evidence can be extremely productive in dealing with a number of major problems of Russian institutional and social history: the impact of the Mongol conquest in
Muscovy; the effects of Peter the Great's adoption of the goals and
methods of contemporary German *Polizeiwissenschaft;* the consequences of taking a peasant, the son of a serf, and dropping him into
the large factory of advanced Western industrialism; or the particular
combination of Russian and Western Marxist elements that went into
Bolshevism.

This approach is hardly an exciting discovery; it is the familiar
province of the historian. But in the present connection two points
need emphasis. First, such an approach, if it is to be fruitful, must be
closely related to the material at hand; the results are illuminating to
the degree that they lead to a concrete historical picture. It is not an
approach that yields sweeping generalizations. Second, while such
study does look beyond Russia's frontiers for some of its evidence and
insights, its central purpose is to advance our understanding of Russia.
Comparative study is a valuable tool to that end, but comparison *per se*
is not the goal.

Indeed, all these approaches that I have mentioned as methods of
looking at Russia and the West move away from direct comparison,

[17] Marc Raeff, "Home, School, and Service in the Life of the 18th-Century Russian
Nobleman," *The Slavonic and East European Review*, XL, No. 95 (June, 1962), 295-307.

either by blurring the comparison through reference to a "spectrum" or by becoming an analysis of the various factors, belatedness or foreign influences, that have contributed to the formation of Russia.

Would this suggest that such a comparison is a fruitless enterprise, that we may be engaged in an impossible endeavor to answer a pseudo problem? In one sense the answer must be yes. If we are asked whether two objects are alike or different, we are immediately impelled to counter: "With respect to what?" or "In terms of what standard?" If we ask whether two maple leaves are alike, we can answer affirmatively if it is a question of contrasting them to oak or elm leaves, or we can answer negatively if it is a question of their being congruent or having identical vein structures. We cannot make a comparison *sans phrase*, without reference to the setting and purpose of the question.

This rather simple but tricky ambiguity in the act of comparison was well analyzed by Kant in a section of his *Critique of Pure Reason*. As he observed, some scholars are interested in and attracted by the principle of "homogeneity," others by the principle of "specification." "Those who are more especially speculative are, we may almost say, hostile to heterogeneity, and are always on the watch for the unity of the genus; those, on the other hand, who are more especially empirical, are constantly endeavouring to differentiate nature in such manifold fashion as almost to extinguish the hope of ever being able to determine its appearances in accordance with universal principles."[18]

According to Kant these differences in attitude have nothing to do with questions of fact or with the nature of reality but with method. In his rather formidable vocabulary similarity and dissimilarity are "regulative principles"—working maxims, both of which are necessary and which describe diverse tendencies and interests of human thought. Difficulties occur when we mistake their function and take them to constitute reality. "When merely regulative principles are treated as constitutive, and are therefore employed as objective principles, they may come into conflict with one another. . . . The differences between the maxims of manifoldness and of unity in nature thus easily allow of reconciliation. So long, however, as the maxims are taken as yielding objective insight, and until a way has been discovered of adjusting their conflicting claims . . . they will not only give rise to disputes but will be a positive hindrance, and cause long delays in the discovery of truth."

My mention of maple, oak, and elm leaves suggests the possibility that we might bring the Russia-West comparison into more manageable shape by establishing the criterion of genus and species, of making our comparison within a hierarchy of classification. The terms of our comparison—Russia, a country, and the West, a group of countries—

---

[18] See *Immanuel Kant's Critique of Pure Reason,* trans. Norman Kemp Smith (London: Macmillan, 1933), pp. 537-49.

would point to just such a classification. In some restricted but relevant areas this kind of classification can be useful. If we wish to compare the Russian language with those of Western Europe, we do have a linguistic structure locating Russian in the Slavic branch of the Indo-European languages, to which French and German, through their respective branches, also belong. Even in the more elusive field of religion we can, by tracing the course of theological disputes and schisms, construct a reasonably workable classification of the branches of Christendom and place Russian Orthodoxy in its appropriate niche.

But these classifications extend only to such relatively well-defined subjects as language and religion; we are here concerned with such vast complexes as national entities, of which language and religion form only a part. How are we to establish classifications that can enable us to make comparisons on this larger scale?

Max Planck, the originator of the quantum theory, remarked that while the introduction of order and comparison is essential to scientific treatment and that order demands classification, "It is important at this point to state that there is no one definite principle available *a priori* and enabling a classification suitable for every purpose to be made. This applies equally to every science. Hence it is impossible in this connection to assert that any science possesses a structure evolving from its own nature inevitably and apart from any arbitrary presupposition. . . . Every kind of classification is inevitably vitiated by a certain element of caprice and hence of onesidedness."[19]

Such a cold douche from the austere natural sciences should make us cautious about the absoluteness of classifications in our rowdy and disheveled political and humanistic disciplines. I am entirely skeptical of any claims for a system of classification that purports to be inherent in the structure of history itself and free of arbitrary presuppositions. I find none of the principles of classification, whether based on geography or geopolitics, religion, ethnic-racial categories, social structure, or political system to be persuasive in providing an *objective* basis for ordering and comparing such complex congeries as nations. For example, to take the familiar Orthodox–Roman Catholic division of Christendom, while granting the enormous importance of this division as a historical influence, it would appear to me, after periods of residence in Moscow, Bucharest, and Athens—all Orthodox capitals—that this religious factor is, at least in the twentieth century, altogether inadequate as a principle of classification, though obviously of value in helping to explain many attitudes.

If we concede that we are not likely to find a purely objective order of classification that will enable us to compare Russia and the West, then we are driven back to the view that difference and similarity,

19 Max Planck, *The Philosophy of Physics*, trans. W. H. Johnston (New York: Norton, 1936), pp. 13 and 14.

homogeneity and heterogeneity, are tools to serve our diverse intellectual interests. As such they are necessarily tied to and get their
meaning from our purposes and concerns in making the comparison.
This is not to say that they conveniently produce answers we feed into
them, but that, depending upon the questions which we bring to bear
in our comparisons of Russia and the West, we will get a multitude of
answers, indicating widely varying degrees of similarity and dissimilarity, each perhaps valid in its own setting, but only there. An anthro-
pologist interested in the whole range of humanity's social organizations would probably regard the Russia-West contrast as relatively
narrow. The political theorist, working within the framework of
highly articulated and sophisticated political systems, would find the
contrast, say, between autocracy and democracy very great indeed, perhaps representing the extreme ranges of his particular scale.

If we could be satisfied with such a modest and circumscribed role
for comparisons of Russia and the West, there would be much less
acrimony and controversy on this subject. But there's the rub; as we
have seen, the motives that have impelled both Russians and Westerners into such endless debate and wrangling are powerful and urgent.
Although we can hold, with Kant as our guide, that attempts to make
absolute comparisons will produce intellectual confusion and error, I
am afraid it is certain that efforts will continue to be made to find in a
comparison of Russia and the West either support for normative positions on the *political* relations of the Soviet Union and the Western
Powers or the basis for a prediction on the outcome of this relationship
in the future.

With respect to the range of ideological, diplomatic, and moral
issues that currently divide us from the Soviet Union, I should certainly not underestimate their reality and importance or question the
need for us to defend our own positions. But while we have all become
used to employing the term "West" as a kind of shorthand for "our
side," it would be well if we based our policies on the preservation of
values and principles because we believe in them and not because they
are "Western."

As for the future, I do not believe that the outcome, whatever it may
be, is prefigured in the comparison of Russia and the West. If we look
back to the decade or two preceding the outbreak of the First World
War, we have the impression that for a brief period the old debate over
Russia's relationship to the West was losing its intensity and was perhaps beginning to appear irrelevant. These were the years of that profound intellectual and cultural eruption (Einstein, Freud, postimpres-
sionism, etc.), the consequences of which are still jolting us and which,
in a half century's retrospect, seems to have been one of the great historical watersheds. Russia in its "Silver Age" entered fully and immediately into that movement, its creative talents were at the forefront,

there was no significant time lag. In this breakthrough, initially on a narrow front of thought and art, the traditional Russia-West debate seemed out of place, not resolved but overtaken by new challenges and horizons. The First World War and the Russian revolutions interrupted and in considerable measure obscured this development, and as we have seen the old antithesis reappeared in the harsh form of communism versus "imperialism."

While this antagonism has by no means played out, it is becoming increasingly evident that the new world adumbrated at the beginning of the century is coming on apace, and whether we prefer to symbolize it by $E = mc^2$, or automation, or the return of the repressed, or abstract expressionism, it is a strange world. While Russia and the West will probably respond to it in different fashions, there is a distinct danger that by keeping our attention focused on Russian-Western relations and comparisons we may be quite unprepared to meet the challenge of novelty. If we think of the Western tradition as a kind of comfortable interest-bearing inheritance that we can bank on for the future, we are in for serious trouble.

Russia's Perception of Her Relationship with the West

MARC RAEFF

The old French adage *comparaison n'est pas raison* indicates that comparison (contrast, too, for that matter) is never made for its own sake but only to lead to some conclusion. That is why the habit of comparing, or contrasting, the history of one country with that of another (or several others) gives rise to such vexing problems and generates such intense passions—and in turn feeds on them. We are dealing here not only with a "scientific" problem, whose solution would be an acquired truth, but with the attitudes of the participants and spectators of historical events as well. Unlike the scholar who is supposed to search only for truth, social and political thinkers and littérateurs engage in comparative analysis and reasoning in order to indulge whatever lies closest to their hearts at a given moment. In his paper Mr. Roberts has concentrated on the problems facing the scholar-scientist. His scientific similes and epistemological caveats are therefore neither mere literary embellishments nor a challenge to C. P. Snow's dichotomized view of the contemporary intellectual but quite deliberate and telling evidence that his main preoccupation is to clarify the methodological issues involved. In this very essential and laudable enterprise he has cut away much of the underbrush that all too often obscures comparative analysis and politically (or culturally or religiously) motivated contrasts. But in so doing he has perhaps allowed himself to lose sight of the reasons that made the question of Russia's relationship to the West an issue of such momentous concern for generations of Russians as well as Europeans—and now for Americans too. By taking up the discussion from the questions of method which Mr. Roberts has elucidated so well, we may be able to come to grips with the problem of attitudes and clarify a bit more the nature of the specific comparative issue with which we are concerned.

It may be worth recalling that the starting point of any judgment of comparison or contrast is a recognition, usually tacit, of identity. We do not compare or speak of the differences between two objects that have no elements in common. We do not compare pebbles and leaves. The question of the comparability of Russia and the West must perforce begin with a recognition—however unconscious—of some underlying identity that makes a comparison meaningful and possible, even if its result should be negative. Except for the obvious and unproduc-

MR. RAEFF *is professor of Russian history at Columbia University.*

371

tive awareness that both Russians and West Europeans are human beings, the question "Is Russia part of the West?" had no meaning, say, at the time of Ivan III.[1] Western travelers described Russia's condition and people in a detached way, much as modern anthropologists might describe some Samoan or Indian tribe, or—at most—with the incredulous indifference of Montesquieu's Parisian: "comment peut-on être persan?" The question of Russia's relationship to the West therefore arose only after some judgments of identity had been first made by either the Russians or the West Europeans.

For the Russians, no doubt, this recognition of some identity with the West took place in two steps. First, during the Times of Troubles, when in their political distress some Russians turned for succor to their Western neighbors, offering the throne to Wladyslaw of Poland and identifying as much as they could with Polish cultural influence (e.g., Khvorostinin). The Western (mainly Polish-Catholic) answer was an attempt at incorporating Russia in such a way as to destroy its traditions and identity. Russia reacted by withdrawing and erecting a psychological wall between itself and the West. And yet it remained conscious of some identity with Western Europe, if only in contrast to its perception of Turkey or China as utterly alien.

The second step, of course, was taken by Peter the Great in his energetic and conscious efforts to make Russia into a Western state. How right he was and how well he succeeded need not be considered at this point. He obviously had more than a little success, as shown by the rapid westernization of the Russian elite and the fact that he enlisted the support of a fair number of persons in Russia for whom the underlying identity between Russia and the West, which had to be brought out, was axiomatic.[2] More significant in our context was the fact that Peter's reforms or transformation split Russian society and consciousness. In the first place, we see a break between the upper classes—the educated westernized elites—and the common people, who remained relatively untouched by the process of modernization. This phenomenon has been commented upon often enough not to bear repetition here. It does, however, point up one interesting aspect involved in the problem of comparison or contrast between Russia and the West: for *whom,* from *whose* point of view is, or is not, Russia part of the West? The Slavophiles (and some populists) were quite right when they stressed the existence of "two nations" in Russia and when they put the question of "Russia and the West" in terms of the relevance and differing meaning it had for each of these nations.[3]

---

[1] Even if a consensus on what is the "West" could have been reached by contemporaries (a task that would not have been much easier then than it is today).

[2] Н. Павлов-Сильванскій, *Проекты реформъ въ запискахъ современниковъ Петра Великаго* (St. Petersburg, 1897).

[3] I am, of course, well aware that the dichotomy between the two parts of the Russian nation was not quite as sharp and fixed as the Slavophiles and others believed; otherwise

The second split created by Peter the Great is even more important for our purpose. The Russian educated elite experienced a radical break with the nation's past (the experience was very likely shared by the people to some extent, though conclusive evidence is lacking). The educated nobleman of the eighteenth century found himself doubly cut off: from his own people's past, which he had learned to scorn and reject, and from Western Europe, which had not yet fully accepted him and of which he still did not feel the equal.[4] For the educated Russian the question of "Russia and the West" thus became the double problem of his sense of alienation and his need of identification. He felt alienated from Russia to the extent that its common people, its social system, its form of government were unlike those of France, England, and Germany. And the sense of alienation from that which, after all, was very close, in truth part of their very existence and being, produced the angry *ressentiment* and passionate rejection of Russia we find among many members of the intelligentsia. Is this not one of the reasons for Chaadaev's rejection of Russia's past and his denying that Russia had a civilization? And what other feelings could give rise to the unparalleled, nay shocking, admission of Pecherin that it is "sweet to hate one's fatherland"?[5] As to identification, the educated *intelligent* hoped to find it by becoming a West European and by feeling at one with all Western values. This proved difficult—if not impossible—for the more sophisticated. Conscious desire to identify with someone creates an idealized image of that which one aspires to be, an image which direct experience with reality tarnishes all too easily. The model proved to be a will-o'-the-wisp; the "land of holy wonders" turned into a stench-filled cemetery. Herzen, Bakunin, and so many others experienced (to varying degrees) this shock of recognition, a shock that led them to reject and hate what they had worshiped from afar.

The very existence—and the anguished character—of the question whether Russia belonged to the West or not stemmed therefore from the double alienation experienced by the Russian elite in the eighteenth and nineteenth centuries (and *mutatis mutandis* perhaps still experienced by the Soviet intelligentsia of the twentieth). Alienated

---

it would be difficult to account, for example, for the popularity and assimilation of the great Russian classic writers of the nineteenth century by the common people as soon as the latter had learned to read.

4 We only need to recall the satirist's description of the young fop in Catherine II's time whose body belonged to Russia but whose soul was French, or that other *petit-maître* who bewailed the fact that under Russian conditions it was impossible to reach the exalted level of cultural sophistication of his dear Parisian models. And even the fad for Russian history at the end of the eighteenth century was but a form of westernization. Cf. Hans Rogger, *National Consciousness in Eighteenth Century Russia* (Cambridge, Mass., 1960).

5 "Kak sladostno otchiznu nenavidet'! / I zhadno zhdat' eia unichtozhen'ia! / I v razrushenii otchizny videt' / Vsemirnogo dennitsu vozrozhden'ia!" Cited by M. O. Гершензонъ, *Исторія молодой Россіи* (Moscow, 1908), p. 105.

from both their own past and their people, they could not identify with a Western Europe that did not conform to their idealized image and failed to fulfill their hopes and aspirations.

The evolution of the West European (or American) view of the question offers a counterpart to the Russian picture. At first we can discern a growing sense of discovering an identity between Russia and the West. This was due either to a spreading belief that—in contrast to Asia, at any rate—Russia had been *basically* European for a long time or to the fact that, in appearance at least, Russia had become more Western with every generation since Peter had dramatically proven its European stature by his victory over Charles XII. The growth of the belief that Russia was becoming European and should participate in the affairs of the world as part of Europe is plainly evident in the dispatches of French diplomats and agents in Russia in the eighteenth century.[6] The change in Western opinion is well summarized in the latter part of the century in the words of a French diplomat: "Nous nous étions représentés les Russes comme des barbares [i.e., completely different and not subject to comparison—M.R.], nous les voyons aussi maniérés et aussi bien élevés que les hommes les plus policés."[7] A factor in the rapid acceptance of Russia as a *nation policée* (and of members of its elite in Western European intellectual circles) was the eighteenth-century belief in the uniformity of human nature (and process of civilization), on one hand, and the discovery of the radically different cultures of China and India, on the other. By virtue of being men, the Russians were obviously part and parcel of humanity, while as a country and as a culture Russia was quite clearly closer to Europe than to China or India, hence it was European. The problem of "Russia and the West" (Russia versus the West, rather), did not exist therefore in the eighteenth century, except as an occasional by-product of war propaganda.[8] On the contrary, the *philosophes* looked to Russia as potentially outdoing Western Europe in bringing solutions and values that would enrich the future of mankind.[9]

Whether Russia belonged to the West became a serious question only in the middle of the nineteenth century for both Russians and Europeans. That it remained a live issue throughout the nineteenth

[6] Basile G. Spiridonakis, *Mémoires et documents du Ministère des Affaires Etrangères de France sur la Russie* (Quebec: Faculté des Arts, Université de Sherbrooke, n.d.).

[7] Sabatier de Cabre, memoir of July 31, 1772, Archives du Ministère des Affaires Etrangères, *Mémoires et Documents, Russie*, Vol. LXXXV, Supplement No. 6 (1769-1772), p. 227.

[8] It is interesting to note that the problem did not even arise during the Napoleonic wars and Russia's occupation of France in 1814-15.

[9] Cf. Albert Lortholary, *Les "Philosophes" du XVIIIe siècle et la Russie: Le mirage russe en France au XVIIIe s.* (Paris, 1951); Dieter Groh, *Russland und das Selbstverständnis Europas: Ein Beitrag zur europäischen Geistesgeschichte* (Neuwied, 1961) and supporting documentation in Dmitrij Tschiževskij and Dieter Groh, eds., *Europa und Russland: Texte zum Problem des westeuropäischen und russischen Selbstverständnisses* (Darmstadt, 1959).

and into the twentieth century was mainly due, I think, to the fact that the cultural values which the Russian elite had absorbed from Western Europe (and by which it judged the West) were those of the eighteenth and early nineteenth centuries; and having been raised in Russia to the status of absolutes, they could not be made to fit into the changing reality of a Western Europe that was becoming increasingly industrialized, materialistic, and ugly. To be sure, many West Europeans—and some Americans—felt the same way (from the Romantics through Carlyle to Nietzsche), and their anti-Western "cultural despair" frequently echoed the cries of anguish and anger of Herzen, Dostoevsky, or Leontiev. Obviously what distinguished the "Europeans" from the latter was that they did not (except in a few extreme cases) have the experience of alienation from their own people and country that was so characteristic of the Russians. Hence the more traumatic, more immediately relevant, more easily politicized aspect of the debate on Russia's relationship to the West in Russia.

In the West the debate was usually provoked and carried by waves of Russophobia (Russia is not part of Europe and should be treated as a dangerous barbarian intruder), which were the by-products of developments in foreign policy. As a great power Russia was the adversary of many European states; its threat was heightened in the minds of those who recognized in it aspects of Europe's political structure that stood condemned and that, it was hoped, would soon disappear, for example, serfdom and political tyranny in an age of liberalization. This was the notorious message of the Marquis de Custine, for example. The twentieth-century fear of Russia in the West derives largely from the realization that Russia may be showing up the very essence of modern industrial society and the latter's inherent threat to Western traditions and values.

An essential element of historical comparability, therefore, is the question: who experiences the identity or difference, and for what purposes is this experience used? The preceding pages have dealt with the experiences of the Russian elite and of West European intellectuals. Naturally, if the question of Russia's belonging to the West were put to peasants in the eighteenth or nineteenth century, it either would be meaningless or produce reactions quite at variance with those we have been discussing and with which we are all familiar from our readings. Furthermore, the question may be meaningful to different groups at different times. It is most likely that a factory worker in France, Italy, or England today would feel that Russia is quite part of "his" world, by whatever adjective we may choose to describe this world; the Russian worker probably feels the same way with respect to the West. But this may not be true at all if we could put the question to a French or Italian peasant, on the one hand, and a Russian or Ukrainian collective farmer, on the other. In the nineteenth century, the question of Russia's relationship to the West was given different answers by the intelligentsia and by members of the "establishment." Many members of the intelligentsia doubted that Russia belonged to the West, but it never entered the mind of an official to think and act on this idea. To my knowledge, businessmen in both Russia and the West were quite indifferent to the problem around, say, 1900, and felt that both belonged to the same progressive, technologically oriented European civilization.

Mr. Roberts has quite rightly stressed that for purposes of analyzing and understanding the relations between two events or processes of development, one has to isolate specific institutions, factors, and trends. In analyzing them one discovers that their homogeneity is more apparent than real and that their variety permits a high degree of discrimination and differentiation; the result may be an ordering of national manifestations as if on a continuum. This type of historical analysis (which has been begun with reference to feudalism, serfdom, industrialization, etc.) has been—and will be in the future—very fruitful in insights and meaningful results.[10] The fault of so many alleged comparative analyses has been that one of these categories has been taken as an unchanging and rigidly definable concept and then used rather mechanically in differing historical contexts: if phenomenon X is present in both A and B, the latter must be similar, if it is absent, they cannot be the same. Besides making for very sterile (as well as questionable) results, such an approach flattens our perspective of the past. It fails to take into account the obvious fact that no human institution or activity remains the same for any period of time and that it may play quite different roles depending on its relation to other elements of the culture or polity.

Men do not accept passively and obey blindly institutions, cultural values, aesthetic preferences, or mental attitudes—all the elements we make use of when we compare or contrast historical processes and realities. Men live in them and make use of them, and thereby constantly transform them and their functions. The mechanical and static comparison of institutions, for example, fails to do justice to their dynamic functional relationships. For instance, a "progressive" economic technique or practice may—in the context of serfdom—acquire a most "reactionary" effect and even hamper the modernization of the country's economy.[11] It is the task of the comparative historian to detect and interpret the variety of functions and relationships which an institution, a style of thought or art, an administrative or economic structure, or a political system may have had in the context of the

---

[10] See Dietrich Gerhard, *Alte und neue Welt in vergleichender Geschichtsbetrachtung* (Göttingen, 1962); Otto Brunner, *Neue Wege der Sozialgeschichte* (Göttingen, 1956).

[11] See Michael Confino, *Domaines et seigneurs en Russie vers la fin du XVIIIe siècle: Étude de structures agraires et de mentalités économiques* (Paris, 1963), pp. 136 ff.

periods and cultures studied. The elements may have been the same in Russia and Western Europe (or Asia for that matter), but did they play the same role, did they belong to a pattern that made for similar effects? Could it not be that similar elements would have opposite historical effects in different contexts?

All of this brings me back to the final and essential point so forcefully made by Mr. Roberts. The quest for comparisons and contrasts without well-defined and historically meaningful questions in mind is a sterile occupation, fraught with many methodological pitfalls. To sharpen our understanding of the past, to shed light on the interplay of forces, on the pulls and stresses to which people have been subjected in a given situation, comparative historical analysis must deal with elements that are comparable and selected according to criteria that are relevant to the times and conditions studied. It must further be kept in mind that the contemporaries' perception of reality is a basic constituent element of the picture and that it rarely remains the same for long, either in space or in time. Only by being constantly aware of the complexity of reality, the delicacy of his tools of analysis, as well as the ever changing nature of his subject matter can the comparative historian arrive at results that are historically true and intellectually meaningful.

The Historical Limits of the Question
of Russia and the West

MARC SZEFTEL

Professor Roberts' study is an impressive methodological achievement. The more one meditates on it, the less one finds to disagree with. The task of this writer is rather a frustrating one, for how can one bring new points of view to supplement such a thorough treatment?

Professor Roberts pointed out that the future of the dilemma under study will hardly be dominated by the issue "Russia versus the West," for it will be overshadowed by more powerful factors which have dominated the life of both the West and Russia since the beginning of our century (Russia up to 1917!). I would be tempted as a historian to go one step further, and question our ability to see, or consciously to shape, the future. First of all, many new factors may appear. Second, we do not know the relationship and proportional weight of factors that will continue from the present into the future. So I would eschew the consideration of the future altogether.

Is it possible, however, to look with the same eye in the directions of both the present and the past of our problem? The answer must be negative. The method of studying the present is different from that of studying the past. The latter is a part of history; the former belongs to the social sciences, such as political science, sociology, economics, and so forth. I firmly believe that Clio should not be confused with the still unnamed Muse of the sciences of the present.

In our particular problem the confusion between the premises drawn from the observation of the present and those drawn from the study of the past is particularly damaging. The very terms of comparison with which we are preoccupied have undergone a fundamental change since the fateful events of October, 1917, and especially since 1945. "West" used to mean primarily "Western Europe," while before 1917 no one used the terms "Russia" and "East" indiscriminately. At the present time the two latter terms are synonymous in the language of political information, and even political literature, while the term "West" as applied to our dilemma means primarily the United States. On the other hand, the geographically conditioned terms "West" and "East" have lost most of their geographical meaning because of the global

MR. SZEFTEL is professor of history at the University of Washington.

character of the existing antinomy between "the Western world" and Russia. In the daily language of political information "the West" (led by Washington, D.C.) means a group composed of many countries both Western and Eastern geographically: all European countries to the West of the "Iron Curtain," all countries of the Western hemisphere (except Cuba), the British Commonwealth overseas, and the Asian countries actively opposing the Communist bloc. The "East" (led by Moscow), in this language, means the Communist countries, whether in Europe, Asia, or, in one instance, the Western Hemisphere. Between "the West" and "the East" there are the "noncommitted" countries of different geographical location.

It would not be too difficult to demonstrate, on the basis of generally known historical information, that the political groupings of the present that have been mentioned have no common historical past. To avoid any temptation of anachronistic interpretation, the historian's wisdom would prompt also the removal of the present from the task of our comparison. Let the social scientist proceed to this comparison; for him it may be valid. The historian should remain with Clio.

In our case it may involve an important limitation. The drama begun in Russia in October, 1917, is still being acted. Who is able to say what the remaining acts will be, and what will be the final word of the drama? It may become most important in our understanding of the phenomenon called "the history of Russia," and it may revise all our assumptions based on its history as of 1917. However, we are on more solid ground as historians if we base our judgment of Russian history on the events we can judge with adequate perspective, namely, on those before 1917.

These are severe limitations: no scrutiny of the future, no fixation on the present, looking backwards from the vantage point of 1917. They will make the inquiry much narrower, but it may be then conducted far from the hopes and fears inspired by the contemplation of the future, and far from the din of the battles of the present. It may then become cool and objective, and be conducted with due perspective. Within these limitations, a twofold comparison may be attempted. One deals with the past of Russia and the United States, the leaders of the two blocs which face each other, subject to re-evaluation by historians specializing on the latter country; the other with Russia and the rest of Europe.

The striking formula coined by de Tocqueville in his *Democracy in America* is generally known. It concerned at the time the future development of the United States and Russia, and it might have been influenced by the existence of serfdom in Russia at the time it was written. De Tocqueville's identification of the United States with freedom and of Russia with the servitude of man concerned the growth of both countries as great powers in the future more than the study of their civilizations in the past. However, there was much historical truth in it, and this becomes obvious if one focuses not on the future (an elusive and uncertain "reality" to observe!) but on the past perspectives of historical development. The formula gains special strength because of the existence of common historical factors between the two nations.[1]

Three factors can be observed in the history both of the United States and Russia. One of them is that both histories developed in a big continental setting, with a relatively small ratio of the population to the size of the territory. Another is the mobility of the population, which passed, in a relatively short span of time, from "frontier" to "frontier," with, in both cases, the Pacific Ocean as the ultimate boundary. The third common factor is the basic Mediterranean cultural roots (Christian religion and classical antiquity), which led to the participation of both nations in the European culture of the modern era.

The factors mentioned have served some historians and political philosophers as the basis to explain why free economic and political institutions developed on the soil of the United States. Why did not the same factors lead to the development of similar institutions in Russia?

An answer may be given by acknowledging the existence of three basic differences in the premises underlying the development of the two nations. One difference concerned external security. In the case of Russia, since its origin much of its national economic and political energy was absorbed by the necessities of military defense (with aggressive overtones). As to the United States, it is difficult to calculate how much energy was saved for peaceful pursuits by a territorial configuration which ensured stable peace to the nation without any necessity of a strong military establishment. Another difference lay in the *immediate* cultural background of the two nations at the time of their consolidation. In the case of Russia, it was Imperial Byzantium, the country from which it took Christianity. In the case of the United States, it was seventeenth-century England. The third factor was the origin of the population. It was based on immigration in both cases. However, the immigration from the Dnieper region that formed the basis of the Slav population in northeastern Rus' had purely economic motives (or military, in the case of the princes' and boyars' retinues). The population of the United States was formed by a selective immigration, to a great extent because of religious and political persecutions first in the British Isles and, later, in other countries of Europe; it provided a natural milieu for ideas emphasizing religious and political freedom.

[1] Alexis de Tocqueville, *Democracy in America,* trans. Henry Reeve (London, 1947), pp. 242-43. This formula concludes the chapter "Future Prospects of the United States." Since the book was published in 1835, when Europe stood in the shadow of Nicholas I's ostensible military power, one wonders whether de Tocqueville's forecast was not inspired by the impression of this power. One knows how fallacious this impression became in 1854!

The result was a basic institutional difference between the United States and Russia: emphasis on the individual's freedom in the former, emphasis on the state's initiative and pre-eminence in the latter.[2]

Comparison between the historical past of Russia and that of the rest of Europe is far more difficult. It is even possible that the present state of historical knowledge does not yet justify such a comparison. It involves two phenomena, of which only one has been studied thoroughly, namely, the historical past of Russia. As to the synthesis of the historical past of the rest of Europe, it has not yet been accomplished. Moreover, if it is easy to ascertain what is meant by "Russia" in this comparison (one basically agrees that it should not be taken in the sense of the multinational political formation called the Russian Empire or, lately, the Soviet Union, but in that of the Great Russian ethnic group), there is no agreement at all on whether the rest of Europe represents historically a homogeneous unit.

There are many points of view concerning the geographical and national limits of the "European community" historically defined. First of all there is the Ranke definition limiting this community to Germanic and Romance nations alone.[3] This criterion obviously excludes all the Slavic peoples as well as the Baltic countries (among them Finland), Hungary, and Greece. There is a broader point of view, expressed by Gonzague de Reynold, which embraces in one European community all nations, whatever their linguistic or racial background, who shared the Roman Catholic faith before the great split of the Reformation.[4] This particular criterion leaves outside "l'Europe européenne"[5] all those nations who took their Christian faith not from Rome but from Byzantium. Finally, there is Professor Oscar Halecki's approach, which identifies "European history" as that of all nations of geographical Europe except Russia.[6] One must point out that the latter approach is similar to that developed by the so-called Eurasian ideology formulated by some Russian scholars abroad in the decade following the Revolution of 1917.[7] The complexity of the problem is

[2] These ideas are offered for discussion only, for the author realizes their relativity: factors considered as more pertinent may be adduced, and the factors offered here may be given a different weight, by specialists of American history. Different conclusions may be arrived at in this case.

[3] Leopold von Ranke, *Geschichte der romanischen und germanischen Völker von 1494 bis 1514* (Berlin, 1825), pp. 1 and 3 of the English translation by Ashworth (London, 1889): cited in Oscar Halecki, *The Limits and Divisions of European History* (New York, 1950), pp. 90 and 217.

[4] Gonzague de Reynold, *La Formation de l'Europe*, Vol. I: *Qu'est-ce que l'Europe?* (Fribourg, Switzerland, 1944), p. 54.

[5] *Ibid.*, p. 55.

[6] The idea is expressed in several places in Halecki, *op. cit.*, especially in Chapter 5, "The Geographical Limits: The Great Eastern Isthmus."

[7] Cf. Prince Dmitri Mirsky, "The Eurasian Movement," *The Slavonic and East European Review*, V (1927), 311-12. The basis underlying Professor Halecki's statements differs from that of the Eurasian school, whose argumentation is primarily geopolitical and anthropological. Halecki based his conclusion mostly on historical analysis, using the

enhanced by the circumstance that even within the generally accepted Europe of Germanic and Romance nations (Ranke's Europe) identification with "l'Europe européenne" has not been taken for granted by all its participants. As Professor Roberts pointed out so pertinently, the absolute value of such an identification has been questioned not only in Germany but even in Great Britain and Romance Italy—France alone being free of doubts.[8]

Which criterion should one follow? Although all of them exclude Russia, it is not at all irrelevant whether Russia *alone* is placed outside the European community or is considered one of a more numerous group of European nations, this group consisting, dependent upon the criterion, of all Eastern Slavs (i.e., also the Ukrainians and the Belorussians), of all Orthodox Christian nations of Europe, or even of all nations of Europe other than Germanic and Romance nations. As long as this problem had not been solved, all sweeping comparison of the historical past of Russia and the rest of Europe will remain in the realm of speculation.

If it were even possible to draw, as Professor Halecki does, a rigid line differentiating the historical development of Europe on both sides of "the Great Eastern Isthmus" with the "pre-War limit . . . running approximately from Petsamo to Cetatea Alba"[9] or even farther, to the Eastern boundaries of Belorussia and the Ukraine,[10] much difficulty would still be presented by the absolute claim of the proposed discrimi-

Tatar invasion, and the prolonged separation from the rest of Europe that resulted from it, as his main argument (pp. 92-95). In this connection it is interesting to recall a much earlier thesis which excludes Russians from the Slavic race on the grounds that they are "Turanians" who only adopted (and distorted) the Church Slavonic when they were converted to Christianity; the Ukrainians and Belorussians, being genuinely Slavic, should be included in the European community, the border of which should be traced to the east of their habitat. Such is the idea expressed by Franciszek Duchiński (1817-80) in a series of books published in Polish and French between 1858 and 1864. See Jan Ignacy Baudouin de Courtenay, *Z powodu jubileuszu profesora Duchińskiego* (Krakow, 1886). Quite lately Duchiński's views have been revived in Henryk Paszkiewicz's works *The Origin of Russia* (London and New York, 1954) and *The Making of the Russian Nation* (London, 1963) with much more sophistication and an impressive scholarly apparatus.

[8] Cf. Henri Massis, *Défense de l'Occident* (Paris, 1929), where the idea has been expressed that Germany, a latecomer on the road of human culture, is only incompletely and artificially connected with "the body of the West," for it wavers between Asian mysticism and Latinity (p. 19). Quoting Badler, *Le Romantisme berlinois* (1921), Massis pointed out the heterogeneous character of the German culture, the Romanized southwest of which evolved toward humanism and classicism, while its Slavicized northeast espoused individualistic mysticism and romanticism. And he emphasized that the map of Roman Catholic Germany almost exactly coincides with the limits of the Roman *Germania* (p. 66, n. 1). The underlying idea of this statement is that the Eastern limit of the true Western world corresponds to that of the Western Roman Empire!

[9] Halecki, *op. cit.*, p. 101. This line would leave the Left Bank Ukraine on the Russian side!

[10] In his subsequent book, *Borderlands of Western Civilization: A History of East Central Europe* (New York, 1952), Professor Halecki considered the Ukrainians and the White Ruthenians (i.e., Belorussians) as such borderland populations, part of East Central Europe to the west of Russia proper (pp. 412-16 and, esp., p. 473).

nation. First, there is the chronological difficulty. It is impossible to see all of the Russian past as basically different from that of the rest of Europe at all periods. One should not be hypnotized by the fatal cleavage of the October Revolution. When it occurred Russia already had a long historical past, and there was much variety in that past in relation to the rest of Europe. There were periods when the pattern of Russian political, economic, social, and cultural life was based on the very same principles as that of non-Russian Europe. In the eighteenth century, Russia's mercantilism and serfdom were shared with the rest of continental Europe, while its absolutism was by far the most prevalent form of government in Europe. Culturally, from the 1740's on, Russia was, like all other countries of the continent, save the Ottoman Empire, a province of the French Enlightenment. In the following century, until 1848, Russia shared absolutism, serfdom, and the role of the state in the economic life with the Germanic countries to the west of it, such as Prussia and Austria; while again in its cultural life it was, without any doubt, a part of Europe. A lag that began in 1848 did not last long, for serfdom was suppressed in 1861, and the first limitation of absolutism was undertaken three years later by the Judicial Reform of 1864.[11] Much of it still subsisted, however, until 1905, when, with the new constitutional government, Russian life aligned itself, until 1917, in all respects with the rest of Europe![12]

There were other epochs when there were differences in some major aspects, while in other aspects, also major, there were none: between 1878 and 1905, among the Christian nations of Europe, Russia was the only one that still preserved an absolute monarchy, but its economic and legal institutions, its social system, and its cultural activity were based on principles common to the rest of Europe of that time. There were again periods when to West or Central European observers there seemed to be fundamental differences in institutions, mores, and cultural life. Such was the long period of Muscovite history from the end of the fifteenth to the end of the seventeenth century. However, even at that time not all was different: cultural life, on the same religious basis, was shared with other Eastern Christian countries of Europe (Greece, Serbia, Bulgaria, Rumania); serfdom (complete in Russia only since 1649) was characteristic of the whole of continental Europe, and most of the latter lived, like Muscovy, under an absolute monarchy. Like other countries during this period Muscovy evolved its Estates-

---

[11] A certain degree of limitation was also provided by the Ordinance on Local Self-Government (zemstvos) of 1864. See on those limitations, Marc Szeftel, "The Form of Government of the Russian Empire prior to the Constitutional Reforms of 1905-1906," in *Essays in Russian and Soviet History*, ed. John Curtiss (New York, 1963), pp. 105-20.

[12] On the increasing degree of parliamentarism during this period see Marc Szeftel, "The Representatives and Their Powers in the Russian Legislative Chambers (1906-1917)," forthcoming in *Studies Presented to the International Commission for the History of Representative and Parliamentary Institutions*, Vol. XXV.

General *(Zemskie Sobory)* and its form of elective monarchy, while under Alexis Mikhailovich and his successors the mercantilist theory became official policy of the Muscovite government: not all was different in Muscovy from the rest of Europe in that transitional seventeenth century![13]

Thus the problem of mutual relationship differs from epoch to epoch, and, undoubtedly, it is misleading to look for *one* label covering it for the whole span of Russian history up to 1917 (and even beyond, with the outlook into the future!). Given the incertitude about what "European community" means geographically and ethnically and the absence of a meaningful and solidly established synthesis of such a community, and considering also the chronological diversity of the possible relationship of this community, however we define it, to Russia's historical development, it seems that the only realistic approach to the comparative study of our problem can be to proceed step by step by partial comparisons. This can be done in two ways. One is to compare the Russian development with that of other European countries one by one: Russia and France, Russia and Germany, Russia and Poland, and so on. When this comparison is made, after a thorough inquiry into all aspects of the parallel historical processes, only then can a general conclusion be drawn regarding differences and similarities between the history of Russia and that of the rest of Europe (or any part of it). And, obviously, this inquiry should be undertaken period by period.

This vertical method is not easy, for it requires a solid knowledge of the history of both countries compared. It should be done by two specialists jointly, and not the same ones country by country. Easier may be the horizontal method—the comparison of the parallel development in all European countries of the same historical phenomenon, again one by one and period by period: the development of serfdom in different countries of Europe, the development of private industry, that of absolute monarchy, that of public education, of literary forms, of art, and so forth. This study would provide material for synthesis in a meaningful context. The understanding of the nature of the phenomenon may be in this instance as important as that of the knowledge of a national history as a whole; that is why each phenomenon should be studied by a comparative-minded specialist, then all of them may be drawn into a final synthesis by a group of historians. There are many nations in Europe, and there are many phenomena to investigate: I am afraid that the hour of synthesis is remote, but there is no other way to arrive at it.

Such being the case, does it mean that no ideas can be considered as

[13] See Marc Szeftel, "La monarchie absolue dans l'État moscovite et l'Empire russe (fin XVe s.–1905)" and "La participation des assemblées populaires dans le gouvernement central de la Russie avant 1800," forthcoming in *Recueils de la Société Jean Bodin pour l'histoire comparative des institutions* (Brussels), Vols. XXI and XXIV.

pertinent pending this meticulous and difficult inquiry? All ideas are interesting, even those whose pertinency is not considerable from the point of view of historical evidence, let alone those that have some evidence. Among the ideas expressed on the philosophy of Russian history (what else are the sweeping comparisons offered to us on "Russia and West" to be called?), some are based on considerable evidence. I prefer, however, to consider them only as interesting and stimulating speculations as long as the problems of comparison are not completely clarified, and the inquiry which I propose not accomplished. Until then they may offer excellent opportunities for the formulation of untested and self-gratifying hypotheses, but hardly much more.

Reply

HENRY L. ROBERTS

I suspect that my commentators were overly indulgent with my methodological preoccupations—all egg crate and no eggs—but I am pleased that my piece should have elicited their own interesting observations on the theme. Taking advantage of their forbearance I shall limit my comments to just a few reflections on the points they have raised.

Mr. Raeff's concern is chiefly with the subjective plane—that of attitudes and awareness—and I would agree that it is probably at this level that we must seek for the explanations why, historically, Russia's relationship to the West has seemed an "issue of such momentous concern." Certainly a felt *sense* of difference may affect behavior more decisively than any number of "objective" points of similarity. (Witness the contrasting, even antithetical, roles that a pair of identical twins may come to adopt.) Still, even on the subjective level similarity and contrast must be placed in some setting, and I would not agree that the awareness of a common human status—*homo sum*—while obvious, is unproductive, especially in a pre-Darwinian age. Moreover, the sense of participating in Christendom, even a Christendom riven by schism and heresies, does, it seems to me, give a particular flavor to Russian-Western relations from the outset. Hence I should be inclined to argue that there was a somewhat more substantial context for presumptions of identity, at a somewhat earlier time, than Mr. Raeff indicates. And while it may be true that by the late sixteenth century the idea of the "slave-born Muscovite"[1] was beginning to establish itself in English literature, it is also true that in the mid-seventeenth century, John Milton spoke of Muscovy "as being the most northern region of Europe reputed civil."[2]

Mr. Raeff's central interest, however, is with the consequences—at the level of consciousness—of Russia's westernization and modernization from the time of Peter on. He has provided a suggestive sketch of the complex pattern of splits that ensued: between the upper classes and the rest of the population, the rupture with the Russian past, and finally the not infrequent disillusionment with the West itself. There is no doubt that such a "double alienation" was experienced by mem-

[1] The phrase is Sir Philip Sydney's, cited in M. S. Anderson, *Britain's Discovery of Russia, 1553-1815* (London: St. Martin's Press, 1958), p. 24.

[2] John Milton, preface to *A Brief History of Muscovy*, in *The Prose Works of John Milton* (London, 1881), V, 394. One has the impression that in this time a North-South rather than an East-West division seemed the more significant.

bers of the Russian elite, or that it contributed to the "anguished character" of the question whether Russia belonged to the West or not. Yet precisely the reality of this sense of alienation leads one to ask what is sufficient to account for it in the historical process of westernization. Was it simply that the objective (i.e., institutional, social, etc.) differences between Russia and the West were so great that an attempt at westernization by forced draft was bound to be uprooting and dislocating? Or, was it rather a particular quality *within* Russian society that was activated by the challenge of "westernization"? It is difficult to provide a certain answer from a scrutiny of Russian history alone, but the nature of the problem might be illuminated by comparative study. For example, there have been other cultures—the Japanese comes to mind—standing at a great distance from the West which also undertook precipitous westernization. Did this experience lead to a corresponding "double alienation"? My impression is that it did not, though this might be an interesting topic for closer inquiry. On the other hand, the United States has always been "westernized," yet many West European observers have commented, some with concern, others with relish, on a quality of alienation that American intellectuals seem to have shared with their Russian counterparts, including periodic waves of expatriation. If there is something to these comments, and I am not sure how much there is, then clearly the problem of alienation at the level of awareness stems from something other than mere cultural distance, and the rupture of abrupt transformation.

I am entirely in agreement with Mr. Szeftel's doubts about the historian, as historian, dabbling in the future; the attempt to use the categories and insights of the historian's craft as a means of probing the future is like pushing with a string (which is not to deny that there may be other intellectual disciplines that may appropriately be concerned with aspects of the future). I am not sure, however, that the distinction between history and the social sciences is between past and present. Does it not lie rather in the different approaches of these disciplines to the process of events through time, whether it be seen as the heart of the inquiry or as ancillary to other, usually generalizing, concerns?

I should also be reluctant, even out of deference to Clio, to exclude, for purposes of historical inquiry or comparison, a recent period of time, even so unruly and difficult a subject as post-1917 Russia. Treacherous as the ground may be, given all the problems of sources, passion, and uncertain perspective, I would submit that historical study has an important intellectual role to play for the Soviet period and for trying to comprehend the connections, or discontinuities, between Russian past and Soviet present.

Nor am I sure that even if we limit our comparisons to the period before 1917, we can avoid our involvement in the present. Indeed Mr. Szeftel's comparison of the United States and Russia, the "leaders of the two blocs which face each other," suggests that at least the nature of the questions raised may often and inevitably be tied to our present vantage point. I personally see no disadvantage to this; it is entirely proper for our present concerns to pose questions of the past. It is when we start feeding the answers into the past that we corrupt history.

All this, however, is merely an aside—or rather it opens a vast but different topic: the issue of present-mindedness in historians. I was particularly gratified that Mr. Szeftel should have extended a plea for both "vertical" and "horizontal" comparisons, whether by pairs of nations or by periods, for I am increasingly persuaded that in practical terms, that is, in our tasks as students of history, it is only through such acts of articulation, or modulation, that the gross and vexing issue of Russia and the West can be reduced to workable dimensions.

Selected Bibliography

1. The Nature of the Soviet System

Arendt, Hannah. *The Origins of Totalitarianism*. New York: World, 1962.

Armstrong, John A. *The Soviet Bureaucratic Elite*. New York: Praeger, 1959.

Brzezinski, Zbigniew K. *Ideology and Power in Soviet Politics*. New York: Praeger, 1962 (and Paperback).

Fainsod, Merle. *How Russia is Ruled*. Rev. ed. Cambridge, Mass.: Harvard University Press, 1963.

Friedrich, Carl J. and Brzezinski, Zbigniew K. *Totalitarian Dictatorship and Autocracy*. Cambridge, Mass.: Harvard University Press, 1956 (and Praeger Paperback).

Hazard, John N. *The Soviet System of Government*. Chicago: University of Chicago Press, 1960.

Kornhauser, William. *The Politics of Mass Society*. Glencoe, Ill.: Free Press, 1959.

Meyer, Alfred G. *Leninism*. Cambridge, Mass.: Harvard University Press, 1957 (and Praeger Paperback).

Moore, Barrington, Jr. *Soviet Politics—The Dilemma of Power*. Cambridge, Mass.: Harvard University Press, 1950.

Talmon, Jacob L. *Political Messianism*. New York: Praeger, 1960.

Tucker, Robert C. *The Soviet Political Mind*. New York: Praeger, 1963 (and Paperback).

2. The Structure and Organization of the Soviet Economy

Bergson, Abram. *The Real National Income of Soviet Russia Since 1928*. Cambridge, Mass.: Harvard University Press, 1961.

Bergson, Abram and Kuznets, Simon, eds. *Economic Trends in the Soviet Union*. Cambridge, Mass.: Harvard University Press, 1963.

Campbell, Robert W. *Soviet Economic Power*. Boston: Houghton Mifflin, 1960 (Paperback).

Holzman, Franklyn D., ed. *Readings on the Soviet Economy*. Chicago: Rand McNally, 1962.

Nove, Alec. *The Soviet Economy: An Introduction.* New York: Praeger, 1961 (and Paperback).

Wiles, P. J. D. *The Political Economy of Communism.* Cambridge, Mass.: Harvard University Press, 1962.

87th Congress, 2nd Session, Joint Economic Committee. *Dimensions of Soviet Economic Power.* Washington, D. C.: Government Printing Office, 1962 (Paperback).

3. The Development of Modern Russian Literature

Mathewson, Rufus W., Jr. *The Positive Hero in Russian Literature.* New York: Columbia University Press, 1958.

Mirsky, D. S. *A History of Russian Literature from the Earliest Times to the Death of Dostoevsky (1881).* London: Routledge. New York: Knopf, 1927.

————. *Contemporary Russian Literature, 1881-1925.* London: Routledge. New York: Knopf, 1926.

A combined version of the above two volumes, edited and abridged by Francis J. Whitfield, was published by Knopf in 1949 under the title: *A History of Russian Literature.* A part of this abridged version is available in paperback under the title: *A History of Russian Literature from Its Beginnings to 1900.* New York: Vintage, 1958.

Struve, Gleb. *Soviet Russian Literature, 1917-50.* Norman: University of Oklahoma Press, 1951.

4. The Problem of Old Russian Culture

Blagoi, D. D., ed. *Istoriia russkoi literatury.* 3 vols. Volume I. Leningrad: USSR Academy of Sciences, 1958.

Kliuchevsky, V. O. *A History of Russia.* 5 vols.; esp. vols. III and IV. Trans. by C. J. Hogarth. London: J. M. Dent & Sons, 1911-31. (A new translation of Vol. IV is available in Vintage Paperback.)

Likhachev, D. S. *Kul'tura russkogo naroda, X-XVII vv.* Leningrad: USSR Academy of Sciences, 1961.

————. *Kul'tura Rusi epokhi obrazovaniia Russkogo Natsional'nogo Gosudarstva (konets XIV—nachalo XVI veka).* Leningrad: State Publishing House of Political Literature, 1946.

————. *Kul'tura Rusi vremeni Andreia Rubleva i Epifaniia Premudrogo (konets XIV—nachalo XV v.)* Moscow: USSR Academy of Sciences, 1962.

Miliukov, Paul N. *Outlines of Russian Culture.* Edited by M. Karpovich. Philadelphia: University of Pennsylvania Press, 1948 (and Perpetua Paperback, 3 vols.).

Picchio, Riccardo. *Storia della letteratura russa antica.* Milan: Nuova Accademia Editrice, n.d.

Riasanovsky, Nicholas V. *Russia and the West in the Teaching of the Slavophiles.* Cambridge, Mass.: Harvard University Press, 1952.

Sorokin, Pitirim A. "Toynbee's Philosophy of History," in *The Pattern of the Past: Can We Determine It?* Boston: The Beacon Press, 1949. Pp. 95-126. Reprinted from the *Journal of Modern History*, Sept., 1940.

Tschiževskij, D. and Groh, D., eds. *Europa und Russland: Texte zum Problem des westeuropäischen und russischen Selbstverständnisses.* Darmstadt: Wissenschaftliche Buchgesellschaft, 1959.

5. The Nature of Imperial Russian Society

Bill, Valentine T. *The Forgotten Class: The Russian Bourgeoisie from the Earliest Beginnings to 1900.* New York: Praeger, 1959.

Black, C. E., ed. *The Transformation of Russian Society.* Cambridge, Mass.: Harvard University Press, 1960.

Blum, Jerome. *Lord and Peasant in Russia from the Ninth to the Nineteenth Century.* Princeton, N. J.: Princeton University Press, 1961.

Florinsky, Michael T. *The End of the Russian Empire.* London: Oxford University Press, 1931 (and Collier Paperback).

Hans, Nicholas A. *History of Russian Educational Policy, 1701-1917.* London: P. S. King & Son, 1931.

Kliuchevsky, V. O. *Peter the Great.* Trans. by Liliana Archibald. New York: St. Martin's Press, 1958 (and Vintage Paperback).

Korkunov, N. M. *Russkoe gosudarstvennoe pravo.* 2 vols. St. Petersburg: Stasiulevich, 1909.

Pares, Sir Bernard. *The Fall of the Russian Monarchy.* London: J. Cape, 1939 (and Vintage Paperback).

Raeff, Marc. *Michael Speransky, Statesman of Imperial Russia, 1772-1839* The Hague: M. Nijhoff, 1957.

Robinson, Geroid T. *Rural Russia Under the Old Regime.* London: Longmans, 1932.

Seton-Watson, Hugh. *The Decline of Imperial Russia, 1855-1914.* London: Methuen, 1952 (and Praeger Paperback).

Treadgold, Donald W. *The Great Siberian Migration.* Princeton, N.J.: Princeton University Press, 1957.

Von Laue, Theodore. *Sergei Witte and the Industrialization of Russia.* New York and London: Columbia University Press, 1963.

Wallace, Sir Donald Mackenzie. *Russia.* London: Cassell, 1912 (and Vintage Paperback: *Russia: On the Eve of War and Revolution*).

Weidlé, Wladimir. *Russia: Absent and Present.* London: Hollis & Carter, 1952 (and Vintage Paperback).

Yarmolinsky, Avrahm. *Road to Revolution: A Century of Russian Radicalism.* London: Cassell, 1957 (and Collier Paperback).

6. The Role of the Ukraine in Modern History

Armstrong, John A. *Ukrainian Nationalism.* 2nd ed. New York: Columbia University Press, 1963.

Borys, Jurij. *The Russian Communist Party and the Sovietization of Ukraine: A Study in the Communist Doctrine of the Self-Determination of Nations.* Stockholm, 1960.

Dmytryshyn, Basil. *Moscow and the Ukraine, 1918-1953: A Study of Russian Bolshevik Nationality Policy.* New York: Bookman Associates, 1956.

Doroshenko, Dmytro. *History of the Ukraine.* Translated from the Ukrainian and abridged by Hanna Chikalenko-Keller. Edited and introduction by G. W. Simpson. Edmonton, Alberta: Institute Press, 1941.

Doroshenko, Dmytro. "A Survey of Ukrainian Historiography," by Dmytro Doroshenko. "Ukrainian Historiography, 1917-1956," by Olexander Ohloblyn. *The Annals of the Ukrainian Academy of Arts and Sciences in the U.S.,* vol. 5/6, 1957. New York, 1957.

Hrushevsky, Michael. *A History of Ukraine.* Edited by O. J. Frederiksen. Preface by George Vernadsky. New Haven, Conn.: Yale University Press, 1941.

Kononenko, Konstantyn. *Ukraine and Russia: A History of the Economic Relations Between Ukraine and Russia, 1654-1917.* Milwaukee, Wis.: Marquette University Press, 1958.

O'Brien, C. Bickford. *Muscovy and the Ukraine: From the Pereiaslavl Agreement to the Truce of Andrusovo, 1654-1667.* Berkeley: University of California Press, 1963 (Paperback).

Reshetar, John S. *The Ukrainian Revolution, 1917-1920: A Study in Nationalism.* Princeton, N.J.: Princeton University Press, 1952.

Sullivant, Robert S. *Soviet Politics and the Ukraine, 1917-1957.* New York: Columbia University Press, 1962.

Ukraine: A Concise Encyclopaedia. Prepared by Shevchenko Scientific Society. Editor-in-chief Volodymyr Kubijovyč. Preface by Ernest J. Simmons. Toronto: University of Toronto Press, 1963- . 2 vols.

Vernadsky, George. *Bohdan, Hetman of Ukraine.* New Haven, Conn.: Yale University Press, 1941.

7. The Problem of Unity in the Polish-Lithuanian State

Halecki, Oscar. *Dzieje Unii Jagiellońskiej.* 2 vols. Krakow: Akademia Umiejetnosci, 1919-20.

————. *From Florence to Brest (1439-1596).* Rome: Sacrum Poloniae Millennium. New York: Fordham University Press, 1958.

Hrushevsky, Michael. *A History of Ukraine.* Edited by O. J. Frederiksen. New Haven, Conn.: Yale University Press, 1941.

Kaplan, Herbert H. *The First Partition of Poland.* New York and London: Columbia University Press, 1962.

Kutrzeba, Stanislaw. *Historia ustroju Polski w zarysie: Korona.* 8th ed. rev. by Adam Vetulani. Warsaw, 1949.

Liubavsky, Matvei K. *Ocherk istorii litovsko-russkago gosudarstva.* 1st ed. Moscow, 1910. 2nd ed. Moscow, 1915.

Lord, Robert H. *The Second Partition of Poland: A Study in Diplomatic History.* Cambridge, Mass.: Harvard University Press, 1915.

Reddaway, William F., et al., eds. *The Cambridge History of Poland.* 2 vols. Cambridge, Eng.: Cambridge University Press, 1950-51.

Rutkowski, Jan. *Historia gospodarcza Polski.* 3rd expanded ed. Poznan, 1947.

Vernadsky, George. *Bohdan, Hetman of the Ukraine.* New Haven, Conn.: Yale University Press, 1941.

―――. *Russia at the Dawn of the Modern Age.* New Haven, Conn. and London: Yale University Press, 1959.

8. Russia and the East: A Comparison and Contrast

Kliuchevsky, V. O. *A History of Russia.* Trans. by C. J. Hogarth. 5 vols. London: J. M. Dent & Sons, 1911-31.

―――. *Peter the Great.* Trans. by Liliana Archibald. New York: St. Martin's Press, 1958 (and Vintage Paperback).

Mavor, James. *An Economic History of Russia.* 2 vols. New York: Dutton, 1914.

Miliukov, Paul N. *Outlines of Russian Culture.* 3 vols. Philadelphia: University of Pennsylvania Press, 1948 (and Perpetua Paperback, 3 vols.).

―――. *Russia and Its Crisis.* Chicago: University of Chicago Press, 1905 (and Collier Paperback).

Plekhanov, George. *Selected Philosophical Works.* Vol. I. Moscow: Foreign Languages Publishing House, n. d. London: Lawrence and Wishart, 1961.

Sumner, B. H. *Survey of Russian History.* London: Gerald Duckworth & Co., 1947.

Vernadsky, George. *The Mongols and Russia.* New Haven, Conn.: Yale University Press, 1953.

Wittfogel, Karl A. *Oriental Despotism: A Comparative Study of Total Power.* New Haven, Conn. and London: Yale University Press, 1963 (and Paperback).

9. Russia and the West: A Comparison and Contrast

Anderson, M. S. *Britain's Discovery of Russia, 1553-1815.* London: Macmillan, 1958.

Custine, Astolphe Louis Léonard, marquis de. *La Russie en 1839, par le marquis de Custine.* Paris: Amyot, 1843. (English trans. by Phyllis Penn Kohler. *Journey for Our Time.* New York: Pellegrini & Cudahy, 1951.)

Danilevsky, N. *Russland und Europa.* Stuttgart and Berlin: Deutsche Verlags-Anstalt, 1920.

Groh, Dieter. *Russland und das Selbstverständnis Europas: Ein Beitrag zur europäischen Geistesgeschichte.* Neuwied: Luchterhand Verlag, 1961.

Halecki, Oscar. *The Limits and Divisions of European History.* London and New York: Sheed & Ward, 1950.

Riasanovsky, Nicholas V. *Russia and the West in the Teaching of the Slavophiles.* Cambridge, Mass.: Harvard University Press, 1952.

Rogger, Hans. *National Consciousness in Eighteenth Century Russia.* Cambridge, Mass.: Harvard University Press, 1960.

Tschiẑewskij, D. and Groh, D., eds. *Europa und Russland: Texte zum Problem des westeuropäischen und russischen Selbstverständnisses.* Darmstadt: Wissenschaftliche Buchgesellschaft, 1959.

Index